Matthew E. Gordley

Teaching through Song
in Antiquity

Didactic Hymnody among Greeks, Romans,
Jews, and Christians

Mohr Siebeck

MATTHEW E. GORDLEY, born 1972; 2000 M.Div; 2006 PhD; currently assistant professor of religious studies and chair of the Department of Religion and Philosophy, Regent University (Virginia).

PN
1401
.G67
2011

ISBN 978-3-16-150722-9
ISSN 0340-9570 (Wissenschaftliche Untersuchungen zum Neuen Testament, 2. Reihe)

Die Deutsche Nationalbibliothek lists this publication in the Deutsche Nationalbiblio-graphie; detailed bibliographic data are available on the Internet at *http://dnb.d-nb.de*.

The book was printed by Laupp & Göbel in Nehren on non-aging paper and bound by Buchbinderei Nädele in Nehren.

Printed in Germany.

Wissenschaftliche Untersuchungen
zum Neuen Testament · 2. Reihe

Herausgeber / Editor
Jörg Frey (Zürich)

Mitherausgeber / Associate Editors
Friedrich Avemarie (Marburg)
Markus Bockmuehl (Oxford)
James A. Kelhoffer (Uppsala)
Hans-Josef Klauck (Chicago, IL)

302

To David E. Aune
My teacher, mentor, and friend

Preface

The idea for this volume grew out of my earlier volume on the Colossian hymn (*The Colossian Hymn in Context* [Mohr Siebeck, 2007]). In that volume I argued that Col 1:15–20 could be best understood as a quasi-philosophical prose-hymn utilized for purposes of instruction and exhortation in the context of the epistle. In other words, Col 1:15–20 was a didactic hymn. In the course of that study I encountered many hymns, psalms, and prayers that, while not specifically related to the Colossian hymn in any direct way, shared similar dynamics in that they utilized hymnic style or form for purposes of instructing a human audience. While specialized studies of many of those texts were plentiful, I noted that there was not one monograph that explored the vast variety of ways that ancient poets, in many times and places, utilized hymns in order to teach a human audience and shape a community's understanding of itself. It occurred to me that such a broad-ranging comparative survey would provide a foundation for further study of these texts, as well as reveal something of the inter-relatedness of the traditions of Judaism and Christianity as well as Greek and Roman traditions. This volume has emerged as my contribution to this topic, and I hope it will result in further efforts to engage more fully with these fascinating ancient texts that both praise and instruct.

Here I would like to express my deep appreciation to the professors who have contributed so much to my personal and professional development as a student of Scripture and other ancient texts. In particular I am grateful to David E. Aune who read through drafts of multiple chapters and offered insightful suggestions and critiques in many places. It is to David that this volume is gratefully dedicated. Naturally, many of my professors from my time at the University of Notre Dame continue to inspire and influence my work, especially James VanderKam, Hindy Najman, Greg Sterling, Jerry Neyrey, Mary-Rose D'Angelo, and Robin Darling Young. I would also like to acknowledge the ongoing influence of James Charlesworth, Ross Wagner, and Don Juel from the time I spent at Princeton Theological Seminary. I thank William V. Crockett of Alliance Theological Seminary for igniting in me a passion for the world of the New Testament, and also David Denyer and Bryan Widbin of ATS for their ongoing influence.

I would also like to thank the organizers of the numerous SBL sections that allowed me the opportunity to present portions of this research in recent years, particularly the Pseudepigrapha section, the Qumran section, the Hellenistic Judaism section, the Disputed Paulines section, the Johannine Literature section, and the Construction of Christian Identities section. In particular, I want to thank the following individuals for their comments, questions, and suggestions in these forums that contributed to my thinking as I completed this volume: Judith Newman, Hindy Najman, Esther Chazon, Eileen Schuller, George Brooke, Daniel Falk, Angela Kim, Jack Conroy, and Michael Daise. In addition, my appreciation is due to my colleagues Bill Lyons and Steve Sherman in the Department of Religion and Philosophy at Regent University for their comments and suggestions in the context of these presentations. Thanks also to Ardea Russo and Kindy De Long for allowing me access to their exceptional monographs on Revelation and Acts respectively, prior to their publication. Many thanks are due also to Jörg Frey for helpful, critical comments on an ealier version of this volume and for ultimately including this final version in this series.

In addition I count it a privilege to thank a number of people and organizations that have supported my work on this volume. I am grateful to Gregory Nagy and Kenny Morrell at Harvard University's Center for Hellenic Studies who selected me to participate in a week-long seminar on Homeric Hymns and the poetry of Hesiod in summer 2008. My thanks are due also to the Council of Independent Colleges which sponsored the seminar. I am grateful to Regent University for awarding me three faculty research grants over the course of the 2007–8, 2008–9, and 2010–11 academic years. My thanks are due as well to Beth Doriani who granted me research release time in the early stages of this project. Several graduate students, notably Laura Latora, Alicia Eichmann, and Ryan Cooper, provided stellar research assistance at various stages of this project. Anthony Lipscomb did a tremendous job of proofreading the entire manuscript and compiling the indices, eliminating many errors and inconsistencies.

Finally, I want to warmly acknowledge my family for their love and support and for making my life all that it has been during the course of this research project. My wife Janine is the light of my world and has always supported and encouraged my research and writing in every way possible, even in the midst of difficult times. My sons, Jack, Aidan, and Noah, have been a constant source of refreshment and have helped me maintain my sanity (such as it is!) even in the midst of intense periods of research and writing. Completing this volume gives me a good excuse to put into print a few words of gratitude to the ones who mean the world to me. Thank you.

Table of Contents

Chapter 1

Beginning a Study of Ancient Didactic Hymns, Prayers, and Poems

A. Introduction

A primary purpose of most ancient hymns was the offering of praise, thanks, requests, or some combination of these, to the divine. That is, generally speaking, what hymns do. However, what unites the diverse and varied hymnic compositions under consideration in this volume is the way they employ hymnic forms and features from a variety of styles for a different primary purpose: instruction.

This study will argue that some poets, psalmists, and hymn-writers in antiquity took on a much more humanistic (and perhaps more difficult) task than praising a god or invoking the favor of a deity. They took on the task of molding and shaping the imaginations, thoughts, and perspectives of their audiences. They embraced the challenge of showing their hearers, through the medium of words, a world in which supernatural forces were at work. Often they confronted what their listeners could see in the world around them, creating a verbal portrait of the unseen world and bringing it into contact with the reality their community was experiencing. Through their compositions these psalmists and poets expressed a particular view of the world, of their community's place in it, and of the larger purposes of the divine among them. They espoused a way of seeing the world that was not always self-evident. In simplest terms, they took on the role of teachers and they taught through their hymns.

Of course, it is fair to say that all hymns and poems teach on some level. One could analyze any hymn and consider what values are inscribed within it, what it claims about the one being praised, and what it teaches about the position and status of the one reciting the hymn. One can also consider how a given hymn models praise and teaches the human audience about the nature of praise through its example. Even as hymns offer praise to a deity, they offer some amount of instruction to a human audience. Some hymns, however, indicate that teaching a human audience is a primary function of the hymn and not just a by-product. In some cases this is explicit while in others this teaching function, though primary, may only be implied. Either way, the hymns that manifest this primary emphasis on teaching are those that we are calling "didactic hymns."

This study makes three related claims. First, didactic hymnody, carefully defined, is a recognizable and widespread phenomenon in Greek, Roman, Jewish, and Christian traditions of antiquity. Second, by attending to the specific contents, style, and strategies of a given didactic hymn, we can gain insight into issues facing a community and how the didactic hymn contributes to an ongoing process of identity formation for that community. Third, by comparing the use of didactic hymnody in a variety of cultural traditions in antiquity, we can gain a greater appreciation and understanding of the instructional dynamics of these texts and the strategies they employed as they functioned in the ancient world.

Though didactic hymns cannot be considered a distinct literary genre (as we will see, these texts are often found within a number of different genres), many hymnic and poetic praise texts show this primary concern for instruction and communal formation for a human audience. Didactic hymns, prayers, and praise poetry conveyed such things as knowledge of the past, perspective on the present, as well as beliefs, values, and ideals central to a community's self understanding. These compositions created a picture of reality in which a human audience could locate itself and find its identity. In light of these claims, we will articulate a broad definition of didactic hymnody and provide a broad survey of didactic hymns and prayers in Greek, Roman, Jewish, and Christian contexts. We will also examine a selection of didactic hymns from each tradition showing how poets and authors used a variety of strategies to instruct and engage their human audiences in considering the world and their place in it. The ultimate aims of this study, then, are a richer understanding of the individual compositions, a clearer picture of some of the authors and communities that produced and treasured these compositions, and a fuller appreciation of the ways that hymns and prayers functioned within the instructional landscape of Greco-Roman antiquity.

With these aims in view, the present volume contributes to recent scholarly discussions relating to the process of identity formation, the construction of identity, and the dynamics of communal formation among religious and social groups of antiquity. This field of study has emerged in recent years as an important and growing area of research for scholars of early Judaism and Christianity in particular.[1] For example, the recent volume of

---

[1] Several recent volumes attest to the interest of scholars in these kinds of issues as well as the kinds of results that such an approach can yield: Zeba A. Crook and Philip A. Harland, *Identity and Interaction in the Ancient Mediterranean: Jews, Christians and Others: Essays in Honour of Stephen G. Wilson* (New Testament Monographs 18; Sheffield: Sheffield Phoenix Press, 2007); Jörg Frey, Daniel R. Schwartz, and Stephanie

essays edited by Holmberg and Winninge in particular highlights a number of approaches and methods for examining identity formation within the New Testament and other early Christian writings. Their volume is to be commended for its variety of approaches including post-colonial criticism, intertextual analysis, consideration of literary techniques, and gender analysis. It also is helpful in providing some foundational understandings of identity.[2] Nevertheless, the Holmberg and Winninge volume shows a surprising omission in the consideration of hymnic, poetic, or other liturgical texts as aspects of identity formation for early Christians. This is regrettable since in the introduction to the volume the editors note that "among other things liturgy functions as an expression and a celebration of the distinctive norms, values, and ideals of the worshipping community."[3] While communal worship and its contribution toward the formation of identity is not addressed in their important volume, the present study is positioned precisely in the middle of this conceptual category.

Accordingly, we will look closely at how a certain kind of hymnic composition – didactic hymnody – instructs its audience and uses a number of strategies to contribute to a sense of communal identity among its listeners. We will see that didactic hymns are complex, artistic creations that use a variety of approaches to show forth a vision of reality that goes beyond what the audience could readily observe in the world around them. Hymns in particular were well-suited to bring into focus the work of the divine in the context of the earthly.

An exploration of instructionally oriented praise compositions from antiquity faces a number of challenges that are readily apparent to any serious student of the ancient world and its texts. The problems relate to terminology, selection of texts, and methodology, as well as the broad religious and cultural scope of the study. Recognizing these challenges, this

---

Gripentrog, *Jewish Identity in the Greco-Roman World = Jüdische Identität in der griechisch-römischen Welt* (Leiden: Brill, 2007); Philip A. Harland, *Dynamics of Identity in the World of the Early Christians: Associations, Judeans, and Cultural Minorities* (New York: T & T Clark, 2009); Bengt Holmberg and Mikael Winninge, *Identity Formation in the New Testament* (WUNT 227; Tübingen: Mohr Siebeck, 2008); Carol A. Newsom, *The Self as Symbolic Space: Constructing Identity and Community at Qumran* (STDJ 52; Leiden: Brill, 2004).

[2] For example, the editors are careful to note that identity concerns much more than texts: "Identity is a larger, more complex social reality with both cognitive, ritual, and moral dimensions, crystallized into social relations and institutions, and developing in both predictable and surprising directions over time." Holmberg and Winninge, *Identity Formation*, vii.

[3] Ibid. In the conference that spawned this volume one of the seminar groups was apparently intended to consider how liturgy contributed to the formation of identity ("liturgy as identity formation"). Its focus apparently ended up being broader than liturgy with the result that liturgical concerns are not represented in the conference volume.

first chapter addresses the following issues in turn: a definition of didactic hymnody; identification of didactic hymns; and the scope and approach of this study. Next a discussion of methodology highlights a number of tools that we will use to explore the multiple levels of didactic impact of a given hymn. We will conclude this chapter by discussing features of didactic hymns that enable some degree of classification of these compositions.

B. A Definition of Didactic Hymnody

A significant challenge is that of defining the kinds of texts we are considering in this study. The term used in the title – didactic hymnody – has been used by other scholars. However, it has not been well-defined and has no consistent use within the scholarly literature that treats the kinds of texts that are under consideration in this study. Given that some degree of instruction is an inherent part of most expressions of song (in the modern world as well as the ancient), it is surprising that not one monograph has been devoted to the study of the didactic use of song in the ancient world.[4] The lack of scholarly discussion of this particular category, with definitions of the scope, contents, and function of texts within this category, simply means that those essential concepts need to be discussed here. In this section we first provide a definition of didactic hymnody that is as succinct as possible and at the same time allows for the complexity of the phenomenon being explored here. We follow this definition with discussion of some related terminology in order to clarify both what this study is and is not examining.

While each tradition employs a range of terminology for its praise texts this study recognizes that a number of different kinds of poetic or religious compositions can be considered didactic hymns when their contents register a didactic tone and their style participates in hymnic conventions. In light of this understanding, we propose the following definition:

---

[4] To be sure, some specialized studies on one particular text or one particular tradition have raised the issue. Some recent examples include: Stephen E. Fowl, *The Story of Christ in the Ethics of Paul: An Analysis of the Function of the Hymnic Material in the Pauline Corpus* (JSNTSup 36; Sheffield: Sheffield Academic Press, 1990); Terry Giles and William Doan, *Twice Used Songs: Performance Criticism of the Songs of Ancient Israel* (Peabody, Mass.: Hendrickson, 2009); Jan Liesen, *Full of Praise: An Exegetical Study of Sir 39, 12–35* (JSJSup 64; Boston: Brill, 2000); Newsom, *The Self as Symbolic Space*; Johan C. Thom, *Cleanthes' Hymn to Zeus* (STAC 33; Tübingen: Mohr Siebeck, 2005). In spite of the excellent contribution of each of these studies, not one takes a broad enough view to be able to situate the didactic function of that one text or set of texts within the larger framework of instructional song in antiquity.

Didactic hymns, prayers, and religious poetry are those compositions which employ the stylistic and/or formal conventions of praise and prayer, but whose primary purpose was to convey a lesson, idea, or theological truth to a human audience.

Though somewhat unwieldy, the phrase "didactic hymns, prayers, and religious poetry" gives both the breadth needed in terms of genres while at the same time placing the emphasis on teaching and instruction within those genres. As a shorthand expression we will use the more manageable phrase "didactic hymnody," though the reader must bear in mind the broad sense in which we use the term "hymnody," particularly as it is discussed in the following paragraphs.

A number of other terms suggest themselves as good candidates for a category that reflects the scope of this study. Some terms are indeed relevant to our study, though they may not be suitable to describe the phenomenon as a whole. For example, the terms "instructional psalmody" and "didactic poetry" open the discussion to a number of relevant texts and get us moving in the right direction. We are concerned here with religious poetry that was written to instruct. However, in light of the broader scope of this project, which aims to encounter this phenomenon in antiquity in several religious and cultural traditions, these terms are not completely satisfactory. The term "psalmody" tends to be restricted to Jewish and Christian compositions and is therefore too limiting.[5] Similarly the expression "didactic poetry" refers to a phenomenon that is already closely associated with Greco-Roman literary traditions, and is therefore too restrictive for our broad survey.[6] The term is also too restrictive in that some of the didactic compositions we will examine here as hymns cannot technically be regarded as poetry. I refer here to the little studied prose hymns of antiquity, some of which explicitly claim that they are *not* poetry (cf. Aristides, *Or.* 45.1–14). In addition, didactic poetry as a category can also be considered to be too broad in the sense that its subject matter extends far beyond the religious contexts which are the primary focus of this study. While didactic poetry may employ didactic hymnody at times (e.g., the hymn to Zeus that makes up the proem of Aratus's *Phaenomena*), didactic poetry as a genre can cover anything from farming to astronomy. The term "didactic hymnody" is also broad, but in the more useful sense that it can include any number of ancient religious traditions; Jews, Christians, Greeks, and Romans all made use of hymnody, albeit in various forms. Further, the

---

[5] Cf. Martin Hengel, "Hymns and Christology," in *Between Jesus and Paul* (London: Fortress Press, 1983), 78–96. Hengel observes, "The Jewish *psalmos* was fundamentally different from the traditional Greek hymn to the gods with its strict metre, dependent on the variation between stressed and unstressed syllables" (78).

[6] Peter Toohey, *Epic Lessons: An Introduction to Ancient Didactic Poetry* (London: Routledge, 1996).

broad understanding of hymnody adopted here allows for inclusion of a wide range of texts within this category.[7] Though more specialized uses of the term are also attested in antiquity, the broadest definition of hymn relevant here is that which refers to any composition in honor of a god.[8]

Nevertheless, the idea of a hymn can take several manifestations, some of which are more specific or more technical in their meaning; not all of these are in line with our use of the term here.[9] In the study of the canonical book of Psalms, for example, form-critics distinguish hymns as one type of psalm among others (e.g., laments, songs of thanksgiving, songs of ascent, etc.) depending on the classification scheme used. A number of psalms have clear didactic emphases and yet do not fall into the form-critical category of "hymns." In order to avoid limiting the scope of this volume and excluding valuable comparative material, we include a variety of religious poetry and hymnic compositions which lay claim to didactic purposes. These include: psalms, prayers, poems, songs, and hymns. Each of these kinds of compositions can be crafted with the goal of communicating with a deity, and in many cases, this is understood to be one of their main purposes. But each of these kinds of compositions can also take on a didactic function – a function which may even be the primary purpose of the composition.

What we are most interested in are those compositions which have the appearance of being written to render praise to a deity (i.e., hymns) or to communicate with a deity (i.e., prayers), but which at the same time also teach a human audience, whether the individuals in the audience are passive listeners or active participants. In this study, then, we explore hymns, psalms, and prayers that have a didactic function. We also explore those compositions that employ the conventions of these categories to a significant extent. Thus we do include religious poetry at times even if it is technically not a hymn. Though religious poetry may not be cast in the form of

---

[7] Note the range of uses of the hymn in the entries in Therese Fuhrer, "Hymnus III. The Christian Hymn," in *Brill's New Pauly* (ed. Hubert Cancik and Helmuth Schneider; Boston: Brill, 2005), col. 622–625.

[8] Cf. R. C. T. Parker, "Hymns (Greek)," in *Oxford Classical Dictionary* (3rd revised ed.; Oxford: Oxford University Press, 2003), 735–736. For a similar discussion of a broad definition of hymnody in antiquity see Josef Kroll, *Die christliche Hymnodik bis zu Klemens von Alexandria* (2nd ed.; Darmstadt: Wissenschaftliche Buchgesellschaft, 1968), 8–12.

[9] See the further discussion in Parker, "Hymns (Greek)." He notes three meanings of ὕμνος, all of which employ the idea of song in honor of a god. Yet he also notes a broader use of the term as he writes that in our period "many hymns were also composed that were not, in all seeming, intended for performance: instances are as diverse as the hymns of Callimachus, Cleanthes' Hymn to Zeus, hymns to fortune and to nature and to Rome, and in due course epideictic compositions such as the prose hymns of Aelius Aristides" (736).

a prayer or hymn, it often takes advantage of the conventions of prayer and praise to convey its message.

A brief example illustrates the complexity of this issue and also our approach in addressing it. In the Jewish tradition, Wisdom of Solomon 10 is a discourse on the saving role of Wisdom in Israel's history from the creation of Adam through the exodus from Egypt. Though not formally a hymn (there is no hymnic opening; it is not found in the context of a collection of psalms but rather is incorporated into a protreptic discourse; etc.) the passage does include a number of hymnic features in terms of both style and content. Further, there is no question that a major purpose of this chapter is to convince the listener of the value of aligning oneself with the powerful figure of Wisdom, clearly reflecting the Jewish historical and theological tradition. This passage is included in this study since a case can be made that it is a composition in hymnic style (if not form) with a heavy didactic emphasis. In that broad sense, Wis 10 may be considered to fall into our category of didactic hymns, prayers, and religious poetry.

Having briefly noted this example, it may appear to make sense to refer more broadly to "didactic religious poetry." However, the phrase "didactic religious poetry" is not appropriate here since there is a strong tradition of prose prayer and even prose hymnody in antiquity.[10] Moreover, since the publication of James Kugel's *The Idea of Biblical Poetry* several decades ago, many scholars have called into question the clear-cut distinction between poetry and prose, at least within the Hebrew Bible.[11] While the present study recognizes a distinction between poetry and prose (however that is defined), both poetic and prose prayers and hymns fall within the scope of this study. Poetic form, rhythm, and meter are recognized as several features that may be indicative of a hymnic style. Nevertheless, the label "poetry" is not the only feature associated with hymnody nor is it determinative of a hymn in any case.

The term "didactic" as a descriptor is easier to defend as it emphasizes the primary function of the hymns in question here: instruction. This term is often used in distinction from other terms such as "cultic" or "liturgical," each of which suggests a primary purpose of giving praise, thanks, honor, or some form of verbal offering to a deity in the context of a worship ceremony or sacrifice. Of course, we must recognize that these categories are not mutually exclusive; didactic hymns could have been used in these kinds of communal worship settings. Even so, Sigmund Mowinckel

---

[10] D. A. Russell, "Aristides and the Prose Hymn," in *Antonine Literature* (ed. D. A. Russell; Oxford: Clarendon Press, 1990), 199–216.

[11] James L. Kugel, *The Idea of Biblical Poetry: Parallelism and its History* (New Haven: Yale University Press, 1981); James L. Kugel, "Some Thoughts on Future Research into Biblical Style: Addenda to The Idea of Biblical Poetry," *JSOT* 28 (1984): 108–117.

made a distinction when he spoke of "learned psalmography," a subset of Jewish psalms associated less with temple worship and more with the house of instruction. In using this terminology Mowinckel indicated something of the origin and authorship of a selection of psalms: those which appear to have originated within wisdom circles.[12] However, wisdom poetry and even "learned psalmography" as a phenomenon are really a subset of our larger category of didactic hymnody, and as such will be explored at some length. By referring to a larger category of didactic hymns, psalms, and prayers, the emphasis in this study is not on their authorship or origin (whether from wisdom circles or cultic circles) but on their content and function (how they function in their literary or social context).

Naturally, it must be admitted that it is usually extremely difficult to identify the origin of any ancient poem. Identification of the author is, in many cases, impossible. Even the idea of discerning the *intent* of the author in a given text is fraught with difficulty. However, from clues based on the form, contents, and the later collection and preservation of many of these psalms, hymns, or prayers, it is possible to speak of their didactic function as at least one purpose among several. A goal of this study will be to explore the kinds of lessons and instructions that were given through this medium of hymnody. Observations about the varieties of forms which these songs could take, in comparison with one another, will also be significant. For example, in the Jewish tradition, what kinds of lessons are conveyed through hymns that review history as opposed to wisdom poems? Or in the Greek tradition, what kinds of lessons are conveyed through a hymn to a deity as opposed to compositions in praise of a human ruler?

One other possible way of describing these kinds of texts brings out an additional challenge for this study. As a category "didactic religious discourse" is close to getting to the heart of the issue, since it combines the didactic function with a religious perspective. However, this phrase would suggest that the compositions are limited here only to the realm of the religious, which may imply a distinction between religious and other discourses such as philosophical or political discourse. No such distinction is intended in this study, though the texts chosen for study here do generally register a religious tone as a primary feature. Yet that overriding tone does not serve to remove political, social, or philosophical issues from the purview of their didactic designs. In addition, though we will concern ourselves with questions relating to discourse analysis (see below on method) the general term "discourse" is much too broad. The texts under consideration here tend to be shorter discrete units, a factor which needs to be kept

---

[12] S. Mowinckel, "Psalms and Wisdom," in *Wisdom in Israel and in the Ancient Near East Presented to Professor Harold Henry Rowley* (ed. M. Noth and D. Winton Thomas; Leiden: Brill, 1960).

in mind as well. In light of the above discussion, the admittedly cumbersome expression "didactic hymns, prayers, and religious poetry" does justice to the concerns of this study.

C. Identification of Didactic Hymns

A second challenge we face from the outset is the recognition that within each of the cultural-religious complexes under discussion here (Greco-Roman, early Jewish, early Christian) many texts of different types and styles could lay claim to being both "didactic" on some level and "hymnic" to some extent. Selecting representative didactic hymns from among this wide range of potential texts is thus a major difficulty. The parameters of our definition of didactic hymnody serve as a starting point for these judgments. From there the specifics of which texts really ought to be considered didactic can and should be debated. However, the advantage of a broad survey such as this is that even if one, two, or ten texts are omitted which should have been included, the impact they would have on the overall thesis should not be too great. Likewise, space does not allow for a full analysis of all of the hymnic or prayer texts we might consider didactic. I have thus tried to select those texts which have potential to open up our understanding of the phenomenon, showing a variety of approaches to hymnic instruction. This section outlines the features that enable us to identify a hymn as didactic.

As we have already noted in passing, some ancient hymns made their teaching function explicit. This is most easily observable when the poet invites the human audience to hear and learn as the poet speaks or when the hymn makes prominent use of the language of instruction. For example, Psalm 78 begins with the call: "Give ear, my people, to my instruction; incline your ear to the words of my mouth."[13] When compositions with those kinds of didactic features employ a hymnic form or at least a hymnic style, it is clear that they fit our conception of didactic hymnody. Didactic hymns vary in the degree to which they make their teaching explicit and in the degree to which they address the audience directly. For those whose teaching is less clearly on display, it is often the context or other indicators that suggest the hymn should be considered among what we are calling "didactic hymns."

In many instances the teaching function of an ancient hymn is far less explicit and must be more carefully discerned. A number of factors can indicate the priority of a hymn's didactic purpose, even if the language of

---

[13] Unless otherwise noted, translations of biblical passages are my own.

instruction is absent. First of all, direct address to the human audience, even in portions of the hymn, can signal that the hymn-writer has as a primary goal the conveying of ideas, information, or values to the human audience. This can be done in connection with or in addition to praising the divine; the tasks of praise and teaching are not mutually exclusive. However, when the poet addresses the audience directly, we should at least consider that the hymn may be intended to shape the perceptions and thoughts of that audience.

A second indicator of the didactic nature of a hymn is the extent to which it makes direct claims about the nature of the one being praised and/or about the community offering the praise. Direct claims about the deity, his powers, and his characteristics at least reveal something of the theology of the hymn. Likewise comments about the worshippers (whether they are blessed, specially favored, etc.) reveal the perspective of the hymnist about the community. It is possible, of course, that these claims may be incidental and subsumed under a main purpose of praising the divine. In such instances the didactic role of such claims may be less significant. However, at times the direct claims about the deity become the focal point of the hymn, enabling us to identify a major purpose of that hymn as instruction. Again, instruction may not be the only purpose, but it is a primary one when a central aspect of the hymn is making claims about the deity that the audience is expected to accept.

A third indicator is related to the second. When the hymn, in the form of narrative, recounts events of the mythic past or recent past, we should be aware that a didactic purpose may be present. A didactic role may be seen particularly clearly when the narrative about the recent, distant, or mythic past relates to the present concerns of the community from which the hymn comes. While that is not always the case (i.e. a narrative may be included for reasons other than teaching a lesson), the presence of narrative elements in a hymn should at least be considered one clue to the purpose of that hymn. The didactic function of such a narrative is rendered more certain when the hymn also addresses the audience directly at times and makes explicit claims about the deity and/or the audience.

The indicators noted above are elements within the hymn that enable us to consider that it may have been composed, in part, for purposes of teaching a human audience in addition to praising the divine. However, we will also see that some hymns, whose original purpose may not have been primarily didactic (i.e. they do not contain language of instruction, do not address the audience directly, and do not have direct claims or didactic narrative as a primary element), *become* didactic when they are preserved and used by later generations in new contexts. In some cases a hymn whose primary purpose may have originally been praise and whose teaching purpose was only a secondary concern, can be employed in a new context which renders the didactic purpose as the primary function. This is particularly the case for hymns and psalms embedded in narrative and epistolary contexts of which there are numerous examples in the Hebrew Scriptures, the New Testament, and other early Jewish and Christian writings. Even the collecting of hymns together in one document provides a new context for each hymn and may serve to cause the teaching purpose to be highlighted, depending on the use of the larger document within a given community. For example, if a psalm from the Jewish Psalter was originally composed primarily as a vehicle for praise of God, when collected with other psalms it may retain that focus when the Psalms are used as a prayer and praise book. But when Psalms is read as a prophetic text, the content of a given psalm is then considered much more instructional than praise-oriented. Accordingly we must be aware of the possibility of multiple uses and functions of a text depending on its context and the disposition of the community that is composing it, reciting it, or reading it.

In some cases, a hymn or poem may be found in the context of a larger composition whose purposes are instructional. For example, Lucretius's didactic poem *On the Nature of the Universe* contains a number of hymnic passages. Likewise, Hesiod's *Works and Days* begins with a hymnic prelude as does Aratus's *Phaenomenon*. In cases like these, the didactic focus of the larger composition enables us to consider hymns it contains as potentially didactic as well. Questions about the didactic function of such hymns would center on how the themes and emphasis of the hymn contribute to the teaching of the larger composition. As we will see, many poets made effective use of hymnic forms to prepare audiences to receive their instruction.

In this volume we examine hymns that place a primary emphasis on teaching a human audience some kind of lesson (theological, historical, moral, political) whether that is explicit or implicit. Or, if the hymn itself does not suggest the primacy of a teaching function, its placement in a particular context indicates that it was understood by a later community to carry a didactic function. We thus recognize that didactic hymnody is not a monolithic category but a way of viewing certain kinds of hymnic texts found in a wide range of literary genres.

D. Scope and Approach of this Study

In light of our definition of didactic hymnody and our goal of exploring hymns with didactic emphases in a number of genres, a third challenge for the present study arises from the diversity of the cultural and religious background of the texts we consider to be didactic hymns. It is an under-statement to say that the literary traditions of ancient Judaism, early Christianity, and Greco-Roman cultures are incredibly diverse. In light of that reality we must consider whether there is much value in attempting to compare such a wide range of texts. What value will accrue, for example, from putting Psalm 105 and Cleanthes' *Hymn to Zeus* on the same playing field? What insights will come from bringing the *Hodayot* of Qumran and the "star hymn" of Ignatius of Antioch into conversation? In short, though each tradition can and should be considered in its own right, a volume that was limited to just one (or even two) of these cultural traditions would be at risk of missing valuable data for comparison and contrast. It is easiest, perhaps, to see how the Christian tradition is dependent on earlier Jewish traditions. However, the Christian tradition of didactic hymnody must also be understood within the larger Greco-Roman context in which it developed and to which it is also indebted. To examine the early Christian use of didactic hymnody apart from other expressions of didactic hymnody (forms which were surely familiar to the first and second-century Christians) would severely limit our ability to appreciate the dynamics affecting their use of hymnic material, themes, and styles. Likewise, comparisons between Jewish and Greco-Roman expressions of didactic hymnody can shed light on the complex inter-relationship of these cultures, particularly in the Hellenistic period and beyond.[14] Even within one tradition later manifestations of hymnic praise need to be understood in light of hymnic conventions that have been passed down from earlier poets.

Accordingly, the scope of the present volume is a safeguard against isolating each tradition unnecessarily from influencing factors within its surrounding environment. More sharply focused investigations into the deployment of didactic hymnody within one particular tradition or within one particular work will surely continue to be desirable. This volume is intentionally focused more broadly as it aims for the insights that a wide-angle view can generate. As a result of this survey, subsequent specialized studies will be able to position themselves within this larger playing field, as they also add depth, nuance, and/or correction to the findings presented here.

This study offers close readings of specific texts within the context of a broader survey in order to more adequately hear what the texts have to say and to assess their significance as hymns and prayers within a specific community. Our approach is two-fold. On the one hand, we employ a wide-ranging survey and comparative analysis to situate each text within

---

[14] Unfortunately, the comparison of ancient Israelite didactic poetry with the poems and hymns of the Ancient Near East falls outside the scope of even this wide-ranging survey.

some of its larger contexts (literary, cultural, religious, historical, etc.). This approach leads to the overall structure of the work and results in conclusions that go beyond observations about one particular text or tradition, and serves to highlight more general features and trends of didactic hymnody and its functions in the ancient world. On the other hand, we selectively utilize detailed textual analyses of individual hymns, drawing on the tools supplied by a number of critical methodologies. This aspect of our study leads to insights regarding specific texts that arose within specific communities. These close readings of a number of representative texts feed into the comparative analyses with the result that the survey aspect of this volume is not merely descriptive. The broad-ranging survey is itself a means of drawing attention to the complex and multi-faceted use of hymns, prayers, and poems for religious instruction and identity formation in antiquity.

Each of the three main sections of this book explores the phenomenon of didactic hymnody in one major tradition and thereby contributes to a greater appreciation of this instructional method and its deployment over time within that cultural context. Part one (chapters two through four) looks at examples of didactic hymnody from a wide variety of Greco-Roman authors. Since literary and textual evidence in this case does not permit a focus on the development of one specific tradition over time, it is necessary to explore a number of didactic hymns and poems from diverse times and places. The intention is not to create a monolithic picture of "Greco-Roman didactic hymns." Such a picture would likely be more of a distortion of the evidence rather than an accurate reflection of it. Instead, study of examples from many corners of the Greco-Roman world will allow for some significant conclusions about the varied nature and use of didactic hymns in the Greco-Roman world. The Homeric Hymns and the poetry of Hesiod provide a starting point for our considerations since their influence in later Greco-Roman hymnody cannot be over-rated (chapter two). A chapter on the use of didactic hymnody within philosophical settings will show how the medium of hymnic praise, influenced by traditional hymnody, was used to paint a portrait of reality which a student would be invited to embrace (chapter three). A third chapter in this vein explores the Greco-Roman practice of praising exceptional humans, whether victors or rulers, as it developed from Pindar and his victory odes in the fourth century BCE to Pliny the Younger and his *Panegyricus* at the beginning of the second century CE (chapter four). Like the philosophical hymns in the same time period, these praises of human subjects invited listeners to see the world and their place in it in a certain way as the hymn-like praise situated the honoree in the larger context of the divine and human worlds. Such a broad survey will also allow for a greater appreciation of the variety inherent in these didactic compositions as well as the way they functioned within specific social and cultural circumstances. We will see that Greek and Roman hymns contributed to an ongoing process of formation of and reinforcement of a particular communal identity focused on values and ideals that were central to a particular community. In the Greco-Roman world these didactic hymns often related to negotiating the relationship between the human and divine worlds.

The main focus for part two, early Judaism, is the writings of the Second Temple period. However, the hymns and psalms of Second Temple Judaism reflect earlier hymnic and exegetical traditions to such a great extent that they can only be fully appreciated in light of those earlier traditions found in the Hebrew Bible. We therefore devote a chapter to the examination of didactic hymns of the Hebrew Bible as they are found within a number of literary contexts including psalm collections, narratives, Wisdom literature, and prophetic writings (chapter five). As we move on to explore the Jewish writings of the Second Temple period we will encounter further developments in didactic hymnody within the same broad range of genres (chapter six). A specific chapter on didactic hymnody within the Dead Sea Scrolls will enable us to consider the role of instructional psalmody in one specific community (chapter seven). The scope of this section is therefore quite broad in order to adequately explore the phenomenon of Jewish didactic hymns in antiquity. As we examine the broad reach of this tradition we will see that Jewish poets and teachers utilized didactic hymns to reflect on present realities in light of the past, and to situate themselves in the larger story of the ongoing work of the God of Israel among his people.

Part three (chapters eight through ten) explores didactic hymnody within the New Testament and other early Christian writings. The scope of this section is limited to the first two centuries because of the complexity and variety of this material. Drawing, as much of it does, on the earlier Jewish traditions of instructional psalmody, it is important to recognize the extent to which Jewish models are in view and the extent to which Christian writers chart their own paths in this area. In addition, later Christian hymnody is influenced by the New Testament model and the growing canon-consciousness of what Christians will come to conceive of as the Old and New Testaments. Accordingly the focus on the earliest Christian writings (chapter eight on the epistles; chapter nine on gospels and the apocalypse) will be important as foundational work for further study of the employment of didactic hymns and prayers in Christian writings of the second century CE (chapter ten). In particular we will consider the setting of each of these early Christian didactic hymns within the broader cultural context of the Roman Empire. We will see that the early Christians made frequent use of hymnic forms to paint a portrait of reality in which Jesus is the agent of God in God's work of the redemption of humanity.

As we have seen, in surveying and assessing these kinds of didactic hymns, prayers, and religious poetry, it will be necessary to move at the intersection of several spheres of literary and generic categories. Recognition of the level of complexity of the material covered in this study serves as a caution against conclusions which are too neat or too simple. This complexity points to the need for an analytical approach that is multi-faceted and that can be adapted for a variety of texts. It is to such an approach that we now turn.

E. Methodological Considerations

While situating texts by attending to historical-critical issues and issues of genre and literary form, we also draw on some of the insights, sensitivities, and questions raised by reader-response criticism, discourse oriented analysis, mnemohistorical analysis, and performance criticism. These method-ologies provide tools that enable us to consider the ways that hymns and prayers convey meaning, shape the thought-world of their communities, create a portrait of reality, alter the needs and possibilities of their readers, reinforce or challenge cultural norms and values, and/or portray the world to their audiences. In simplest terms, these approaches help us to consider not merely what these texts *say* to their readers or hearers, but also what these texts *do* within their communities. Though this volume is not governed by any one of these methodological approaches, the kinds of questions raised by these types of analyses provide a mix of tools that will be particularly helpful for exploring the wide range of texts under consideration here.

1. Discourse Oriented Analysis and Reader-Response Criticism

One methodological approach that has proven useful for our detailed analyses has been discourse oriented analysis. Two features of discourse oriented analysis which are most helpful in the context of the current study are the focus on the text itself and the concern for the communication from author to hearer.[15] While sources and influences on the text are surely sig-

---

[15] McKnight explains, "Discourse oriented analysis is a productive way of coordinating New Critical and socio-historical emphases. Discourse oriented analysis is an advance on source oriented analysis in that the text is the focus instead of some realities behind the text...The discourse is the center of attention because it embodies the intention of the speaker and guides the response of the hearer," Edgar V. McKnight, *Postmod-*

nificant, this study will place more emphasis on the discourse of the text itself within a particular context and community (or a particular community to the best of our ability to reconstruct it). We will concern ourselves with the multiple levels of meaning that are conveyed in the text, as well as how those meanings are conveyed, and how a reader would have encountered them. One way of approaching discourse analysis is to consider what it means to encounter the world of the text.

The idea of encountering the world of the text is distinct from exploring the religious and cultural world in which the text was composed or read, though these concerns cannot be completely isolated from one another. Nevertheless, by the "world of the text" we refer to the values, worldview, and view of reality that is inscribed in the text and that the text invites the reader or hearer to embrace. The concept is thus more of a literary one than an historical-critical one. McKnight is helpful in outlining some of the features of this issue, distinguishing the world of the text from the facts contained in it, particularly as this relates to biblical texts:

> The sort of knowledge that is provided by the Bible as literature may be seen as different from the sort of knowledge provided by the Bible as theology or history. This is not simply knowledge of facts that can be determined from the biblical narrative and discourses, detached from the texts, and then reattached to dogmatic and historical systems of the reader's own day. The knowledge gained is the kind that is obtained by viewing biblical texts in the light of their integrity as linguistic and literary creations, by examining the world disclosed in the texts and the world of values and meanings presupposed by the world of the text.[16]

In this study we employ this approach specifically with didactic hymns and prayers. We explore what they teach as well as how they teach, what world of values and meanings they presuppose, and what vision of reality they paint for their communities.

The preceding discussion sets the stage for another dimension of this kind of analysis: consideration of how the ancient reader or hearer in his or her community would have experienced and responded to the world of the text. The interaction of text and reader is often an experience that challenges or redefines the reader's understanding of the world. McKnight explains:

> The text often challenges the conceptions and ideologies with which the reader begins, and the reader's world is modified or recreated ideologically. Since world and self do not exist in isolation, however, the reader's self is being redefined in the process. Experience

---

ern *Use of the Bible: the Emergence of Reader-Oriented Criticism* (Nashville: Abingdon Press, 1988), 142–43.

[16] Ibid., 176.

with the text is an experience that alters needs and possibilities. The reader is then creating a world affectively in experience with the text.[17]

By historical and cultural study of the early history of the text in its community, we can explore ways that early readers of the text would have experienced the text with its capacity to recreate their world. This approach has been utilized effectively with psalms and prayers in several contexts (e.g., the *Hodayot* texts from Qumran, Homeric Hymns, and several New Testament hymns). In this study we apply the insights from this kind of analysis to a broader range of ancient didactic hymns. If it is clear that the hymns in this study have an instructional role, this particular method of analysis considers the way the instructional aims of the composition would have impacted the members of the community that read and preserved a given hymn.

Naturally, this aspect of the approach cannot be applied the same way for each text or tradition in this study. For some of our texts, we can recreate and consider an original community or group of communities that would have treasured the composition and been open to receiving its didactic impact. The *Hodayot* hymns of the Qumran community provide such an example. However, for other hymns we are on less firm ground. For instance, the Psalms of the Hebrew Bible were read and studied in numerous communities over many centuries. We could potentially consider the response of a reader/hearer in the time when a given Psalm was composed, in the time when it was collected in the Psalter and used in association with Jewish cult, or in the era when the Psalms were used by Christians in developing their understanding of Jesus. To an individual in each of these different eras, the didactic impact of one Psalm would be experienced in quite different ways.

Other texts present similar challenges with regard to considering their use in a specific hypothetical community. The *Hellenistic Synagogue Prayers* were quite clearly written, used, and edited over a number of generations. They reflect both early Jewish traditions and explicitly Christian concerns that have been overlaid upon the earlier Jewish prayers. In order to appreciate prayers like these, we can consider only the broad religious and cultural milieu in which these were written and adapted. However, we are still able to consider the world of the texts themselves, as this is inherent within the text. From that consideration we can consider how, perhaps as early as the second century, Jewish and Christian communities may have utilized these traditional prayers, and thus how they may have responded to the contents of these texts. For a hymn like Cleanthes' *Hymn to Zeus* we can situate it generally within the period of its composition and

---

[17] Ibid., 177.

within the framework of the philosophical and religious issues faced by early Stoic philosophers. While a more specific setting cannot be ascertained, this method of analysis allows us to consider at least how a Stoic student or potential student may have encountered the world of this particular text.

One result of this discourse oriented approach is that, although it does not resolve it altogether, it minimizes the problematic issue of determining authorial intent. It is quite possible and even likely that many of these hymns came to mean something to later generations that went well beyond anything the original author intended. As an example consider the early Christian use of what some understood as "messianic" Psalms.[18] Another example is seen in some of the non-sectarian prayers preserved in the Dead Sea Scrolls which were presumably used at Qumran because they were seen to lend support to the sectarian views of that community. Regardless of the intention of the original authors, these texts were appropriated by later communities and meant something distinct and important to them. The approach we follow here allows us the possibility of considering the meaning of a text in several contexts, including (when possible) a reconstructed original context. Of particular interest is how the values and teaching inscribed in a given poetic or hymnic text come to be perceived and appreciated by later generations.

2. Mnemohistory and the Construction of Identity

The approach we utilize here bears some resemblance to what Jan Assmann has referred to as mnemohistory, the process of studying the dynamics of cultural memory. He explains, "Unlike history proper, mnemohistory is concerned not with the past as such, but only with the past as it is remembered. It surveys the story-lines of tradition, the webs of intertextuality, the diachronic continuities and discontinuities of reading the past."[19] While Assmann uses mnemohistorical analysis to explore how cultures from ancient to modern times have remembered Moses, the present study is much more broadly conceived. Rather than exploring one particular theme which could be properly studied diachronically, this study explores one of the artistic means by which diverse cultures and peoples have inscribed and passed on their cultural memory: didactic hymnody.

Assmann's methodology opens up the possibility of exploring the meaning and significance of past events for a particular community without con-

---

[18] Donald Juel, *Messianic Exegesis: Christological Interpretation of the Old Testament in Early Christianity* (Philadelphia: Fortress Press, 1988), 99–117.

[19] Jan Assmann, *Moses the Egyptian: The Memory of Egypt in Western Monotheism* (Cambridge, Mass.: Harvard University Press, 1997), 9.

fusing such an approach with an evaluation of the historical reality of the past deeds or events which are being recalled.[20] Alain M. Gowing has recently used this kind of methodology to examine how writers in the early imperial period represented the Republic in their compositions.[21] In each instance, the role of memory appears to have less to do with keeping the facts straight (modern concerns) and more to do with attitudes to the past and present in light of the author's present political and cultural realities under the principate.

Many of the didactic hymns under consideration here are filled with remembrances of past events that provide perspective and meaning to the present reality of the community in which they were composed. Regarding the dynamic function of remembrance Assmann explains,

Seen as an individual and as a social capacity, memory is not simply the storage of past 'facts' but the ongoing work of reconstructive imagination. In other words, the past cannot be stored but always has to be 'processed' and mediated. This mediation depends on the semantic frames and needs of a given individual or society within a given present.[22]

The present study considers this process of constructive imagination as inscribed within a text, together with what we know of the historical circumstances and cultural community in which a text was written and preserved. These texts can thus be explored in terms of what may be called "social memory."[23]

3. Performance-Criticism

Performance criticism is a method of analysis that has potential to illumine some of the texts under consideration here. Various aspects of theatrical, dramatic, and social-drama frameworks have been successfully applied to the songs of the Hebrew Bible that are embedded in narrative contexts.[24] These methodologies have also been applied to the Homeric Hymns and other poems likely composed for public performance. But, since many of

---

[20] Ibid., 14–15.

[21] Alain M. Gowing, *Empire and Memory: The Representation of the Roman Republic in Imperial Culture* (Cambridge: Cambridge University Press, 2005). Regarding Roman *historia*: "Its aim was likewise not so much the accurate or 'truthful' recording of the past as the preservation and even the creation of memory" (11).

[22] Assmann, *Moses the Egyptian*, 14.

[23] For more on this concept see James Fentress and Chris Wickham, *Social Memory* (Oxford, UK: Blackwell, 1992), 1–39. See also Doron Mendels, *Memory in Jewish, Pagan, and Christian Societies of the Graeco-Roman World* (LSTS 45; London: T & T Clark, 2004), esp. chap. 2, "Recycling the Past: Fragmented Historical Memories, Comprehensive and Collected Memories," pp. 30–47; Michael A. Signer, *Memory and History in Christianity and Judaism* (Notre Dame, Ind.: University of Notre Dame, 2001).

[24] Giles and Doan, *Twice Used Songs*.

the hymns and prayers we are looking at were not composed for performance (or their original performative setting is unknown) not all of these compositions lend themselves equally well to performance criticism. Nevertheless, performance criticism does raise some important questions that can be applied to each of our texts, even those that do not suggest a dramatic or theatrical presentation.

The concept of a "performative mode of thought" allows us some leverage to be able to consider how a hearer/reader as audience would respond to the text. The audience is the individual or group that is listening to the reading of the text or reading it directly. Though in most cases we will not be able to concern ourselves with an original performance prior to the written text that we possess, we can consider the performance of the text as it is being read in its context. For example, while it is possible to consider the Johannine hymn (John 1:1–18) as a preexisting hymn which may have been "performed" in a communal worship context (a position which would need to be argued), our concern for what it teaches and how it teaches will be governed by its context as the opening of the Fourth Gospel. Accordingly, the performative mode of thought enables us to consider the reading of the prologue in the context of a reading of the Fourth Gospel. The *Hymn to Christ the Saviour* that concludes Clement of Alexandria's *Paedagogus* could also be examined as a hymn that was performed or sung in some kind of worship or teaching setting. However, we will consider its impact in its literary context as the ending of the *Paedagogus*. In this context, it functions as the conclusion of the performance of reading or hearing the *Paedagogus* as a whole.

4. Multiple Levels of Didactic Impact

The approaches outlined above serve as a set of tools that will help us discern the multiple levels of impact that these complex and multi-faceted hymnic and prayer texts would have had on the readers/hearers. None of these specific approaches are novel in and of themselves. However, when applied together, these approaches help us gain a much richer appreciation for the way these texts would have functioned within the communities that treasured them. These angles also allow us to discern differences in approach and strategy among different texts, as we will see when we begin to compare one text with another within distinct traditions and across traditional lines.

In bringing together the methodological considerations noted above, our approach for assessing the multiple communicative levels of psalms, hymns, and prayers includes the following kinds of questions:

1. The *content* of the text. What does the text say explicitly?
2. The *theology* or *ideology* of the text. What does the content mean as part of a larger system of thought or belief?
3. The *values* inscribed in the text. What does the text say implicitly about who "we" are, what "we" value, and what "we" do?
4. The *conflict* suggested in the text. What competing ideas does the text challenge either explicitly or implicitly?
5. The *vision* of the text. What ultimate picture of reality does the text invite the hearer to embrace? This is where we look not *at* the text, but *with* the text, and consider the picture the author is endeavoring to paint. The vision of the text may relate to the present reality, the future, the community's memory of the past or a combination of these.
6. The *strategy* of the text. How does the text utilize the dynamics of hymn, prayer, or religious poetry to contribute to its context(s)? The strategy of the text is the place where the question of liturgical or other use can be raised, since the performative context of the prayer contributes to a fuller understanding of the strategy of the text.

This brief list, though not exhaustive, highlights the multiple angles from which we assess the hymns and prayers under consideration. While we begin with descriptive considerations related to what the text says and how it says it, this approach enables us to move on to what I take to be the more significant questions of meaning, function, and, ultimately, possible contributions made by the text in the context of an ongoing process of the development of religious and cultural thought within a particular tradition. Taken together, these analytical angles show promise for examining and appreciating the didactic aspects of any given hymn or prayer.

These angles of analysis also provide the possibility of comparing the use of didactic hymnody across cultural lines. This study finds that for Greeks and Romans, as well as for Jews and Christians, the art of the poet and the heart of the teacher converge in these multifaceted texts that I am calling didactic hymns.

F. Classification of Didactic Hymns, Prayers, and Religious Poetry

Didactic hymns create a verbal portrait of reality, whether human or divine, and invite the reader or reciter to locate him or herself within that portrait. As we employ our methodology across a wide-range of didactic hymns in each tradition, we will begin to see patterns and trends. As written compositions these hymns have a number of features which could provide us with several possible means of classifying them according to a system.

In terms of categorizing these texts, the focus and content of the hymn is one place to begin. Didactic hymns can center their content on a number of different planes relative to the one being praised, the individual from which the praise comes, and the community to whom the instruction is directed. In this regard we can also think of multiple registers almost like a variety of keys in which a hymn can be sung. Some hymns will be situated primarily in one register while others will modulate to tap into the dynamics of multiple registers. For our purposes we should be aware of the kinds of chords the hymns strike and the registers in which they are played. The kinds of registers we will observe in many hymns include: temporal register (mythic past, recent past, current events, near future, distant future), spatial/geographical register (earthly spaces such as temples, battlefields, or exile, as well as heavenly spaces), and attributive/narratival register (a focus on attributes of the one being praised or a narration of deeds). We will also consider what we might call the imperative register (degree of focus on the response required of the audience) and cognitive register (direct claims about the nature of reality in light of the claims about the one being praised).

By tapping into a variety of these registers, didactic hymns create a multi-textured vision of reality which the listening or reciting audience is invited to embrace. The performance of the hymn, whether in reading, reciting, chanting, or singing, creates the opportunity for the audience to perceive this vision of reality in what we might call the "deictic moment." The nature of the god, the community, and the larger world is on display at some level through the didactic hymn. At that moment and in light of it, it is possible for the audience members (individually and collectively) to consider how this vision of reality enables them to have a new or renewed perspective on the reality they perceive around them.

1. Temporal Register

One way of classifying these hymns is by attending to the temporal register of each text. Though a didactic hymn functions to provide meaning for the community in the present, its vision may be focused primarily on the mythic past, the recent past, the present, or the future. In terms of temporal register we will observe:

Hymns that bring a vision of the mythic past to bear on the present.[25]
Hymns that craft a portrait of the recent past in a way that reflects on the concerns of the present community.[26]

---

[25] For example the *Hymn to Demeter*; *Hymn to Apollo*; *Hymn to Hermes*; Wis 10; John 1:1–18; the Song of Moses (Deut 32:7); the Prayer for the Time of War in the *War Scroll*.

[26] See Lucretius's praises of Epicurus in *De rerum natura* 5.2–54; Pindar, *Pyth.* 1; Isocrates *Evagoras*; the Song of Moses in Deut 32; *Hel. Syn. Pr.* 7; Sir 44–50; 1QH^a 13:7–21; the Star Hymn of Ignatius (Ign. *Eph.* 19:1–18).

Hymns that create a vision of the present in which the present is infused with divine
   meaning. These may focus more on the community or more on the divine realm.[27]
Those that craft a vision of the future as it relates to the concerns of the present.[28]

In addition, many didactic hymns operate in multiple temporal registers as
part of their overall strategy. For example Hesiod's *Theogony* and *Works
and Days* both reflect the poet's recent past (inspiration by the Muses) and
the mythic past (deeds of Zeus) as well as infusing the present with divine
significance (*Works and Days*, lines 3–8). Aristotle's *Hymn to Virtue* connects the recent past with the mythic past. Cleanthes' *Hymn to Zeus* presents divine reality in the present together with future hope.[29] Some hymns
show an awareness and a confidence that future generations will remember
the one being honored.[30] Interestingly, post-New Testament early Christian
hymns and Gnostic hymns focus on the mythic and recent past but show
little concern for the future.[31]

2. Spatial/Geographical Register

As an aspect of their didactic emphasis, hymns can situate the one being
praised, or the narrative aspect of the praise, in a particular spatial and/or
geographical locale. The Homeric *Hymn to Apollo* manifests a dual focus
on two different oracular sites for the temple of Apollo. Hesiod praises
"high thundering Zeus, who dwells in the loftiest mansions" (*Works and
Days* 8). The Homeric *Hymn to Demeter* describes Demeter's sojourn
among the people of the town of Eleusis. Aratus claims that streets, havens, and market-places are full of Zeus (*Phaen.* 2–4). Pindar's victory
odes in particular situate the victories they describe and the victors who are
praised in very precise geographical locations.

In this regard Horace's *Odes* in praise of Augustus make interesting use
of space. *Odes* IV.5 describes the longing of the Romans when Augustus is
absent, and the blessings they experience when he is present. *Odes* IV.15
describes threats from people of other lands (IV.15, lines 21–24). Pliny can
attribute to the emperor a god-like role in bringing peace between rival cit-

---

[27] For example Lucretius's Hymn to Venus in *De rerum natura* 1.20–53; Callimachus'
Hymn to Zeus; Theocritus, *Encomium of Ptolemy Philadelphus*; Horace *Odes* IV.5 and
15; Pliny's *Panegyricus*; Ps 49; *Pss. Sol.* 5; Bar 3:9–14; *Hel. Syn. Pr.* 7:2; Clement's
Hymn to Christ the Saviour.

[28] See Isa 42:10–13; Horace *Odes* IV.5; Dan 3–4; Tob 13:1–18; Bar 54:21.

[29] Other hymns that tap into multiple temporal registers include John 1:1–18; the
prayers of the Qumran *War Scroll*; Phil 2:6–11; the Magnificat and Benedictus of Luke
1–2; the hymns of Rev 4–5.

[30] See Theocritus, *Encomium of Ptolemy*, 136–137; Pindar, *Pyth.* 1:92–100.

[31] E.g., the Naassene Hymn; *Odes Sol.* 16.

ies as he makes his presence known wherever it is needed (*Panegyricus*, 80.3).

We will see that issues of geographical register figure significantly in the didactic hymns in the Jewish tradition. In biblical texts Isa 42:10–13 calls for praise from sea, plains, and hills. In the book of Daniel, king Nebuchadnezzar acknowledges the sovereignty of God in heaven as well as amongst the inhabitants of the earth (Dan 4:31–32), as does Enoch (1 En 84:2–3a). *Pss. Sol.* 5 shows God's provision in the wilderness to every living thing. Tobit situates God's people in the land of exile, but teaches that even there God will gather his people if they turn to him (13:1–18). Baruch likewise reflects on the location of the people of Israel in exile (Bar 3:9–14). The author of the Qumran *Hodayot* hymns saw himself in the land of exile before God rescued him (1QH^a 13:7–21). Fourth Ezra and many Second Temple Jewish texts tap into both a spatial and temporal register as they recall the exodus from Egypt and the sojourn of the people in the wilderness as a paradigmatic aspect of the past of the people of Israel.[32]

In the Christian traditions several hymns focus on a variety of spatial registers. The hymn in Philippians 2 paints a portrait in which the Lordship of Christ impacts creatures in heaven, on earth, and under the earth. The Gnostic Naassene Hymn pictures a heavenly redeemer, Jesus, who leaves the Father, descends to earth, passing through the aeons, to reveal secrets of the holy way to Psyche. In many instances it can be seen that the use of a particular spatial register, or multiple spatial registers, plays a role in the didactic purposes of the hymn.

3. Attributive/Narratival Register

Another dimension of didactic hymns is the nature of the specific claims being made about the one being praised. Hymns vary greatly in the manner in which they portray the deity or exalted human. Some describe the individual through descriptive phrases and attributes (attributive register). Others employ narratives of varying length to praise the subject through the telling of his or her accomplishments in heaven or on earth (narratival register). As with the other categories of classification, many hymns tap into multiple registers as they seek to engage their audience. For example, the Homeric *Hymn to Demeter* works primarily in the register of descriptive narrative regarding the events in which Demeter was involved from her kidnapping to her establishing of her rites. However, when Demeter reveals herself to humans the hymn taps into the attributive register as she

---

[32] *Fourth Ezra* 9:29; 4Q434 1 i.

claims to be "the honored one, one who is the greatest boon and joy to immortals and mortals" (lines 268–269).[33]

The hymns of the heavenly throne room of Revelation 4–5 connect descriptive attributes with descriptive narrative. The primary attributes ascribed to God are holiness ("Holy, Holy, Holy Lord God Almighty," Rev 4:8b), eternal existence ("who was and who is and who is to come") and worthiness to receive glory, honor, and power (4:11a). The attribute of worthiness is expressly tied to narrative praise: "For you created all things, and according to your will they exist and were created" (Rev 4:11b). Similarly the Lamb is ascribed worthiness (5:9a) in relationship with the narrative of his universal redemptive accomplishments through his death (5:9b–10).

In the letters of Ignatius, the Star Hymn offers its praise and teaching about Christ through descriptive narrative, while the other two hymns in his letters (Ign. *Eph.* 7:2; Ign. *Pol.* 3:2) make their contribution through the description of attributes and characteristics of Christ with little reference to narration of his deeds. By attending to the specific attributive/narratival register of a hymn we can discern a variety of approaches to conveying meaning to the human audience that reads or hears the hymn.

4. Other Registers

Several other registers provide us with some other means of classifying didactic hymns. As we have already noted, didactic hymns vary with regard to whether they make their teaching explicit or allow it to remain implicit and allusive.[34] To the extent that a hymn makes direct claims about reality (direct teaching), we may say that it is tapping into a cognitive register as it engages the thoughts of the audience. Hymns whose instruction is less explicit utilize other more subtle means to convey their teaching, perhaps in ways that may have less cognitive content but more emotive force (e.g., allusion; suggestion; narration).

A related aspect we can consider for purposes of classification and analysis is the manner and extent of the address to the community if there is any explicit recognition of the community at all. For example, Pliny acknowledges an audience and its duties as he asks rhetorically, "Is there any proper return we can make to you to match all you have done for us?"

---

[33] Trans. is from M. L. West, *Homeric Hymns, Homeric Apocrypha, Lives of Homer* (LCL 496; Cambridge, Mass.: Harvard University Press, 2003).

[34] Explicit teaching: "I myself will instruct you" (*Hymn to Demeter* 274); "we are his offspring" (Aratus's hymn to Zeus; *Phaen.* 5); "He is the image of the invisible god" (Col 1:15). Implicit teaching: "as if a god were their leader" (Isocrates *Evagoras* 29); "polluted by no stain, the home is pure" (Horace *Odes* IV.5.21); Aristotle's *Hymn to Virtue*.

(*Panegyricus* 93.3).[35] At times the audience will be addressed directly with imperatives (e.g., Ps 34:11). The degree to which the audience is addressed or exhorted can be considered the imperatival register.

Also significant is the extent to which the hymn employs language or stylistic features that evoke or echo sacred writings or revered traditions of the community. When hymns tap into language that is sacred, they teach (implicitly) the sacred nature of the subject matter. We will see this in both praises of human rulers, and early Christian praises of Christ.

The preceding discussion suggests the wide variety of ways that hymns convey their teaching and gives us some possibilities for classifying texts from diverse traditions, particularly when they utilize a similar combination of strategies. However, the range of possibilities that we have identified (temporal register; spatial register; attributive/narratival register; cognitive register; imperative register) should also caution us against expecting to be able to create an all-encompassing system of a classification. This is even more true when we consider the variety of genres within which we find didactic hymns (free-standing poems and hymns; narrative contexts; epistolary contexts; wisdom writings; didactic poems; philosophical discourses; etc.). So while we will appreciate when different hymns utilize similar strategies for conveying their teaching, we can also recognize the ways the context, contents, and setting of hymns set them apart from one another and reflect the specific needs of a given audience.

G. Summary

In this chapter we have provided a working definition of didactic hymnody, addressed issues relating to identifying didactic hymns, and outlined our approach to this study. We also articulated a methodology for discerning multiple levels of didactic impact. Finally, we noted some possible categories for classifying didactic hymns across the traditions as they tap into a variety of registers to paint their verbal portrait of reality. After we explore some specific texts in these traditions (chapters two through ten), the final chapter of this study will draw together the most significant conclusions with regard to the practice of teaching through song in each tradition. At that time we will review the major themes and approaches of each tradition in light of the broader portrait of ancient didactic hymnody that the volume as a whole has presented. The conclusion will also provide opportunity to reflect on features and themes that were common to all traditions. Taken together, the hymns, prayers, and poems surveyed here will demon-

---

[35] Trans. from Pliny, *Letters and Panegyricus* (trans. Betty Radice; LCL 59; Cambridge: Heinemann, 1969).

strate that the hymn-writers and psalmists of antiquity often kept their human audiences in view even as they appeared to offer praise and prayer to a divine or exalted audience. Teaching through song was not accidental or incidental – it was a central aspect of the creative output of visionaries and teachers in Greek, Roman, Jewish, and Christian traditions.

Chapter 2

Homeric Hymns and Hesiodic Poetry

A. Introduction

The thirty-three hymns associated with Homer and referred to as the Homeric Hymns, together with the major surviving works of Hesiod, provide some of the earliest written witnesses to ancient Greek practices of hymnody as well as Greek understandings of the nature and powers of the gods.[1] As a starting point in our study of didactic hymns, this chapter will explore a few of the dynamics of the Homeric Hymns and Hesiod's poetry, looking specifically at the kinds of lessons these poems offered their audiences. This analysis will also give us some historical and literary perspective so we can observe how the hymns and prayers of later centuries drew on these precedents to accomplish their own time-bound and culturally-situated aims.

Naturally there are a number of lenses that may be used to explore and appreciate the Homeric Hymns and the poetry of Hesiod. The stories or myths about the gods that make up the bulk of the hymns and a good portion of the poetry of Hesiod are one aspect of the value of these hymns. They shed light on ancient understandings of the gods, their attributes, their titles, their abilities, and their gifts to humanity.[2] For example, as we will see the *Hymn to Hermes* narrates Hermes' invention of the lyre and also reveals a number of details about the personalities of the gods and their relationships with one another. The references to the cultic worship of the gods in specific locations are a second angle from which the hymns may be explored. For example, the *Hymn to Demeter* may be read with an ear for the evidence it provides for the Eleusinian mysteries and their prac-

---

[1] Scholars attribute the Homeric Hymns to a variety of anonymous epodes and typically date the Homeric Hymns to the 6th and 7th centuries BCE. Karl Arno Pfeiff, Gerd von der Gönna, and Erika Simon, *Homerische Hymnen* (Tübingen: Stauffenburg, 2002), ix. Glenn W. Most dates the poetry of Hesiod to the end of the 8th or beginning of the 7th centuries BCE. Glenn W. Most, *Hesiod: Theogony, Works and Days, Testimonia* (LCL 57; Cambridge, Mass.: Harvard University Press, 2006), xxv.

[2] These kinds of understandings are also evident in the *Iliad* and the *Odyssey*, though the gods are not the primary focus of those epics. Cf. Emily Kearns, "The Gods in the Homeric Epics," in *The Cambridge Companion to Homer* (ed. Robert Fowler; Cambridge: Cambridge University Press, 2004), 59–73.

tice.[3] Third, the hymns may at times be profitably explored for what they reveal about the political and cultural realities that impacted the lives of the singers or participants in the cult. The *Hymn to Apollo*, with what may be two distinct hymns joined together, can be seen to reflect some very challenging cultural realities during a time when Athens was seeking to assert itself as a center for Greek culture.[4] The pan-Hellenic impulses represented in the *Hymn to Demeter* may likewise reflect similar political and social realities.[5]

But cult, myth, and political context are not all that the hymns offer to the careful reader. The hymns may also be explored for the cultural and societal values and ideals that are inscribed within them. Proper reverence for the gods is certainly paramount among these, but other ideals are represented and taught as well. In this sense Homeric Hymns may be considered not just epic poetry but didactic as well. They teach – both in their story and in their substance – truths, ideals, and morals that Greeks embraced and valued.[6] As Gregory Nagy explains, "The explicitly narrative structure of epic, as is the case with myth making in general, frames a value system that sustains and in fact educates a given society."[7] This understanding of Homer and Hesiod is not a novel one, for at least one ancient reader recognized the value of these poets in articulating the essential ideas of Greek religious thought. Nagy points out, "In the fifth century B.C., Herodotus was moved to observe (2.53.2) that the Greeks owed the systematization of their gods – we may say, of their universe – to two poets, Homer and Hesiod."[8] Nagy goes on to argue that "the poems of Homer and Hesiod were the primary artistic means of encoding a value system common to all Greeks."[9] Reading the Homeric Hymns and Hesiod along these lines of thought, one can consider the hymns in terms of what values and ideals they conveyed to their audiences, and also how they contributed to those audiences' sense of communal identity.

We may also consider what the hymns reveal about the skill of the poet in crafting the hymn; this may include the rhetorical features of the hymn,

---

[3] Other examples may be given as well: the *Hymn to Apollo* describes the festival at Delos (lines 140–164); the *Hymn to Hermes* describes the sacrifice to the twelve Olympian gods (lines 112–137).

[4] Gregory Nagy, *Homer the Preclassic* (University of California, 2009), 10.

[5] Helene P. Foley, *The Homeric Hymn to Demeter: Translation, Commentary, and Interpretive Essays* (Princeton: Princeton University Press, 1994), 169–178.

[6] Though not the focus of this chapter, the *Iliad* and the *Odyssey* themselves also provide a rich repository of cultural and social values inscribed in narrative.

[7] Gregory Nagy, *Greek Mythology and Poetics* (Myth and Poetics; Ithaca, N.Y.: Cornell University Press, 1990), 36–37.

[8] Ibid., 36.

[9] Ibid.

its meter, its form and the way the form is adapted for unique purposes in each instance, as well as what the hymns reveal about the way the poet sees himself.[10] Further, we may find value in thinking about the function of the hymn from several of the vantage points mentioned above: telling a mythological tale in a particular performative context in a particular way can be seen as a means of accomplishing larger political or cultural aims, as we will see. Finally, we can and should also consider the original use of the hymn along with its later use, or how the hymn functions differently over time within the communities that preserved it.

The varied perspectives noted above do not constitute an exhaustive list with respect to how one can read this poetry. But the variety of lenses through which one can view these ancient hymns should be kept in mind as the hymns, their themes, and their purposes, are received and appropriated in later time periods, in different cultural settings, for different purposes. It is in this way that the Homeric Hymns and Hesiodic poems can serve as a starting point for exploring didactic hymnody in the Greco-Roman world. For though they pre-date the later hymns to which this study points, their features, themes, and contents are certainly reflected in later literature. The dynamics that classicists have identified in these hymns continue to be at play in the hymnody of later eras – especially the hymns of the Greek-speaking world. Greeks, Romans, Jews and Christians found themselves in this world – a world which looked to the past for ideals and inspiration for the present.

B. The Homeric Hymns

The collection known as the Homeric Hymns provides a window into a number of aspects of religious thought and poetic practice in the Hellenic world. By considering the didactic aspects of the *Hymn to Demeter*, the *Hymn to Apollo*, and the *Hymn to Hermes*, we will observe several ways that ancient poets created a grand vision of reality with implications for the present even as they recounted deeds of the mythic past. Some comments on the nature of the Homeric Hymns in general will set the stage for more detailed analyses of these three hymns.

Dating from the seventh to the fifth centuries BCE, the Homeric Hymns were composed by anonymous poets in a variety of geographical loca-

---

[10] On the role of the singer (*aoidos*) in Homer in general see, for example, Walter Pötscher, "Das Selbstverständnis des Dichters in der homerischen Poesie," *Literaturwissenschaftliches Jahrbuch* 27 (1986): 9–22; Charles Segal, "Bard and Audience in Homer," in *Singers, Heroes, and Gods in the Odyssey* (ed. Charles Segal; Ithaca, N.Y.: Cornell University Press, 1994), 113–141.

tions.[11] Unlike many hymns that survive from the ancient world the Homeric Hymns were, for the most part, not written as cult hymns; i.e., they were not written to be sung in the context of religious cult.[12] Instead, from both internal and external evidence, it seems that many of the hymns were composed to be performed as preludes to epic poetry recited in the context of competitive performance. Furley and Bremer outline several major reasons for this view.[13] First, most of the hymns conclude with an indication that they will remember the deity as they turn to another song or continue in song. Second, the hymns themselves contain references to competitive performance (e.g., *Hymn to Aphrodite*, 19–20). Third, at least one later writer refers to these hymns as preludes: Thucydides (3.104.4) refers specifically to the Homeric *Hymn to Apollo* as a προοίμιον.[14] Fourth, other writers such as Pindar (*Nem.* 2.1) and ps. Plutarch (*Mus.* 6.1133c) supply evidence that it was customary for competitive singers to sing a hymn at the beginning of their performances in order to secure the favor of a particular deity.[15] Richardson, who also cites the witness of Pindar, summarizes this perspective well when he writes, "It is thus reasonable to conclude that it was customary at a poetic recitation, and perhaps especially in a contest, for the poet to preface his epic narrative with a hymn to whichever deity was appropriate to the place and circumstances of composition."[16] As reasonable as this conclusion may appear, it does require some qualification.

The main problem with this line of thought that sees the Homeric Hymns as a whole as preludes to the recitation of epic poetry is the matter of the length of some of the major hymns. It is difficult to imagine a setting in which the 495 line *Hymn to Demeter* or the 546 line *Hymn to Apollo* could be sung as preludes to another performance. Because of this Allen, Halliday, and Sikes suggested that only the shorter hymns really functioned as preludes to recitations of Homer. Still, they recognized that the formulaic consistency in the opening and closing of the hymns does indeed mark them all as belonging to the same genre. They concluded, "There is

---

[11] M. L. West, *Homeric Hymns, Homeric Apocrypha, Lives of Homer* (LCL 496; Cambridge, Mass.: Harvard University Press, 2003), 5–6.

[12] William D. Furley and Jan Maarten Bremer, *Greek Hymns: Selected Cult Songs from the Archaic to the Hellenistic Period* (2 vols.; STAC 9–10; Tübingen: Mohr Siebeck, 2001), 1:41.

[13] Ibid., 1:41–42.

[14] For full discussion of references to the Homeric Hymns in antiquity, as well as the significance of these references, see T. W. Allen, W. R. Halliday, and E. E. Sikes, *The Homeric Hymns* (Reprint of 1936 ed.; Amsterdam: Adolf M. Hakkert, 1980), lxiv–lxxxii.

[15] Furley and Bremer, *Greek Hymns*, 1:41–42.

[16] N. J. Richardson, *The Homeric Hymn to Demeter* (Oxford: Clarendon Press, 1974), 4.

nothing incongruous in supposing Homerid rhapsodes at one time prefac-
ing their recital of portions of Homer with invocatory verses of their own,
and at another reciting, at ἀγῶνες and festivals, longer independent compositions in honour of the God of the place."[17] This caveat allows for the
complexity of the hymns, their varying length, and the likelihood that their
individual idiosyncrasies may reflect the fact that they were composed and
performed in a wide range of settings.[18]

The debate over the genre and occasion of the Homeric Hymns, since
they are preserved as a collection, is largely due to our lack of concrete
knowledge about the original use of the hymns as well as the disparity in
length of the hymns. As a way of moving past this issue, Nagy has suggested that the Homeric Hymns, as closely related to epic as they are, may
have developed in a way similar to epic poetry. In other words, just as epic
narratives evolved, and were expanded and embellished over time, it is
possible that the same process could have occurred with some of the
hymns originally composed as preludes.[19] In this regard he compares the
Theogony of Hesiod with the Homeric Hymns, noting that all the hymns,
even the longest ones, still maintain the formal characteristics of a prelude.
He explains, "Despite the monumental size of the larger *Hymns*, however,
the point remains that they maintain the traditional program of a functional
prelude, one that is worthy of pan-Hellenic performance."[20] The traditional
program of a prelude includes:

1. The invocation proper; naming of the god.
2. Application of the god's epithets, conveying either explicitly or implicitly his/her effi-
cacy on the local level of cult.
3. A description of the god's ascent to Olympus, whereby he/she achieved pan-Hellenic
recognition.
4. A prayer to the god that he/she be pleased with the recognition that has been accorded
him/her so far in the performance.
5. Transition to the rest of the performance.[21]

Not all of the Homeric Hymns contain these elements in the same propor-
tion or to the same extent. Some hymns omit the narrative portion (#3 in
this list) while others do not contain a prayer or request (#4 in this list).
Nevertheless, there is enough consistency in the collection to suggest that
formally they belong to the same genre. Nagy's observations help us to see
how the Homeric Hymns, even the longest and most fully developed, are

[17] Allen, Halliday, and Sikes, *The Homeric Hymns*, xcv.
[18] Along these lines, Furley and Bremer do recognize that the hymns' identification as
preludes does not preclude the possibility that they could indeed have been performed at
occasions other than rhapsodic competitions. Furley and Bremer, *Greek Hymns*, 1:43.
[19] Nagy, *Greek Mythology and Poetics*, 54.
[20] Ibid.
[21] Ibid., 55.

closely related to one another and participate in the conventions of hymnic preludes.

Having spoken in general about the nature of the Homeric Hymns and where they fall on a spectrum of ancient hymnody, preludes, and poetic texts, it is possible now to move beyond those observations in order to explore the specific didactic emphases of select hymns. Consideration of the nature of the hymns and their generic characteristics is but one of several important steps in achieving this goal. In addition, the time and place of performance is also quite significant in assessing the didactic impact of a given hymn. Certain hymns, due to their performative context and their subject matter, more directly reflect on a particular set of issues and thus lend themselves to "teaching" different kinds of lessons and functioning in different ways.

In the survey that follows, we will see how within the framework of a prelude the hymns convey perspective on ritual aspects of ancient Greek life (mystery rites, sacrificial rites, festivals, banquets, hymnic performances, etc.). Though they do not always necessarily teach directly about these kinds of events, the way in which these events are incorporated into larger narratives about the god or goddess with whom they have to do often does have an implicit teaching function. A narrative about the origin of a ritual reinforces and reminds the hearers that these ritual aspects that are part of their lives are full of deep and timeless significance since they find their origins in the actions and purposes of the gods themselves. By skillfully incorporating the rituals themselves into mythic tales of the gods, the poets effectively remind the listeners that the very much time-bound and spatially-limited activities (whether a banquet, a sacrifice, or a festival) are actually part of a larger reality. These ritual activities bring humans into contact with the realm of the divine and bridge the gap between the human world and the world of the immortal gods.

Aside from whatever ritual experiences are reflected in the hymns, the narratives themselves teach directly about the gods and goddesses. At the simplest level they reveal the names, attributes, and characteristics of the gods. They bring into focus the strengths, abilities, and special areas of influence with which each god or goddess is concerned. At a more profound level the narratives also explain why things are the way they are in the current era. Clay observes, "Each hymn describes an epoch-making moment in the mythic chronology of Olympus and, as such, inaugurates a new era in the divine and human cosmos. The state of the cosmos at the end of each of the hymns differs from that at its beginning; the intervening narrative explains the character of that change and how it came about."[22] In this sense the hymns are seen to be overtly theological, "containing some of the most sustained and systematic theological speculation of the archaic period."[23] Within the Olympian framework the narratives reveal the appropriate manner for humans to avail themselves of the god's blessings in the era inaugurated by the birth of the god. At this point, of course, the theology of the hymns spills over into the sphere of ritual again, for these rites and practices are the primary means of securing the blessing of the god.

Along with explicit teaching about the gods and their rites through direct statement, or implicit teaching through narrative, the hymns also instruct as their content is adapted by the singer and brought into the context of a specific performance at a specific place and time. As Nagy reminds, "The medium of transmitting the Homeric and Hesiodic poems was consistently that of performance, not reading. One important traditional context of poetic performance was the institution of pan-Hellenic festivals, though there may well have been other appropriate public events as well."[24] For example, Plato's *Ion* recounts the story of a singer who traveled to Athens to compete in the festival known as the Panathenaia.[25] An awareness of the context of the performance of each hymn brings the themes and expression of the hymn into contact with political and social realities – factors which are notoriously difficult for modern readers to appreciate. Regardless of the difficulty, it will be useful to at least consider the scholarly reconstruction of the performative contexts of each hymn and the political and cultural dynamics that would have come into play in the complex interaction between singer, song, audience, and setting.

Related to the specific context of the performance are the broader cultural realities affecting the cities of the Hellenic world. Clay notes the emergence of a unifying impulse or "centripetal force" among the diverse Greek cities in the eighth century BCE. She explains,

It manifests itself in the emergence of the great Panhellenic shrines, like Olympia, Delphi, Delos, and Eleusis, which draw Greek speakers from every city and community. It also manifests itself in the great Panhellenic epics of Homer and Hesiod and, above all, in the creation of a Panhellenic Olympian religion.[26]

The Homeric Hymns very much reflect these cultural dynamics in their tendency to treat the gods and goddesses from a pan-Hellenic perspective

---

[22] Jenny Strauss Clay, *The Politics of Olympus: Form and Meaning in the Major Homeric Hymns* (2nd ed.; Bristol Classical Paperbacks; London: Bristol Classical, 2006), 15.

[23] Ibid., 267.

[24] Nagy, *Greek Mythology and Poetics*, 38.

[25] Ibid.

[26] Clay, *The Politics of Olympus*, 9.

in contrast to a specific localizing perspective. Along these lines Nagy observes,

[Homeric poetry] synthesizes the diverse local traditions of each major city-state into a unified pan-Hellenic model that suits the ideology of the polis in general, but without being restricted to the ideology of any one polis in particular. Perhaps the clearest example is the Homeric concept of the Olympian gods, which incorporates yet goes beyond the localized religious traditions of each polis; the pan-Hellenic perspective of Homeric poetry has transcended local phenomena such as the cult of gods, which is functional only on the local level of the polis.[27]

With this understanding in mind, it is possible to consider how even the perspective of the hymn may serve as a vehicle of instruction, providing a certain theological outlook that was not necessarily inherent in the origins of the mythical narrative itself.

1. Hymn to Demeter

One of the longest of the Homeric Hymns, the 495 line *Hymn to Demeter* is unique among the Homeric Hymns for a number of significant reasons. Its themes and its contents relate to an important sacred narrative that was widely accepted by the Greeks, namely, the story of Demeter and Persephone. In addition to its narrative force, its contents shed light on a number of aspects of ancient Greek life and thought, dating as it does to the late seventh or early sixth century BCE.[28] Allen, Halliday, and Sikes comment, "Great as is the poetical value of the Hymn, perhaps its chief interest lies in the fact that it is the most ancient document bearing on the Eleusinian mysteries."[29] Though there are many angles from which this hymn has been explored and could be explored, this section will explore the *Hymn to Demeter* with an ear to what may be learned about its didactic function.

While this hymn was most certainly composed to be sung and performed, possibly as the rites of the mysteries were being practiced, the hymn itself provides instruction on several levels. Two are of great importance here, among others. First, the hymn teaches about the nature of the gods as well as the relationship between gods and humans. It conveys a very clear theological perspective. Second, and closely related, the hymn teaches about the origins of the Eleusinian mysteries and sheds light on their practice. Thus, in terms of its teaching, the hymn has both an aetiological function as well as a (broadly) theological one.

---

[27] Nagy, *Greek Mythology and Poetics*, 10.
[28] West, *Homeric Hymns*, 9. West dates the *Hymn to Demeter* to the first half of the sixth century. For a dating at the end of the seventh century see Pfeiff, Gönna, and Simon, *Homerische Hymnen*, 95.
[29] Allen, Halliday, and Sikes, *The Homeric Hymns*, 118.

In addition, though not as directly related to the purposes of this study, the hymn sheds light on women's roles in some ancient Greek religious practices, as well as indirectly on women's experience in general (e.g., suffering, powerlessness, marriage, child-rearing, mother-daughter relationships, etc.).[30] It also exhibits a pan-Hellenic outlook reflective of the dynamic of social and political changes going on in the period in which the hymn was recited and adapted. Though these last two issues (women and pan-Hellenic) are not directly related to didactic emphases, they do serve to instruct by their very presence in the hymn, and thus are worth considering here as well. After a brief synopsis of the hymn, each of the above points will briefly be examined below.

The *Hymn to Demeter* opens in a manner typical of Homeric Hymns with the singer identifying the goddess about whom he will sing (lines 1–3).[31]

Of Demeter the lovely-haired, the august goddess first I sing,
Of her and her slender-ankled daughter, whom Aidoneus
seized. (lines 1–3)

From here the hymn leads immediately into the narrative portion of the hymn which is set in the mythic past (lines 3–489). Lines 3–37 recount the manner in which Persephone was given unwillingly to Hades. Beginning in line 38 Demeter begins to search for Persephone after discovering what has happened. Demeter, in deep grief, withdraws from the company of the gods and enters the world of humanity, coming eventually to Eleusis and taking on a disguise. The daughters of Keleos meet her at a well and invite her to their home where she remains in disguise and consents to care for and raise the infant Demophoön (lines 105–241). Demophoön thrives under Demeter's care, and we learn that he was on the way to becoming immortal himself until his mother intervened, angering Demeter (lines 231–254). At this point Demeter begins the speech in which she reveals her true identity and instructs the people to build a temple and perform the rites that she will reveal:

For I am Demeter the honored one, who is the greatest
boon and joy to immortals and mortals.
Now, let the whole people build me a great temple with an altar
below it, under the citadel's sheer wall,
above Kallichoron, where the hill juts out.

---

[30] For a fuller development of these ideas see Ross Shepard Kraemer, *Her Share of the Blessings: Women's Religions among Pagans, Jews and Christians in the Greco-Roman World* (New York: Oxford University Press, 1992), 24–29.

[31] Unless otherwise indicated, line numbers and translations of the Homeric Hymns are from West, *Homeric Hymns*.

As to the rites, I myself will instruct you on how in future
you can propitiate me with holy performance. (lines 268–275)

After the speech, Demeter reveals her glory and the family responds (lines
275–293). The people of Eleusis obey and build the temple (lines 293–
302), while Demeter remains aloof from the immortals, wasting away in
grief, and bringing a horrible famine upon the earth (lines 303–309).

At this point in the narrative, Zeus takes notice and sends Iris to persuade Demeter to rejoin the immortals (lines 310–333). When this approach fails, Zeus dispatches Hermes to bring Persphone back from Hades
(lines 334–341). Hades allows her to go but stealthily gives her a pome-
granate seed to eat, thus ensuring that she would return to the underworld
(lines 342–385). After their reunion (lines 386–440), the hymn recounts
the arrangement that Zeus makes for Persephone to be with her mother for
two-thirds of the year and to be with Hades one-third of the year (lines
441–469). Through the mediation of Rheia, Demeter accepts the arrangement, allowing crops to grow again and revealing the mysteries to the
kings (lines 470–479). The singer expounds on the blessings of those who
participate in these rites (lines 480–482), then recounts the return of the
goddesses to Olympus (lines 483–486). The singer returns to the blessings
given by the goddesses (lines 486–489), then transitions to the final two
elements typical of Homeric Hymns: a request (lines 490–494) and a transition to further singing (line 495).

While this rich hymn touches on a number of issues (marriage, mother-
hood, women's roles, relationships between the gods and humans, etc.) its
primary focus is on placing the origins of the Eleusinian mysteries within
the mythical tradition of Demeter and Persephone. Thus the hymn recounts
a story about the goddesses that results in the revelation of the mysteries to
humanity. As a multifaceted composition, the hymn taps into multiple
temporal and spatial registers. In this regard Foley has pointed out the way
that the hymn concerns itself with two kinds of events: those that occur on
the divine sphere and those that occur in the human realm. For example,
the divine sphere is considered in lines 3–89, and 310–470 (and arguably
483–486 as well). Events in the human realm are discussed in lines 90–
309. Lines 471–494 consider how humans can enjoy the blessings of the
gods through divinely established means and thus address both the human
and divine realm at the same time. Foley notes that the poem is "framed" at
the beginning and end by the divine story: "The structure of the poem thus
emphasizes the primacy of the framing divine story, the intersection between divine and mortal experience in the central episode, and the final
result of that intersection, the Mysteries."[32] One lesson of the hymn is that,

---

[32] Foley, *The Homeric Hymn to Demeter*, 83.

though humans and gods may have had direct interactions in the mythic past, the present means for securing the blessing of the goddess is through participation in the rites Demeter established.

This lesson is illustrated in Demeter's failure to immortalize De-mophoön. Because of Demeter's care for the child, the child "grew miracu-lously fast; he was like the gods" (241). However, when Metaneira spies and sees Demeter placing Demophoön in the fire, she cries out, causing Demeter in anger to cast the child to the ground. Demeter, in her anger, says, "I would have made your child immortal and ageless forever; I would have given him unfailing honor. But now he cannot escape death and the death spirits" (lines 260–262). All this because mortals are ignorant and foolish and "incurably led by [their] folly" (lines 256–258). On this ex-change Foley observes, "The Demophoön episode sets the stage for the Mysteries, in that Demeter has failed to immortalize a mortal and can only mitigate death by another route."[33] In the end, the rites are the key to a bet-ter lot in the next life: "Blessed is he of men on earth who has beheld them, whereas he that is uninitiated in the rites, or he that has had no part in them, never enjoys a similar lot down in the musty dark when he is dead" (lines 480–482).[34] Thus it may be seen that an implicit didactic aim of the story itself is to point to the divinely appointed means for experiencing the blessing of the goddess, a blissful immortality. More direct means of con-tact with the gods are not possible due to the folly of mortal perspectives that cannot understand or appreciate the presence of divine power. The rites are sufficient, appropriate, and themselves a gift from the goddess.

With regard to these rites, the *Hymn to Demeter* is our earliest written source relating to the Eleusinian mysteries, widely recognized as the most significant and influential of the Greek mystery cults of antiquity.[35] Foley explains, "The *Hymn*, like many of the hymns, is an aetiological poem; that is, it explains how Demeter and Persephone came to have the honors that they have in the universe and how the Mysteries were founded."[36] What does it reveal about these honors? Allen, Halliday, and Sikes give this cau-tious answer:

Of the actual details of this, the most famous religious ceremony of antiquity, very little is known. About the preliminary proceedings up to the moment of the arrival of the pro-

---

[33] Ibid., 48.
[34] For further discussion of the relationship between Demophoön and the mystery ini-tiate see Ibid, 48–50.
[35] Ibid., 64–65.
[36] Ibid., 84.

cession of worshippers from Athens at Eleusis we are fairly well informed, but as to what took place at the great service of the *telesterion* we are almost completely in the dark.[37]

Hints of rites associated with the Eleusinian mysteries may be seen in the hymn, but other than the two passages announcing their institution, there can be little certainty that any feature of the poem reflects a rite of the mysteries.[38] Determining the substance of the rituals or the "content" of the mysteries remains difficult because of the emphasis on secrecy within the mysteries together with the fact that many of our earliest sources are from those hostile to the mysteries. Nevertheless, as Foley notes, "It seems clear then, that the secret rites did not pass on any secret doctrine or worldview or inculcate beliefs, but that its blessings came from experiencing and viewing signs, symbols, stories, or dramas and bonding with fellow initiates."[39] It is this ritual experience that the hymn reflects at times.

The experiential aspect of the mysteries is emphasized in a number of places. One is in the way the poem emphasizes seeing. Foley notes, "The *Hymn* privileges seeing, and especially seeing with understanding and pleasure, over hearing, and the highest level of initiation in the Mysteries is *epopteia*, or seeing."[40] For example, the scene in which the daughters of Keleos *see* Demeter by the well (line 105) is bracketed by references to the difficulty that humans have *seeing* and recognizing gods and goddesses (line 94–95, 111).[41] Emphasizing the importance of seeing, line 480 reads, "Blessed is the mortal on earth who has seen these rites." Foley notes, "Both Demeter and mortals progress toward sight/insight in the course of the poem."[42] What exactly the initiates would have seen in the practice of the rites is not known, though ancient sources make it clear that the rites did indeed involve seeing some secret image.[43] Aside from seeing, ancient sources reveal that the Eleusinian mysteries involved a number of other preparatory and purifying practices. References to these experiential ritual

---

[37] Allen, Halliday, and Sikes, *The Homeric Hymns*, 118. Foley concurs, "The Hymn itself refers in detail only to the mythical origins of preliminary rites at Eleusis that could be revealed to outsiders and culminates with the founding of the cult and veiled references to the promises it offered to the initiate," Foley, *The Homeric Hymn to Demeter*, 65.

[38] Allen, Halliday, and Sikes, *The Homeric Hymns*, 120.

[39] Foley, *The Homeric Hymn to Demeter*, 70.

[40] Ibid., 39.

[41] For further examples, see Ibid., 38–39.

[42] Ibid., 39.

[43] See the collection of relevant documents in Marvin W. Meyer, *The Ancient Mysteries: A Sourcebook* (Philadelphia: University of Pennsylvania Press, 1999), 18–19.

practices of the mysteries may be seen in lines 47–48, 211, 371–373, though the exact connection with actual rites is debated.[44]

Aside from providing insight into the mysteries and into Greek thought, the *Hymn to Demeter* also provides some insight into the pan-Hellenic impulse that was developing during this time period.[45] This is seen most clearly in a tendency to appeal to what was common in Hellenic culture as opposed to what was local and unique. Foley has explored the nature of the *Hymn to Demeter* as pan-Hellenic poetry and points out a number of pan-Hellenic qualities of the hymn.[46] First, in general we are aware of a pan-Hellenic movement in poetry by the end of the eighth century BCE when the major Homeric epics were composed. Second, by emphasizing the collective nature of Demeter's gifts to humanity rather than one particular group of people, the poem itself supports the idea that it was written for more than just a local audience. Third, this version of the Hymn does not necessarily oppose local myths, but presents the myth in a way that would appeal to more than just a local Eleusinian audience. Along these lines one can note the archaizing style of the poem, which accounts for its lack of any mention of Athens.[47] Foley writes, "The Panhellenic context in which the Homeric hymns were probably presented would further encourage an archaic Greek poet to avoid or downplay regional versions of the myth and local details."[48] Further, the hymn "deftly avoids choosing among different local claims about which mortals were the first to inform and help the goddess, through bypassing that version altogether in favor of divine witnesses

---

[44] For example, the account in lines 47–48 may be more closely associated with the *Thesmophoria* than with the Eleusinian mysteries themselves. Cf. Allen, Halliday, and Sikes, *The Homeric Hymns*, 136–137.

[45] Nagy provides a concise definition of this concept of pan-Hellenic together with the role of the anonymous performers of Homeric poetry: "This process of ever widening dissemination [of forms of oral poetry that correspond to what was later known as Homeric and Hesiodic poetry], in the context of ongoing recomposition-in-performance, can be described as pan-Hellenization. Correspondingly, the poets who were identified with these forms of poetry, Homer and Hesiod, became more and more pan-Hellenic" (4). Nagy is careful to point out, however, that the term pan-Hellenic in the context of Homeric and Hesiodic poetry and performance is used in a relative sense, not an absolute one. Nagy explains, "To relativize pan-Hellenic is to recognize that the pan-Hellenization of Homer and Hesiod, just like other aspects of pan-Hellenism, cannot be described in absolute terms of universalization. Despite the totalizing ideology implicit in the term pan-Hellenic, the pan-Hellenization of Homer and Hesiod was not an absolute: it was merely a tendency toward a notional absolute;" Gregory Nagy, "Hesiod and the Ancient Biographical Traditions," in *Brill Companion to Hesiod* (ed. A. Rengakos and Ch. Tsagalis; Leiden: Brill, 2008), 4–5. The term itself is actually used in Hesiod, *Works and Days* 528 referring to "all the Greeks."

[46] Foley, *The Homeric Hymn to Demeter*, 175–178.

[47] Ibid., 169–175.

[48] Ibid., 176.

and locating the abduction at the ends of the earth."[49] For example, one can observe that in line 17 the location of the abduction is vague and mythical as opposed to later versions of the myth which place it in thirteen different sites.[50]

Reading the *Hymn to Demeter* in light of this pan-Hellenic trend allows readers to appreciate the number of levels on which the hymn functioned. While teaching the origins of the Eleusinian mysteries, the hymn also presumably served to teach and attract Greeks from nearby Athens and beyond to become initiates into the mysteries. Clay's insights about the doctrinal dynamics at work in the hymn are relevant here, particularly in light of the fact that Demeter is a chthonic deity and, as such, was excluded form the Olympians. She notes,

> Eleusis always offered a potential antagonism to Olympus, and its doctrine posed a possible threat to the Olympian *theologoumenon*, as is abundantly confirmed by the later adoption of Eleusis by the anti-Olympian Orphics and other sects. As a whole, the *Hymn to Demeter* may be understood as an attempt to integrate, and hence absorb, the cult of Demeter and the message of Eleusis into the Olympian cosmos.[51]

Obviously, this kind of teaching is more implicit than explicit, but an awareness of cultural, social, and political trends that were at play during the time when this poem was performed helps us to hear both the explicit teaching and the implicit teaching as well. Given the complex and polyvalent ways that the hymn communicates its meaning, it is probably more accurate to speak of didactic functions as well as political/rhetorical functions. While these may merge at times, in most instances the political/rhetorical functions (such as legitimizing claims to cultural dominance or universalizing local traditions for trans-local purposes) are more subtle than the explicit didactic aims. The political/rhetorical functions also require more subjective hypotheses to discern their existence and their significance.

2. Hymn to Apollo

The *Hymn to Apollo* is perhaps the oldest hymn in the collection of Homeric Hymns.[52] It is commonly dated to the early sixth century BCE, though dating the hymn is difficult since it appears to join together two hymns of differing dates and origins.[53] As was the case with each of the Homeric hymns, the *Hymn to Apollo* was a hymn that was performed and thus came

---

[49] Ibid., 177.

[50] Ibid., 36.

[51] Clay, *The Politics of Olympus*, 265.

[52] Allen, Halliday, and Sikes, *The Homeric Hymns*, 183.

[53] Pfeiff, Gönna, and Simon, *Homerische Hymnen*, 111; West, *Homeric Hymns*, 10.

to life in the context of a socially situated event. Though the exact nature of the performative event at which it was sung is not known, readers can discern didactic emphases and major themes that, regardless of the imagined performance setting, would likely have been a part of the impact of the hymn. Like the *Hymn to Demeter* the Homeric *Hymn to Apollo* can be viewed from a number of different angles, each of which yields significant insights into aspects of Greek thought, worship, and political history. It also presents its own share of mysteries as to how it was composed and how it came to reach its current form. After a short synopsis of the *Hymn to Apollo*, this section examines the hymn from several vantage points. First, I explore the explicit teaching of the hymn in terms of its narrative and the function of that narrative within the whole, noting that the instructional emphasis relates primarily to the cult and the founding of places of worship of Apollo. Second, I reflect on the theological perspective of the hymn which addresses to some extent the idea of prophecy in the Hellenic world. Third, I comment on the political realities that may be reflected in this hymn which appears to be two hymns joined together. This analysis will show that, by means of a hymnic form which taps into multiple temporal, spatial, and cognitive registers, the *Hymn to Apollo* affirms a pan-Hellenic Apollo who is able to dispense counsel to humankind through his oracular sites.

The *Hymn to Apollo* begins with the hymnist's declaration to remember Apollo, who is first presented to the reader in a scene in which he is welcomed home at Zeus' house (1–18). The hymn opens in the present tense temporal framework of the poet:

Let me call to mind and not neglect Apollo the far-shooter,
at whose coming the gods tremble in Zeus' house. (lines 1–2)

After the introduction, what appears to be a Delian hymn (i.e., a hymn performed at Delos in honor of Apollo)[54] begins with a narrative about the mythic past that runs from line 19 through line 164. The narrative opens with a typical question on the part of the singer:

How shall I hymn you, fit subject as you are in every respect? (line 19)

In the following narrative Leto chooses Delos as the place to give birth to Apollo, thus placing a particular emphasis on geographical locale. Once he is born and eats of the divine food, Apollo speaks of his inventions and benefactions to mankind including the lyre, the bow, and prophecy (lines 131–132). At the end of this narrative is a colorful description of the Delian festival in honor of Apollo (lines 140–164). This particular hymn ends (or gives the appearance of ending) with a request that the god would be

---

[54] West, *Homeric Hymns*, 9.

favorable and allow the singer to be remembered by the celebrants as their favorite singer (lines 165–178).

The second of two hymns within this larger composition begins in a very similar way to the first with a general description of the joy of the gods over Apollo after he goes from Delos to Pythos and then returns to Olympus (lines 179–206). At line 207 the singer repeats the question that opened the first hymn:

How shall I hymn you, fit subject as you are in every respect? (line 207)

The narrative of the hymn then focuses on how Apollo chose a site for his oracle at Delphi, the spatial register again shifting from the heavenly to the earthly realm. The hymn discusses a number of places that Apollo did not choose for a variety of reasons (lines 216–277). He ultimately declares where he will build his temple and will "dispense unerring counsel to them all, issuing oracles in my rich temple" (lines 292–293). The narrative shifts to discuss how Apollo shot Typhaon with his bow, how Pythos thereby received its name, and also how Apollo receives honor in Telphousa under the title Telphousios (lines 300–387). The remainder of the hymn recounts Apollo's selection of his servants, how he took the form of a dolphin, jumped on board a ship, and commissioned the sailors to become his servants (lines 388–543). The hymn concludes with an ending that is typical of the Homeric Hymns:

So I salute you, son of Zeus and Leto.
And I will take heed both for you and other singing. (lines 545–546)

From a straightforward reading of the text it is evident that the hymn as a whole has a strong emphasis on explaining the origins of the worship of Apollo at both Delos and Delphi. The rich description of the festival in honor of the god at Delos (lines 146–164) provides a glimpse into the dynamics of the performative setting of this and other Homeric Hymns. Singing, dancing, boxing, processions involving the participation of men, women, and children were all a part of the setting in which the hymn would have been performed. Likewise, Apollo's instructions to his newly recruited temple servants (lines 474–501; 531–544), and the description of their actions (lines 502–519) reflect aspects of the cult in honor of Apollo at Delphi. The celebration would have included sacrifice, prayer, libation, feasting, singing, dancing, and processions. One can imagine that the recitation of a hymn (or hymns) like this at a festival in honor of Apollo would serve several purposes. First, the performance of the hymn itself would be a part of the festivities and presumably a source of joy and even pride for those listening (lines 160–161). Second, the content of the hymn would reinforce the importance of all the external aspects of the celebration. Third, it would remind the hearers that what they are doing is rooted in tradition that is grounded in the past of their cultural memory. West suggests that the precise setting for this particular hymn would have been the combined Delian and Pythian festival on Delos in honor of Apollo in 523 BCE, held by Polycrates.[55] Whether this is correct or not, one can at least imagine that a setting like that would be the kind that would allow for a multi-faceted hymn like the *Hymn to Apollo*.[56]

In spite of the references to aspects of the cult of Apollo, the primary concern of the hymn is not necessarily with providing the origins of a set of cultic practices. Nevertheless, the hymn can still be considered aetiological, though in a manner somewhat different from that of the *Hymn to Demeter* with its explanations of various ritual activities relative to the Eleusinian mysteries. Miller explains, "The poet's interest lies not in the particularities of Delphic rite and custom but in the general question of how and why, in what spirit and with what purpose the Pythian oracle was founded."[57] In other words, it answers the question as to why Delos and Delphi were cult centers of Apollo. In the context of this interest, the narrative about the birth and early days of Apollo are included in the hymn as a way of setting the stage for the climax of the hymn, the founding of the Delphic oracle.

The *Hymn to Apollo* conveys a distinct theological perspective, particularly as it relates to the benefactions of Apollo and human access to divine revelation. Certainly his association with the lyre and music is affirmed (line 131; 179–206), as is his identification with archery (lines 1–13). Clay points out the "triple *timai*", the three honors which Apollo takes for himself, and how these feature in the narrative. Shortly after Apollo is born and eats of the divine food he declares, "I want the lyre and the crooked bow as my things. And I shall prophesy Zeus' unerring will to humankind" (lines 131–132). Though all three *timai* are affirmed in the hymn, perhaps the most significant as it relates to human interaction with the gods is his association with prophecy. Clay points out the way that Apollo's declaration "has important consequences for both gods and men."[58] As for the gods, she notes, Apollo "allies himself unambiguously with his Father and the Olympian regime whose spokesmen he will be."[59] As for humanity, Apollo will be a mediator between Zeus and mortals, bringing to an end

---

[55] Ibid., 11. See also Nagy, *Homer the Preclassic*, 13–14.

[56] More than a century later, Thucydides' quotes from the *Hymn to Apollo* as he describes in detail the festival at Delia in 426 and how it is not an innovation but rather a revival of an ancient festival. Nagy, *Homer the Preclassic*, 8–12.

[57] Andrew M. Miller, *From Delos to Delphi: A Literary Study of the Homeric Hymn to Apollo* (Mnemosyne 93; Leiden: Brill, 1986), x–xi.

[58] Clay, *The Politics of Olympus*, 44.

[59] Ibid.

the era in which mortals lived in ignorance of the divine will.[60] The hymn, as it recounts the birth of Apollo and the new order it initiates, reinforces the supreme rule of Zeus as it teaches a theological lesson about how humans can access the will of Zeus.

The details of the narratives relating to the cultic sites of Apollo likewise emphasize the oracular power of Apollo. When Leto announces to Delos that it will be the site for the birth of Apollo, Delos makes a request. She asks that the goddess would "swear a powerful oath that this will be the first place he makes his beautiful temple to be an oracular site for men, and that (only) after that (will he go) all over the world, since indeed his name will be widely known" (lines 79–82). This request reflects the reality that there were of course many temples in which Apollo could be honored and his oracles secured; it is therefore a way of asserting the priority of the temple at Delos. Behind this apologetic effort on behalf of Delos stands the widely held belief that Apollo was the god of divination who had founded certain locations for seeking the divine will in this way.[61] This understanding is reiterated elsewhere in the hymn as well. In seeking a site for his oracle he tells Telphousa, "Here I am minded to make my beautiful temple as an oracle for humankind. . . . And I would dispense unerring counsel to them all, issuing oracles in my rich temple" (lines 247–254). He makes the exact same declaration at Crisa (lines 287–293), thus emphasizing by repetition a primary point of the hymn. As far as its teaching then, the hymn explicitly reinforces a particular view of Apollo, his gifts, and the benefactions associated with him. Humans can obtain unerring counsel by seeking Apollo in the prescribed manner.

Beyond the specific actions of the cultic worship of Apollo or the origins of the oracle at Delphi, a prominent feature of the hymn is the concept of remembrance. The hymn begins with the hymnist's declaration to remember (line 1). The people at the festival in Delos remember Apollo in their celebrating (line 150). The singers also "turn their thoughts to" (i.e., remember) the men and women of old (line 160). The hymnist himself wants to be remembered (line 167). He will remember again as well (line 546). Similarly, the hymn ends with Apollo's instructions to the priests he has chosen to watch over his temple: "You have your instructions; it is for you to guard them" (line 544). Though the verb "guard" comes from a different root, West translates the idea of the expression as, "It is for you to remember them" (line 544). This emphasis on the notion of remembrance,

---

[60] On the place of prophecy in the Greek world and for details on the oracular tradition associated with Apollo, see chapter 2, "Greco-Roman Prophecy: Oracular Places and Persons," in David E. Aune, *Prophecy in Early Christianity and the Ancient Mediterranean World* (Grand Rapids: Eerdmans, 1983), 23–48.

[61] There were more than 30 Apolline oracles. Ibid., 27.

in this hymn and in ancient hymnody in general, is tied much more closely with the dynamics of the performative events than modern readers may appreciate.

In a recent study Bakker has discussed the opening lines of this hymn with their references to remembering in light of the concept of memory in Homer. He notes,

> Memory not only provides access to a reality that is ontologically prior; it also makes that reality present and is, as such, a strong mental experience. . . . Memory in Homer is not a retrieval of stored facts, but a dynamic cognitive operation in the present, a matter of consciousness, or more precisely of the *activation* of consciousness.[62]

The Homeric concept of "remembering" thus has a much more dynamic connotation than simply accessing information about the past. In these references to remembering within the context of the *Hymn to Apollo* we gain a glimpse of the potential for hymnic discourse to function as a means of cultural memory. The values and meanings that are encapsulated in the narrative of the hymn are brought into the foreground of the audience's consciousness in the act of performance. The idea of performance of a hymn as a part of the dynamic of cultural memory is a means of gaining a better understanding of the function of the Homeric Hymns as a group as well.

A final note should be made about the presumed origins of this particular hymn. Scholars have attempted to explain the fact that this hymn appears to join a newer Delian hymn with an older Pythian hymn.[63] Some of the indicators are fairly straightforward: its apparent ending phraseology at lines 177–178, its apparent new beginning at line 179, and its dual geographical focus are the most obvious indicators. As mentioned above, some have suggested that a combined Delian and Pythian festival in 523 BCE gave the singer Cynaethus the opportunity to conflate two earlier hymns. One can imagine this kind of festival as a performative setting in which it would have made sense for a singer to join together two versions of a *Hymn to Apollo* in order to affirm earlier local traditions, while at the same time using them as a means of unifying a larger populace within a pan-Hellenic framework.[64]

Taking a different approach, other scholars argue for the unity of the work, explaining that the features unique to this hymn could certainly have come about in the process of oral composition in which the singer compos-

---

[62] Egbert J. Bakker, *Pointing at the Past: From Formula to Performance in Homeric Poetics* (Washington, D.C.: Center for Hellenic Studies, 2005), 141.

[63] For a summary of the issue see West, *Homeric Hymns*, 9–11. For a fuller examination see the discussion in Miller, *From Delos to Delphi*, 111–117.

[64] See the discussion in Nagy, *Homer the Preclassic*, 57–58. Nagy suggests some of the dynamics relating to varying traditions that may have led to such a composition.

es in the act of performance, expanding portions of the narrative as appropriate to the audience.[65] While the resolution of this issue is well beyond the scope of this volume, the problem does relate to our interest in the hymn's teaching. More precisely this issue of the hymn's origin and performative context relates to the hymn's function. If indeed the hymn reflects this particular time period then it is possible to consider how recounting a mythological tale in this hymnic form accomplishes larger political/cultural/legitimizing aims of the sponsoring power. Further, if the hymn as we have it joins two earlier hymns, then in order to fully appreciate the results we need to consider the impact of the hymns as originally performed in their respective cities, as well as the impact of the hymns when joined together and performed in a later context.[66]

To conclude this discussion of the *Hymn to Apollo* a few comments on the hymn's pan-Hellenic tendencies are appropriate, particularly as these relate to the spatial and geographical registers of the hymn. Clay writes,

The presentation of Apollo in the hymn is thoroughly Olympian in its perspective. The poem's Olympianism goes hand in hand with its Panhellenic orientation... Throughout, the hymn conveys Apollo's universality by means of the geographical catalogs that cumulatively cover the whole Greek world.[67]

The poet presents an Apollo who is worshipped everywhere (lines 81–82). Likewise, as in the *Hymn to Demeter*, the poet limits the influence of local versions of the myth. On a related note, Clay provides an intriguing suggestion about the structure of the hymn:

The poet adopts a peculiar strategy that precludes *all* local exclusivity, by singling out not one, but two cult places: Delos *and* Delphi. Moreover, both sites are emphatically characterized as having *no* local traditions at all but being purely Apolline and Panhellenic.[68]

Thus the shape of the hymn as we have it, whether composed in whole or from the joining of previously composed hymns, can be seen to reflect the pan-Hellenic impulses represented in other Homeric Hymns as well.

---

[65] Miller, *From Delos to Delphi*, 186.

[66] At this point the discussion becomes more hypothetical than we may be comfortable with (drawing conclusions from theories which themselves are highly debatable). Nevertheless, the notion that a hymn can have one function when originally composed and then a different one when it is appropriated by later generations is very relevant to this study. This idea is one that must be kept in mind in evaluating the didactic impact of any hymnic or poetic composition.

[67] Clay, *The Politics of Olympus*, 92–93.

[68] Ibid., 93.

3. Hymn to Hermes

In the Homeric *Hymn to Hermes*, the latest of the longer Homeric Hymns,[69] we learn of the cunning and exploits of baby Hermes as he invents the lyre and steals the cattle of Apollo. The narrative of the hymn is an engaging tale full of humor and playfulness. Yet in spite of its liveliness and wit, the Homeric *Hymn to Hermes* is arguably one of the most challenging of the hymns in terms of identifying a main theme.[70] By reading the *Hymn to Hermes* in light of the dynamics of the other major Homeric Hymns, Clay has argued that this hymn aims to show how Hermes came to acquire his *timai* and his proper place among the other Olympians. She suggests, "Like the *Hymn to Apollo*, *Hermes* recounts the birth of a new god who at first appears to threaten the stability of the established pantheon but who ultimately accedes to his prerogatives and takes his destined place within the divine order."[71] By means of its narrative the hymn explains the origins of one aspect of the systematic framework of the Olympian gods with which the readers would have been quite familiar. In the following pages, after discussing the performative context and summarizing the content of the hymn, I will treat several of its themes as they relate to the didactic emphases of the overall hymn. We will see that the *Hymn to Hermes* teaches important lessons to adolescents who themselves are negotiating a place in the world of adults.

For purposes of this discussion I will follow the recent suggestion of Johnston who claims that the unifying center of the hymn is best understood in light of its performative context: "The poet's primary task was to craft a hymn that articulated the concerns expressed by the festival at which he performed and the functions of the god whom that festival honored."[72] Her conclusion is that the hymn was composed for performance at the Hermaia, an athletic contest honoring Hermes, and that it is aimed at the concerns of young men transitioning into adulthood.[73] Accordingly the hymn adapted a theme for that particular audience as it "expressed con-

---

[69] Pfeiff dates it to the later part of the 6th c. BCE; Pfeiff, Gönna, and Simon, *Homerische Hymnen*, 136.

[70] Sarah Iles Johnston, "Myth, Festival, and Poet: *The Homeric Hymn to Hermes* and Its Performative Context," *CPh* 97 (2002): 109–132. Johnston claims that this hymn "has proven to be one of the most interpretively difficult of all Greek poems" (109).

[71] Clay, *The Politics of Olympus*, 96.

[72] Johnston, "Myth, Festival, and Poet," 111.

[73] Johnston explains, "Athletic festivals called Hermaia, which eventually were celebrated all over the Greek world, particularly stress Hermes' connection to maturing males in this setting, for in cases where we have more than a passing reference to Hermaia, it becomes clear that they focused on παῖδες, νεανίσκοι, νέοι, and ἔφηβοι," Ibid., 116. See 128–130 for her discussion of which Hermaia may have been the occasion for the *Hymn to Hermes*.

cerns that were most immediately relevant to young males, whom Hermes was expected to protect and guide during their maturation."[74] Reading the hymn within the framework of such a context sheds light on the way this hymn would have functioned and also on what it may have taught its hearers. Though Johnston's theory cannot be proven with certainty, it should be noted that her view does align well with the internal dynamics of the hymn as observed by other scholars.[75] Though not the only place in ancient culture where movement across boundaries is necessary, the movement from child to adult may at least be seen as one critical place where such movement occurs. The adolescent themes and references in the hymn likewise support a reading that brings the hymn to bear on the issues of adolescents crossing the boundaries into the adult world.

The hymn begins as other hymns do, identifying the god who will be sung, and invoking the muses (line 1). It moves immediately into recounting Hermes' birth and first day. The description is worth quoting in full as it sets forth the main emphases of the rest of the hymn:

She gave birth to a son resourceful
and cunning, a robber,
a rustler of cattle, a bringer of dreams,
a night watcher, a gate-lurker,
who was soon to display deeds
of renown among the gods:
born in the morning, by mid-day he was playing the lyre,
and in the evening he stole the cattle of far-shooting Apollo –
on the fourth of the month,
the day the lady Maia bore him. (lines 13–19)

He invents the lyre from a tortoise (lines 20–61) and from this description we get a glimpse of the practice of impromptu singing at dinners:

The god sang beautifully to it, impromptu, experimentally,
as young men at dinners make ribald interjections:
(he sang) about Zeus son of Kronos
and fair-shod Maia,
how they used to talk love in companionable intimacy,
and declaring his own renowned lineage. (lines 54–59)

---

[74] Ibid., 111.

[75] For example, Clay has noted that Hermes introduces a dynamic of movement into the otherwise static pantheon. She writes, "To find his place on Olympus, Hermes must discover his particular sphere of activity – the traversing of boundaries – and, appropriately, he must wrest his privileges from the god whose business it is to ensure those boundaries. Hermes, then, introduces dynamic movement and vitality into what might otherwise be a beautifully ordered but static cosmos." Clay, *The Politics of Olympus*, 102.

In the narrative about stealing the cattle of Apollo (lines 62–153) we learn that Hermes was resourceful enough to invent fire (lines 108–114) and we also witness firsthand the process of sacrificing two bulls (lines 115–137). In the ensuing conversations, accusations, and investigation with Apollo and Zeus we learn of the cunning nature of Hermes. Hermes ultimately appeases Apollo by singing a song with the lyre and then giving it to Apollo (lines 434–512), after which the two brothers' relationship goes on to be one of mutual respect and love (lines 574–575). Apollo ultimately recognizes Hermes' abilities and sees to it that he is welcomed into the company of the immortals and receives the honor that he is due.

The lyre plays a significant role in the hymn on several levels. Two are of direct relevance with regard to discerning the didactic import of the hymn. First, the invention of the lyre and Hermes' two performances frame the cattle raid scene, thus suggesting that the two performances are related but also different due to what has transpired in between. The comparison of the two performances suggests that Hermes has changed as a result of his success in stealing the cattle of Apollo. Johnston notes that the first song (lines 54–59, cited above) is limited to exalting his mother, his birth, and his home. By contrast, she explains,

> His second song, performed after the raid, is quite different: it takes in the entire cosmos and all of its divine inhabitants, the maturing god's proper *milieu*. It is the raid, and its consequent effects, that have enabled Hermes to move from the small domestic sphere of his birth into the larger social sphere of the gods, where he is determined to make his career.[76]

This dynamic of changing, maturing, and moving into the larger social sphere through a test of skill and cunning is a process with which the young male participants at the athletic contests of the Hermaia would identify. This is one way that the poet draws the listener into the story and enables the young male listener to identify with Hermes.

A second role played by the performances on the lyre is the two-fold function of reinforcing current social practices and implicitly modeling proper performance and its goals. The singer is very careful to point out the manner in which Hermes sang as well as the order of his composition:

> Remembrance first of the gods he honored in his song,
> the mother of the Muses,
> for she had Maia's son in her province,
> and then the rest of the immortal gods
> Zeus' splendid son honored according to seniority and affiliation,
> relating everything in due order,
> and playing the lyre that hung from his arm. (lines 429–438)

---

[76] Johnston, "Myth, Festival, and Poet," 124.

Hermes here implicitly provides a model for appropriate and orderly remembrance of the gods in song. Apollo likewise brings the current social
world into view when he says, "I have never thought of anything like this –
like the passing to the right at young men's feasts" (lines 453–454). Johnston suggests that such descriptions are proleptic: "The poet reminds his
audience of how the lyre is used at contemporary symposia."[77] Indeed they
are, but there may be a further dynamic here as well, as Hermes models for
the listeners the appropriate way to praise gods, and by extension, heroes,
ancestors, and so forth. In the first performance of Hermes, the hymn reflects the coarseness and joking that can be a part of symposia (cf. lines
55–56). By contrast, the second "more mature" performance emphasizes
the orderly way in which Hermes composes his song as well as the authoritative and lovely sound of his voice (lines 425–427). To emphasize the didactic import of this model Hermes likewise gives Apollo, and indirectly
the audience, some advice on using the lyre effectively: "If one questions
her with skill and expertise, she speaks all kinds of lessons to charm the
fancy, easily tickled with tender familiarity, avoiding tiresome effort. But
if a novice questions her roughly, then she will utter useless discordant
nonsense" (lines 482–488). From these references it is clear that the hymn
not only gives the origins of the lyre, but implicitly and explicitly urges
those in the audience to play it well and to sing appropriately according to
the occasion.

In the process of negotiating his place in the world of the immortals,
Hermes trades the lyre with Apollo for the role of caring for cattle (lines
436–512). In this exchange Apollo raises the issue of divination and indicates that he cannot give him the prophetic art (lines 533–568). It is in the
context of this conversation that the hymn contains a very pointed didactic
moment. Apollo does grant Hermes a lesser form of divination in which he
will discern the movements of bees and relate the meaning of those movements to humans (lines 552–566).[78] Yet before he grants this source of
prophecy to Hermes, Apollo speaks about his own gift of prophecy and the
proper way for humans to seek the divine will (lines 533–549). Apollo explains, "He will profit from my utterance who comes on the cry or the
flights of valid omen bird: that man will profit from my utterance, and I
shall not deceive him" (lines 543–545). Further, humans can come to harm
by seeking prophecy through invalid channels or seeking too much divine
knowledge (lines 546–549). Hermes on the other hand may bring luck to
humans who will listen to him (lines 565–566), but, as the singer points
out later, only rarely does he bring profit (line 577). The message is clear:

---

[77] Ibid., 123.
[78] On the distinction between the two kinds of prophecy and how these function within the narrative see Clay, *The Politics of Olympus*, 146–148.

Hermes may be sought for a specialized kind of oracle, but Apollo alone is the source of the divine will.[79] Thus while the focus of the hymn is ostensibly on Hermes, with whom adolescents may identify, there are also some serious and direct teachings; particularly regarding the proper place of Apollo and a human's proper relationship with him.

Interestingly, as we explore the didactic impact of the *Hymn to Hermes*, several of the key strategies of the *Hymn to Demeter* and the *Hymn to Apollo* are absent.[80] As we have seen, the *Hymn to Demeter* contains, among other things, references to certain ritual practices which the initiates themselves would be performing. It also details the selection of Eleusis as the cultic site. The *Hymn to Apollo*, while it does reflect some ritual practices, recounts the selection of the site for the temple of Apollo, presumably a place where the hearers are gathered to honor the god. The *Hymn to Hermes* takes a different strategy as it neither discusses the founding of his rites nor the practices his worshippers would perform. Johnston explains, "The poet endeavors to transform the listeners into virtual participants in the mythic drama he narrates, virtual doublets of Hermes. Public recitation of the myth, then, almost functions as a ritual itself, as listeners negotiate the tensions that the myth expresses."[81] In other words, the interplay between the myth and the performative context would create a dynamic in which the hearers would sense themselves to be caught in the same kinds of struggles Hermes was undergoing. By identifying with him as he resolves those struggles and is accepted into the company of his elders (especially Apollo), presumably the participants in the Hermaia would find encouragement and hope in their own struggle for acceptance. This particular transformative function is one we have not encountered in the other Homeric Hymns which we have examined.

In addition to the kinds of didactic lessons we have looked at already there is, however, at least some indication of ritual practice. After Hermes steals the cattle of Apollo, he sacrifices two of them in a scene which has given rise to a number of interpretations (lines 112–137). It is noteworthy that Hermes divides the sacrifice into twelve portions, a detail that has lead many to see here a reference to the Olympic cult of the Twelve Gods.[82]

---

[79] For a fuller discussion of the distinctions reflected in this exchange see Gregory Nagy, "Ancient Greek Poetry, Prophecy, and Concepts of Theory," in *Poetry and Prophecy: The Beginnings of a Literary Tradition* (ed. James L. Kugel; Ithaca, N.Y.: Cornell University Press, 1990), 56–64.

[80] This point is raised by Johnston, "Myth, Festival, and Poet," 126–127.

[81] Ibid., 127.

[82] Ibid., 125; West, *Homeric Hymns*, 123. For an alternative reading that sees this as Hermes' cooking a meal for his fellow gods, see Clay, *The Politics of Olympus*, 117–121. It is not my aim to adjudicate between the merits of different views here, but simply to

Johnston makes the point that Olympus is the site not only of a sanctuary of Zeus but also of the Olympic games. She suggests a number of associations that this scene would bring to mind for the ancient listener. First, the poet situates the act of Hermes within the context of athletic contests, possibly the contests that were the occasion for this very hymn.[83] Second, by abstaining from the meat in spite of its appeal (lines 130–133), Hermes not only plays the proper role of a god, he also follows the rule of the athletes competing in the games. Again, this marks one of several points of identification between Hermes and the hearers. Third, by offering a sacrifice at Olympus, Hermes participates in (or perhaps initiates, from the point of view of the narrative) a practice that later victors would emulate. The sacrifice now marks Hermes as victor after his successful cattle raid.[84] In pointing out these various associations, Johnston asserts, "Hermes' actions would have brought to mind a complex of associations concerning both what it meant to compete at the grandest of all athletic games and what it meant to win there."[85] Further, "By refusing the meat in the *Hymn* and enjoying only the smell of its smoke, he claims what the audience already knew to be his rightful place not only among gods in general but specifically among the gods whom the most successful athletes would worship."[86] To sum up, while the scene most certainly does contain an "aetiological element relating to the cult,"[87] it also may function on a more sophisticated level, serving to heighten the male listener's association with Hermes as well as to mark his claim for his rightful place among the older gods.

The narrative scenes and careful development of the *Hymn to Hermes* function on several levels as far as making a point, teaching key lessons, and reinforcing social processes. Like the *Hymn to Demeter* there is reference to rites and perhaps events that the listeners are experiencing. Like the *Hymn to Apollo*, there is direct teaching about the abilities and special areas of oversight of the god. But this hymn contains an added dynamic which enables the young male hearer to identify with Hermes and the qualities that he demonstrates throughout his first two days of existence. In the context of the performance, the hearer would be encouraged to emulate Hermes where needed and to navigate the changing social roles from

---

point out some of the ways in which the hymn may have communicated its message to its hearers.

[83] Johnston, "Myth, Festival, and Poet," 125.

[84] Ibid.

[85] Ibid., 126.

[86] Ibid.

[87] West, *Homeric Hymns*, 13.

childhood to adulthood.[88] If the athletic contests associated with the Hermaia are at hand, then the young men would be inspired to prove their abilities in that sphere as a part of showing that they had what it takes to be a part of the world of adult males.

4. General Conclusions Regarding Didactic Emphases of the Homeric Hymns

From this brief look at several Homeric Hymns, it is already possible to note some common characteristic features of the didactic elements of the hymns. First, a good portion of the instructional impact of the hymns comes through the narrative(s) about the god's origins, powers, and the establishment of cult centers. These narratives often explain the current state of affairs by showing that the way things are now is a result of actions and events in the divine and human realms in the timeless mythic past. Presumably, much of the material in the narratives was traditional so that the hearers were not necessarily learning something new. Nevertheless, the repetition and retelling of sacred narratives does serve to reinforce the aetiological function as well as to reemphasize what is most important about the god or goddess under consideration and how humans ought to regard and respond to that deity. In this way the hymns serve as a part of an ongoing communal process relating to cultural memory.

Second, a part of the instructional impact would have come through the specific context in which the hymn was performed. The nature of the festival, what god or gods were being honored, what city it was being held in, and also what ruler or other entity had arranged it, surely added texture and meaning to aspects of the hymn. For example, reading the *Hymn to Hermes* as addressing the concerns of young males participating in athletic contests and navigating the transition to adulthood lends a depth to the narrative of the hymn that would be lacking if such a context were not considered in the interpretive process. As important as they are, these contextual aspects which affected how the hymn would have been perceived and received by the audience are the ones which are perhaps most difficult for modern readers to discern.

Third, in addition to the narrative itself and the performative context, the hymns often taught in even more direct ways through explicit statements. We observed the editorial comments by the hymnist in the *Hymn to Demeter*: "Blessed is he of men on earth who has beheld them, whereas he that is uninitiated in the rites, or he that has had no part in them, never en-

---

[88] Though the young hearers would not necessarily be encouraged to steal cattle, they would find encouragement to display the cunning and skill of Hermes as they find their own place in society.

joys a similar lot down in the musty dark when he is dead" (480–482). In the *Hymn to Apollo* it is Apollo himself who makes a direct statement about where and how to receive his unerring counsel through oracles (lines 287–293). Likewise in the *Hymn to Hermes* it is Apollo who gives a most explicit teaching for the human audience to take to heart, though ostensibly spoken to Hermes: "He will profit from my utterance who comes on the cry or the flights of valid omen birds: that man will profit from my utterance, and I shall not deceive him. But he who puts his trust in omens of vain utterance, and wants to enquire after a prophecy beyond my intention, and to know more than the eternal gods, I declare he will journey for nothing, though I shall take his offerings" (543–548). Whether in the context of the narrative or as a comment by the hymnist, these kinds of direct statements reveal an explicit instructional emphasis of the song.

If we had the opportunity to explore the remainder of the Homeric Hymns, we would encounter still other instructional elements and other means of conveying such teaching. The narrative in the *Hymn to Dionysus* implicitly urges the reader to take care to show proper reverence and care toward the god. The *Hymn to Aphrodite* is lacking in references to the goddess's birth and the founding of the cult, yet through its narrative the hearer learns how and why humans have lost their earlier intimacy with the world of the gods.[89] We could even explore the song of Demodokos in *Odyssey* 8 as an example of a song in narrative epic that is at least analogous to what we have seen in the Homeric Hymns as a group.[90] As a whole then, the Homeric Hymns manifest a masterful diversity of content, themes, and didactic intent while remaining within the constraints of their hymnic form and their primary function as prooimia.

C. Hesiodic Poetry and Hymnody

The hymnic traditions and styles represented in the Homeric Hymns also find representation in the works of Hesiod. The *Works and Days* begins with what is, in essence, a ten-line hymn to Zeus. The *Theogony* opens with a longer hymn to the Muses (lines 1–115), and it has been suggested that the entire composition can be classified and examined as mirroring the

---

[89] "By explaining and justifying our loss of intimacy with the divine, the *Hymn to Aphrodite* bids us come to terms with our mortal lot," Clay, *The Politics of Olympus*, 201.

[90] See chapter 4 of Nagy, *Homer the Preclassic*, esp. pp. 63–77. Nagy writes, "I argue that the second song of Demodokos is an older form of poetry embedded within a newer form of poetry as represented by the Odyssey: this older form is analogous to what we know as the Homeric Hymns" (72).

forms of a Homeric hymn. In this section we examine the hymnic preludes
to the *Theogony* and the *Works and Days* in order to assess their didactic
emphases and their functions within their respective works. The following
analyses of the prelude to *Works and Days* and of the *Theogony* trace the
didactic emphases of these works and the poetic means which Hesiod has
used to teach his audience.

Though the *Theogony* and the *Works and Days* are quite different from
one another in terms of genre, contents, and emphasis, it is possible to read
them together as presenting a comprehensive picture of early Greek
thought. Clay argues that these works are reflective of ancient Greek theology, by which she means "the speculation inherent in those works concerning relations between gods and men and, since those relations have
changed in the course of time, their evolution to the world's present
state."[91] In her view the theology of the early Greeks is inscribed in and
recounted through the poetic telling of mythical narratives about the gods
and heroes.[92] Taken together, the *Theogony* and the *Works and Days* reflect
a comprehensive theological system which accounts for the origins of the
gods, the order of the world, and the proper way for humans to live within
it. Clay summarizes, "The *Theogony* offers an account of the genesis of the
cosmos and the gods and culminates in Zeus's final and permanent order of
that cosmos; in the *Works and Days*, Hesiod advises his wayward brother
Perses how best to live in the world as it is constituted under Zeus's
rule."[93] Granted, this view does not explain away all of the challenges related to articulating the relationship of the two works. However, for the
purposes of this chapter, Clay's approach helps us to be aware of didactic
emphases of the individual compositions as well as some ways that they
work together to present an even grander pan-Hellenic perspective on the
cosmos.

1. Hesiod's Theogony

Hesiod's *Theogony* is possibly the oldest Greek poem to have survived to
the present.[94] As a theogony proper it is part of a broader literary tradition
which deals with cosmic and divine origins and with events of the mythic

---

[91] Jenny Strauss Clay, *Hesiod's Cosmos* (Cambridge: Cambridge University Press,
2003), 1.

[92] "Unlike other ancient societies, the theology of the ancient Greeks was developed
neither by priests nor holy men, but by the poets. These, in turn, did not expound dogma
or religious doctrine, but recounted myths about the gods as well as stories of the famous
deeds of the heroes of old," Ibid.

[93] Ibid.

[94] M. L. West, *Hesiod: Theogony* (Oxford: Clarendon Press, 1997), 46.

past that shape the present.[95] Running over one thousand lines, the scope of Hesiod's particular *Theogony* is immense.[96] In his wide-ranging account Hesiod incorporates, accommodates, and synthesizes a number of local traditions into a larger, systematic pan-Hellenic framework that accounts for the realities of the world that Hesiod and his contemporaries experienced.[97]

As far as its form is concerned, the *Theogony* is a self-contained poem, much longer than any of the Homeric Hymns, and clearly not intended as a prelude to another kind of performance. Nevertheless, by looking at the five elements of preludes noted above (i.e., invocation, epithets, narrative, prayer, farewell), the *Theogony* can be seen as a complex prelude, at least from a formal perspective.[98] The idea of a "complex prelude" is in contrast to the Homeric Hymns which can be considered "simplex preludes" in that they address only one god. In this view the *Theogony* is a longer hymn that, rather than invoking one god, invokes all of the gods in the context of a larger work.

While it is possible to treat the entire work as a complex hymn, this section has a much more modest aim. It will examine the proem of the *Theogony* (lines 1–115), which manifests both the form and the function of an actual prelude in that it really does serve as an introduction to the poem that follows. This opening section is formally a hymn addressed to the Muses. A brief synopsis of the prelude will be followed by a discussion of some of the key didactic emphases of the hymn. We will see that this hymn creates a vision of reality in which Zeus reigns supreme and Hesiod is an inspired poet and herald.

It is fairly clear that lines 1–115 form a distinct unit and function as a prelude within the larger work of the *Theogony*.[99] Line 1 opens in a very typical hymnic fashion identifying the subjects of the hymn: the Muses. Line 2 begins with a relative pronoun and goes on to describe the Helikonian Muses more fully.[100] The whole section comprised of lines 1–21 offers an opening description of the Muses dancing, washing, walking, and

---

[95] Ibid., 1.

[96] Most summarizes, "Hesiod's *Theogony* provides a comprehensive account of the origin and organization of the divinities responsible for the religious, moral, and physical structure of the world, starting from the very beginning and culminating in the present regime, in which Zeus has supreme power and administers justice." Most, *Hesiod*, xxvi.

[97] Cf. Clay, *Hesiod's Cosmos*, 4.

[98] Nagy, *Greek Mythology and Poetics*, 54.

[99] Line numbering and translations of the works of Hesiod are taken from Most, *Hesiod*.

[100] On lines 1–2 West notes, "These opening lines, while not formally an invocation, have much in common with invocation structure." West, *Hesiod: Theogony*, 152. However, the formal invocation actually occurs at the end of the hymn in lines 104–115.

singing of Zeus and all of the other immortals. In the next major section of the prelude, lines 22–34, Hesiod describes his own encounter with the Muses, an encounter in which he is authorized as a poet. The Muses teach Hesiod, giving him a staff and a divine voice, and commanding him to "sing of the race of the blessed ones who always are, but always to sing of themselves first and last" (lines 33–34). Line 35 marks a transition from the narrative of his own gifting and calling to the theogony proper.[101] At this point in the hymn, lines 36–52 describe the Muses and their singing; lines 53–67 describe their birth; lines 68–74 recount their first song as they ascended Olympus; lines 75–80 discuss their names; and lines 81–103 describe the gifts of the Muses to humans. Lines 104–115 constitute "the invocation properly speaking" as Hesiod requests of the Muses that they tell him of the origins of the gods and of the earth from the beginning.[102]

Several key themes of this prelude suggest the didactic emphases of the larger work. First, the person and role of the poet in relation to the Muses is of great importance at the outset. Second, the central focus of the work is the nature of the cosmos and how things came to be the way they are. These themes both are related to the cultural realities impacting ancient Greek cities – realities which are reflected in Hesiod's role as a pan-Hellenic poet articulating a worldview that transcended localized traditions as it placed them under the reign of Zeus.

The relationship between Hesiod and the Muses is a fascinating one that has much to tell us about how the ancient poet conceived of himself and his work in relation to the divine world. Whether one understands his vision and revelation of the Muses (lines 22–34) as an autobiographical account, a literary convention, or a combination of both, the account is rich with meaning both for the poet, his theology, and the way his hearer's should understand his message.[103] Though much could be said about each aspect of the account, I will focus here on lines 30–34. Most renders these,

They plucked a staff, a branch of luxuriant laurel,
a marvel, and gave it to me;
and they breathed a divine voice into me,
so that I might glorify what will be and what was before,
and they commanded me to sing

---

[101] Line 36, "let us begin from the Muses," echoes lines 1–2 in a more concise form. It could be argued that this is the beginning of another discrete hymn that runs from 36–104. But, compared to a hymn like the Homeric *Hymn to Apollo* with its various starts and "restarts", it makes sense to view the entire section from 1–115 as a self-contained hymn. Lines 1–35 merely serve as the extended opening to the larger hymn.

[102] Clay, *Hesiod's Cosmos*, 70–71.

[103] West, *Hesiod: Theogony*, 158–160. See the in-depth treatment of the issue of the relationship between Hesiod and the Muses in Clay, *Hesiod's Cosmos*, 49–72.

of the race of the blessed ones who always are,
but always to sing of themselves first and last. (lines 30–34)[104]

The gifts of the Muses, the staff of laurel and the divine voice, are most
certainly intended to demonstrate the authorizing and empowering of Hesiod to proclaim divine truths. First, the staff (σκῆπτρον; line 30) can carry a
wide range of connotations directly related to speaking. West points out,
"The word elsewhere denotes the staff carried by kings, priests, and prophets as the symbol that they are a god's representatives; also by heralds and,
temporarily, by anyone who stands up to speak in the assembly of leaders."[105] With these associations in view, the Muses are empowering Hesiod
to speak as their representative. Second, the laurel is associated in particular with Apollo, who himself is explicitly connected with the Muses later
in line 94. In the Homeric *Hymn to Apollo* the laurel or bay is specifically
associated with Apollo's oracle (line 396).[106] This allusion to Apollo and
his oracle, by which the will of Zeus is mediated to mortals, goes hand-in-
hand with the idea that Hesiod has been empowered to speak on behalf of
the gods.

In addition, the breathing into Hesiod a divine voice (lines 31–32)
serves to make explicit what the gift of the staff and laurel suggested: Hesiod is a divinely empowered poet and prophet. West suggests that the two
offices of poet and prophet are closely connected in line 32 which speaks
of Hesiod glorifying things to come along with things that have already
happened. He explains, "The phrase expresses the close connexion between poetry and prophecy which is widespread in early literature. In the
absence of written records, the ability to see into the distant past is no less
marvellous than the ability to see into the future, and there is no reason for
a sharp distinction between the two."[107] However, some scholars dispute
the idea that two separate and distinct tasks (recounting the past and fore-
telling the future) are in view here. Clay, for example, suggests that line 32
refers to one single class of proclamation: "The Hesiodic phrasing refers to
one category of things that both will be and were before."[108] For purposes
of our discussion, neither interpretation eclipses the main point. Regardless
of how one interprets the phrase, the primary emphasis is on the fact that
Hesiod is empowered by the Muses to speak things that he could not otherwise have known apart from their inspiration.

Nagy develops the idea that Hesiod is here portraying himself as more
than a singer of songs, and that he is indeed to be seen as embodying the

---

[104] Most, *Hesiod*, 5.
[105] West, *Hesiod: Theogony*, 163.
[106] Ibid., 164.
[107] Ibid., 166.
[108] Clay, *Hesiod's Cosmos*, 66.

functions of a herald of the gods and a prophet. During the time of composition of the *Theogony* these functions were not yet differentiated as they
would be in later eras.[109] In a way similar to the older and newer traditions
that meet in the Homeric *Hymn to Hermes*, Nagy explains, "Hesiod's relationship with the Helikonian Muses represents an older and broader poetic
realm that the poet then streamlines into the newer and narrower one of a
pan-Hellenic theogony by way of synthesizing the Helikonian with the
Olympian Muses."[110] Interestingly, Hesiod the poet necessitates the services of both the local and the Olympian Muses for his poetic purposes.
Nagy notes,

> The figure of Hesiod requires these local Muses in order to compose a theogony, but he
> also requires the Olympian Muses in order to compose pan-Hellenic poetry. His own im-
> plicit reward for assimilating the Helikonian Muses into the Olympian is that his local
> gifts, a staff and a voice that are both appropriate to a local theogony, become in a pan-
> Hellenic context the emblems that establish his ultimate authority as poet, emanating
> from the ultimate authority of Zeus as king.[111]

We will see a similar authorizing dynamic in Hesiod's references to the
Muses in the *Works and Days*. Ultimately, the force of the encounter with
the Muses authorizes Hesiod and also lends credibility to Hesiod's *Theogony* as a whole as well as the pan-Hellenic theology inscribed within.[112]

Hesiod's encounter with the Muses enables him to begin the *Theogony*
in an authoritative manner in the plural: "Let us begin to sing from the Hel-
iconian Muses" (line 1). Clay observes, "From the beginning, then, the poet considers his song a collaborative production; it is not simply his alone,
but, insofar as his is an inspired voice, it is joined with, and indissociable
from, the voice of the Muses."[113] This idea is further emphasized in line
75. In the lines preceding, Hesiod has summarized the content of the song
of the Muses in his own words. At line 75 he attributes the song to them,
indicating that at some level his voice has become identified with that of
the Muses.[114] This implicit claim is a significant part of the strategy of the
hymnic proem. As Hesiod hymns the Muses and describes his encounter

---

[109] Nagy, *Greek Mythology and Poetics*, 59. Nagy points to the *Hymn to Hermes* and
the process of differentiation suggested there between Apollo and Hermes. Hermes (the
"newer" god in the view of the hymn) actually represents the older local tradition which
is being assimilated into the newer pan-Hellenic Olympian framework.

[110] Ibid., 60.

[111] Ibid., 60–61.

[112] Nagy explains, "The encounter of Hesiod with the Helikonian Muses leads to the
poet's glorifying them with the *Theogony*, which is technically a pan-Hellenic hymn to
the Muses; in this way the local goddesses of Helikon are assimilated into the pan-
Hellenic goddesses of Olympus," Ibid., 58.

[113] Clay, *Hesiod's Cosmos*, 51–52.

[114] Ibid., 69.

with them, he presents himself as one authorized by the Muses to speak on their behalf.

While the proem serves to authorize Hesiod as spokesperson for the Muses, it also serves to portray the framework of the universe which the entire work will elaborate. Lines 71–74 render the cosmic framework as under the authority of Zeus:

He is king in the sky, holding the thunder and blazing thunderbolt himself,
since he gained victory in supremacy over his father Cronus;
and he distributed well all things alike to the immortals
and devised their honors. (lines 71–74)

Reflecting the supremacy of Zeus, the Muses themselves begin their singing with Zeus (line 11). Likewise, when they sing of him they relate "how he is the best of the gods and the greatest in supremacy" (line 49). The prelude thus establishes the theme of Zeus's supremacy by referencing it in several ways at key points in the development of the hymn. Ultimately, the *Theogony* as a whole will give the details for how this state of affairs came to be as the Muses fulfill the request of Hesiod (lines 104–115).

In this short survey of the prelude to the *Theogony*, we have focused on two of its major themes: the authorization of Hesiod and the supremacy of Zeus. Both ideas are conveyed explicitly through the medium of the hymn. Implicitly, the pan-Hellenic Olympian orientation of the cosmos is also being promoted in contrast to the particular myths and narratives of local deities. All of these emphases are inscribed into the prelude of the *Theogony*. As Clay explains, "The *Theogony* constitutes an attempt to understand the cosmos as the product of a genealogical evolution and a process of individuation that finally leads to the formation of a stable cosmos and ultimately achieves its *telos* under the tutelage of Zeus."[115] As we turn to the *Works and Days* we will encounter a complementary view of the cosmos that focuses primarily on the place of humans under the kingship of Zeus.

2. The Prelude to Works and Days

If the *Theogony* provides a systematic account of the origins of the gods and how the cosmos came to be under the rule of Zeus, the *Works and Days* shifts the focus to the sphere of human endeavors and human relationships. In the *Works and Days*, Hesiod presents his perspective on a deep-seated conflict between himself and his brother Perses, who comes into view at several places in the composition. Though the work is directly aimed at Perses (line 10), it is quite clear that Hesiod's teachings have a

---

[115] Ibid., 13.

much broader application.[116] Recognizing this didactic tone of the *Works and Days*, as well as the wide range of material it contains, scholars have attempted to compare it with other kinds of instructional literature (e.g., Wisdom literature; instructions to kings; catalogue poetry; etc.).[117] Though not conclusive, such comparisons serve to shed some light on the work's conventions, contents, and the way it presents traditional material within its larger framework.

While it cannot be shown that Hesiod relies heavily on one particular literary precedent, it has been argued that the *Works and Days* itself sets the standard for didactic poetry as a genre. Toohey suggests the following way of understanding this genre:

Within the culture of classical antiquity there were a variety of elastic, ill-defined, but nonetheless recognizeable subspecies or subgenres of epic: mythological or narrative epic is one; but so too was the small-scale epic practiced by the Alexandrian writers in the third century BCE (which could include pastoral); there was even a comedic or parodic epic; alongside these stands didactic epic which can deal with subjects as varied as science, philosophy, religion, and agriculture.[118]

Toohey takes the *Works and Days* to be the standard example of this genre against which all later didactic epic can be measured. In his view the two central features of didactic epic are the implicit or explicit presence of an instructor's voice and of an addressee, both of which are present in the *Works and Days*.[119] Notwithstanding the pitfalls that surround attempts to classify ancient compositions into discrete generic categories (even elastic and ill-defined ones), it is at least fair to note that the *Works and Days* does indeed convey a strongly didactic impression. We can agree that it was composed for purposes of instruction.

The ten lines that open the *Works and Days* of Hesiod are of interest in our study since they are, in essence, a brief hymn to Zeus. We know from the *Theogony* that Hesiod could have provided a much longer prooimion to this work. West explains, "He might have made it a long hymn by telling of the god's birth (the commonest narrative theme in such hymns), or of how he established his rule in heaven. . . . Instead he contents himself with a brief but powerful statement of Zeus' supremacy over man."[120] Though functionally this hymn invokes the presence and blessing of Zeus in all that

---

[116] Clay observes, "While the *Works and Days* is addressed to the specific individual, Perses, its teaching casts a far wider net. And it is precisely this combination of the general and the specific that gives the poem its validity as a protreptic," Ibid., 36.

[117] For discussions of Wisdom Literature in the ancient world and the relationship of *Works and Days* with these other writings see M. L. West, *Hesiod: Works and Days* (Oxford: Clarendon Press, 1978), 3–30.

[118] Toohey, *Epic Lessons*, 6.

[119] Ibid., 21.

[120] West, *Hesiod: Works and Days*, 136.

follows, it plays a didactic role as well, situated as it is at the beginning of a long didactic poem and focusing as it does on Zeus's supremacy. This section will explore the hymn in terms of its form, content, and function, showing that it introduces key themes which will be developed throughout the *Works and Days*.

This hymn contains a typical hymnic opening invoking the Muses and calling them to hymn their father Zeus:

Muses, from Peiria, glorifying in songs,
come here, tell in hymns of your father Zeus. (lines 1–2)

This hymning of Zeus is reminiscent of the prelude of the *Theogony*, especially lines 44, 47, and 53.[121] This opening is different from the *Theogony*, however, since that composition began with what was in essence a hymn to the Muses, while this one is most clearly a hymn to Zeus. The relative pronoun at the beginning of line 3 serves as the transition to the body of the hymn where the powers and epithets of Zeus are expounded in a descriptive rather than narrative style (lines 3–8):

through whom mortal men are unfamed and famed alike,
and named and unnamed, by the will of great Zeus.
For easily he strengthens, and easily he crushes the strong,
and easily he straightens the crooked and whithers the manly –
high-thundering Zeus, who dwells in the loftiest mansions. (lines 3–8)

The hymn contains no narrative (also making this quite different from *Theogony* 1–115), making it more similar to some of the shorter Homeric Hymns which lack a narrative about the god or goddess.[122] The hymn concludes (lines 9–10) with a request of Zeus as well as a declaration on the part of the poet to move to another poetic task:

Give ear to me, watching and listening, and straighten the verdicts with justice
Yourself; as for me, I will proclaim truths to Perses. (lines 9–10)

Unlike the hymnic preludes that we saw in the Homeric Hymns, Hesiod's task is not singing another song but instead it is proclaiming truth to Perses.

Since the hymn as we have it is in the context of a much larger work, it is clear that the hymn does indeed function as a prooimion (i.e., a hymnic prelude to a poetic recitation that will follow). Its integral connection with all that follows strongly suggests that this particular hymn was specifically composed for this purpose. Though reflecting traditional forms, epithets, and content, as a prooimion the hymn serves at least two important func-

---

[121] Ibid., 137.
[122] For example, hymn 21 (to Apollo), 22 (to Poseidon), 23 (to Zeus), 24 (to Hestia), and 25 (to the Muses and Apollo).

tions. First, it invokes the presence of Zeus and places all that will follow in the context of a hymn; the following performance is thus rendered sacred by the presence of the god. Second, it introduces themes and ideas that will be more fully developed in the remainder of the composition. Four such themes will be briefly mentioned here.

The prelude introduces a number of important ideas that will be further developed throughout the poem. First, the supreme greatness of Zeus is emphasized as a guiding theme of the hymn and the entire composition as well. He is "great Zeus" (line 4) and "high thundering Zeus, who dwells in the loftiest mansions" (line 8). West notes that as far as the geography of Olympus goes, "Zeus' house is the highest up. But the phrase can also be taken more generally of his dominant position above the world."[123] It is this dominant position that is surely in view here; all that follows in the composition thus occurs under the realm of Zeus. This is certainly a foundational assumption for Hesiod, as seen a few lines later in line 18 and also in *Theogony* 529, where Zeus "rules on high." The supreme ruling power of Zeus is likewise reflected in the human sphere, where he "easily" exerts control (lines 5–7). This explicit focus on the supreme reign of Zeus is one reflection of the pan-Hellenic tendencies of Hesiod as a poet.[124]

Second, Hesiod's calling on the Muses to aid him, a common opening *topos*, implies their inspiration of what he will declare. Verdenius explains that "divine inspiration is always presupposed in Hes[iod]'s poetry, and conversely the words of the Muses are always spoken by the poet himself at the same time."[125] We have already observed this to be the case in the proem of the *Theogony*, especially as it is spelled out in lines 22–34. But this idea is also elaborated later on in the *Works and Days*. In lines 661–662, Hesiod says, "Even so I shall speak forth the mind of aegis-holding Zeus, for the Muses taught me to sing an inconceivable hymn." Though not stated explicitly in the prelude, Verdenius is correct to find reference to this idea that the Muses will glorify Zeus through the mouth of the poet. Verdenius concludes, "This ambitious claim [that anything said by the poet should be understood as a manifestation of the will of Zeus] is also implied in the proem: the fact that the Muses are called on to celebrate Zeus means that the whole of the poem will be a song of praise to Zeus."[126] Taking this argument one step further, this idea that the whole composition be seen as

---

[123] West, *Hesiod: Works and Days*, 141.

[124] Nagy notes other aspects of Hesiod's pan-Hellenic outlook in terms of the political realities reflected in the Works and Days: "The vantage point is pan-Hellenic, in that all the cities of the Hellenes are reduced to two extreme types, the polis of *dikē* (225–237) and the polis of *hŭbris* (238–247)," Nagy, *Greek Mythology and Poetics*, 67.

[125] Willem Jacob Verdenius, *A Commentary on Hesiod: Works and Days, vv. 1–382* (Mnemosyne. Supplementum 86; Leiden: Brill, 1985), 3.

[126] Ibid.

a song of praise to Zeus connects the proem with the Homeric Hymns. As prooimia their purpose was to invoke the god's presence and favor in the recitation that would follow. The remainder of the performance that followed would thus be an offering of praise to the god. Such a perspective – that the poet is inspired by the Muses to recite his poem in honor of the supreme Zeus – serves to remind as well as to instruct the audience in the ultimate sources of divine knowledge and the nature of the performance which they are witnessing.

Third, the hymn brings into focus the variety of fates of men as they experience the strengthening, increasing power of Zeus or the crushing, diminishing power of Zeus. Human prosperity and the lack thereof are ultimately set within the will of Zeus (lines 4–8). Verdenius suggests that there is a notion of rectification in these middle lines of the hymn. He explains, "Whenever Zeus intervenes in human life, strengthening the weak or weakening the strong, this always implies a correction either of direction (ἰθύνει) or of magnitude (κάρφει)."[127] This perspective is most likely correct, as Hesiod's request to Zeus in line 9 suggests. The poet asks Zeus to "straighten the verdicts with justice yourself" (lines 9–10). West's view here is that "Zeus is being asked here to make sure that the judgments given [by the human ruling authority] are straight, shaped by δίκη."[128] These ways in which Zeus is said to intervene in human affairs in the prelude suggest a significant theological concept that is central to the larger composition: Zeus can bring about justice and is ultimately responsible for prosperity and poverty as these circumstances come to humans in the course of their lives.

Finally, the occasion of the poem is introduced as the poet declares that he will "proclaim truths to Perses" (line 10). This idea is resumed early on in the *Works and Days* as the poet pleads with Perses, "Let us decide our quarrel right here with straight judgments, which come from Zeus, the best ones" (lines 35–36). The quarrel, whether real or a literary fiction, provides the opportunity for Hesiod to speak forth the judgments of Zeus (cf. lines 661–662).

Though each of these themes may be traced throughout the larger poem, it is not necessary to do so here. Rather, it is sufficient at this point to note the integral connection between the contents of the opening hymn and the larger work and to recognize the way that the hymn functions to raise these issues in this emphatically didactic context. Comparison of *Works and Days* 1–10 with the scope and themes of *Theogony* 1–115 reveal both similarities and differences in the use of a hymnic prelude to begin a longer

---

[127] Ibid., 8. Other scholars see a punitive dimension in lines 7–8 as well, e.g., Clay, *Hesiod's Cosmos*, 77.

[128] West, *Hesiod: Works and Days*, 141.

composition.[129] In both cases, major themes are introduced, issues of the authority of the poet are raised and addressed, and the entire composition is placed under the rule of Olympian Zeus.

D. Conclusions

By viewing the hymnody of Homer and Hesiod through a variety of lenses, it has been possible to gain insight into several aspects of Hellenic life and thought. At a very general level, readers of this poetry are confronted with a highly developed literary tradition with roots firmly planted in oral performance. The originally oral nature of this poetry brings into view the questions of when these poems were composed, for what purposes, and for whom they were performed. Knowledge of ancient Greek festivals (such as the Pan-Atheneia, the Hermaia, and others) and cultic rituals (the Eleusinian mysteries) helps us to imagine settings where this poetry would have been performed. Awareness of these festivals also brings into view a variety of social and political factors which are reflected in the poems. As I argue in other chapters of this study, along with the timeless element of hymnic praise of the divine, many ancient hymns reflect the realities of life as experienced by the author of the hymns and/or the communities that treasured them.

Considering the hymns more closely, a number of themes have emerged – themes which will be reflected in later hymnody as well. These themes include the powers of the gods, the establishment of the cult of the gods, and also explanations for realities of human life in this world. Further, these poems raise issues of the authority of the poet as herald of divine truths, often implicitly teaching the audience about the nature of the poetic and/or prophetic task. Finally, the hymns of Homer and Hesiod reflect the ongoing process of theological reflection through sacred narrative that finds order and structure in the cosmos under the reign of Zeus.

As we turn our attention to later developments in didactic hymnody, we can continue to consider the complex relationship between the historical and social setting of the author, the possible performative context of the presentation of the hymn, and the cultural and political context of the various members of the audience. We have seen that hymns provide a powerful way of rehearsing and remembering (and creating) the past in a way that

---

[129] Clay overstates these differences and places these two passages in too sharp of a contrast with one another (cf. *Hesiod's Cosmos*, 80). She claims that *Works and Days* presents the human viewpoint directly without the need for a divine intermediary. However, reading the passages in light of each other has allowed us to see how they function in similar ways in spite of the different subject matter of the compositions that follow.

gives meaning to the present. As a form of social memory, they are a powerful tool for casting a vision of ultimate reality that can look beyond what is seen in the present. For later generations of Greeks (and Romans as well), the poetic and hymnic traditions they inherited established patterns in which they could inscribe their cultural, social, and theological views in hymnic form for their own generation.

Chapter 3

Didactic Hymns and Prayers in the Service of Philosophy

A. Introduction

The development and growth of philosophical thought within the Greek world was a complex and multi-faceted process facilitated by the contributions of many individual thinkers and schools of thought, as well as the influences of cultural and historical factors.[1] The many philosophical writings that have survived from the ancient world represent only a small portion of the works that philosophers, writers, and scholars actually produced. The present chapter explores one specific segment of these ancient philosophical compositions: hymns and prayers.

The fact that we are aware of a number of philosophical hymns and prayers from antiquity suggests that we ought to begin with the recognition that both philosophical thought and religious beliefs were interrelated to some degree. That is, philosophy was done within the context of the very religious culture of the Greeks – a culture in which deities were worshipped through cultic sacrifice. On the other hand Greek religion, a congeries of practices, values, and beliefs, came to be viewed, by some, through philosophical lenses. As philosophy developed, it certainly did not replace religious practice or do away with it. In fact, it has been argued that Greek and Roman philosophy served at some times to supplement religion, and at other times to correct its misapplication. Most explains, "The fundamental tendency of the vast majority of ancient Greek and Roman

---

[1] For a brief account of Hellenic and Hellenistic philosophy within the particular context of a monumental study of Stoicism see the opening chapter of M. Pohlenz, *Die Stoa: Geschichte einer geistigen Bewegung* (Göttingen: Vandenhoeck & Ruprecht, 1948). For convenient summaries of schools of thought, key figures, and themes see the essays in Anthony A. Long, *The Cambridge Companion to Early Greek Philosophy* (Cambridge Companions to Philosophy; Cambridge: Cambridge University Press, 2006); D. N. Sedley, *The Cambridge Companion to Greek and Roman Philosophy* (Cambridge Companions to Philosophy; Cambridge: Cambridge University Press, 2003).

philosophers is not at all to debunk religion, but to reinforce religiosity."[2] He notes that philosophy often attempts "to satisfy needs and answer questions which, because of the peculiar nature of the ancient religions, these did not seem to them to be able to supply themselves in a satisfactory manner."[3] In other words, Greek and Roman cults and their myths were not necessarily able to address the kinds of questions philosophers and other intellectuals were asking. In those cases philosophy was better suited to provide more satisfactory answers. On the other hand, philosophy at times served as a corrective to religion, "modifying those features of traditional myths, cults and beliefs which most clearly violated what were seen to be the demands of reason or of morality, and thereby producing a more philosophically acceptable version of traditional religion."[4] In light of these realities, we should be careful to avoid oversimplifying the relationship between religion and philosophy in the ancient world on the basis of false dichotomies.

Along these lines one can note that philosophers and philosophical schools were quite comfortable in developing and reflecting on what scholars today would consider "theological" ideas. In particular their writings are often concerned, even more so than Greek religious texts, with cosmology, eschatology, and ethics. Most notes, "In all three of these areas, ancient philosophers seem from the beginning to have discovered a relative deficit on the part of ancient religion and to have recognized therein a particularly fruitful opportunity to fill gaps and to answer questions."[5] When we come to explore the ways in which ancient philosophers utilized the literary forms of hymns, we can look for ways that these compositions went beyond the traditional understandings of the deities, their myths, and their cult in order to address areas of concern to contemporary, albeit limited, audiences.

We begin with Aristotle's fourth century BCE *Hymn to Virtue* as possibly the earliest hymn to fit the description "philosophical hymn." We move on to two hymns that are closely related to one another in that they reflect Stoic ideas and come from roughly the same time period as each other: Aratus's hymn to Zeus and Cleanthes' *Hymn to Zeus*. Finally, in the Roman literary and philosophical tradition we examine some later examples of Epicurean didactic hymnody in Lucretius's *On the Nature of the Universe*.

---

[2] Glenn W. Most, "Philosophy and Religion," in *The Cambridge Companion to Greek and Roman Philosophy* (ed. D. N. Sedley; Cambridge: Cambridge University Press, 2003), 300–321, here 307.

[3] Ibid., 307.

[4] Ibid., 308.

[5] Ibid., 310.

Several general questions will guide our study. First, how do these hymns draw on earlier hymnic traditions in terms of their form, content, and function? Second, where can we observe adaptation and innovation relative to the earlier hymnic traditions, and what do these developments suggest in terms of the teaching of the poem? Third, how can we account for the choice of a hymnic and/or poetic form on the part of the author? In other words, what was it about the subject matter, the instructional aims of the author, and the medium of hymnody that led the philosopher to choose this particular means of communication? As we explore these diverse examples of didactic philosophical hymns, we will see that philosophers made creative and strategic use of hymnic forms to convey their teaching in attractive ways to their followers and potential followers. Their hymns reflected central values of their philosophies and key elements in their teaching in a manner that blended traditional hymns with poetic innovation.

B. Aristotle's *Hymn to Virtue*

Aristotle's *Hymn to Virtue* is an intriguing specimen of poetry put into the service of instructional discourse. Written in 338 BCE after the death of his friend Hermias, the poem both celebrates excellence (ἀρετά) and honors Hermias for his passionate devotion to excellence.[6] As for its performative context the hymn was recited within the private context of a communal meal, in what might be considered a philosophical community. Nevertheless, in spite of its hymnic features, the precise generic identification of this composition has been debated.

Scholars have sought to compare the *Hymn to Virtue* with a variety of ancient hymnic compositions. Furley and Bremer suggest that the hymns of Pindar are the closest precedent. They write, "Aristotle chose the form of a Pindaric hymn addressed to Areta, the personification of human excellence. That he wanted his poem to sound like a hymn is clear from the repeated second person address."[7] Bowra, on the other hand, suggested that the poem should not be considered a hymn, since Areta was not a goddess but an abstraction. He suggested that the *Hymn to Virtue* compared favorably to Ariphron's *Hymn to Hygeia* and was influenced in a number of ways

---

[6] Furley and Bremer, *Greek Hymns*, 1:262–263.

[7] Ibid., 1:265. The odes of Pindar could be examined for their didactic qualities as well, particularly in the virtues they promote. Furley and Bremer note, "Pindar had also often started his epinikia with a hymnic invocation to a divinity before passing on to a mythical paradigm of heroic valour and celebrating the excellence of his laudandus" (265).

by that composition.[8] However, while the *Hymn to Hygeia* was a paean, Bowra notes that Aristotle's composition was not. Hygeia was associated with Asclepius and, by extension, Apollo, who was the proper recipient of paeans. Furthermore, Hygeia had a cult, while Areta, at the time, did not.[9] So while the *Hymn to Virtue* was possibly influenced by the paean of Ariphron, it was not itself technically a paean. Bowra went on to suggest that an ancient kind of burial song, the θρῆνος, which was sung at the tomb and also at a yearly festival of remembrance, was a model for Aristotle.[10] He concluded, "Aristotle modeled his poem on the Paean but added to it some characteristics of the θρῆνος, and addressed it to a power who meant a great deal to him but was not officially in the Greek pantheon."[11] In these respects (i.e. combining several poetic forms and addressing the composition to an abstraction), Aristotle reflects some of the tendencies of his century. For the purposes of this study it is sufficient to note that Aristotle's composition reflects features of earlier hymnic compositions, while at the same time giving evidence of Aristotle's own originality.

As for the structure of the hymn, it divides neatly into three main sections. Lines 1–8 offer hymnic praise of Areta in descriptive style, making claims about Areta. Lines 9–12 provide proof of the claims of the first section by offering heroic examples from the mythic past. Lines 13–18 shift the temporal register of the hymn to the recent past as they describe Hermias and his achievements.[12] In English translation the hymn in its entirety reads:

Excellence, for human beings hardest-earned,
    most coveted prize of a life-time's hunt,
for your sake, like a pretty girl's,
    even dying is considered in Greece a desirable fate,
and also putting up with crushing, endless tasks.
    So precious is the fruit you nurture in the mind:
godlike, it surpasses gold
    and parents and soft-eyed sleep.

For your sake Zeus' son Herakles and the sons of Leda
laboured at their numerous tasks

---

[8] C. M. Bowra, *Problems in Greek Poetry* (Oxford: Clarendon Press, 1953), 139–142. On the *Hymn to Hygeia* see Édouard Des Places, "Hymnes grecs au seuil de l'ère chrétienne," *Bib* 38 (1957): 113–129; Furley and Bremer, *Greek Hymns*, 1:224–227. Furley and Bremer minimize the connections between the two hymns as they argue for a later date for the *Hymn to Hygeia*.

[9] Bowra, *Problems in Greek Poetry*, 144. Ariphron may have composed his *Hymn to Hygeia* to inaugurate her cult in 420 BCE. Cf. Des Places, "Hymnes grecs," 114–115.

[10] Bowra, *Problems in Greek Poetry*, 145.

[11] Ibid.

[12] Furley and Bremer, *Greek Hymns*, 1:266.

(thirsting) for your power.
And out of sheer desire for you Achilles and Aias
    descended to Hades' house.

Passion for your beauty led the native son
    of Atarneus to leave the light bereft.
Therefore his achievement is praiseworthy,
    and the Muses, daughters of Memory,
will promote him to immortality,
celebrating the awesome power of Zeus, god of friendship,
and the distinction of lasting loyalty.[13]

The teaching of the hymn may be seen to operate on several levels. First, one can observe the direct claims made about Areta. It is worth great sacrifice and effort to earn it; its value surpasses the most valuable things in the world. In this arena, Aristotle may reflect the influence of Prodicus, among others.[14] Second, one can note the ways that heroes (Herakles, the sons of Ledo, Achilles, and Aias) are provided as models. They illustrate the truth of the claims just made by reminding the audience of the lengths to which individuals have gone to obtain her. Though not a direct exhortation, there is an implicit one in these examples in that they are held up as models to be imitated. The imitation is not, however, of their exact deeds, but of the desire for excellence that drove them to labor at impossible tasks. Third, by placing Hermias in the company of these heroes, Aristotle conveys the high view he has of Hermias both in his life and death. Hermias is remembered alongside heroes of the mythic past. In particular it is faithfulness and the power of friendship that are singled out for praise and connected with the lasting fame Hermias will enjoy. His immortality is connected with the work of the Muses in inspiring songs like this one which commemorate Hermias and his own pursuit of excellence.

As for the philosophical orientation of the poem, the abstract nature of the deity along with the emphasis on the pursuit of Areta are perhaps the most philosophical aspects. Of course, deified abstractions were not unknown in earlier Greek literature, as the *Theogony* of Hesiod readily illustrates.[15] What is of interest here is that Aristotle devotes an entire hymn to this abstract deity. Still, that does not necessarily point to a philosophical orientation for the hymn as a whole. Along these lines Bowra suggested, "It is perhaps unwise to look for philosophical ideas in this poem. Such

---

[13] Ibid., 1:262–263.

[14] Areta was also personified in Hesiod's *Works and Days* 289–293. Bowra, *Problems in Greek Poetry*, 146–148.

[15] The *Theogony* is replete with examples. See, for example, *Theogony* 901 where we encounter Eunomia (lawfulness), Dike (justice), and Eirene (peace). I am grateful to David Aune for drawing my attention to the early existence of personified abstractions in Greek mythology.

ideas as it does contain are largely traditional . . . He was writing in honour of a dead friend; he was concerned with an individual."[16] When we examine other examples of philosophical hymns, we will indeed see that the later hymns are more explicit in revealing their philosophical orientation. Nevertheless, while not promoting a particular philosophical agenda, it is clear that the *Hymn to Virtue* promotes and fosters key values (i.e., friendship, loyalty, hard work, the value of excellence) that are central to the philosophical way of life. In this sense the remembrance of Hermias in the context of a *Hymn to Virtue* serves as a form of communal memory even as it contributes to the formation of communal identity. In hymnic form it inscribes a particular set of values as worthy of striving for, even to the point of death.

C. Aratus's Hymn to Zeus

The Hellenistic poet Aratus (born c. 310 BCE) begins his didactic poem *Phaenomena* with an eighteen-line introduction in the form of a hexameter hymn to Zeus.[17] This hymn taps into multiple temporal and spatial registers as it makes a number of claims about Zeus and his relationship with the world of humanity. The hymn reads:

From Zeus let us begin; him do we mortals never leave
unnamed; full of Zeus are all the streets
and all the market-places of men; full is the sea
and the havens thereof; always we all have need of Zeus.
For we also are his offspring; and he in his kindness unto men
giveth favourable signs and wakeneth the people to work,
reminding them of livelihood. He tells what time the soil is best
for the labour of the ox and for the mattock, and what time the seasons are favorable
both for the planting of trees and for casting all manner of seeds.
For himself it was who set the signs in heaven,
and marked out the constellations, and for the year devised
what stars chiefly should give to men right signs of the seasons,
to the end that all things might grow unfailingly.
Wherefore him do men ever worship first and last.
Hail, O Father, mighty marvel, mighty blessing unto men.
Hail to thee and to the Elder Race! Hail, ye Muses,

---

[16] Bowra, *Problems in Greek Poetry*, 150.

[17] For commentary on the hymn see Douglas Kidd, *Aratus: Phaenomena* (Cambridge Classical Texts and Commentaries 34; Cambridge: Cambridge University Press, 1997), 161–174.

right kindly, every one! But for me, too, in answer to my prayer
direct all my lay, even as is meet, to tell the stars. (lines 1–18)[18]

In very traditional style he hymns Zeus and recounts his benefactions to
humanity particularly as they relate to the signs that Zeus has appointed in
the stars (lines 1–15). He also invokes the Muses and asks that they would
guide his song as he tells of the stars (lines 16–18). All of this serves as a
fitting proem for the larger composition that follows.

Many aspects of Aratus's hymn are intrinsically interesting and a number of these relate directly with the concerns of this chapter, namely, didactic hymnody in the Greco-Roman world. Aratus quite consciously imi-
tates the literary precedents he has inherited.[19] At the same time, he infuses
those forms with new ideas and new meanings. That is, he uses traditional
forms to express current ideas, particularly those of Stoic philosophy, although his work cannot be considered a Stoic treatise by any means.[20] In
this project he adapts aspects of earlier hymnic traditions, and creates a
composition that reflects both tradition and innovation.[21] Kidd suggests
that Aratus seeks to improve on Hesiod "by bringing his genre up to
date."[22] He claims that Hellenistic readers were "expected to appreciate the
ingenuity with which the source material is often differently treated."[23] For
purposes of the present study it will be instructive to observe some of these
dynamics in the hymn and in the *Phaenomena* as a whole. These observations will be particularly important since the hymn itself has had some significant influence on later writers (e.g., Paul and others). As we will see in
both Jewish and Christian hymnody and poetry, the dynamics which are
reflected in both imitation of and innovation relating to earlier texts often
have much to do with presenting the intellectual, social, and cultural ideas
of the past in such a way that they shed light on contemporary challenges
that the community is facing. These dynamics appear to be in play in the
poetry of Aratus as well.

In order to appreciate the role of the proem, a few words need to be said
about the *Phaenomena* as a whole. The 1,154 line poem deals primarily

---

[18] English translations of this hymn are from Aratus, "Phaenomena," in *Callimachus, Hymns and Epigrams; Lycophron; Aratus* (trans. A. W. Mair and G. R. Mair; Cambridge, Mass.: Harvard University Press, 1977), 183–299, here 207.

[19] Christos Fakas, *Der hellenistische Hesiod: Arats Phainomena und die Tradition der antiken Lehrepik* (Serta Graeca 11; Wiesbaden: Reichert, 2001), 221.

[20] A. W. James, "The Zeus Hymns of Cleanthes and Aratus," *Antichthon* 6 (1972): 28–38. James compares Aratus with Cleanthes and notes, "Aratus…was only incidentally concerned with contemporary philosophy in his *Phaenomena*, which may be character-ized as a versified technical treatise tinged with Stoicism" (28).

[21] See the fuller development of this idea in Fakas, *Der hellenistische Hesiod.*

[22] Kidd, *Aratus*, 8.

[23] Ibid.

with the constellations of stars, how to recognize them, and how to gain insight into the proper times for agricultural labor by observing the movements of the stars, moon, and sun. The final third of the poem deals with signs relating to weather conditions in particular as these relate to sailing.[24] Composed in the Hellenistic period, an era which witnessed the emergence of prose handbooks and treatises on matters ranging from medicine to rhetoric to military tactics, the *Phaenomena* corresponds in some ways with the ideals of earlier times represented by Hesiod. In that context, Toohey suggests that Hellenistic didactic epic, of which Aratus is a prime example, "represents an attempt to counterpoise the strangeness of a long-defunct epic language and meter with the (artificial) novelty of the popular, contemporary literature of the handbook."[25] Even as Aratus presents a comprehensive account of astronomical and atmospheric phenomena derived from scientific advances of the Hellenistic period, he does so in a form and with language that marks his composition as a participant in an ancient and revered form of teaching.[26]

As for the overall teaching of the *Phaenomena*, it is offered within the framework of the overriding authority of Zeus. As Hesiod began his *Works and Days* by appealing to Zeus, and as the Muses in the *Theogony* begin and end with Zeus, so Aratus begins with Zeus. But as one learns in the course of the composition, Aratus's poem features an updated Zeus. Kidd notes, "While the character and language of the proem are clearly Hesiodic, its content strongly reflects the cosmic beliefs of the contemporary Old Stoa, especially as they are expressed in Cleanthes' *Hymn to Zeus*."[27] While we will turn our attention to Cleanthes later in this chapter, for now it is important to note that Aratus at least reflects Stoic doctrine, whether or not he aims to present a fully integrated Stoic view of the cosmos. By reflecting the Stoic concept of a rational God, Aratus's poem is in implicit contrast with Hesiod's portrayal of Zeus. In this way Aratus can be said to highlight the progress of Greek civilization, particularly in understanding the phenomena of the natural world.[28] The *Phaenomena* as a whole thus

---

[24] Kidd outlines the *Phaenomena* in five sections: A. 1–18 Proem; B. 19–461 The constellations and how to recognize them; C. 462–757 The passage of time and how to estimate it by observing the constellations and the moon and sun; D. 758–1141 Local weather signs observable in natural phenomena and the behaviour of birds and animals (with 758–777 serving as a second proem); E. 1152–1154 Conclusion: a summing-up of the principal lessons; Ibid., 5–7.

[25] Toohey, *Epic Lessons*, 51.

[26] For a full treatment of the extent to which Aratus seeks to embody and emulate the style and genre of Hesiod's poems, see Fakas, *Der hellenistische Hesiod*.

[27] Kidd, *Aratus*, 10.

[28] Ibid., 12. Along these lines, James observes, "There is little affinity in detail between Hesiod's praise of Zeus and Aratus'," James, "Zeus Hymns," 35.

reflects the orderly nature of the universe and Zeus's beneficence to humanity in revealing the signs of the seasons and of the weather to humanity.

With this understanding in mind one can better appreciate the crucial role played by the proem as it introduces the main theme and the universal framework for what will follow. Like the work as a whole, the proem "owes its form to the traditions of Hesiodic epic and its content to the contemporary themes of Stoicism."[29] We can observe a number of poetic and hymnic aspects of the proem as well as numerous places where the language of Homeric epic and Hesiodic poetry are reflected. As for the subject matter, particularly as it relates to the idea of the divine, that is where one sees some of the Hellenistic and philosophical innovation. Kidd explains, "There is no reference to the old myths at all. Instead we have the Stoic concept of Zeus as the πνεῦμα that pervades the cosmos, the source of all life, an intelligence that reveals its divine πρόνοια in making the universe intelligible and favorable."[30] Aratus thus presents what formally appears to be a very traditional hymn but what in reality reflects more recent understandings of the nature of the divine.

This hymn serves several purposes in this context. First, if we take it at face value, it invokes the presence of Zeus and the Muses to empower Aratus to speak of the stars. As we have seen in the Homeric Hymns and the poetry of Hesiod, this was a common *topos* in ancient hymnody. Second, it sets his entire composition within the context of a prayer/hymn. Third, it introduces the subject and themes of the larger composition (as Hesiod did in his *Works and Days*, though his subject and themes were different). Fourth, through its use of epic phrases and motifs, as well as through its hymnic form, it places itself in the Hesiodic tradition, setting a tone and an expectation among the hearers.

As for the explicit teaching of the hymn, it is possible to identify seven lessons which the hymn brings into focus for the listener or reader. These can be discerned as one moves through the hymn section by section. First, line 1, "From Zeus let us begin; him do we mortals never leave unnamed." This line contains an implicit message as it reflects the practices of the day. In other words, it is a reflection both on how things are done as far as current practice, and how they ought to be done.[31] The hymn values and reinforces contemporary practice as it relates to praising Zeus in many contexts.

---

[29] Kidd, *Aratus*, 161.

[30] Ibid., 162.

[31] Kidd points to and rejects the possibility raised by some scholars that this line may suggest the setting is an address to friends at a symposium or at least that the language is suggestive of such an occasion. Ibid., 163.

Second, lines 2–4, "Full of Zeus are all the streets and all the market-places of men; full is the sea and the havens thereof." These lines contain direct and explicit teaching regarding the presence of Zeus everywhere. It is here that the reader begins to be confronted with Stoic thought as dis-tinct from the mythological narratives of the earlier hymnic traditions rep-resented by the *Homeric Hymns* and Hesiod's hymnic preludes. It is possi-ble that by having specific locations such as roads and marketplaces as well as sea and havens filled with Zeus, Aratus has given Zeus areas that are the province of Poseidon and Apollo. As Kidd notes, "The Stoic Zeus has now supplanted the older gods, and the cosmos is now monotheistic."[32] This "Stoic Zeus" will be treated more fully by Cleanthes in his longer but roughly contemporary *Hymn to Zeus*.[33]

Third, line 4, "Always we all have need of Zeus. For we also are his offspring." Here again we observe explicit instruction through direct state-ment rather than narrative. This line in particular will have lasting impact as placed on the lips of Paul in Acts 17:28. The claims at this point in the hymn relate to human dependence on Zeus and the nature of the human relationship to him. Repeated use of the terms "all" and "always" reflect the totality of Zeus and the totality of our need of him. Though not named as father until line 15, the idea here is a crucial part of the argument that the hymn sets out regarding the relationship of humans to Zeus and the stars he set in place.[34]

Fourth, lines 5–13 recount the benefactions that Zeus has given to men due to his kindness. Zeus gives signs to humanity; he wakens people to la-bor; he tells when the soil is best and when the seasons are favorable for planting. He set stars in heaven and marked the constellations, devising what stars would prevail at different times of the year. The style of re-counting the deeds of Zeus continues to be descriptive rather than narrati-val. Zeus's purpose in doing this is taught directly in line 13: "to the end that all things might grow unfailingly." The goal of all the aforementioned deeds of Zeus: all things would grow well for the benefit of humanity.

Fifth, line 14, "Wherefore him do men ever worship first and last." In this point Aratus circles back to the beginning. It is because of the benefac-tions of Zeus that men begin their works with him and also why he is never left unnamed (line 1). This line again reinforces the propriety of giving honor to Zeus at all times. The worship that Zeus receives is not out of du-ty or fear or compulsion. Humans honor Zeus because of their inherent re-

---

[32] Ibid., 165.

[33] See the brief comparison of the presentation of Zeus in the two works in Pohlenz, *Die Stoa*, 169.

[34] Kidd, *Aratus*, 166.

lationship with the deity ("we are his offspring," line 4) and because of his benefactions to humanity.

Sixth, line 15, "Hail, O Father, mighty marvel, mighty blessing unto men. Hail to thee and to the Elder Race!" In these lines which reflect the traditional manner of addressing the deity at the end of a hymn, the teaching about the relationship of Zeus with humanity is made explicit: Zeus is indeed a father to the human race. He is a great wonder, and great blessing to humanity. Though the meaning of the "Elder Race" is debated (there are at least seven possibilities), it is not crucial to make a determination of the meaning of this phrase for our present purposes.[35]

Seventh, lines 16–18: "Hail, ye Muses, right kindly, every one! But for me, too, in answer to my prayer direct all my lay, even as is meet, to tell the stars." Just as the poem throughout has reflected aspects of earlier hymnody, the ending does as well. As Hesiod took leave of his hymn to Zeus at the opening of the *Works and Days* so that he could speak truth to Perses, so Aratus concludes his hymn and turns to recounting the stars. This particular form of ending places the passage clearly within the tradition of hymnic prooimia: it addresses the Muses, and seeks divine aid for the poet as he turns to another task.

As we have seen, Aratus has written a prologue for his work in the form of a hymn to Zeus. The hymn reflects a didactic purpose on a number of levels. Most obviously, the hymn is set at the beginning of a didactic poem, the *Phaenomena*. Beyond that, the hymn itself teaches its own lessons in several ways. As far as explicit teaching, the hymn makes claims about the universality of Zeus's rule and all of humanity's dependence on him. It also establishes the connection between Zeus, the signs of the heavens and earth, and human labor. But the hymn also conveys truth in more implicit ways. By beginning his poem in this way, Aratus hearkens back to ancient traditions of prooimia, setting his poem in a venerable line of poetry including the *Works and Days* of Hesiod. Such a move indicates to the reader or hearer how the remainder of the work should be read. Further, by calling upon the Muses for inspiration, the hymn conveys that the words that follow are not those of Aratus alone. As the Muses guide his singing, Aratus will give divine insight into the signs that Zeus has given to humanity.

---

[35] Kidd (172–173) gives the possibilities and argues that it refers to the group of immortals of which Zeus is a part. "From the Stoic point of view as presented in the *Phainomena* there are only the two races, the divine and the human, and A. here may be seen to have updated Hesiod by eliminating the ἡμίθεοι of *Op.* 160 and promoting Hesiod's phrase to the divine level," Ibid., 173.

D. Cleanthes' *Hymn to Zeus*

Cleanthes of Assos, an early Stoic teacher and philosopher, penned among other things a *Hymn to Zeus* in the third century BCE.[36] Like many of the hymns we explore in this study, Cleanthes' *Hymn* includes both traditional hymnic material as well as elements that are more indicative of his own context and interests. Many of its expressions show the influence of Homeric and Hesiodic hymns as does the overall choice to compose in hexameter, the typical meter for the Homeric Hymns and a marker of the special status of the composition.[37] The *Hymn to Zeus* has been classified as a philosophical hymn, since the figure of Zeus is not the traditional Olympian deity but rather the universal reason of the Stoic universe.[38] Yet in spite of its philosophical orientation and content, the *Hymn* also conveys what seems to be a genuine sense of reverence and awe, so that many interpreters view it as an authentic prayer of Cleanthes and not merely a philosophical teaching tool. This study finds that, as with many other ancient hymns, it can be profitably explored on a number of levels including that of its teaching, both explicit and implicit. After a brief summary of the contents of the *Hymn*, this section will explore several of the didactic aspects of this fascinating composition showing how Cleanthes utilized tradition and innovation in hymnic form to teach about universal reason, humanity, the problem of evil, and the nature of the good life.

The original purpose of the *Hymn* is unknown, and a variety of possibilities have been suggested. Even the basic question as to whether it was written as a genuine hymn of praise to Zeus or whether it was more of a literary creation on the part of a philosopher who appreciated the medium of poetry for conveying philosophical truth, is still debated. Scholars have proposed several possibilities regarding the function of the hymn in Cleanthes' day, none of which is decisive. For example, it may have been intended for recitation at a symposium, or for use as a table prayer, or perhaps for inaugurating a series of lectures. In more of a literary vein, the *Hymn* could have been written as a prooimion to another work, or perhaps as an interlude between the author's prose works.[39] Thom, the most recent major commentator on the *Hymn*, suggests that because of the centrality of the prayer, a religious setting should be preferred to a purely literary one. However, he notes that this setting does not negate the likelihood that the

---

[36] Thom, *Cleanthes' Hymn to Zeus*, 7.

[37] Ibid., 9, 24. Cf. Glenn W. Most, "The Poetics of Early Greek Philosophy," in *The Cambridge Companion to Early Greek Philosophy* (ed. Anthony A. Long; Cambridge: Cambridge University Press, 2006), 332–362, esp. 353.

[38] Thom, *Cleanthes' Hymn to Zeus*, 9.

[39] Ibid., 11–13.

hymn also had a "pedagogic function, reinforcing Stoic ideas."[40] He claims that it functioned on at least two levels: the internal communication between the singer and Zeus, and the external level between the poet and his human audience. In this section, we will explore what the *Hymn to Zeus* conveyed to the human audience that encountered it in some kind of instructional context.

The structure of the hymn is quite traditional as it opens with a six-line invocation, a feature which is typical of the earlier hymnic traditions. In English translation, the hymn begins:

Noblest of immortals, many-named, always all-powerful
Zeus, first cause and ruler of nature, governing everything with your law,
greetings! For it is right for all mortals to address you:
for we have our origin in you, bearing a likeness to God,
we, alone of all that live and move as mortal creatures on earth.
Therefore I shall praise you constantly; indeed I always sing of your rule. (lines 1–6)[41]

The first two lines identify the subject of the hymn with epithets and descriptions. The manner of address in these opening lines, and the entire hymn, is composed in the second person; i.e., the whole hymn is spoken directly to Zeus. Lines 3–6 reflect on the appropriateness of praising Zeus in light of his strength and in light of the close relationship that humans have with him. This idea echoes what we saw in Aratus's hymn to Zeus, with its explicit development of the notion that Zeus is a father and humans are his offspring.

The main portion of the hymn (the argument) runs from lines 7–31. It is this section that is most unlike earlier hymns. Though he uses much that is traditional in terms of expressions and style, Cleanthes does not compose this section around the typical themes of the mythical deeds of the god, his origins, or the origins of the cultic worship of the deity. Instead, Cleanthes turns to a philosophically oriented recounting of the power of Zeus (lines 7–20) and the problem of evildoers (lines 14, 21–30). Zeus's complete control over nature by the common reason is presented in sharp contrast to the folly of humans who disregard the will of Zeus, striving for happiness apart from the universal law.

As one might expect, the *Hymn* concludes with a lengthy prayer in lines 32–39. However, this prayer is somewhat different than what we have encountered at the conclusion of other hymns:

But all-bountiful Zeus, cloud-wrapped ruler of the thunderbolt,
deliver human beings from their destructive ignorance;
disperse it from their souls; grant that they obtain
The insight on which you rely when governing everything with justice;

---

[40] Ibid., 13.
[41] English translation of this hymn is that of Johann C. Thom. Ibid., 40–41.

so that we, having been honored, may honor you in return,
constantly praising your works, as befits
one who is mortal. For there is no other greater privilege for mortals
or for gods than always to praise the universal law in justice. (lines 32–39)

Unlike other Greek hymns that we have examined, the prayer in this hymn
is not for Cleanthes himself, that Zeus might favor him as he recites another song, or that he might grant him prosperity. Rather, the prayer is universal, asking Zeus to "deliver human beings" from the folly he has just discussed and to give them insight so that humans may repay Zeus with honor
as they praise his works and sing of his law. The prayer thus asks that Zeus
would save humans from folly and allow them to live in accordance with
the divine reason.

Though the form and structure of the hymn is quite reflective of earlier
precedents, the preceding summary indicates that the *Hymn* goes beyond
earlier Greek hymnody in terms of its content and its portrayal of Zeus.
The main section of the *Hymn*, which in the longer *Homeric Hymns* is generally concerned with mythical history, the deeds of the god, his origins,
his inventions, etc., is here concerned with reflection that is much more
theological and philosophical than narratival. The uniqueness of this section is further underscored by the way that Cleanthes maintains a second-
person address throughout the composition. Many of the Greek hymns we
have looked at relate their mythical narrative in third-person style. This
was certainly the case with the hymnic preludes to both the *Theogony* and
Works and Days. Though direct address was a feature of the closing request of these hymns, the narrative was provided in a third-person descriptive style. By crafting the whole hymn as if it were spoken directly to the
deity, Cleanthes enhances the impression of a personal relationship to the
deity.

The hymn teaches in a fairly direct manner, rather than by recounting a
narrative that must be interpreted for its applicability to a contemporary
audience. In terms of what the *Hymn* communicates to the human audience, Thom observes, "The *Hymn to Zeus* serves to remind people of, and
implicitly exhorts them to achieve, their true goal in life, namely, to live in
accordance with the divine *logos* manifest in nature. As such, it also functions as an expression of Stoic doctrine."[42] One can easily imagine that the
Hymn and its prayer could serve as a convenient reminder for students of
Stoic philosophy of what their ultimate aims are, as well as the things that
can deter them from achieving those aims. Thom suggests, however, that
Cleanthes may have had a more general audience in mind as well. He
writes, "Some kind of public performance, whether at a symposium or before a public lecture, would be more suitable for this function than as an

---

[42] Ibid., 13.

insert in a philosophical treatise."[43] In view of the prayer at the end, it is possible to see this hymn in the tradition of hymnic preludes. Cleanthes' prayer, while universal in scope, includes both himself (as teacher) and his audience (as students and potential students). The prayer could be answered in the lecture or reading that followed the recitation of this *Hymn*. Though Cleanthes does not use any of the traditional expressions that end hymnic preludes (e.g., Homeric *Hymn to Demeter* 494–495, *Works and Days* 11, *Phaenomena* 18), he does end by introducing a particular subject matter. The final lines read, "For there is no other greater privilege for mortals or for gods than always to praise the universal law in justice" (lines 38–39). One could imagine the poet turning his attention then to an exposition of universal law in the form of a lecture (if this were considered in the setting of a public performance), or a written treatise on Stoic doctrine (if this were considered in the context of a literary work).

In terms of its specific teaching the *Hymn* conveys three important aspects of Stoic doctrine and ethics: the nature of the universal reason and human connectedness to it, the problem of evil, and the proper way for humans to live.

The string of epithets that open the *Hymn* (lines 1–2) presents a wide range of perspectives on the identity and power of Zeus and introduces the main themes of the hymn. Cleanthes teaches in these opening lines that Zeus is, among other things, many-named, all-powerful, the first cause and ruler of nature, and the one who governs everything. The term "many-named" is a common epithet used to honor ancient deities. But it also carries philosophical meaning as well.[44] Thom suggests, "Cleanthes is deliberately using the term in a literal sense to convey the Stoic notion that Zeus, as the active principle in the universe, may be viewed from multiple perspectives: the universe as a unity, reason, fire, fate, or providence."[45] James presents a similar explanation, arguing that the term, in this context, "has a philosophical weight of meaning, referring to the Stoic pantheistic notion of Zeus as cosmic νόμος, λόγος and πῦρ, an identification that soon becomes apparent to the attentive reader."[46] Each of these opening epithets and phrases is carefully chosen and reflects both traditional meanings as well as specifically Stoic overtones.[47] They convey Stoic teaching about who Zeus is and how he governs the world.

---

[43] Ibid.
[44] Pohlenz, *Die Stoa*, 108.
[45] Thom, *Cleanthes' Hymn to Zeus*, 46.
[46] James, "Zeus Hymns," 29.
[47] Thom, *Cleanthes' Hymn to Zeus*, 44–52.

These ideas reflect well the physics of Stoic philosophy.[48] As Brunschwig explains, "Above all else, Stoic physics is a grand vision of the world as a perfect unity, a divine living being governed by its own omnipresent and providential reason."[49] Certainly this is the perspective reflected in lines 1–2, 7–8, 13–15, and infused throughout the hymn. In Stoic philosophical texts this active principle is often expressed through the idea of fire.[50] This idea is reflected in the *Hymn* as well in the image of the "the two-edged, fiery, ever-living thunderbolt" (line 10). Here, traditional language and imagery in reference to Zeus takes on a philosophical reference as well.[51] The thunderbolt is symbolic of Zeus's power in directing all things: "With it you direct the universal reason" (line 12). The belief in this active principle which directs the universe through reason leads to a deterministic view of history. This idea is reflected clearly enough in line 15, "Not a single deed takes place on earth without you, God," as well as in lines 7–8, "This whole universe, spinning around the earth, truly obeys you wherever you lead, and is readily ruled by you." The *Hymn* clearly paints a portrait of Zeus and the world that promotes the particular Stoic perspective that the world is governed by all-powerful divine reason.[52]

Another facet of the hymn's teaching has to do with the relation of humanity to Zeus. Humans have their origin in Zeus (line 4), bear his likeness (line 4), and have the privilege and responsibility of praising Zeus (lines 6; 36–39). Stoic texts often emphasized a close relationship between the divine and humanity, indicating that humans share with the deity both rationality and virtue.[53] Thom notes, "Cleanthes in his description of the relationship between God and mortals (v. 4) combines traditional mythological terms of genealogy and resemblance between father and child with the more technical philosophical terminology of participation in deity."[54] The strategy of Cleanthes in describing the relationship of Zeus and humans is similar to the strategy he employed in speaking of the characteristics and powers of Zeus in lines 1–2. Cleanthes uses familiar language and brings in technical and philosophical meanings as well.

The deterministic view of God and the world noted above points ahead to two further aspects of Stoic teaching which occur in the *Hymn*: the prob-

---

[48] For a detailed analysis of Stoic physics see Pohlenz, *Die Stoa*, 64–110. For a summary picture see Jacques Brunschwig and D. N. Sedley, "Hellenistic Philosophy," in *The Cambridge Companion to Greek and Roman Philosophy* (ed. D. N. Sedley; Cambridge: Cambridge University Press, 2003), 151–183, esp. 169–172.

[49] Brunschwig and Sedley, "Hellenistic Philosophy," 169.

[50] Ibid., 170–172.

[51] James, "Zeus Hymns," 32.

[52] Brunschwig and Sedley, "Hellenistic Philosophy," 172.

[53] Thom, *Cleanthes' Hymn to Zeus*, 21.

[54] Ibid., 21, 64.

lem of evil, and the proper human response to the divine order of the world. Thom suggests this is, in fact, the major theme of the *Hymn* as a whole: "The main theme of the *Hymn to Zeus* is not simply the praise of Zeus, but the problem posed by human folly and disobedience that disrupt both God's rule and the appropriate praise of his rule."[55] The presence of evil in the world became a point of difficulty for the Stoics, who, as we have seen, asserted that the whole world was governed by all-powerful divine reason. Sandbach points out that the *Hymn* aims to provide an explanation for evil by declaring "that Zeus wills everything except the actions of bad men, but that these are fitted by him into his scheme."[56] Zeus's power is reflected in his ability to integrate those bad choices into his good universe. Sandbach explains, "The bad man appears as an independent originator of some happenings which God, who had no hand in devising them, is clever enough to turn to serve his purposes."[57] Lines 15–31 elaborate on the choices made by "bad people" and the way that Zeus is even able to fit these into his plans. It appears then that the choices of "bad people" fall outside of the determined course of history.[58]

Finally, the hymn exhorts the hearer to the best way of life, a life that is lived in harmony with divine reason. Line 25 provides the clue to the good life. The preceding lines discuss the bad people who do not listen to or heed the universal law, which, if they obeyed it, would have enabled them to "have a good life with understanding" (line 25). Sandbach summarizes the ethic this way: "The whole world is ruled by God and nothing in it happens without its being his will. So the good man will accept everything, knowing that it is not only unalterable, since Fate determines all, but also the work of God, the perfect being."[59] Zeno's expression for this ethic is "living in agreement with nature."[60] Other fragments of Cleanthes also express this view. The following prayer to Zeus preserved in Epictetus and attributed to Cleanthes reflects similar themes to the *Hymn to Zeus* but in a more personal manner:

Lead me, O Zeus, and lead me thou, O Fate,
Unto that place where you have stationed me:

---

[55] Ibid., 18.

[56] F. H. Sandbach, *The Stoics* (2nd ed.; Bristol: Bristol Press, 1989), 101.

[57] Ibid.

[58] The extent to which this explanation is philosophically satisfactory is open to debate. Sandbach suggests that Cleanthes' successor, Chrysippus, saw the inherent difficulty in this position and endeavored to defend it. Ibid., 101–110.

[59] Ibid., 37.

[60] Brunschwig and Sedley, "Hellenistic Philosophy," 172.

I shall not flinch, but follow: and if become
Wicked I should refuse, I still must follow.[61]

The Stoic ethic is thus a personal one, and the audience to the *Hymn* is exhorted to listen to and heed the universal reason so that they may enjoy a "good life with understanding." Thom summarizes the ethical teaching of the *Hymn* by stating that a good or happy life "is obtained when insight and understanding are combined with obedience to the universal law, that is, when one's own mind and actions are in harmony with the events unfolding in nature."[62]

What does the choice of poetic form convey? Sandbach argues that, for Cleanthes, the *Hymn* "expresses the exaltation he felt as he recognized God's omnipotence and his own kinship to this marvelous power."[63] As a genre, hymnody is well-suited to portray grandeur, awe, and greatness and to convey that kind of impression to a human audience, certainly more so than a prose treatise or other kind of composition. Sandbach, again, notes, "Although philosophic thought could sufficiently explain things divine as well as human, prose did not possess phrases to go with divine greatness; but meter and tune and rhythm matched the truth to be found in the consideration of the divine."[64] The choice of hymnic form is appropriate to the lofty subject matter which Cleanthes wished to treat in this composition.

Poetic forms played a role in philosophy not only in Cleanthes but also with other early Greek philosophers. Early philosophers such as Xenophanes, Parmenides, Empedocles, and Heraclitus utilized dactylic hexameter, a meter that carried with it an association with the divine. In assessing the significance of this phenomenon, Most explains,

Parmenides not only in general made novel use of the divine status associated with metrical form in order to legitimate a philosophical discourse transcending human capabilities, but also in particular exploited the linguistic and metrical possibilities of traditional epic in a creative and imaginative way so as to put into this archaic form doctrines that were quite new and foreign to it.[65]

From our analysis it is clear that Cleanthes employed a similar strategy, or at least that some of these dynamics are at work in his choice of poetic form.

In addition to the ethos associated with meter, Most has observed the implicit influence of poetry on early Greek philosophy.[66] Because of their

---

[61] Frag. 527, H. von Arnim, *Stoicorum Veterum Fragmenta* (3 vols.; Stuttgart: B.G. Teubner, 1964), 1:118. English translation is from Sandbach, *The Stoics*, 37.

[62] Thom, *Cleanthes' Hymn to Zeus*, 127.

[63] Sandbach, *The Stoics*, 110.

[64] Ibid.

[65] Most, "Poetics of Early Greek Philosophy," 355.

[66] Ibid., 342.

success and their influence, Homer and Hesiod created a set of expectations that any serious discourse within the Greek culture needed to meet. The works of Homer and Hesiod reflected what Greek audiences expected in their serious public discourse and also shaped those expectations as well. Most argues that Homer and Hesiod "represent a heritage and a context of expectations that the early Greek philosophers could only have ignored at their own risk – and one that they quickly learned with considerable sophistication to exploit to their advantage."[67] Most discusses this discursive framework, cultural expectations, and how early poets worked within these constraints to a large extent. Again, we have seen that Cleanthes himself was able to work within the "discursive framework" he inherited from earlier Greek poets in order to effectively and powerfully portray a set of philosophical ideas in a hymnic form.

Ultimately, Cleanthes was able to compose a hymn that was at the same time a reflection of many fundamental and traditional aspects of Greek culture, as well as more recent Stoic philosophical ideas. The extent to which the *Hymn* was intended to reinforce Stoic thought among students or to promote Stoic ideas among a wider audience is debated. Regardless, as we have seen, Stoic thought is most certainly creatively inscribed in this *Hymn* in a traditional style of poetic composition.

E. Lucretius's *On the Nature of the Universe*

The most striking and sophisticated use of hymnic form in the service of philosophical thought is found in the massive didactic poem of Lucretius. The first-century BCE Roman poet begins several of the six books of *On the Nature of the Universe* with passages that are, in essence, hymns. At the very least these passages can be considered hymnic in that they invoke a divine being and offer praise for accomplishments or prayer for divine aid. Lucretius explicitly and directly invokes Venus (1.1–49) and the Muse Calliope (6.91–95). Further, in four passages he praises Epicurus, the originator of the philosophy that the poem expounds, as one deserving to be honored as a god (1.62–79; 3.1–30; 5.1–54; 6.1–41). In light of the traditions of didactic hymns and prooimia that we have considered, none of these passages seems particularly strange. In fact, they are of interest for the ways that they very much reflect the earlier literary and hymnic precedents. But what is of more interest in this case is that hymnic praise of gods and prayers for divine aid are part of a didactic poem whose aim is to help people realize that gods are not involved in human or earthly affairs.

---

[67] Ibid.

According to the poem, the gods do not answer prayer or direct the course of nature, so devotion to the gods is misguided at best and harmful at worst. It would seem then that Lucretius's deployment of hymnody undermines or at least contradicts the main thrust of his whole composition. It is this tension between Epicurean beliefs and the theology that underlies traditional hymnic forms that makes this particular didactic poem so intriguing. As we will see, Lucretius's use of hymnic styles is not incidental nor is it an unconscious mistake on the part of Lucretius. Rather the use of hymnody in *On the Nature of the Universe* serves a number of important communicative functions within the larger didactic context.

Lucretius's didactic epic is the first multi-book poem of its kind. In terms of its length, style, and purpose it represents an innovative approach to the genre of didactic poetry.[68] At the same time, Lucretius seems to draw inspiration from earlier Greek poets, particularly the philosophical poetry of Parmenides and Empedocles.[69] Sedley explains, "Lucretius is the servant of two masters. Epicurus is the founder of his philosophy; Empedocles is the father of his genre. It is the unique task of Epicureanism's first poet to combine these two loyalties."[70] Complicating matters, Lucretius composed his work in Latin for a Roman audience, so that his work can be considered "an endeavour of both linguistic and cultural translation, the propagation of a Greek philosophical doctrine with the intention of changing radically the way that Lucretius's Roman audience thinks and lives."[71] Accordingly, as we examine the poetry of Lucretius, we can look for the influence of Greek poetic and philosophical precedents as well as indications of Lucretius's Roman context.

As a poem that expounds on and translates the doctrines of Epicurus into Latin, Lucretius's poem has a strongly didactic and philosophical tone. Like other philosophical schools of the day, the Epicureans were concerned with the practical therapeutic effects of their teaching in the lives of those who would adopt their philosophical way of life.[72] The Epicureans had a particularly high regard for the genius of their founder. Accordingly,

---

[68] Toohey, *Epic Lessons*, 88–90.

[69] Monica Gale, *Myth and Poetry in Lucretius* (Cambridge Classical Studies; Cambridge: Cambridge University Press, 1994), 50–74.

[70] D. N. Sedley, "The Empedoclean Opening," in *Lucretius* (ed. Monica Gale; Oxford: Oxford University Press, 2007), 48–87, here 87.

[71] Stuart Gillespie and Philip R. Hardie, "Introduction," in *The Cambridge Companion to Lucretius* (ed. Stuart Gillespie and Philip R. Hardie; Cambridge: Cambridge University Press, 2007), 1–15, here 2.

[72] Anthony A. Long, "Roman Philosophy," in *The Cambridge Companion to Greek and Roman Philosophy* (ed. D. N. Sedley; Cambridge: Cambridge University Press, 2003), 184–210, esp. 192.

Lucretius praises Epicurus for showing not only what the highest good was but also the path to achieve it:

With words of truth he purged men's hearts
And set a limit to desire and fear.
He showed the nature of that highest good
For which all mankind strives, and showed the way,
The strait and narrow path which leads to it
If we go forward with unswerving steps. (lines 24–29)[73]

The Epicureans aimed to help people find peace of mind, which Epicurus had referred to as *ataraxia*, "being undisturbed."[74] Part of the philosophical journey to *ataraxia* involved gaining a correct understanding of the gods as far removed from the world of humanity.[75] These insights lead to the elimination of fear of the gods as well as fear of death (3.31–93). As an Epicurean composition, then, its purpose was to enable people to experience peace by doing away with incorrect perceptions of reality that lead to fear and anxiety, and to replace those with correct Epicurean physics and theology. Lucretius wished to bring the life-giving teaching of Epicurus to his people during a time of particularly great turmoil near the end of the Roman Republic (1.29–43).[76]

We examine here two examples of hymnic passages within *On the Nature of the Universe*: the opening section of book 1, a hymn to Venus, and the opening section of book 5, a passage in praise of Epicurus. In the course of our examination of these passages, we will need to consider several other passages that will help to illumine Lucretius's strategy in making such significant use of hymnic styles.

Book 1 opens with what, on the surface, appears to be a very traditional hymnic prooimion in lines 1–49 of the longer prologue comprised of lines 1–149. The hymnic portion of the prooimion divides naturally into four sections. The hymn addresses Venus (lines 1–5), recounts her deeds in the bringing of spring (lines 6–19), and ends with two requests: a request on

---

[73] English translations are from Lucretius, *On the Nature of the Universe* (trans. Ronald Melville and with notes and introduction by Don Fowler and Peta Fowler; Oxford: Oxford University Press, 1999).

[74] In their introduction Don Fowler and Peta Fowler explain, "The metaphysics, the physics, the epistemology, the psychology, the theology were all designed to provide this peace" (Ibid., xvii).

[75] *On the Nature of the Universe* 1.44–49; 3.18–24; 5.146–154.

[76] Long suggests, "[Lucretius] looks to Epicureanism as the antidote to the strife and competition that were wrecking the Roman Republic" ("Greek and Roman Philosophy," 192). For further details on the historical developments in Rome at this time see Alessandro Schiesaro, "Lucretius and Roman Politics and History," in *The Cambridge Companion to Lucretius* (ed. Stuart Gillespie and Philip R. Hardie; Cambridge: Cambridge University Press, 2007), 41–58, esp. 53–58.

the part of Lucretius regarding his poem (lines 20–28) and a second request of Venus regarding bringing peace and putting an end to war (lines
29–49).[77] The hymn "masterfully uses the full palette of ancient hymnic
convention to produce a stunning picture of the power and beauty of the
traditional goddess of love and her effects."[78] The powerful hymnic portion
of the proem is followed by an address directly to Memmius, the listener to
whom the work is directed (lines 50–61).

The structure and content of this hymnic opening is very much in keeping with the opening sections of earlier didactic poems. In particular, there
are clear affinities with Hesiod's *Works and Days* and *Theogony*, as well as
Aratus's *Phaenomena*.[79] As the preludes of those works ended with requests of the deity, so does this opening passage in Lucretius. The first request, lines 20–28, comes after a recitation of the deeds and powers of Venus:

Since you and only you are nature's guide
And nothing to the glorious shores of light
Rises without you, nor grows sweet and lovely,
You I desire as partner in my verses
Which I try to fashion on the Nature of Things,
For Memmius, my friend, whom you have willed
At all times to excel in every grace.
For his sake all the more endow my words,
Goddess divine, with everlasting charm. (lines 20–28)

Lucretius here appears to be seeking the direct aid of the goddess as he
embarks on his instructional task, much like Hesiod invoked Zeus as he
addressed Perses in the *Works and Days*.

As many scholars have noted, it is surely surprising and perhaps a bit
confusing to observe the traditional invocation of the goddess here at the
beginning of this poem, especially since Lucretius will argue for the irrele-
vance of the gods to human existence.[80] Can we then regard this as mere
literary convention? Lucretius himself gives us part of the answer in another passage that occurs twice in this composition. Near the end of book 1

---

[77] Elizabeth Asmis, "Lucretius' Venus and Stoic Zeus," in *Lucretius* (ed. Monica
Gale; Oxford: Oxford University Press, 2007), 88–103, here 96.

[78] Gillespie and Hardie, "Introduction," 6.

[79] For a fuller list of parallels and connections with earlier hymns and poems see Gale,
Myth and Poetry in Lucretius, 209–211; idem., "Lucretius and Previous Poetic Traditions," in *The Cambridge Companion to Lucretius* (ed. Stuart Gillespie and Philip R.
Hardie; Cambridge: Cambridge University Press, 2007), 59–75, esp. 61–66; Hans
Schwabl, "Aus der Geschichte der Hymnischen Prooimien: Homer, Hesiod, art, Lukrez –
und ein Blick auf den Zeushymnus des Kleanthes," *Wiener humanistische Blätter* 43
(2001): 39–105.

[80] Gale, *Myth and Poetry in Lucretius*, 206.

in lines 926–950, Lucretius claims to be traveling a path that has not yet been taken.[81] In these lines he will mention the Muses three times, though not to invoke them directly.[82] Rather, he refers to their abilities to explain to the reader why he has chosen to write poetry instead of a prose treatise:

My purpose is
With the sweet voices of Pierian song
To expound my doctrine, and as it were to touch it
With the delicious honey of the Muses;
So in this way perchance my poetry
Can hold your mind, while you attempt to grasp
The nature of the world, and understand
Its value and its usefulness to men. (lines 19–25)

The poetry of Lucretius is thus designed to make the teaching of Epicurus more pleasant to the taste, at least initially. He compares his approach to doctors who smear honey on the rim of a cup in order to give loathsome medications to children (lines 11–19). If we use this as a clue to understanding Lucretius's hymnic passages, we can recognize that these are intended, at least in part, to make the whole presentation more acceptable initially. His Roman audience, which surely did believe in the presence and power of the gods in human life (this was one of the problems the poem seeks to address), would have appreciated and even expected such a poem to begin with the invocation of a divine being. They would likewise expect the direct invocation of a Muse, which we find in book 6:

Calliope, most skilful of the Muses,
Solace of men, delight of gods, do you
Now go before me as the last lap I run
And point the way to the white winning post
Marked out for me, that led by you renown
May greet me as I win the victor's crown. (lines 91–95)

Far from reflecting his belief in the power of the gods to grant him an answer to his request, the passages about inspiration and the Muses serve other purposes.[83] One purpose is that of reflecting his use of earlier traditions and also his innovations to his audience. However, as one commentator notes, "This does not tell the whole story of the role of poetry in *On the Nature of the Universe*, but it stressed how the verse both brings the reader

---

[81] The same passage is found in book 4.1–25, with the only difference appearing in the final line.

[82] In part through these references, Lucretius places his own composition within a particular stream of tradition including that of his Roman predecessor Ennius whom he had already referenced in 1.117–118. Cf. Gale, "Lucretius and Previous Poetic Traditions," 59.

[83] Diskin Clay, "The Sources of Lucretius' Inspiration," in *Lucretius* (ed. Monica Gale; Oxford: Oxford University Press, 2007), 18–47, esp. 26–31.

to drink and holds the reader in its grip while the 'medicine' of philosophy does its work."[84] Accordingly, we can see that Lucretius expected that his poetic form and his hymnic expressions would give him an opening with his audience that he might not have had if he had begun with the non-traditional principles of Epicurean philosophy.

In addition to the role of "sweetening the cup," the hymn to Venus also functions on several other levels. The multiple affinities with earlier didactic and epic poetry serve to position the work within those traditions. Gale observes that *On the Nature of the Universe* as a whole is "an extremely self-conscious work, which continually reflects, at both explicit and implicit levels, on its own poetics and its place in the literary canons and hierarchies of the ancient world."[85] The literary and hymnic connections, the employment of generic conventions, and the intertextual echoes in the opening proem are but several aspects of the reflections of Lucretius's sophistication as an author in the first century BCE. These ideas and echoes would not have been lost on Lucretius's educated audience, and we can assume that Lucretius's work would have conveyed to its readers the work's seriousness and its rootedness in tradition by means of these explicit and implicit markers of style and genre.

It is also the case that the opening of book 1 suggests the didactic role of all that follows. As Lucretius teaches Memmius, the reader will also learn as he or she overhears and participates in the dialogue between Lucretius and Memmius.[86] But the goal of the work goes beyond simply teaching to the more difficult task of persuading. Lucretius urges Memmius:

And now good Memmius, receptive ears
And keen intelligence detached from cares
I pray you bring to true philosophy;
Lest you should scorn and disregard my gifts
Set out for you with faithful diligence
Before their meaning has been understood. (lines 50–53)

In these lines we see the possibility that Memmius may reject the teaching of Lucretius before he gives it a fair hearing. Lucretius must persuade him to give it a fair hearing. This challenge again brings to mind the metaphor of honey on the edge of a cup of bitter medicine. In this regard we can see that the persuasive goal is one that is furthered by the poetic form of the

---

[84] Don Fowler and Peta Fowler in Lucretius, *On the Nature of the Universe*, 223. The reference to honey and medicine is a philosophical one as well, one that has its origin in Plato, *Laws* 2. 659e.

[85] Monica Gale, "Introduction," in *Lucretius* (ed. Monica Gale; Oxford: Oxford University Press, 2007), 1–17, here 16.

[86] Ibid., 13–14.

whole composition.[87] The work aims to create a response in the hearer or reader. Gale explains, "The *DRN* is to be read as a protreptic work, in which the poetry itself helps to draw the reader in and has a functional role to play in the process of conversion."[88] This happens as the poem unfolds, as, for example, the deeds ascribed to the goddess Venus in the opening hymn are reassigned to other natural forces.[89]

Given the multi-faceted roles played by the poetry of the whole composition and the hymn that opens book 1 in particular, what can be said about the teaching of the hymn itself? Does the hymn implicitly teach the value of praying to the goddess even as the whole work speaks against such a belief? Most scholars agree that Venus in the opening of book 1 should be taken as a symbol of pleasure or perhaps nature, so that seeking the deity through prayer and praise is not at issue here.[90] Along these lines, though, one key to understanding the teaching of the hymn may come in comparing the Venus of Lucretius to the Zeus of the Stoics, and of Cleanthes in particular. Asmis compares the two hymns in terms of the attributes and characteristics of the supreme deity they describe.[91] She finds that Lucretius has taken the powers attributed to Stoic Zeus and, whether he has gotten them from Cleanthes' *Hymn* directly or not, has applied them to Venus, with the result that the supreme goddess Venus is shown to represent the Epicurean ideal. In view of this understanding, it is worth noting the particular emphases of the hymn itself. The hymn emphasizes light (lines 5, 9, 21–22, cf. 136–149), as well as the eagerness and willingness with which nature and living things follow the goddess (lines 15–16, 18). These emphases contrast with Cleanthes' *Hymn to Zeus* where even the actions of bad people are brought into alignment with the divine will by the forceful power of Zeus, and Zeus wields the thunderbolt amidst dark and ominous clouds. Of Cleanthes' *Hymn to Zeus* Asmis explains, "The overall view of Zeus which emerges from the poem is that he is a supremely powerful rul-

---

[87] Gale notes a recognition among scholars "that the poetry of the *DRN* [*De rerum natura*] is in itself a kind of rhetorical tactic – that is, that the poem's language is designed not just to *explain* the principles of Epicurean philosophy, but to *persuade* the reader of the validity of the system and, ultimately, to make a convert of him or her" (Ibid., 5). On the rhetoric of the whole composition and its persuasive aims, see also E. J. Kenney, "Lucretian Texture: Style, Metre and Rhetoric in the *De rerum natura*," in *The Cambridge Companion to Lucretius* (ed. Stuart Gillespie and Philip R. Hardie; Cambridge: Cambridge University Press, 2007), 92–110.

[88] Gale, "Introduction," 5. For another example of didactic hymnody in the service of protreptic discourse see the hymn by a Hellenistic Jewish author in Wisdom of Solomon 10.

[89] Idem, *Myth and Poetry in Lucretius*, 211–215.

[90] Idem, "Introduction," 17.

[91] Asmis, "Lucretius' Venus."

er who has absolute control over the structure of events, even though there is resistance by mankind."[92] The portrait of Venus offered by Lucretius is thus much more positive as Venus guides and directs all things in a much different way. Summing up the presentation of Venus in the hymn of book 1, Asmis writes, "Venus . . . was conceived in part as an allegorical rival to Stoic Zeus: she stands for pleasure in a world ordered by its spontaneous impulses, as opposed to Stoic Zeus who stands for divine might and a world bound by an inexorable divine will."[93] In this regard we can see that Lucretius's portrayal of Venus in these terms is not only a positive statement about an alternative view of reality; it is also an implicit contrast with the Stoic understanding of the divine.

Asmis' observations and comparisons with Stoic Zeus certainly serve to illuminate important aspects of the meaning of the Venus imagery in the proem. Nevertheless, other interpretations suggest that the complexity of the Venus symbol cannot be reduced to any one idea in particular. Gale reviews other symbolic interpretations which interpret Venus as symbolizing the onset of spring or the creative forces of nature or pleasure itself.[94] In taking a more integrative view of this symbol, Gale writes, "In the figure of Venus, then, Lucretius has created a great mythological symbol for all that is positive, creative, and attractive in the natural world and in man. . . . This, then, is the Epicurean reading of the invocation which Lucretius suggests to his reader by means of verbal echo and reapplication of imagery."[95] Accepting this larger view of the symbol, we can recognize the power of poetry to convey a variety of interrelated meanings through its use of earlier traditions in a new context for a new purpose.

In concluding our look at the hymn to Venus in book 1, we can now note several aspects of its didactic purpose and function. First, as a hymnic proem it lays out the themes of the work and sets the generic expectations on the part of the reader. Second, as a poem and a hymn, Lucretius intended for it to sweeten his composition and make the less flavorful Epicurean teachings easier to swallow, as it were. Third, by using traditional imagery to present Venus as the ruler of all, in implicit contrast with the Stoic Zeus, Lucretius makes a case for an alternative vision of reality – a distinctly Epicurean vision which unfolds throughout the remainder of his composi-

---

[92] Ibid., 93.

[93] Ibid., 89. Asmis goes on to note, "The portrait of Venus . . . is a highly complex allegory, in which the traditional goddess of sexual pleasure has been transformed into a cosmic ruling force who has various attributes corresponding to those of Stoic Zeus. As the goddess of pleasure, Venus becomes the supreme creator, and the goddess of freedom and peace; and as such Lucretius claims her as his own source of inspiration and as a goddess to be venerated by the Romans" (100).

[94] Gale, *Myth and Poetry in Lucretius*, 217–223.

[95] Ibid., 223.

tion. Fourth, the specific choice of Venus conveys much in terms of her association with pleasure, and the delight which humans can experience as they embrace the Epicurean understanding of reality. These four aspects of the teaching function of the hymn, while certainly not exhausting the avenues for examining the didactic impact of the hymn, provide sufficient context to enable us to move on to explore another hymnic passage within Lucretius's didactic poem.

One of the striking features of *On the Nature of the Universe* is the high view of Epicurus. A number of passages praise Epicurus for his accomplishments and accord to him the honors normally reserved for gods and heroes. Taken together, these passages play an important role in the development of the poem, as the teachings of Epicurus enlighten the hearer and do away with the more traditional conception of the gods and their involvement in the world of humanity. Gale argues that the "*Remythisierung* of Epicurus is a systematic process, spanning the whole poem, whereby the philosopher is shown to supplant the traditional gods of Graeco-Roman religion and mythology."[96] In light of this overall strategy, we will examine one particular passage below, the proem to book 5.

Of the passages that praise him for his wonderful gifts to humanity, lines 1–54 of book 5 are the most striking in that they enumerate in hymnic style the reasons that Epicurus ought to be considered divine. The opening rhetorical questions are reminiscent of earlier hymns, and of poets searching for the right words and narratives with which to praise the deity (aporia):

Who can find fit words
To praise the man who left us such great treasures
Born from his breast and searched out by his mind? (lines 2–4)

As a rhetorical strategy the use of aporia serves to connect the praise of Epicurus with the traditional praise of the gods. As the passage unfolds Lucretius states his claims about Epicurus in language that is in every way appropriate to the praise of a god:

He was a god, a god indeed, who first
Found out that rule and principle of life
Which bears the name of Wisdom, and by his skill
Brought life from such mighty waves and darkness
And placed it in such calm and light so clear. (lines 8–12)

Like any good hymn of praise, the passage describes the discoveries and accomplishments of the deity who is the subject of the hymn. Here we see that Epicurus was the first to discover Wisdom (lines 8–10). He was also a

---

[96] Ibid., 192.

source of life in the midst of chaos (lines 11–12). These are the primary accomplishments that justify calling Epicurus a god (line 8).[97]

If the claims Lucretius makes about Epicurus were not shocking enough, he goes on to compare the discoveries of Epicurus with those of other gods (lines 13–21) and the deeds of Epicurus with those of other heroes (lines 22–44). In these comparisons, the discoveries of Epicurus are more praiseworthy than the discoveries of Ceres or Bacchus, and the deeds of Epicurus deserve more renown than those of Hercules. His comparisons are aimed to show that Epicurus' accomplishments are greater than those who are considered gods by the rest of humanity. In lines 13–14 of book 5 he writes,

Only compare the things that others found
In ancient time, and earned the name divine. (lines 13–14)

In the course of the comparison, Lucretius argues that even the crops of Ceres and the wine of Bacchus are not necessary for human life. However, he argues, a good life cannot be had without the teaching of Epicurus.

In a similar vein he compares the deeds of Hercules to the deeds of Epicurus. As impressive as were the victories of Hercules over wild beasts, they were not nearly as important for human life as the victories of Epicurus over the mental troubles of humanity. Gale explains, "The philosopher's purification of men's hearts (43) parallels Hercules' purification of the world from monsters: this enables the poet to present him as a new and better Hercules, who relied on words, not physical prowess (50)."[98] The final lines of the passage serve to summarize the themes of the hymn as they recount his blessings to humanity:

He therefore who has mastered all these vices
And cast them from the mind by words, not arms,
Will it not then be right to find him worthy
To be counted in the number of the gods?
Especially since in words from heaven inspired
He used to teach about the gods themselves,
And all the nature of the world make plain. (lines 49–54)

His words were inspired even as he taught about the gods themselves. Lucretius himself claims to utter "oracles more holy and more surely true" than any others in the ancient world (5.110–125). In these passages, reli-

---

[97] On the provocative line 8, Don Fowler and Peta Fowler write, "The Epicureans liked to shock by playing with the exaggerated language of praise used for rulers and other supposed benefactors (which sometimes passed over into real cult); so, for instance, the young Epicurean Colotes is said to have prostrated himself before Epicurus (Plutarch, *Against Colotes* 1117b–c). This was justified by the magnitude of Epicurus' blessings for mankind" (Lucretius, *On the Nature of the Universe*, 250).

[98] Gale, *Myth and Poetry in Lucretius*, 202.

gious language is used to assert the authority and origins of the teaching, while at the same time religion itself is undermined by the content of the teaching.[99]

As with the opening hymn to Venus, praising Epicurus as a god with unique accomplishments seems odd, particularly for a teacher who sought to show that the gods were far removed from the sphere of human existence. However, two aspects of the larger context of these claims help us appreciate their role. First, this exalted view of Epicurus can be seen as part of an older philosophical tradition in which the philosopher is seen as a *theois aner*. Gale notes, "Certain philosophers (especially Pythagoras) were credited with superhuman and divinely inspired wisdom and even domination over nature, or accorded divine honors."[100] In this light, praise of Epicurus is appropriate as part of the tradition of inspired philosophers. Second, when seen as part of the overall rhetorical strategy of the entire poem, Lucretius's point about Epicurus can be seen more clearly. The gift of *ataraxia* that Epicurus offers humanity through his teaching is better than any gifts of the gods. Further, the *ataraxia* that he achieved places Epicurus himself in the category of the gods who themselves dwell apart from the world in perfect tranquility. If one honors the traditional gods for their gifts, or if one honors deified humans for their accomplishments, or if one would honor the Epicurean gods who exist in perfect peace, how much more ought one to honor Epicurus whose gifts were superior to the others in every way? Taking this idea further, Gale explains, "Lucretius sets Epicurus up as a replacement for the traditional gods: the process is part of his overall strategy of investing the truths of Epicurean philosophy with the beauty and attractive power of images derived from myth."[101]

What does the presence of these hymnic passages, and the hymnic eulogizing of Epicurus do for the composition? Toohey suggests that, at least on the surface, the use of mythological imagery and references to the gods is to be expected in this type of composition. Toohey explains,

The use of mythology is generically conditioned. Here, however, is a poem built upon the premise of independence from the gods of human life, yet its demonstration of this very point is periodically driven to utilize myth as illustrative materials.[102]

---

[99] On this dynamic Gale notes, "His intention is undoubtedly polemical, and the passage serves both to enhance the poet's praise of his master and, in the long run, to undercut the very assumptions on which it appeared to rely." Ibid., 80.

[100] Ibid., 192. For examples, see the note on p. 192. Divine honors are noted in Diogenes Laertius 1.114; 8.68, Diodorus Siculus 9.9.9, Porphyry *Vit. Pyth.* 20, Iamblachus *Vit. Pyth.* 30. Further, the "near-idolisation of its founder" is a distinguishing characteristic of the Epicurean school. Cf. Gillespie and Hardie, "Introduction," 3.

[101] Gale, *Myth and Poetry in Lucretius*, 207.

[102] Toohey, *Epic Lessons*, 106.

He goes on to point out that even the choice of poetry as a means of communication creates some dissonance between the content of the larger work:

Lucretius' passionate language sabotages his Epicurean standpoint in very much the same way as does his evocation of Epicurus, or his excessively empathetic use of mythology. The conflict between the Lucretian medium and message has its reconciliation, again, in voice. This conflict may offend the logician, but it thrills the aesthete.[103]

In other words, Lucretius creates a work of great aesthetic value as he expresses the then ancient views of Epicurus in an ancient medium for a contemporary audience.

Toohey has suggested five qualities which didactic epic needed in order to succeed. These are, "voice, vivid, even sensational material (to offset the dryness of the didactic instruction), generic or at least textual variety (dramatic tonal oscillations, for example), conceptual simplicity, and a spirit of playfulness balancing the instruction."[104] The expression of Epicurean truths in poetic and even mythological style creates a dynamic in the composition as a whole that makes it compelling and enables it to succeed as didactic epic. Toohey further suggests that it is the "voice" of Lucretius that makes this poem work:

Despite Lucretius' having based his lore on the quiescent teaching of Epicurus, his voice seems to catch the timbre of that of the extravagant Empedocles. The manifest attractions of Empedocles' voice – the vigour, the hyperbole, the apparent self-confidence, the propensity for overstatement – are shared in many ways by Lucretius.[105]

Together with with this voice, the poetic expression and Epicurean content create a vivid and compelling portrait of reality as seen through Epicurean eyes.

Along these lines, Long points out the dynamic tension created by the pure Epicurean doctrine and the poetic form in which it was expressed:

Like all Epicureans, he looks back to Epicurus as his unique authority; he has no interest in doctrinal innovation or substantive deviation from the texts he takes to be canonical. Yet, while Lucretius has rightly been called a 'fundamentalist' Epicurean, his work is immensely creative not only in its poetic form but also in its rhetorical and emotional power and social relevance.[106]

---

[103] Ibid., 107.

[104] Ibid., 98.

[105] Ibid., 98–99. On the pre-Socratic poet Empedocles: "Empedocles . . . is one of the most astonishing of the ancient didactic poets. The key aspects of his work, his inimitably vigorous and vatic voice, his sensationalism, and his startling adversarial optimism, and his belief in some sort of an abstract, immortal, controlling, immanent principle (396–7 KRS) would mark his poetry out in any tradition" (47).

[106] Long, "Greek and Roman Philosophy," 195.

In this regard, the creativity of Lucretius is seen not in his adaptation of the doctrines of Epicurus, as much as in his persuasive presentation of that doctrine in poetic form.

F. Conclusions

Our survey of major philosophical hymns reveals several common characteristics. First, in each case we have noted that the hymnic expression of philosophical ideas was rooted in traditional styles, forms, and/or terminology that can be traced back to the Homeric Hymns and the poetry of Hesiod. Second, the choice of such a form appeared to be part of an overall communicative strategy designed to present the teachings of philosophy in ways that would have been readily understandable to students or potential students within a philosophical context. Third, our knowledge of the philosophical school in which each hymn arose enabled us to see connections between the teaching of the hymn and some of the main ideas of the philosophical system. Fourth, the contents of the hymns we explored tended to avoid mythological narrative, focusing instead on descriptions of the characteristics, powers, and accomplishments of the one who was the subject of the hymn.

In spite of these common features, each of the hymns we looked at also used some unique strategies to convey their teaching through praise. Aristotle's *Hymn to Virtue* was unique in its form, reflecting aspects of a paean and a θρῆνος, and addressing abstraction rather than an Olympian deity. Its teaching was, for the most part, implicit as it portrayed core values of Aristotle's philosophical way of life through the form of a hymn. Aratus employed the traditional form of the hymn to Zeus to begin his larger didactic composition and to position it within the tradition of didactic poetry stretching back to Hesiod himself. Cleanthes likewise employed the form of a hymn to Zeus but for a self-contained, stand-alone hymn that was not necessarily associated with a larger composition. Though its precise performative context is not known, its expression of Stoic philosophical ideas in traditional hymnic language creates a compelling portrait of the Stoic view of ultimate reality. Perhaps most striking was Lucretius's use of hymns to espouse the Epicurean philosophical system, a system that undermined the need for hymnic praise of the gods. Not only his use of hymns but his selection of subject matter (Venus and Epicurus) was of critical importance in achieving his didactic aims. In each of these instances we have seen that these poets were able to utilize traditional forms and styles of expression from ages past in innovative ways in order to achieve a didactic purpose for their day and age. As we will see in the next chapter, it was not only philosophy that made use of traditionally-styled hymnic praise for instructional purposes. Praise of exalted humans in hymnic style had an increasingly important place in the political and social world of the Greeks and Romans.

Chapter 4

Didactic Aspects of the Praises of Human Rulers

A. Introduction

The gods were not the only ones who received praise and honor in the ancient world of the Greeks and Romans; the giving of honor through verbal expressions of praise was an important aspect of many strata of ancient society. Rulers, benefactors, and heroes were praised for their accomplishments, their victories, their virtues, and their generosity.[1] Through hymnlike compositions known as encomia, honor was given to those who were thought deserving of it by those who were recipients of their benefactions or by professional poets who were commissioned to write poems of praise.

This ancient practice intersects with our study of didactic hymns in several ways. First, the ancients themselves tell us that, in terms of composition, contents, and themes, there is very little difference between praise of god (a hymn) and praise of a person (an encomium).[2] The primary difference in terminology relates to the nature of the one addressed. In order to more fully appreciate what we observe in the hymnic traditions, we would do well to consider the closely related encomiastic traditions.

Second, as was the case with many hymns in praise of gods, the compositions in praise of humans often conveyed much more than praise. Like hymns to gods, the encomia created a portrait of reality that the writer would have the hearers embrace on some level. In other words, like didactic hymns, the praises of rulers and other exalted humans often had a significant teaching function for their communities. The goal of the present chapter is to discern some of the didactic aspects of praises offered to hu-

---

[1] See for example the wide-ranging collection of honorary inscriptions with translation and commentary in Frederick W. Danker, *Benefactor: Epigraphic Study of a Graeco-Roman and New Testament Semantic Field* (St. Louis, Mo.: Clayton Pub. House, 1982).

[2] In his 1st c. CE *Progymnasmata*, Theon writes about encomia, "The term is now specifically applied to praise of living persons whereas praise of the dead is called an *epitaphios* and praise of the gods a hymn; but whether one praises the living or the dead or heroes or gods, the method of speaking is one and the same" (trans. is taken from George Alexander Kennedy, *Progymnasmata: Greek Textbooks of Prose Composition and Rhetoric* [SBLWGRW 10; Atlanta: Society of Biblical Literature, 2003], 50).

mans in the Greek and Roman world. This chapter will show that praises of humans, like didactic hymns directed toward the gods, often functioned as a strategy of instruction and at times, persuasion. In these compositions, traditional ideas or, occasionally, ideas that have not yet been fully embraced by a community, were portrayed in forms and styles that conveyed to the audience the sacred nature of these ideas and that helped the hearers to connect the ideas with more traditional religious and cultural associations.

As is the case with this volume as a whole, it is not possible to provide detailed analyses of all the texts that could possibly be included in a chapter on the praise of rulers and exalted humans in the Greco-Roman world. This chapter highlights examples from several different settings, providing these in chronological order. By arranging them in this way I do not mean to suggest there is dependence from one text to another. Rather, through these few examples we can observe some of the dynamics of praise of humans and its didactic functions, noting similarities as well as developments or divergences from one text to the next.

We begin with Pindar and his poetic compositions in praise of individuals who were victorious in athletic contests. Next we move to Isocrates who praises the ruler Evagoras in a prose encomium exhibiting hymnic features and themes. From there we will explore a hymn of Callimachus which praises both Zeus and Ptolemy II Philadelphus. This text leads naturally to a consideration of Theocritus' encomium of the same ruler. These texts reveal a good deal about how the conventions of hymnic praise that we have observed in earlier chapters are brought to bear on human rulers. The fact that each composition is closely connected with a specific time, place, and circumstance allows us to consider some of the larger purposes for which they are composed. Specifically, we will see how a vision of past and present are brought to bear in a process of identity formation for a particular community and its highly honored member.

The second half of the chapter looks at selected compositions and inscriptions in praise of Roman rulers. We begin with two compositions of Horace: *Odes* IV.5 and 15. In these *Odes* Horace praises Caesar Augustus in a manner that paints an ideal portrait of the Roman Empire under Augustus while at the same time inviting the reader to consider his or her place in it. Next we provide a very brief overview of some of the dynamics of the imperial ideology as it developed in the first centuries BCE and CE. By considering some key elements of the Roman imperial ideology, we will be better able to appreciate the ways that later texts and writers negotiate the challenges of the imperial context. We conclude with a brief look at Pliny's *Panegyricus*. As with the earlier Greek compositions, we will be able to see how these praise texts invite the readers or hearers to see themselves within the specific vision of the world that has been painted by the writer. In the Roman world in particular, we will see that didactic praise provided a means of negotiating the relationship between the most powerful individual in the world and those who found themselves to be beneficiaries of that individual.

B. Pindar's Victory Odes

Pindar, composing in the fifth century BCE, is best known for his epinician odes – the primary surviving specimens of his much larger and wider ranging corpus of poetic compositions. It is widely known that these were written to praise victors in the four major pan-Hellenic athletic festivals in Olympia, Delphi, the Isthmos, and Nemea, and that they blend hymnic and mythic elements together with didactic concepts as they give praise to the individual being honored.[3] Accordingly, most epinician odes deal with the athletic victory of the person honored, a myth that is related to the person (whether or not it is related to the specific victory), and moral and theological instruction, partly related to the myth.[4] Pindar's odes are neither pure hymns addressed to gods, nor are they merely poetic recitations of the praiseworthy deeds of individual humans. In light of their uniqueness as compositions of praise, what about Pindar's epinician odes is significant for this study of didactic hymnody?

First and foremost, epinician odes are, broadly speaking, part of the trajectory of praise in the ancient world. They utilize features and components of the hymnic tradition to cast their vision of ultimate reality and to position the athletic victor and his community within it. More specifically, Pindar's odes often include passages that are considered hymns in and of themselves, even if no one ode is considered to be purely a hymn (cf. *Nem.* 7.1–9; *Ol.* 12.1–14; *Isthm.* 7.1–21). These hymns function in a number of ways to provide the context and landscape in which to view the accomplishments of the human victor. While the epinician odes reflect earlier traditions of hymnic praise of gods, they also manifest innovation and development as they join these to praises of living men. Thus, Pindar's odes

---

[3] For general introductions to the world of Pindar see, for example, D. S. Carne-Ross, *Pindar* (New Haven: Yale University Press, 1985); Simon Hornblower and Catherine Morgan, *Pindar's Poetry, Patrons, and Festivals: From Archaic Greece to the Roman Empire* (Oxford: Oxford University Press, 2007); M. M. Willcock, *Pindar: Victory Odes* (CGLC; Cambridge: Cambridge University Press, 1995).

[4] Albrecht Dihle, *A History of Greek Literature: From Homer to the Hellenistic Period* (London: Routledge, 1994), 68–69.

give us insight into the ways that humans receive praise, and how this fits within the ancient Greek mythical framework.

Second, Pindar's praise of humans in close connection with divine myths reflects a time period before humans received more explicit hymn-like praise directly. Later writers will praise kings and rulers (even philosophers!) in god-like terms, using language once reserved for deities in order to express the greatness of the accomplishment of these exalted humans. Pindar never goes that far with his praise. However, Pindar, composing in the fifth century BCE, clears conceptual space for such a later practice as he brings the praise of human accomplishments and the praise of the divine into the same composition.

Third, though written to praise a victor, the epinician odes manifest a very strong didactic tendency as well, as noted above. They teach about the victor (his praiseworthy qualities) and about the gods (how the victor's accomplishments reflect an aspect of the mythic world of the gods and heroes), and they offer direct exhortation to the implied audience, whether that is the victor himself or the larger community of listeners. Unlike many of the other texts considered in this study, the didactic function is not the primary aim of these odes; nevertheless, in light of the complex cultural and political context of these odes, the didactic function – the way the odes paint a portrait of reality and invite the listener to embrace it – remains a significant feature of these compositions. The didactic lessons of the odes include such topics as reflections on the nature of the gods and the nature of humanity (*Nem.* 6.1–6; *Isthm.* 5.14–16), the source and significance of human success (*Ol.* 8.12–14; *Pyth.*1.41–42), the concept and nature of the afterlife (*Ol.* 2.53–80), the nature of the highest possible human achievements (*Nem.* 9.44–47; 7.54–58; *Pyth.* 1.99–100; 10.22–29; *Isthm.* 5.12–16), and the importance of ruling with virtue (*Pyth.* 1.81–98). The odes are also known for giving Pindar's perspective on the poet's task and the significance of praise.[5]

In the present study on didactic hymnody (broadly conceived), it could be enlightening to discuss several aspects of Pindar's epinician odes. His use of hymns in praise of gods within his odes, and the purposes of such components, would certainly be relevant.[6] Likewise, the specific vocabulary and style of expression used to praise the human victors would be of interest. The performative context of the odes and the variety of settings they seem to represent (symposia; private performance; public display;

---

[5] Cf. *Isthm.* 7.16–21; *Nem.* 3.6–12; 6.28–30; 7.9–16; 7.61–79; 9.6–7.

[6] William H. Race, *Style and Rhetoric in Pindar's Odes* (Atlanta: Scholars Press, 1990), 85–117.

etc.) is another angle from which the odes might be considered.[7] However, the focus of the following few pages will be to consider the didactic functions of these odes. What – in the context of praise of a human victor, in the context of divine myth, in the presence of a particular audience – did Pindar teach? Naturally, a fully satisfying answer to this question would necessitate a complex and multi-faceted study that would fill a volume of its own. Nevertheless, since Pindar's manner of "teaching through song" is highly relevant to this larger study, we will attempt to gain some perspective by examining one text, *Pythian* 1, that will enable us to consider some of the didactic aspects of Pindaric praise.

1. Pindar's Pythian *1*

As one of Pindar's more famous odes, *Pythian* 1 provides a good example for the present study as it showcases Pindar's method of blending divine and human praise, while at the same time casting a vision of reality that offers instruction to the audience.[8] In this ode of five strophes of 20 lines each, Pindar praises Hieron, who was victorious in the chariot race in 470 BCE. But the ode gives very little attention to Hieron's athletic achievement – just a few lines (lines 32–33; 59). Instead it focuses on his military victories and his civic achievements as the founder of Aitna. These achievements are celebrated in an ode that places in the foreground the divinely ordained peace and calm that Zeus is responsible for (represented by the golden lyre, lines 1–12) and that he achieved by defeating Typhon (lines 13–28). Accordingly, the military victories and civic peace that Hieron is responsible for are seen within the context of the larger story of Zeus's peace-bringing work in the world. As one would expect, there is no sense in which Hieron is ascribed any kind of divine power – his are human powers that are given to him by the gods. Nevertheless, the astute listener will have recognized the high praise that Pindar was giving Hieron through this kind of comparison, as he placed the achievements of Hieron on the same stage as the divine myth.

The ode opens with a hymn to the golden lyre (lines 1–12), reminiscent of earlier hymns which began with a scene in the dwelling place of Zeus (e.g., the Homeric *Hymn to Apollo*). Pindar begins:

Golden Lyre, rightful possession of Apollo
and the violet-haired Muses, to you the footstep listens
as it begins the splendid celebration,

---

[7] Bruno Currie, *Pindar and the Cult of Heroes* (Oxford: Oxford University Press, 2005); Simon Hornblower, *Thucydides and Pindar: Historical Narrative and the World of Epinikian Poetry* (Oxford: Oxford University Press, 2004), 33–36.

[8] For an overview of some of the significant features of this ode see Carne-Ross, *Pindar*, 101–111.

and the singers heed your signals
whenever with your vibrations you strike up
the chorus leading preludes.
You quench even the warring thunderbolt
of ever-flowing fire; and the eagle sleeps
on the scepter of Zeus,
having relaxed his swift wings on either side,
the king of birds, for you have poured
over his curved head a black-hooded cloud,
sweet seal for his eyelids. And as he slumbers,
he ripples his supple back, held in check
by your volley of notes. For even powerful
Ares puts aside
his sharp-pointed spears and delights his heart
in sleep. (lines 1–12)[9]

The hymn thus opens with references to Apollo and the Muses as it celebrates the peace and calm in the heavenly realm that the lyre brings about.
The thunderbolt of Zeus is quenched (line 5), the eagle on the scepter of
Zeus is relaxed and sleeping (lines 6–10), and the god of war himself sets
his spears down and rests (lines 10–12). There is order and peace in the
realm of Zeus. But, as later philosophical hymns and songs will note (cf.
chapter three of this study), not every aspect of the universe submits willingly to the reign of Zeus. Lines 12–28 recount the terror that overtakes the
enemies of Zeus as they hear the heavenly song. An extended description
of Zeus's enemy Typhos and his imprisonment beneath Mt. Aitna culminates in a painful description of his final fate – jagged rocks scrape the entire length of his back (line 28).

These graphic descriptions of restful peace and forced and painful submission culminate in Pindar's first request: that Zeus be pleased with him
(line 29). In a skillful maneuver Pindar uses the request to introduce the
subject of this victory ode:

Grant, O Zeus, grant that I may please you,
you who rule that mountain, the brow of
a fruitful land, whose neighboring city that bears
its name [i.e., Aitna] was honored by its illustrious founder [i.e., Hieron],
when at the racecourse of the Pythian festival
the herald proclaimed it [i.e., Aitna]
in announcing Hieron's splendid victory
with the chariot. (lines 29–33)

The prayer shifts focus to the city of Aitna near the base of Mt. Aitna, and
to the "illustrious founder" and his victory. This transition to the victory of

---

[9] All translations are from Pindar, *Olympian Odes; Pythian Odes* (trans. William H.
Race; LCL 56; Cambridge, Mass.: Harvard University Press, 1997).

Hieron allows Pindar to go on in lines 33–38 to suggest that this recently founded city will enjoy great future fame, based on the success it has enjoyed in its early days. Pindar joins to that hope his second prayer to Apollos:

Lord of Lykia, O Phoebus, you who rule over Delos
and who love Parnassos' Kastalian spring,
willingly take those things to heart and make this a land of
brave men. (lines 39–40)

Thus by the end of the second strophe, Pindar has introduced major mythic themes of peace and conflict, as well as the athletic victory of Hieron and the valor of the city he has founded. Pindar has also demonstrated his ability to tap into multiple temporal registers (mythic past, recent past, future) and spatial registers to craft an ode which is grand in scope and vision. These dynamics continue in the remainder of the ode as well.

As Pindar moves on in his task of praise, he takes the opportunity to reflect on the military victories of Hieron, comparing him to Philoktetes in the expedition against Troy (lines 47–57). Then he introduces yet one more significant theme: the son of Hieron, Deinomenes, the current king of Aitna. Pindar does this through a third prayer, this time to the Muse:

Muse, at the side of Deinomenes too
I bid you sing the reward for the four-horse chariot,
for a father's victory is no alien joy.
 Come then, let us compose a loving hymn for Aitna's king
for whom Hieron founded that city. (lines 58–61)

At this point Pindar has introduced the full range of themes which he will weave together in the remaining two strophes of the ode.

In the fourth strophe, a prayer to Zeus asking for his help in creating "harmonious peace" for the people (lines 67–72) is sandwiched between two historical reviews of ancient and recent battles. The Doric conquest of Greece is outlined in lines 61–66. Two recent victories of Hieron are placed beside two more famous battles in lines 73–80. Again we see that Pindar moves effortlessly across space and time as he creates a multi-textured verbal portrait of reality in this ode.

In the fifth strophe Pindar's praise of Hieron concludes with words of advice and wisdom on ruling well. From one point of view, these are words of praise since they imply that these are the traits that already marked the reign of Hieron and that now mark the reign of his son.[10] But these may also be seen as explicit exhortations to both the king and any others in positions of power, showing the didactic nature of this praise poem. It is noteworthy that Pindar's words contain not just exhortation but

---

[10] Carne-Ross, *Pindar*, 108.

also the rationale as to why each word of advice is wise. For example, he writes,

Do not be deceived,
O my friend, by shameful gains,
for the posthumous acclaim of fame
alone reveals the life of men who are dead and gone
to both chroniclers and poets. The kindly
excellence of Croesus does not perish,
but universal execration overwhelms Phalaris, that man
of pitiless spirit who burned men in his bronze bull,
and no lyres in banquet halls welcome him
in gentle fellowship with boys' voices. (lines 92–98)

In this injunction the advice is supported by a reason (posthumous praise is what carries on when a man has died) and by two examples, one positive (Croesus) and one negative (Phalaris). Pindar takes this opportunity to advise the ruler and to reflect in his poem the power of the poet to ensure lasting fame or disgrace.

The first Pythian ode concludes with a fitting summary of the life and achievements of Hieron, couched in a straightforward lesson for all listeners:

Success is the first of prizes; and renown the second portion; but the man who
meets with both and gains them has won the highest crown. (lines 99–100)

Pindar would have Hieron and his broader audience accept the idea that Hieron has won the highest crown. It is of interest to note that in line 50 Pindar already explained how Hieron, with divine help, had won a "rich and lordly crown" in victory.[11] Now he has also won the highest crown, since he has both victory and renown. Carne-Ross suggested that the rich and lordly crown might serve as the emblem of the entire ode.

This repetition of a key word or idea is notable elsewhere in the ode. For example, Zeus defeats his enemy Typhon, who is explicitly termed his enemy in line 15. Hieron and his brother defeat their enemies in line 80. The use of the same word invites the hearer to see a connection between the divine victory and the human conquests. In a similar way, the request that Zeus help Hieron and his son to bring about "harmonious peace" (line 70) reminds one of the peace-inducing song of the heavenly lyre hymned in lines 1–12. On many levels, then, the comparison between the achievements of Hieron on the human plane, and the achievements of Zeus in the divine realm are brought together. Zeus is the source of human achievements and giftings (lines 41–42; 67–68); Hieron has been a recipient of divine help (line 48) and, if Zeus wills, will continue to be (lines 56–57).

---

[11] Ibid., 105.

This has been but a quick sketch of the contents and ideas of *Pythian* 1, yet even this brief look has suggested the level of complexity of the way that Pindar interweaves human and divine themes and motifs. In other odes we would discover themes and ideas that complement what we found here and indicate the power of epinician odes to create a world of meaning for the human audience. But for now, we can simply note that Pindar has brought together praise of the divine and praise of human achievements in one kind of composition. Race summarizes the many themes of this ode:

> The ode celebrates that founding in a broader context of harmonious peace, achieved in the polis by good governance, maintained against foreign aggression by resolute warfare, and, on a cosmic scale, gained and held against the forces of disorder by Zeus' power, exemplified by Typhos' confinement under Mt. Aitna.[12]

In bringing these ideas together, Pindar has used his art to paint a vivid and allusive portrait of reality that gives meaning and depth to something as concrete and seemingly as simple as an athletic victory. He has used the opportunity to provide his audience a view of the world and of humanity's place in that world – particularly the place and role of humans who have been granted skill, ability, wealth, and power in this world. Pindar's ode instructs both implicitly (through narrative and comparison) and explicitly (through direct address of the human audience).

As we move on to explore the development of praise poetry in later centuries, we will note that the influence of Pindar is quite significant. This becomes particularly clear in Horace who, in addition to the panegyric compositions that we will explore, composes a number of odes in praise of Roman military victories (cf. *Odes* IV.4 and 14). But Pindar's influence can also be observed in other praise compositions that place the accomplishments of human subjects in the context of divine myths and thereby offer lasting significance to the achievements of these human rulers. Finally, we can observe the continuing development of the self-conscious portrayal of the poet as an individual who is uniquely suited to guarantee lasting fame for the *laudandus* through his inspired words.

C. Hymnic Praises of Rulers

1. Hellenic and Hellenistic Practices

As we move from Pindar's praises of athletic victors to later Greek practices of praising rulers and kings, it is important to recall that the practice of giving honor to those who were thought to be deserving of it went far

---

[12] Race's comment is from LCL 56 (Pindar, *Olympian Odes; Pythian Odes*), 210.

beyond the composition of poems or speeches. Honor could be ascribed through inscriptions, statues, festivals, tax-relief, citizenship, and civic decrees in honor of praiseworthy individuals. The Greeks in particular participated in elaborate systems of cultic worship of both heroes and gods. From these institutions involving sacrifice, priests, and festivals among other things, it is possible to see a connection with the later developments of Hellenistic ruler cults and the kinds of verbal praise and honorific language associated with them. Though hero cult, divine cult, and ruler cult, along with their inter-relationship, fall outside the scope of this study, a brief sketch of the developments in ruler cult in the Hellenistic period will help to provide some context for the kinds of verbal praises we will encounter below.[13]

Hero cult and divine cult were two ways of honoring humans and deities in the Greek world. A series of political, cultural, and historical factors opened the way to a new kind of cult, ruler cult, in the era of Alexander the Great and his successors.[14] As it developed, it is possible to see two distinct kinds of ruler cult in the Hellenistic period. The first was a cult of a single ruler initiated by an individual city, which tended to be a way of honoring an individual for his benefactions on behalf of the city. These benefactions were often associated with the deeds of a god who had saved, delivered, or exercised other divine functions on behalf of the city. Fishwick notes, "In founding a cult as a token of esteem, a city might hope to encourage continued benefactions on the part of the individual honored . . . As a result, ruler worship grew into a diplomatic exercise that served the various purposes of the interested parties."[15] This practice with its corresponding diplomatic outcomes continued to grow and remained a part of the imperial cult into the Roman era. As we explore instances of praise of rulers, we can consider the extent to which these kinds of dynamics – negotiating the interests of the ruler and the ruled – are at play.

The second kind of worship is seen in dynastic cults imposed on the state as a whole by a ruler of a powerful Hellenistic kingdom. This is particularly associated with the Seleucids and the Ptolemies.[16] Fishwick notes, "Whereas divine honours had earlier been granted in recognition of services rendered by an external liberator, now cult was paid to the king *qua* king, independently of his personal qualities; divinity, that is, became a

---

[13] On the development of hero cults and their reflection in Pindar see Currie, *Pindar and the Cult of Heroes*, esp. 57–59. For a broader survey of the development of hero and ruler cult see Duncan Fishwick, *The Imperial Cult in the Latin West: Studies in the Ruler Cult of the Western Provinces of the Roman Empire* (2 vols.; Études préliminaires aux religions orientales dans l'Empire Romain; Leiden: Brill, 1987), esp. 1.1.

[14] Fishwick, *Imperial Cult in the Latin West*, 1.1:3–11.

[15] Ibid., 1.1:11.

[16] Ibid., 1.1:13–20.

characteristic of absolute monarchy."[17] Fishwick explains, "The king, now a universal benefactor and saviour, is portrayed as god made man, one who participates in divinity and exercises on earth a divine kingship corresponding to that of the highest god of the universe."[18] In this system, divinity is attributed not only to the king, but also to his family, including his wife, children, and, at times, even his parents. The development of this process can be seen very clearly within the succession of Ptolemaic rulers from Ptolemy I Soter down through Ptolemy IV Philopator.[19] The praises of Ptolemy II Philadelphus below fall into this line of development.

As we consider compositions of praise in these contexts of ruler cult, it will be useful to keep in mind the broader functions of the ruler cult within these Hellenistic kingdoms. Price suggests that the ruler cults developed out of the divine cults (not the hero cult) as a response to supreme power.[20] Price explains,

> The key to an historical explanation of the cults which goes further than the statements of the actors without imposing modernizing observer categories is that the cults be seen as reactions to power. It was by solving the crucial problem of classification that the Greeks were able to represent to themselves otherwise unmanageable power, whether of the king or of local citizens.[21]

In other words, part of the transition in the Hellenistic period involved cities and their inhabitants coming to grips with an individual who had absolute power in nearly every sense of the word. Price continues showing how the ruler cult is closely connected with the idea behind the divine cult:

> This solution to the problem of power over the city is no less religious a phenomenon than the cults of the traditional gods. These too were conceived in terms of honours and can also be analysed as the representations of power. The significance of the classification of the ruler in divine terms is that it disguised the novelty of the monarchies and formed a significant element in the relationships of power between subject and ruler.[22]

In the end, the ruler cult allowed the cities a means of negotiating with and dealing with the power that now presented itself over them. Religious language and ideas provided a preexisting system for dealing with this kind of superhuman power.

We will return to Price's notion of negotiating power when we consider the development of imperial ideology within the Roman Empire. For now we turn to several examples of praise of Hellenistic rulers that teach even

---

[17] Ibid., 1.1:13.

[18] Ibid.

[19] Ibid., 1.1:13–15.

[20] S. R. F. Price, *Rituals and Power: The Roman Imperial Cult in Asia Minor* (Cambridge: Cambridge University Press, 1986), 32–33.

[21] Ibid., 52.

[22] Ibid.

as they praise. We can observe that an aspect of the teaching of these compositions deals with just what Price has suggested: how to negotiate power, whether from the perspective of the ruled or, at times, of the ruler.

D. Isocrates' *Evagoras*

In the centuries after Pindar, we encounter some new developments in the art of praise, particularly with regard to the praises of men. As we observed, Pindar praised athletic victors who were often wealthy aristocrats or, as in the case of Hieron, rulers. With Isocrates' *Evagoras* in the fourth century BCE we encounter the example of praise for a king after his death. The occasion was a festival given in honor of the murdered king of Salamis by his son Nicocles some time after his death.[23] The aged Isocrates, an orator-philosopher of the court, had known Evagoras well and took the opportunity to "worthily recount his principles in life and his perilous deeds" with the hope that this would immortalize the deeds and achievements of Evagoras in the most fitting way (§§2–3).[24] In taking the approach he does, he indicates that the goals of his composition were both rhetorical and didactic.

Three aspects of this composition are of interest here. First, Isocrates takes on the task of praising Evagoras in prose rather than poetry and so provides a very early example of the prose encomium.[25] Isocrates claims to be the first to attempt such a task and offers a lengthy and valuable description of the challenges facing the orator in comparison with the poet (§§8–11). Yet in spite of the difference in genre, the qualities and accomplishments for which Evagoras is praised show a great deal of continuity with the praises that Pindar offered his athletic victors. Second, as we will see, this composition is unreservedly didactic as it offers exhortation and instruction to Nicocles, the son of Evagoras, on how he might live up to the example of his father. In this way Isocrates reflects the hortatory impulses of Pindar who found epinician odes a suitable venue for offering instruction on matters such as ruling well, the nature of human success, or the Greek view of the afterlife. Isocrates also thereby takes on himself the role of "philosopher as political adviser," a role which is reflected else-

---

[23] LaRue Van Hook, *Isocrates. In Three Volumes* (LCL 373; Cambridge, Mass.: Harvard University Press, 1968), 3:2–3.

[24] Translations of Isocrates are those of LaRue Van Hook found in LCL 373.

[25] For discussion of the development of this tradition in later writings see Edgar Krentz, "Epideiktik and Hymnody: The New Testament and Its World," *BR* 40 (1995): 50–97; Russell, "Aristides and the Prose Hymn."

where in his writings as well, but particularly so in this composition.[26] Third, though neither a hymn nor a poem, this composition is very relevant to the present study in that it shows how praise of humans is brought into contact with praise of the divine, yet in a more direct and less allusive way than Pindar. Thus it sets the stage for later compositions that will praise men in more explicitly hymnic terms.[27]

In this section we will briefly examine the qualities for which Evagoras is praised, the ways that the realm of the human and divine are brought into contact, and the ways that the composition teaches and instructs even as it praises.

1. Praiseworthy Qualities

Isocrates is concerned to highlight the praiseworthy character traits of Evagoras and so notes these along with his accomplishments and natural gifting. For example, as a child Evagoras possessed beauty, strength, and modesty (§22). As an adult he added to these manly courage, wisdom, and justice so that he demonstrated excellence (ἀρετή) of body and mind (§23). He maintained greatness of soul, even in exile, taking as his guiding principle to act only in self-defense and not as an aggressor (§§27–28). The way he overthrew the tyrant and secured his throne (with bravery, piety, and justice, among other things) shows that Evagoras is in a class by himself and deserving of praise greater than any other king (§§33–39). Beyond military exploits and natural gifting, Evagoras cultivated his mind and applied it to both public and private affairs (§§41–42). In his governing "he never acted unjustly toward anyone but ever honoured the good" (§43). He ruled justly and fairly, worked at those things which were most important, cultivated friendships through benefactions, and inspired fear through his excellent character (§§44–45). Isocrates sums up his praiseworthy characteristics by noting "in general, he fell in no respect short of the qualities which belong to kings" (§46). Isocrates has painted a portrait of the king who demonstrates arête in every respect.

To the list of personal attributes and character qualities noted above Isocrates adds a series of descriptions of the accomplishments of Evagoras, both civic and military, and the ways he advanced not only his city but the whole region (§§47–64). He asks, "In truth, how could one reveal the courage, the wisdom, or the virtues generally of Evagoras more clearly than by pointing to such deeds and perilous enterprises?" (§65). The deeds clearly serve as a way of highlighting the virtues of Evagoras. Isocrates then adds a lengthy summary of the accomplishments of Evagoras, ulti-

---

[26] Dihle, *History of Greek Literature*, 207.
[27] See the discussion of the development in Danker, *Benefactor*, 27.

mately suggesting that, if one were to claim that any human was a god among men, it would not be inappropriate to make that claim about Evagoras (§72). This particular claim leads us to a brief consideration of the ways that Isocrates alludes to the near-divine status of Evagoras.

2. God-like Characteristics

Isocrates never directly claims divine status for Evagoras. However, through several kinds of comparison and comment, Isocrates suggests that Evagoras at least manifested many traits that took him out of the realm of common humanity. Throughout the composition Isocrates hints that he is moving in this direction. Evagoras is, of course, descended from the demigods, the sons of Zeus (§§12–18). His men follow him "as if a god were their leader" (§29). He achieved supreme power which is the greatest of all blessings "whether human or divine" (§40). When compared with the heroes celebrated in song, his exploits are far greater than even the legendary heroes of Troy (§65). Finally, Isocrates is forced to conclude that, if anyone has attained to immortality, Evagoras has:

Therefore, I believe that, if any men of the past have by their merit become immortal, Evagoras also has earned this preferment; and my evidence for that belief is this – that the life he lived on earth has been more blessed by fortune and more favored by the gods than theirs. (§70)

In the view of Isocrates, the unique blessing and divine favor Evagoras enjoyed in life would suggest that in death he was granted immortality by the same gods who so esteemed him in life. At the very least, if other men were granted this honor – and who really knows anyway – surely Evagoras would be a most likely candidate for immortality.

Isocrates saves his most explicit statement about the nature of Evagoras for his conclusion to the review of his deeds alluded to above. In paragraph 72 he concludes:

In view of these facts, if any of the poets have used extravagant expressions in characterizing any man of the past, asserting that he was a god among men, or a mortal divinity, all praise of that kind would be especially in harmony with the noble qualities of Evagoras.

The beauty of this statement is that Isocrates does not come right out and claim that Evagoras was a mortal divinity or a god among men. He does not wish to make that claim nor does he need to for the purposes of his speech. But he does say that if ever there was a person to whom this descriptor might apply, Evagoras would be a prime candidate. It is through this kind of comparison that Isocrates offers Evagoras the highest praise that a human might receive, yet he does so without crossing a line of propriety that would ignore the fact that the deceased Evagoras was most certainly mortal and not divine. It is statements like these which will provide the context for our understanding of praises of later rulers who will, it seems, be explicitly identified as divine.

3. Didactic Emphases

In addition to his goal of ensuring that the deeds and qualities of Evagoras were "never to be forgotten among all mankind" (§4), Isocrates admits of another primary goal for this composition: exhortation and instruction to current and future generations. He states this goal at the outset (§5), but makes it most explicit in the final paragraphs of his oration. He explains,

> For these reasons especially have I undertaken to write this discourse because I believed that for you, for your children, and for all the other descendants of Evagoras, it would be by far the best incentive, if someone should assemble his achievements, give them verbal adornment, and submit them to you for your contemplation and study. For we exhort young men to the study of philosophy by praising others in order that they, emulating those who are eulogized, may desire to adopt the same pursuits. (§76)

Evagoras here makes the connection between praise and exhortation that Aristotle notes when the latter compares epideictic rhetoric and deliberative rhetoric. Praise can be closely aligned with direct instruction just by a slight shift in emphasis: the qualities that one praises in one individual are the very qualities one wishes to recommend to the listeners.[28] In this instance the exhortation is being given directly to Nicocles and indirectly to the wider audience. Evagoras is not afraid to speak quite frankly to Nicocles. After assuring him in good rhetorical style that he is not reproaching him but merely urging him to continue on with the course he has already chosen, he says,

> It is my task, therefore, and that of your other friends, to speak and to write in such a fashion as may be likely to incite you to strive eagerly after those things which even now you do in fact desire; and you it behooves not to be negligent, but as at present so in the future to pay heed to yourself and to discipline your mind that you may be worthy of your father and all your ancestors. (§80)

The ultimate end for Isocrates is that Nicocles live a life that is worthy of his father and his ancestors, embodying the praiseworthy qualities of Evagoras as he now rules the people. As the final line of the oration indicates, Isocrates intends that Nicocles become the man it is fitting he should be (§81).

In assessing this oration as both praise and instruction, it is evident that Isocrates had both functions in mind. He had his eye on the deeds and qualities of Evagoras, but he also had his thoughts on what Nicocles needed to know and do. He utilized the prose encomium to paint a vivid and

---

[28] Aristotle, *Rhet.* 1.35–36.

glowing portrait of the kind of ruler and leader that Evagoras had been. He used the same medium to charge Nicocles publicly to live up to his heritage.

In this composition we thus observe the power of praise to work on several levels at once as the poet crafts a description of the individual within a framework that includes both the human and divine realms. In such a composition there is room for giving honor where it is due and also for exhorting the audience to conduct itself in accordance with the ultimate vision of reality that the poet creates. The lesson for Nicocles is to use his power in a way that aligns with the good example of his father. The lesson for the broader audience, however, is to recognize and honor the ruler that has been divinely appointed and divinely empowered. Whether or not Nicocles received the exhortation to himself, he surely would have appreciated the underlying message about the legitimacy of his kingship and the appropriateness of the power he wielded.

E. Praises of Ptolemy II Philadelphus by Callimachus and Theocritus

Our survey of the praises of rulers and men continues into the third century BCE with two compositions in praise of Ptolemy II Philadelphus who ruled 287–245 BCE. Callimachus composed a hymn to Zeus which reflects on the reign of Ptolemy as it praises Zeus and recounts his birth and ascension to the throne. Theocritus, in Idyll 17, composed an innovative hexameter encomium of Ptolemy with many of the marks of a more traditional hymn to Zeus. Both compositions provide opportunities for us to examine ways that hymnic praise and encomiastic style are joined to paint larger-than-life portraits of a powerful human subject. Both likewise suggest that it was not only praise but also instruction that was one of the primary goals of these texts.

1. *Callimachus's* Hymn to Zeus

Callimachus, a scholar and poet from Alexandria, worked in the famous library of that city in the third century BCE.[29] Ancient sources attribute over 800 works to him along with poems in every meter.[30] He catalogued the entire collection at Alexandria, and Dihle describes his scholarly career

---

[29] Dihle, *History of Greek Literature*, 256.
[30] A. W. Mair, *Callimachus, Hymns and Epigrams. Lycophron* (LCL 129; Cambridge, Mass.: Harvard University Press, 1977), 1.

as "almost unimaginably prolific."[31] His works were marked by a depth of erudition and a breadth of allusion and literary awareness to such an extent that only those in his circle of literary colleagues could fully appreciate the richness of his work. Though steeped in the poetry of the past, Callimachus was not content to simply mirror the great works of the past in his own work. Instead he preferred short and highly polished poetry to the more expansive style of epic poetry of the past.[32] His hymns thus reflected traditional style along with the literary innovations of his own era.

In a study of tradition and innovation in Hellenistic poetry, Fantuzzi and Hunter identify aspects of a common language of praise, influenced by Hesiod and Homer, that can be found throughout the Hellenistic world. Regarding Callimachus they note, "Callimachus' six hymns are not only rewritings of archaic poetry, principally of the major poems of our collection of 'Homeric Hymns', but they also mark themselves off against this *lingua franca*, requiring us to notice both similarity and difference."[33] The *Hymn to Zeus* is a good example of several of these features of his work.[34]

The hexameter *Hymn to Zeus*, following the traditional style and form of the Homeric Hymns, runs for 95 lines and may be outlined in the following sections:

Traditional style hymnic opening (1–9)
Birth and infancy narrative (10–53)
Growth and ascension to the throne (54–68)
First Request (68)
Kingship as the special area of Zeus (69–84)
Ptolemy II as an illustration (84–89)
First hymnic salutation (90–92)
Second hymnic salutation and requests (93–95)

Clearly Zeus is the focus of the hymn as it recounts his birth, rise to power, and area of special concern drawing on traditional mythical motifs and accounts. However, Callimachus brings the focus of the hymn from the mythical past into the present when he turns his attention to Ptolemy II Philadelphus as a specific illustration of Zeus's care for kings. Interestingly, once Ptolemy II comes into view, one realizes that the earlier parts of the poem that appeared to be solely concerned with Zeus are actually part of a network of associations that are intended to show a close connection between Zeus and the human ruler.

---

[31] Dihle, *History of Greek Literature*, 256.

[32] Mair, *Callimachus*, 3.

[33] Marco Fantuzzi and R. L. Hunter, *Tradition and Innovation in Hellenistic Poetry* (Cambridge: Cambridge University Press, 2004), 353.

[34] Dihle discusses this hymn in *History of Greek Literature*, 257–258.

The connections between Zeus and Ptolemy occur on at least two levels. First, the accession of Zeus to the throne may be brought into view to reflect on the way that Ptolemy assumed the throne. Second, the two are connected in that Zeus appoints and oversees the kings, and has clearly especially favored Ptolemy Philadelphus.

After recounting the birth of Zeus, the hymn goes on to discuss his maturation and ascension to the throne as a result of his exceptional qualities.[35] Though Ptolemy is not mentioned in this section and Zeus is the sole subject at this point, once Ptolemy is brought into focus near the end of the hymn, it becomes conceivable that a comparison is being made here between the way Zeus received his rule and the way Ptolemy received his. Ptolemy likewise was made sovereign because of his deeds along with his power and strength. Callimachus does not state this outright, but in a way that is, perhaps, more rhetorically effective, he merely places the idea on the minds of his reader through the power of suggestion or allusion. Callimachus does not make the claim; the reader comes to see the truth about Ptolemy for himself or herself.

Ptolemy II Philadelphus and Zeus are shown to be closely associated in another way as the hymn develops. In this vein, Zeus's area of particular oversight is kingship:

But from Zeus come kings; for nothing is diviner than the kings of Zeus. Wherefore thou didst choose them for thine own lot, and gavest them cities to guard. And thou didst seat thyself in the high places of the cities, watching who rule their people with crooked judgments, and who rule otherwise. And thou hast bestowed upon them wealth and prosperity abundantly; unto all, but not in equal measure. (lines 78–84)

Though Zeus gives king both cities and wealth, he does not give these things equally to all kings. The hymn then moves to a more specific example of Zeus's appointing a ruler and granting prosperity to the greatest extent possible:

One may well judge by our Ruler, for he hath clean outstripped all others. At evening he accomplisheth that whereon he thinketh in the morning; yea, at evening the greatest things, but the lesser soon as he thinketh on them. But the others accomplish some things in a year, and some things not in one; of others, again, thou thyself dost utterly frustrate the accomplishing and thwartest their desire. (lines 84–89)

---

[35] Callimachus notes that Zeus grew swiftly to manhood and displayed amazing qualities even as a child (lines 54–56) with the result that his siblings were pleased to have him rule heaven, even though they were older: "Wherefore thy kindred, though an earlier generation, grudged not that thou shouldst have heaven for thine appointed habitation" (lines 57–58). With this narrative he corrects the erroneous view of earlier poets and alerts the audience to this fact: "Thou wert made sovereign of the gods not by casting of lots but by the deeds of thy hands, thy might and strength which thou hast set beside thy throne" (lines 65–66).

In other words, everyone knows that Zeus does not favor all kings the same way – but consider how well he has favored Ptolemy! We may consider what such hymnic praise of Zeus would teach a human audience about the reign of Ptolemy II Philadelphus. The audience learns that his reign is ordained by and especially blessed by Zeus. Everything comes from Zeus, but Ptolemy has received from Zeus abundantly – more than the rest.

The associations made between Zeus and Ptolemy can be better appreciated when they are understood in comparison with other hymns which identify a close relationship between a god and a human ruler. For example, Isidorus draws on a Hesiodic theme and claims that Isis (here portrayed as Greek Demeter) grants wealth and prosperity to "sceptre-bearing kings" if they heed her (Isidorus 3.1–18). Successful and prosperous rule is a gift of the deity and thus evidence of divine favor. This idea is clearly an aspect of Callimachus's *Hymn to Zeus* as well. However, Callimachus goes further than his predecessors in associating Ptolemy with Zeus. Comparing Isidorus and Callimachus, Hunter and Fantuzzi observe,

> Both poets use Hesiodic reminiscence to confirm the very close link between the *basileus* here on earth and his heavenly protector; whereas, however, in Poem 3, Isidorus maintains a clear distinction between the heavenly 'queen' (v. 12) and the ruler she most favours, Callimachus all but runs the heavenly and earthly 'Zeuses' together.[36]

While these authors may be overstating the case to make a point, nevertheless this close association of Zeus and Ptolemy constitutes a central aspect of the vision of reality put forth by Callimachus.

The hymn ends with a typical hymnic salutation and a request of Zeus. This request may also be considered hortatory:

> Hail! Father, hail again! and grant us goodness and prosperity. Without goodness wealth cannot bless men, nor goodness without prosperity. Give us goodness and weal. (line 95)

In this regard, Callimachus has praised Ptolemy II Philadelphus as specially favored by Zeus. It may be here that he is encouraging Ptolemy himself to be a person of ἀρετή. Alternatively, as Dihle suggests, Callimachus may be taking a stand on a philosophical issue of the day, the question of whether one needs both wealth and ἀρετή. Either way, the implicit exhortation to the listener is to be mindful of both without neglecting one or the other. Also, the reader is exhorted to recognize what the highest good is – both wealth and ἀρετή together.

---

[36] Fantuzzi and Hunter, *Tradition and Innovation*, 353.

2. *Theocritus's* Encomium of Ptolemy Philadelphus

Theocritus, a poet of the same generation as Callimachus, is perhaps the most influential of Alexandrian poets and is arguably the only poet of the period who was a match for Callimachus's inventiveness, taste, and skill.[37] In a work that reflects a close relationship to Callimachus's *Hymn to Zeus*, Theocritus likewise exploits the connections and the differences between hymn and encomium to highlight the greatness of Ptolemy II Philadelphus. Though best known for his pastoral poetry, Theocritus composed poems in a wide variety of genres and styles.[38] The breadth of subject matter and allusions to places and individuals in Theocritus's poetry suggests that he was a professional poet who traveled from city to city throughout his career: "The poetry of Theocritus will suggest a whole world of poetic and personal relations stretching from Syracuse to the coast of Asia Minor."[39] Nevertheless, in the 270's BCE in particular, Theocritus apparently worked within the sphere of Ptolemaic patronage as Idylls 14, 15, and 17 suggest.[40] In 273 BCE he composed an encomium of Ptolemy II Philadelphus, a text which is preserved for us as Idyll 17.

In a form that is very similar to the Homeric Hymns, the hexameter *Encomium of Ptolemy* praises Ptolemy II Philadelphus using many of the standard categories for encomiastic praise. Unlike Callimachus's *Hymn to Zeus* (which praises a living ruler indirectly in a work that is primarily addressed to a god) or Isocrates' *Evagoras* (a prose encomium which is emphatically not a hymn but praises a deceased ruler in ways that suggest his divine status), in the *Encomium of Ptolemy* we have an example of a hexameter hymn praising a living ruler. As with other hymns, we can examine the ways that this composition uses hymnic conventions and form to create a portrait of reality that will enable the hearer to appreciate both Ptolemy and the poet. After a brief review of the contents of the hymn, we will examine the opening, the birth omen, and encomiastic *topoi* employed in this text in order to clarify the impact and meaning of the hymn. We will also consider the role of the poet and his relationship with the *laudandus*. This hymn not only teaches of the power of Ptolemy, it also reminds the hearer of the power and importance of the poet.

Like many ancient hymns, the *Encomium of Ptolemy* begins with a proem (lines 1–12) and ends with a salutation (lines 135–137). The body of the hymn treats a variety of standard encomiastic topics related to Philadelphus: his father (13–33); his mother (34–57); his birth (58–76); his ter-

---

[37] Dihle, *History of Greek Literature*, 272.

[38] R. L. Hunter, "Introduction and Notes," in *Idylls* (New ed.; Oxford: Oxford University Press, 2008), xviii–xx.

[39] Ibid., x.

[40] Ibid., ix.

ritory (77–94); his wealth (95–120); and his wife (121–134).[41] These are standard topics of encomiastic rhetoric according to the ancient hand-books.[42] It is noteworthy, however, that Theocritus leaves out many other standard topics such as the deeds of Ptolemy, his military achievements, and his embodiment of virtues.[43] While readers may speculate as to what significance the absence of some of these may have, we will limit our brief discussion to the topics Theocritus chose to treat.

The opening of the hymn places it unmistakably within the tradition of hexameter hymns going back to Homer and Hesiod. It begins,

From Zeus let us begin, Muses, and with Zeus let us end,
When we make our songs, for he is pre-eminent among the gods.
But among mortals, let Ptolemy be reckoned first,
First and last and in between, for he is supreme among men. (lines 1–4)[44]

By opening this way, Theocritus positions the piece in the tradition of hexameter hymns, while at the same time creating an interesting dynamic between Ptolemy and Zeus. Zeus is first among the gods, but Ptolemy is first among mortals. In some ways this creates a contrast between the two (Zeus is divine; Ptolemy is mortal), but the more significant effect is that of creating a comparison between the two: as Zeus is to the gods, so Ptolemy is to humans. As Hunter notes, the opening with Zeus and not Ptolemy becomes more significant as the hymn develops: "This comes to be seen as a first move in a poetic game about the relation of the Olympian Zeus to Ptolemy."[45] The relationship between the two supreme figures will be further developed as the hymn unfolds.

The hymnic opening does more than introduce Zeus and Ptolemy onto the same stage, however. It also serves as the first opportunity for the poet to introduce himself and to begin instructing the audience on the value of his art:

Heroes of former times, children of demigods, had skilful poets
To celebrate their glorious deeds; I too possess that art,
And it is Ptolemy I must celebrate in my hymns –
For hymns are a reward even among the gods. (lines 5–8)

Through this explanatory section of four lines, Theocritus positions not only the hymn but himself in the long line of skilled poets who celebrated

---

[41] Idem, *Theocritus: Encomium of Ptolemy Philadelphus* (Berkeley: University of California Press, 2003), 19–20.

[42] Quintilian 3.7.10–18. Cf. also the *progymnasmata* of Hermogenes, Theon, and Aphthonius.

[43] Hunter, *Theocritus: Encomium*, 23–24.

[44] Translations of Idylls 17 are taken from Theocritus, *Idylls* (trans. Anthony Verity; New ed.; Oxford World's Classics; Oxford: Oxford University Press, 2008), 54–58.

[45] Hunter, *Theocritus: Encomium*, 8.

the glorious deeds of heroes, demigods, and gods. Further, he reminds the audience that a hymn itself is a kind of reward that the gods themselves appreciate. We may begin to see that perhaps Theocritus is painting a picture not only of Ptolemy but also of the poet's task, his own skill, and Ptolemy's need for what he can offer. As if to demonstrate his skill, the hymnic opening concludes in lines 9–12 with a standard hymnic device, that of searching for where to begin when the subject of praise offers so many possible starting points. At this point the reader is prepared for a hymn celebrating Ptolemy, the supreme king. The audience may also suspect that they will be hearing more from the poet about his own abilities as well.

The hymn proceeds to discuss Ptolemy's father, Ptolemy I, and then his mother, Berenice, both of whom have been deified. References to Zeus and other gods and mythical heroes figure prominently in these accounts. In fact, Zeus has granted Ptolemy I "equal honor with the immortal gods" and a throne in the house of Zeus right next to that of Alexander and opposite to the throne of Heracles (lines 15–20). Further, both Alexander and Ptolemy I are said to be descendants of Heracles, and are now regarded as immortals (lines 21–25). High praise is next offered to Berenice who was especially cared for by Aphrodite, who "set her up in your temple, and shared your honours with her" (line 50). Theocritus' encomium thus brings the mythic past and recent past into contact, as well as the realms of the divine and the human.

Praise of Berenice leads naturally into a section on the birth of Ptolemy II on Cos in 308 BCE (lines 58–76). Many features of this section are noteworthy, particularly for their mythic references and comparisons with the birth of Apollo on Delos.[46] The sign of the eagle is particularly important. The hymn reads,

And high above it a mighty eagle shrieked three times in the clouds.
This is the bird of fate, and surely it was Zeus, Cronos' son, who
Sent the sign, Zeus who watches over revered kings, but chiefly those
He has loved from their moment of birth. Great wealth goes hand in hand
With such a man, and his rule spreads far abroad over land and sea. (lines 71–75)

This passage again reinforces a connection between Zeus and Ptolemy II. Zeus, as everyone knows, watches over kings and grants them wealth and success. Callimachus made such a point in his *Hymn to Zeus*. In this case, Theocritus goes farther to suggest that Zeus has shown a particular preference for Ptolemy II Philadelphus, sending an eagle to shriek at the time of his birth. This is particularly significant since Callimachus also regarded the eagle of Zeus as a sign of favor. In the *Hymn to Zeus* the rehearsal of

---

[46] Hunter notes, "Theocritus, like Callimachus in his *Hymn to Delos*, suggests an analogy between the birth of Ptolemy and that of Apollo on Delos as described in the Homeric *Hymn to Apollo*" (Hunter, "Introduction and Notes," 109).

Zeus's birth, maturation, and ascension to the throne concludes with a request:

And the most excellent of birds thou didst make the messenger of thy signs; favourable to my friends be the signs thou showest! (lines 67–68)

In the *Encomium of Ptolemy* Theocritus capitalizes on this belief and uses it to further elaborate on the unique relationship between Zeus and Ptolemy.

The *Encomium of Ptolemy* goes on to describe the extent of Ptolemy's land and wealth that was alluded to in lines 74–75. The discussion of how Ptolemy uses his wealth is quite interesting as Theocritus praises him for his open-handedness, claiming that he gives generously to the gods, to mighty kings, to cities, and to his noble companions (lines 107–110). To this list of beneficiaries, Theocritus adds the singers at the Dionysian contests:

No singer proficient in the clear-voiced song at Dionysus' sacred contest
Fails to receive the present which his art deserves, and Ptolemy's
Liberality is praised by the Muses' sacred speakers. (lines 111–113)

The *Encomium of Ptolemy* itself is an example of the kind of art Theocritus refers to here. And in this vein he hearkens back to a theme introduced in the opening of the hymn: the importance of songs of praise to ensure the lasting reputation of a ruler. The hymn goes on:

What more splendid
Aim can a rich man pursue than to win a glorious reputation here on earth?
Even the sons of Atreus' fame is secure, though the boundless wealth
They amassed at the sack of mighty Priam's palace is now lost, hidden
Somewhere in the misty darkness from which there is no return. (lines 113–117)

The clear implication here is that wealth that is horded is lost, but wealth that is spent on the support of a skilled poet will lead to lasting and glorious fame on earth. The hymn would have the reader know that Ptolemy is wise enough to recognize this. Further, if it was the case that Ptolemy recognized this, the hymn then encourages the continuation of that reality. If Ptolemy had not yet embraced that philosophy, then the hymn could be seen to be instructing Ptolemy on the wise use of his wealth. Theocritus wants the hearer to embrace the reality that there is no aim more splendid for a rich man than to win a glorious reputation through praise (line 113–114).

Theocritus concludes his praise of Ptolemy by noting his uniqueness in founding shrines for his father and mother, and by comparing he and his praiseworthy wife and sister to Zeus and Hera. The formulaic ending of the hymn takes leave of the subject ("Farewell, lord Ptolemy") and promises further songs ("you shall be my hymn's theme no less than other demigods"). In place of the typical request (be gracious; grant me fame; etc.) the poet asserts his belief that his words will be remembered: "I believe my words will not be disregarded by men to come" (lines 136–137). His concluding statement urges Ptolemy to seek Zeus for excellence (ἀρετή). It is instructive that where Callimachus ended with a prayer to Zeus for excellence and wealth, Theocritus ends differently. In this hymn he has taught the hearer to seek Ptolemy for wealth but to seek Zeus for ἀρετή.

As we conclude our overview of these third century BCE Alexandrian poets, we can see that the divide between hymn and encomium, and praise of gods and praise of men, has become blurred. This process has been aided by the deification of rulers upon their death, and by the recognition of the special favor Zeus has for kings together with the analogous role in their respective places as superior over others. Further, having descended directly from mythical heroes like Heracles and indirectly from Zeus himself, such a move is not surprising. This process occurs within the social framework of a poet who seeks reward for his poetry even as he guarantees fame and glory to those he praises. It is not surprising then to see that these compositions reinforce the legitimacy of the powerful ruler they address. Like other aspects of the developing ruler cult, verbal praise teaches the audience how to view their ruler and provides them a framework in which they can see themselves as beneficiaries of their king and of Zeus who gave them their king. We will see that Roman poets dealt with some of the same ambiguities as they navigated the praises of the emperor in the first centuries BCE and CE.

F. Praise of Rulers in the Roman Era

1. Emerging Imperial Ideology

In the Roman world the individual who was the focal point of praise and honor was, of course, the emperor. The imperial cult, which honored the emperor, was the culmination of a number of practices and underlying ideas that served to preserve and promote a particular Roman imperial ideology. This imperial ideology was itself a complex of ideas that centered around legitimating and augmenting the emperor's claims to power.[47] For

---

[47] On Roman imperial ideology in general see Clifford Ando, *Imperial Ideology and Provincial Loyalty in the Roman Empire* (Classics and Contemporary Thought 6; Berkeley, Calif.: University of California, 2000); Karl Galinsky, *Augustan Culture: An Interpretive Introduction* (Princeton: Princeton University Press, 1996); Gowing, *Empire and Memory*; Ittai Gradel, *Emperor Worship and Roman Religion* (Oxford Classical Monographs; Oxford: Clarendon Press, 2002); Price, *Rituals and Power*. As it impacted the New Testament, see among others, the studies by Adela Yarbro Collins, "The Worship of

the purposes of this chapter several inter-related elements of the ideology of Empire are significant: the worship of the deified emperors, the emperor as a divinely empowered bringer of universal peace, and the emperor as restorer of virtue to the Roman world. The compositions of Horace and Pliny that we will explore below attest to the power of this imperial ideology and will illustrate one way it was promoted. Before we examine those compositions, a few words about the divine status of the emperor are in order.

The divine status of the emperor is one component of the imperial ideology that was still evolving during the first century BCE. It began with the deification of an individual after his death, as in the case of Julius Caesar, whose deification was established in 42 BCE by the Roman Senate, two years after his death.[48] Interestingly, there is evidence that divine honors were decreed for Julius Caesar during his lifetime as early as 44 BCE, though these were not fully implemented until after his death.[49] Either way, his adopted son/grandnephew Octavian could thus refer to himself as "son of god," or more specifically, son of the deified Julius. This appears to have been a title that Octavian actively promoted. In his study of the development and expansion of the imperial cult Fishwick notes,

> From increasing use of the title on coins there can be little doubt that Octavian did make political capital out of the fact that he now had a god for a father, a unique relationship that helped establish the legitimacy of his claim to rule and consolidate his power by winning over the adherents of Caesar.[50]

Octavian thus actively promoted the divine status of Julius Caesar, and was likewise part of a conscious effort to establish the cult of Divus Iulius throughout the provinces.[51]

During his reign Augustus adopted a policy that would enable him to be the focal point of honors appropriate from a Hellenistic point of view while at the same time avoiding claims to being a divine monarch that would have offended Roman Republican sensibilities. While he refused to be di-

---

Jesus and the Imperial Cult," in *The Jewish Roots of Christological Monotheism: Papers from the St. Andrews Conference on the Historical Origins of the Worship of Jesus* (ed. Carey C. Newman, James R. Davila, and Gladys S. Lewis; Leiden: Brill, 1999), 234–257; Steven J. Friesen, *Imperial Cults and the Apocalypse of John: Reading Revelation in the Ruins* (New York: Oxford University Press, 2001); Richard A. Horsley, *Paul and Empire: Religion and Power in Roman Imperial Society* (Harrisburg, Pa.: Trinity Press International, 1997); Brian J. Walsh and Sylvia C. Keesmaat, *Colossians Remixed: Subverting the Empire* (Downers Grove, Ill.: InterVarsity Press, 2004).

[48] See the review of this precedent and its evolution in Gradel, *Emperor Worship*, 263–370.

[49] See the discussion in Fishwick, *Imperial Cult in the Latin West*, 1:66–75.

[50] Ibid., 1:76.

[51] Ibid., 1:76–77.

rectly worshipped as a god, he allowed many kinds of honors which were already associated with divine kingship through Julius Caesar and through earlier Hellenistic monarchs, especially in the eastern provinces. Further, his personal qualities were closely associated with divine abstractions such as Pax Augusta, Victoria Augusta, and Concordia Augusta.[52] He also fostered close connections between himself and key state deities such as Jupiter and Mars Ultor.[53] Fishwick observes, "Officially divinity was something Augustus would attain only after death, but unofficially there are signs he was not averse to the more open ascription of divinity to himself already in his lifetime."[54] In this way it appears that Octavian shrewdly navigated the competing social and political forces that Caesar had been unable to overcome.[55]

Aside from official Roman decrees and policies, we read of rulers being acclaimed and referred to as divine in many other contexts during their lifetimes. This was particularly true in the East where the association of kings with gods was well-accepted. For example, as early as 48 BCE, while Julius Caesar was still alive, an inscription from the town council of Ephesus speaks of the dictator as "the God made manifest, offspring of Ares and Aphrodite, the common saviour of human life (τὸν ἀπὸ Ἄρεως καὶ Ἀφροδε[ί]της θεὸν ἐπιφανῆ καὶ κοινὸν τοῦ ἀνθρωπίνου βίου σωτῆρα)."[56] Caesar Augustus, son of the divine Julius, was likewise acclaimed a god as is seen in papyri and inscriptions that refer to him as "god of god," "saviour," and a "benefactor," who had outdone even the Olympian gods.[57] Even so, at least in the West, it was not until after his death that he received divine honors including temples built in his honor, sacrifices performed to him, and a priesthood – *minister Augusti* – or servants of the Imperial cult. In the poetry of Horace we are fortunate to be able to observe some aspects of the development of the praises of Augustus. Horace capably draws on hymnic and other poetic traditions in order to paint a vivid verbal portrait of Augustus and also of Rome under his rule.

---

[52] Ibid., 1:85–87.

[53] Ibid., 1:87–88.

[54] Ibid., 1:90.

[55] On the recognition of the divinity of Augustus within his lifetime see Gradel, *Emperor Worship*, 271–282.

[56] Dittenberger, *Syll.* 3:760, cited in Adolf Deissmann, *Light from the Ancient East* (trans. Lionel R. M. Strachan; New and completely rev. ed.; Grand Rapids: Baker Book House, 1927; repr. 1978), 344.

[57] Price, *Rituals and Power*, 55.

G. Horace's *Odes* and Praise of Augustus

Horace lived and wrote in a time of dramatic cultural and political transition during the reign of Octavian. Among his surviving works are poems that reflect many features of ancient hymns, particularly the mythical contents along with encomiastic praise of living persons.[58] Several of his poems may be considered epinikia (i.e., victory odes) in that they celebrate military victories and draw mythical comparisons in a way that is roughly comparable to Pindar (e.g., *Odes* IV.4, 14). In the present context we are specifically concerned with the ways that Horace praised the living ruler of the Roman world, Caesar Augustus. We are particularly interested in what Horace may have taught through his poetic praise of the *princeps*. As with other ancient poets, we will examine how Horace used the medium of praise to craft a vision of reality that the audience was invited to embrace. In particular, we will attend to ways that Horace "complicates" the praise he gives and thus invites the hearers into an interpretive dialogue regarding the identity of the Roman emperor and the Roman Empire.

Though there are many points in the *Odes* where we could observe Horace's presentation of Augustus, we will examine here *Odes* IV.5 and 15, which both directly focus on the praiseworthy accomplishments of the emperor. Both of these *Odes* are closely related to one another in terms of content and the ultimate picture of reality they portray. In terms of their context and time of composition, they reflect two different settings. *Odes* IV.5 reflects a time period when Augustus is absent from Rome on a military campaign, though perhaps it was written upon his return to Rome in 13 BCE.[59] *Odes* IV.15 reflects a later time, perhaps as late as 9 BCE, when Caesar is in his city and peace is secure.[60] Both hymns portray a grand vision of the god-like Augustus and his divine accomplishments while at the same time inviting a Roman audience to see their role and construct their identity in the world ruled by Caesar.

---

[58] On Horace's life and works in general see Gordon Willis Williams, *Horace* (Greece & Rome: New Surveys in the Classics 6; Oxford: Clarendon Press, 1972). More specialized studies can be found in Timothy S. Johnson, *A Symposion of Praise: Horace Returns to Lyric in Odes IV* (Wisconsin Studies in Classics; Madison, Wisc.: University of Wisconsin Press, 2004); Michèle Lowrie, *Horace's Narrative Odes* (Oxford: Oxford University Press, 1997); Elizabeth H. Sutherland, *Horace's Well-Trained Reader: Toward a Methodology of Audience Participation in the Odes* (Studien zur klassischen Philologie 136; Frankfurt am Main: Peter Lang, 2002). See also the essays collected in S. J. Harrison, ed., *Homage to Horace: A Bimillenary Celebration* (Oxford: Clarendon Press, 1995).

[59] Williams, *Horace*, 48.

[60] Ibid.

1. Horace Odes IV.5

In *Odes* IV.5 Horace offers what might be considered a prime example of panegyric. Following up on the military epinikion of *Odes* IV.4, this metrical hymn of ten stanzas of four lines each focuses on the blessings of peace enjoyed by the Roman world because of Augustus. Modern readers have taken a variety of approaches to interpreting this composition ranging from seeing this as Horace fulfilling (without his earlier poetic creativity) a task he was commissioned to do by the emperor, to seeing the poem as Horace's heartfelt praise of the emperor and his accomplishments. Johnson provides a compelling case that Horace employs his poetic power within this composition to reflect on some of the more complex dynamics of the new age in which he and Rome find themselves.[61]

A major theme of the present ode is the absence of the emperor. Ostensibly, the occasion of the hymn is the emperor's extended absence from Rome in 16–13 BCE on a military campaign from which he has yet to return.[62] But it is also possible that Horace is using the occasion to point to the larger question of what Rome will do without the presence of Augustus in the future after his death. The poem casts a constructive answer that finds the power for Rome's continued success in the simple people of Rome, cultivating their land, and raising up a libation to Augustus. In this way the process of divinization seen in the panegyric accentuates not only the greatness of Augustus but also the source for the present and future stability and well-being of Rome. The scope of the poem thus goes beyond Caesar to include the Roman people and their role and identity in Rome's ongoing existence.

The hymn begins with high praise for its subject, identifying his divine lineage and also identifying the setting of the hymn – the absence of the leader:

Sprung from the blessed gods, best guardian
of the race of Romulus, too long already art thou absent.
Come back, for thou didst pledge a swift return
to the sacred council of the Fathers.

To thy country give again, blest leader, the light of thy presence!
For when, like spring, thy face has beamed

---

[61] Johnson, *Symposion of Praise*, 114–133. For more on this *Ode* see I. M. Le M. Du Quesnay, "Horace, *Odes* 4.5: *Pro Reditu Imperatoris Caesaris Divi Filii Augusti*," in *Homage to Horace: A Bimillenary Celebration* (ed. S. J. Harrison; Oxford: Clarendon Press, 1995), 128–187; Michael C. J. Putnam, *Artifices of Eternity: Horace's Fourth Book of Odes* (Ithaca, N.Y.: Cornell University Press, 1986).

[62] Du Quesnay, "Horace, *Odes* 4.5," 131–135.

upon the folk, more pleasant runs the day,
and brighter shines the sun. (lines 1–8)[63]

The opening stanzas are rich with allusions to earlier Latin literature, so in this regard it strikes chords familiar to an educated Roman audience.[64] These ideas are now applied by Horace directly to Augustus as the new Romulus, who is sprung from the gods to be the guardian of his people. But while Romulus led his people to shores of light, in Horace's poem Augustus himself is light. While the hymn thus opens with high praise of Augustus, the tone of the hymn is not entirely positive. Already from the opening lines we observe that the absence of Augustus is now extending beyond what might have been expected. The light of his presence is needed once again.

To further highlight the two themes (the greatness of the emperor and the problem of his absence) the hymn moves to a picture of a distraught mother whose son is away at war (lines 9–14). The mother calls to her son with vows, omens, and prayers, but the forces of the world continue to keep him away (lines 9–14). Nevertheless she continues to look from the shore and will not turn her face away from the sea as she yearns for his return.[65] In the same way, Rome longs for its ruler: "So, moved by loyal love, his country yearns for Caesar" (lines 15–16). All of Rome desires the return of its ruler, whose name is finally and climactically given in line 16.

The hymn moves from this picture of longing to a rehearsal of the accomplishments of Caesar in stanzas five and six. The accomplishments are most impressive. In addition to physical safety and security there is agricultural bounty, safe commerce, moral purity in the home, and punishment of the guilty.[66]

---

[63] Unless otherwise noted, translations of Horace's *Odes* taken from Horace, *The Odes and Epodes* (trans. Charles E. Bennett; revised ed.; LCL 33; Cambridge, Mass.: Harvard University Press, 1927; repr. 1978), 303–305, 345–347.

[64] For an excellent and accessible commentary on this Ode and its literary and cultural allusions see Du Quesnay, "Horace, *Odes* 4.5." This particular poem in praise of Augustus places itself in a long tradition of praise poetry of gods and men as a first move in its formative role for the audience. Scholars agree that Horace is echoing the words of Ennius in reference to Romulus: "O Romulus, blessed Romulus, what a guardian of the fatherland did the gods beget in you! O father, o begetter, o blood sprung from the gods! You have led us within the shores of light" (Ennius, *Ann.* 110–4V[3]) cited in Putnam, *Artifices of Eternity*, 103–104.

[65] The picture here is vivid of the mother longing for the return of her son from war, and again Horace is drawing on literary antecedents that would have been familiar to his audience. Putnam, *Artifices of Eternity*, 105–106. Putnam points specifically to Propertius 3.7.9–12, 45–46.

[66] This list of blessings may be a sustained allusion to Hesiod's description of the blessings enjoyed by a city which thrives under a good leader (cf. *Works and Days* 225–237); Du Quesnay, "Horace, *Odes* 4.5," 164–165. In addition, they reflect the standard

For when he is here, the ox in safety roams the pastures;
Ceres and benign Prosperity make rich the crops;
safe are the seas o'er which our sailors course;
Faith shrinks from blame;

polluted by no stain, the home is pure;
custom and law have stamped out the taint of sin;
mothers win praise because of children like unto their sires;
while Vengeance follows close on guilt. (lines 17–24)

Interestingly, while several factors serve to associate Augustus with the gods (he is now the recipient of a hymn; he is addressed with second person pronouns appropriate to deities in lines 32–33; and he is the object of cult in lines 35–36) the hymn avoids one central feature of ancient hymnody: a narrative. Though Augustus may be praised as divine (line 1), he is not accorded a mythical narrative as would be appropriate for a deity. Instead Horace lists a state of affairs, indirectly teaching that Augustus is responsible for having brought these about.[67]

Further, as Horace spells out in non-narrative style the praiseworthy achievements of the emperor, the focus is subtly drawn from the emperor to the citizens of Rome:

On his own hillside each man spends the day,
and weds his vines to waiting trees;
thence gladly repairs to the feast, and
at the second course invokes thee as a god.

Thee with many a prayer, thee with pure wine
poured from bowls, he worships; and mingles thy majesty
with his household gods, like Greece mindful of Castor
and great Hercules. (lines 29–36)

The blessings of Augustus's reign directly impact the common Roman vinedresser, who responds accordingly, honoring Augustus as a god. Interestingly, the worship of Augustus does not require the physical presence of Augustus. In fact, physical presence is irrelevant. What matters in this *Ode* is the ritual act of worship of the vinedresser who, like all Romans, can invoke the presence of Augustus at the end of the day as he attends to his household gods. Johnson explains,

When the vinedresser pours the libation and invokes the god Augustus, through his prayer Augustus unbounded by any distance or manner of separation, even death, does return (*praesens*), and the celebration spreads from the rustic's private house to the public ban-

---

topoi of the Augustan ideology particularly as reflected in the *Res Gestae*. Cf. Johnson, *Symposion of Praise*, 201.
  [67] Lowrie, *Horace's Narrative Odes*, 335–337.

quet. The vinedresser averts the crisis of separation by wedding Augustus permanently to sympotic celebration through ritual.[68]

Horace's description of this ideal scene thus inscribes key values and practices of Roman life and links them with the ongoing treatment of Augustus as a god.

Aside from what this hymn teaches about the great deeds of Augustus, or the kinds of ways he is honored by common citizens, the panegyric addresses a fundamental uncertainty of Augustus's phenomenal reign. By dealing with a temporary absence of Augustus from Rome, the poem can address the anxiety about what will happen when he is permanently absent. In this regard, *Odes* IV.5 paints a portrait of reality that includes not just Augustus, but also all of Rome. To the extent that the hearers embrace this image and find themselves in it, the potential for the continued well-being of the empire is assured. But it is not assured through the emperor's lasting stay on earth. Rather, it is assured through the people of Rome working in their fields and invoking the emperor as the people of Greece invoked both gods and heroes. Augustus is (arguably) presented as both hero and god, and can be remembered as both, even when he is physically absent. The hymn itself then cannot simply be seen as Horace merely fulfilling a poetic obligation to praise the ruling power, nor can it be seen as a critique of Augustan ideology. As Johnson notes, "It transcends these boundaries by investing the simple country folk with the creative ritual needed to restore brokenness: libation, which is the poet's panegyric song."[69] Seen in this light, Horace has utilized the medium of panegyric not only to praise the emperor but to invest in his readers and invite them to see their role in the construction of Rome's identity.

2. Horace Odes *IV.15*

Odes IV.15 concludes the fourth book of *Odes* and, like *Odes* IV.5, follows immediately upon the heels of a victory poem in honor of Augustus, Tiberius, and Drusus. It is most striking for the way that it follows the topical and thematic focus of Augustus's *Res Gestae*. In English translation it reads:

Thy age, O Caesar,
has restored to farms their plenteous crops
and to our Jove the standards
stript from the proud columns of the Parthians;
has closed Quirinus' fane

---

[68] Johnson, *Symposion of Praise*, 132.
[69] Ibid., 133.

empty of war;
has put a check on licence, passing righteous bounds;
has banished crime
and called back home the ancient ways

whereby the Latin name and might of Italy
waxed great, and the fame and majesty
of our dominion were spread from
the sun's western bed to his arising.

While Caesar guards the state, not
civil rage, nor violence,
nor wrath that forges swords,
embroiling hapless towns, shall banish peace.

Not they that drink the Danube deep
shall break the Julian laws, nor Getae,
Seres, faithless Parthians,
nor they by Tanais born. (lines 4–24)

In this *Ode*, the claims of peace and restoration of Rome under Augustus illustrate the fundamental aspects of Roman imperial ideology.[70]

One interesting feature of this praise is the way that Caesar Augustus and his accomplishments transcend the limitations of time. While in the present Caesar has reversed the decline that had been occurring in previous ages, the poem shifts to predict the future under the protection of Augustus. As long as the rule of Augustus lasts, there will be peace with no threat of internal or external conflict. By tapping into multiple temporal registers Horace suggests that Augustus's accomplishments transcend the present moment. Johnson explains, "The greatness of Augustus in c.15 is his ability to unite in the present Rome's past and future, and for doing so he will be immortalized through the songs of his people. Caesar is as divine as the sympotic lyric poet could portray him without the overt use of a title."[71] Taking this assessment seriously, we see that here Horace has pushed the limits of Roman poetry in praise of an exalted human as far as they could go in this time period.

After the recitation of the accomplishments of Caesar, the poem shifts its focus to the response of the Roman people. The final lines of the poem, lines 25–32, read,

On common and on sacred days,
amid the gifts of merry Bacchus,
with wife and child
we first will duly pray the gods;

---

[70] For detailed analysis see the commentary in Putnam, *Artifices of Eternity*, 262–306.

[71] Johnson, *Symposion of Praise*, 203.

then after our fathers' wont, in measures
joined to strains of Lydian flutes, we will hymn
the glories of the heroic dead, Troy and Anchises
and benign Venus' offspring.

All commentators note the shift from the "I" of the poet at the opening of the poem to the "we" of the Roman people at the end of the poem. A number of explanations have been offered with regard to interpreting this shift. One view sees the concluding "we" of the poem as indicating the poet subsumed or absorbed into society; Horace is no longer speaking as the ego we encounter in the rest of his *Odes*.[72] This move is part of his way of negotiating the challenge of writing panegyric in the Augustan era.[73] However, this perspective does not do justice to the skill and effort of Horace that he has displayed throughout the remainder of his works.

Taking seriously the larger context of the entire book IV of the *Odes* along with the sympotic nature of the *Odes* brings out a different perspective: Horace is not disappearing into a crowd but inviting others into community. Johnson explains, "While insisting on the power of his lyric voice, he complicates the imperial panegyric and then concludes with an open invitation to a banquet where the poet and the Roman people will sing together the praises of their founders and leaders."[74] The result is a poem that "requires an interpretive community to actively engage the song and negotiate its meaning through their voices."[75] Seen in this perspective the switch to "we" is thus not Horace disappearing into the crowd, but Horace inviting the community to gather and celebrate. Horace's strategy "incorporates competing and complementary vantage points (*dubia*) and insists on the power of individuals to overcome the pains of mortality when they come together to share songs."[76]

Johnson goes on to explain that Horace does not allow any single voice to dominate the whole. He summarizes,

Horace does not resolve the ode's panegyric conflicts (*dubia*) by allowing any single voice in the *recusatio* to dominate the others no matter how powerful or necessary to the panegyric process these individuals may be: the god Apollo, the poet, or Caesar Augustus. Horatian panegyric culminates in the plural, a symposion of praise: the Dionysiac authority of the Roman community that closes the ode.[77]

---

[72] Lowrie, *Horace's Narrative Odes*, 347–348.
[73] Ibid., 350–352.
[74] Johnson, *Symposion of Praise*, 201.
[75] Ibid.
[76] Ibid., 211.
[77] Ibid.

When viewed in this way we are able to see the power of the *Ode* to paint a picture of reality that invites and requires the voices of a larger community to participate and interpret the portrait.

3. Conclusions Regarding Horace's Praise of Augustus

We may conclude our consideration of Horace's imperial praise by noting two observations that relate the praises of Caesar with the present project. First, we can agree with the assessment of Dihle. Horace was a man who "as much as he supported the newly founded order, was not in the least blind to the deep shadows in the picture which the new rulers presented of their characters, and their actions."[78] These two *Odes*, with their high praise of Augustus, can be read in such a way that they paint a complex portrait of reality (albeit one that is colored by Augustan ideology) that invites and necessitates the involvement of the Roman people in the ongoing peace and prosperity of the empire. Both *Odes* certainly present a shift of focus from the one being praised to the people who are the beneficiaries of his rule, a move which must be considered significant in interpreting the meaning of each *Ode*.

Second, following Johnson we have been able to read the *Odes* of book IV within the context of Horace's persona of books I–III as sympotic poetry. Showing that Horace connects panegyric with the sympotic persona he developed in his earlier poetry, Johnson notes, "Horatian panegyric depends on an invitation to community rather than a confrontational relationship of a poet facing an audience and attempting to persuade them to adopt a particular position toward a *laudandus*."[79] In this regard the *Odes* of Horace are quite unique when we compare their didactic techniques with those of other didactic hymns. Johnson concludes, "Horace's lyric praise requires and nurtures a collective interpretive process that transforms panegyric into a vibrant communal activity."[80] Horace has utilized hymnic styles and elements to construct and create a medium for communal formation. His contemporaries could reflect on their place in Caesar's world as they engaged with the issues and themes of his sympotic praise poetry.

---

[78] Albrecht Dihle, *Greek and Latin Literature of the Roman Empire: From Augustus to Justinian* (London: Routledge, 1994), 34.

[79] Johnson, *Symposion of Praise*, xix.

[80] Ibid., xx.

H. Imperial Praise after Horace

Before fast-forwarding to Pliny's *Panegyricus* in 100 CE, it will be valuable to note some of the developments of imperial praise and imperial ideology in the first century CE. In this section some of these changes will be noted along with recent scholarly analyses of the forms and functions of the imperial ideology.

In spite of Augustus's stated policy of moderation in receiving divine honors, eventually some Roman emperors would allow themselves to be worshipped as divine in their own lifetime. A prime example of this development was Caligula, who reigned 37–41 CE and was notorious, according to ancient sources, for his desire to receive divine worship.[81] That Caligula had crossed the line in the eyes of the Romans is evident from the fact that the senate never voted to approve his deification or require that he be given divine honors. As we will see below, Pliny will contrast Trajan with these earlier excesses (an encomiastic *topos* in itself) and show that Trajan restored what was lost during the reign of less-moderate rulers.

While the question of exactly to what extent Roman citizens considered their emperor to be divine is worth asking, it is important to consider here that the Imperial ideology had more to do with the status of the emperor than with his nature in a philosophical or theological sense. Gradel writes,

> The honours, such as temple, priest, the title of Divus Julius, the inscription to Caesar as 'Deus Invictus' after Munda, should be seen as an expression of relative divinity, that is, divine *status* in relation to all other men. The words obviously did not exclude that Caesar really was a god in an absolute sense, but this question, one of dogma, was simply irrelevant.[82]

In other words, the emperor held a position which placed him above all other men. Particularly in terms of his unlimited power in the world, Caesar was much closer to the realm of the divine. Further, his benefactions to

---

[81] Suetonius wrote of Caligula in his *Lives of the Caesars*, "But on being reminded that he had risen above the elevation both of princes and kings, he began from that time to lay claim to divine majesty; for after giving orders that such statues of the gods as were especially famous for their sanctity or their artistic merit, including that of Jupiter of Olympia, should be brought from Greece, in order to remove their heads and put his in their place, he built a part of the Palace as far as the Forum, and making the temple of Castor and Pollux its vestibule, he often took his place between the divine brethren, and exhibited himself there to be worshipped by those who presented themselves; and some hailed him as Jupiter Latiaris. He also set up a special temple to his own godhead, with priests and with victims of the choicest kind. In this temple was a life-sized statue of the emperor in gold, which was dressed each day in clothing such as he wore himself" (*Cal.* 22), cited in Suetonius, *Suetonius* (trans. John Carew Rolfe; Rev. ed.; LCL 38; Cambridge, Mass.: Harvard University Press, 1998), 449.

[82] Gradel, *Emperor Worship*, 72.

humanity went beyond what might be expected from any human. As we have seen, it was thought that through Caesar Augustus (and future emperors) a time of peace had been bestowed on humanity, which resulted in the restoration of the world in what amounted to being, in essence, a new creation.

Though we have already encountered several aspects of this imperial ideology in the *Odes* of Horace, inscriptions from outside of Rome also attest to this complex of beliefs. An inscription from Asia Minor captures this well, calling Augustus a "savior who put an end to war and established all things" and referring to his arrival as "good tidings (*euangelion*)." This inscription also records the decision of the people:

> Whereas the birthday of the god [Augustus] marked for the world the beginning of good tidings [*euangelion*] through his coming... We could justly hold it [the birthday of Caesar] to be equivalent to the beginning of all things, and he has restored at least to serviceability, if not to its natural state, every form that had become imperfect and fallen into misfortune; and he has given a different aspect to the whole world, which blithely would have embraced its own destruction if Caesar had not been born for the common benefit of all.[83]

Caesar's arrival in the world was good news indeed in that it brought about the restoration of all things.

Further, through Caesar it was understood that a new era of order and morality was instituted in the world.[84] Caesar was the ultimate father, and the Roman world was his well-ordered household.[85] This family was an example of this good order to the Romans and to the rest of the world.[86] We have encountered references to the moral order of the Augustan age already in Horace. By the second century CE such ideas were still preva-

---

[83] *OGI* 2, 458, decree of Paulus Fabius Maximus, proconsul of Asia, cited in Price, *Rituals and Power*, 55.

[84] See the discussion about Augustus's moral legislation and its role in justifying Roman conquest and expansion as a civilizing force in the world in Galinsky, *Augustan Culture*, 128–140.

[85] Note the following claims: "Our fatherland which is safe and secure with you as its parent . . . father of our country," Ovid, *Tristia*, 2.157, 181; "Augustus, the founder of the empire, did not wish to be called *dominus*, for that is the name of God. I will openly call the emperor *dominus*, but only in a mundane fashion, and only when I am not compelled to call him *dominus* as if he were a *deus*. . . . He who is *pater patriae*, how is he its *dominus*? Surely the name suggesting piety and not power is the more pleasurable. Even the fathers of families are called *patres* rather than *domini*," Tertullian, *Apol.* 34.1–2. These citations are from Ando, *Imperial Ideology*, 401–402.

[86] Deborah Sawyer notes, "The macrocosm for the family structure in the Roman world was the imperial household itself, headed by the Emperor-god, and underpinned by the constant hearth fire of Vesta. This was the overarching superstructure, which was emulated by microcosmic family units," (Deborah F. Sawyer, *God, Gender, and the Bible* [London: Routledge, 2002], 132).

lent as witnessed by Aelius Aristides comments on the Roman Empire and its ruler.[87] To summarize, major aspects of imperial ideology included the idea that the emperor, by divine authority and power, had brought great blessings to humanity including universal peace and the renewal of all things including agriculture and morality.

This ideology was promoted throughout the empire in a variety of ways that permeated every aspect of society. In addition to inscriptions, royal decrees, and other forms of verbal communication, there was a focused effort to promote the imperial ideology through images. The image of the emperor was ubiquitous, not just in temples and city squares, but also in public buildings, baths, theatres, and forums. It was found on their coins, and archaeological remains suggest that the image of the emperor found a prominent place in many homes.[88] It also appears that individuals included the genius of the emperor (a representation of his spirit) among their household and personal gods, so that the image of the emperor was a part of private family life and religion.[89]

It is the omnipresent nature of the imperial ideology along with the extravagant claims of this ideology that would make it seem almost impossible that an inhabitant of the Roman world in the early centuries of this era would not have known of these imperial claims. The degree to which a response was required would of course vary from region to region and from urban centers to rural locales.

In light of this brief sketch, three broader themes may be seen to coalesce in the institution of the imperial cult: power, honor, and ideology. Other themes and ideas are relevant in a consideration of the imperial cult, but these three (power, honor, and ideology) provide three angles from which we can explore the phenomenon.

---

[87] "Therefore they [provincial governors] believe that he has more knowledge of their actions than they do of themselves, and they have more fear and respect for him than anyone would for the presence of his master who was supervising and giving orders. No one is so confident in himself that he is able to remain calm after only hearing his name. But he stands up, praises, and reverences him, and offers a double prayer, one to the gods on the emperor's behalf, the other concerning his personal affairs to the emperor himself. If they should have even some small doubt over suits and the legal privileges of their subjects, either public or private, whether any are entitled to these privileges, they immediately send to him, asking what should be done, and they wait for his signal, no less than a chorus waits upon its teacher." Aristides, *Or.* XXVI Regarding Rome (trans. C. A. Behr, *Aelius Aristides: The Complete Works* [2 vols.; Leiden: Brill, 1981] 2:80).

[88] Price, *Rituals and Power*, 170–206. For a creative "first-hand" description of the ubiquitous nature of the imperial cult see the fictitious letter in Walsh and Keesmaat, *Colossians Remixed*, 49–64.

[89] This is suggested in Horace *Odes* IV.5 among other places. Cf. Fishwick, *Imperial Cult in the Latin West*, 2.1:375–387.

In terms of power, scholars have long since moved away from exploring emperor worship as only a religious phenomenon and have recognized its political aspects as well. Gradel's notion of relative divinity is relevant here:

What mattered was power, again *relative* divinity, and Caesar's power was at this stage unquestioned, as was Jupiter's. Absolute power entailed divinity and vice versa. Caesar's heavenly honours express his new status far above the position of any other man, past or present, in the Roman republic.[90]

Thus it was the power of the emperor that was in view in the eyes of those who honored him through various forms of worship.

Also recognizing the importance of the power of the emperor, Price suggests that the ruler cult created a complex "system of exchange" that linked Greece and Rome and enabled the provinces to deal with this power in profitable ways.[91] He explains,

To avoid feeling an inferior element of the empire they needed to create a positive relationship with the centre. . . . In this enterprise the imperial image was of particular significance. The image, which emanated from and represented the centre, was omnipresent and widely venerated. By it, above all, the charisma of the central power was diffused, transformed, and incorporated into the Greek world.[92]

In general, it can be argued that honor was an appropriate response to power regardless of whether that power was human or divine (or both). Imperial cult was just one part of a spectrum of honors, albeit the highest point possible for humans.[93] Honoring those who were thought to be deserving of it because of their superior power was considered to be the natural and appropriate response. Citizens thus gave honor to the emperor; the emperor (and others so honored) in turn utilized their power beneficently on behalf of the people. Gradel explains, "The fact that this notion was apparently so obvious and widespread lends strong support to the view that

---

[90] Gradel, *Emperor Worship*, 72. Gradel explains that the same approach applied to the gods: "In cultic life, given authority by the weight of tradition, the *mos maiorum*, rituals, primarily sacrifices, were what mattered. In this system of gift exchange, gods were cultivated simply because of their power, and out of that power were obliged to return the honours bestowed on them with benefactions. Imperial honours, whether cultic or not, functioned along the same lines. No sane person could, or did, doubt the enormous power of the ruling emperor" (334).

[91] Price, *Rituals and Power*, 65–77.

[92] Ibid., 206.

[93] Davies explains, "What we call imperial cult is, in the narrative at least, in fact only the apex of a pyramid of potential honours: the *diui* are not the only eminent dead and their lesser counterparts can be honoured religiously on a lesser scale." Jason P. Davies, *Rome's Religious History: Livy, Tacitus, and Ammianus on their Gods* (Cambridge: Cambridge University Press, 2004), 182–183.

divine honours were simply the 'natural' response to absolute power in antiquity."[94]

This system of relating to the power of Rome makes good sense in light
of the Roman imperial ideology which promoted a worldview that citizens
were called to embrace. This ideology insisted that the power of the emperor was a gift to humanity for the reconciliation and redemption of the
world, and that everyone in the empire was a recipient of the results of this
gift. In such a world grateful honor was thus the appropriate response of
every person in the Roman world.

Having introduced the imperial cult and the ideology with which it was
integrally related, we may now consider the way in which verbal praise of
the emperor fit into the picture. On the one hand, it was appropriate as a
response to the greatness of the emperor. As we have noted above, a benefactor deserved the praise of those who had benefited from his services. On
the other hand, verbal praise of the emperor reinforced the central components of imperial ideology. To the extent that it did so in the traditional
kinds of language normally offered in praise of gods, it gave the impression that worship of the emperor was itself an ancient and culturally acceptable practice.

As we asked with several other texts, we might ask, what did praise of
the emperor *do*? To begin with it positioned the worshipper in a favorable
position relative to the supreme power. It placed the worshipper in a position of one who had already received the benefactions of the emperor and
was able to respond with the appropriate degree of gratitude and thanks.
This conveyed to the emperor that the worshipper would continue to respond favorably were the emperor to continue in his kindness to the worshipper and his community (city, region, or province). Second, praise of
the emperor negotiated the position of the one who authorized the praise
(the governor, the council, the wealthy patron) relative to the rest of the
community. Third, as it modeled an appropriate response to divine benefactions it also taught the listener the appropriate way to view the emperor.

In one sense then, the system of emperor worship created a kind of implicit social contract between the emperor and the citizens. Gradel explains, "This was the basic reason behind all honours, whether to gods,
rulers, or patrons: by receiving such honours, the emperor was morally
obliged to return benefactions, that is, to rule well."[95] Such an analysis can
be seen to fit both the praise of Augustus offered by Horace and the praise
of Trajan offered over a century later by Pliny. It is to Pliny's panegyric of
Trajan that we now turn.

---

[94] Gradel, *Emperor Worship*, 269.
[95] Ibid., 369.

I. Pliny's *Panegyricus*

At the beginning of the second century we encounter an expansive and fully developed panegyric of the emperor Trajan (ruled 98–117 CE) in the writings of Pliny the Younger.[96] Pliny composed and delivered his panegyric at the request of the senate when he was consul in 100 CE, and then later published it for a wider audience (cf. *Ep.* III. 13.1). The purpose was to praise the emperor for his many good qualities, accomplishments, and benefactions to the Roman world. But as we have seen, praise is often joined with other purposes such as instruction, encouragement, and exhortation. With regard to these kinds of didactic goals, Pliny's *Panegyricus* does not disappoint. Pliny himself explains:

> But now I must bow to the decree of the Senate which in the public interest has declared that under the form of a vote of thanks delivered by the voice of the consul, good rulers should recognize their own deeds and bad ones learn what theirs should be. (4.1)[97]

While the form is an expression of thanks to the emperor, the purpose goes beyond simply expressing thanks to include facilitating recognition on the part of good rulers and learning on the part of bad ones. In other words, the *Panegyricus* has an explicit didactic focus. The ultimate aim, however, is the promotion of the best interest of the public. Pliny accomplishes this by praising Trajan (the good ruler) for his virtues, deeds, and policies and by contrasting his reign with that of earlier rulers, especially Domitian (a bad ruler). In this way Trajan, who is presented as the ideal prince, is encouraged to continue his policies. Likewise the senators and consuls are exhorted to live up to the responsibilities that have been granted them by Trajan.

Formally Pliny's *Panegyricus* is not a hymn, nor does it claim to be. Nevertheless it contains hymnic elements such as an opening invocation addressed to Jupiter, suggestive comparisons between Trajan and Jupiter, and a closing prayer. These contribute to the overall aims of the composition as a whole as Pliny uses his panegyric to paint a portrait of reality for his hearers and readers. He would have them see in the person of Trajan a return to the Augustan ideal of a ruler who is specially given to Rome by the gods for the good of the world. Further, Pliny paints a picture in which Trajan's reign marks a return to the state of affairs in the Republic when the senators and consuls had real authority and power. This picture of the

---

[96] For an overview of Pliny's writings see Michael von Albrecht and Gareth L. Schmeling, *A History of Roman Literature: From Livius Andronicus to Boethius* (trans. Ruth R. Caston and Francis R. Schwartz; 2 vols.; Leiden: Brill, 1997), 2:1146–1157; Dihle, *Greek and Latin Literature*, 224–226.

[97] Translations of the *Panegyricus* are from Pliny, *Letters and Panegyricus* (trans. Betty Radice; LCL 59; Cambridge: Heinemann, 1969).

world is contrasted with the reign of Domitian which is portrayed as a dark period of history for the Roman people. This historical background enables Pliny to cast Trajan in an even better light as he restores the Republic (though now a principate) and embodies the virtues that Domitian was lacking. Those who accept this view of things are then exhorted to live in accordance with this vision and not as though they were still under the oppressive reign of a tyrant. In this section I will briefly trace out several of these key themes of the panegyric in order to show how praise, instruction, and exhortation are woven together in this composition as Pliny offers a verbal portrait of reality under the emperor.

1. Associations with the Gods: Trajan is a Gift of the Gods to Humanity

In the opening of the *Panegyricus*, as one might expect, Pliny introduces a major theme of the entire composition: the close connection between Trajan and the gods. After noting the wise custom of beginning all speeches with a prayer to the gods he asks the rhetorical question, "What gift of the gods could be greater and more glorious than a prince whose purity and virtue make him their own equal?" (1.3) The implication is, of course, that there is no gift that could be greater. But in asking this question, Pliny has suggested both that Trajan himself is a gift of the gods, and that in his purity and virtue he should be considered an equal of the gods. In the remainder of the speech Pliny will not go so far as to make any straightforward equation of Trajan with the gods (he is after all a fellow-citizen! Cf. 2.3), but he will also continue making associations between Trajan and Jupiter throughout the composition.[98]

The divine choice of Trajan as emperor is a theme about which there is no question for Pliny. He writes,

> If it were still in doubt whether the rulers of the earth were given us by the hazards of chance or by some heavenly power, it would be evident that our emperor at least was divinely chosen for his task; for it was no blind act of fate but Jupiter himself who chose and revealed him in the sight and hearing of us all. (1.4–5)

Trajan is hand-selected by Jupiter himself, a theme which is echoed elsewhere in the panegyric (5.1–2; 52.2, 6). Here Pliny refers to the historical circumstances in which Nerva announced the adoption of Trajan as his son and his choice of Trajan to succeed him. His revelation to the people of Rome is given in imagery suggestive of the epiphany of a god.

---

[98] For a discussion of the way these associations work in combination with Pliny's assertions that he will not flatter Trajan in this way see Shadi Bartsch, *Actors in the Audience: Theatricality and Doublespeak from Nero to Hadrian* (Revealing Antiquity 6; Cambridge, Mass.: Harvard University Press, 1994), 162–166.

Not only does Pliny claim that Trajan is a gift of the gods, but Pliny praises Trajan for his god-like ability to settle disputes and to bring about peace and reconciliation through the application of reason. First he explains that actions like these are the work of princes and gods:

This is indeed the true care of a prince, or even that of a god, to settle rivalries between cities, to soothe the passions of angry peoples less by exercise of power than by reason: to intervene where there has been official injustice, to undo what should never have been done: finally, like a swift-moving star, to see all, hear all, and be present at once with aid wherever your help is sought. (80.3)

We could note here the didactic tone of these lines as they reflect on some of the primary concerns of princes and gods. The audience is being instructed with regard to the qualities and deeds they should expect to see in their prince. Pliny goes on to show that these aptitudes are abundantly present in their ruler. He argues that because of Trajan's god-like skill in these matters Jupiter no longer needs to concern himself with the earthly portion of his responsibilities; Trajan has things well under control.

It is thus, I fancy, that the great Father of the universe rules all with a nod of the head, if he ever looks down on earth and deigns to consider mortal destinies among his divine affairs. Now he is rid of this part of his duties, free to devote himself to heaven's concerns, since he has given you to us to fill his role with regard to the entire human race. And you are filling it, worthy of his trust in you: since every passing day brings every advantage for us and the greatest glory for you. (80.4–5)

Though this may be exaggerated rhetoric the point is clear. Trajan's skill in the administration and running of the empire is of such quality that it may be compared to the way Jupiter cares for the affairs of the whole world. In this way a major theme of the panegyric is reinforced: the gods have given Trajan to the Romans and he is fulfilling his role gloriously. In fact, no one could possibly do it better.

Trajan's relationship with the gods is further developed elsewhere as Pliny unfolds the details of Trajan's appropriate reverence of the gods. This is particularly the case with regard to his honoring of his father, Nerva.

You gave your father his place among the stars with no thought of terrorizing your subjects, of bringing the gods into disrepute, or of gaining reflected glory, but simply because you thought he *was* a god. (11.2)

In contrast to other emperors who gave their fathers divine honors out of ambition or other impure motives, Trajan did it to give honor where honor was due. Later Pliny discusses the moderation Trajan employs with respect to the placement of his own statues and the practice of praying to his genius.[99] Trajan's devotion to the gods and his moderation with respect to seeking honor are among the reasons why the gods have given him all the power he has. Along these lines Pliny explains,

> With the same reverence for the gods, Caesar, you will not allow public thanks for your benevolence to be addressed to your genius, but direct them to the godhead of Jupiter Best and Highest; to him, you say, we owe whatever we owe you, and your benefactions are the gift of him who gave you to us. (52.6)

Claims about the way the *laudandus* reveres and honors the gods are a standard part of encomiastic praise.[100] In the case of Trajan, however, worship of the gods is shown to be part of a larger network of relational ties between the divine world and the human emperor. Trajan is a gift of the gods, who rules with divine skill and enjoys divine favor because of his own moderation and reverence of the gods.

2. Trajan's Accomplishments Include Restoration of the Blessings of the Republic

Along with claims about Trajan's connections with the divine world, Pliny aims to lay out the ways in which the emperor has brought the empire into a new era – an era that is in many ways a restoration of better days of the past. Here we can note Gowing's discussion of *historia* and *memoria* in Pliny's *Panegyricus*. In general, Gowing observes,

> The Roman view of *historia* and *memoria* inevitably leads to a refashioning of the meaning of the past, requiring authors to give it meaning in the present and decide not only *what* to remember but *how* it should be remembered. This is why from one regime to the next the use of Republican history varies significantly.[101]

By the time of Pliny, the Roman Empire possessed enough imperial history that Pliny can refer to more distant Republican themes as well as more recent history under the Principate. Both aspects of *memoria* serve to present Trajan as an ideal ruler who champions ideals of the Republic (the authority of the senate; honor to Roman families with distinguished history; freedom of speech among the senate) and who is the antidote to the bad emperors who have ruled since Augustus.[102]

---

[99] "You enter the sanctuary only to offer your own prayers – for you the highest honour is to have your statues placed outside the temples, on guard before the doors. This is why the gods have set you on the pinnacle of human power: they know that you do not covet their own" (52.2).

[100] Cf. Theocritus's praises of Ptolemy II Philadelphus who created temples for his parents (*Idylls* 17.121–125).

[101] Gowing, *Empire and Memory*, 10.

[102] On the theme of restoration see Ibid., 121–123.

Of course, as Pliny strikes certain notes about the restoration of the Republic it is clear that Trajan has not actually restored the Republic. Trajan is indeed the emperor, but Pliny incorporates this fact into his Republican rhetoric by showing that what Trajan has brought about is better than the Republic, even as it is better than any period since Augustus. Gowing explains the ultimate purpose of remembering the past in the *Panegyricus*:

> Trajan's memory (as well as that of Pliny) has now been added to – and in some measure has displaced – the memory of Rome's Republican past. *That* past warrants remembering not for what it can teach or as a model for present and future behavior, but rather as a reminder that so long as the Principate is held by a man such as Trajan, Rome is better off than it was under the Republic.[103]

Rome under the rule of Trajan has the best of both worlds: the cultural and political freedoms of the Republic preserved by the power and rule of a virtuous, god-given prince.

By presenting Trajan in contrast to rulers in more recent history, Pliny is able to show that Trajan truly is the best and that he will certainly be remembered by future generations as such.[104] Trajan has restored the Republic to what it was like before this long period of corruption and even before the days of emperors (53.1; 93.3). Trajan's person and deeds can be contrasted with Domitian in particular as is done in several sections regarding moderation in allowing himself to be worshipped, as well as in sections relating to Trajan's physical and military prowess. Pliny also addresses the troubling times in the reign of Domitian, contrasting the two rulers with regard to the social and political climates they engendered within Rome.[105]

One clear example of this approach is seen in chapter 47, where Trajan is presented as a champion of the arts: "Under you the liberal arts are restored, to breathe and live in their own country – the learning which the barbarity of the past punished with exile, when an emperor acquainted with all the vices sought to banish everything hostile to vice" (47.1). In the next chapter Pliny discusses how the senators enjoy lingering in the halls of Trajan as if they were in their own home:

> We stay behind to linger on as if in a home we share, though this is the place where recently that fearful monster built his defences with untold terrors, where lurking in his den he licked up the blood of his murdered relatives or emerged to plot the massacre and destruction of his most distinguished subjects. (48.3)

---

[103] Ibid., 130.

[104] Trajan is called Optimus, a title which not so subtly brings to mind the god Jupiter Optimus Maximus.

[105] Cf. 90.5–6 where Pliny references the murder of his friends under Domitian.

The memory of the vices of previous emperors provides opportunity to showcase the many good qualities of Trajan. Indeed, for Pliny the contrast of good and bad is a major part of his approach to panegyric. He himself writes,

Indeed, eulogy is best expressed through comparison, and, moreover, the first duty of grateful subjects towards a perfect emperor is to attach those who are least like him: for no one can properly appreciate a good prince who does not sufficiently hate a bad one. (53.2)

But mere appreciation is not Pliny's only goal in praising Trajan in this way. His speech suggests that he desires to encourage specific actions in various members of his audience.

3. Exhortation

The language of praise is often closely connected with exhortation. Pliny's praise of the emperor and his policies, far from being a simple record of his achievements, undoubtedly serves to encourage the emperor to continue on with his policies. Further it encourages the consuls to boldly fulfill their duties to the public. Near the conclusion of his speech Pliny spells this out clearly as he praises the emperor and exhorts the consuls along these lines:

So far as it rests with our prince, the consuls are free to fill their role as they did before the days of the emperors. Is there any proper return we can make you, to match all you have done for us? Only perhaps by remembering all our lives that we have been consuls, your consuls; by ensuring that our opinions and pronouncements are worthy of the office we once held; by playing an active part in public affairs to show we believe that the republic still exists; by not withholding our aid and counsel, and by not imagining ourselves rid of the consulate and dismissed from office, but believing ourselves always closely bound up with it in some way. (93.3)

Here three themes of the panegyric are brought together: Trajan's benefactions to the Roman people ("all you have done for us"), restoration of the republic ("before the days of the emperors"), and exhortation to the consuls ("remembering that we have been your consuls;" "playing an active part in public affairs"). In the picture of the present state of affairs that Pliny paints, both emperor and senate have a vital role to play in preserving that state of affairs. Since the *Panegyricus* is delivered so early in the reign of Trajan it is also likely that Pliny is describing the way he hopes that things will turn out under Trajan's rule in the long run. The portrait painted in this composition may thus reflect not only one view of present reality in 100 CE but also the hopes of Pliny for the future as well. Painting such an attractive picture (at least for emperor and senate) would undoubtedly have served a role in promoting the kinds of values and policies that are praised in this text.[106]

In his praises of the emperor Pliny provided perspective on the person and accomplishments of Trajan. But this was not merely for informational purposes. Nor was it only to register the gratitude of the senate for all of his benefactions, though that was certainly a part of the impulse behind this speech. Judging by the contents and development of the *Panegyricus*, Pliny had much more elaborate aims in view as well. He hoped to encourage the emperor to continue on with his good policies (87.1; 93.1) and to discourage him from any actions which would resemble his less praiseworthy predecessors. He was also interested in exhorting the consuls to serve according to the ideals of the new era and not the terrors of the old era. Ultimately he painted a portrait of a new reality in which the emperor was a gift of the gods, one who ruled with moderation as he restored the glories of earlier days and undid the damage of less praiseworthy rulers.

J. Conclusions

Verbal praise of rulers, emperors, or deified emperors was a practice which we have seen is both religious and political in its orientation: "religious" in the sense that it was a response to a power that was understood to be superhuman; "political" in the sense that it functioned to promote the interests of the one being praised as well as the one(s) offering the praise. In the Roman Empire, praises of the emperor were just one part of the propagation of an imperial ideology through other means (visual, legal, architectural, monetary, etc.). To the extent that we have evidence for the practice, praise of emperors was offered in language nearly identical to praise of the gods. Though not always explicitly praised as a god, the close associations with the gods in terms of the ruler's birth, appointment, deeds, virtues and accomplishments certainly place the ruler closer to the realm of the gods than the realm of the average mortal. The purpose of such elevated language was related to the need of individuals, cities, and communities to negotiate power in a changing and emerging political system. In this setting it is not surprising that encomia of rulers would praise the ruler even as they instruct the community about the nature of this new reality. The fact that each of the compositions we examined in this chapter can be placed in a specific time and place aids us in imagining the impact they

---

[106] That is, if Pliny's remarks were considered sincere by his audience. The issue of Pliny's sincerity in praising the emperor is another leitmotif of the *Panegyricus*. See the discussion in chapter 5 ("The Art of Sincerity: Pliny's *Panegyricus*") in Bartsch, *Actors in the Audience*, 148–188.

might have had on their communities as their authors painted a verbal portrait of a reality in which the ruler exceeds the expectations for what a mere mortal might accomplish.

However, as we have seen, the praise of the emperor did not always aim to instruct the community alone. In some cases it appears that the poet or writer aimed to instruct and exhort not only the audience but also the *laudandus*. This was at least the case with Isocrates' *Evagoras* and Pliny's *Panegyricus*. In other instances, Horace in particular, we observed that praise invited the community to interpret and evaluate claims about what was of ultimate and lasting value.

Having considered these dynamics at some length, we are now in a position to have our ears attuned to hearing when imperial chords may be sounded in other hymnic compositions from the Greco-Roman world. This will be seen most clearly in several of the early Christian hymns in which accomplishments and honors are ascribed to Jesus which were normally ascribed to the emperor himself, or only to the gods. We can also be attuned to ways that these kinds of praise compositions offer instruction or invite interpretation within the context of an audience which may be receiving other imperially oriented messages as well. In all cases we can consider how the act of verbal praise plays a role in the formation of the community in which the praise originates.

Chapter 5

Didactic Hymns in the Hebrew Bible

A. Introduction

The psalmists and songwriters of ancient Israel had many reasons for producing their compositions. Praising God, giving thanks to him, seeking him in time of need, seeking deliverance, repenting of wrongdoing, or lamenting in times of trouble are among the most obvious. However, some biblical psalms also indicate another reason for their composition and recitation: teaching. The psalmists do not conceal this purpose, but at times make it quite plain. For instance, Ps 78 begins

Give ear, my people, to my instruction;
incline your ear to the words of my mouth.[1]

In a similar manner, Ps 34:11 reads,

Come, children, listen to me;
I will teach you the fear of the LORD.

The authors of these psalms evidently intended to convey instruction to their hearers even as they praised God through their compositions.[2]

---

[1] Translations of the Hebrew Bible are mine unless otherwise noted.

[2] Some scholars refer to these more didactically oriented psalms as "wisdom psalms" since in many ways they indicate the influence of Jewish wisdom traditions. However, this label is not necessarily helpful in that it may obscure the close connection that these psalms share with other psalms. Samuel Terrien, "Wisdom in the Psalter," in *In Search of Wisdom: Essays in Memory of John G. Gammie* (ed. Leo G. Perdue, Bernard Brandon Scott, and William Johnston Wiseman; Louisville, Ky.: Westminster John Knox, 1993), 51–72, 113. For example, von Rad pointed out that, as far as their *Gattungen*, these didactic psalms rightly belong to the genres of the psalm-types that they imitate (hymns, laments, thanksgiving songs, etc.). They do not make up their own genre of psalm and there is no definitive set of formal criteria for identifying these didactic prayers. In this line of thinking, these instructionally oriented psalms are traditional psalms in terms of form, but didactic psalms in terms of content and purpose. Von Rad writes, "It is, rather, a general impression, one of a certain erudition and didactic quality, of a preponderance of theological thoughts, etc., which entitles us to separate these psalms from the great body of predominantly cultically orientated psalms." Gerhard von Rad, *Wisdom in Israel* (trans. James D. Martin; Nashville: Abingdon Press, 1972), 48.

In order to gain a greater appreciation of the ways that psalm-like texts were used to convey religious instruction to their readers, the present chapter will survey those hymns, prayers and poems in the Hebrew Bible whose chief purpose was to teach and instruct.[3] We will also be sensitive to instructional passages which employ aspects of hymnic style to convey their message. After some general observations about the kinds of didactic hymns and prayers in the Hebrew Bible, this chapter will review where these compositions occur in several contexts: the book of Psalms, Wisdom literature, narrative, and prophetic and apocalyptic literature. Through this survey we will observe the ways that these didactic hymns tap into multiple temporal and spatial registers and employ a variety of modes of presentation from descriptive to narrative in order to instruct the readers or hearers in the ways of God.

B. Didactic Hymns in the Hebrew Bible: An Overview

In surveying early Jewish literature for didactic hymns (broadly conceived), this study casts a wide net to consider passages that blend a didactic purpose with hymnic form. Accordingly we will examine hymns, prayers, and poems that register an implicit or explicit instructional purpose as well as didactic passages that utilize hymnic forms and styles. In the Hebrew Bible compositions that fall within these loose constraints can generally be classified within the following categories:

1. Hymns, psalms, and prayers that include direct exhortation to the listener. In these the instructional purpose is straightforward, with some kind of instructional outcome clearly indicated (e.g., Ps 34 and Prov 8).
2. Hymns, psalms, and prayers that provide wisdom and instruction but whose exhortation is more implicit than explicit (e.g., Pss 1 and 49, and Job 28).
3. Hymns, psalms, and prayers that narrate history. In the course of praise, the narration of God's deeds, while serving as the content and reason for praise, is also at the same instructing the hearer or the reader with regard to what God has done (e.g., Pss 78, 105, and 106). Hymnic passages in later Wisdom writings also take this approach (e.g., Wis 10; Sir 44–50).

---

[3] We should recall here that while some psalms are unmistakably didactic in nature, it is also certainly true to say that all psalms have a didactic function to some extent. Even psalms whose primary purpose is to give praise or thanks to God may also be said to serve an instructional function in teaching those who hear them about the praiseworthy character and deeds of God. They also serve as models to be imitated in later compositions. And, of course, many psalms share these multiple purposes of praise joined with instruction. Nevertheless, this chapter focuses specifically on that subset of psalms that give an indication that teaching and instruction is one of their primary purposes. These are the didactic hymns of the Hebrew Bible.

4. Hymns, psalms, and prayers that play a role in narrative. The literary function of these compositions may be varied, but in some way they are instructive. They may serve to reinforce or highlight a central theme (Song of the Sea [Exod 15]; Song of Hannah [1 Sam 2:1–10]) or model the righteous response to God's intervention (Song of Judith; Song of the Three Young Men in the Greek version of Daniel).
5. Hymnically influenced instructional passages. These are passages that do not technically meet the formal criteria for a hymn, but that nevertheless utilize hymnic styles of expression to convey their message. Numerous passages in Isa 40–55 reflect this quality (e.g., Isa 40:12–31) as do passages in Wisdom literature (Wis 7:22–8:1).

These five categories are not so tightly defined that there is no overlap. Rather, the boundaries are fluid so that they provide more of a spectrum for the major ways that didactic purposes are achieved through hymns or hymnic styles. Hymns that narrate history may or may not also provide explicit exhortation. Hymns that play a role in narrative may be quite similar to hymns that narrate history in that they mention historical events, but their placement in a narrative context gives them a different function and purpose.

Although these didactic hymns share some common features, those features are not enough to allow us to refer to "didactic hymnody" as a specific genre in the Hebrew Scriptures. Instead it seems to have been but one of a number of modes of instruction and teaching. Von Rad observed, "One cannot speak of a particular *Gattung* of didactic prayers, only of a common language and motif."[4] Thus it is more correct to say that a number of different kinds of poetic compositions can be considered didactic hymns when their contents register an instructional tone and their style participates in hymnic conventions.[5]

As the five categories noted above indicate, hymns and psalms written for purposes of instruction are found throughout the Hebrew Bible and, likewise, in the later writings of Second Temple Judaism. Some are independent songs found in larger collections, such as those in the book of Psalms, the *Psalms of Solomon*, or the Hodayot. Others are found embedded in larger literary contexts, whether Wisdom literature, narrative, or prophetic writings. This chapter will explore these contexts separately. For each of these contexts one or more illustrative examples will be singled out

---

[4] von Rad, *Wisdom in Israel*, 48.

[5] Gunkel, for example, spoke of wisdom poetry in the Psalms and noted that "the thoughts and forms of wisdom literature even penetrated the characteristically lyric generes" including the hymn; Hermann Gunkel and Joachim Begrich, *Introduction to Psalms: The Genres of the Religious Lyric of Israel* (trans. James D. Nogalski; MLBS; Macon, Ga.: Mercer University Press, 1998), 297–298. For the influence of hymns on wisdom see pp. 60–61. Of Psalm 78 in particular, Gunkel notes, "The hymnic poet begins the wisdom poem with the celebratory form of the introduction because he wants to recite his material, the sacral history, not only to honor God, but also to teach subsequent generations" (60).

for more detailed analysis and commentary. Though none of these contexts are completely independent of one another, this way of dividing up the material will serve to highlight the different ways that didactic hymnody functions in the various settings.

C. Didactic Hymns in the Psalter

Though a full-scale treatment of didactic hymnody with the Psalms falls outside the scope and purpose of this monograph, it will be valuable to survey those Psalms which convey the impression that teaching a lesson was their primary purpose. While these Psalms are of interest in their own right, they are also important for assessing the use of didactic hymns and psalms in other books of the Hebrew Bible.

Sigmund Mowinckel identified ten psalms which he believed were not written for cultic purposes: 1, 34, 37, 49, 78, 105, 106, 111, 112, 127.[6] His contention was that these particular psalms were not written for recitation or use at the temple sacrifices, while the remainder of the psalms most likely had some kind of ritual setting in which they were used. He referred to these kinds of non-cultic psalms as "learned psalmography," suggesting they derive from wisdom circles and show the influence of the wisdom schools.[7] These psalms, with their strong emphasis on instruction, provide an excellent starting point for understanding the phenomenon of didactic hymnody. They also introduce us to an ongoing debate in psalms scholarship: what constitutes a "wisdom psalm" and is this even a valid category?[8]

The issue of defining what is meant by "wisdom psalm" is complicated by several different views on what constitutes the wisdom tradition in Israel.[9] Murphy considers wisdom psalms to be a distinct literary form with distinct characteristics in style, contents, and themes. He notes that other psalms incorporate wisdom elements and exhibit didactic purposes, but these, he claims, remain formally something else (hymn, thanksgivings,

---

[6] S. Mowinckel, "Psalms and Wisdom," in *Wisdom in Israel and in the Ancient Near East* (ed. M. Noth and D. Winton Thomas; Leiden: Brill, 1955), 205–224, here 213. Mowinckel later added an eleventh in Ps 19B; S. Mowinckel, *The Psalms in Israel's Worship* (trans. D. R. Ap-Thomas; 2 vols.; Reprint of 1962 ed.; Grand Rapids: Eerdmans, 2004), 111.

[7] Mowinckel, "Psalms and Wisdom," 213.

[8] For an overview of wisdom in the Psalms see the chapter "Wisdom Poetry in the Psalms" in Gunkel and Begrich, *Introduction to Psalms*, 292–305.

[9] See J. A. Grant, "Wisdom Poem," in *Dictionary of the Old Testament: Wisdom, Poetry & Writings* (ed. Tremper Longman and Peter Enns; Downers Grove, Ill.: IVP Academic, 2008), 891–894.

etc).[10] Terrien, on the other hand, finds that it is not easy to make a distinction between wisdom psalms and other psalm genres. He explains that one can observe "that each of the so-called wisdom psalms belongs in fact to several *Gattungen* and includes a great variety of theological motifs, which in turn are expressed in diverse styles."[11] These perspectives are only the tip of the iceberg of the scholarly debate over wisdom psalms. Much more has been written on the issue of whether or not wisdom psalms is a valid category and why it matters.[12]

Thus it is at least clear for our purposes that not all scholars have agreed with Mowinckel's view of these non-cultic didactic psalms. Some have suggested that, in spite of the presence of wisdom elements and the lack of liturgical indicators, it is still likely that these psalms found a place in the worship practices of faithful Jews.[13] The difficulty with making generalizations about the cultic or non-cultic use of the psalms has to do with the fact that the concept of "cultic use" changed dramatically from the pre-exilic period to the post-exilic period and into the Second Temple period. For example, the rise of synagogues as a place of prayer and instruction in which psalms would find a prominent place complicates the playing field adding a new context for their use.[14] At any rate, cultic and non-cultic use of the psalms is a discussion which varies dramatically depending on the historical era one is considering. Further, Holm-Nielsen suggests, "Properly speaking there is no reason to doubt that they [biblical and non-canonical psalms and hymns] were used for instructional purposes, but this does not preclude the possibility that they were used at the divine service in the synagogue."[15] It must surely be granted that there was a multi-modal use of these psalm-like texts in the Second Temple period at least, with the Temple, synagogue, school, and home being likely locations for their reading.

---

[10] Roland Murphy, "A Consideration of the Classification 'Wisdom Psalms,'" in *Studies in Ancient Israelite Wisdom* (ed. James L. Crenshaw; New York: Ktav Pub. House, 1976), 456–467, here 467.

[11] Terrien, "Wisdom in the Psalter," 55.

[12] James Crenshaw, "Wisdom Psalms?," *Currents in Biblical Research* 8 (2000): 9–17; James Crenshaw, "Gold Dust or Nuggets? A Brief Response to J. Kenneth Kuntz," *Currents in Biblical Research* 1 (2003): 155–158; J. Kenneth Kuntz, "Reclaiming Biblical Wisdom Psalms: A Response to Crenshaw," *Currents in Biblical Research* 1 (2003): 145–154.

[13] Svend Holm-Nielsen, "The Importance of Late Jewish Psalmody for the Understanding of Old Testament Psalmodic Tradition," *ST* 14 (1960): 1–53, here 7–9. Gunkel thought that wisdom poetry did not originally have a place in the worship service but was later incorporated into that setting (Gunkel and Begrich, *Introduction to Psalms*, 303).

[14] Holm-Nielsen, "The Importance of Late Jewish Psalmody," 8–9.

[15] Ibid., 9.

Aside from their cultic and non-cultic use, another important issue with specifically didactic hymns relates to their origin. Were these written by a special class of learned sages of Israel so that they can be separated out from the more traditional psalms based on this criteria? Terrien points out that wisdom songs should not necessarily be understood as their own category of psalm composed by other writers than the rest of the psalms. He notes that it is unlikely that the psalmists, scribes, and wisdom teachers would have been completely isolated and cut off from one another. Instead, he suggests that they would most likely have influenced one another in a number of ways.[16] He explains, "Sapiential words and expressions abound in numerous psalms, but similarities in terminology and phraseology indicate only that the wise and some sacred musicians moved in the same social circles."[17] His concern is to demonstrate that the wisdom psalms do not necessarily indicate that a class of wisdom teachers composed their own psalms, some of which are now found in the Psalter. The presence of wisdom elements may simply be a result of the influence of wisdom teachers on psalmists and musicians. The picture that emerges then is not one of sharp distinctions, but of a complex inter-relationship between the psalms that are preserved in the biblical Psalter and in other contexts.

The present investigation does not require a definitive conclusion about the liturgical or non-liturgical use of each psalm, or even what kind of person (scribe, wisdom teacher, temple liturgist, etc.) composed it. Instead, based on the indicators within a particular psalm, the nature, themes, and purpose of instruction are the primary concern here.

The eleven psalms typically identified as wisdom psalms are often broken down further on the basis of their contents, primary themes, and form. Psalms 78, 105, and 106 are historical surveys ("hymnal legends").[18] Of these three, Ps 105 takes a positive spin on the history of Israel, while the outlook of the other two is more somber. Other kinds of non-cultic poems are those that provide general, universal, wisdom precepts (e.g., Pss 1, 19, 49, and 127)[19], with a sub-category being acrostics (Pss 34, 37, 111, 112). Terrien discusses the Torah psalms (Pss 1, 19, and 119) as examples of sapiential instruction.[20] Mowinckel speaks of Torah psalms as well, and notes, "The zeal for the law sometimes finds expression in a hymn to the law of Yahweh, to which is now attributed nearly all the power-filled and

---

[16] Terrien, "Wisdom in the Psalter," 53.

[17] Ibid., 55.

[18] These show a close affinity with later hymns that review history. It can be argued that they influenced the kinds of historical reminiscences we find in passages like Wis 10, Sir 45–50, the prayers in the War Scroll (1QM 10–14), and John 1:1–18.

[19] I add Ps 128 to this list even though it is more of a blessing.

[20] Terrien, "Wisdom in the Psalter," 57–63.

saving qualities, for which the hymn used to praise Yahweh."[21] Terrien also notes that contemplation of the cosmos in a number of psalms is evidence of wisdom's influence in the psalms.[22]

To provide an example of the kinds of didactic psalms within the Psalter, we will briefly explore three different kinds of didactic psalms: 34, 49, and 105. We will observe that although they utilize a range of approaches to their task, in each case the psalmist uses his craft to create a compelling verbal portrait of ultimate reality which the audience is urged to embrace.

1. Psalm 34

Psalm 34, an acrostic poem, combines elements of a variety of psalm types. It is included here as an instance of a psalm that offers direct instruction to the listener. Goldingay suggests that it is a psalm of personal testimony that gives way to more general teaching about God and his relationship to his people.[23] Along with an intention to praise (vv. 1–2), it includes the more hymnic imperatival call to praise (v. 3).

I will bless the LORD at all times;
his praise shall continually be in my mouth.
My soul makes its boast in the LORD;
let the humble hear and be glad.
O magnify the LORD with me,
and let us exalt his name together. (vv. 1–3 NRSV)

These declarations are followed by a recounting of personal deliverance (vv. 4–6). The psalm contains direct statements about the goodness of the Lord and his acts of redemption and deliverance. It also contains direct commands to look to the Lord (v. 5), fear the Lord (v. 9), listen to the psalmist (v. 11), as well as commands about how the righteous ought to live (vv. 13–14). Mowinckel notes,

Here the style and ideas of the wisdom poetry with its exhortatory and religious moral instruction, and its reference to the experiences of the teacher, make themselves felt. The thanksgiving song may become mainly instructive, and approximate to the didactic poem, as is the case in Ps 34.[24]

---

[21] Mowinckel, *Psalms in Israel's Worship*, 113.

[22] Terrien does not classify these as a separate category but mentions Ps 19; 104; Prov 8:22–31; Job 26:7; 37:4–18; 19–24; Ps 8:19; 89:12–13; 102:26; 113:1–3; 136:6; cf. Terrien, "Wisdom in the Psalter," 70–71.

[23] John Goldingay, *Psalms 1–41* (Baker Commentary on the Old Testament: Wisdom and Psalms; Grand Rapids: Baker Academic, 2006), 477.

[24] Mowinckel, *Psalms in Israel's Worship*, 112.

Psalm 34 thus provides a good example of a biblical psalm in which instructional concerns dominate. That this is a didactic psalm is made clear in v. 11 which is the central line of the psalm:

Come, children, listen to me;
I will teach you the fear of the LORD.

Of particular interest in Ps 34 is the addition to the acrostic of an extra line beginning with the letter *pe*. Anthony Ceresko notes that the result is that the line beginning with *lamed* is found in the exact middle of the psalm. The psalm hereby inscribes the consonants of the letter *aleph* (*aleph, lamed, pe*) through the first letter of the first line (*aleph*), the first letter of the central line (*lamed*), and the first letter of the final line (*pe*).[25] Additional acrostic-related devices have been identified in this psalm as well.[26] Ceresko suggests that these instances of "play" on the part of the wisdom writers are not merely attempts at aesthetic beauty. Instead, they are informed by the larger concerns of wisdom writers to reflect order and symmetry in the social world of the Israelites.[27] Certainly Ps 34 itself reflects the reality of chaos, pain, difficulty, and affliction even for the righteous (e.g., vv. 15, 17, 18, 19). But it also reflects the ultimate order of the world in which God is in control and invites the listener to learn to trust fully in the Lord who is good (v. 8) and cares for those who take refuge in him (vv. 8, 22). Through its acrostic order the psalm visibly represents the truths it teaches about the order and regularity of the world.[28] Through the central placement of v. 11, the psalm teaches that the Lord's goodness can be experienced by those who are willing to learn.

2. Psalm 49

Psalm 49 reflects on the shortness of life and the certainty of death for wise and foolish alike. Unlike typical hymns of praise or other psalms, it begins with a call to hear (vv. 1–2) and a declaration on the part of the psalmist that he will speak wisdom (vv. 3–4).

Hear this, all you peoples;
give ear, all inhabitants of the world,
both low and high,

---

[25] A. R. Ceresko, "The Sage in the Psalms," in *The Sage in Israel and the Ancient Near East* (ed. John G. Gammie and Leo G. Perdue; Winona Lake, Ind.: Eisenbrauns, 1990), 217–30, here 225–226.

[26] Victor Hurowitz, "Additional Elements of Alphabetical Thinking in Psalm xxxiv," *VT* 52 (2002): 326–333.

[27] Ceresko, "The Sage in the Psalms," 224–225.

[28] Note also how this practice reflects a willingness to exploit the potential of language in its written form in particular; Ibid., 226.

rich and poor together.
My mouth shall speak wisdom;
the meditation of my heart shall be understanding.
I will incline my ear to a proverb;
I will solve my riddle to the music of the harp. (vv. 1–4 NRSV)

Rather than containing a review of history or a series of imperative commands, the remainder of the psalm is more of a meditation on the realities of life and death, using wisdom terminology.[29] Verses 10–12 read,

When we look at the wise, they die;
fool and dolt perish together
and leave their wealth to others.
Their graves are their homes forever,
their dwelling places to all generations,
though they named lands their own.
Mortals cannot abide in their pomp;
they are like the animals that perish. (vv. 10–12 NRSV)

Crenshaw offers this as an example of a psalm which connects strongly with the impulses of Wisdom literature.[30] While we need not decide here whether to argue that Psalm 49 is a wisdom psalm, clearly its theme and the way it develops the theme connect at a deep level with the fundamental concerns of the wisdom tradition.

In terms of didactic function, this psalm achieves its impact through direct statements that convey a picture of reality with an authoritative tone (vv. 10–12; 17–20). In particular, the affirmation of God's ransoming and receiving the psalmist (v. 15) is offered without supporting reason; it is simply affirmed as reality. The temporal register of the psalm has both a present and a future aspect, observing the present state of the rich while at the same time pointing to the futility of wealth to save one from the grave forever (vv. 5–9). Similarly, the psalm points to two different spatial realities: the space of present existence, and the space of the grave to which the foolhardy will descend and where there is decay and darkness (vv. 13–14; 19). The audience is in view throughout the psalm and is addressed directly in vv. 1–2 and v. 16, and indirectly in v. 10. Taken together, the dynamics identified here work together to create a compelling portrait of a wise and sober assessment of the relative value of wealth and the certainty of death

---

[29] Samuel L. Terrien, *The Psalms: Strophic Structure and Theological Commentary* (The Eerdmans Critical Commentary; Grand Rapids: Eerdmans, 2003), 65. He compares this kind of meditation with what we encounter in Job and also Pss 73 and 139.

[30] He notes this psalm as an example of one that assesses reality through philosophical reflection: "A few Psalms also broach this issue, either to deny that any problem exists, as in Psalm 37, or to forge new insights, as in Psalms 49 and 73," James Crenshaw, *Education in Ancient Israel* (ABRL; New York: Doubleday, 1998), 55.

– an assessment that falls squarely within the wisdom tradition of ancient Israel.

3. Psalm 105

Psalm 105 provides an excellent example of a didactic hymn in the form Mowinckel calls a "hymnal legend."[31] More commonly, this psalm is classified within the category of "historical psalm" along with Pss 78, 106, and perhaps 44, 81, 135, 136, and 137 as well.[32] However, as Holm-Nielsen points out, such a classification gives attention to the content only and not to the form, style, or original setting.[33] Nevertheless, regardless of classification schemes, the beginning of the psalm is written in hymnic form (vv. 1–4), and the contents of this psalm constitute a review of history in the form of a hymn of praise with the clear aim of teaching a lesson to a human audience.

As a whole the psalm reviews the history of Israel from the time of Abraham to the exodus, wanderings, and promised land in light of the covenant. It represents a call to the people of God to remember his deeds (v. 5) and observe his laws (v. 45), in light of the fact that God always remembered his covenant and brought his promises to be. The major theme, stated early in the psalm and at the end, is that God remembers his covenant (v. 8) and his holy promise (v. 42) with Abraham, and has acted in history in accordance with that promise.

The psalm taps into multiple temporal registers as it exhorts the community in the present day to recall the distant past of history. It also taps into multiple spatial registers as it mentions all the earth (v. 7), the land of Canaan (v. 11), wandering from nation to nation (v. 13), Egypt (v. 23), and the giving to Israel of the lands of the nations (v. 44). As a review of history its manner of address is primarily narratival, rather than descriptive, as it teaches its lessons through a narration of the deeds of God on behalf of his people.

Childs notes the all-encompassing reach of this psalm and explains, "Ps. 105.8, 42 views Israel's redemptive history as the result of God's remembering his covenant."[34] As for the theology of what it means for God to remember the past, Childs notes,

His remembering is not conceived of as an actualization of a past event in history; rather, every event stems from the eternal purpose of God. Only from Israel's point of view is

---

[31] Mowinckel, "Psalms and Wisdom," 214.

[32] Svend Holm-Nielsen, "The Exodus Traditions in Psalm 105," *ASTI* 11 (1962–63), 22.

[33] Ibid.

[34] Brevard S. Childs, *Memory and Tradition in Israel* (Naperville, Ill.: A. R. Allenson, 1962), 41.

each remembrance past. God's memory is not re-creating of the past, but a continuation of the selfsame purpose.[35]

This perspective helps shed light on the way that a historical psalm like Psalm 105 is rich with meaning for the "present" community of listeners. It is not simply a rehearsal of events of the past but a declaration of who God is and how he has worked and continues to work in history in light of his character.

Childs' observations on the role of memory in Israel are pertinent in this context and help to shed light on this particular psalm and on historical psalms in general. He notes, "Each successive generation in Israel witnessed in faith to a reality which it encountered when remembering the tradition."[36] The tradition constitutes the shared communal memory of Israel; psalms like this one gave opportunity to express that tradition and bring its realities into focus in light of present realities. Childs continues,

Each generation reinterpreted the same determinative events of the tradition in terms of its new encounter. This gives the biblical witness its peculiar character. It consists of layer upon layer of Israel's reinterpretation of the same period of her history, because each successive generation rewrites the past in terms of her own experience with the God who meets his people through the tradition.[37]

As we will see, this ongoing process of interpreting the past continues to be a significant element in the writings of the Second Temple period.

Attempts to return to the original setting of the Psalms are notoriously difficult. Nevertheless, as for a general time period Holm-Nielsen suggests this psalm is viewing events of the exodus from the perspective of the exile and was perhaps even written in the post-exilic period.[38] In the case of this particular psalm, using examples from history as a warning is not the main purpose (as it is in Pss 78 and 106). Instead, it aims to proclaim "the Lord's unconditional salvation of his people."[39] In this way the didactic aim is more implicit than explicit. From the perspective of the exile or the post-exilic period, this didactic aim can be seen to be critical. As Childs explains,

According to the psalmist redemptive history does not end, because the present events which stem from God's memory are not different in quality from the former. God's memory encompasses his entire relationship with his people. His memory includes both the great deeds of the past as well as his continued concern for his people in the future.[40]

---

[35] Ibid., 42.
[36] Ibid., 88.
[37] Ibid., 89.
[38] Holm-Nielsen, "The Exodus Traditions in Psalm 105," 27.
[39] Ibid.
[40] Childs, *Memory and Tradition*, 42.

This view of God and human history would conceivably be of great encouragement to faithful Jews in times of historical uncertainty.

4. Conclusions Regarding Didactic Hymns in the Psalter

Each of these didactic psalms (34, 49, and 105), rather than praising God or even addressing God directly, are addressed to the listener, with the clear goal of imparting wisdom. That wisdom may be related to lessons of history, an understanding of God's nature and how he wants his people to live, or more general lessons about the nature of life itself and the order of the world. The extent to which these didactic hymns can be considered wisdom psalms is open for debate. Partly this depends on how one defines the wisdom tradition.[41] Whether a psalm is termed a wisdom psalm or not, the important issue is really a question of the extent to which each composition participates in biblical wisdom, and the extent to which its contents indicate that it participates in other different but complementary aspects of Jewish discourse.[42] Our aim here has been less to argue for the existence of wisdom psalms and more to recognize that many psalms exhibit characteristics of didactic hymnody. By examining a few such psalms, we have been able to appreciate the purposes for which these didactic hymns were written. We have also observed the way they tap into multiple temporal, spatial, and cognitive registers as they craft a complex portrait of reality in psalm form. Whether through direct claims or narrative retellings, these psalms teach as they offer a vision of ultimate reality for the listener wise enough to accept it. When we encounter didactic hymns outside of the Psalms, we will be able to consider the ways that they reflect the kinds of instruction that are inscribed within the traditional praises of the people of Israel.

D. Didactic Hymns Outside of the Psalms

Didactic hymns and prayers are not limited to the Psalms just as the poetry of the Hebrew Bible is not restricted to what is found in the Psalter. The Hebrew Scriptures contain an extensive selection of Hebrew poetry in a

---

[41] James Crenshaw, *Old Testament Wisdom: An Introduction* (Louisville, Ky.: Westminster John Knox, 1998), 11.

[42] For more on this problem, see Crenshaw, "Wisdom Psalms?." He writes, "Perhaps we should limit ourselves to what can definitely be affirmed: some psalms resemble wisdom literature in stressing the importance of learning, struggling to ascertain life's meaning, and employing proverbial lore. Their authorship and provenance matter less than the accuracy and profundity of what they say" (15).

broad range of literary contexts.[43] In the second half of this chapter we examine a selection of didactic hymns found in literary contexts other than
the Psalms. First, we will look at didactic hymnody within Wisdom literature, looking specifically at the influential wisdom poem in Prov 8 as an
example. Next we will examine didactic hymnody in narrative contexts,
exploring the Song of the Sea (Exod 15) and the Song of Moses (Deut 32)
as two examples. We will address didactic hymnody in prophetic contexts
through a brief look at hymnic passages in Isa 40–55. Finally, we will conclude with a look at didactic hymnody in the book of Daniel.

1. Didactic Hymns in Wisdom Writings

While the focus of the preceding section was on psalms with strong didactic emphases (which included so-called wisdom psalms), the focus of
this section is on Wisdom literature proper, and, in particular, didactic
wisdom poetry written in hymnic style. Like the Psalms the Wisdom writings of ancient Israel have received a great deal of attention over the years.
In discussing the forms of wisdom von Rad distinguishes between the
shorter "literary proverb" or maxim, and "other forms of didactic poetry"
which included numerical sayings, autobiographical stylization, long didactic poems, dialogue, fable, allegory, and prayers.[44] The aspect of Jewish
Wisdom literature that is of interest in this study are the didactic poems,
particularly those that employ aspects of hymnic style.

Crenshaw has suggested a development from the shorter forms of wisdom discourse to the longer and more complex forms. He writes,

The popular saying, often only a half-line, commanded assent by its content alone. Instructions relied on motivation clauses and warnings to persuade others that their teachings were valid. This extended discourse developed into didactic poems, which treated
single themes at greater length than occurred in sayings and instructions.[45]

He continues, "Didactic poems delve into the wonder and majesty surrounding the creative process, both the divine act by which everything
came into existence and the human intellectual adventure that endeavors to
make sense of reality as it presents itself to inquiring minds.[46] It is at this
point in particular where didactic poems, with their emphasis on wisdom
and reflection, come into contact with psalms and hymns, with their emphasis on the praise of God for his wonderful works.

---

[43] For a survey of this material see S. E. Gillingham, *The Poems and Psalms of the
Hebrew Bible* (Oxford Bible Series; Oxford: Oxford University Press, 1994), 91–169.

[44] von Rad, *Wisdom in Israel*, 24–50.

[45] Crenshaw, *Education in Ancient Israel*, 59.

[46] Ibid.

As noted in the earlier section, the precise nature of the relationship between wisdom poems and didactic hymns is debatable. It is safe to say that
writers of wisdom poetry generally have instruction as a primary goal. Yet
they are not insulated from the influences of psalmody and hymnody. Their
poetry often takes on a hymnic tone and style as they extol the value of
wisdom and praise the life of the righteous or the deeds of God. In fact, as
most scholars will grant, it is most likely that the various classes of people
involved in Israelite religious life (scribes, psalmist, priests, temple personnel, etc.) were closely connected and influenced one another.[47] This is
one way of explaining the presence of wisdom elements in the psalms, and
the psalm-like elements in wisdom writings.

1.1 Proverbs 8

The didactic poem in Prov 8 represents a masterpiece of ancient didactic
poetry as well as a source of inspiration for a long tradition of Jewish wisdom speculation in the Second Temple period. It has been called "the most
important and subsequently most influential theological contribution of the
Book of Proverbs."[48] This section will briefly examine Prov 8 in order to
explore the way that this passage accomplishes its didactic purposes by
means of its poetic and hymnic style. We will see that the hymnic style of
the passage facilitates the author's didactic purpose exceptionally well.

Proverbs 8:1–36 can be divided into a number of shorter sections, although there is good reason for seeing the entire chapter as a coherent and
unified whole (consisting of several sections).[49] Perdue arranges the chapter in five sections:

The Sage's Introduction to Woman Wisdom (vv. 1–3)
Wisdom's Call (vv. 4–11)
Wisdom's Providential Rule (vv. 12–21)
Wisdom's Place in Creation (vv. 22–31)
Wisdom's Instruction of Life (vv. 32–36)[50]

In this analysis, two sections (vv. 12–21 and 22–31) can be viewed as
"hymns of self praise." Hymns of self-praise are unprecedented in the Hebrew Bible, though they find representation in other ancient cultures, par-

---

[47] Mowinckel, *Psalms in Israel's Worship*, 2:104.
[48] R. B. Y. Scott, *Proverbs, Ecclesiastes* (AB 18; Garden City, N.Y.: Doubleday,
1965), 27.
[49] Ibid., 71.
[50] Leo G. Perdue, *Wisdom and Creation: The Theology of Wisdom Literature* (Nashville: Abingdon, 1994), 84.

ticularly Mesopotamia.[51] From Egypt, Isis aretalogies also make use of this first person self-praise format.[52]

The purposes of these two hymnic passages in Prov 8 where Wisdom recounts her unique relationship with God stemming back prior to creation are best understood within the context of the passage as a whole. Taken as a unified composition, chapter 8 is an appeal by Wisdom the teacher to recruit students (this is abundantly clear in 8:1–11 and 32–36). Perdue observed, "More than likely, this protrepsis, or invitation to study, reflects a school setting where a teacher offers to impart to the untutored the ways of wisdom."[53] In this context the two passages of hymnic self-praise present the reasons why one should heed the appeal of Lady Wisdom and become her pupil; these passages serve as Wisdom's resume, so to speak.

As we have observed with other didactic hymns, these hymns of self-praise use a variety of means to convey their lesson. While vv. 12–21 have a descriptive style, vv. 22–31 utilize a more narratival style as they narrate Wisdom's creation and her involvement in God's acts of creation. The hymn in vv. 12–21 emphasizes present time as it elaborates on the qualities and gifts of wisdom; the hymn in vv. 22–31 hearkens back to the mythic past, enhancing the authority of Wisdom by recounting her origins. Waltke notes that the passage "establishes that wisdom's precedence in rank and dignity over the rest of creation is both qualitative (i.e., begotten, not created) and temporal (i.e., existing "before" any other creature). As a result she is competent to counsel and authoritative when she speaks."[54] The chapter as a whole is intended to persuade, and it does so not only through logos (the reasons presented) but also through ethos and pathos (the emotions that the hymnic style evokes about the speaker through the composition itself). The hymns of self-praise contribute effectively to these aims.

As a didactic poem the entire chapter functions on several levels. On one level it is a straightforward call to the listener or reader to learn the ways of Wisdom. On another level, while Wisdom rehearses her credentials, the listener learns fundamental truths about Wisdom's providential and positive role in human affairs (8:12–21) as well as Wisdom's antiquity relative to the created world (8:22–31). In this sense the content of Prov 8 is didactic with regard to the nature of Wisdom. Finally, on a still deeper level, the hymnic style of Wisdom's self-praise, along with the content of

---

[51] Bruce K. Waltke, *The Book of Proverbs: Chapters 1–15* (NICOT; Grand Rapids: Eerdmans, 2004), 392.

[52] For detailed description and bibliography of extant Isis aretalogies from the 1st c. BCE to the 4th c. CE see Yves Grandjean, *Une Nouvelle Arétalogie d'Isis à Maronée* (EPRO 49; Leiden: Brill, 1975), 8–11.

[53] Perdue, *Wisdom and Creation*, 85.

[54] Waltke, *Proverbs*, 408.

her speech, suggests the divine nature of Wisdom in a powerful, emotive way that direct speech alone could not have accomplished. The didactic poem thus accomplishes its purposes by working on several levels at one time – a feature we will see at work in much of the didactic hymnody under examination in this study.[55]

2. Didactic Hymns in Narrative Contexts

The hymns and prayers embedded in narrative contexts within the Hebrew Bible have been studied extensively and continue to be the object of scholarly inquiry.[56] Though they do not always align precisely with specific psalm *Gattungen*, many of them have a primary emphasis on praise of God for his deeds. In this way they can be broadly classified as hymns of praise, even though more precise generic categories are often suggested (e.g., song of thanksgiving, victory hymn , etc.). The most widely studied hymns in narrative contexts are Hannah's song (1 Sam 2:1–10), the Song of the Sea (Exod 15:1–18), the Song of Moses (Deut 32:1–43), the Song of Deborah (Judg 5), and David's thanksgiving (2 Sam 22). Other psalms are found in narrative portions of prophetic writings (e.g., Hezekiah's psalm in Isa 38:9–20; Jonah's psalm in Jonah 2:3–10) and apocalyptic literature (e.g., Daniel's praise in Dan 2:20–23; the praises of Nebuchadnezzar in Dan 4:34–37 and Darius in Dan 6:26–27).

While earlier studies tended to focus on the language, form, and background of the hymns, more recent studies focus on how they are utilized in their literary contexts and for what purpose. In general it is the case that in the narratives of the Hebrew Bible, the presence of hymns does not serve a role in advancing the plot. Rather, their literary function appears to be that of emphasizing key themes and overarching principles for the sake of the reader. James Watts suggests that they serve to "deepen the theocentric orientation of books and internal characterization of individuals, and actualize the narratives by eliciting reader participation in the songs."[57] Generally, the psalms themselves do not narrate history, although, some of these

---

[55] For yet another perspective on the way this passage teaches, one that problematizes the symbolic world that Prov 1–8 creates, see the study by Carol A. Newsom, "Woman and the Discourse of Patriarchal Wisdom," in *Reading Bibles, Writing Bodies: Identity and the Book* (ed. Timothy K. Beal and D. M. Gunn; New York: Routledge, 1997), 116–131.

[56] See for example, Giles and Doan, *Twice Used Songs*; James W. Watts, *Psalm and Story: Inset Hymns in Hebrew Narrative* (JSOTSup 139; Sheffield: JSOT Press, 1992); Steven Weitzman, *Song and Story in Biblical Narrative: The History of a Literary Convention in Ancient Israel* (Indiana Studies in Biblical Literature; Bloomington: Indiana University Press, 1997).

[57] Watts, *Psalm and Story*, 197.

psalms do narrate historical events and so are didactic both in terms of their own content and in terms of their interpretive function within the larger narrative. The Song of the Sea, the Song of Moses, the Song of Deborah, and later, the Song of Judith (Jdt 16) and the Song of Tobit (Tob 13) all contain mention of historical events and thus include within their content some form of narrative. Whether the hymns in narrative context contain historical narrative or not, in all cases their placement within a narrative serves as theological commentary on the events that have preceded within the larger narrative.

The practice of placing hymnic materials in narrative contexts is not a uniquely Jewish phenomenon. Though the ancient Near Eastern precedents for the incorporation of hymns in narrative falls outside the scope of this volume, it is important to recognize that early Jewish writers and redactors were utilizing literary conventions that would potentially have been readily identifiable. As Watts claims, "The Hebrew practice of placing psalms in narrative contexts is in basic continuity with the use of hymnic poetry in the narrative literatures of ancient Mesopotamia and Egypt."[58] In a similar vein Weitzmann draws attention to the ways that songs within biblical narratives draw on ancient Near Eastern traditions in ways which vary depending on the context.[59]

Looking beyond these influences to the way these passages influence later writings, we see that these texts themselves become a mark of standard, biblical style in and of themselves. The result is the phenomenon of "scripturalizing revisions" and also direct imitation. In Dan 3 the Song of the Three Young Men provides an example of a scripturalizing revision that was intended to bring a biblical text into line with the expectations created by a developing canon-consciousness on the part of faithful Jews.[60] As a further development of this impulse, Weitzman notes later Jewish practices of imitating these biblical models. He explains how Jewish authors "sought to emulate biblical genres and styles in their own literary and liturgical compositions, as if the Bible's form was as sacred as the events which it described."[61] Though intended to provide the original readers a theological perspective on events in the narrative, these songs in narrative contexts in the Hebrew Bible also provided a model for later readers in terms of both their biblical form and their biblical content.

---

[58] Ibid., 196. See his Appendix, 206–220, "Hymns in Other Ancient Narrative Traditions."

[59] E.g., Exod 15 and Judg 5 share similarities with military literature and victory songs; Deut 32 shows connections with the last-words topos (Weitzman, *Song and Story*, 36–39).

[60] Ibid., 94.

[61] Ibid., 92.

Two examples, the Song of the Sea (Exod 15:1–18) and the Song of Moses (Deut 32) will illustrate two different ways these psalms function. The Song of the Sea provides a thematic focus to the narrative context, connecting the events of Exod 14 with the larger concerns of the Pentateuch. The Song of Moses functions differently, providing a memorable summary of the teaching of Deuteronomy.

2.1. The Song of the Sea (Exod 15)

After the crossing of the Red Sea and the drowning of the army of Pharoah in Exod 14, Moses and the Israelites sang a song to the Lord. The words of this hymn are recorded in Exod 15:1b–18 in one of the earliest poetic passages in the Hebrew Bible. While scholars have investigated many critical issues associated with this passage, the purpose of this section is to examine the didactic function of the use of this psalm in its current literary context. After a brief discussion of issues of form, structure, and origin, I will turn to the issue of the function of this hymn in its narrative context, showing that in its literary context the hymn teaches a way of remembering the past and thereby of understanding the present as well.

In terms of the form of the passage, it has been referred to as a hymn, enthronement psalm, litany, victory psalm, and a combination of a hymn and thanksgiving psalm.[62] Though the Song of the Sea reflects aspects of each of these forms, it is fair to say that no one specific form accounts for the unique features of the Song as a whole. Noteworthy features include the way it switches person, verb tenses, subject matter, speaker, topic, and meter.[63]

The Song of the Sea has been resistant to yielding the date or circumstances of its origins. On the one hand it has been dated to as early as the twelfth century BCE.[64] Frank Moore Cross argued that in terms of style and structure it fit the pattern of old Canaanite poetry as well as the earliest Hebrew poetry.[65] While the original song predates the narrative context in which it is placed, the Song of the Sea appears to have been added to its

---

[62] Brevard S. Childs, *The Book of Exodus: A Critical, Theological Commentary* (OTL; Philadelphia: Westminster Press, 1976), 243.

[63] Thomas Dozeman, "The Song of the Sea and Salvation History," in *On the Way to Nineveh: Studies in Honor of George M. Landes* (ed. Stephen L. Cook, George M. Landes, and Sara C. Winter; Atlanta: Scholars Press, 1999), 96–113, here 96–101.

[64] Frank Moore Cross and David Noel Freedman, *Studies in Ancient Yahwistic Poetry* (New ed.; The Biblical Resource Series; Grand Rapids: Eerdmans, 1997), 31–33. This date has recently been defended by Brian D. Russell, *The Song of the Sea: The Date of Composition and Influence of Exodus 15, 1–21* (Studies in Biblical Literature 101; New York: Peter Lang, 2007), 96.

[65] Cross and Freedman, *Studies in Ancient Yahwistic Poetry*, 86.

context at a later stage of editing.[66] Many features of the passage indicate
that before its incorporation into Exod 15 it existed as a liturgical song that
would have been used at a festival and so was part of Israel's cultural heritage.[67] This position can be supported by an appeal to the influence of this
song on later writings including the Psalms and prophets. However, it is
difficult to argue the direction of dependence in many cases. Further, some
scholars see the features that point to an early date as representing an intentionally archaizing style used by a later author; these scholars have argued for a much later date, as late as the fifth century BCE.[68]

A major critical question among scholars is the compositional unity of
the Song of the Sea. In spite of recent analyses and persuasive arguments
on both sides of the issue, no consensus has emerged.[69] By comparing the
Song of the Sea with Ugarittic victory hymns, Dozeman has suggested an
original pre-exilic hymn that consisted of vv. 1–12 and v. 18.[70] The literary
version of the hymn, edited in the monarchical or exilic period, adds vv.
13–17. What is compelling about Dozeman's analysis is the way he aligns
themes of Exod 15:1–12, 18 with a particular sub-set of Canaanite victory
hymns, and likewise the way he aligns Exod 15:13–17 with another sub-set
of Canaanite hymns. The result appears to confirm the understanding that
Exod 15 is a composite song. However, the results of Dozeman's survey
really only show that the Song of the Sea centers around two distinct subject matters (divine victory and conquest), themes which were common in
other ancient Near Eastern hymns. This two-fold focus of the passage is
evident from reading Exod 15 by itself without reference to Ugaritic texts.
The ancient Near Eastern parallels neither confirm nor disconfirm the thesis that the Song of the Sea is a unity.

This matter of the unity of the Song of the Sea is significant in assessing
recent explorations of the function of the hymn in its narrative context. For
example, Giles and Doan have explored the Song of the Sea as an example
of a "twice used song," a song that was originally performed as an independent song and that was later modified and incorporated into a prose
narrative context.[71] Based on this understanding they interpret both the hy-

---

[66] For relationship to the compositional history of Exod 1–15 see Watts, *Psalm and Story*, 55–60.

[67] G. W. Coats, "The Song of the Sea," *CBQ* 31 (1969): 1–17, esp 9–10; Cross and Freedman, *Studies in Ancient Yahwistic Poetry*, 31.

[68] Georg Fischer, "Das Schilfmeerlied Exodus 15 in seinem Kontext," *Bib* 77 (1996): 32–47, here 43.

[69] Compare Dozeman, "Song of the Sea," 96 with J. P. Fokkelman, *Major Poems of the Hebrew Bible: At the Interface of Hermeneutics and Structural Analysis: Vol. 1: Ex. 15, Deut. 32, and Job 3* (SSN 37; Assen, Netherlands: Van Gorcum, 1998), 30-32.

[70] Dozeman, "Song of the Sea," 100.

[71] Giles and Doan, *Twice Used Songs*, 49–66.

pothetical original and the significance of its modification and placement in the exodus narrative. Their analysis depends on identifying the precise form of the original song (they accept Dozeman's analysis). However, if the song is taken as a unified composition, a similar method of analysis can still be applied, but with different results. The Song of the Sea would still be considered a "twice-used song," but in this case the whole song would have been used in a liturgical setting previously, before its current use in a literary setting.

In terms of its structure many proposals have been made. The song narrates, but not in order, events including God's delivering the Israelites and destroying Pharoah's army, the inhabitants of the land being seized with fear, and the Israelites' being brought into the land. As a hymn embedded in narrative the Song of the Sea serves a number of significant functions. Most importantly by contributing to Israelite cultural memory it serves a major role in the ongoing process of communal formation for the Israelites.

As for the Song of the Sea in its current context, one way of viewing the structure is as follows:

Introductory declaration of intent to praise (v. 1b)
Hymnic expansion of the introduction (vv. 2–3)
Epic narration of Yahweh's deeds (vv. 4–10; break between vv. 5 and 6)
Hymnic coda (v. 11)
Epic narration of Yahweh's deeds (vv. 12–17; break between vv. 13 and 14)
Hymnic coda (v. 18)[72]

Regardless of whether one accepts this particular structure, an important element is the change in theme that occurs at v. 11. While the earlier verses focus on the victory of Yahweh over Pharoah and his armies, the later verses of the song switch the focus to the conquest (vv. 12–17). As many scholars note, this change of focus is somewhat surprising given the literary context of Exod 15 in which those events had not yet occurred. Such an observation is suggestive of a possible function for this material: it draws the contemporary audience (which is already in the land of promise) into the events of the narrative to join with the Israelites of Exod 15 in singing the praise of Yahweh, the victorious one.[73]

Another function of the material is brought to light by comparing this song with ancient Near Eastern parallels. In comparison with the Piye Stela, Weitzman explains:

The insertions of the songs in Exodus 15 and Judges 5 within their respective narrative settings may simply represent independent manifestations of a single conventional form of closure taken over from Egyptian battle accounts. As it was originally developed, the form was intended to promote the king as invincible ruler and to render him the hero of

---

[72] Coats, "The Song of the Sea," 7.
[73] Watts, *Psalm and Story*, 54–55, 60.

battles in which he did not personally participate. As it was adapted by the authors of biblical narrative, it served to promote God as invincible ruler and to render him the hero of battles in which his participation was difficult to represent.[74]

The psalm thus serves as a means of highlighting the theological lesson of the narrative. It also provides a model of a godly response to divine deliverance – a model which will be imitated many times throughout biblical history.

Giles and Doan suggest that the song utilizes what has been called an "iconic mode of representation."[75] An iconic mode of presentation (in contrast to a dialectical mode of presentation) has three primary characteristics. First, it is marked by "embodiment" as it emphasizes being rather than becoming. Second, it is marked by an "unfolding display" as it emphasizes ritual enactment and display rather than development. Third, it produces an effect of "illumination," moving an audience into awe and insight.[76] By participating in an iconic mode of presentation the Song of the Sea puts Yahweh's victories on display and enables the audience to participate in celebrating those victories. Giles and Doan write, "In its pre-Exodus incarnation, the Song of the Sea provided an iconic means of communal solidarity in which both performer and spectator celebrated a social memory."[77] While we can only speculate about how the song was used prior to its use in Exodus (if at all), the idea of an iconic mode of representation does fit the contents of the hymn.

Interestingly, with the song now found in a narrative context, the same dynamics are at work, but in a different way. Giles and Doan explain that the Song of the Sea in its narrative context is an embodiment of cultural memory. "It retells, recalls, and reestablishes memory and the experience of memory as the site of cultural experience for the people of Israel."[78] The memory is not just of the victories but also of the celebration of the victories in song. "The function of the song is not to further the narrative story of the exodus but to draw the reader (or listener) into the drama of the story by presenting a device whereby the reader (or listener) can 'sing along' and so be part of the telling of the story."[79] Whether or not the audience actually joined in the song, hymnic praise of God would surely have been a memorable part of the retelling of this foundational story in a communal context.

---

[74] Weitzman, *Song and Story*, 35–36.
[75] Giles and Doan, *Twice Used Songs*, 52–56.
[76] Ibid., 53–54.
[77] Ibid., 57.
[78] Ibid., 63.
[79] Ibid., 66.

In this case, the distinction between the performed song and the recycled version in the narrative context is not particularly illuminating. Far more compelling is the reading of Watts who notes the effect of extending the temporal perspective of the song in vv. 12–17. He explains, "The characterization of Israel is expanded beyond the people on the banks of the Reed Sea to include future generations, including that of the readers themselves, who witness and commemorate Yahweh's acts of salvation."[80] This move serves to strengthen the readers' sense of identification with the Israel of the exodus. In this reading, "The psalm's identification of the readers with the ancient Israelites actualizes the event and its meaning for a contemporary congregation."[81]

The Song of the Sea thus contributes on a number of levels to achieving the larger purposes of the narrative in which it is embedded. Blenkinsopp has set out the purpose of the central three books of the Pentateuch as centering around "the broad theme of the creation of a people with a special relationship to God (YHWH) who nurtures it into viable existence, preserves it, and prepares it to play its preordained role among the nations of the world."[82] The Song of the Sea makes it clear to readers of any later generation that the events of Exod 14 were indeed the works of God alone and were paradigmatic for his larger purposes of nurturing, preserving, and preparing the Israelites for his purposes.

In terms of its function within the narrative, it plays at least four interrelated roles. First, it concludes the exodus account. Second, it recaps major themes of the narrative. Third, it connects with earlier praises of God in the narrative, showing that it is in the exodus that God most clearly reveals who he is.[83] Finally, it presents Moses as a song-writer and song-leader.

As we move to the Song of Moses in Deut 32, we will see that similar dynamics are at work in terms of engaging the contemporary reader and contributing to the ongoing development of communal memory. However, the context and content of that song reveal that other purposes are at work as well.

2.2. The Song of Moses (Deut 32:1–43)

Deuteronomy 32:1–43 is essentially a summary of the teaching of Deuteronomy in the form of a song. It is referred to as a song in its immediate context both before and after Moses recites it (31:19, 22, 30; 32:44). As for its formal, generic designation it has been referred to as a poem, a hymn, a

---

[80] Watts, *Psalm and Story*, 54.

[81] Ibid., 60.

[82] Joseph Blenkinsopp, *The Pentateuch: An Introduction to the First Five Books of the Bible* (ABRL; New York: Doubleday, 1992), 135.

[83] Fischer, "Schilfmeerlied," 46–47.

prophetic lawsuit, a last-words literary piece, or the conluding part of a
larger ancient Near Eastern treaty pattern.[84] Most scholars recognize that it
is a poem which contains features of several different generic categories
including hymns, poems, and psalms, as well as wisdom and prophetic influences.[85]

In terms of its content it opens up with a clear statement of its didactic
purpose (32:1–2) that moves into a call to the Israelites to ascribe greatness
to God in hymnic style (32:3; cf. Ps 96:7–8).

Give ear, O heavens, let me speak;
Let the earth hear the words I utter!
May my discourse come down as the rain,
My speech distill as the dew,
Like showers on young growth,
Like droplets on the grass.
For the name of the LORD I proclaim;
Give glory to our God! (vv. 1–3 JPS)

These opening verses together form the exordium.[86] The Song goes on to
describe God's faithful nature in contrast to the faithlessness of his children (vv. 4–6).

The Rock! – His deeds are perfect,
Yea, all His ways are just;
A faithful God, never false,
True and upright is He.
Children unworthy of Him –
That crooked, perverse generation –
Their baseness has played Him false.
Do you thus requite the LORD,
O dull and witless people?
Is not He the Father who created you,
Fashioned you and made you endure! (vv. 4–6 JPS)

Together these verses serve as the thesis for the entire song.[87]

From there the Song unfolds in two lengthy sections which review the
history of God's dealings with Israel (vv. 7–25) and God's decisions to
punish and also to limit Israel's punishment and punish Israel's enemies
(vv. 26–42). The body of the Song begins with a call to remember:

Remember the days of old,
Consider the years of ages past;

---

[84] Giles and Doan, *Twice Used Songs*, 110.

[85] Jeffrey Howard Tigay, *Deuteronomy: The Traditional Hebrew Text with the New
JPS Translation* (The JPS Torah Commentary; Philadelphia: Jewish Publication Society,
1996), 509.

[86] Ibid., 299.

[87] Ibid.

Ask your father, he will inform you,
Your elders, they will tell you. (v. 7 JPS)

The psalm then reviews some aspects of history and God's deeds on behalf of Israel (vv. 8–14); Israel's turning away (vv. 15–18); the Lord's jealousy, anger, and wrath (vv. 19–35); and the Lord's compassion (vv. 36–42). It closes with a final call to the heavens to give praise and celebrate God's redemption of his people (v. 43). Following the psalm, in v. 46 the people are urged to take these words to heart.

This psalm, with its gloomy outlook and focus on instruction and teaching, is quite different from the Song of the Sea. It also takes on a different role in the narrative than did the Song of the Sea. Watts explains what the psalm accomplishes and how it does so. He notes

> The psalm does provide a summary of Deuteronomic themes in a memorable form. The psalm's position in the narrative of Moses' last days and its highly emotional language also create a climactic effect at the end of Deuteronomy (and the Pentateuch). The intention seems to have been to bring home to readers as forcefully as possible the message of the book as a whole.[88]

In regard to the function of providing a forceful summary of the message of the book, didactic hymnody would seem to be a good choice. By its style and form it is set off from the remainder of the narrative. It also stops the flow of the narrative and allows for a period of reflection on what has preceded.

Though he does not use the term "didactic hymnody," Watts summarizes the importance of didactic hymnody, using Deut 32 as a focal point. He writes,

> The text makes clear the important role that psalms played in religious instruction. They provided a medium whereby theological notions could be imparted to and remembered by the people. This didactic role which psalmody played in Israelite religion may have contributed to redactors' willingness to use psalms to bring out and emphasize the theological concerns of Hebrew narrative texts.[89]

As with the Song of the Sea, the Song of Moses promotes theological lessons. However, while the Song of the Sea provided a theological perspective on an event that had just occurred in the narrative, the Song of Moses in Deut 32 serves more of a summative role for the book as a whole.

One theme emphasized in Deut 32 is the importance of remembering the past (Deut 32:7; cf. v. 18). As Childs has suggested, the community envisioned by the author of Deuteronomy was far removed from the traditions about Moses and the events of the Pentateuch. Childs explains, "Now memory takes on central theological significance. Present Israel has not

---

[88] Watts, *Psalm and Story*, 80.
[89] Ibid., 81.

been cut off from redemptive history, but she encounters the same covenant God through a living tradition. Memory provides the link between
past and present."[90] The incorporation of hymns and songs into the narrative serves to strengthen this link of the present with the past, for each new
generation.

Theories about the origins and compositional history of the Song lend
even greater weight to Childs' observations about the way memory links
the past and the present. As we observed in earlier chapters, particularly in
the poetry of Homer and Hesiod, poetry provided a means of navigating
tremendous change in the order and structure of society. Various attempts
have been made to locate the time period of both the composition of the
Song of Moses as well as the time of its incorporation into Deuteronomy,
the most recent proposal being that of Mark Leuchter.[91] Leuchter has offered a series of arguments that affirm the view that the Song could have
been written as early as the tenth century BCE. He suggests that it was a
liturgical song originating in the Northern Kingdom, but one that was included in an editorial revision of Deuteronomy prior to a later redaction.[92]
He follows Holladay in claiming that the song was incorporated into Deuteronomy in a pre-exilic edition, a version that was edited during the period of the Josianic reforms.[93] The purpose of the addition of the song, a
northern song, was "to hermeneutically transform a Jerusalemite document
into a program consistent with ancient northern Levitical tradition, and indeed to present the Deuteronomic program as the fullest expression of ancient northern Levitcal interests."[94] Thus the inclusion of the Song in Deuteronomy can be said to serve "propagandistic purposes" related to Josi-
ah's program of reform.[95]

Of interest for our purposes is consideration of multiple audiences for
the Song of Moses. On Leuchter's view there is the original northern audience that sang the song in their own liturgy. There is also the audience that
would have read the Song in its Deuteronomic context in the days of Josi-
ah. Finally, there is the audience that would have read the Song in the final
version of Deuteronomy in the days of the exile and beyond. Each performative context (whether sung, recited, or heard by an audience) would
have a unique set of social, cultural, and theological challenges. A further
task might be to study the way that the song would have contributed to

---

[90] Childs, *Memory and Tradition*, 55.

[91] Mark Leuchter, "Why is the Song of Moses in Deuteronomy?," *VT* 57 (2007): 295–
317.

[92] Ibid., 300.

[93] Ibid., 306.

[94] Ibid., 314.

[95] The details of the case are complex and do not need to be repeated here.

each of these contexts. We can simply note here that the song itself conveys a certain immediacy in its context, as a song authored not only by Moses but commissioned and composed by God himself (31:16–22). The Song of Moses itself does not require any one particular context for it to convey its meaning.[96] In any of the settings above, it brings God and his plan before the eyes and ears of the human audience so that they may respond to him appropriately and "take to heart" all that Moses had said.

3. Praise in Prophetic and Apocalyptic Writings

As was the case with Wisdom literature and narrative, a form of hymnody finds a place in the prophetic writings as well. It is well-known that the prophets often conveyed their message in the medium of poetry. Whether offering a message of reproof, admonition, consolation, or restoration, the poets utilized the medium of poetry as an evocative way of helping their audiences imagine their world and their place in it.[97] Though they are in no sense a collection of psalms, prophetic writings do employ hymnic forms and styles on occasion. Occasionally they contain psalms as part of a developing narrative (e.g., Isa 38:9–20; Dan 2:20–23; 4:34–37; 6:26–27). More frequently, however, the prophets' language and expression resonate with hymnic precedents elsewhere in the Hebrew Bible.[98] The use of hymnic style, coupled with the instructional aims of the prophets in those particular passages, suggest that they are exploiting the potential of didactic hymnody to instruct their hearers. In order to highlight these dynamics this section will focus on select instances of hymnic forms employed for didactic purposes in Isa 40–55.

3.1. Hymns in Isaiah 40–55

Though contained within the larger work named after the prophet Isaiah, scholars have found a number of reasons for considering chapters 40–55 as a unified composition with unique features and its own historical outlook.[99] One prominent feature is the way that the salvation oracles of Isa 40–55

---

[96] Giles and Doan, *Twice Used Songs*, 108.

[97] Robert Alter, *The Art of Biblical Poetry* (Edinburgh: T&T Clark, 1990), 141–142.

[98] Marjo C. A. Korpel, "The Demarcation of Hymns and Prayers in the Prophets (2)," in *Psalms and Prayers: Papers Read at the Joint Meeting of the Society of Old Testament Study and Het Oudtestamentische Werkgezelschap in Nederland en België, Apeldoorn August 2006* (ed. Bob Becking and Eric Peels; Leiden: Brill, 2007), 141–157; Marjo C. A. Korpel, "The Demarcation of Hymns and Prayers in the Prophets (1)," in *The Impact of Unit Delimitation on Exegesis* (ed. Raymond de Hoop, Marjo C. A. Korpel, and Stanley E. Porter; Leiden: Brill, 2009), 114–145.

[99] Klaus Baltzer, *Deutero-Isaiah: A Commentary on Isaiah 40–55* (Hermeneia; Minneapolis: Fortress Press, 2001), 1; Claus Westermann, *Isaiah 40–66: A Commentary* (OTL; London: SCM Press, 1976), 8.

make extensive use of features that connect them with the praise of God in the Psalms.[100] The prophet employs a number of psalm forms to convey his message of eschatological hope, but makes particular use of hymns (40:9–11; 42:10–13; 43:14–21; 44:23; 45:7; 52:7–10; 54:1–3, 4–8, 9–10; 55:12–13). Some more specific genres may be noted including Zion hymns (Isa 40:9–11; 52:1–2, 7–10) and kingship hymns (40:21–23; 44:6–8; 49:22–26; 51:4–6), along with the related servant songs (42:1–4; 49:1–6; 50:4–7; 52:13–53:12).[101] By emphasizing praise so strongly in these oracles, Westermann suggests that the author aims to "resuscitate the praises of Israel" in order to return their focus on God in the days of the Babylonian exile. He explains, "What Deutero-Isaiah is seeking to do by this means is, in the time of his people's deep affliction, to make them recapture the vision of God as great and majestic; for only such a God can be imagined powerful enough to bring about the new miraculous deliverance."[102] In the context of exile, hymnic passages offer the prophet the medium with which to paint a compelling picture of reality in which God is not only in firm control but also able, willing, and planning to redeem his people.

While Westermann offers one perspective which is particularly sensitive to the use of hymnic styles, another proposal has been made by Baltzer. Though he would agree with Westermann on the unity of the composition as a whole and on the importance of hymnic styles within it, Baltzer has recently proposed reading Deutero-Isaiah as liturgical drama composed in Jerusalem in the late fifth century BCE.[103] As a liturgical drama, Isa 40–55 falls into six acts introduced by a prologue and followed by an epilogue. Hymns mark the conclusion of Acts I–V and much of the language of the acts can be seen to be in the form of "hymnal dialogue." This liturgical drama is thus closely aligned with Israel's worship. In reviewing the connections between drama and cult, Baltzer surveys Babylonian, Egyptian, and Attic drama as well as later Jewish drama evidenced by the *Exagoge* of Ezekiel the Tragedian.[104] He claims, "In the ancient Near Eastern world there has been 'drama' within the framework of the cult since time immemorial."[105] Of particular interest for scholars who note the disparate character of much of the material in Isa 40–55 is the recognition that drama is well-suited to incorporate a variety of different smaller genres or literary units.

---

[100] Cf. Benjamin D. Sommer, *A Prophet Reads Scripture: Allusion in Isaiah 40–66* (Stanford, Calif: Stanford University Press, 1998); Westermann, *Isaiah 40–66*, 108–131.

[101] Gillingham, *The Poems and Psalms of the Hebrew Bible*, 140–169.

[102] Westermann, *Isaiah 40–66*, 14.

[103] Baltzer, *Deutero-Isaiah*, 7–32.

[104] Ibid., 7–14.

[105] Ibid., 7.

While an intriguing proposal, and one with some precedent, the liturgical drama theory has come under severe criticism.[106] Though it is well beyond the scope of this section to resolve the disparity between these two particular views (Westermann's "resuscitating praise" model and Baltzer's "liturgical drama" model), it is possible here to note some points of continuity between the two views. In terms of the function of hymnody within the larger composition, the two theories may not be as far apart as they appear. First, both recognize the significance of the Psalms and of the traditional language of praise for this composition. Second, both also recognize the importance of assessing the message of Isa 40–55 as a unity. Third, neither asserts that preexisting hymns are incorporated into Isa 40–55 at a later stage. Accordingly, at least as far as the text itself is concerned, in either compositional scenario it is possible to examine the use of Jewish hymnic styles and themes within the context of the larger unified composition of Isa 40–55. The interpretation of the significance of the findings of such an examination will vary, however, depending on the historical situation of the community to which these chapters are addressed.

Here we might also consider the issue of the audience: exiles in Babylon in the sixth century BCE or the poor and weak in Judah in the fifth century BCE. While Westermann and many others accept that Isa 40–55 was written from Babylon, Baltzer makes the case for a fifth century date and a location within the land of Israel.[107] Goulder has recently laid out a case for reading the entire composition as being composed in the land of Israel and addressed to the inhabitants of Jerusalem in the time period immediately after the exile.[108] While this dispute cannot be adjudicated here, it is fair to note that the themes that are hymnically traced out in Isa 40:12–31 would be appropriate to either of these settings. Goulder explains that the Jews living in Judah "are likely to have been even more dispirited than their fellow Jews in exile. They too were prone to fall into idolatry, and needed reassurance that Yahweh was supreme God, indeed the only God, the sole creator."[109] Goldingay's suggestion, that the audience is a more general "Judean community" both in Babylon and in Jerusalem, seems to treat the textual evidence most fairly. In this reading the poems "can be read as addressing Judeans in Babylon who had been transported there at the beginning of the sixth century, and their descendants, but also as addressing Judeans in Palestine who had not been transported there, and their descend-

---

[106] John G. F. Wilks, "The Prophet as Incompetent Dramatist," *VT* 53 (2003): 530–543.

[107] Baltzer, *Deutero-Isaiah*, 30-31.

[108] Michael Goulder, "Deutero-Isaiah of Jerusalem," *JSOT* 28 (2004): 351–362.

[109] Ibid., 362.

ants."[110] We can merely note here that it is conceivable that Jews at either location in either time period would be in need of Deutero-Isaiah's message that emphasized God's power as both creator and redeemer of his people – a message that was rooted in their past traditions of history and liturgy.

In light of these considerations, we will explore two examples of hymnically styled passages, Isa 40:12–31 (a descriptive psalm of praise) and Isa 42:10–13 (the first of several eschatological psalms of praise), within their immediate contexts. Together they show how the author can tap into multiple spatial, temporal, and cognitive registers to paint a compelling portrait of ultimate reality for the audience.

Isaiah 40:12–31 is a passage that reflects on the incomparable greatness and majesty of God (vv. 12–26) together with his care for his people even in their powerlessness (vv. 27–31). By emphasizing these two themes this complex passage provides a theological foundation on which the prophet can build his message of hope.

Formally, the passage is not a hymn, but rather a compilation of four disputations. Nevertheless, the contents, themes, and movement of the whole are modeled on the descriptive psalms of praise.[111] Each section (vv. 12–17, 18–24, 25–26, and 27–31) draws on themes and emphases of the psalms to make the case that the God of Israel is the incomparable creator, the Lord of history, and one who cares for his people.[112] These echoes of psalm traditions are not surprising: the tone of the whole passage suggests that these are truths that the Israelites have known from the beginning through their liturgical traditions (cf. Isa 40:21, 28).

Westermann suggests that the hymnic praise that infuses this poem is in part guided by a response to the lament of the Israelites in exile. Verse 27 provides the lament of the Israelites as the climactic focus of the series of four disputations. The prophet grounds his response to their lament and complaint in the language and ideas of hymnic praise to God who is the creator and redeemer.[113]

---

[110] John Goldingay and David F. Payne, *Isaiah 40–55: Volume 1* (ICC; London: T&T Clark, 2006), 33.

[111] Westermann, *Isaiah 40–66*, 62.

[112] Westermann suggests Psalm 33 as an example of a psalm which provides this same overarching theme. Ibid., 49, 61–62. In his discussion of Ps 33 Goldingay notes its affinity with the message of Deutero-Isaiah; Goldingay, *Psalms 1–41*, 469. Sommer suggests that Isa 40:12–31 echoes some of the major themes of Ps 82. These include the idea that God is mightier than the nations, that people neither know nor understand, concerns related to the divine court, and the issue of how human leadership relates to divine leadership; Sommer, *A Prophet Reads Scripture*, 122–124.

[113] Westermann, *Isaiah 40–66*, 59–60.

For Westerman this hymn follows the prologue (40:1–11) and ends by returning to themes that are enunciated in it. In this way the entire chapter is a unity introducing major themes of the whole composition.[114] In Baltzer's litrugcial drama, the whole chapter serves as the prologue to the drama, and is composed of a number of separate units (including the hymn of vv. 12–17 and the hymnal dialogue of vv. 21–31) that work together as a unity to announce the themes of the work, provide the setting for the drama, and introduce the main characters of the drama.[115] In either view, the greater part of Isa 40:12–31 reflects patterns and forms of traditional hymnic praise derived from the Psalms and the cultic worship of Israel.[116] The thematic focus centers on God as creator, Lord of history, and as the one who can provide strength for his weary people. Whether for the literary work or the performed liturgical drama, the hymn(s) contribute to setting the stage for all that will follow in Isa 41–55.

In concluding our discussion of Isa 40:12–31 we can agree with Goldingay's observation that the language and style of Isa 40–55 as a whole is marked by a blend of poetry as well as "prophetic rhetoric."[117] Poetic imagery and hymnic style are but one part of the strategy and composition of the overall message that the prophet is attempting to deliver to his audience.

In contrast to the hymnically-styled teaching in Isa 40:12–31, Isa 42:10–13 makes a quite different use of hymnic styles. In the form of a hymn of praise, it opens with an imperative call to praise (v. 10a) and goes on to call all the inhabitants of the earth to give glory to the LORD and declare his praise (vv. 10b–12). Finally it provides the reason for this praise with the description of the LORD who goes forth like a warrior (v. 13). The text reads:

Sing to the LORD a new song, his praise from the end of the earth!
Let the sea roar and all that fills it, the coastlands and their inhabitants.
Let the desert and its towns lift up their voice, the villages that Kedar inhabits;
let the inhabitants of Sela sing for joy, let them shout from the tops of the mountains.
Let them give glory to the LORD, and declare his praise in the coastlands.
The LORD goes forth like a soldier, like a warrior he stirs up his fury;
he cries out, he shouts aloud, he shows himself mighty against his foes.
(vv. 10–13 NRSV)

Though clearly related to earlier psalm traditions, Westermann describes this passage as the first of a new psalm form that is characteristic of the author of Isa 40–55, the eschatological hymn of praise. Rather than offer-

---

[114] Ibid., 61.

[115] Baltzer, *Deutero-Isaiah*, 47–48.

[116] Cf. chapter 4 of Sommer, *A Prophet Reads Scripture*, 108–131.

[117] Goldingay and Payne, *Isaiah 40–55: Volume 1*, 24.

ing praise for some aspect of God's goodness and majesty, these hymns offer praise for the future deliverance of God. Westermann explains, "In this specific hymn-form, Deutero-Isaiah summons his audience, his fellow-countrymen in exile, even now to strike up jubilation at the event which, while it lies ahead of them all, is already a settled fact in the mind of God, the return which he himself brings about."[118] This dynamic of advance praise for future deliverance is seen in other declarations of praise as well in which the heavens and earth are called upon to celebrate God's compassion and redemption for his people (e.g., 44:23; 49:13).[119]

The precise function of this hymn in its context is, in this case, a little more dependent on the literary genre of the whole. As the first of several eschatological hymns of praise, it can be seen to initiate the divine action of God as he "goes forth" (v. 13). God's eschatological victory is thus set in motion, though not yet accomplished. The later eschatogical hymns will speak of his redemption and comforting of his people as accomplished facts (44:23; 49:13). In Baltzer's view the hymn takes on additional significance as it serves to signal the conclusion of Act I. Further, as a song by the chorus it is an essential element in the dramatic build-up of the whole.[120] It is possible to argue that in either scenario, literary/poetic or dramatic, the employment of eschatological hymns both here and elsewhere in Isa 40–55 play a role in creating a heightening of tension in the work – a tension which is only fully resolved in the final chapter when the people of Israel go out in joy and are led back in peace (Isa 55:12).

This brief look at two passages in Isa 40–55 suggests that the author employed hymnic forms and styles for several purposes. As we have seen, in ancient Israel hymns were a common means of reflecting on the works of God in the past and the unchanging nature of God for all generations. By drawing on this tradition in 40:12–31, the author was able to tap into an element of the collective memory of Israel in order to remind the downtrodden audience that God was indeed supreme and that he still cared for his people. Further, in Isa 42:10–13 the author employed hymnic elements to call on all creation to burst forth in praise to God because of his coming deliverance. In the midst of exile, such eschatological praise served as a call to the audience both to recall and affirm their understanding of God as the Divine Warrior who had fought for his people in the past, and was on

---

[118] Westermann, *Isaiah 40–66*, 102.

[119] When we examine the hymns of the Lukan infancy narrative, we will observe one way that these hymnic passages are taken up and interpreted within early Christian traditions. The heavenly host in Luke 2 responds to these Isaianic imperatives and the heavens literally give glory to God for his redemptive work through the birth of Jesus. In this way, Luke utilizes hymns as one part of a strategy of indicating the fulfillment of these prophecies of Isa 40–55.

[120] Baltzer, *Deutero-Isaiah*, 138.

the verge of delivering them again. These hymnic elements served as one tributary to the author's vision of ultimate reality – a view of the world from the perspective of faith, and a view that stood in marked contrast to the present circumstances of the Israelites.

3.2. Didactic Hymns in Daniel

Turning to the book of Daniel, the reader is confronted with an exciting array of genres and styles: narrative, prophecy, court tales, didactic tales, apocalyptic imagery, and more. In this diverse text, hymnic praise of God is not absent. In fact, the narrative portions of Daniel are marked by praise, both on the part of Daniel and, surprisingly, on the part of gentile rulers. Further, the later Greek version of Daniel provides a lengthy hymn in the midst of the narrative of the men in the fiery furnace. The Song of the Three Men is thus another instance of a hymn in a narrative context which serves to highlight a theological truth as well as to model a godly response to divine deliverance.

Within the Aramaic sections of Daniel are four poetic passages that convey praise to God from the perspective of a character in the narrative. In 2:20–23 Daniel renders thanks to God for answering his prayer and revealing the dream and its interpretation. In 3:31–33 Nebuchadnezzar offers praise to God in the opening section of the letter he sends to all of his people. Toward the end of this letter, in 4:31–32, Nebuchadnezzar again offers praise to God. Finally, in 6:26–28 Darius offers praise in a letter he sent to all of his people.[121] These several instances where pagan kings verbalize the praises of the God of Daniel are worth reviewing briefly as we conclude this study of didactic hymnody in the Hebrew Bible.

Towner offered what has become the standard treatment of all four passages in the Aramaic section of Daniel.[122] After devoting a significant amount of attention to the song of praise by Daniel in chapter 2, he then treated the final three poetic passages as a group under the umbrella of 3:31–33. He explains his rationale, "This is possible because of the similarity of their form and content; furthermore, all three serve to sum up and reflect upon the significance of the narratives to which they are attached."[123] Towner then noted a number of similarities in form and function that were helpful as far as they went. Ultimately, the greatest contribu-

---

[121] Space will not allow for a discussion of the ordering and alteration of these units in the Old Greek. Collins discusses this issue and observes that the variations in order and content suggest that this whole unit (3:31–6:28) may have circulated independently since a divergent text emerged only for these chapters. John Joseph Collins, *Daniel: A Commentary on the Book of Daniel* (Hermeneia; Minneapolis: Fortress Press, 1993), 220.

[122] W. Sibley Towner, "The Poetic Passages in Daniel 1–6," *CBQ* 31 (1969): 317–326.

[123] Ibid., 320.

tion of Towner was in drawing attention to the way these four passages
function similarly within the larger work and serve as a unifying feature of
the narrative.

Space will not allow us to provide an analysis of all four of these hymnic passages. Instead, we will briefly explore the praise to God that opens
and closes the letter of Nebuchadnezzar to all people, nations, and tongues
in Daniel 3. The letter recounts Nebuchadnezzar's frightening dream and
its fulfillment. It begins with a brief introduction in 3:31 and 32. The introduction is not unlike other Aramaic epistolary introductions and each
part of it can be seen to resemble portions of the letters found in the Aramaic portions of Ezra and other surviving examples of ancient epistolary
technique. In English translation the letter begins, "King Nebuchadnezzar.
To all the peoples, nations, and language groups who are dwelling in all
the land. May your peace increase."[124] Following this greeting, Nebuchadnezzar explains the purpose of his letter. Verse 32 reads, "The signs and
wonders that the most high God performed with me, it seemed good to me
to declare." These two verses have just set the stage then for what will follow in chapter four. In fact, one might reasonably expect the letter to move
right into the narrative of the events from this point. Instead, the author
includes what Collins refers to as "a very short hymn" before moving forward with the details.[125] Verse 33 reads as follows:

His signs – how great!
His wonders – how mighty!
His kingdom is a kingdom forever,
and his sovereignty exists with generation after generation.

The narrative of events then picks up in 4:1 immediately following this
short hymn of praise.

This short passage is rich with suggestive terminology, and though written in Aramaic almost every word can be explored with regard to equivalent forms used within the Hebrew Bible. References to "signs and wonders" appear in Exodus, Deuteronomy, Nehemiah, Psalms, and Jeremiah.[126]
With regard to the eternality of God's kingdom, the obvious connection
with Psalm 145:12 cannot be missed. It reads, "Your kingdom is a kingdom forever, and your rule is from generation to generation." The richness
of this passage may be further appreciated when one notes that a number of
key concepts and ideas are introduced here and are then developed further

---

[124] Translations of Daniel are my own.

[125] Collins, *Daniel*, 222. As for the proper terminology with which to refer to these
passages, Towner uses "poetic passages" or "hymns." The phrase "psalm-like units" is
surely safe, if not a bit boring.

[126] Exod 7:3; Deut 4:34; 6:22; 7:19; 26:8; 29:3; Neh 9:10; Ps 78:43; Ps 105:27; Ps
135:9; Jer 32:20–21; Cf. Acts 7:36.

in the succeeding narrative. Four terms are particularly relevant: 'great', 'mighty', 'kingdom', and 'sovereignty.' These terms spell out the theme of the letter as a whole, i.e., that God is the great and mighty one who is ultimately in control of even the mightiest kingdom on earth. Goldingay puts it this way, "The chapter concerns the question, who is king? – but by its form it gives us the answer before we begin."[127] In this way, the short hymnic passage paves the way for the message that follows.

Following this introductory hymnic section, the letter proceeds to narrate the miraculous events that occurred to Nebuchadnezzar – his dream, its interpretation, his humiliation, and ultimately his restoration. The second hymnic passage in this letter occurs at the end of the epistle after Nebuchadnezzar is restored. In verse 31, Nebuchadnezzar explains what happened and then turns to praise. He explains in 4:31–32,

And at the end of the days I, Nebuchadnezzar, lifted up my eyes toward heaven and my knowledge returned to me,
And I blessed the most high, and praised and glorified the one who lives forever,
For his reign is a reign forever,
And his kingdom is with generation after generation.
And all the inhabitants of earth are considered as naught,
and as he wishes he does with the force of heaven and the inhabitants of earth.
And there is no one who will stay his hand
or even say to him, "What are you doing?"

Both on a broad thematic level and on the level of individual words, some clear connections are apparent between this passage and the hymn that began the letter. Where the first passage refers to the deity as "the most high God" here he is "the most high" and "the one who lives forever." Where the first passage notes the eternal nature of his kingdom and reign, this passage does as well, but with the order of kingdom and reign reversed. Thus the context of the psalms noted above may be seen to be in view here as well. Beyond that, this passage expands on the idea of God's sovereignty with the addition of the idea that earth's inhabitants are considered as nothing and that God does what he wants in both heaven and earth. God's purposes cannot be resisted and no one exists who can even question him. In other words, God's authority is without limit and is incapable of being compromised by the activities of humanity. The language here is reminiscent of Isa 40:17 and 45:9–10, where similar ideas are expressed. In addition the language again resonates with aspects of Ps 135, particularly v. 6.

These hymns leave no doubt about their thematic and didactic intent: they convey that God is the one who is in charge, and that no one – not even unbelieving kings – can thwart his plans. More than this, in an unprecedented narrative move even some of the unbelieving kings come to

---

[127] John Goldingay, *Daniel* (WBC 30; Dallas, Tex.: Word Books, 1989), 91.

perceive this truth and worship God because of it. Though simple in theme, the way the message is conveyed in this larger unit is quite complex. It involves dreams, proclamations, letters, threats, mental illness, lavish banquets, a lion's den, writing on walls, and hymns – all over the span of the reign of three kings. In addition to its complexity, we can note also that the account is time-bound as well as timeless. The setting in the specific reigns of three kings, and the recounting of specific details give the accounts a very historic quality. The manner of telling evokes the narrative accounts in other historical books of the Hebrew Bible, with a concrete setting in time and place. Yet, as with all of history, the account is not intended to convey information about the past – at least not as its final goal. If one assumes that these were composed many years after the reigns of the kings in question, it is beyond question that the point conveyed in the narrative and its hymns is a point that is intended for the audience of the author of the accounts.

Thus, we may conclude that the point of this story from the past with its hymnic elements is to teach that the God of the impossible in the days of Daniel is the same sovereign God in the impossible situations of the present. As a lesson intended for the people of God in an era far removed from the events recorded, the narrative conveys clear instruction to later generations. It invites the people of God to see their circumstances in light of the eternal reign of God – a reign which will have no end and which will never be destroyed. The narrative employs hymnody to sharpen the point in unprecedented ways. As we will see in later Second Temple Jewish writings, this theme becomes more prominent in hymns of all kinds.

E. Conclusions

Within the writings of the Hebrew Bible, psalms, hymns, and prayers serve a number of purposes in a wide range of contexts. In this chapter we have explored the didactic functions of a number of these compositions. In several cases the didactic intent was explicit (e.g., Wisdom psalms), but often it was more subtle (e.g., songs in narrative contexts). Assessing the didactic impact of these hymns and psalms requires sensitivity to their contents, form, style, and context. It also requires some degree of historical imagination as we place ourselves in the position of the audience hearing these hymns in their historical context or, later, hearing them in their literary context.

As we appraise the uses of didactic hymnody in the Hebrew Bible it will be helpful to compare these texts to other didactic texts within ancient Israel. Davies' insights about how didactic stories functioned for Israel can

offer some helpful perspectives on how didactic hymns may have functioned as well. This is particularly true for those hymns that relate an historical event or a series of events. Two points are of particular relevance.
First is the issue of the way these texts (whether narrative or hymn) impart
their lessons. Davies explains, "Narrative texts construct a world: and
however much that world represents itself as the real one of the reader's
experience, the story world is not the world of experience for it is ordered
into an author's narrative."[128] In a similar vein, didactic hymns paint a picture of reality that may or may not align with the perceived reality of the
audience. The effectiveness of the hymn may be in part related to its ability
to create a vision of reality that is compelling to the audience.

A second related issue is the way these texts engage the reader or hearer. Regarding didactic stories Davies explains, "Stories function by engaging the interest of the reader in the plot, the characters or the point of view:
devices such as suspense, irony, humor and pathos address the emotions
and the intellect of the reader."[129] Again, the application to didactic hymnody is similar. Didactic hymns engage the emotions as well as the intellect as they paint their portrait of reality in light of the divine reality perceived by their authors. They create a lyrical world within which the reader
can locate himself or herself. They also provide a context for reflection on
current issues and events in light of significant overarching themes and
truths of the tradition.

Central themes in the didactic hymns of the Pentateuch were God's
faithfulness, his power, his mercy towards his people, and the response of
his people to his deeds (whether good or bad). Within the Psalms, didactic
hymns emphasized wise living, reflections on life, and the work of God in
the world and in history. Isaiah's use of hymnic styles and motifs served at
least two purposes. First, it drew attention to God's identity by means of
concepts and ideas already in the cultural memory of the Israelites. Second, it pointed to both the uniqueness and the certainty of the coming deliverance by picturing all creation responding in praise to God's redemptive work.

In his *Art of Biblical Poetry*, Robert Alter suggested, "Poetry . . . is not
just a set of techniques for saying impressively what could be said otherwise. Rather, it is a particular way of imagining the world."[130] In each of
the instances we have examined in this chapter, the didactic hymn, psalm,
or prayer creates a lyrical world and invites the reader to accept that por-

---

[128] Philip R. Davies, "Didactic Stories," in *Justification and Variegated Nomism. Vol.
1, The Complexities of Second Temple Judaism* (ed. D. A. Carson, Peter T. O'Brien, and
Mark A. Seifrid; Grand Rapids: Baker Academic, 2001), 99–133, here 99.

[129] Ibid., 99.

[130] Alter, *The Art of Biblical Poetry*, 151.

trait of reality. It also invites the reader to see himself or herself within that world as an heir to those traditions and as a recipient of God's mercies in history. As we will see, later Jewish (and early Christian) psalms and hymns can only be fully appreciated when they are read in the context of these earlier traditions they are reflecting, imitating, and, at times, transforming.

Chapter 6

Didactic Hymns in Jewish Writings from the Second Temple Period to the Second Century

A. Introduction

Many of the devout Jews represented by the writings of the period of the Second Temple saw themselves as participants in the plan of God and as recipients of the promises of the covenant. They viewed their religious, political, and ethical life as being intimately connected with the traditions they inherited in the writings that came to make up the Hebrew Bible. Yet even as they looked back to the work of God in their midst in earlier generations, they also faced new and unprecedented challenges in their own time. Faithful Jews sought to understand the promises and plan of God as revealed in the Torah, the prophets, and the writings and in particular what these meant for their corporate existence in the present. Their writings testify to the extent to which they valued those earlier writings and sought to live in accordance with them in their own time. Accordingly, we find in the writings of the Second Temple period many of the same kinds of writings that would later make up the Hebrew Bible: narrative, history, poetry, psalmody, Wisdom literature, prophecy, and apocalyptic.[1]

Of interest in this study are the ways that hymnody and psalmody are used for purposes of teaching and instructing the latest generation in the ways of God. As with the earlier writings, didactic hymns form a subset of hymns and psalms, most of which were still written primarily for purposes of expressing praise to God or making a request of God.[2] Yet certain

---

[1] For overviews of these writings and their themes see the standard treatments in George W. E. Nickelsburg, *Jewish Literature between the Bible and the Mishnah: A Historical and Literary Introduction* (2nd ed.; Minneapolis: Fortress, 2005); Michael E. Stone, *Jewish Writings of the Second Temple Period: Apocrypha, Pseudepigrapha, Qumran, Sectarian Writings, Philo, Josephus* (CRINT. Section 2, Literature of the Jewish People in the Period of the Second Temple and the Talmud 2; Assen, Netherlands; Philadelphia: Van Gorcum; Fortress Press, 1984); James C. VanderKam, *An Introduction to Early Judaism* (2nd ed.; Grand Rapids: Eerdmans, 2003).

[2] See the overviews of this material in James H. Charlesworth, "Jewish Hymns, Odes, and Prayers (ca 167 BCE–135 CE)," in *Early Judaism and its Modern Interpreters* (Philadelphia: Fortress Press, 1986), 411–436; David Flusser, "Psalms, Hymns, and Prayers,"

psalm-like and hymn-like texts in this period appear to be primarily concerned with teaching a lesson to a human audience in addition to (or at times instead of) directly praising God. These are found in collections of psalms, in narrative contexts, in Wisdom literature, and in apocalyptic writings. This chapter will explore examples of each to show how these didactic hymns utilize the language and form of hymnic praise to convey instruction to their readers.

Since the didactically-oriented hymns, psalms, and prayers of this period are found in a wide range of literary contexts, it is important to recall several of the underlying principles guiding the identification of didactic hymns in this study. As we have noted, all hymns and prayers can be considered didactic to some extent. That is, hymns teach their audiences as they either model a way of communicating with or about the divine, or, in the process of communicating verbally with the divine, the human audience encounters certain truths about the one who is the subject of the hymn or prayer. While it would be of general interest to consider the teaching or theology of any hymn from these two angles, this study has a more specific focus. Our aim is to consider those psalms and hymns in which teaching a human audience is a *primary* purpose of the composition. Instruction may not be the only purpose of such compositions – the hymn or psalm may be genuinely directed to the deity – but in hymns where engaging the human audience in reflection about the nature and ways of God is a main focus, we can consider such a hymn a didactic hymn. Indications that a particular hymn or prayer is didactic can be seen in explicit references to what the hymn will teach or through implicit indicators such as the subject matter of the hymn (historical review, emphasis on wisdom, meditation on aspects of creation, etc.). Those indicators are particularly important for hymns that stand alone apart from a larger literary context. In the Hebrew Bible that was the case with the Psalms; in this chapter it will be the case with the *Psalms of Solomon* and the Jewish prayers lying behind the *Apostolic Constitutions*. For hymns, prayers, and psalms embedded in another kind of writing (narrative, Wisdom literature, apocalypse) we can consider the hymn to be didactic to the extent to which it contributes to or supports the instructional aims of the larger composition. These embedded hymns and prayers also may contain explicit or implicit indications of a teaching function, but the fact of their inclusion in another kind of writing is in itself an indication of a didactic role. We saw this to be the case with the Hebrew Bible in such passages as Exod 15, Deut 32, Prov 8 and Isa 40. In this chapter we will examine hymns in the context of Wisdom literature (Wis-

---

in *Jewish Writings of the Second Temple Period: Apocrypha, Pseudepigrapha, Qumran Sectarian Writings, Philo, Josephus* (ed. Michael E. Stone; Philadelphia: Fortress Press, 1984), 551–577.

dom of Solomon; Wisdom of Ben Sira), in the context of narrative writings (Tobit; Baruch), and in the context of apocalyptic literature (*1 Enoch*; *4 Ezra*; *2 Baruch*; *Apocalypse of Abraham*).

At this point one may rightly ask if there are any poetic or prayer compositions that would fall outside of this broad understanding of didactic hymnody. Indeed there are, for this study is focused primarily on those texts which take on this didactic function (explicit or implicit) in the form of hymnic praise of the divine. In the texts of the Second Temple period, many prayers, laments, blessings, curses, and other kinds of poetic passages can be found which have very little emphasis on praise of God or his ways. We are interested here in passages composed as a hymn or reflecting a hymnic style and that contain a teaching function as a primary purpose or one of several primary purposes.

In examining these particular texts we will consider both what these hymns teach and how they teach it. Further, when we can situate a given text within a particular time period and social setting (which is sometimes possible) we can consider how the passage contributes to a community's understanding of itself and its God within that setting. Didactic hymns were well-suited for painting a portrait of reality in which a community may find its identity and purpose clarified in the face of competing views or challenging circumstances. The Second Temple period offered no shortage of either of these for Jews seeking to live as the people of God in those times.

B. Didactic Hymns in Psalm Collections

As was the case in the Hebrew Bible, didactic hymns may be found in psalm collections of the Second Temple period. Two such collections will be discussed here. First, this section will explore the first-century BCE or first-century CE collection known as the *Psalms of Solomon*. Second, this section will explore the Jewish hymns and prayers found in the *Apostolic Constitutions*. Though the latter composition reached its final edited form as a Christian composition in the fourth century CE, some of the material was of Jewish origin and was likely composed in the second and third centuries CE. Composed in different centuries in diverse political and cultural environments, we will see the degrees of variety these hymns and psalms exhibit. We will also observe specific examples of didactic hymnody within each composition, considering both what they teach and how they convey that instruction. Finally, we can consider how these didactic hymns contributed to the development of a sense of communal identity for the groups that composed and preserved them.

1. Psalms of Solomon

The *Psalms of Solomon* is a prime example of a collection of psalms from the middle of the period under discussion here. Unlike the other hymnic texts in this section, these psalms and prayers represent a unified and independent collection, though likely written by a number of authors, possibly in different generations of the community. With direct allusions to Pompey and his invasion of Jerusalem in 63 BCE (in *Pss. Sol.* 2, 8, and 17), but no reference to the destruction of the temple in 70 CE, the *Psalms of Solomon* were probably composed in Hebrew in the mid to late first century BCE, reaching their final edited and translated form before 70 CE.[3] The eighteen psalms collected under this title reflect a mixture of second and third person psalms, hymns, and prayers. Some appear to be directed to God in prayer and praise while others are clearly directed toward the listener with a didactic emphasis.

The general historical circumstances that provide the background to these psalms are fairly easy to discern.[4] References to the corruption of the Hasmonean Sadducees as well as descriptions of Pompey's taking of Jerusalem place the composition of many of the psalms in a time of great turmoil and difficulty for faithful Jews. As Flusser observes, "The eighteen psalms reflect the dramatic events of Jewish history in that period and criticize the various Jewish groups."[5] The historical context along with the contents of the psalms cause scholars to consider this as "crisis literature."[6] As the authors of these psalms seek to understand the justice of God in light of the success of the enemies of the people of God, theodicy becomes a prominent theme.[7] The hope of the community associated with these compositions is not found in the present circumstances. Rather, the community's hope arises from belief in the justice of God and the future arrival of the Messiah, who, as God's eschatological agent, will reverse the for-

---

[3] R. B. Wright, "Psalms of Solomon: A New Translation and Introduction," in *The Old Testament Pseudepigrapha, Vol. 2.* (ed. James H. Charlesworth; New York: Doubleday, 1985), 639–670, here 640–641. For detailed analysis and commentary on the *Pss. Sol.* as a whole see Kenneth Atkinson, *I Cried to the Lord: A Study of the Psalms of Solomon's Historical Background and Social Setting* (JSJSup 84; Leiden; Boston: Brill, 2004); Joachim Schüpphaus, *Die Psalmen Salomos: ein Zeugnis Jerusalemer Theologie und Frömmigkeit in der Mitte des vorchristlichen Jahrhunderts* (ALGHJ 7; Leiden: E.J. Brill, 1977).

[4] A majority of scholars at least recognize that some of the *Pss. Sol.* reflect the events of the Pompeian era. See Atkinson, *I Cried to the Lord*, 5. The earliest clear allusion is to Pompey's 63 BCE invasion of Jerusalem (recounted in *Pss. Sol.* 2:1–2; 8:18–22; 17:7–9), with the latest allusion being to his assassination in 48 BCE (*Pss. Sol.* 2:26–27).

[5] Flusser, "Psalms, Hymns, and Prayers," 573.

[6] Wright, "Psalms of Solomon," 646.

[7] Cf. *Pss. Sol.* 2:1, 15–18; 3:3–5; 4:8; 8:3, 23–26; 9:2; Ibid.

tunes of the faithful followers of God. In this respect the *Psalms of Solomon* share the concerns of many of the compositions we will consider in this chapter.

Though the general historical context of these psalms appears quite straightforward, the provenance and social setting of these compositions are much more difficult to determine.[8] Written before the destruction of the temple in 70 CE, the negative views expressed toward the temple personnel render it highly unlikely that they were intended for use in the sacrificial rites. Nevertheless, while it is unlikely that they were written for cultic purposes, a communal worship setting is still possible. Atkinson proposes that these psalms belonged to a sectarian Jewish community within Jerusalem:

> Their present arrangement was likely undertaken to meet the needs of the redactor's community which sought to use these poems in their worship services. Although the historical problems reflected in many of the *Psalms* had undoubtedly passed by the time these poems were gathered together, their focus on sin and suffering made them relevant for later generations to use for liturgical purposes.[9]

In Atkinson's view the *Psalms of Solomon* found a place in the synagogue worship of one particular community.[10]

While a liturgical setting is possible, some scholars reject such a setting and instead envision a more pointedly instructional context, favoring an educational setting related to the synagogue or private instruction. Flusser explains, "The aim of the *Psalms of Solomon* is didactic, polemical, and theological. It is difficult to assume that they were written for liturgical purposes or later became part of any liturgy."[11] Though Flusser may be right about the difficulty in assigning a liturgical purpose to these psalms, Holm-Nielsen has cautioned scholars about drawing conclusions too hastily about the original or later setting of a given psalm-like composition. He writes,

> In post-Exilic and Late Jewish times the temple remained the home of the psalms. But at the same time when in all probability the *Psalms of Solomon* and the Psalms of Qumran were composed, there existed, besides the temple, synagogues in which the people gath-

---

[8] Atkinson, *I Cried to the Lord*, 3–11.

[9] Ibid., 1–2.

[10] Here we cannot assess the variety of views regarding the specific Jewish group from which these psalms came, though many scholars view them as representing Pharisaic concerns to some degree. For a review of research on the possible background of the *Pss. Sol.* see Schüpphaus, *Die Psalmen Salomos*, 1–20. More recently see Atkinson, *I Cried to the Lord*, esp. 211–222. While Atkinson argues for a sectarian origin, for a reading that views the *Pss. Sol.* as a Pharisaic document and places its themes in conversation with Pauline literature see Dieter Lührmann, "Paul and the Pharisaic Tradition," *JSNT* 36 (1989): 75–94.

[11] Flusser, "Psalms, Hymns, and Prayers," 573.

ered, at any rate, on the Sabbath. . . . Properly speaking there is no reason to doubt that they were used for instructional purposes, but this does not preclude the possibility that they were used at the divine service in the synagogue.[12]

Holm-Nielsen is describing the interconnectedness of the various settings where psalms – didactic or otherwise – were composed, read, and treasured. Efforts to isolate one setting from another may not be completely defensible based on the nature of these institutions in the Second Temple period as well as on the nature of our evidence, which is very limited.

In light of that complex situation, the present study looks within the psalms themselves for indications of the nature and function of certain psalms. Earlier scholars have sought to classify individual psalms from the *Psalms of Solomon* based on their degree of conformity to biblical categories.[13] Such observations and comparisons are valuable in that they show the ways that the *Psalms of Solomon* are not an isolated literary phenomenon. However, the present study recognizes the value of viewing the *Psalms of Solomon* and other Second Temple psalm-like compositions as more than just imitations of earlier standard styles. The *Psalms of Solomon* in particular exhibit much more than just conscious imitation, echo, and mixing of psalm types. These eighteen psalms remind us that psalm composition was alive and well in its own right, and provided one way to reflect on and teach about the current realities facing the Jewish community. The author is not looking *back* to older models as much as he is looking *around* at his current situation and responding to it in a living and vital mode of discourse. The older models have surely played a significant and formative role in making the psalmist who he was in his day; that is, they shaped his sensibilities about what constituted "good" religious poetry. However the psalms and prayers this psalmist composed were much more than simply an imitation of the "righteous" way to respond to such a crisis.

This study further recognizes that the choice of a given form itself communicates something to the reader. The psalmist could have chosen to reflect on this national tragedy through other forms including epistles, Wisdom literature, prophetic, apocalyptic, or narrative. Yet psalms were chosen as the medium for his message. Even within the realm of psalmody, didactic hymnody may take on diverse forms, reflecting styles of praise or

---

[12] Holm-Nielsen, "The Importance of Late Jewish Psalmody," 8–9.

[13] Wright identifies hymns (2:30, 33–37; 3:1f.); individual and community laments (2:19–25; 7; 8:22–34; 16:6–15); thanksgiving songs (8:1–4; 15:1–6; 16:1–5); and didactic poems (3:3–12; 6), as well as a more prevalent "mixing of psalm types than in the psalter," Wright, "Psalms of Solomon," 646. Wright also notes the many "echoes" of the Jewish Scriptures explaining, "Conceptual constructs, individual ideas, and snatches of phrases from the Old Testament lie behind the *Psalms of Solomon*." Wright, "Psalms of Solomon," 647. See also Kenneth Atkinson, *An Intertextual Study of the Psalms of Solomon* (Lewiston, N.Y.: E. Mellen Press, 2001), 402–404.

lament or even wisdom if needed. The nature of the style and content of the teaching of the *Psalms of Solomon* will be explored below with the analysis of some individual psalms. Surprisingly, this kind of analysis has not yet been fully conducted with regard to the *Psalms of Solomon*. Atkinson, for example, devotes a paragraph to discussing the blending of poetry and history in *Psalms of Solomon* and other psalm traditions. He concludes, "Since ancient authors did not write with our modern notions of genre in mind and did not always separate history and poetry, the *Psalms of Solomon* must be viewed as both a poetic composition and a historical work that recounts the sufferings of a pious Jewish community in Jerusalem."[14] While correct as far as he goes with this, Atkinson does not follow through to explore the implications of an author's choice of a particular style or form to communicate his message to his audience.

In this section we review and summarize a number of the *Psalms of Solomon* that convey their instruction in a hymn or at least in a hymnic style. We will see that *Pss. Sol.* 3 and 5 convey their teaching in timeless forms in ways that resonate with biblical hymns of praise. *Psalms of Solomon* 8 and 9 review recent historical events in ways that align with didactic historical psalms. *Psalms of Solomon* 17 and 18 tap into multiple temporal registers as they review key events in biblical history and recent history, and make claims about the future. This brief overview will show that, through a variety of means, these hymns promote a view of God and of reality that would encourage a Jewish audience to trust in the goodness and mercy of God even in times of great turmoil.

Psalms of Solomon 3 and 5 are perhaps the closest to "hymns" in the form-critical sense of the term. Yet both diverge from that idealized form to present didactic instruction to the reader or listener. *Psalms of Solomon* 3 has an opening that is reminiscent of classical hymns. The opening question, "Why do you sleep, soul, and do not praise the Lord?" (3:1a), is followed by an imperative call to praise, "Sing a new song to God, who is worthy to be praised" (3:1b).[15] Verse 2 extends the imperative and expands it to include not just singing but watching or awareness "of how he is aware of you." After v. 2 the psalm shifts from addressing the soul directly to speaking in the third person. The remainder of the psalm contrasts the righteous and the sinner in what is clearly recognizable as a didactic poem along the lines of Ps 1 with its contrast of the righteous and the wicked. In particular the focus of this psalm is on the response of the righteous to the

---

[14] Atkinson, *I Cried to the Lord*, 9.
[15] Translations of *Psalms of Solomon* are from Wright, "Psalms of Solomon."

Lord's discipline and to their own stumbling.[16] Also like Psalm 1, without direct exhortation, listeners are motivated to imitate the righteous and their way of life with its promising end: "Those who fear the Lord shall rise up to eternal life" (3:12).[17] Atkinson notes that there is no historical allusion within this psalm that would allow modern scholars to pinpoint its date of composition.[18] Accordingly, one can observe that this particular psalm thus presents instruction and teaching in a timeless form that would have applied to the generation of the author as well as future generations who cherished this psalm. In a similar way *Pss. Sol.* 5 conveys views about God's care for people in a way that is timeless and applicable to all generations of faithful Jews.[19] *Psalms of Solomon* 3 and 5 provide the closest connection in form to what may be considered a hymn in the biblical sense of the term. Yet the didactic concerns of the author overshadow any level of commitment to consciously imitate biblical hymns.[20]

Psalms of Solomon 8 and 9 connect with biblical psalmody in a different way. Rather than imitating hymnic forms, they provide a review of and commentary on historical events, connecting them with the didactic historical psalms (e.g., Pss 78, 105, and 106). *Psalms of Solomon* 8 poetically

---

[16] Lührmann views this psalm in light of the traditions about Job, showing that it addresses a question common to Wisdom literature, namely, the "qualitative difference between sin and righteousness;" Lührmann, "Paul and the Pharisaic Tradition," 82.

[17] Compare Ps 1:6 with *Ps. Sol.* 3:11.

[18] See Atkinson's discussion of the social and historical setting of this psalm in Atkinson, *I Cried to the Lord*, 193–7.

[19] *Pss. Sol.* 5 resembles an individual song of praise addressed directly to the Lord. It begins with the intention of the psalmist: "Lord God, I will joyfully praise your name among those who know your righteous judgments" (5:1). Like the psalms of praise it then provides the justification for the praise with the transitional "for": "For you are good and merciful, the shelter of the poor" (5:2). The psalm unfolds the ways and deeds of God, with an emphasis on God's provision for his people. Verses 9–10 utilize language about God's provision in his creation. There is also mention of God's providing pasture in the wilderness: "You feed the birds and the fish, as you send rain to the wilderness that the grass may sprout to provide pasture in the wilderness for every living thing" (5:9–10b). The second person form of address ends in v. 15 which may have made a fitting ending to the psalm: "Lord, your mercy is upon the whole world in goodness." However, after that line there is a brief reflection, in the third person, on the blessing of moderate wealth. Verse 18b returns to the second person form saying, "In your kingdom your goodness is upon Israel." The psalm ends with an affirmation of praise and the community's collective relationship with the Lord: "May the glory of the Lord be praised, for he is our king." Though there have been some attempts to link the references to hunger with the famine brought on by the siege of Jerusalem in 63 BCE, there really are no clear historical references within this psalm. Ibid., 185.

[20] Lührmann notes that the hymn specifically teaches that fasting is the means of atonement (v. 8), a clear connection with Pharisaic teaching. Lührmann, "Paul and the Pharisaic Tradition," 83–84.

describes the taking of Jerusalem by Pompey.[21] The descriptions of the siege are colored by biblical allusions that point to the author's belief that this siege is an instance of divine judgment on the city.[22] Like the historical psalms, this psalm clearly aims to review events of history in order to draw out a lesson for the present moment. After the events are described the psalm turns to an explanation of God's justice in all of this (vv. 23–26), a request for God's mercy and compassion (vv. 27–30, 33), and a declaration of commitment and praise (vv. 31–34). As Atkinson observes, "Throughout the *Psalm*, the writer encourages his community to accept God's discipline and to recognize that their present suffering is an opportunity to appeal to God's mercy (8:23–28)."[23] The author of this psalm reflects on recent events in language reminiscent of the biblical past, in order to teach, explain, evaluate, and understand these events. One can readily grasp the didactic purpose for both the present generation experiencing these things and for future generations who would look back on those events.

Psalm of Solomon 9 is likewise historical in that it discusses the exile (vv. 1–3) for the purpose of drawing out a theological truth for the present. The discussion of the exile is followed by the author's reflection on the timeless reality of God's goodness and mercy toward the righteous (vv. 4–7), and his affirmation of the present relationship of God with his people (vv. 8–11). Though it likely relates to a military assault in the current world of the psalmist, there are no clear historical allusions that would allow modern readers to place this particular psalm more precisely within the period in which these psalms were written.[24]

Together *Pss. Sol.* 8 and 9 provide examples of historical psalms with didactic emphases. These psalms review current national events in light of biblical history and show the reader how to view these events from the proper perspective. In this way they can be seen to function as a part of the social memory of the Jewish community that produced these psalms. Assmann's notion of social memory is highly relevant here. He suggests,

Seen as an individual and as a social capacity, memory is not simply the storage of past 'facts' but the ongoing work of reconstructive imagination. In other words, the past cannot be stored but always has to be 'processed' and mediated. This mediation depends on the semantic frames and needs of a given individual or society within a given present.[25]

---

[21] Schüpphaus, *Die Psalmen Salomos*, 45–46.
[22] See the review of the historical details in Atkinson, *I Cried to the Lord*, 55–87. For the biblical allusions and their function see 60–61.
[23] Ibid., 58.
[24] Ibid., 193.
[25] Assmann, *Moses the Egyptian*, 14.

It was the present need of the Jews of this period that required them to reflect on the events of their recent past in light of the inherited traditions of their more distant history. *Psalms of Solomon* 8 and 9, among others, provide a first-hand example of the mediating and processing of cultural history in light of present challenges.

Psalms of Solomon 17 and 18 continue to reflect this dynamic of social memory while at the same time shifting the emphasis to the future and the blessings that the Israelites will experience when the Messiah begins to reign. Such a future hope is cause for praise and for reaffirmation of central truths of Jewish belief. Before turning to a lengthy description of the coming days of the Messiah, *Pss. Sol.* 17 reviews some key events in the history of Israel in a manner not unlike the historical psalms in the Hebrew Bible and also elsewhere in *Psalms of Solomon*. This particular psalm begins (and ends) with a declaration of God as king (17:1–3, 45–46). Following this opening declaration the author reviews God's provision of David, as well as the fall of the monarchy and the taking of Jerusalem. It is thought that in v. 7 we have a direct reference to Pompey, who fits the description of a gentile ruler from the west (vv. 12–14).[26] Throughout the process of historical remembrance (vv. 4–20), the emphasis falls on the problem of sin and God's justice in dealing with it.[27] The downfall of the Davidic kingdom was the sin of the people (v. 5), the downfall of the Hasmonean dynasty was sin and arrogance (vv. 5b–6), and the downfall of the current gentile ruler will be his sin and arrogance (v. 13, 20). The author uses shared cultural memory and his interpretation of God's judgment in the past to express his confidence in God's coming judgment on the current ruling dynasty. Having established this perspective by reviewing the past (vv. 4–20), the psalm transitions into a prayer for and a description of the coming Messiah who will be the son of David and will rule in the time known only to God (v. 21).[28] His rule will be marked by righteousness and holiness (vv. 26, 29, 32, 36, 40, 41). In fact, in contrast to all the preceding rulers and kingdoms which faced judgment because of sin, "He himself (will be) free from sin" (v. 36). Verses 45–46 close with a prayer and a reaffirmation of God as their king (cf. v. 1). Taken as a whole, this particular psalm promotes a particular view of the past, present, and future that em-

---

[26] Wright, "Psalms of Solomon," 641, 666.

[27] There is a similar emphasis on the historical pattern of sin and punishment in *Pss. Sol.* 1 and 2. Nickelsburg, *Jewish Literature*, 241.

[28] This passage is noteworthy as it contains the first reference to the Messiah as the "son of David," cf. Wright, "Psalms of Solomon," 647. For a full discussion of the messianic content of this passage in relation to other facets of early Judaism and Christianity see Atkinson, *I Cried to the Lord*, 129–179.

phasizes the righteousness of God, his justice in punishing sin, and his ultimate plan to deliver his people.

Psalms of Solomon 18 is a prayer that reaffirms the response of the righteous to times of trouble. It begins by declaring the mercies of the Lord in the second person, rehearsing God's mercies in prayer to him.[29] At v. 5 the psalm shifts to third person discourse and describes the day of the Messiah (through v. 9), emphasizing that God will at last provide the Messiah who will reign and do good things for the coming generation. The psalm closes with a collective declaration of the greatness of God and his control of the stars (vv. 10–12), presumably a reminder that God is ultimately in control, regardless of the appearance of the present moment when their enemies are prospering and they are oppressed. The psalm teaches as it unfolds central elements of Jewish theology – elements that the author must have considered essential for he and his fellow Jews to be able to endure the oppression of foreigners. The multiple themes and apparent lack of unity of this final psalm have lead some scholars to suggest that *Pss. Sol.* 18 was composed of bits and pieces of the other seventeen psalms as a way of closing the collection. Regardless of how it was composed, *Pss. Sol.* 18 certainly seems appropriate as a concluding psalm. Atkinson notes,

> The poem also serves as a balance to *Psalms of Solomon* 1, which describes a crisis, since it concludes with a message of hope that the messiah is coming and that God controls the universe. In this way, the *Psalms of Solomon* begins with distress and ends with a message of hope that the messiah will soon arrive and remedy the present crisis.[30]

Atkinson's observation suggests the likelihood that there is a didactic function to the collection as a whole in its final edited form, in addition to the teaching of the individual psalms noted above.

Though these psalms cannot easily be placed in one precise social setting (synagogue, private study, school setting, etc.), their didactic concerns are quite clear. Their teaching emphasizes the need for the righteous to remain faithful to God in spite of his judgment that has come upon the unrighteous Jews. The *Psalms of Solomon* reaffirm that God is in control and that he cares for and watches over his faithful children. Likewise, the *Psalms of Solomon* affirm that better days are on the way – the days of the Messiah, the son of David, who will "be a righteous king over them, taught by God" (17:32). Rather than teaching through exhortation or direct instruction, these compositions promote their theological agenda in the form of hymns and prayers. Nevertheless, the forms do not mitigate against the

---

[29] Among the truths that are emphasized: God is merciful (v. 1); he shows goodness to Israel (v. 1); his eyes are on them (v. 2); his ears hear their prayers (v. 2); his compassionate judgments are over the whole world (v. 3); his love for the Israelites remains (v. 3); and his discipline is intended for his children for their good (v. 4).

[30] Atkinson, *I Cried to the Lord*, 209.

instructional nature of these psalms. These forms suggest instead that the author or authors were aiming not only at the minds of the listeners but also at their emotions.

On the whole the *Psalms of Solomon* teach a view of suffering and foreign conquest that is rooted in confidence in the covenant and on God's justice toward both faithful and unfaithful Jews. The subjects for which God is praised are foundational theological truths that factor into the community's understanding of recent historical events and their own relationship with God.[31] The psalms that review history to any degree address key biblical events (founding of the Davidic monarchy in *Pss. Sol.* 17, the exile in *Pss. Sol.* 9) and current or recent events (the siege of Jerusalem in *Pss. Sol.* 2, 8, and 17). More distant events provide examples to show how and why God has acted or allowed certain events in the present.

Like many of the hymns found embedded in the apocalyptic literature of this period and later, the *Psalms of Solomon* also teach a confidence in the justice of God who will deliver his people in times to come. Unlike the apocalyptic literature, it does not appear that this deliverance by God's agent is imminent, nor is there reference to a particular revelation to the author regarding when these hopes would be fulfilled.[32] The author(s) of the *Psalms of Solomon* declared their understanding of the times and painted their verbal portrait of reality without appeal to direct revelation.

2. Hellenistic Synagogal Prayers

The prayers and psalms known as the *Hellenistic Synagogal Prayers* are a collection of Greek prayers found within the fourth-century Christian work the *Apostolic Constitutions*. In spite of the overtly Christian perspective of the *Apostolic Constitutions*, and the fact that it was compiled in its final form around 380 CE, scholars believe that it contains as many as sixteen prayers in books seven and eight which are remnants of Jewish synagogal prayers originating between 150 and 300 CE.[33] These prayers reflect the

---

[31] The same could well be said of the didactic hymns and prayers of the Dead Sea Scrolls, some of which reflect the same historical period and the same concerns with the Jerusalem Temple.

[32] Nickelsburg, *Jewish Literature*, 243. In the hymnic prayers of *2 Baruch*, for example, note that God's revelation to Baruch is an important subject (cf. *2 Bar.* 54:6–7, 20).

[33] David A. Fiensy, "Hellenistic Synagogal Prayers: Introduction," in *The Old Testament Pseudepigrapha, Vol. 2.* (ed. James H. Charlesworth; New York: Doubleday, 1985), 671–676. More reserved are the findings of van der Horst and Newman who suggest that only the prayers in *Apos. Con.* 7.33–38 should be considered Jewish; Pieter W. van der Horst and Judith H. Newman, *Early Jewish Prayers in Greek* (Commentaries on Early Jewish Literature; Berlin: Walter de Gruyter, 2008), 27–28. On the basis of parallels from Qumran, Chazon has argued that the prayer in *Apos. Con.* 8.6.5–8 reflects a Jewish original; E. G. Chazon, "A 'Prayer Alleged to be Jewish' in the *Apostolic Constitutions*,"

styles and contents of the biblical Psalter in many ways and also indicate the composers' full knowledge of the Jewish Scriptures.[34] Further, these prayers also reflect some of the forms and ideas found in the much later Wisdom of Solomon as well as more general Hellenistic philosophical ideas.[35] Taken together, these prayers can be used to provide some insight into Jewish thought and worship practices of the second century CE.[36]

The task of identifying as much as possible the earliest strata of these prayers falls well beyond the scope of the present study. For the purposes of this study, the conclusions of Fiensy will serve as our starting point for reading the *Hellenistic Synagogal Prayers*. In his view the individual prayers are the result of several generations of Jewish worshippers who composed and passed on these prayers orally in the context of synagogue worship, until they found their way, via Christians, to the compiler of the *Apostolic Constitutions*.[37] Fiensy concludes, "The theology of the prayers is in the main that of the Hebrew benedictions and of rabbinic thought, and the prayers were probably an example of the Syrian synagogal Sabbath morning service in the late second to early fourth centuries A.D."[38] Based on this scenario, the reconstructed synagogue prayers witness to some connection with second-century Jewish synagogue traditions, even if they are not as reliable as unedited primary witnesses would be.[39]

---

in *Things Revealed: Studies in Early Jewish and Christian Literature in Honor of Michael E. Stone* (ed. Esther G. Chazon, David Satran, and Ruth A. Clements; Leiden: Brill, 2004), 261–277.

[34] Fiensy, "Hellenistic Synagogal Prayers: Introduction," 674.

[35] Van der Horst and Newman, *Early Jewish Prayers in Greek*, 26–27.

[36] The study of these prayers as witnesses to Jewish thought and worship practice of the second century is beset with a number of challenges. If they were originally Jewish prayers, explicitly Christian content has been added by later editors to some of these prayers with the result that attempts at peeling away the redactional layers are extremely challenging. However, several factors cause many scholars to believe it is possible to remove the Christian interpolations and identify original Jewish compositions. As a collection the *Apostolic Constitutions* as a whole makes use of other sources which are still in existence. By examining the editorial tendencies of the compiler, scholars can get a clearer sense of the kinds of additions, subtractions, and alterations the fourth century compiler made. Exploring the ways the compiler uses and edits the *Didascalia*, the *Didache*, *Apostolic Tradition*, and the *Clementine Liturgy*, it becomes clear that the compiler depends heavily on source material, and also that he edits in a certain limited number of ways. David A. Fiensy, *Prayers Alleged to Be Jewish: An Examination of the Constitutiones Apostolorum* (BJS 65; Chico, Calif.: Scholars Press, 1985), 19–25.

[37] Ibid., 210. For a description of several possible means of transmission of the prayer in *Apos. Con.* 8.6.5–8 see Chazon, "A 'Prayer Alleged to be Jewish'," 271–274.

[38] Fiensy, *Prayers Alleged to be Jewish*, 234.

[39] The following observations on the didactic features of these prayers are based on the reconstructed *Hellenistic Synagogal Prayers* and translation by D. R. Darnell, "Hellenistic Synagogal Prayers: Translation," in *The Old Testament Pseudepigrapha, Vol. 2.*

As we explore the didactic features of these prayers, we will see that these prayers utilize a variety of hymnic approaches to convey their vision of reality to the human audience. Indicators of a primary didactic function can be observed in these prayers through their emphasis on knowledge and instruction, their content which centers on direct claims about God and the community, and their direct address to the community about the nature of the task of praise. In particular, a prominent feature of the prayers is the hymnic review of history in which key events from the past are recounted in such a way that they function as communal memory for the Diaspora community which used these prayers.[40]

In general all of the prayers are infused with a concern for knowledge relating to who God is and what he has done for his people. Prayer 1 is a prayer of thanksgiving, which includes praise for God's holy name encamping among the community, and for "knowledge, faith, love, immortality" given to the community.[41] Among the qualities or deeds for which God is praised are: his creation of the world; his creation of the natural law; his relationship with Abraham, Isaac, and Jacob; that he is powerful, faithful and true; that his promises are without falsehood. Such descriptions not

---

(ed. James H. Charlesworth; New York: Doubleday, 1985), 677–97. I reference the prayers by number according to the scheme used in Charlesworth, *OTP II*: 1. A Prayer of Thanksgiving Following Communion (*Apos. Con.* 7.26.1–3); 2. A Prayer of Praise to God, the Universal Savior and Fighter on Behalf of Abraham's Race (*Apos. Con.* 7.33.2–7); 3. A Prayer That Meditates upon God's Manifold Creative Power, Which Comes to Sinful Man in Redemption (*Apos. Con.* 7.34.1–8); 4. A Prayer That Joins with All Nature in Praising the One and Only Great and Merciful God (*Apos. Con.* 7.35.1–10); 5. A Prayer Praising God for His Redemptive Deeds for Israel, Old and New, and for the Institution of Days Set Apart for Worship (*Apos. Con.* 7.36.1–7); 6. A Prayer of Invocation, Calling upon God, Who Has Always Accepted the Worship of His People, to Accept the Present Prayers of His New People (*Apos. Con.* 7.37.1–5); 7. A Prayer of Thanksgiving to God for His Continuing Acts of Redemption in the Past, and Now in Christ; and for His Manifold Gifts to Man, the Rational Animal (*Apos. Con.* 7.38.1–8); 8. Instruction for Catechumens (*Apos. Con.* 7.39.2–4); 9. A Prayer of Praise to God for His Greatness, and for His Appointment of Leaders for His People (*Apos. Con.* 8.5.1–4); 10. A Prayer on Behalf of the Catechumens (*Apos. Con.* 8.6.5–8); 11. A Prayer of Entreaty for God's Mercy upon the Penitent (*Apos. Con.* 8.9.8f.); 12. A Prayer of Praise to God, Rehearsing the Grounds in Redemption and in Creation Which Make Praise So Fitting for God's Redeemed Creature, Man (*Apos. Con.* 8.12.6–27); 13. A Prayer of Praise and Benediction, Spoken by a Bishop at the Close of the Eucharistic Service (*Apos. Con.* 8.15.7–9); 14. A Portion of a Prayer Prayed at the Ordination of Presbyters (*Apos. Con.* 8.16.3); 15. A Prayer to Accompany the Offering of Firstfruits (*Apos. Con.* 8.40.2–4); 16. Funeral Prayer for the Dead (*Apos. Con.* 8.41.2–5).

[40] On the series of examples, or *Beispielreihe*, in these and other prayers see van der Horst and Newman, *Early Jewish Prayers in Greek*, 47.

[41] Unless otherwise noted, translations are those of Darnell, "Hellenistic Synagogal Prayers: Translation."

only serve the purpose of praising God, but clearly have the purpose of reminding the community of these fundamental truths. These themes are developed further in other prayers as well. Prayer 2 uses Abraham and other patriarchs as examples, but in particular it is the fact that God taught Abraham that is singled out: "You guided him by a vision and taught him what (life in) this world really is (about). From that knowledge came forth his faith, and the covenant was the consequence of his faith."[42] Along with this emphasis on knowledge, several prayers include a long list of titles, deeds, or descriptions of God.[43]

Of interest in the context of this study are the ways that some of these prayers provide reviews of history as part of their content.[44] Prayer 6 taps into multiple temporal registers as it reviews how God accepted the prayers of the righteous in previous generations and asks the Lord to receive the prayers of his people in the present. The review of the righteous begins with Abel (6:4), ends with Mattathias and Jael (6:12), and includes thirty-four biblical characters from at least fifteen books including 1 Maccabees. Prayers 7 and 12 likewise draw on biblical history in order to make their main point, and are worth considering a little more fully.

Prayer 7 (*Apos. Con.* 7.38.1–8) is a prayer of thanks to God in the form of a hymn of praise. Like the typical hymn of praise in the second person, it begins, "We give thanks to you for all things, O Master Almighty." The opening is followed by justification for the thanksgiving: "because you have not forsaken us with your mercies and compassions; but generation after generation you save, rescue, lay hold of, (and) shelter" (7:2). The psalmist thanks God for his work of saving, rescuing, laying hold of, and sheltering his people in all generations, and thus sets the stage for a review of history. Examples are given from history beginning with Enos and

---

[42] Trans. of *Apos. Con.* 7.33.4 taken from van der Horst and Newman, *Early Jewish Prayers in Greek*, 46.

[43] These are in some ways reminiscent of what one finds in Wis 7 and 9. Prayer 4 is notable with its praise by negation (4:29–37, 42–43). Prayer 9:1–8 lists many positive and negative traits as well, emphasizing God as the one and only. Cf. 13:1–13.

[44] This is particularly the case in prayers 2, 3, 5, 6, 7, 9, and 12. Prayer 2 begins its review of history with Abraham (2:14–16), discusses Isaac (2:17–18) and Jacob (2:19–20), and ends with Moses (2:21–22). Prayer 3 reviews the creation of the world (3:1–17), the creation of man (3:18–21), and, after further praise of God's continuing work in nature (3:22–23), concludes with reflections on the fall of man and the death that resulted (3:24–27). It begins, "Blessed are you, O Lord, King of the ages, who made everything, and in the beginning ordered that which was unprepared." In the final Christianized version one can note the interpolations of "through Christ" and "through him"; see discussion in *OTP* 2:678–679. Prayer 5 begins with creation and advances to the deliverance from Egypt. Both historical events are discussed with reference to their providing the justification for Sabbaths (5:18–19). Prayer 9:10–16 describes the provision of specific priests throughout history.

Enoch and progressing through to "the days of Judah Maccabeus and his brothers" (7:3). Among the later Christian additions (in lines 4, 7, 14, 15, and 18) is the mention of Jesus Christ in this review of historical eras in which God laid hold of his people (v. 4).[45] In this regard we can see an instance where the history of God's work among his people is remembered in similar but also strikingly different ways by Jewish and Christian groups.

After the review of these historical figures, the psalmist returns to reflections on the appropriateness of giving thanks to God. The author notes that God himself gave man his voice along with every other bodily ability (7:7–8), and that God teaches man in this life and promises resurrection in the next (7:9–11). Because of all these things, even eternity is not sufficient to give thanks to God (7:12). The psalmist comes close to offering an exhortation to the audience as he notes: "To do so worthily would be impossible, but (to do so) according to (our) ability is holy" (7:13). Thus, in the course of thanking God for these many blessings, the psalmist teaches the hearer/reader the vital importance of thanksgiving in the life of the faithful.

Prayer 12 (*Apos. Con.* 8.12.6–27), the longest of the prayers, combines the features of most of the prayers noted above. In the form of a hymn, it begins, "It is truly worthy and right before all things to sing a hymn to you" (12:1). The opening sections give titles, deeds, and attributes of God, then move on to God's creation of all things including spiritual beings (12:14) and all that is seen (12:15–34). The creation of man is described in 12:35–40. An extended review of history beginning in Eden and ending with the entry into the promised land under the leadership of Joshua occurs in 12:41–79. The final section of the prayer begins with an ascription of glory: "Glory is yours, because of all these things, O Master Almighty!" (12:80). This acclamation is followed by a brief description of heavenly worship by innumerable armies of angels leading to the recitation of the *kedushah* of Isa 6:3 together (12:81–85).[46] The style and contents of this hymn suggest that it would certainly have enjoyed circulation and use in a liturgical format. For example, v. 84 interrupts the description of heavenly worship and enjoins, "And all the people together, let them say." Further, the whole prayer is framed as a hymn sung to God (v. 1). In other words, it

---

[45] Here van der Horst and Newman suggest the compiler took an early Jewish hymn addressed directly to God ("you delivered us, etc.") and revised it to focus on Jesus ("he delivered us, etc."); van der Horst and Newman, *Early Jewish Prayers in Greek*, 89–90.

[46] On the significance of the inclusion of the *kedushah* here see Judith H. Newman, "Holy, Holy, Holy: The Use of Isaiah 6.3 in *Apostolic Constitutions* 7.35.1–10 and 8.12.6–27," in *Of Scribes and Sages: Early Jewish Interpretation and Transmission of Scripture* (ed. Craig A. Evans; 2 vols.; London: T & T Clark, 2004), 2:123–134.

is a hymn which has as one of its primary goals the singing of praise to God for all of his deeds. However, another primary goal is surely to instruct the worshipper. The didactic component is seen as this prayer offers a grand vision of reality, tapping into multiple temporal and spatial registers (note the heavenly worship), reinforcing for the worshipper a particular way of understanding God's work in history and his relationship with his people. This composition embodies didactic hymnody in the way it draws on the lessons and content of Jewish theological reflection as the reason for the praise it calls forth from the assembly.

As they communicate praise and prayer to God, the *Hellenistic Synagogal Prayers*, like the *Psalms of Solomon*, teach some very clear and pointed lessons to the present generation: God is the only true God, the creator, the sustainer and rescuer of his people throughout history. He is the source of knowledge and wisdom and the giver of the natural and the written Law (cf. 7:10; 11:3; 12:69). He is also the source of eternal life and the resurrection (cf. 3:24–27; 7:11). Unlike the *Psalms of Solomon*, however, there are more indications in the *Hellenistic Synagogal Prayers* of their actual liturgical use. Further, these synagogue prayers do not give the sense that they are written in a time of crisis. Emphasis on the saving and rescuing power of God does suggest that the community encounters difficulties of many kinds and needs reminding of God's ability to save. But without the pointed historical references to specific enemies, attacks, or invasions, these prayers and psalms carry more of a timeless feel.

One shared feature of the two collections discussed in this section is the prominent use of historical examples as a focal point for both praise of God and instruction in his ways. The scope of these examples varied by collection, presumably based on the emphasis of the author or authors. *Psalms of Solomon* showed a historical interest focused primarily on the monarchy, the exile, and Pompey's taking of Jerusalem either as examples from the past or as current or recent events requiring theological reflection and discussion. As we noted, the fruit of this kind of reflection was the assurance that God would soon judge the unrighteous rulers who were over his people (as he had always done), and that he would do this through the coming Messiah. The *Hellenistic Synagogal Prayers* offered more sweeping views of history from creation through the Maccabean period, highlighting key figures along the way and emphasizing God's active, saving role in the lives of his people throughout history.

The particular historical focus of a given work reflects the little that we do know about the social setting of each of these collections. The *Psalms of Solomon* are most obvious in that as 'crisis literature' they address historical precedents and causes for the very real and very current crisis that the community was facing. The *Hellenistic Synagogal Prayers*, with their broader focus on history from creation through the Maccabean period along with their use of some philosophical ideas, reflect quite clearly the concerns of diaspora Jews, in contrast to those remaining in Palestine. The Greek-speaking diaspora communities, rather than needing to reflect on the status of Jerusalem or the temple, needed to remain connected to their historical roots. God had worked powerfully and mightily in the lives of their ancestors; the Jews of the diaspora needed to maintain a sense of personal connection with these ancient events and with the God who had acted in them. The medium of psalms, hymns, and prayers provided a convenient, memorable, and powerful way to rehearse these historical deeds, as well as to teach fundamental truths of Jewish theology.

C. Didactic Hymns in Wisdom Writings

The Jewish wisdom tradition was alive and well in the Second Temple period.[47] The two best known wisdom writings of this period, the Wisdom of Solomon, and the Wisdom of Jesus Ben Sira, both contain unique examples of hymnic forms that were used for didactic purposes. In some respects these hymnic passages reflect themes similar to those we observed in the *Psalms of Solomon* and the *Hellenistic Synagogal Prayers*. However, because of their particular interests and the needs of their communities, together with their presence in Wisdom writings, they also have some unique features. In the following sections we will examine one particular didactic hymn in the Wisdom of Solomon (an ode to Wisdom's saving role in history in Wis 10) as well as three didactic hymns in the Wisdom of Ben Sira (24:1–22; 39:12–35; 44:1–50:24).

1. Wisdom of Solomon

Wisdom of Solomon is a *logos protreptikos*, a form of philosophical hortatory discourse, written in Alexndria in the first century BCE or first century CE. The book is notoriously difficult to date since there are no direct references to the actual author, the intended audience, or to precise historical events in the time period of composition. This feature appears to have been one part of the rhetorical strategy of the author. Nevertheless, scholars have been able to identify possible allusions to historical events, and

---

[47] For an introduction to the literature connected with this tradition see John Joseph Collins, *Jewish Wisdom in the Hellenistic Age* (OTL; Louisville, Ky.: Westminster John Knox, 1997); Leo G. Perdue, *The Sword and the Stylus: An Introduction to Wisdom in the Age of Empires* (Grand Rapids: Eerdmans, 2008).

several theories for the date have been defended.[48] To the extent that one can identify a more specific social setting, it is possible to read certain passages as directly addressing precise historical events within Alexandria. Even apart from being able to identify a specific time period, it is clear that the work as a whole is aimed to encourage a Hellenistic Jewish readership to maintain their loyalty to the God of Israel in spite of opposition they are facing within the larger non-Jewish society.

As a *logos protreptikos*, Wisdom of Solomon aims to encourage its readers to adopt a particular approach to life. As with other instances of this genre, it can employ a number of other kinds of genres to make its case both for the benefits of the way of life it is promoting, as well as of the negative features of competing philosophical approaches. As Hübner points out, in terms of the ancient rhetorical categories for speeches (judicial, deliberative, and epideictic), a *logos protreptikos* is a written composition that employs all three kinds of rhetoric. It does not represent one specific rhetorical genre.[49]

Though there is some disagreement among scholars as to exactly where one section ends and begins, there is general agreement that Wisdom of Solomon exhibits a three-fold structure. The first section concerns Wisdom's gift of immortality (1:1–6:21). The second discusses Wisdom's nature and source (6:22–11:1). The third considers God's work in Israel's history in the exodus (11:2–19:22). As part of the unfolding of this didactic exhortation, the author employs what many scholars have referred to as a hymn or "Ode to Wisdom's Saving Role in History" in Wis 10.[50] In the context of this instructional composition, this hymnic passage plays a pivotal role, and is a fascinating example of didactic hymnody as defined in this larger study.

Wisdom of Solomon 10 is marked by many traits that show a connection with Hellenistic hymnic conventions. In particular, the passage shows marked similarities with praises of Isis.[51] While not all scholars agree on

---

[48] Hans Hübner, *Die Weisheit Salomons* (ATDA 4; Göttingen: Vandenhoeck & Ruprecht, 1999), 14–19; David Winston, *The Wisdom of Solomon: A New Translation with Introduction and Commentary* (AB 43; Garden City, N.Y.: Doubleday and Company, 1979), 20–23. On the broader cultural and historical context see Perdue, *The Sword and the Stylus*, 292–355.

[49] Hübner, *Die Weisheit Salomons*, 26–27.

[50] Winston, *Wisdom of Solomon*, 210.

[51] For features and examples of Isis hymns, see for example Vera Frederika Vanderlip, *The Four Greek Hymns of Isidorus and the Cult of Isis* (ASP 12; Toronto: A. M. Hakkert, 1972). Reese suggested that Wis 10 was part of a larger section that imitated Isis aretalogies in terms of form and contents. James M. Reese, *Hellenistic Influence on the Book of Wisdom and Its Consequences* (Analecta Biblica, 41; Rome: Biblical Institute Press, 1970), 43–50.

the precise nature of these associations, Kloppenborg has shown that there is a pattern of attributes in Wis 10 that resonates with the major patterns of the theology of Hellenistic Isis who is savior of all.[52] These include:

Emphasis on saving power (Wis 10:1, 4, 5, 6, 9, 12, 13, 15; P.Oxy. 1380 lines 20, 55, 70, 92; Maroneia Inscription [M] 11; Isidorus [Inscription from Medinet Madi] 1.26–34)

Piloting the ark (Wis 10:4; P.Oxy. 1380 lines 15, 61, 69, 74, 187–188; M 15; Isidorus 1.32–34)

Guiding the righteous (Wis 10:10, 17; P.Oxy 1380 lines 121–122; Isis is *epitropon kai odegon*; compare to the verb in Wis 10:10 and 17)

Causing increase or decrease (Wis 10:10 in contrast with 10:7; P.Oxy. 1380 lines 174–177, 194–195; M 7; Isidorus 2.15–19; 3.14–15; cf. Isis the "fruitbringer" in *SIRIS* 379)

Giving wealth (Wis 10:11; Isidorus 1.1; 2.5–6; 3.3–6)

Giving victory in contests (Wis 10:12; P.Oxy. 1380 line 78)

Releasing a captive from prison and causing justice to be done (Wis 10:13–14; M 34–38, 48; Isidorus 1.29, 34)

Giving glory (Wis 10:14; M 40)

Giving strength to rule and providing a scepter (Wis 10:2, 14; P.Oxy. 1380 lines 121, 265–266)

Providing the light of stars (Wis 10:17; P.Oxy. 159–160, 248–249; M 13; Isidorus 2.11)

Engendering joy and praise for benefactions (Wis 10:20–21; P.Oxy. 1380 lines 162–163; M 4–5; Isidorus 2.24–28)

Further, one can observe in at least one Isis inscription a stylistic commonality: the use of anaphora, in this case the repetition of αὕτη.[53]

Of all of these elements, the overall emphasis on Sophia as a savior provides the strongest connection to the claims made by and for Isis. Secondarily, some of the ways that Sophia has demonstrated her saving role in the lives of the righteous show some degree of interaction with Isis traditions.[54]

---

[52] John S. Kloppenborg, "Isis and Sophia in the Book of Wisdom," *HTR* 75 (1982): 57–84, here 67–72. I agree with Kloppenborg that Reese's comparisons are forced on the one hand, and also do not take into account the fact that Wis 10 is its own literary unit and not part of a larger aretalogy.

[53] While in Wis 10 it occurs 6 times, in one Isis inscription it appears 3 times in a row. "She with Hermes discovered writing; and of this writing some was sacred for initiates, some was publicly available for all. She instituted justice, that each of us might know how to live on equal terms, just as, because of our nature, death makes us equal. She instituted the non-Greek language for some, Greek language for others, in order that the race might be differentiated not only as between men and women, but also between all peoples," (G. H. R. Horsley, "A Personalized Aretalogy of Isis," *NewDocs* 6 [1981]: 10–23, here 11). It also appears as a feature in Kore Kosmou; cf. Reese, *Hellenistic Influence*, 48.

[54] The connections are strong enough so that Winston can claim "the author of Wisd skillfully adapted the Isis aretalogies for his own use in describing Sophia" (37). And also that "It was only fitting that the author of Wisd reclaim the falsely appropriated *aretai* for 'Her' to whom they truly belonged" (Winston, *Wisdom of Solomon*, 38).

However, even if parallels can be identified for each section, or many sections of Wis 10, one could argue that this is still not determinative of influence from Isis, as much as that both traditions utilize shared imagery and forms of expression. For example, consider the imagery of making Jacob fruitful in Wis 10:10. Isis is hailed occasionally as fruitbringer and also claims that she made the earth produce food (cf. line 36 of the Maroneia inscription). Pseudo-Solomon and the authors of the aretalogies are dealing with similar phenomena in similar ways. Pseudo-Solomon is not necessarily imitating Isis aretalogies here, as much as using common terminology to express related concepts about what a divine being has accomplished.

Further, most Isis aretalogies, though not all, were composed in the first person. To more powerfully imitate and re-appropriate for Sophia the claims of Isis, one might expect a first person discourse by Sophia. Given the precedent in Prov 8, it is perhaps surprising that we do not find one here in Wis 10.

These considerations suggest that praises of Isis are not necessarily the only influence, or even the primary influence, on Wis 10. Among Greek compositions the passage connects just as strongly with Hellenistic hymnic traditions in general. For example, the use of the emphatic pronoun αὕτη which occurs in Wis 10 and at least one aretalogie is "one form of the encomium to the gods in Greek literature" as Norden has shown.[55]

Beyond matters of style, one can observe the expectations for the contents of hymns as reflected in the rhetorical handbooks. For example, Quinitilian says, "With gods, in general, the first thing will be to show veneration of the majesty of their nature; next to expound the power of each and discoveries of his which have benefited humanity. . . . Next we must mention any exploits of theirs known to history."[56] Other rhetorical handbooks and progymnasmata reflect similar understandings that the nature of the deity, her powers, and her deeds in history are crucial components of a hymn.[57]

When one looks beyond the rhetorical theorists to actual examples of ancient hymns, it could be argued that Wis 10 is more like the Homeric Hymns in some regards. In particular, in comparison with cultic hymns,

---

[55] Ibid., 212. See Eduard Norden, *Agnostos Theos: Untersuchungen zur Formengeschichte religiöser Rede* (Stuttgart: B.G. Teubner, 1956), 163–165, 223–224.

[56] Quintilian, *The Orator's Education* (trans. D. A. Russell; LCL 124–127, 494; Cambridge, Mass.: Harvard University Press, 2001), 3.7.7–9.

[57] Aelius Theon writes, "Encomion is language revealing the greatness of virtuous actions and other good qualities belonging to a particular person. The term is now specifically applied to praise of living persons whereas praise of the dead is called an epitaphios and praise of the gods a hymn; but whether one praises the living or the dead or heroes or gods, the method of speaking is one and the same" (trans. Kennedy, *Progymnasmata*, 50).

the Homeric hymns are somewhat less personal in that they intend to sing about the god, are often in the third person, and are not as concerned with making a request as they are with detailing the god's attributes and achievements. The recitation of the saving and rescuing deeds of Sophia on behalf of the righteous connects to a large extent with this kind of hymnic tradition in general.

In addition to connections with Hellenistic hymns, one can observe some degree of commonality with Greek prose writings that use a series of examples to illustrate a point. Schmitt cites examples of Greek literature in which authors provide reviews of history and argues that these compositions served as models for the author of Wisdom of Solomon.[58] However, most of these prose examples reveal little about the origin of Wis 10. Rather, these help us appreciate the way in which such a series of examples from history (positive and negative) would be understood. They also demonstrate a literary precedent for using examples as proof of some kind in a larger composition.

Aristotle discusses the appropriate use of historical examples in constructing speeches. He points out that if the actions are well-known they do not need to be described in detail.[59] In deliberative speeches he explains that narrative is not common, "because no one narrates future events. But if there is narrative, it is of events in the past, in order that being reminded of those things the audience will take better counsel about what is to come (either criticizing or praising)" (3.16.11). Further, as far as placement of examples in a speech he suggests, "When the paradigms are put at the end they become witnesses, and a witness is everywhere persuasive" (2.20.9).

These comments and comparisons regarding the contents and style of Wis 10 suggest that this passage participates in hymnic and rhetorical conventions that were prevalent in the Hellenistic world. The literary context of this passage makes it clear that these conventional styles are deployed for didactic purposes.

In addition to parallels with Hellenistic writings and praise techniques it can also be argued that Wis 10 connects on a number of levels with tradi-

---

[58] Von Armin Schmitt, "Struktur, Herkunft und Bedeutung der Beispielreihe in Weish 10," *BZ* 21 (1977): 1–22, esp. 13–20. Schmitt cites: Lysias in his Oration 19, "On the Property of Aristophanes" (see lines 45–49); Isocrates *Antidosis* (231–235); *Iliad* 5.381–402; *Odyssey* 5.118–120, 121–129; Pindar, *Nem.* 10.1–3, 4–18. Schmitt (19–20) also cites examples of characterizing (for example, the characters of Theophrastus) and syncrisis (in Plutarch and in Pindar's *Pythian Odes* 1.94–98; 2.15–17 and 21–24). See also Winston who suggests that chapter 10 (and 4:10 as well) reflects the "evocation of mythological heroes or wise men" which is one diatribal feature among many found in Wis (Winston, *Wisdom of Solomon*, 20).

[59] In an epideictic speech: "Well known actions should only be recalled [not described in detail]" (*Rhet.* 3.16.2).

tions of didactic hymns represented in the Hebrew Bible and Septuagint. Though verbal parallels and allusions to specific verses have been suggested, it is much more significant to note the overall similarity to patterns found within certain Psalms, specifically those Psalms which provide a review of history in order to make their point.[60]

Among the so-called historical psalms, Psalm 105 provides the closest connection on several levels.[61] First, as a whole Ps 105 has a similar thematic emphasis/purpose.[62] In both Ps 105 and Wis 10 the emphasis is not so much on the successes or failures of God's people as it is on the faithfulness of God to his people. Second, there is a significant degree of overlap in terms of content (at least in terms of Abraham, Joseph, Moses and Israel in Egypt and the exodus).[63] Third, two specific verses in Wis 10 reflect a knowledge of traditions in the LXX of Ps 105 which are not found in Exodus.[64] In other words, Ps-Solomon reads Exodus in light of Ps 105 LXX in at least two places. These points make a strong case that at least one historical Psalm, Ps 105, was influential in Ps-Solomon's description of Wisdom's saving role in history in Wis 10.[65]

---

[60] Skehan observes connections with specific Psalms but this does not indicate influence on the whole composition, as much as in individual verses. See Patrick W. Skehan, "Borrowings from the Psalms in the Book of Wisdom," *CBQ* 10 (1948): 384–97.

[61] Schmitt discusses Pss 78, 106, and 136 and concludes that while there is great thematic affinity between these historical Psalms and Wis 10, these psalms do not provide the structural model on which Wis 10 is based. Surprisingly, though he mentions Ps 105 in a footnote, he does not discuss it. Nor does he explore any of these Psalms in Greek in order to see just how close the connections are. Schmitt, "Struktur, Herkunft und Bedeutung der Beispielreihe in Weish 10."

[62] Compare Ps 105:8 and Wis 10:9; cf. also Wis 9:18 and 11:1.

[63] But to be fair, Psalm 105 does not include Adam, Cain, Noah, Lot, or Jacob.

[64] In at least two places the traditions in Ps 105 (104) come into play: "kings" in 16:b and the cloud as a shelter in 17c. Peter Enns, *Exodus Retold: Ancient Exegesis of the Departure from Egypt in Wisdom 10:15–21 and 19:1–9* (Atlanta: Scholar's Press, 1997), 52, 59.

[65] Overall however, Ps. Solomon does not seem to be expressly copying or emulating Ps 105. When he discusses similar events he often seems to use different terminology. For example, in the Joseph story: no verbal connections with Ps 105:16–22; in v. 21 he becomes lord and ruler; in Wis 10:14 he receives the scepter of a kingdom and authority over his masters. The same idea is expressed with completely different terminology. Enemies are called *ekthrous* (104:24) in 104 but in the parallel place in Wis 10 they are *thlibontas* (10:15). Enemies are also mentioned in Wis 10:12, 19. Moses is described differently as a servant of the Lord in both writings (*ton doulon autou*, Ps 104:26 but *therapontos kuriou* in Wis 10:16). Only in discussing the signs and wonders that Moses performed in Egypt do the authors use the same terms (Ps 104:27; Wis 10:16). The other psalms which review history for didactic purposes show even greater shades of difference from Wis 10 in terms of their tone, emphasis, and coverage of history. For example, Pss 78 and 106 emphasize the failures of the people of God in spite of God's actions in history. They demonstrate fewer thematic or verbal parallels as well.

At the level of the retelling of each specific incident in Wis 10's review of history, it is possible to argue that a connection with Isis traditions, Hellenistic writings, or earlier Jewish traditions is more or less likely. Regardless of the influences on each specific line, the overall framework and the way the individual pieces are brought together suggest a connection with both the tradition of the historical psalms, and the recitation of the deeds of Greek gods found in Hellenistic hymns, as represented by the Isis aretalogies.[66] From both a Greco-Roman and Jewish perspective, then, this passage can be viewed as a didactic hymn.

Given that this passage fits a broad understanding of didactic hymnody, what are its instructional aims and how are they achieved? The primary subject is Wisdom. The individual heroes are examples but not the primary focus, as their anonymity suggests. Wisdom of Solomon 10:9 provides the summary: "But Wisdom rescued from distresses those who attended upon her." The passage is thus an *explicit* call to appreciate the saving power of Wisdom (6:22, 23, 25) and also an *implicit* call to be counted among the righteous who experience the benefits of Wisdom. It is thus not only about Wisdom or only about the righteous; it is about both Wisdom and the righteous and the life-giving relationship between the two.

The instructional aim is achieved in an interesting fashion. Surprisingly, it is not done through allegory. Nor is it accomplished through direct instruction. Rather the didactic aim is achieved through a compilation of well-known examples from history interpreted anew and expressed in hymnic style.[67] While the interpretation of authoritative texts was an important aspect of Hellenistic philosophy, Wis 10 is more about framing Israelite history in light of Wisdom's saving work than it is about exegeting texts. While both exegesis and reframing history are on the table, it appears to me that exegesis is employed in service of the primary function of retelling and reframing history for the present day.

---

[66] This passage lacks the opening call to praise or closing request typical of most ancient hymns. In this regard, it is somewhat less than a hymn or psalm. However, in light of its contents expressed in hymnic style and brought to bear for a larger didactic purpose, it is also more than a hymn: it is a didactic hymn.

[67] This observation corresponds to some extent with the observation of Enns. He claims that Wis as a whole represents a change in the sage's 'job description': no longer simply gaining wisdom from observing creation, but also looking to history and exegeting Scripture to apply lessons to people who were struggling and looking to God for answers in hard times (Enns, *Exodus Retold*, 215). In another context David Aune has noted that exegesis of authoritative texts was an important feature of Hellenistic school activity; in fact, a related phenomenon occurs in Romans 9–11 which some would accept is part of a larger *logos protreptikos* which gives order and meaning to the book of Romans as a whole (David E. Aune, "Romans as a Logos Protreptikos," in *The Romans Debate* [ed. Karl P. Donfried; rev. and expanded ed.; Peabody, Mass.: Hendrickson, 1991], 278–296).

Additionally, the choice of a hymnic style itself communicates something. One fourth-century BCE rhetorician wrote, "If you wish to write a pleasing speech, be careful as far as possible to adapt the character of your speech to that of your public."[68] We can deduce from Ps-Solomon's choice of contents and style that his public was well aware of both Greek and Jewish religious and philosophical concepts and terminology. They knew what kinds of entities typically received this kind of praise. To praise Wisdom in this way, by a recitation of her deeds, would presumably have had a powerful impact on such an audience.[69]

We noted above that although scholars agree on a threefold division of Wisdom of Solomon, the precise section divisions are debated. In terms of the overall composition of Wisdom of Solomon as a whole, this study supports the view that sees Wis 10 as the culmination of the second main part of the work. In this regard, one can note Aristotle's suggestion about the power of examples to serve as witnesses: "When the paradigms are put at the end they become witnesses, and a witness is everywhere persuasive" (*Rhet.* 2.20.9). As a conclusion to this portion of the book, the examples from history in hymnic style serve two purposes. First, they illustrate the claims made previously (particularly in 9:18). Second, they demonstrate from history the truth of these claims.

2. The Wisdom of Ben Sira

The Wisdom of Ben Sira provides the teaching of a Jerusalem sage, Joshua Ben Eleazar Ben Sira, from the early part of the second century BCE.[70] This work provides an extensive range of examples of didactic poetry and didactic hymns. Hymns of praise and thanksgiving are found throughout Ben Sira. Mowinckel observes, "In addition to the actual 'words of wisdom,' and exhortative and didactic poems on the pattern of 'wisdom', Sirach also composed psalms in the traditional psalm style, but with recognizable elements taken from the ideas and forms of 'wisdom'."[71] These psalm-like passages include hymns in praise of God (1:1–10; 18:1–7; 39:12–35; 42:15–43:33; 50:22–24; 51:1–12), in praise of Wisdom (24:1–33), and in praise of virtuous leaders (44:1–50:24).[72] The number of hymns

---

[68] *Rhetorica ad Alexandrum*, 1434 b 28–30 (trans. H. Rackham; LCL).

[69] In a similar vein we noted in chapter 3 that Lucretius's use of hymns in *On the Nature of the Universe* put hymnody in service of protreptic discourse.

[70] Nickelsburg, *Jewish Literature*, 53. The work can be dated more precisely between 196 and 175 BCE (Ibid., 62–63). On the background and contents of this work in its cultural context see Perdue, *The Sword and the Stylus*, 256–290.

[71] Mowinckel, *Psalms in Israel's Worship*, 116.

[72] Patrick W. Skehan and Alexander A. Di Lella, *The Wisdom of Ben Sira: A New Translation with Notes and Commentary* (AB 39; New York: Doubleday, 1987), 27–28.

and the variety of forms make Ben Sira a fascinating source for studying the use and function of didactic hymnody in Second Temple Judaism.

As Wisdom literature, the book as a whole is a collection of wise sayings, hymnic reflections, and wisdom poetry. The primary literary genres are: *mashal*, hymn of praise, prayer of petition, autobiographical narrative, lists or onomastica, and didactic narrative.[73] Skehan and Di Lella explain, "In composing his book, he simply employed the forms of expression and literary styles he found ready-made in the Scriptures, especially the Wisdom literature, of which Proverbs was his overwhelming favorite."[74] Further, though biblical literature was his primary source, Ben Sira also notably employs non-Jewish writings in his overall attempt to "inspire the Jews of his day to remain faithful to their heritage and to resist the blandishments of Hellenistic culture and religion."[75]

The aim of the book as a whole is clear. Ben Sira's grandson explains its purpose in the prologue: "By becoming familiar also with this book those who love learning might make even greater progress in living according to the law."[76] The book also opens with the implied exhortation to fear the Lord. Fear of the Lord is mentioned ten times in 1:11–30, though not as an imperative. It is closely associated with wisdom, blessing, glory, joy, and gladness, so that from the very beginning of the book the reader is offered a vision of reality in which the fear of the Lord (understood as keeping his commandments; vv. 26–27) is held up as the centerpiece of a good life.

Because Ben Sira makes liberal use of psalm-like and hymn-like passages in his quest to help students progress in living according to the law, a comprehensive study of these is not possible in this context. This section will look at three very different passages in Ben Sira to explore the ways that this particular author teaches foundational lessons in hymnic style. The first is Wisdom's hymn of self-praise in 24:1–22. The second, 39:12–35, is the passage in Ben Sira that looks most like a classical hymn of praise. The third passage is 44:1–50:24, a "Hymn in Honor of Our Ancestors." In each of these, though the form is that of hymnic praise, the didactic function is primary. We will observe that Ben Sira makes creative use of hymnic praise in a range of styles to teach his audience important lessons about wisdom, Torah, the world, and God's work in history.

---

[73] Ibid., 21.
[74] Ibid.
[75] Ibid., 50.
[76] English translations of Ben Sira are from the NRSV.

2.1. Sirach 24:1–22

In chapter 24 Wisdom praises herself in first person style reminiscent of
Prov 8. Skehan and Di Lella claim, "In this chapter, the most famous part
of the whole book, Ben Sira is at his best in displaying his poetic skills."[77]
The passage opens with allusions to Prov 8:6–8 with the declaration that
"Wisdom praises herself, and tells of her glory in the midst of her people.
In the assembly of the Most High she opens her mouth, and in the presence
of his hosts she tells of her glory" (vv. 1–2). Clearly a setting in the presence of God is envisioned and the verbs are those of praise and worship.
She tells of her origins (vv. 3–7), her dwelling among the people of God
(vv. 8–12), her growth (vv. 13–17), and her benefits (vv. 19–22). The temporal registers of Wisdom's self-praise range from the mythic past of pre-
creation, to the distant past of her taking up residence in Jerusalem, to her
call to people in the present day to come to her for a banquet. In a similar
way, the spatial registers of the hymn are multiple as Wisdom speaks of
herself in the presence of God, the highest heavens, the abyss, the sea, and
the earth. She also makes specific references to Zion, Jerusalem, Lebanon,
Hermon, En-Gedi, and Jericho. Through the use of multiple temporal and
spatial registers, this passage creates the impression of offering a sweeping
vision of a world in which God's timeless Wisdom is incomparable and is
to be found in Jerusalem among the people of Israel.

In terms of the audience, this passage does contain explicit address to
the audience through the use of an imperative. Wisdom calls out, "Come to
me, you who desire me, and eat your fill of my fruits" (v. 19). The poem
thus functions as a call to recognize the value of Wisdom and respond. The
passage closes with the claim, "Whoever obeys me will not be put to
shame, and those who work with me will not sin" (v. 22). This kind of final statement is an implied exhortation to obey Wisdom and work with her,
which is the thrust of the entire passage. It is noteworthy here that the first
verse that follows this hymn provides some interpretation which is not
found in the hymn itself: "All this is the book of the covenant of the Most
High God, the law that Moses commanded us as an inheritance for the
congregations of Jacob" (v. 23). Here Ben Sira makes explicit what he
suggested in the first chapter: that keeping the commandments is wisdom
(1:26). Later in this chapter we will see that other didactic hymns of the
Second Temple period make a similar identification of Torah and wisdom
(cf. Bar 4:1; *2 Bar.* 48:24).

---

[77] Skehan and Di Lella, *Wisdom of Ben Sira*, 331.

2.2. Sirach 39:12–35

Sirach 39:12–35 is the passage in this work that comes closest to an actual hymn in that it opens with a hymnic call to praise (vv. 12–15) and closes with an imperative as well (v. 35). Skehan and Di Lella explain, "Its theme is the goodness and purposefulness of creation and divine providence, which are manifest to the wise, who are invited to sing the praises of the Creator."[78] The call to praise is much more embellished and more artistic than the biblical models. Ben Sira begins with poetic imagery to indicate that what he has to say will cause his listeners to "blossom like a rose growing by a stream of water" (v. 13). He ultimately leads to his call to praise which is more reflective of the traditional psalm style:

Sing a hymn of praise; bless the Lord for all his works.
Ascribe majesty to his name and give thanks to him with praise, with songs on your lips, and with harps. (vv. 14b–15b)

Ben Sira makes an interesting addition, however, in that he prescribes what they ought to say: "This is what you shall say in thanksgiving" (v. 15c). The text that follows is the "body" of the hymn which reflects on the goodness of all the works of the Lord in creation. This body of the hymn is an extended meditation on the thesis of v. 16 that "all the works of the Lord are very good." Through a series of examples in creation and among humans – examples which tap into a variety of temporal and spatial registers – Ben Sira affirms the goodness of God (cf. vv. 25, 27, 33, 34). The psalm closes with another imperative: "So now sing praise with all your heart and voice, and bless the name of the Lord" (v. 35).

As the most clearly hymn-like passage in Ben Sira, this text raises the question as to the primary function of this passage. Was this first and foremost a hymn composed to be used in a worship service, whose teaching function was only secondary? Or was this hymn composed in order to teach, and only delivered in the form of a hymn for rhetorical impact? These questions prompt us to revisit the definition of a didactic hymn and reconsider the distinctions that we are making in this study. While we recognize that all hymns convey a degree of teaching in some form (either by their content or as they model "good" praise for their audience), we are specifically interested in hymns that indicate that their didactic purpose is a primary purpose. In this case, it can be argued that this passage has instruction as a primary purpose both by its contents (it teaches some very explicit lessons about God and his ways in the world) and by its context (it is found within a larger work which is explicitly instructional in nature). These observations do not exclude the possibility that this psalm might also have been chanted in worship of God in some communal context. But as

---

[78] Ibid., 458.

we have the text preserved for us, we consider it to have a sufficiently strong didactic focus that it can be considered a didactic hymn.

In support of this approach, Liesen argues that the wisdom elements in this passage are primary, and that the hymnic form of the passage is simply the means that Ben Sira has chosen to convey his teaching. He explains,

> It seems best then to assume that 39, 12–35 as a whole has the literary form of a wisdom instruction. This didactic text contains (in 39,16–31) a wisdom poem (Lehrgedicht) that through a frame (in 39, 12–15; 32–35) has been consciously presented as a hymn, so that one could perhaps speak of a *hymnic wisdom poem*, or a *didactic hymn*.[79]

In other words, the substance of the passage is a wisdom poem, and only the opening and closing elements are hymnic. Similarly, Skehan and Di Lella summarize their view of the content and purpose of the hymn as essentially in line with the wisdom tradition: "This long poem has as its deep intent to provide a theodicy, and so can be compared to the books of Job and Qoheleth."[80] Yet, the choice of a hymnic frame for this passage is not without consequences, and in this particular instance suggests that there is a further purpose. Liesen has identified both an explicit and an implicit purpose. This is particularly the case with the invitation to praise in 39:12–15. The explicit purpose is praise of God's name, while the implicit purpose, discerned in the imagery and context of the invitation, is to increase the wisdom of Ben Sira's disciples.[81]

In this particular instance praise itself is connected with true wisdom. It is not only that the content of the hymn is the content of wisdom. Rather, the relationship of individuals with God that would lead to praise is a fundamental condition for the increase of wisdom in a person's life. As Liesen explains,

> The educational strategy of Ben Sira in 39,12–35 consists in presenting his wisdom not only as a reflection on the nature of God's work, but as a *practice of praise*. By enfolding his reflection about the goodness of God's work in an actual praise of God, Ben Sira draws his disciples into a relationship with God, which is the condition for true wisdom (1,1–10.14–20; 19,20.22).[82]

So Ben Sira teaches about the work of God, but also models the proper response of the individual to gaining this insight. The didactic impact of this hymn comes through in its content as well as its form.

---

[79] Liesen, *Full of Praise*, 39.
[80] Skehan and Di Lella, *Wisdom of Ben Sira*, 461.
[81] Liesen, *Full of Praise*, 189.
[82] Ibid., 281.

2.3. Sirach 44:1–50:24

Ben Sira 44:1–50:24 offers an extensive hymnic review of history.[83] This hymnic review of history opens with what could itself be considered a hymnic prologue (44:1–15). The historical review then begins with Enoch (44:16), Noah (44:17–18), and Abraham (44:19–23), and continues all the way through to Simon the high priest (50:1–21). The encomium closes with a call to bless the God of all (50:22–24). The form of 50:22–24 is itself hymn-like with a call to praise, a list of God's deeds (he works wonders, he fosters growth, he shows mercy), and a closing request (50:23–24). The closing request serves to link this closing section to the rest of the hymn of praise asking for "peace in our days in Israel, as in the days of old" (50:23).

According to Mack, Ben Sira's encomium must be understood in light of the wisdom myth. Ben Sira's encomium, like Wis 10, represents a scholarly and literary response to social crises which threaten conventional wisdom.[84] Mack argues that in both cases "a wisdom mode of reading the Pentateuch as a primal and archetypal history has enabled the modeling."[85] Such a reading and re-telling of archetypal history served to reaffirm and encourage the faith of their contemporary Jewish readers. Skehan and Dilella explain, "This portrait gallery drawn from Israel's sacred history is meant to reinforce the conviction and courage of Ben Sira's contemporaries"[86] Both texts thus represent a similar mode of reading history and a similar overall goal of presenting traditional Jewish belief in light of their current cultural moment.

However, in spite of those major similarities the focus was somewhat different in Wis 10 than in Sir 44–50. Skehan and Dilella note, "In these chapters Ben Sira emphasizes God's gracious call and election of Israel and the divine covenant with Abraham and his descendants."[87] While Ben Sira's encomium emphasized God's faithfulness to his covenant through exemplary leaders, in Wis 10 it was Sophia's rescuing power for the righteous and not the covenant that was emphasized. Taken together, these two

---

[83] For literature on this passage, see for example Burton L. Mack, *Wisdom and the Hebrew Epic: Ben Sira's Hymn in Praise of the Fathers* (Chicago Studies in the History of Judaism; Chicago: University of Chicago Press, 1985). More recent studies on this passage can be found in Renate Egger-Wenzel, *Ben Sira's God: Proceedings of the International Ben Sira Conference, Durham, Upshaw College 2001* (Berlin: De Gruyter, 2002); Maurice Gilbert, Núria Calduch-Benages, and J. Vermeylen, *Treasures of Wisdom: Studies in Ben Sira and the Book of Wisdom: Festschrift M. Gilbert* (BETL 143; Leuven: Leuven University Press, 1999).

[84] Mack, *Wisdom and the Hebrew Epic*, 143–144.

[85] Ibid., 186.

[86] Skehan and Di Lella, *Wisdom of Ben Sira*, 500.

[87] Ibid.

hymnic reviews of history provide examples of how remembering the past provides a specific set of meanings for the community that owns this history.

Here once again we see the hymnic review of history employed for the purpose of providing meaning in the present. In this case, the present day of the author is linked with biblical history through an unbroken chain of examples of God's provision of exemplary leaders for his people in fulfillment of his covenant promises to Israel.

D. Didactic Hymns in Narrative Contexts

Just as hymns, psalms, and prayers were a regular feature of narrative within the Hebrew Bible, they also play a role in the Jewish narratives of the Second Temple period. After Judith cut off the head of Holofernes, she and the people of Israel sang a song of praise (Jdt 16:1–17) that was reminiscent of the Song of the Sea (Exod 15) and the Song of Deborah (Judg 5). In the Greek additions to Daniel, Azariah offers an extended prayer to the Lord (Pr Azar 2–22) and the three men in the furnace sing a song of praise (Sg Three 28–68). In a similar vein the Greek additions to Esther record prayers of Mordecai (13:8–17) and Esther (14:3–19), both of which include praise of God for his character, power, and rule. Prayers are included in *Joseph and Aseneth*, both on the lips of Joseph (8:10–11) and Aseneth (25:10–21).[88] Hymns, prayers, laments, and contemporary poems find a place in the historical books of the Maccabees.[89] The *Biblical Antiquities* and the *Testament of Job* likewise include prayers and hymns at key moments in support of the overall didactic aims of the larger composition.[90]

In this section I examine the didactic aspects of the song of praise found in Tob 13. I will then briefly examine several psalm-like passages in the book of Baruch in terms of their instructional content. These passages convey their teaching in different ways, but in both cases the authors utilize concepts of space relating to being in the land of exile in order to reflect on the shortcomings of the people of Israel and how they need to respond in the present.

---

[88] Aseneth's psalm, entitled "Hymn of Confession of Aseneth to the Most High," is a psalm of repentance and so not directly associated with the kinds of hymnic praise we are interested in in this study.

[89] 1 Macc 1:24–28, 36–40; 2:7–13; 3:3–9, 45, 51–53; 7:37–38; 14:4–15; 2 Macc 1:24–29; 14:35–36; 15:22–24; 3 Macc 2:1–20; 6:1–15; 4 Macc 18:6b–19.

[90] Flusser, "Psalms, Hymns, and Prayers," 563–564, 574–575.

1. Tobit 13:1–18

The book of Tobit uses the form of a story set in the Assyrian Diaspora in the eighth century BCE, to reflect on concerns facing faithful Jews during the period of its composition between 225 BCE and 175 BCE.[91] Its narrative setting in Nineveh and several other cities suggests that it was composed from the context of the eastern Diaspora in Mesopotamia. However, geographical inconsistencies in the book, together with the book's interest in Jerusalem, have led some scholars to see the book as originating within the sphere of Palestinian Judaism.[92] Regardless of the precise origin of the work, scholars agree that it emphasizes both the greatness and mercy of the God of Israel within the framework of Deuteronomic retribution.[93] Specifically, the story emphasizes God's care for righteous Jews even in times of suffering.[94]

Generally recognized as a fictional account reflecting some historical details, Tobit has been referred to as a "multifaceted didactic novel."[95] Of interest for the present study is the fact that this account contains several hymns of praise and multiple prayers uttered by the characters in the story. Prayers and thanks are offered by Tobit (3:2–6; 11:13–15; and 13:1–18), Sarah (3:11–15), Tobiah (8:5–8), and Raguel (8:15–17).[96] In this section we will briefly examine Tobit's hymn of praise in chapter 13 as an instance of a hymnic text with strong didactic flavoring.

Tobit's hymn divides naturally into two main sections, each of which are expressed in general language of praise and show little direct reference to the events of the narrative. In vv. 1–8 Tobit praises God for his rule as king as well as for his judgment and mercy. Fitzmyer sees this first part as being composed along the lines of the Song of the Sea (Exod 15:1–18) as it reflects similar themes. In vv. 9–18 Tobit continues in praise of God for his divine kingship but with an emphasis on the future restoration of Jerusalem. In this section future responses of praise are described as well as the importance of praising God in the present.

Blessed is the God who lives forever, and his kingdom.
For he scourges but then has mercy.
He casts down to the deepest grave,

---

[91] Joseph A. Fitzmyer, *Tobit* (Commentaries on Early Jewish Literature; Berlin: Walter de Gruyter, 2003), 50–52.

[92] Ibid., 52–54.

[93] Ibid., 46–47.

[94] Nickelsburg, *Jewish Literature*, 33–34.

[95] Ibid., 34.

[96] Fitzmyer, *Tobit*, 47. On prayers in Tobit see also Carey A. Moore, *Tobit: A New Translation with Introduction and Commentary* (AB 40A; New York: Doubleday, 1996), 27–30.

And he brings up from the abyss.
There is no one who can escape his hand.
Israelites, acknowledge him before the nations,
For he has scattered you among them.
Even there he has shown you his greatness.
Therefore exalt him in the presence of every living being,
Because he is our Lord, and he is our God;
He is our Father, and he is God forever.
Though he will scourge you for your iniquities,
He will also have mercy on all of you.
He will gather you from all the nations
    among whom you have been scattered.
If you will turn to him with all your heart and
all your soul, acting honestly toward him,
Then he will turn to you
And will no longer hide his face from you.
So now see what he has done for you.
And praise him with full voice.
Bless the Lord of righteousness
And exalt the King of the ages.
In the land of my exile I acknowledge him,
And make known his power and majesty to a sinful nation:
"You sinners, turn and do what is right before him.
Perhaps he may look with favor upon you and show you mercy."
I will exalt my God,
And I will rejoice in the King of Heaven.
Let all men speak of his majesty
And acknowledge him in Jerusalem. (13:1b–8)[97]

From verse 8 the psalm turns its focus toward the future restoration of Jerusalem, a restoration that culminates in hymns of joy (v. 18).

Clearly, issues of physical location are a primary concern of the psalm as it explicitly cites multiple spatial realities including heaven (v. 7), the grave (v. 2), the abyss (v. 2), the land of exile (v. 6), and Jerusalem (v. 8). The centerpiece of the psalm, the promise of return from exile, is concerned with space as well: "He will gather you from all the nations among whom you have been scattered" (v. 5b). Likewise, the psalm taps into multiple temporal registers. The eternality of God is emphasized (vv. 1, 4, 6), along with God's judgment in the past (vv. 3, 5), his desired response in the present (vv. 3, 6), and his promise for the future (vv. 5–6). Like many Jewish didactic psalms, the psalm paints a grand vision of reality which has the potential to offer hope to an audience in difficult circumstances.

Scholars have long recognized that the prayers and psalms in Tobit are found at key points in the narrative and that they provide a means of interpretation, enabling the reader to understand the events of the narrative

---

[97] Translation from Moore, *Tobit*, 275–276.

from a larger theological perspective.[98] Like many hymns in narrative contexts within the Hebrew Bible, the hymns and prayers in Tobit also contribute to the characterization of the individuals within the narrative.[99]
However, De Long has recently shown that responses of praise within the
narrative have an even more significant function for the story as a
whole.[100]

By means of literary analysis of the internal development of the story,
De Long examined the connection between healing and joyous responses
of praise in the narrative. She has shown that Tobit goes through a transformational process which includes not only his physical healing from
blindness to sight but also from an inability to praise to the ability to offer
joyous praise in response to a total transformation that is both physical and
spiritual. Further, this transformation is extended and shown to be representative of the Jewish community as a whole, as seen in Tobit's hymn of
praise in 13:1–18. De Long explains,

> Tobit's hymn uses the praise motif to set Tobit's experience of healing, recognition, and
> praise in parallel with his people's plight in exile (in the present) and with the eschato-
> logical transformation expected for Jerusalem (in the future). Tobit's story shows that
> God is working to heal (save) even when divine mercy seems absent, so the people ought
> to praise continually, even in exile.[101]

In light of this interpretation, it can be seen that Tobit's hymn may be considered didactic on several levels. First, it contributes to the overall message of the didactic novel as a whole as the contents of the hymn correspond with the overall aims of the story. Second, it makes explicit the connection between Tobit's experience in the story and the experience of Israel as a whole in exile. Third, it teaches that God is ultimately in control
and that, as Tobit was restored, so Jerusalem will be restored. This assurance is a cause for praise not just in the future when it happens (13:18), but
in the present (13:8, 13).

Another productive method of exploration is examination of intertextual
allusions between Tobit and its biblical predecessors. This kind of analysis
also offers further insight into the didactic role of the hymn of Tobit. By
looking at intertextual connections between Tob 13–14 and Deut 31–32,
Weitzman has shown that the author of Tobit has carefully portrayed Tobit
in a role similar to that of Moses at the end of his life. Both narratives describe songs written and spoken by pious sages just before the end of their
lives. The setting of both accounts is outside of the land of Israel. The con-

---

[98] Fitzmyer, *Tobit*, 47.

[99] Watts, *Psalm and Story*, 177–178.

[100] Kindalee Pfremmer De Long, *Surprised by God: Praise Responses in the Narrative of Luke-Acts* (BZNW 166; Berlin: Walter de Gruyter, 2009), 75–104.

[101] Ibid., 104.

tents of the songs are closely connected as well, as they praise God not only for what God has done but also what he will do in the future. Weitzman
observes, "The effect of the allusions is to suggest that its protagonist's life
perpetuates or repeats historical patterns established in the biblical past."[102]
Further, the biblical pattern is quite interesting for Jews living in exile in
the days of the writing of Tobit, for shortly after the death of Moses in the
biblical account, the Jews entered the land of Israel. Weitzman suggests
that one implication of the story of Tobit and the parallels he identifies is
that Israel would return to the land of Israel soon after the death of Tobit.[103] Weitzman explains, "By emulating the past, early Jewish authors
were in effect recreating the present, licensing religious and cultural innovations . . . by representing them as continuations of the biblical past."[104]
This is a case, then, where a new understanding of the present is offered in
a way that connects closely with views and traditions that are already well-
established in the communal history of the audience.

Weitzman's analysis relates closely to the notion of cultural memory
that we have employed earlier in this study. The memory of God's dealings
with Israel in the Pentateuch is here brought to bear in a story that remembers the exile. The memory of both time periods "haunts" the present of
the author and his community who, like the Jews of old, needed to know of
God's scourging and of his mercy, and needed to be encouraged to maintain their Jewish identity whether they were in the land of Israel or in the
Diaspora.

2. Baruch

The book of Baruch presents itself as being composed in Babylon after the
destruction of Jerusalem in 586 BCE (1:1–2). The date of Baruch has been
quite difficult to determine, and has been proposed as anywhere from the
middle of the second century BCE (at least portions of it) up to the period
between 70 and 135 CE.[105] It is composed of several sections that may
have originally been independent of one another and composed at different
times. However, as Nickelsburg notes, "The various component parts,
whatever their origin, have been edited into an almost seamless unity."[106]
Though not exactly a narrative, the collection of materials contained in Baruch are connected by a narrative setting, so it is appropriate to consider
the didactically-oriented hymnic materials in this section of this chapter.

---

[102] Weitzman, *Song and Story*, 68.

[103] Ibid., 70.

[104] Ibid.

[105] Carey A. Moore, *Daniel, Esther and Jeremiah: The Additions* (AB 44; New York:
Doubleday, 1985), 260.

[106] Nickelsburg, *Jewish Literature*, 96–97.

The narrative introduction (1:1–14) is followed by a prose prayer of confession (1:15–3:8), a wisdom poem (3:9–4:4), and a poem of consolation (4:5–5:9). The wisdom poem may share some connections with Sir 24, Job 28, and other passages. The psalm of consolation is marked with the language of Deuteronomy but also depends heavily on Isa 40–55. Both convey a particular message to the reader and thus lay claim to a didactic purpose.

Moore calls the hymn in 3:9–4:4 "A Poem in Praise of Wisdom as Embodied in the Law."[107] The passage begins:

Listen, O Israel, to the commandments that mean life;
Hear and learn what wisdom means.
Why, Israel, why is it that you are in the land of your enemies,
that you are growing old in a foreign country,
that you have been polluted with the dead,
that you are numbered with those who go down to the grave?
It is because you have abandoned the spring of wisdom!
If you had walked in God's way,
you would have always lived in peace.
Learn where wisdom is, where strength, where understanding is,
and so learn where longevity and life are,
where there is light for the eyes, and peace. (3:9–14)

In language reminiscent of Job 28, the poem goes on in vv. 15–31 to discuss the difficulty of finding wisdom. God is extolled as the one who knows wisdom, who discovered her, and gave her to Israel (vv. 32–37). The poem concludes by identifying wisdom with Torah:

She is the book of the commandments of God,
the Law that will last for ever.
All who keep her will live
while those who abandon her will die.
Turn back, Jacob, and seize her;
approach the radiance of her light.
Do not surrender your glory to another,
or your privileges to a foreign people.
Israel, we are happy
because we know the things that please God! (4:1–4)

Moore notes the many intertextual echoes in the poem, particularly the resemblance to Job 28, Sir 24, and Wis 9.[108] The point of view of the whole is clearly didactic more so than prophetic (although, as we have seen, prophetic writings make frequent use of hymnody to teach their readers as well).

---

[107] Moore, *Daniel, Esther and Jeremiah*, 295. The translation provided here is that of Moore.

[108] Ibid., 303.

The didactic purpose of the poem is evident, as it opens with the imperatives "listen," "hear," and "learn" (v. 9), and repeats the command to learn two more times in v. 14. The other imperatives are found at the end where Jacob is exhorted directly to turn back and seize her (4:2), and the reader is implicitly encouraged to keep the Law and live (4:1). The poem teaches the reader both what wisdom means (3:9, 14; 4:1) and how the current state of exile represents a failure to properly attend to the spring of wisdom (3:10–12). It conveys its teaching by tapping into significant spatial registers, through direct address of the audience, and through a cognitive approach that teaches explicitly and directly (rather than implicitly through a narrative).

E. Hymnic Contributions to Apocalypses

Not surprisingly, hymns, psalms, and prayers play prominent roles in apocalyptic writings during the Second Temple period. As was the case with the prophetic and apocalyptic writings of the Hebrew Bible, it will not always be possible to identify a specific passage as a hymn in a formal, technical sense. In some instances passages will fit our definition of didactic hymnody defined in the broadest sense as passages whose contents and style utilize hymnic conventions for the purpose of conveying instruction. Our awareness of the ways in which hymnic styles, themes, and ideas are used in the earlier texts of the Hebrew Bible enables us to see ways that later apocalyptic writings employ prayers and hymn-like passages in order to contribute to their teaching.[109]

While it may be possible to draw forth a lesson from any poetic composition or song, this study examines those passages which focus their discussion on the divine. Thus compositions in praise of God, directed to God, or about God, can be considered. Some prayers can be considered, particularly when their contents go beyond request or petition to include a rehearsal of God's deeds or qualities. Further, in the case of apocalyptic writings (as with narratives), the inclusion of a hymn or prayer is likely to be instructional simply by the fact of its presence within a larger genre of writing. Recall that for collections of psalms, the didactic nature of a particular psalm had to be determined from its content. In the case of a song

---

[109] For an introduction to Second Temple apocalyptic literature see John Joseph Collins, *The Apocalyptic Imagination: An Introduction to Jewish Apocalyptic Literature* (2nd ed.; The Biblical Resource Series; Grand Rapids: Eerdmans, 1998); Michael E. Stone, "Apocalyptic Literature," in *Jewish Writings of the Second Temple Period: Apocrypha, Pseudepigrapha, Qumran, Sectarian Writings, Philo, Josephus* (ed. Michael E. Stone; Assen, Netherlands; Philadelphia: Van Gorcum; Fortress Press, 1984), 383–441.

or psalm in narrative or other kind of writing, the very fact of its inclusion suggests its didactic purpose, or at least a purpose of furthering the development of understanding of the larger composition.

In this section we briefly review the presence and purpose of hymns and prayers in the Dream Visions of *1 Enoch*, and in *4 Ezra*, *2 Baruch*, and the *Apocalypse of Abraham*. Rather than providing a detailed analysis of any particular hymn, in this section we review the general contributions of each hymn to the teaching of the whole composition.

1. 1 Enoch *84*

The books of *1 Enoch* are a rich and complex arrangement of apocalyptic material and visions composed between the fourth century BCE and the first century CE and later joined in one collection.[110] The main divisions are the Book of the Watchers (chapters 1–36), the Parables of Enoch (chapters 37–71), the Book of Luminaries (chapters 72–82), the Dream Visions (chapters 83–90), the Epistle of Enoch (chapters 91–107), with one chapter concluding the collection (chapter 108).

Hymns and prayers do not play a prominent role in *1 Enoch*, though Enoch is described as blessing God on occasion, particularly in the Book of the Watchers (12:3; 22:14; 25:7; 27:5; 36:4). In the Parables of Enoch, Enoch blesses God (71:11–12) as do the inhabitants of the heavens (40:3–6; 41:7). The spirits of the righteous dead bless God in the final chapter (108:9). In one instance a prayer of moderate length is recorded in the Dream Visions. In response to the vision recounted in *1 En.* 83, Enoch describes how he blessed God (vv. 2–4), and prayed to him to sustain the righteous even as he destroys the wicked (vv. 5–6).

The hymn opens in a manner typical of praise of God in the Second Temple period, praising God as King and creator of all.

Blessed are you, O Lord, King,
great and mighty in your majesty,
Lord of all the creation of the heaven,
King of kings and God of all eternity.
Your power and your reign and your majesty abide forever and forever and ever,
and to all generations, your dominion.
All the heavens are your throne forever,
and all the earth is your footstool forever and forever and ever.

---

[110] George W. E. Nickelsburg, *1 Enoch 1: A Commentary on the Book of 1 Enoch, Chapters 1–36; 81–108* (Hermeneia; Minneapolis: Fortress Press, 2001), 1. See also James C. VanderKam, *Enoch: A Man for All Generations* (Studies on Personalities of the Old Testament; Columbia, S.C.: University of South Carolina Press, 1995). For a standard introduction and translation of the Ethiopic text see E. Isaac, "1 (Ethiopic Apocalypse of) Enoch," in *The Old Testament Pseudepigrapha, Vol. 1, Apocalyptic Literature and Testaments* (ed. James H. Charlesworth; Garden City, N.Y.: Doubleday, 1983), 5–89.

For you have made and you rule all things,
and nothing is too difficult for you.
Wisdom does not escape you,
<and it does not turn away from your throne,> nor from your presence.
You know and see and hear all things,
and there is nothing that is hidden from you. (84:2–3)[111]

While the praise portion of the psalm is not critical to the movement of the book, it does provide a concise statement of theological themes that are central to the work as a whole. These include God's majesty, greatness, and authority, the eternity of his kingdom, his creative power, and his present and lasting rule of the world. In addition to God's power and reign, the final lines emphasize the wisdom of God and his knowledge of all things. We will observe that many of these themes are central components of later apocalypses as well.

Enoch's praise of God is closely connected with the hymnody of the Second Temple period. The emphasis is on the divine kingship of God which endures for all generations together with his role as creator of all things. These two themes are connected in similar fashion in the prayer in *2 Bar.* 21:4–11. Similarities to the themes and contents of the hymns of Revelation have also been noted.[112]

2. Fourth Ezra

Composed at the end of the first century CE, *4 Ezra* is a series of apocalyptic visions in which the seer, Ezra, dialogues with God and the angel Uriel about God's treatment of his people. The book was composed in response to the Roman destruction of Jerusalem, but is set in the time of the Babylonian destruction of Jerusalem in the sixth century BCE.[113] Its content is closely related to *2 Baruch (Syriac Apocalypse)* and *Apocalypse of Abraham* both of which were also dealing with the reality of the destruction of Jerusalem.[114]

Fourth Ezra is organized in seven sections, each of which centers on a revelatory vision.[115] The whole composition contains numerous prayers of Ezra as he inquires about the justice of God and the plan of God for his people. Many of the prayers of *4 Ezra* reflect the conventions of national

---

[111] George W. E. Nickelsburg and James C. VanderKam, *1 Enoch: A New Translation: Based on the Hermeneia Commentary* (Minneapolis: Fortress Press, 2004), 119.

[112] David E. Aune, *Revelation 1–5* (WBC 52a; Dallas: Word, 1997), 317.

[113] Nickelsburg, *Jewish Literature*, 270.

[114] For good coverage of the critical issues in the *4 Ezra* see Michael E. Stone, *Fourth Ezra: A Commentary on the Book of Fourth Ezra* (Hermeneia; Minneapolis: Fortress Press, 1990), 9–47.

[115] Nickelsburg, *Jewish Literature*, 271.

lament (e.g., 5:23–30).[116] In one instance (13:57) Ezra comes to the place where he is able to respond with praise to God, although the content of his praise is not provided. *Fourth Ezra* contains nothing that might be considered a hymn in its own right. There are no imperative calls to praise or declarations of blessing that are typical of hymns. However, many of the prayers begin with content that is very rich in terms of its theological orientation and that reflects the rehearsal of God's deeds that is often found in hymns of praise. At times he focuses on God's work in creation (6:38–54), the glory of the Law of Moses (9:29–37), or God's divine qualities (7:132–140; 8:20–23). These psalm-like meditations and rehearsals of God's deeds may be considered didactic in that they rehearse the deeds and qualities of God as a foundation for the questions that follow. They also contribute to the pedagogical aims of the composition as a whole. In this sense we may explore some of the prayers of *4 Ezra* as participating in the practice of didactic hymnody.

The passage in 6:1–7 is unique in that it contains a fourteen-line poem (vv. 1–6) in which God himself responds directly to Ezra. The focus of this passage is on God being the sole agent both of creation and of the final visitation.[117] Its language and imagery is reminiscent of Prov 8:22–29 and it reflects the general theme of other ancient hymnic creation compositions.[118] In this context the creation language drives home the point that God has planned everything, including the details of the final eschatological events. By bringing the past work of creation into connection with the coming work of consummation in this way, one effect of the whole is to minimize the significance of the intervening time in which Ezra and his contemporaries find themselves. Ultimate reality is seen in the plans of God that cannot be thwarted.[119]

Ezra's address to God in 6:38–59 reviews the six days of creation (vv. 38–54) leading up to Ezra's questions about why God created this world for his people, although they do not possess it and are dominated by other nations (vv. 55–59). The first part of the passage recasts the Genesis 1 creation account in direct address to God, giving the passage something closer to a hymnic style than Genesis 1. The second part relates the election of Israel and reflects a widespread motif: the idea that creation exists for the sake of Israel.[120]

---

[116] Jacob Martin Myers, *I and II Esdras* (AB 42; Garden City, N.Y.: Doubleday, 1974), 199–200.

[117] Stone, *Fourth Ezra*, 147.

[118] See the discussion in Ibid., 155–159.

[119] Myers, *I and II Esdras*, 201.

[120] Stone, *Fourth Ezra*, 184.

Fourth Ezra 7:132–140 provides a series of seven attributes of God including that he is merciful, gracious, patient, bountiful, and abundant in compassion. This passage has been interpreted as a Midrash on Exod 34:6–7.[121] The emphasis is clearly on the goodness and compassion of God, with the implication that, in spite of the evil inclination of humans, there will yet be salvation.[122]

Of great significance for later Christian liturgy, 8:20–36 is a prayer for mercy in which Ezra asks God not to look on their sin (vv. 26–30). He begins his prayer with an opening doxology, a rehearsal of the attributes of God noting his greatness, eternity, glory, and so on (vv. 20–23). In particular, the prayer references the certainty of God's word (v. 22). Verses 24–25 provide Ezra's call for attention, with the body of the prayer provided in vv. 26–35. As the prayer begins, so it closes with a doxology as well (v. 36).[123] Stone, noting that Israel is not mentioned by name here, suggests that the thrust of the prayer is a call for divine mercy on all humans.[124] This prayer, later known as the "Confession of Ezra," is quoted in the *Apostolic Constitutions*, a sign of its importance in early Christian liturgy.[125]

Taking a different theme as its focus, 9:29–37 rehearses the glory of the Law of Moses. It begins with the wilderness, the reception of the Law, and the lasting glory of the Law in spite of the failure of the Israelites to keep it or observe it. It begins,

O Lord, thou didst indeed show thyself to our fathers in the wilderness when they came out of Egypt and when they came into the wilderness which is untrodden and unfruitful. (v. 29)

But though our fathers received the law, they did not keep it, and did not observe the statutes; yet the fruit of the law did not perish – for it could not perish, because it was thine. (v. 32)[126]

By reviewing God's dealings with his people along with their failures, the passage reflects ideas similar to historical psalms such as Pss 78 and 106. It also reflects ideas that are seen in later writings about the glory and value of the Law (cf. Sir 24:1–29 esp. v. 23; Bar 4:1–4).[127]

---

[121] Ibid., 256–257.

[122] Myers, *I and II Esdras*, 257.

[123] Stone, *Fourth Ezra*, 270–275.

[124] Ibid., 271.

[125] Myers, *I and II Esdras*, 258–259.

[126] Translation is from Stone, *Fourth Ezra*, 306.

[127] Later additions to *4 Ezra* (chapters 15–16) include similar kinds of passages in which Ezra rehearses deeds and qualities of God. In a section in which the author calls on the reader not to think he can hide his sins from God, the author rehearses God's deeds in creation and in the creation of man (16:53–67).

All of these passages reflect hymnic themes and ideas, though they are not formally hymns but merely part of Ezra's direct address to God in dialogue. The one explicit reference to Ezra's praise of God in *4 Ezra* deserves a brief comment. It is precisely in this kind of place that one might expect the insertion of a hymn, one that gave voice to the praise to which the narrative refers. We observed such a hymn in Tob 13, where the theological truths of the larger composition are made explicit. However, in the case of *4 Ezra*, the author merely provides a description of the praise:

Then I arose and walked in the field, giving great glory and praise to the Most High because of his wonders, which he did from time to time, and because he governs the times and whatever things come to pass in their seasons. (13:57–58)[128]

Though not a hymn, the subject of the praise is summarized. In this case it has to do with God's wonders (his deeds of the past) and God's control of history (his deeds of the present and future). It is this assurance, together with the content of the earlier prayers reflecting on God's mercy and on his Law, that conveys the lesson of the work as a whole. Ezra himself has moved from grief and despair (3:1–3) to praise of the Most High (13:57). The author would have the reader come to this place of embracing God's mercy and placing confidence in the God who controls the times and has the good of his people in mind.

In *4 Ezra*, though praise is not prominent, hymnic reflection on the deeds, qualities, and ways of God in the past, present, and future are one means of directing the reader to consider a way of dealing with the way things appear on the earthly level in a desperate time of national crisis.

3. 2 Baruch

Like *4 Ezra*, *2 Baruch (Syriac Apocalypse)* is an apocalypse dating from the late first or early second century CE. It too situates itself in the sixth century BCE. Also like *4 Ezra*, this work contains laments (e.g., 4:6–19; 35:2–4), visions (e.g., 36:1–37:1; 53:1–12), and prayers.[129] It contains other elements as well including addresses to the people (chapters 31–34; 44–46; 77), and a letter (chapters 78–87).[130]

---

[128] Bruce M. Metzger, "Fourth Ezra," in *The Old Testament Pseudepigrapha. Vol. 1, Apocalyptic Literature and Testaments* (ed. James H. Charlesworth; Garden City, N.Y.: Doubleday, 1983), 525–559.

[129] The prayers are found in *2 Bar.* 21:4–25; 48:2–24; 54:1–22; and 75:1–8.

[130] A. F. J. Klijn, "2 (Syriac Apocalypse of) Baruch," in *The Old Testament Pseudepigrapha. Vol. 1, Apocalyptic Literature and Testaments* (ed. James H. Charlesworth; Garden City, N.Y.: Doubleday, 1983), 621–652, 615.

A characteristic of each of the four prayers is a section that Nickelsburg refers to as an "extended doxology."[131] In these sections God is addressed with regard to key characteristics and qualities that are pertinent to the concerns of the author. It is in these extended doxologies with their thematic emphases that we can discern a strong didactic purpose as well. For our purposes it will be instructive to review the emphases of the final three prayers of *2 Baruch*.[132]

The prayer of Baruch in 48:2–24 is offered after fasting and waiting seven days in Hebron (cf. 43:3). The prayer opens with direct address to God about his knowledge and wisdom (vv. 2–10). At v. 11 the prayer transitions to petition, specifically for the Lord to protect and help his chosen people (vv. 18–20). The prayer ends with a meditation on the place of the Law among the Israelites. This meditation has clear didactic overtones:

In you we have put our trust, because, behold, your Law is with us,
and we know that we do not fall as long as we keep your statutes.
We shall always be blessed; at least, we did not mingle with the nations.
For we are a people of the Name;
we, who received one Law from the One.
And that Law that is among us will help us,
and that excellent wisdom which is in us will support us. (vv. 22–24)[133]

Here, as in *4 Ezra* 9:29–37, the special place of the Law in Israel's life and the importance of the Law for Israel's well-being is brought into view. It is interesting to observe here that the Law and wisdom are equated through the parallelism of v. 24. This equation of wisdom and Torah is reflected elsewhere in the writings of this period, as we have already noted in Sir 24 and Bar 4.

The prayer of Baruch in 54:1–22 comes in response to the vision of the clouds in chapter 53. Like the earlier prayers it opens with direct address to God in praise of his knowledge and power (vv. 1–5). The prayer transitions to petition with v. 6: "You showed this vision to your servant; open to me its exposition also." In vv. 7–12 Baruch reflects on the proper way to honor and praise God verbally. He writes,

Blessed is my mother among those who bear,
and praised among women is she who bore me.
For I shall not be silent in honoring the Mighty One
but with the voice of glory I shall narrate his marvelous works. (vv. 10–11)

---

[131] Nickelsburg, *Jewish Literature*, 279.–281.

[132] The first prayer of Baruch (21:4–25) is less clearly didactic though it does teach that God is creator, ruler, one who knows the end before it happens, and so on (vv. 4–8). Though not formally a hymn, the extended opening reflects ideas that are typical of hymnic praise in apocalyptic literature.

[133] Translation by Klijn, "2 (Syriac Apocalypse of) Baruch."

From there Baruch goes on to narrate God's reign over his creation, the value of the Law, and the justice of God's judgments (vv. 13–16). In this section he discusses the idea that even though Adam sinned and brought death to all, even so each individual is responsible for believing or rejecting the ways of God (vv. 15–19). Implicit in this praise is a reminder to the listener to make a wise choice:

For at the end of the world, a retribution will be demanded with regard to those who have done wickedly in accordance with their wickedness, and you will glorify the faithful ones in accordance with their faith. (v. 21)

This prayer thus reminds us that hymnic discourse can have not only an instructional element but can contain an implicit exhortation to the human audience.

The prayer of Baruch in 75:1–8 is different than the three preceding prayers. This prayer is offered in response to the explanation of the apocalypse. Unlike the other prayers it contains no request or petition. Its focus is on the incomprehensible goodness and mercy of God (vv. 1–6) and the importance of subjecting oneself to "him who brought us out of Egypt" (vv. 7–8). It opens with a series of questions:

Who can equal your goodness, O Lord?
for it is incomprehensible.
Or who can fathom your grace
which is without end?
Or who can understand your intelligence?
Or who can narrate the thoughts of your spirit?
Or who of those born can hope to arrive at these things,
apart from those to whom you are merciful and gracious? (vv. 1–5)

This focus on the inability of humans to fathom God's ways is reminiscent of similar questions in Isa 40:13–14. The focus on God's abundant mercy continues (v. 6) and is reminiscent of some of the hymnic passages in *4 Ezra*.[134] A person may recognize this reality and subject oneself to God which will lead to rejoicing (v. 7). Or a person may remain ignorant, reject the sovereignty of God, and experience grief (v. 8).

As was the case with *4 Ezra*, hymnic styles and forms are utilized at times in the course of a narrative to highlight themes that are central to the overall message of the book. In *2 Baruch* major themes included God's control of all things, his justice, the value of the Law, the importance of verbal praise, and, ultimately, God's goodness and mercy.

---

[134] Cf. *4 Ezra* 7:132–134; 8:31–32, 36.

4. Apocalypse of Abraham

Composed in the period after the destruction of the temple in 70 CE, the *Apocalypse of Abraham* reflects aspects of the apocalyptic traditions we have already encountered in *4 Ezra*, and *2 Baruch*. Like these other apocalypses it includes a main character/visionary who is an important figure from the history of Israel (Abraham), a narrative set in the distant past (chapters 1–8), visions and dialogues (chapters 9–32), and assurance that the God of Israel is in control of history and will indeed bring about justice for his people. The *Apocalypse of Abraham* differs from *4 Ezra* and *2 Baruch* in significant ways as well, particularly in terms of its analysis of the causes of the destruction of Jerusalem, as well as its emphasis on Abraham's ascent and throne vision.[135] The latter aspect places the *Apocalypse of Abraham* in a closer connection with the traditions originating in *1 En.* 1–36.

Neither hymns nor prayers play a prominent role in the *Apocalypse of Abraham*. Nevertheless, there is one unique instance of a song: Abraham's angelic guide teaches him the words of a heavenly song which he then recites with the angel in 17:8–21. In chapter 18 the reader learns that many other heavenly creatures were reciting this song as well (cf. 18:1–3). References to angelic worship around the throne are a common feature of apocalypses.[136] Hymns and angelic praise are often referred to and even described in detail (e.g., *Mart. Ascen. Isa.* 9:27–10:5). However, the actual content of the hymns is rarely provided.[137]

The song of the angel in *Apoc. Ab.* 17 begins with a series of names of God then a series of attributes of God. It is reminiscent of the description of Wisdom in Wis 7:22–8:1. The attributes progress to focus on God's mercy and compassion (v. 12). Again, the song circles back to names of God (v. 13) and attributes of God (vv. 14–15). It then describes God as one who receives petitions, redeems his people, and who causes light to shine (vv. 16–19). Verse 17 hails God as

Redeemer of those who dwell in the midst of the wicked ones,
of those who are dispersed among the just of the world, in the corruptible age. (v. 17)

---

[135] R. Rubinkiewicz and H. G. Lunt, "The Apocalypse of Abraham," in *The Old Testament Pseudepigrapha. Vol. 1, Apocalyptic Literature and Testaments* (ed. James H. Charlesworth; Garden City, N.Y.: Doubleday, 1983), 781–705, here 685.

[136] The perpetual heavenly liturgy is represented in *2 En.* 18:8–9; 19:3; 42:4; *Apoc. Zeph.*, frag. A; *T. Job* 51:1–4; 52:12; *3 En.* 24–40; *Apoc. Ab.* 18:3; *T. Ab.* 20:12; *T. Isaac* 6:1–6, 24; *T. Adam* 1:4 as noted in Aune, *Revelation 1–5*, 316.

[137] Ibid. A few exceptions are found in the short acclamations of praise in *3 En.* 20:2 and 39:2. As we will see in the New Testament, Revelation provides the content of the angelic worship in an unfolding sequence of hymns which contributes directly to the overall aims of the author.

This prayer concludes with a request to God to receive his prayer (v. 20) and to receive him favorably: "Teach me, show me, and make known to your servant what you have promised me" (v. 21).

In many ways this song is unique in apocalyptic literature.[138] In spite of its unique setting and features, it demonstrates some key themes of other apocalyptic songs: God's nature and his attributes, particularly his mercy and his compassion for his people.

5. Conclusions about Hymns in Apocalyptic Writings

The hymns and prayers in apocalyptic writings serve at least three didactic functions. First and foremost they focus attention either on attributes of God or deeds of God, and so, like many hymns and prayers, communicate not just to God but to the reader about God. The primary emphases include God's supremacy, kingship, rule over creation, rule over history, justice in judgment, as well as his mercy and compassion.

Second, they focus attention on the responses of God's people to him. These responses are both in the past (often cited as negative examples) and the present, where the option is available to respond with trust in God and, at times, the Law he has provided. This trust is expressed through praise focused on God's deeds in the past and future, faithfulness to the Law, and holding on to the Jewish identity even in the place of exile.

Third, they contribute to the grand vision of reality that the overall work creates. Unlike some of the didactic hymns that stand alone (Ps 105) or are found inserted into narratives (Song of the Three Young Men), all the hymnic portions and prayers in apocalypses that we examined appear to be composed as part of the process of composition of the larger writing. Though they surely reflect liturgical practices of their communities, they were not actual prayers of those communities. Rather, they depict the seer as praying in a certain way as part of the narrative development and theological emphasis of the apocalypse.

In these ways hymns in apocalyptic writings teach about the rule and reign of God who created all and rules all. They also teach about the divine plan that cannot be thwarted. They emphasize the importance of the Law for the people of Israel. They warn about the judgment that will come on the unrighteous who forsake God's law. Finally, they teach about the mercy and compassion of God.

---

[138] Flusser counts this among the broad category of "mystical prayers," among which see also *T. Job* 25; Flusser, "Psalms, Hymns, and Prayers," 563–566.

F. Conclusions

While it is no surprise that hymns, psalms, and prayers continued to be composed in the period of the Second Temple and in the aftermath of the temple's destruction, the prevalence of hymnic passages and psalm-like texts in almost every kind of writing is striking. What is of most interest here is the didactic tenor of these hymns. Through their contents (making direct claims about wisdom, the Law, God's deeds in history, etc.) and/or through their placement in the context of another kind of writing (in narrative, apocalyptic, and wisdom contexts), many of these hymns betray a didactic emphasis. It is fascinating to observe many of the same emphases emerge time and again in hymnic praise: the greatness of God, God as creator, God as ruler of all, God as merciful, God as just, God as the source of knowledge and wisdom, God as the source of the life-giving Law. All of these themes called forth hymnic celebration by Jewish writers composing their works in times of current or impending upheaval.

These hymns painted a portrait of reality that went beyond the visible world to deal with the world as perceived by the eyes of faith. Hymns and prayers addressed to God or about God provided a means of tapping into a higher register of reality for the poet/writer and his or her audience. Didactic hymns, psalms, and prayers provided a way of rehearsing the past as an exercise in communal memory with implications for the present.

Chapter 7

Didactic Hymns in the Dead Sea Scrolls

A. Introduction

An assumption of the present study has been that all prayers, hymns, and religious poems are didactic on some level. Whether through the content of the prayer or the example it provides of how one is to approach a deity, any prayer could be studied with an eye for its teaching. This is true even of prayers that were expressly intended for liturgical or personal use in communicating with God in praise, petition, supplication, or lament. However, in some hymnic texts, the instructional purpose takes on a greater prominence, becoming as important as, or perhaps even more important than, the purpose of praising or petitioning a god. These instructionally-oriented texts are referred to as didactic hymns and are the focus of the current study.

It is well known that the Dead Sea Scrolls contain an abundance of hymns and prayers. These tell us a great deal about how the members of the Qumran community praised God and prayed to God. They also reveal a great deal about the theology and beliefs of the community. Some Qumran hymns and prayers provide clear indicators that they were written to be recited at certain festivals or on certain days (e.g., the Songs of the Sabbath Sacrifice). The explicit instructions within those hymns and prayers themselves make that quite clear. Others lack specific instructions and contain no explicit indicators of their intended use. Many of the hymns and prayers of the Dead Sea Scrolls that are without specific instructions for their use reflect the features of didactic hymnody as defined above. These compositions employ the stylistic and/or formal conventions of praise and prayer, but their primary purpose was to convey a lesson, idea, or theological truth to a human audience. This chapter examines three Qumran compositions to explore how didactic hymnody is represented and also how it may have functioned in this particular Jewish community. The hymns in focus here come from the War Scroll (1QM), *Barkhi Nafshi* (4Q434–4Q437), and the Hodayot (1QH^a).

The main sections of this chapter will provide a survey of the kinds of hymns and prayers in each composition, and will also explore a selection of specific texts in more detail. The purpose of the survey and analysis is to provide for a keener appreciation of the purposes of the many hymns and prayers found among the Dead Sea Scrolls. This chapter will show that the poets and psalmists of Qumran made careful and probably quite effective use of hymnic forms to convey their distinctive sectarian theology.

A note on method is needed at the outset of this chapter. As was the case with the prayers and psalms of the Hebrew Bible and Second Temple Jewish writings, it is often quite difficult to determine the function or purpose of the prayers and psalms of Qumran. The fragmentary nature of many of the texts and the need for creative scholarly reconstructions of the social organization and history of the Qumran community make it quite challenging to speak with any certainty about the origin, use, and significance of a particular group of prayers to the Qumran community as a whole.[1] For the prayers and hymns being examined here, some discussion of the setting and use will be important. Though the texts under consideration register quite high in terms of their didactic features, any conclusions about the extent to which the didactic purpose overshadows the purpose of communicating with the divine will necessarily be tentative. On the one hand, that cannot be helped; due to the nature of these compositions we cannot expect certainty about an exact purpose for each psalm or hymn. On the other hand, it should be kept in mind that conclusions about the original purpose of a hymn, tentative as they are, are not the most significant results of this study. Instead, conclusions relating to the instruction that each hymn actually provides and the manner in which it is conveyed are where this study makes its contribution. The results of that kind of analysis are on much firmer ground since they are based on the message of the individual psalms and the ways that they emphasize certain aspects of the sect's theology and teaching.

The following survey and analysis will show that the War Scroll, *Barkhi Nafshi*, and the Hodayot all use didactic hymnody in similar ways to convey a distinct set of ideas that are central to the Qumran community. Part of the didactic function of each hymn is to teach about the nature of the Qumran community itself as well as the nature of those outside of or hostile to that community. Reinforcing communal identity is a common thread in each distinct set of hymns. However, each composition also has its own unique perspectives, as well as unique strategies for reinforcing this communal perspective. These emphases and strategies will be seen quite clear-

---

[1] Esther Glickler Chazon, "Hymns and Prayers in the Dead Sea Scrolls," in *Dead Sea Scrolls after Fifty Years: A Comprehensive Assessment* (ed. James C. VanderKam and Peter W. Flint; Leiden: Brill, 1998), 244–270; Eileen M. Schuller, "Some Reflections on the Function and Use of Poetical Texts among the Dead Sea Scrolls," in *Liturgical Perspectives: Prayer and Poetry in Light of the Dead Sea Scrolls* (ed. Esther G. Chazon; Leiden: Brill, 2003), 173–189.

ly when the individual hymns are analyzed in terms of their message and how they communicate it through the medium of psalmody. Taken together, the commonalities and differences within the didactic strategies of these hymns suggest that didactic hymnody played a vital role in the development of the community and its members' self-understanding, view of God, and view of the world.

B. Hymns and Prayers in the War Scroll (1QM)

The hymns and prayers of the War Scroll are fascinating. As they exist now within the context of the War Scroll they do have clear instructions on when they were to be used: at the final eschatological battle of the war of the sons of light against the sons of darkness. To the extent that these prayers contain clear instructions for the time and manner of their use, the prayers of the War Scroll might be considered liturgical.[2] On the other hand, Nitzan refers to them as "eschatological prayers," terms which reflect the eschatological content of some of the prayers, but even more so the eschatological setting of these prayers within the larger document.[3] These prayers come with explicit instructions for their recitation at various times before, during, or after the battle of the sons of light and the sons of darkness. Before that battle, however, one can imagine that these prayers were written, studied, and utilized for purposes of preparing for that great battle.[4] Davies has suggested that the prayers and hymns in the War Scroll existed independently and were collected together along with the specific instructions for the war.[5] Offering a slightly more nuanced explanation, Duhaime compares the work as a whole to Greco-Roman tactical treatises. Based on these comparisons and also on additional fragments found in Cave 4, Duhaime concludes, "Such evidence makes it likely that the *War*

---

[2] Jean Duhaime, "War Scroll," in *The Dead Sea Scrolls: Hebrew, Aramaic, and Greek Texts with English Translations. Volume 2: Damascus Document, War Scroll, and Related Documents* (ed. James Charlesworth; Tübingen: Mohr (Siebeck), 1995), 80–141, 87. Among the possibilities for how the text functioned, "it could have been a work for initiates only, a genuinely utopian product written for liturgical purposes or for personal meditation" (87).

[3] Bilha Nitzan, *Qumran Prayer and Religious Poetry* (STDJ 12; Leiden: Brill, 1994), 201–226.

[4] Duhaime, "War Scroll," 87. Duhaime suggests another use: "As a work of propaganda, it could have been the means through which a group of frustrated priests were opposing the way rival Jewish leaders, religious or civilian, were conducting the war" (87).

[5] Philip R. Davies, *1QM, the War Scroll from Qumran: Its Structure and History* (Biblica et orientalia 32; Rome: Biblical Institute Press, 1977), 123.

Scroll is a compilation of at least three different documents (cols. 2–9; 10–14; 15–19), which may have been transmitted in various recensions and modified more than once."[6] Most recently, Brian Schultz has explored the compositional history of 1QM and related texts, arguing that the War Scroll contains two distinct kinds of materials relating to two different wars.[7] While we cannot assess these varied views in the context of the present study, we can agree that in any of these scholarly reconstructions, the hymns of the War Scroll would thus represent the theology of the community as it developed over at least a century or perhaps even longer.

The recognition of this complex history of the War Scroll leads to interesting results in terms of the prayers and hymns. When looking at these as potentially didactic in function one must consider three distinct contexts. The first is the context of the original writing of each prayer and the use of each of these prayers independent of the war texts as a group. The original authors and members of their community likely used these for a variety of purposes. The second context is the community that read these prayers once they were incorporated into 1QM. In this context these prayers are no longer discrete units nor are they independent. Their meaning is found in the context in which they are placed in 1QM. Further, in this context the eschatological war is still in the future. The prayers are studied then as models in preparation for a war that is coming in the future (though perhaps in the very near future). The third context would be that of the actual use of these prayers before battle, in battle, and after the battle. This is the intended context, or the context in which the writer of 1QM imagines they will be used. The function of this same group of prayers will be viewed somewhat differently depending on which of the three contexts is envisioned.

For the purposes of this study, these prayers will be examined in the second context, i.e., the context of the community that now has these prayers as part of a document that gives them instruction on how to conduct themselves in the war that is still in the future. The first context, these prayers circulating independently of the war texts, is beyond our ability to reconstruct save by hypotheses that compare these prayers with other prayers for which we know the setting. The third context, while intrinsically interesting, goes beyond the scope of this particular study. While those two con-

---

[6] Duhaime, "War Scroll," 84.

[7] Brian Schultz, *Conquering the World: The War Scroll (1QM) Reconsidered* (STDJ 76; Leiden: Brill, 2009). In his view cols 1 and 15–19 relate to an initial War against the Kittim, while cols 2 and 3–14 relate to a later War of the Divisions. Further, the prayers in cols 10–14, intended for the War of the Divisions, originated in other contexts. See his analysis of the prayers in cols 10–14 on pp. 255–305. The present study assumes the prayers relate to one expected future conflagration.

texts may be considered from time to time, the perspective of this study is on the community that read and preserved these prayers in the context of 1QM for a battle that was still in the future. The discussion that follows explores the ways that these prayers and hymns would have served a didactic purpose within the Dead Sea sect. As we will see, these hymns functioned like many of the didactic hymns and prayers at Qumran, promoting and enhancing the sense of the unique identity of the community, especially in contrast to outsiders. These hymns also give explicit instruction as to the nature of God and the certainty of the outcome of the final battle, based on God's deeds and words in the past, and on what he has revealed to members of the community in the present.

1. The Prayers

The main collection of prayers is found in cols 10–14 with an additional hymn of thanksgiving in cols 18 and 19 (18:6b–19:8). Because of the fragmentary nature of these columns, it is not always clear where one hymn ends and another begins. Distinguishing between individual hymns and prayers is further complicated by the composite nature of these columns: prayers, rubrics, and scriptural citations appear to have been joined together by the editor of 1QM. Still, it is possible to isolate at least four distinct prayers based on instructions in the text for their recitation (prayers 2, 3, and 4) or on abrupt changes in contents, person, and style from the fragmentary end of one column to the beginning of another (prayer 1). These are: 1) a prayer for the time of war; 2) a prayer after the defeat of the sons of darkness; 3) a hymn on the day after the victory; 4) a thanksgiving at sunset.

Prayer for the Time of War. Though composite in nature, the prayers in cols 10–12 are, in the final redaction of the War Scroll, part of one lengthy prayer.[8] Duhaime calls this the "prayer at the camp."[9] This is likely the "prayer for the time of war" referred to in 15:4–5.[10] I will treat it here as one prayer, though it is already divided into sections even in the scroll itself.[11] These divisions do not necessarily indicate that one prayer is ending

---

[8] Davies, *1QM*, 111–112, 123.

[9] Jean Duhaime, *The War Texts: 1QM and Related Manuscripts* (Companion to the Qumran Scrolls 6; London: T & T Clark, 2004), 17–18.

[10] Yigael Yadin, *The Scroll of the War of the Sons of Light against the Sons of Darkness* (London: Oxford University Press, 1962), 210.

[11] For example, there is a break in the manuscript in 11:12, 12:6 and 12:16. Davies takes these breaks to indicate distinct prayers in each case, though he recognizes that in the final form they may be intended as one long prayer (123). See the compositional analysis by Schultz, who divides the prayers more extensively than previous scholars,

and another is beginning; they may simply indicate the transition from one major section of this lengthy prayer to another.

Prayer after the Defeat of the Sons of Darkness. Prayer two is found in col. 13. This prayer includes a blessing, a curse, and a prayer of thanksgiving that were possibly intended for recitation immediately after the victory (12:17–14:1). Alternatively, Duhaime views these as "prayers for the battlefield" and suggests they are "probably part of the immediate preparation for the engagement on the 'day of battle' (13.14)."[12] The lack of clarity is likely due to the composite nature of the final composition, as was noted above. Regardless of its intended time of recitation, it may be studied for its content and instructional impact.

Hymn on the Day after Victory. The third distinct prayer is found in col. 14:4–15. Although line 2 of col. 14 mentions a "hymn of return," no text for that hymn is provided. It may be that the hymn in col. 13 provides the text of that hymn. Nevertheless, 14:4–15 explicitly provides the text of prayer 3, the hymn of victory to be recited on the day after the victory.

Thanksgiving at Sunset. A fourth prayer text is found in cols 18 and 19. 1QM 18:6b–19:8 provides a separate thanksgiving to be sung as the sun is setting on the day of battle. This fourth prayer falls at about the same time as prayer 2 noted above. There is also some content overlap as well. This redundancy again appears to be a result of the bringing together of several sources in the compilation of the version of the War Scroll that we have. The prayers are similar in their themes, though they are not completely identical.[13]

Taken as a whole these four prayer and hymnic passages are marked by a number of features which suggest their didactic function. Most significantly, they explicitly reference teaching and what was taught in the past (e.g., 10:2; 10:10–11; 11:5, 8). Furthermore, several of these prayers review events of biblical history and recent history shaping them into part of the same overall divine drama. As has been noted in earlier chapters, hymnic reviews of history often corresponded with the didactic purposes of the poet or author. In a similar vein, citations of scripture and clear allusions to scripture suggest the interpretive nature of some of these prayers.[14] Beyond simply communicating with God directly, these prayers rehearse the theological perspective of the community in great detail in a biblical style – a

---

and provides a chart comparing the divisions proposed by himself and others; Schultz, *Conquering the World*, 83–85.

[12] Duhaime, *War Texts*, 18.

[13] For a detailed comparison of the prayers in cols 10–14 and 18–19, see Schultz, *Conquering the World*, 297–305.

[14] For more on this aspect see Dean O. Wenthe, "The Use of the Hebrew Scriptures in 1QM," *DSD* 5 (1998): 290–319, esp. 306–312.

style which itself communicates some level of meaning. Even the idea of reciting prayers before, during, and after battle reflects the biblical precedents that these prayers seek to actualize in the approaching conflict. All of these indicators suggest that a major function of these prayers was instruction.[15]

Recognizing the didactic nature of these hymns, what are their instructional aims and how do they achieve them? Duhaime explains that in these prayers "lessons from the past put the coming war into proper context. One is reminded that the powerful Creator of the heavens and the earth stands in the midst of the Israelite army and does battle for it."[16] In essence, the prayers of the War Scroll use several strategies to convey to the members of the community the idea that they are God's people and that God will show mercy to them in the coming battle and in fact fight the battle for them, as he has done for past generations of his faithful children. As will be seen below, in each prayer combinations of biblical history, recent history, scriptural citations, scriptural allusions, or biblical styles of expression all work together to achieve the instructional purposes of these prayers.

2. The Prayer for the Time of War

Columns 10:1–12:16 contain the first of the series of hymn-like prayers. These hymns address God in second person, and cover a variety of themes as they progress. Because of this variation in theme and contents, some scholars have suggested that these were intended to be viewed as a series of separate prayers. However, whether intended as one prayer or multiple prayers, it is still possible to attend to the didactic features of these prayers both section by section and taken together as a whole.

The text that opens col. 10 in lines 1–8 suggests that this whole section be considered a prayer, especially since it is addressed to God in the second person. But it is also clearly instructional in nature. The general subject matter is the biblical guidelines for warfare. The prayer cites Deut 20:2–5 and, later, Num 10:9. In essence the composition tells God in prayer what they, his people, intend to do in battle and, further, that they intend to fulfill the instructions he had given them through Moses. A key phrase is "and he taught us from of old for our generations saying" (10:2). The direct allusion to what has been taught from of old at the very least causes

---

[15] One other indication of their didactic function is the lack of any petition with the possible exception of 1QM 10:17. See discussion of this phenomenon and the theological issues that led to the minimizing of petitionary prayer at Qumran in Israel Knohl, "Between Voice and Silence: The Relationship between Prayer and Temple Cult," *JBL* 115 (1996): 17–30, esp. 29–30.

[16] Duhaime, "War Scroll," 117 n. 54.

the listener to expect didactic content. The content of the teaching has to do with the teachings of Moses in Deut 20 regarding what God's people must do in order to enjoy the benefit of his promises of deliverance.

The expression of belief in these promises of God along with the accompanying assurance of divine aid and help leads naturally to a response of praise on the part of the writer in line 8. As we will see below, the praise of God focuses on who he is, the people he has chosen, and what God has done in creation and in history.

The opening section of this prayer for the time of war (at least what is preserved of it) is thus didactic on several levels. First, it is provided as instruction on how and what one should pray. Second, its content is a reminder to the community of the teaching of Moses. Though directed toward God, the content of this section serves to remind the ones praying and the ones listening (and, we can assume, the ones studying this in preparation for the coming battle) of the teaching and promises of God given in ancient times. Third, it serves to remind the various audiences that they are part of the redemptive history in which these teachings of Moses are found and in which their God has been at work. In this sense these prayers actualize and fulfill what was spoken in the books of Moses. These prayers inspire the audience(s) to live out the realities about which they are speaking/hearing; in this sense these hymns bear a didactic stamp, teaching the community how to view their present circumstances.

The section which serves as a reminder of past teaching leads naturally to the praise section which opens in 10:8–11 with two rhetorical questions. This section reads:

Who is like you, O God of Israel, in the hea[ve]ns or on earth, to act according to your great works
and your mighty strength? Who is like your people Israel who you have chosen for yourself from among all the peoples of the lands,
the holy people of the covenant, learned in the statute, taught in discern[ment..], hearers of the glorious voice, seers of
the holy angels, open of ear (and) hearers of deep things?[17]

With the two questions (Who is a God like you. . . ? Who is a nation like Israel. . . ?) this prayer participates in the conventions used in biblical contexts such as Deuteronomy (cf. Deut 3:24), Exodus (cf. Exod 15:11, the Song of Moses), and also the Psalms (see Ps 113:5–6; 71:19; 35:10).[18] A.

---

[17] Unless otherwise indicated, translations of the prayers of the War Scroll are from Jean Duhaime, "War Scroll," 97–141.

[18] Yadin, *Scroll of the War*, 304. Interestingly, in Ps 113:7, after rhetorical questions about God's greatness, the Psalm recounts how God raises the poor from the dust and lifts the needy from the ash heap. That kind of language is comparable to what is found in 1QM 13:13–14 where the rhetorical question and reference to the needy strongly sug-

Steudel has observed that, on one level, these rhetorical questions about the uniqueness of God and of Israel suggest that the glory of God "is visible in the exulted status of Israel."[19] On a more subtle level, the rhetorical question about Israel serves to bring into focus the specific characteristics of the Qumran community. They are "holy ones of the covenant, learned in the law, wise in knowledge . . . , hearers of the glorious voice, seers of the holy angels, with opened ears, hearing profound things" (10–11).[20] This prayer thus rehearses key characteristics of the community itself, a reminder not to God but to the participants of just who they are.[21] In this sense it is clear that this portion of the prayer participates in didactic purposes just as the earlier section had. Though without the specific biblical citations, the question "Who is a nation like Israel?" has alluded to foundational narratives of the history of Israel: establishment of the covenant, giving of the Law, angelic encounters and ongoing revelation. The dynamics of "intertextuality" may be seen to come into play here, where the reader in the know is able to encounter the deeper meaning in the text precisely because of the biblical allusions and the interplay between the biblical world of the past and the present reality of the community.[22] Given that intertextuality is a prominent feature in Qumran writings, it is not surprising to see this dynamic at work in hymns and prayers as well.

The prayer goes on to review God's work in creation in 10:11–16, beginning with the creation of the physical world and the spirits (10:11–14a), and moving into events of biblical history and on into eternity (10:14b–16). As this study has already suggested, God's creative work has been a popular subject in Jewish didactic psalms.[23] This was the case in the He-

---

gests influence of Ps 113:5–7 and perhaps also 35:10 on that prayer. In many ways Ps 35:9–10 may be seen to provide a summary of the War Scroll in the space of two verses.

[19] Annette Steudel, "The Eternal Reign of the People of God: Collective Expectations in Qumran Texts (4Q246 and 1QM)," *RevQ* 17 (1996): 507–525, here 522.

[20] Trans. Florentino García Martínez and Eibert J. C. Tigchelaar, *The Dead Sea Scrolls Study Edition* (2 vols.; Leiden: Brill, 1997), 1:129–131.

[21] For the rich tapestry of biblical allusions in these lines and possible allusions to other texts within the Dead Sea Scrolls see Yadin, *Scroll of the War*, 306.

[22] Duhaime notes this well when he explains that biblical Intertextuality is "made of a whole network of quotations (explicit or implicit), references and allusions to various texts, as well as phrases that may have been inspired by, if not borrowed from, one or another part of the Scriptures" (Duhaime, *War Texts*, 114). See discussions of the various manifestations and uses of this textual phenomenon in Moshe J. Bernstein, "Scriptures: Quotation and Use," in *Encyclopedia of the Dead Sea Scrolls* (ed. Lawrence H. Schiffman and James C. VanderKam; 2 vols.; New York: Oxford University Press, 2000), 839–842.

[23] It is also a feature of some liturgical prayers (e.g., 4Q504). D. Falk notes the following prayers which rehearse God's acts of mercy in the past and on the basis of those acts, ask for God's mercy in the present: Dan 9:3–19; Neh 9:6–37; Ps 106; Bar 1:15–3:8;

brew Bible (Pss 8, 19; Prov 8) as well as in Second Temple Jewish writings (e.g., Sir 39; Wis 9). Interest in the work of God in history has also been a prominent feature of didactic poetry (e.g., Pss 104, 105; Sir 44–50; Wis 10). The historical events in focus in col. 10 include: the confusion of tongues (Gen 11:1–9); the separation of the nations; the dwelling of the clans; the inheritance of the lands. This brief review of the works of God in history thus takes the prayers/hearers from the book of Genesis to the time of Joshua and the conquest.

At the beginning of col. 11 either a new hymn or the same hymn moves into declarations of confidence in God for this great battle. The refrain, "For the battle is yours!" is repeated three times (11:1, 2, and 4). This portion reads,

> For the battle is yours indeed! With the power of your hand their corpses have been dashed to pieces with no one to bury (them). Goliath of Gath, a mighty man of worth,
> you did deliver into the hand of your servant David, for he trusted in your great name and not in a sword or a spear. For the battle is yours! The
> Philistines, he humil[i]ated many times by your holy name. You also have saved us many times by the hand of our kings
> on account of your compassion and not according to our works, in which we have done evil, and our sinful deeds. The battle is yours, and the strength is from you,
> (it is) not ours! Neither our power nor the force of our hands have done worthily except by your power and with the vigor of your great worth. (11:1–5)

This passage clearly draws on the Divine Warrior theme of the Hebrew Bible.[24] Historical examples, both specific and general, illustrate the claim that the battle is God's: David and Goliath (11:1–2); many defeats of the Philistines (11:3); many acts of salvation by the hands of their kings (11:3–4). Whether or not the prayers in cols 10 and 11 were composed together, their placement together in this sequence makes sense as the author continues a survey of history that is infused with theological meaning that lends perspective on the present crisis.[25]

Taken as a whole this hymn (or these hymns, if more than one) is appropriate for strengthening the hearts of the soldiers prior to battle. It rehearses historical events in which God demonstrated his complete control

---

Pr Azar 2–22; Esther LXX C 14; *3 Macc.* 2:1–20; 6:1–15. Daniel K. Falk, *Daily, Sabbath, and Festival Prayers in the Dead Sea Scrolls* (STDJ 27; Leiden: Brill, 1998), 71.

[24] This declaration echoes a biblical theme found in Deut 20:2–4 and 2 Chron 20:1–30, esp. v. 15. The divine warrior theme is notable in the conquests under Joshua as well, cf. Josh 10:8, 14, 25; 23:9–10. Richard D. Nelson, *Joshua: A Commentary* (OTL; Louisville, Ky.: Westminster John Knox, 1997), 14–20.

[25] Wenthe comments, "The author presents David's victory as an illustration, in miniature, of how the kings of Israel were victorious (11:4), and how the final eschatological triumph is secure (11:11–12)" (Wenthe, "The Use of the Hebrew Scriptures in 1QM," 310).

of history. Not only does God have control, but he exercises it on behalf of his people. Further, col. 11 expresses confidence in God based on the fact that he has won numerous battles in the past. Davies views this portion of the prayer as "a *Heilsgeschichte,* in fact a record of past military glories attributed to God."[26] The hymn is thus instructional for the listeners in that it draws on events of the past to affirm who God is in the present.

To give further confirmation to the victory that God will bring about, the prayer goes on to cite scriptural texts as proof. The prayer cites Num 24:17–19 and Isa 31:8, explaining that it was through anointed ones that God taught his people the times of these particular wars (11:5–12). Again the prayer takes an opportunity to bring the teaching of God into focus. God himself taught them (11:5, 8). Wenthe explains,

History – past, present, and future – is a continuous and harmonious expression of the truth of Yahweh's strength (11:5) which the author and his associates alone perceive. . . The author views history as a series of divinely appointed epochs. The war of the sons of light against the sons of darkness marks the final epoch.[27]

Through the understanding of history elaborated within this prayer, the author expresses a fundamental conviction and a theological truth which undergirds the entire composition.[28]

A further declaration of confidence in God's ability to defeat the enemy comes in the form of a reference to Pharoah and his officers in the Red Sea (11:9–10): "You shall treat them like Pharoah, like the officers of his chariots in the Red Sea."[29] The implication for the listener is that the Qumran covenant community members are part of the same ongoing story that has its roots in Exodus (cf. Exod 15:4 and Deut 7:18–19). In other words, their story is part of the larger story of God who annihilated Israel's enemies for them in the days of Moses. Because of who God is and who they are, they can be confident that God will act in similar ways in their day.[30]

---

[26] Davies, *1QM,* 96.

[27] Wenthe, "The Use of the Hebrew Scriptures in 1QM," 310.

[28] Duhaime is helpful in summarizing the theology succinctly: "The message which is repeated over and over in the War Scroll is simple and coherent. The final war between good and evil is about to take place and involves both natural and supernatural beings. The God of Israel, who set this time long ago, controls the event from beginning to end. The Sons of Light . . . must remain faithful and stand firm, since the hosts of angels are fighting along with them, and since God has already granted them victory" (Duhaime, "War Scroll," 87).

[29] Trans. García Martínez and Tigchelaar, *DSSSE,* 1:131.

[30] Duhaime shows that the combination of scriptural references in this section points to God fighting for his people. He writes, "The references or implicit quotations of this central unit, then, point especially towards Deuteronomy 7, Exodus 14–15 and Zechariah 12. These three passages are unified by a common theme, found repeatedly in this prayer: God himself is fighting on behalf of his people" (Duhaime, *War Texts,* 112).

The portion of the prayer preserved in col. 11 goes on to emphasize that God is going to bring about victory "by the hand of the poor" (lines 9, 13), "those prone in the dust" (13) and "the stricken of spirit" (10). These terms highlight again the nature of the community and remind the hearers of who "we" are. We will encounter similar self-abasing language and terminology in both the *Barkhi Nafshi* hymns and in the Hodayot. This common thread suggests that the "self-image" of the Qumran community is a major theme of their didactic hymnody.

In a similar vein, this column addresses not only who "we" are but also who "they" are and what "they" are like. The purpose of the victory that God will grant is judgment on sin, specifically, the sins of the opponents (lines 13–14). Along these lines the opponents are characterized as the hordes of Belial (line 8), the seven peoples of futility (lines 8–9), the Kittim (line 11), enemies (lines 8, 13), the powerful ones (line 13), with guilty heads (line 14), and Gog (line 16). The teaching of this prayer centers on the dualistic worldview of the Qumran community and, though the specific terms are not used, hearkens back to the notion in col. 1 that this is indeed the war of the Sons of Light and the Sons of Darkness.

Regardless of how weak or poor the community is or how strong and fierce the opponents are, the column ends with an emphasis on the fact that God himself will "wage war against them from the heavens" (line 17). The theology of the prayer emphasizes the certainty of the victory since its origins are not in the will of man but in the will of God. Divine assistance, in fact, divine carrying out of the war is a conclusion of the writer. The nature of the heavenly army that will bring this about becomes the focus in the first half of col. 12 (lines 1–5).

This prayer for the time of war ends with what Yadin asserts to be the essential part of the prayer: a call for God to arise and fight.[31] After lines 7–10, which praise God and affirm the sufficiency of the armies of Israel in conjunction with the heavenly armies, the prayer appeals to God as the Divine Warrior who will fight for his people:

Arise, mighty one! Take your captives, glorious man! Seize
your plunder, (you) who do worthily! Put your hand upon the neck of your enemies and
your foot upon the piles of the slain! Smite the nations, your foes, and let your sword
devour the guilty flesh. Fill your land (with) glory and your inheritance (with) blessing.
(12:10–12)

Davies refers to these lines as an extended war cry whose biblical origin might well go back to Num 10:35.[32] This portion is followed by a call to Zion and Jerusalem to rejoice and celebrate (lines 13–16).

---

[31] Yadin, *Scroll of the War*, 215.
[32] Davies, *1QM*, 103.

Having reached the climax of the prayer for the time of war, we are in a position to assess its overall message and impact. The work of Brevard Childs on the role of remembrance in ancient Israel can help us make some connections between the disparate sections of this long prayer.[33] The essence of his findings about the biblical era are summarized in a brief sentence: "In times of crisis, when the role of the cult was threatened, Israel's memory assumed a new significance in renewing her tradition."[34] This idea finds illustration in the greatest crisis faced in the history of Israel, the exile. Childs suggests that the prophets of the exile drew on remembrance of the past to create a vision for the present and the future, in spite of the desperation of their circumstances. For example, in Deutero-Isaiah Childs cites two functions of their collective memory:

First, memory of the past links Israel with the one great purpose of God in history which encompasses both past and future (44:21; 46:9f). Even the exile is bracketed within the divine will. Second, Israel need not turn to the past for meaning. God is bringing into existence a new age in which Israel can participate (43:18f; 65:17).[35]

These prayers in 1QM 10–12 may have functioned similarly for the community as they remembered the past (both the deeds of God and the words of God) and found themselves participants in the same divine plan in the present. In this way these hymnic prayers function as a kind of cultural memory. In spite of opposition from powerful enemies, the prayer for the time of war assures the Qumran community that the plans of God for his people would not be thwarted. As we have seen, the prayer also has a good deal to say about who God's people are and what they are like. Accordingly, it is fair to say that the prayer for the time of war conveys a significant amount of theological instruction even as it praises God and seeks his help.

3. Prayer on the Day of Victory

Another series of hymns are found in col. 13:2–18 and appear to be intended for the day of victory. The column begins, "Blessed be the God of Israel. . ." The first part of this series, 13:2–6, is a blessing and a curse in the third person. The next part, 13:7–17, is thematically similar to the first though it returns to the second person style and provides a more expansive treatment of the blessing and curse. This portion begins,

Y[o]u, O God of our fathers, we bless your name forever! We are a people [...]/[...]. You have [est]ablished a covenant with our fathers and confirmed it with their descendants through the appointed ti[me]s of eternity. (13:7–8)

---

[33] Childs, *Memory and Tradition*.
[34] Ibid., 80.
[35] Ibid., 79.

The historical references in this section include both biblical history and, presumably, the recent history of the community. These time periods blend together so that there is no distinction between ancient times and the present time. In terms of biblical history, clear allusions include: establishment of the covenant (13:7–8; cf. Gen 17:19) and remembrance (*zekher*; cf. Ps 111:4) of the covenant to aid the remnant (13:8–9). More recent historical events include the redemption of the Qumran community itself (13:9–10). Among the specific deeds discussed in this prayer are claims that God has: established a covenant (7); ratified it (7); aided the remnant (8); redeemed them (9); made them fall into the lot of light (9); assisted them with the Prince of Light (10). Further, the hymn contrasts those in the lot of Belial and the spirits of his lot (11–12): "We, instead, in the lot of your truth, rejoice in your mighty hand, we exult in your salvation, we revel in [your] aid [and in] your peace. Who is like you in strength, God of Israel, whose mighty hand is with the poor?" (12b–14a).[36] The hymn thus features a review of God's mercies in history on behalf of his people, statements of his appointment of Belial and his spirits for destruction, and rhetorical questions in praise of God's incomparability. Through what amounts to being a "biblical style" of thanking God and declaring confidence in him, each aspect of the hymn in this column contributes to the conviction that the coming battle is in God's hands for the good of his people.

This hymn is thus clearly didactic in two ways: it teaches directly what God is like, and it teaches directly what "we" are like. These hymns emphasize the works of God on behalf of his people and also the fact that this community represents the people of God. Wenthe correctly observes, "The claim to be the true descendants of Israel could hardly be made more explicit."[37] The historical events of God's saving work in the past thus represent the history of *this* community. Presumably a major function of these prayers is not to remind God of these realities but to remind the participants in battle that this is so. In this regard the hymn echoes the ideas and purpose of 11:11–16 which used a variety of terms and images to describe the community of God and the enemies of God. The dynamics of remembrance of the past and actualization of historical events in the present suggest that the function of these prayers is similar to the function of the prayer for the time of war. Whether recited during the coming battle (Duhaime's view) or immediately after the victory, their presence in this scroll indicates that these prayers would have been studied and perhaps used by the community in the generations in which the crisis was brewing and the war was seen to be on the horizon.

---

[36] Trans. García Martínez and Tigchelaar, *DSSSE*, 1:135.
[37] Wenthe, "The Use of the Hebrew Scriptures in 1QM," 311.

4. Prayer on the Day after the Victory

In a similar vein the hymn to be sung the next day after washing and cleansing themselves (14:4–18) has historical references to both the establishment of the covenant (14:8) and preservation of the remnant (14:9–11). The historical actions of God include "guarding the covenant with our fathers" (8); "you have bestowed your mercies to your remnant" (9); "you have chased away from [us] his spirits of destruction" (10); "you protected the soul of your redeemed ones" (10); "you raised the fallen with your strength" (11). These declarations of historical facts have a dual focus on God and on the "us" whom he has favored. The historical references are generic enough that they could be applied to God's dealings with his covenant people in the distant biblical past.[38] They could also be read in the context of the expected victory in battle as specific references to that victory. In terms of communal identity the hymn goes on to provide further clarification for who "we" are and what "we" are like: "We, your holy people, will praise your name for the deeds of your truth, for your mighty deeds we will extol [your] spl[endour, at every] moment and at the times indicated by your eternal edicts"(12–13).[39] These lines contain several indicators of communal identity: holy people; marked by praise; following the times decreed by God. With these kinds of explicit and implicit claims, we conclude that this hymn would play a major role in reinforcing the Qumran understanding of what God has done and who the community is in relation to him.

In the three distinct prayers in cols 10–14, it is interesting to note that as the prayers progress the language becomes less and less specific with regard to historical events and more and more general. The more general language could be seen to describe biblical events *or* the recent victory and dealing of God with his people in this community. The prayer for the time of war alluded to very specific events and people in the history of Israel (Moses, Pharoah, David, Goliath). The second prayer references the establishment of the covenant and aiding the remnant in the distant past. The second and third prayers together speak of God's work in the recent history of the community in much more general biblical terminology.

The fourth prayer, the hymn at sunset in 18:6b–15, also reflects this tendency to praise God for the general ways he has delivered his people and kept his covenant in the past:

---

[38] Wenthe observes of this column, "Again, the description is punctuated with creative adaptations of the Hebrew Scriptures" (Ibid., 311–312). In the opening lines of this column he sees allusions to Ezek 30:13–14, Num 31:21ff., and Deut 7:9.

[39] García Martínez and Tigchelaar, *DSSSE*, 1:137.

Blessed be your name, O God of [god]s, for
you have made great with yo[ur] people [...] to do wonders. You have kept your covenant for us since long ago. The gates of deliverances you have opened many times for us
for the sa[ke of] your [co]venant [...]' our oppression according to your goodness towards us. You, O God of righteousness, have acted for the sake of your name. (18:6b–8)

This prayer contains general comments about God keeping his covenant
with his people from of old, opening up the gates of salvation many times
in the past, etc. In this way, it connects biblical times with the present time,
making the point that God will work (or has worked, from the perspective
of the hymn) on behalf of the Qumran community as he has worked on behalf of his people at all times.

In cols 10–14 of the War Scroll, then, hymns and prayers (which were
to be recited before and after the great battle) functioned on several levels.
On the surface level these prayers were directed toward God in obedience
to the biblical instructions for battle. The prayers fulfill the scriptural man-
date and thus serve to secure God's fullest blessing in the impending conflict. At a more profound level, these particular prayers would serve to inspire and encourage the soldiers as they faced the battle itself. As a form of
collective cultural memory, the contents of the prayers offered reminders
of who God was, who they were, and what God had done for his people in
the past. They also offered assurances that God had ordained the times of
the battle, and also had appointed their enemies to destruction. In particular
they drew upon the Divine Warrior imagery of the Hebrew Bible to remind
the people that the battle was God's, not theirs. On the verge of battle
against a formidable opponent, such reminders would have been most welcome to the ears of the soldiers.

But these prayers can also be seen to function on yet another level. Having been written, copied, and collected into 1QM decades before the expected conflagration, the prayers would undoubtedly have had an instructional purpose for the community that wrote, read, copied, and studied this
document as a key document for the future of the people of God. These
prayers would provide encouragement, exhortation, and instruction to the
current members of the community with regard to the identity of the community and the certainty of its future even in the face of impending war.

In sum, this collection of hymnic prayers has drawn on remembrance of
the past to create a vision that the reader could embrace for the present and
the future. In spite of the unsettling nature of their circumstances, the
community members could remember the past (both the deeds of God and
the words of God) and see themselves as participants in the same divine
plan in the present. The prayer for the time of war conveys a significant
amount of theology even as it praises God for his deeds in the past and
seeks his help for the near future.

C. The *Barkhi Nafshi* Hymns (4Q434–438)

The *Barkhi Nafshi* texts are the fragmentary remains of five copies of the same set of prayers found in Cave 4. They have been described as "hymns of thanksgiving – praising and thanking the Lord for his deliverance and continued grace."[40] Though very little of these scrolls remain, the evidence is enough to indicate that these prayers were very important to the community. First, the fact that there were at least five copies of the text suggests a level of significance. Second, the contents of the scrolls that have survived are reflective of central beliefs of the Qumran community as seen in other writings. The editors of these texts explain, "These hymns display numerous connections with the language and themes of texts that are generally considered to be of sectarian origin, and we would argue that the *Barkhi Nafshi* hymns should also be considered of sectarian origin."[41] Whether or not the text was a composition of the Qumran community, its main ideas support the theology of the community as it came to expression in other Qumran compositions.

Why should these hymns be considered didactic? This study acknowledges that all hymns and prayers have a didactic aspect, even if that is not a primary function of the hymn. But some hymns provide evidence which suggests that this didactic aspect is as important as its communicative function. At the same time, these hymns often lack the indicators that communal recitation is the primary purpose. Taken together, the presence of instructional features and the lack of liturgical features suggest that didactic hymn or didactic prayer are appropriate designations for some texts. This combination of factors fits the evidence we have with regard to the *Barkhi Nafshi* hymns.

As for indicators of a liturgical setting, these hymns contain no refrains or other markers of communal use. Portions address God in the third person and refer to the community as a whole (e.g., 4Q434 1 i). Other hymns address God directly from the perspective of an individual who has experienced God's deliverance (4Q437 2 i). Unlike some other Qumran prayer texts there are no indicators of certain times, days, or festivals in which these prayers would be utilized.[42] Though it is still possible that these hymns were utilized in communal gatherings, the lack of clear indicators

---

[40] David Seely and Moshe Weinfeld, "Barkhi Nafshi," in *Qumran Cave 4.XX: Poetical and Liturgical Texts, Part 2* (ed. Esther G. Chazon et al.; Oxford: Clarendon Press, 1999), 255–334, here 255.

[41] Ibid., 258.

[42] As far as the original setting of these hymns, Schuller points out that the editors of the DJD volume do not address the *Sitz im Leben* at all; Schuller, "The Function and Use of Poetical Texts," 177.

causes us at least to place these hymns in a separate category from those with clear directions for their use. If not intended for worship, then the possibility arises that they were composed for another purpose, possibly instruction, teaching, or private study.

Instructional features of these hymns include historical allusions both to events of biblical history and events in the history of the community, biblical quotations and allusions, and also multiple references to teaching, instruction, and understanding. These kinds of contents, along with the lack of liturgical direction, suggest that it would be valuable to explore these hymns as didactic.

Two *Barkhi Nafshi* hymns will be examined here: 4Q434 1 i 1–14, and 4Q437 2 i 1–16. As the two largest fragments of the composition they provide the most context and thus the most potential for providing an understanding of their overall development and the specific purpose of their individual sections. The discussion below will highlight the didactic aspects of these two hymns noting both similarities and differences. By means of its explicit praise of God for certain of his wonders, the hymn in 4Q434 offers an implicit exhortation toward an attitude of humility and gratitude to God for his mercies that have been shown to the community in a variety of ways. Using a different approach, the hymn in 4Q437 models an individual's grateful response in remembering the works of salvation and deliverance that God has brought about for that person. The hymn teaches that remembering the ways God has worked is the key to facing the future with confidence and hope. Taken together, both hymns bless God for his works of deliverance in the past (either for the community or for an individual) and thereby instruct the hearers in proper attitudes and approaches to their current circumstances.

1. 4Q434 1 i 1–14

This hymn of praise recounts in stylized biblical expressions the abundant mercies that God has shown to a select group of people, specifically, the Qumran community. It addresses God in the third person and also refers to his people in the third person with the exception of the opening line ("Bless, O my soul"). Seely and Weinfeld identify at least five strophes in the column with three of the strophes being marked off in the text by the recurrence of the phrase "in the abundance" (lines 3, 4, 7).[43] In order to appreciate the development of the prayer, the English translation is cited here in full:

Bless, O my soul, the Lord
    for all of his wonders forever.

---

[43] Seely and Weinfeld, "Barkhi Nafshi," 272.

And blessed be his name,
    for he has delivered the soul of the poor,
        and the humble he has not despised,
            and he has not forgotten the distress of the helpless.
    He has opened his eyes to the helpless,
        and the cry of orphans he has heard,
            and he has turned his ear to their cry.

In the abundance of his mercy,
    he has been gracious to the needy,
        and he has opened their eyes to see his ways,
            and their ears to his teaching.
    And he has circumcised the foreskins of their heart,
        and he has delivered them on account of his lovingkindness,
            and he set their feet to the way.

In the abundance of their distress,
    he did not abandon them,
        and he did not give them over into the hand of the violent ones.
            And he did not judge them with the wicked.
    He did not kindle his wrath against them,
        and he did not destroy them in his anger.
    Though all his fiery anger was not exhausted,
        in the fire of (his) zeal he did not judge them.
    vacat

(But) he judged them in the abundance of his mercy,
    the judgements of his mercy in order to test them,
        and in the greatness of his mercy he hid them among the gentiles and [ ]
            man he delivered them.
He did not judge them (amidst) the mass of the gentiles,
    and he did not [ ] them among the peoples.
And he hid them in [ ]
    and he made darkness light before them,
        and (made) the crooked places straight,
            and he revealed to them the laws of peace and truth.
[He set] to measure their spirits,
    he meted out their words by weight
        causing them to sing like flutes.
And he gave them ano[th]er heart,
    and they walked in (his) w[ay]
In the way of his heart he also brought them near
    because they pledged with their spirit.
He sent them and fenced about [them,]
    and he commanded [eve]ry plague not to [touch (them.)]
vacat

His angel encamped arou[nd] (them),
   he watched over them lest [ ] he destroy them. (lines 1–12)[44]

As the hymn unfolds two elements come into focus: the identity of the community and the wonderful things that God has done for them.

On the one hand, the identity of the community is expressed using distinctive terminology. They are the poor (line 1), the helpless (twice in line 2), orphans (line 2), and the needy (line 3). The use of this kind of language to describe the community is well represented in other sectarian texts. For example, in the pesher which interprets Psalm 37:11 (i.e., 4Q171 1–2 ii 8–10) and in the pesher on Psalm 37:22 (i.e., 4Q171 1–2 iii 10) the members of the community are "the poor".[45] Similar terminology is used in the prayers of the War Scroll as well (e.g., 1QM 11:9, 13; 13:14; 14:7). God shows compassion on the poor and fatherless in a similar vein in 1QH[a] 5:20. The self-understanding of the Qumran community is revealed in these terms of weakness and poverty.

On the other hand, the phrase "in the abundance of his mercy" (lines 3 and 7) characterizes the actions of God toward this people. Seely and Weinfeld note that though this is not a biblical phrase, it is found at Qumran in 1QH[a] 7:27 with related phrases in 1QH[a] 7:30; 9:14; 11:28; 14:17. In the poetic and sectarian writings of the community, God's compassion for his lowly people is brought into clear focus in a way similar to what one finds in 4Q434.

The specific verbs used to describe the merciful work of God are instructive. They are both positive and negative. On the positive side, God has delivered (lines 1, 4, 8), opened his eyes (line 2), heard (line 2), been gracious (line 3), opened the eyes and ears of the needy (line 3), circumcised the foreskins of their heart (line 4), set their feet on the way (line 4), judged them in the abundance of his mercy (line 7), hid them (lines 7, 8), made darkness light and crooked places straight (line 9), revealed laws to them (line 9),[46] measured their spirits (line 10), meted out their words (line 10), caused them to sing (line 10), gave them another heart (line 10),[47] brought them near (line 11), and so on. On the negative side, the poet describes what God has restrained himself from doing.[48] Both the positive

---

[44] Ibid., 261–262. This is Seely and Weinfeld's translation and poetic arrangement of the text and not a transcription based on the original lines of the manuscript.

[45] Ibid., 274. See also Leander Keck, "The Poor Among the Saints in Jewish Christianity and Qumran," *ZNW* 57 (1966): 54–78, esp. 68.

[46] Compare to 1QH[a] 13:11–12 where the law is concealed in the teacher.

[47] Compare to the transformative idea in 1QH[a] 13:15–17 where the teacher is refined in crucible.

[48] God has not despised (line 2), has not forgotten (line 2), did not abandon (line 4), did not give them over (line 5), did not judge them with the wicked (line 5), did not kin-

acts and the deliberate restraint of God reflect the mercy and compassion of God for his people.

From this list of divine actions, several major themes emerge. First, the hymn has its primary focus on God's acts of deliverance expressed through the verb "deliver" (lines 1, 4, 8) and related terms both positive and negative. This deliverance has both an active component (he set their feet on the way, line 4; made darkness light, line 9; they walked in his way, line 10) and a more passive component whereby God prevented harm from coming upon them (lines 11, 12). These verbs and descriptions of God's mercies related to deliverance, protection among the gentiles, an angel encamping around them, and God bringing them near evoke the imagery of the exodus as well as that of exile and return.

A second theme, based on frequency of its occurrence, is that of God's judgment (lines 5, 6, 7, 8). God has both withheld judgment (lines 6, 8), and also judged according to his mercy (line 7). A third theme is that of the transforming work of God among the community. Through a variety of bodily metaphors this idea of a spiritual transformation is spelled out: opening of eyes and ears (line 3), circumcision of the heart (line 4), giving them words and causing them to sing (line 10), and giving them another heart (line 10).

In terms of its function at Qumran, as a hymn belonging to the community it is evident that this would serve to reinforce the view that the Qumran community was in some ways the favored people of God. God has treated them in many wondrous ways, not only protecting them physically but also providing for their spiritual transformation. This record of God's dealings with them aligns well with the theology of other documents which trace the origins of the community and its purpose in God's plans.

Though there are no commands or direct exhortations aside from the command to "bless, oh my soul" (line 1), the hymn, by virtue of its focus, implicitly urges the reader to value certain things and not others. The things that are valued are: God's preservation of this people in spite of their lowly state; his preparation of them to receive his teaching; his provision of revelation. With these emphases the hymn reinforces the value of humility before God, thanksgiving for his physical protection, recognition of human inability to apprehend God apart from his intervention, and gratitude for what God has provided his people (law, teaching, etc.). It also serves to distinguish this special group (the needy, despised, poor, orphans who were the beneficiaries of God's mercies) from others (the wicked, the gentiles, enemies).

---

dle his wrath against them (line 5), did not destroy them (line 5), did not judge them (lines 6, 8).

But something more can be said about the vision that the poet creates. The network of allusions and echoes in 4Q434 1 create a fascinating tapestry for discerning readers. The psalmist praises the Lord for his work of deliverance in language that evokes the promise of return from Babylon attested in Isa 40–43, a passage which itself uses imagery of the exodus and of the wilderness. The passage also highlights the miraculous work of God among his people, opening their eyes and ears. One almost has the sense that this is a review of ancient Israelite history: these are things God has done for Israel in the distant past. However, the personal tone of the passage, as well as the use of prominent Qumran imagery, taken together with the autobiographical style of other prayers of this document suggest that this hymn is more about the *recent* history of the community than the deeds of God in the distant past. But by using these allusions and presenting it in this hymnic framework this recent history of the community is understood by the psalmist to be the recent expression of the realities experienced by the Israelites in the exodus, in the wilderness, and in the return from exile.

This hymnic teaching speaks against what may have been a competing view, that the community members' expulsion and subsequent sojourn among the Gentiles referred to in lines 7 and 8 (whether literal or symbolic), was punitive and showed God's displeasure. Instead, the author of this psalm wants to reinforce the sectarian view articulated in other documents that the Qumran community is the locus of God's fulfilling of his promises to Israel. Rather than being punished, they have been preserved; moreover, in their weakness God has done a transformative work within them opening their eyes and ears, and circumcising their hearts. The author invites the community to see itself living out the eschatological promises of Isa 40–43.

By means of its explicit praise of God for certain of his wonders, the hymn in 4Q434 1 i 1–14 offers an implicit exhortation toward an attitude of humility and gratitude to God for his mercies that have been shown to the community in a variety of ways. The hymn blesses God for his works of deliverance in the past and thereby instructs the hearers in proper attitudes and approaches to their current circumstances. With its deliberate echo of the language of paradigmatic biblical texts, it paints a very positive picture of the community's past and present, while it also contests other less favorable interpretations of the community's history.

2. 4Q437 2 i 1–16

This particular column contains the praises of God by an individual for delivering him personally from enemies who were trying to trap him. Seely and Weinfeld refer to this as a "hymn of praise and thanksgiving for divine deliverance."[49] Like other poetry from Qumran which we have looked at there is a major emphasis on a crisis and on God's deliverance through this ordeal.

The deliverance of the poet is expressed in terminology that is reminiscent of scriptural precedents. Seely and Weinfeld observe,

As is typical of much of the poetry at Qumran, the author draws heavily on biblical passages for his metaphors of deliverance. The images are taken from the biblical texts, either directly or in an altered form. . . The poet has also created some original images in conjunction with these well-known biblical images.[50]

The biblical "style" is thus a major feature of this particular psalm as was the case with the prayers of the War Scroll above.

The psalmist's descriptions of what God has done for him are reminiscent of the group experiences described in 4Q434 1 i and noted above. In 4Q437 2 i 1–16 the author blesses God's name for:

Delivering him from the snare of the gentiles (line 4, cf. line 10)
Preserving his soul amidst the gentiles (line 5)
Not forsaking him or hiding his face (lines 6–7)
Seeing his groaning and hearing his voice (lines 7–8)
Hiding him (lines 8–9)
Making him into a sharp arrow (line 9)
Bringing up his soul from the underworld (line 11)
Setting life before him (line 11)
Making the congregation sit in front of him (line 12)
Consoling him (line 12)
Gladdening his soul (lines 12–13)[51]
Enlivening his spirit (line 13)

The references to delivering and to hiding connect this hymn closely with what we observed in 4Q434 1 i. Further, there is a connection between deliverance and the resulting praise. With gladdened soul and enlivened spirit (lines 12–13) the writer moves on to bless the Lord with all his strength (line 13). This is reminiscent of 4Q434 1 i 1 and 10 where blessing the Lord (line 1) and singing like flutes (line 10) are the natural results of God's work of deliverance.

The hymn in 4Q437 2 has several features which make it quite distinct from the hymn in 4Q434 1 i. As the expression of one individual (as opposed to the community) this hymn serves the role of a model for giving thanks to God for deliverance. By reflecting on his experiences in the form

---

[49] Seely and Weinfeld, "Barkhi Nafshi," 308.
[50] Ibid.
[51] Cf. 1QH^a 13:16 where the copyist wrote: "you have changed my soul" for "you have changed the storm." Perhaps the copyist was expecting a note of personal transformation in that hymn as well.

of a hymn, the poet provides encouragement to others to move ahead with confidence in the face of adversity. In lines 14–16 the verb "remember" (זכר) is used three times as the key to his joy, confidence, and hope as he looks to the future. This hymnic use of זכר has biblical precedent and is found in hymns, complaint psalms, and individual thanksgiving psalms (Jonah 2:8). Especially close to this particular usage is its use in the biblical "psalms of trust" (e.g., Ps 119:52 and Ps 56).[52]

Of interest in this connection is the writer's specific use of Pss 63 and 77 in this hymn. The author uses phrases from Ps 63:2, 7, and 9, and Ps 77:13 in lines 15–16. Both psalms share the theme of seeking the Lord by day and by night.[53] These observations lead to a conclusion that, from a didactic perspective, the hymn would teach the value of remembering the works of God at all times.

As was the case with the hymns and prayers of the War Scroll, the *Barkhi Nafshi* hymns use several strategies to emphasize aspects of the identity of the Qumran community over against outsiders. Distinctive in these hymns are references to the transformational work of God in the life of an individual, as well as reflecting on the recent deliverance of an individual and community in biblical terms. The idea that the community is one that remembers the work of God in the past is also in view.

D. Didactic Hymns in the Hodayot (1QH^a)

Because of its length and because of its theological emphases the Hodayot must surely be considered one of the most revealing of the Qumran manuscripts.[54] The Hodayot and *Barkhi Nafshi* share several features. First, they are both hymnic compositions with no clear indicators of liturgical function. Second, they both contain prayers written from the perspective of an individual as well as prayers written from the perspective of the collective community. Third, both compositions seem to lie within a stream of tradition with roots in the Hebrew Bible, while at the same time providing clear indicators of the kinds of theological development that were unique to the Qumran sect. A major difference is the amount of material that has survived from each composition. Because portions of 24 columns of the Ho-

---

[52] Childs, *Memory and Tradition*, 49. Childs also points out the significance of those passages where Israel fails to remember, and the disobedience and curse that results. See also Ps 143:5.

[53] Seely and Weinfeld, "Barkhi Nafshi," 318.

[54] On this history of the Hodayot and the reconstruction of 1QH^a see Hartmut Stegemann, Eileen M. Schuller, and Carol A. Newsom, *1QHodayot^a: With Incorporation of 1QHodayot^b and 4QHodayot^{a-f}* (DJD 40; Oxford: Clarendon Press, 2009), 13–53.

dayot have been preserved scholars are able to get a much better picture of the overall themes and emphases of the Hodayot hymns. As we have seen, the major emphases of the *Barkhi Nafshi* hymns are easy enough to discern. Nevertheless, without more samples of nearly complete hymns it is difficult to speak about the purposes of that composition as a whole with any degree of certainty.

A number of scholars have recognized the heavy didactic emphasis of the Hodayot. Though there is debate as to the practical uses of the Hodayot within the community (were they used for community worship? private devotion? individual study? all of the above?), most scholars would agree that providing instruction in the ways of the community is a primary function.[55] Accordingly, rather than enter into debate about the organization, origins, and use of the Hodayot, in this section it is possible to build on the work of other scholars in appreciating these texts as didactic hymns. I will first comment on the perspective of Bilhah Nitzan whose approach grapples with some of the main issues that have occupied scholars of the Hodayot since their discovery. Along with Nitzan's views, a summary of the approach and findings of Carol Newsom will help bring into focus the didactic functions of the Hodayot. Once these perspectives are outlined, it will be possible to see how they are reflected in an analysis of two of the Hodayot thanksgiving hymns: 9:1–39 and 13:7–21.[56]

Nitzan has explored the Hodayot in comparison with other collections of prayers and religious poetry at Qumran.[57] She finds the Hodayot to be the specific expression of an individual's experience, as opposed to more general prayers composed for use by the community. She explains that in 1QH[a], "The individual songs of thanksgiving served as instruments by which to express personal experiences and feelings, as well as to convey particular religious and ideological messages, which had no place in the fixed prayer or in standard religious poetry."[58] This emphasis on conveying particular religious and ideological messages is one indication, among others, that the Hodayot were not written for the same purposes as many of the fixed prayers at Qumran.

As for their instructional impact, Nitzan concludes, "The theoretical statements intertwined within the words of thanksgiving bear an explicitly sectarian message; in this manner, the songs of the *Thanksgiving Scroll*

---

[55] Émile Puech, "Hodayot," in *Encyclopedia of the Dead Sea Scrolls* (ed. Lawrence H. Schiffman and James C. VanderKam; 2 vols.; New York: Oxford University Press, 2000), 365–369.

[56] References to lines and columns of the Hodayot are from Stegemann, Schuller, and Newsom, *1QHodayot*[a]. See the charts comparing the various reconstructions on pp. 49–53.

[57] Nitzan, *Qumran Prayer and Religious Poetry*, 321–355.

[58] Ibid., 328.

became a vehicle by which the poet made known the ways of God to the members of his sect."[59] Nitzan is pointing here to the many direct statements of theological formulations that are found throughout the Hodayot. These are incorporated into hymns and prayers and, through these, the theological ideas of the community were promoted. Nitzan continues,

> Thus, in addition to the individual expression of religious experience and the articulation of praise and thanksgiving as ends in their own right, they serve the function of instructing and making known the doctrine of the sect among its members, and guiding them in 'the way of the heart' of God.[60]

With this understanding one could expect to be able to read and explore the Hodayot hymns for their distinctive theological emphases with very clear results.

While also recognizing the instructional emphasis of the Hodayot, Newsom has taken a different approach to exploring their didactic impact. By examining the construction of the self in the Hodayot, Newsom looks beyond what the text says to consider what the text does.[61] She examines how the language of the Hodayot helps to structure reality for the community members who embrace this way of thinking about themselves and their relationship with God. She makes a number of important observations in this regard. First, she points out that the focus of the Hodayot on thanksgiving is not incidental. Newsom explains, "The introductory formulas orient the reader to thanksgiving as the paradigmatic mode of experience."[62] She goes on to explain,

> From the variety of relationships between worshipper and God in the repertoire of biblical tradition the Qumran community has selected one – benefaction – as its privileged expression. Although a variety of moods, attitudes, and expressions occur in the Hodayot, they are all subordinated to the fundamental relationship established in the opening words that cast the speaker in the role of recipient.[63]

In other words, one who embraces this way of speaking and reflecting will necessarily see oneself as a recipient of divine favor – favor that is not deserved.

In addition, Newsom explains how the use of traditional biblical language alongside sectarian theological reflection serves to call into question other competing interpretations of the biblical precedents. She notes in particular the effect of the juxtaposition of ordinary language in one sentence with sectarian language (e.g., in 1QH^a 7:16–21): "Its effect is simultane-

---

[59] Ibid., 342.
[60] Ibid.
[61] Newsom, *The Self as Symbolic Space*, 2.
[62] Ibid., 206.
[63] Ibid.

ously to appropriate received religious language, to reinterpret its meaning, and implicitly to contest other understandings."[64] Exegetical traditions embodied in the scriptural allusions of the Hodayot thus mark out a distinct space on the playing field of Jewish biblical interpretation in the Second Temple period.

Newsom further examines how the negative, self-abasing language (part of the sectarian ideology) serves as part of the rhetorical device for constructing the self positively in relation to God. She concludes,

> Despite the many uncertainties concerning their composition and use in the life of the sectarian community, the Hodayot of the community clearly serve as templates for the distinctive experience of the self cultivated in the sect. Both by hearing others describe themselves in these poetic prayers and by the practice of articulating one's own experience in terms of the shaped story of the self in the Hodayot, the sectarian is drawn into a radical reinterpretation of his identity.[65]

Seen in this way one might consider the Hodayot to foster a form of experiential learning that goes beyond simply accepting a set of doctrines about the community and its relationship with God.

Nitzan and Newsom do not represent the complete range of approaches to the study of the Hodayot.[66] Nevertheless, they provide a framework that will enable us here to explore several passages within the Hodayot with an ear for their theological content as well as their didactic function within the community. With the insights derived from our study of didactic hymns in the War Scroll and the *Barkhi Nafshi* hymns we have a good foundation for evaluating the Hodayot texts and their didactic impact.

1. *1QHᵃ 9:1–39*

The hymn in 1QHᵃ 9:1–39 provides an excellent starting place for our analysis since it contains a number of features that are representative of many of the Hodayot hymns. Its position in the larger document is of some interest, as it may be viewed as an introduction to what have been called the Teacher Hymns.[67] The Teacher Hymns are a collection of hymns in cols 10–18 which are marked by several characteristics which suggest they were the product of an influential individual, perhaps the sect's founder,

---

[64] Ibid., 212.

[65] Ibid., 347–48.

[66] For recent studies of the Hodayot with different emphases see Angela Kim Harkins, "Observations on the Editorial Shaping of the So-Called Community Hymns from 1QHᵃ and 4QHᵃ (4Q427)," *DSD* 12 (2005): 233–256; Julie Hughes, *Scriptural Allusions and Exegesis in the Hodayot* (STDJ 59; Leiden: Brill, 2006).

[67] This possibility is suggested in Harkins, "Observations on the Editorial Shaping," 237.

the Teacher of Righteousness.[68] As an introduction to the Teacher Hymns – or at least a transitional psalm between the Community Hymns and the Teacher Hymns – this psalm in col. 9 sets out clearly the didactic emphasis of all that will follow.

Though the beginning of the column is lost, it is clear that the hymn quickly moves to a focus on God's work in creation of all things and pre-determining of all things (lines 9–22). In English translation, this first portion reads,

And in your wisdom [ ] eternity, and before you created them you knew [all] their deeds
for everlasting ages. And [without you no]thing is done, and nothing is known without
    your will. You formed
every spirit, and [their] work [you determine]ed, and the judgment for all their deeds.
    You yourself stretched out the heavens
for your glory, and all [ ] you [de]termined according to your will, and powerful spirits
    according to their laws, before
they came to be ho[ly] angels [and]*m* eternal spirits in their dominions: luminaries ac-
    cording to their mysteries,
stars according to [their] paths, [stor]m [winds] according to their task, shooting stars and
    lightning according to their service, and storehouses
devised for th[eir] purposes [ ] according to their mysteries. You yourself created the
    earth through your strength,
and the seas and the deeps [you] made [through your might and] their [de]signs you es-
    tablished through your wisdom, and all that is in them
you set in or[der] according to your will [ ] for the human spirit that you fashioned in the
    world for all the days of eternity
and everlasting generations for *m*[ ]*l* And according to their seasons, you allotted their
    service throughout all their generations and the jud[g]ement
in the times appointed for it, according to the domini[on and] their ways you determined
    for every generation, and a visitation for their recompense together with
<with> all their punishments[ ]*h*. And you allotted it to all their offspring according to
    the number of the generations of eternity
and for all the everlasting years [ ]*h* And in the wisdom of your knowledge you de-
    term[i]ned their des[t]iny before
they existed. According to your wi[ll] everything [comes] to pass; and without you noth-
    ing is done. *vacat* (lines 9–22)[69]

This section is a meditation on the deeds, wisdom, and power of God in creation of things in heaven and things on earth. M. Endo has explored the use of the creation account in this section and has suggested that the psalmist has taken the phrase "God created the heavens and the earth" and

---

[68] See the discussion of the variety of views and reasons in Puech, "Hodayot," 365-369; Michael Owen Wise, "The Concept of a New Covenant in the Teacher Hymns from Qumran (1QH^A X–XVII)," in *The Concept of the Covenant in the Second Temple Period* (ed. Stanley E. Porter and Jacqueline C. R. De Roo; Leiden: Brill, 2003), 99–128.

[69] Translations of the Hodayot are those of Carol Newsom found in Stegemann, Schuller, and Newsom, *1QHodayot^a* (DJD 40).

explored the creation of things in heaven and things in earth as two distinct subjects.[70] By comparing the creation of earthly things including humans (lines 15–22) with the creation of heavenly things (lines 11–15), the author argues for God's control over both spheres of creation. Endo explains the logic of the hymn in this way, "The creation hymn of 1QH[a] col. 9 emphasizes God's sovereignty over human history, by referring to the unshakable order of God, which is compared with the order (or course) in the astronomical and meteorological phenomena."[71] One important aspect of this claim is that both cosmic and earthly things have been created according to the wisdom of God (lines 6, 16, 21) which orders all things.[72]

This first section of the hymn in col. 9 has a universal focus on God's wisdom, his works and his power in creation. This is somewhat different than the *Barkhi Nafshi* hymns with their emphasis on God's saving work for the community or an individual. The prayers and hymns of the War Scroll did include mention of these kinds of activities in creation as well, but also moved to specific activities of God in history on behalf of his people. This use of specific historical examples to make a point is absent in this hymn. However, there is a move from timeless past to the present in this hymn; it occurs when the focus shifts to the psalmist/teacher himself in line 23.

The hymn shifts abruptly to the psalmist himself when he writes about how he came to this knowledge of God's pre-determining role in human history. The psalmist claims,

These things I know because of understanding that comes from you, for you have opened my ears to wondrous mysteries. (line 23a)

What has preceded (i.e. the "these things") is thus understood as the content of what God has revealed to the psalmist. Newsom has pointed out the central role that revealed knowledge plays in this hymn, particularly with regard to what amounts to the *ethos* of the writer. She explains,

The character created by this voice, which can speak so clearly about the divine will and plan, about the mysteries of the heavens, the orderly structures of the cosmos, and even about events of future judgment, is quintessentially a character who has intimate understanding of the sorts of knowledge that are the provenance of God.[73]

---

[70] Masanobu Endo, *Creation and Christology: A Study on the Johannine Prologue in the Light of Early Jewish Creation Accounts* (Tübingen: Mohr Siebeck, 2002), 48.

[71] Ibid., 49.

[72] This is a prominent theme in the Hodayot as well as other Qumran writings. Matthew J. Goff, "Reading Wisdom at Qumran: 4QInstruction and the Hodayot," *DSD* 11 (2004): 263–288. Goff explains, "The 'mysteries' of the cosmic order reflect the wisdom (hochma) of God, according to 1QH[a] 9:7 and 19" (274). See also 1QH[a] 17:23; 20:13; 4Q491c 3; 1QS 4:18.

[73] Newsom, *The Self as Symbolic Space*, 225.

A cursory reading of the Hodayot would reveal to the reader that possessing this special knowledge is of critical importance to this community,
and especially to the leader.[74]

Yet in spite of the psalmist's possession of this special knowledge the
psalm goes on to recount the weakness and finitude of the psalmist in
comparison with God and his knowledge:

Yet I am a creature of clay and a thing kneaded with water,
a foundation of shame and a well or impurity, a furnace of iniquity, and a structure of sin,
a spirit of error and a perverted being, without
understanding, and terrified by righteous judgements. What could I say that is not already
known, or what could I declare that has not already been told? (lines 23b–25)

This understanding of human limitations is another theme that pervades the
Hodayot. Thus the psalmist himself, though possessing special knowledge
and serving as a model to others within the community, has not been singled out for his own aptitude or promise. The psalmist himself is not to be
glorified or exalted. If an individual knows anything of God it is because
God has had compassion on that person in order that he can use him to recount his ways before all God's creatures. Lines 33–36 make this point:

And you, in your mercy
and your great kindness, you have strengthened the human spirit in the face of affliction
and [the poor] soul you have cleansed from great iniquity
so that it might recount your wonders before all your creatures. And I will recit[e contin-
ually] in their midsts the judgements which have afflicted me,
and to humankind all your wonders by which you have shown yourself strong through
[me before hu]mankind. (lines 33–36)

The psalm has thus moved from divinely revealed knowledge, to the one
through whom that knowledge came, to the purpose for that knowledge.

Finally, the psalm switches its focus from addressing God to addressing
a human audience. In this final section the didactic purpose of the whole is
made explicit:

Hear, O sages, and those who ponder knowledge. May those who are eager, become firm
in purpose. [All who are straight of wa]y, become more discerning.
O righteous ones, put an end to injustice. All you whose way is perfect, hold fast [O you
who are cru]shed by afflication, be patient.
Do not reject [righteous] judgement[s.] (lines 36–39)

Here in the language of the sapiential tradition the audience is identified as
those who are already wise and are already meditating on knowledge. The
audience is the devout and faithful men of the community, and perhaps
those who have not yet joined the community. The psalmist implores them
to listen and learn, again making explicit the didactic aim of this psalm. It

---

[74] Menahem Mansoor, *The Thanksgiving Hymns* (STDJ 3; Leiden: Brill, 1961), 65–74.

is this explicit call to learn that may lend support to the idea that this hymn introduces the hymns of the teacher.

The fact that this hymn draws on wisdom imagery and creation imagery has led scholars to discuss connections with other wisdom writings at Qumran. Matthew Goff has compared the didactic strategies of this psalm and the text 4QInstruction which makes similar use of creation and wisdom themes but in a more explicit genre of wisdom writing (as opposed to hymn). He notes, "4QInstruction and the Hodayot combine pedagogical intent with the theme of revelation. Both compositions echo Prov 1:4 when they state a desire 'to make the simple understand'."[75] However, in spite of their similar intentions Goff suggests that these two texts utilize different pedagogical approaches. The Hodayot "shows more interest in the teacher imparting revelation than in his students studying his disclosures."[76] In this view, it is not so much the specific knowledge that the teacher has, as the fact that he *has* this specific knowledge that is in focus. The psalm seems to place the emphasis on the one who possesses the knowledge more so than on the importance of seeking to attain such knowledge.

This psalm is one that represents Newsom's thesis: it offers a paradigmatic view of the self and of God's beneficence in showing grace and mercy. In addition a psalm like this with its clear didactic emphasis serves to re-actualize the wisdom of the earlier Jewish writings. This psalm implies that the psalm itself, written by one who has received special knowledge, is part of the ongoing revelation of the wisdom and knowledge of God. This idea is not unique to this psalm but is expressed in other Teacher Hymns as well (cf. 12:6).

2. 1QH^a 13:7–21

2. 1QH^a 13:7–21

The psalm in 1QH^a 13:7–21 is considered to be one of the "Hymns of the Teacher." In approaching this psalm, Newsom's insights are particularly helpful. Eschewing questions about the historical identity and events in the life of the presumed Teacher of Righteousness who is portrayed in the Teacher Hymns, she moves toward questions of "how these Hodayot functioned over time, as they were continually read or recited, to shape the ethos of the community and to address perennial questions of sectarian life."[77] With regard to their function she explains, "In their repetition over decades of use they would have come to form the dramatized expression of the habitual functions of leadership within the sectarian community."[78]

---

[75] Goff, "Reading Wisdom at Qumran," 274.
[76] Ibid., 275.
[77] Newsom, *The Self as Symbolic Space*, 288.
[78] Ibid., 298.

Following this approach, we can explore the author's description of his experiences with a sensitivity to the way this text would have functioned within the community. A significant aspect of that function would have been to teach and instruct members of the community through the example of the author as he reflects with thanksgiving on his own experiences.

In this particular psalm of thanks the psalmist rehearses what God has done for him. A driving metaphor in this psalm is deliverance from the mouth of the lions (first referenced in line 9). As with other Qumran hymns we can observe language of deliverance and protection expressed both positively and negatively. The psalm reads:

I thank you, O Lord, that you have not abandoned me when I dwelt with a foreign people
[ ] according to my guilt
did you judge me. You did not abandon me to the devices of my inclination. And you
delivered my life from the pit, and you gave me [es]cape in the midst
of lions appointed for the children of guilt, lions that crush the bones of the mighty and
drink the blood of warriors. You placed me
in a dwelling place among the many fishers who spread a net over the surface of the waters and among the hunters of the children of iniquity. And there, for judgement,
you established me, and the counsel of truth you strengthened in my heart. From this
comes a covenant for those who seek it. And you closed the mouth of the young lions
whose
teeth are like a sword and whose jaw teeth are like a pointed spear. Snake venom – such
is all their scheming. They lie in wait for robbery, but they have not
opened their mouths against me. For you, O my God, have sheltered me against mortals,
and your law you have hidden in [me] until the time
when your salvation is revealed to me. For you have not abandoned me in the distress of
my soul, you have heard my cry for help in the bitterness of my soul,
and the outcry of my misery you have recognized in my groaning. You rescued the life of
the poor one in the dwelling of the lions that whet their tongue like a sword.
And you, my God, have shut their teeth, so that they would not rend the life of the poor
and destitute, and you drew back their tongue
like a sword into its sheath, so that the life of your servant was not [cut off]. And in order
to manifest your strength through me before mortal beings you have acted wonderfully
toward the poor one. You have brought him into the furna[ce] like gold (subjected to) the
action of fire and like silver refined in the crucible of the smelters for sevenfold purity.
The wicked among the peoples rushed against me with their torments, and all day they
crush my soul. *vacat*
But you, O my God, turn the storm into stillness, and the soul of the poor one you have
rescued like a bir[d from the snare, and] like prey from the mouth
of the lions. *vacat* (lines 7–21)

With a multitude of allusions to Daniel in the den of lions, the psalmist rehearses how God has preserved him and prepared him for his role of community leader. The contents and emphasis of this hymn shows many striking similarities to the psalms discussed above from 4Q434 and 4Q437.

Connections include a multitude of references to God's delivering and saving work; similar descriptions of God's people as the poor, needy, or weak; God's hearing the cry of the psalmist; the psalmist's being hidden among the Gentiles; biblical imagery of protection (though different metaphors are used in each psalm); and the purpose of God's deliverance being related to revealing or concealing his law. In addition to these similarities, each psalm also identifies some aspect of transformation in the life of the psalmist as well, though the metaphors differ in each case.

The author of this psalm is not describing events of biblical history but events from the recent past. In particular the author is detailing his own personal experience. This particular hymn illustrates Mansoor's observation about the Hodayot as a whole. The author's "election by God was purely personal, and individual. The emotional experience resulting from his election and from his affiliation with the congregation of the elect, is the central theme of the Thanksgiving Hymns."[79] This hymn exemplifies the focus on God's work in the life of the individual.

Of interest here is the particular way that this individual's experience is described and expressed. As was the case in the *Barkhi Nafshi* hymns, this individual's experiences are cast in the language of biblical history. The end result is that his experiences are understood to be a part of the story of the working of God in Israel in ages past (specifically in the time of Daniel). One implication is that God is working now in the same way he always has in the past. The story of the present community is seen to be an actualization of the story of God in the lives of his people in ages past.

Beyond the Daniel imagery, which is primary to the poem, Kittel notes that other apocalyptic judgment metaphors are utilized in a secondary way. She writes,

The poet also speaks of the hunters and fishers with nets – a theme found in Jeremiah and Habakkuk – and of purifying gold and silver through refinement in fire, as in Malachi. These subsidiary images are neatly enclosed, one in the first half of the poem and one in the second half, by the imagery of the lions. All three images are judgment images.[80]

The imagery recalls Jer 16:16, Hab 1:14–17, and Mal 3:3. Mansoor observes that from the allusion to Jer 16:16 "it is clear that the author here is referring to the divine agents of punishment."[81] In other words, God has delivered the psalmist from the agents of judgment that God has used to punish the wicked and that potentially threatened the psalmist as well.

What is being taught by this combination of biblical judgment imagery? In this case, not only that God delivered this person in a time of judgment,

---

[79] Mansoor, *The Thanksgiving Hymns*, 62.

[80] Bonnie Pedrotti Kittel, *The Hymns of Qumran: Translation and Commentary* (Missoula, Mont.: Scholars Press, 1980), 96.

[81] Mansoor, *The Thanksgiving Hymns*, 133.

but also that through the ordeal he prepared this person for what he would do in the future. Kittel observed,

> The poet's thanksgiving is not for rescue as such, but for God's support by which he achieves salvation. . . The lions attempt to destroy the poet, but cannot because of God's salvific work in the poet. The final stage in the judgment process is like the refining of precious metal, in which the dross is washed away, and the poet's salvation is complete. The lions cannot conquer because of God's declaration of innocence and salvation.[82]

Kittel is correct, but one can go further still to note that the salvation of the poet was not for himself alone; his salvation was for the benefit of all the faithful:

> And there, for judgement,
> you established me, and the counsel of truth you strengthened in my heart. From this comes a covenant for those who seek it. (lines 10–11)

Further, in line 13 he refers to his understanding that God "concealed his law" in him. This represents yet another allusion to the idea that God has revealed special knowledge to the teacher (cf. 9:23; 10:15; 12:6–7). In a later stanza he describes his experience with the image of gold refined in a crucible and silver purified and refined in a furnace (line 18). In this psalm the writer thanks God not only for delivering him but also for preparing him through those experiences. It is because of those experiences that God can now show his greatness through this person before the sons of Adam (line 17). The psalm therefore casts the whole experience not only as an experience of God's protecting work but also of God's transforming work in the life of the psalmist. This is not unlike what we observed in the *Barkhi Nafshi* hymns with their emphasis on personal transformation. Here, however, the transformation of the psalmist legitimates his role as teacher. This psalm thus teaches primarily about the teacher, and, perhaps by extension, about the individual community members who identify with him.

3. Other Qumran Themes in the Hodayot

As we have seen, the didactic hymns and prayers of the War Scroll and *Barkhi Nafshi* represented a number of similar ideas and themes. To what extent do the hymns of 1QH[a] prioritize those same ideas? Two themes will be briefly discussed here: the idea of the coming eschatological victory and the concept of remembrance.

Eschatological conflagration that includes the defeat of the enemies of God plays a significant role in the Hodayot. Puech observes that both the Teacher Hymns (cols 10–18) and the Community Hymns (cols 1–9 and

---

[82] Kittel, *The Hymns of Qumran*, 97.

19–26) share this perspective. He points out, "The allusions to the total eschatological war, the final and decisive judgment in the heights on earth
and in the underworld Abyss . . . are found in both categories."[83] This eschatological war is clearly spelled out in the hymns in 11:33–37 and in
14:24–38.

Discussing the eschatological war referenced in col. 11, Kittel observes,
"This cosmological scheme is indeed borrowed from the OT, but its com-
pleteness and its vividness testify to the continuing development and use of
the OT scheme in this period."[84] The hymnic treatment of this theme indicates some degree of theological development beyond the picture of eschatological warfare painted in the earlier Hebrew Scriptures. Rather than being simply poetic language dramatizing the rescue of the righteous, Kittel
finds that this language describes actual eschatological warfare. She writes,
"It is quite clear from a consideration of the poem as a whole that these
terms are eschatological images drawn from a full-blown dynamic mythology, not simply ancient metaphors designed to provide superlative language for rescue in the present life."[85] In part, then, the didactic function
here would be to remind and exhort the hearer or reader about the reality of
the coming judgment and all that it would entail. This is not completely
different from what we observed in the War Scroll, although in that context, the eschatological elements of the prayers were even more explicitly
emphasized as real warfare.

When we look for instances of historical remembrances in the Hodayot
(as we had seen in the prayers in the War Scroll and *Barkhi Nafshi*) it is
surprising to discover that the concept is not very prevalent. Though present implicitly to some extent, the concept of historical remembrance of
the works of God is not explicitly identified in a very prominent way.

The one explicit reference to the psalmist's remembering of the deeds of
God is found in the hymn in col. 12. The psalmist remembers his own guilt
along with the unfaithfulness of the Israelites in history as a cause for fear
and dread before God (lines 33–35). In 1QH^a 12:35–37 he exclaims,

For I remember my guilty acts together with the unfaithfulness of my ancestors, when the
wicked rose against your covenant
and the vile against your word. And I said, 'In my sin I have been abandoned, far from
your covenant'. But when I remembered the strength of your hand together with
your abundant compassion, I stood strong and rose up, and my spirit held fast to (its) station in the face of affliction. (lines 35-37)

What is most interesting here are the objects of remembrance. In this case
the psalmist is not remembering the great deeds of God from the past. In-

---

[83] Puech, "Hodayot," 368.
[84] Kittel, *The Hymns of Qumran*, 80.
[85] Ibid., 79.

stead the objects of his remembrance are theological truths directly related to God himself: his strength and his compassion. Perhaps the writer is remembering these in the sense of remembering his experience of these attributes of God firsthand when God displayed his strength and showed his compassion to the writer in the past, but those events themselves are not referenced. His calling to mind of the abstract qualities of God's strength and compassion provide the writer with strength and resolve in the face of a new set of afflictions.

Aside from this explicit reference to remembering, there are, as we have seen, a number of references to the work of God in the life of the paradigmatic "I" in many of the hymns of the teacher. These references are historical in the sense that they refer to what God has done in the life of this individual.[86] However, the emphasis in the Hodayot is less on remembering the deeds of God in the past and more on having divinely revealed knowledge in the present (e.g., 9:23, 28). While memory plays some role here, the Qumran psalmist(s) responsible for these hymns wants to emphasize the importance of the knowledge of God – presumably theological insights and ways of understanding the times.[87]

The Hodayot thus provide a picture of a multi-faceted use of hymnic and prayer forms. The psalmist is able to reflect on his own experience in the form of thanksgiving to God in a way that helps him and his readers to view his experiences as a part of the ongoing work of the God of Israel from ancient times. Through this kind of reflection the psalmist draws strength to face ongoing crises in the present. Also he models a godly response to suffering and a humble dependence on God. Through this means he emphasizes certain traits of God (power, control of history, compassion). Further the author teaches, in a somewhat surprising way, how he has come to have the position of authority he now experiences.

To the extent that a member of the community identifies himself with the experience of the writer(s) of the Hodayot, that member affirms some theological truths about himself and his relationship with the Creator. The Creator is all-powerful and all-merciful, while the individual is finite, weak, and incapable of grasping the knowledge of God. Any apprehension

---

[86] For a defense of the idea that these should be read as historical see Wise, "Concept of a New Covenant," 100–108.

[87] Mansoor corroborates this view: "In 1QH we find an even greater emphasis upon knowledge than in the wisdom literature of the Old Testament. Knowledge in this sense means for the members of the Qumran community a prerequisite for salvation, which no one outside the group can share. Only the one whom God has elected for his covenant is capable of such knowledge." Mansoor, *The Thanksgiving Hymns*, 68–69. Further direct support of this perspective can be found in 1QH[a] 6:19–24, 7:12, 12:6, and 20:13–16. While remembrance of God's past deeds is important at Qumran, the special knowledge that God has revealed to the psalmist takes center stage in the Hodayot.

of divine truth is a result of God's goodness and compassion in revealing it to humanity, or more specifically, to the Teacher. The appropriate response to God's revelation of his mysteries through this individual is thanksgiving.

Several lines from the hymn found in 1QH[a] 26 may serve to summarize this discussion as they bring into focus the main themes of the Hodayot as discussed above: "Bless the one who wondrously does majestic deeds and who makes known the strength of his hand, sealing up / mysteries and revealing hidden things, raising up those who stumble and those among them who fall, restoring the steps of those who wait for knowledge / but bringing low the lofty assemblies of the eternally proud" (lines 14–16).

E. Conclusions

This chapter has merely scratched the surface in terms of the rich and varied deployment of hymns and prayers within the Qumran writings. In looking at three Qumran hymnic and prayer compositions we have been able to observe the ways that these texts were used to convey instruction. The contents of the instruction concerned the nature of God (past, present, and future), the nature of humanity, the history of God's specially chosen people, the recent history of the Qumran community, the personal history of the psalmist, and the future work of God on behalf of his people in the eschatological war.

We saw that the prayers of the War Scroll use several strategies to convey to the members of the community the idea that they are God's people and that God will show mercy to them in the coming battle and in fact fight the battle for them, as he has done for past generations of his faithful children. The review of history was one central component in bolstering the confidence of the community in light of the approaching eschatological battle. God's deeds for his people in the past were utilized as a source for confidence in how God would act in the future for his people.

The *Barkhi Nafshi* texts utilized hymnic reviews of history as well, but in a more subtle manner. The prayer in 4Q434 1 i 1–14 gives thanks to God for his deliverance in the past using language that is suggestive of the exodus, the exile, and the return from exile. Because of clues in the other prayers of *Barkhi Nafshi*, it is evident that this first prayer is thanking God for events in recent history, not for his preservation of his people in the original exodus or original return from exile. But the language used portrays the recent events of the community in the categories of biblical experience of return from exile as a new exodus, and of the eschatological time of blessing as promised in Isaiah, now fulfilled in the community. The audience is invited to see its present experience as a part of the story of God revealed in the scriptures and experienced in the present.

Though the prayers of the Hodayot likewise utilized historical events and imagery (cf. 1QH^a 13), we observed that a more pronounced emphasis of these texts was the special knowledge that God has revealed to the psalmist. In each text we looked at we were able to gain perspective on how the different authors drew on traditional Jewish motifs to craft a unique poetic vision for their present communities and to shape the imaginations of their audiences. In each of the prayers, combinations of biblical history, recent history, scriptural citations, scriptural allusions, and biblical styles of expression all work together to achieve instructional and theological purposes for the community.

We cannot know to what extent these texts found a place in a liturgical or communal worship setting. These texts, unlike many liturgical texts at Qumran, do not provide any direct information as to how the community made use of them. Nevertheless, because of their presence in multiple copies, and the ways they reflect key beliefs of the Dead Sea sect, we surmise that these were influential within the thoughts and worldview of the members of the community.

Attending to the didactic features of several Qumran hymns has revealed some areas of continuity with earlier Jewish traditions as well. For example, the quotation of biblical verses, references to events in biblical history, and allusions to biblical phraseology and ideas all reflect the importance of the earlier writings for this particular community. Some of the didactic features of these Qumran texts point to the community's need to supplement that tradition with newer ideas as well. Seeing themselves and their teacher as faithful participants in the covenant community of God was not always easy when they were experiencing oppression, persecution, and rejection from their fellow Jews. The hymns and psalms we have explored here suggest that as they reflected on their experiences in light of biblical precedents, they found the courage and confidence to continue facing adversity and even impending war. The poetic expression of history, theology, and belief found in these didactic hymns served a number of functions for the Qumran poets, teachers, and their community. It has also enabled us to look into the Qumran community and attempt to see the world through the eyes of their poets.

Chapter 8

Didactic Hymns in the Letters of the New Testament

A. Introduction

Though the letters of the New Testament contain the earliest surviving witnesses to the beliefs and practices of the early Christians, no one letter gives us a complete picture of the ways the early Christians conceptualized their faith in Christ or the ways they practiced that faith in the course of their daily lives. Nevertheless, as a whole they witness to the existence of many communities of people who were united by a devotion to Jesus as Lord and who attempted to live out the implications of their beliefs within the diverse and challenging world of the first-century Roman Empire. The present chapter explores these letters with an eye toward what we can learn about the place of didactic hymns, prayers, and poetry among these early Christian communities. In particular we will look at the ways that these kinds of compositions served as instructional tools expressing the foundational commitments of the early Christians and painting a uniquely Christian portrait of ultimate reality. From what the letters of the New Testament indicate, didactic hymnody played a prominent role in the early churches, especially in promoting belief in Jesus as God's unique agent in creation and redemption.

Many scholars have explored the New Testament for evidence and indicators of the worship practices of the early Christians.[1] References to singing "psalms, hymns, and spiritual songs," observing the Lord's supper, baptism, prophecy, and other practices of communal worship suggest that formal and informal gatherings of Christians were a central aspect of the lives of the early believers. Germane to our interests are two strands of this

---

[1] Paul F. Bradshaw, *The Search for the Origins of Christian Worship: Sources and Methods for the Study of Early Liturgy* (2nd ed.; New York: Oxford University Press, 2002); Larry W. Hurtado, *At the Origins of Christian Worship: The Context and Character of Earliest Christian Devotion* (Grand Rapids: Eerdmans, 2000); N. T. Wright, "Worship and the Spirit in the New Testament," in *The Spirit in Worship, Worship in the Spirit* (ed. Teresa Berger and Bryan D. Spinks; Collegeville, Minn.: Liturgical Press, 2009), 3–24. See also the essays in Harold W. Attridge and Margot E. Fassler, *Psalms in Community: Jewish and Christian Textual, Liturgical, and Artistic Traditions* (Atlanta: Society of Biblical Literature, 2003).

kind of research. The first is what the Christians *did* when they gathered. The second strand of research is the content of their worship: the indications from the New Testament of what they *said* (or sung or confessed) in their corporate gatherings. After a brief survey of the landscape of early Christian worship practices (what they *did*) as seen in the letters of the New Testament, this chapter will explore the second of these two aspects (what they *said*) more fully. One section will discuss the place of confessional materials in the New Testament. The bulk of the chapter will be devoted to an exploration of two early Christian hymns: Phil 2:5–11 and Col 1:15–20.

Scholars who have explored the dynamics of early Christian worship have pieced together the limited evidence of the New Testament into a more general picture of what we can know about what the Christians did to express their devotion in a communal context. Though we are concerned specifically with didactic hymns, the work of scholars of early liturgy can provide us the context in which we can situate the confessional and hymnic materials that we will be examining. Larry Hurtado has outlined a number of cultic worship practices of the early Christians that together give us a general idea of what the Christians did when they gathered together. Cultic worship, defined by Hurtado, is "devotion offered in a specifically worship (liturgical) setting and expressive of the thanksgiving, praise, communion, and petition that directly represent, manifest and reinforce the relationship of the worshippers with the divine."[2] For Hurtado what is unique about Christian worship is the startling reality that Jesus was included along with God the Father as a recipient of religious devotion. Recognition of this dynamic leads Hurtado to discuss the concepts of "binitarian worship" and "christological monotheism."[3] This offering of devotion to Jesus Christ is indicated by the following practices: prayer, invocation and confession, the Lord's supper, baptism, prophecy, and the singing of psalms and hymns. The practice of hymn-singing included both the composition of new hymns as well as the chanting and interpreting of the psalms of the Jewish scriptures in light of the life and work of Jesus.[4] With regard to the messianic interpretation of certain psalms, Hurtado reminds us, "The 'exegesis' of these crucially important Old Testament passages was not in a seminar, discussion group or at a desk, but emerged initially in inspired insights

---

[2] Hurtado, *At the Origins*, 69.

[3] Ibid., 70. For more on this issue see the essays in Carey C. Newman, James R. Davila, and Gladys S. Lewis, *The Jewish Roots of Christological Monotheism: Papers from the St. Andrews Conference on the Historical Origins of the Worship of Jesus* (JSJSup 63; Leiden; Boston: Brill, 1999).

[4] In this regard see chapter 8, "The Changing Role of Psalmody," in Paul F. Bradshaw, *Reconstructing Early Christian Worship* (London: SPCK, 2009).

coming in the exalted context of pneumatic worship."[5] As Paul's discussion of communal worship at Corinth suggests, the offering of a hymn, lesson, revelation, tongue or interpretation to the community (1 Cor 14:26) occurred in the context of the working of the Spirit (1 Cor 14:15; cf. 1 Cor 12:1–31).[6] Accordingly, as we interpret the hymns in Philippians and Colossians we will need to keep this context of communal worship in mind if we are to fully grasp the didactic significance of these compositions for the early Christian communities.

Scholars often look to Col 3:16 and Eph 5:18c–20 for some perspective on the role of song in the early church. In these verses "psalms, hymns, and spiritual songs" are closely connected with an instructional emphasis.[7] Hengel observed, "We often find hymnic passages in the New Testament which have a didactic character and partly also serve as paraenesis."[8] Hengel explains,

The hymn to Christ had a quite essential significance for the earliest Christian worship as for the formation of Christology. It contained a narration of the work of Christ, above all his death, the salvation that death achieved, his exaltation and, at a later stage of the tradition . . . his pre-existence, mediation at creation and incarnation.[9]

As for the value of these hymnic summaries of the person and work of Christ, Hengel explains, "In contrast to learned exegesis or long-winded preaching the singing of a song quickly found a place; indeed it could be sung as a whole or in part as a refrain by the community, and thus created community."[10] In this way the rehearsal of theological truths about Jesus in song accomplished something that other forms of discourse could not.

Evidence for the actual practice of singing of songs in early Christian worship is limited in the first century. Aside from the mention of psalms, hymns, and spiritual songs in Colossians and Ephesians noted above, and Paul's mention of singing and the offering of a psalm in the context of Christian worship at Corinth (1 Cor 14:15, 26), there are few outright descriptions of early Christian gatherings. In Jas 5:13 we find the command that those who are cheerful should sing. Further, in the gospel of Mark Jesus and the disciples are portrayed as singing a hymn at Passover (Mark 14:26). The picture hinted at by several of Paul's letters and these other New Testament references is confirmed in later Christian writings as

---

[5] Hurtado, *At the Origins*, 89.

[6] On the significance of this idea see Wright, "The Spirit in Worship."

[7] Martin Hengel, "The Song about Christ in Earliest Worship," in *Studies in Early Christology* (Edinburgh: T&T Clark, 1995), 227–291, esp. 271–276.

[8] Hengel, "Hymns and Christology," 79.

[9] Ibid., 88.

[10] Ibid., 96.

well.[11] The famous reference to Christians singing a song to Christ as a god in an early first-century letter of Pliny the Younger rounds out this picture.[12]

The Christian practice of communal song has often been compared with contemporary Greco-Roman and Jewish practices. With regard to Greco-Roman conventions, music certainly played a role in religious rituals among voluntary associations (i.e., *collegia* and *thiasoi*).[13] In addition, there is evidence that select individuals were granted honorary positions that entailed the composition of hymns and encomia in honor of a deity or of the emperor (i.e. *theologoi* and *sebastologoi*).[14] In light of these realities, it is not surprising that gentile Christians would have been quite comfortable adapting these practices within the early Christian communities.

By contrast, evidence for singing within Jewish synagogues in this time period is severely limited.[15] Wilson explains,

There is no evidence for the musical performance of biblical psalms, their use being restricted to scriptural reading and exposition. The evidence we do have suggests that, inso-

---

[11] In the second century musical imagery is prominent in the letters of Ignatius (e.g. Ign. *Eph.* 4:1–2; Ign. *Rom.* 2:2; Ign. *Phld.* 1:2). In *Acts of John* 94–96 Jesus sings a hymn to the Father holding hands with the disciples and with them responding "amen." Further, in *Acts of Paul* 9 there is reference to a communal meal to the accompaniment of psalms and songs. The *Odes of Solomon* likewise contains references to singing (7:22–23; 16:1–3; 41:1–2, 16). References from *Acts of John*, *Acts of Paul*, and *Odes* are from Stephen G. Wilson, "Music in the Early Church," in *Common Life in the Early Church: Essays Honoring Graydon F. Snyder* (ed. Julian V. Hills and Richard B. Gardner; Harrisburg, Pa.: Trinity Press International, 1998), 390–401.

[12] Pliny, *Ep.* 10.96.7. Cf. Ralph P. Martin, *A Hymn of Christ: Philippians 2:5–11 in Recent Interpretation and in the Setting of Early Christian Worship* (Downers Grove, Ill.: InterVarsity Press, 1997), 1–9. Hengel, "The Song about Christ," 262–264.

[13] See the evidence in Wilson, "Music in the Early Church," 398–401.

[14] Adela Yarbro Collins, "The Psalms and the Origins of Christology," in *Psalms in Community: Jewish and Christian Textual, Liturgical, and Artistic Traditions* (ed. Harold W. Attridge and Margot E. Fassler; Atlanta: Society of Biblical Literature, 2003), 113–123, esp. 122–123.

[15] For a helpful survey of early Jewish liturgy, see Stefan C. Reif, *Judaism and Hebrew Prayer: New Perspectives on Jewish Liturgical History* (Cambridge: Cambridge University Press, 1993), 22–87. The nature of the evidence is such that some scholars have argued that Jews of the 1st c. CE did not gather on the Sabbath for worship at a synagogue at all. This view is argued most extensively by Heather A. McKay, *Sabbath and Synagogue: The Question of Sabbath Worship in Ancient Judaism* (RGRW; Leiden: Brill, 1994). However, this view has not gained wide acceptance. See the extended response by Pieter W. van der Horst, "Was the Synagogue a Place of Sabbath Worship?," in *Japheth in the Tents of Shem: Studies on Jewish Hellenism in Antiquity* (Leuven: Peeters, 2002), 55–82. The more specific question of the place of hymn- and psalm-singing in the worship of the Jews is the issue that is relevant to our study.

far as synagogues were used for common worship, this contained two elements: reading and exposition of the scriptures and prayer.[16]

Surely, Philo's description of the *Therapeutae* indicates the reality that the composition and singing of psalms did occur within at least one Jewish context in this time period, but the evidence does not suggest this practice was widespread.[17] On a related note, new compositions at Qumran, particularly those with clear indicators of their use in liturgy, at least attest to the *use* of psalms and hymns in worship. But as Wilson notes, even these do not give evidence of the musical performance of such psalms in worship.[18]

In this chapter our aim is not to sort out the worship practices of the early Christians or their precise connections with worship practices of other contemporary groups. Efforts to uncover more specific patterns of early Christian liturgy through the writings of the New Testament generally run into the problem of too little evidence to draw firm conclusions. More fruitful has been the comparison of the form, style, and content of early Christian confessions and hymns in light of contemporary Jewish and Greco-Roman praise texts. In a recent study of the liturgical elements of Revelation, Ardea Russo provides an exhaustive survey of research on early Christian worship.[19] She concludes that it is impossible to "peel back the layers" from later tradition to describe a first-century Christian liturgy.[20] The most certain conclusion she offers is that first-century Christians used hymns in the context of their worship, and that the hymns preserved in the

---

[16] Wilson, "Music in the Early Church," 396. Cf. J. A. Smith, "The Ancient Synagogue, the Early Church, and Singing," *Music and Letters* 65 (1984): 1–16. He writes, "There is no evidence that psalmody as an entity on its own, apart from the reading of Scripture, had any place in the synagogue service in the first century" (7).

[17] Jutta Leonhard, *Jewish Worship in Philo of Alexandria* (TSAJ 84; Tübingen: Mohr Siebeck, 2001), 169–171; Smith, "Ancient Synagogue," 10–12. For the impact of Philo on early Christian worship see Peter Jeffery, "Philo's Impact on Christian Psalmody," in *Psalms in Community: Jewish and Christian Textual, Liturgical, and Artistic Traditions* (ed. Harold W. Attridge and Margot E. Fassler; Atlanta: Society of Biblical Literature, 2003), 147–187. He suggests the banquet, rather than the synagogue or temple, was the context in which Jewish hymn-singing and, later, Christian hymn-singing, should be understood (147–155).

[18] Music and song does appear to have been a part of some Jewish social gatherings (e.g., weddings, meals, festivals, associations); there is just no evidence for psalm singing as part of a synagogue liturgy. Smith, "Ancient Synagogue," 8–10.

[19] Ardea Russo, "Behind the Heavenly Door: Earthly Liturgy and Heavenly Worship in the Apocalypse of John" (PhD diss., University of Notre Dame, 2009), 39–102.

[20] She summarizes, "Christian services of worship in the first and early-second centuries did not necessarily have fixed structures with the wording of these liturgies already decided upon. And even if they did in some places, we have no way of peeling back the layers of editing of the texts that we do have in order to recover these early prayers and practices," Ibid., 101.

New Testament reflect that reality even if they are not examples of real hymns.[21]

In light of this conclusion this chapter will explore the role of didactic hymns in the letters of the New Testament. A discussion of the nature of early Christian hymns and confessional materials will set the stage for an analysis of Phil 2:6–11 and Col 1:15–20 as didactic hymns. We will see that these early Christian hymns encapsulated a particular way of remembering Jesus as they put forth a vision of ultimate reality that reinforced what the recipients had already been taught. Further, these hymns promoted a view of the world in which the ethical teaching of the epistle made sense.

B. Confessional Materials in the New Testament Letters

In this section we will begin our exploration of what the early Christians said in their corporate gatherings. As noted above, an aspect of early Christian worship was confession. The letters of the New Testament give some hints as to just what the early Christians would confess, particularly about Jesus. These declarations about the person of Jesus have an authoritative tone and encapsulate key Christian beliefs about who Jesus was. Though their functions within the communal context were multi-faceted, a didactic dimension was surely present to some degree. To begin with, these statements represent the kinds of claims that Christians would affirm when they gathered together.[22] The extent to which these statements take on a didactic function as a primary emphasis will need to be determined in each case by the epistolary context of the confession.

Scholars sort this material out according to a variety of different schemas. A typical way of dividing the material is by length. Shorter passages have been identified using terms and groupings such as confessions, proclamation formulae, acclamations, eulogies, and grace-sayings. Longer passages share thematic emphases with these shorter ones, but are called hymns when they demonstrate a fullness of expression that is not seen in the shorter expressions.[23]

Longenecker prefers to speak of single-statement affirmations, *homologiai* (formulaic prose portions), and hymns (poetic portions), recognizing

---

[21] Ibid., 102.

[22] See the discussion and cautions about identifying these materials as liturgical in Hengel, "The Song about Christ," esp. 277–284.

[23] This understanding is developed most fully in Reinhard Deichgräber, *Gotteshymnus und Christushymnus in der frühen Christenheit* (SUNT 5; Göttingen: Vandenhoek & Ruprecht, 1967), 106–117.

that these are all "confessional materials" at some level.[24] Single-statement affirmations are often seen in titles ascribed to Jesus such as Christ, Lord, and Son of God.[25] *Homologiai* are best illustrated by the tradition Paul has received and passed on in 1 Cor 15:3b–5.[26] New Testament hymns include hymns of God (e.g., Rom 11:33–36) as well as hymns of Christ.

In addition to simply classifying these confessional materials by length, some scholars have argued that the shortest expressions are the earliest, while the lengthier forms represent later developments. For example, it has been suggested that Paul inherited earlier confessional statements which were essentially passion formulae. Paul then added to these a focus on the incarnation with the result that we find several kinds of incarnational statements in Paul. The fullest elaboration can be seen in the "summaries of the incarnation" such as Rom 10:6–9, and the two longer christological hymns.[27] These forms of expression are developed further by later writers as seen in Heb 1:1–3 and John 1:1–18 with their cosmic focus. In this view, a brief confession like 1 Cor 8:6 can be described as "an immediate ancestor" of Col 1:16.[28]

Bauckham has recently re-examined the evidence for worship of Jesus alongside the one God of Israel in the context of early Christianity.[29] In addition to the hymns that are the subject of the remainder of this chapter, he focuses on doxologies as an expression of early Christian devotion. Bauckham identifies two kinds of doxologies in the New Testament and early Christian writings: strict doxological form and an acclamatory doxology. Following Deichgräber he identifies the four elements of a strict doxology as: identification of the person praised, a word of praise, an indication of time (e.g., forever), and a concluding "amen." While typically addressed to God, doxologies could be adapted to Christian purposes by adding the phrase "through Jesus Christ."[30] Further, there are three instances of doxologies to Christ alone in the New Testament, while more numerous

---

[24] Richard N. Longenecker, *New Wine into Fresh Wineskins: Contextualizing the Early Christian Confessions* (Peabody, Mass.: Hendrickson, 1999), 7–24.

[25] For example, Mark 8:29b; John 11:27; Acts 9:20; 1 Cor 12:3; Rom 10:9.

[26] Others include Rom 1:3b–4; 3:24–26; 4:25; 1 Cor 1:17–18, 23; 2:2; 2 Cor 5:19a; Gal 1:4; 3:13; 3:26–28; 4:4–5; 1 Thess 4:14a; Heb 1:3; Heb 5:7–9; and maybe Rom 8:33–39; 14:9; 1 Thess 1:9–10; Heb 4:12–13 (Longenecker, *New Wine*, 17–19).

[27] Ethelbert Stauffer, *New Testament Theology* (trans. John Marsh; London: SCM Press, 1955), 246–247.

[28] Petr Pokorný, *Colossians: A Commentary* (Peabody, Mass.: Hendrickson, 1991), 78.

[29] Richard Bauckham, *Jesus and the God of Israel: God Crucified and Other Studies on the New Testament's Christology of Divine Identity* (Grand Rapids: Eerdmans, 2009), 127–151.

[30] Rom 16:27; Jude 25, and *Did.* 9:4; Ibid., 133.

examples are found in the second century and later.[31] The acclamatory doxology (i.e., "Glory to . . .") is used in honor of God alone in the New Testament, though later Christian writings employ this in honor of Jesus.[32] Bauckham notes just one doxology in the New Testament that is addressed to both God and Christ together: Rev 5:13.[33]

Other more specific kinds and categories of confessions and creedal or quasi-creedal statements have been identified. Deichgräber treats εἶς-acclamation formulae as distinct from hymns.[34] He identifies three kinds of these acclamations. The first are those that reflect one God (Mark 10:18; Rom 3:30; Jas 2:19; Gal 3:20). The second are those that contain two parts connecting Christ and God (1 Cor 8:6 and 1 Tim 2:5). Ephesians 4:4–6 represents a third kind of εἶς-acclamation. As we will see, an adaptation of this kind of expression is utilized outside of the New Testament in the writings of Ignatius (Ign. *Eph.* 7:2–3).[35]

In addition to the identification and classification of these materials, scholars have sought to explore the purposes of these confessions. Nils Dahl suggested that a major purpose of these materials was remembrance. He identified two aspects or modes of early Christians' memory of Jesus in the epistles: commemoration of Jesus as savior, and memory of his words as rules of conduct.[36] It is the first mode of memory, commemoration of Jesus as savior, which is reflected in the contents of the early Christian confessions and exhibits characteristics of didactic hymnody in particular. Dahl's insights into the function of these remembrances are worth exploring further.

First, Dahl discusses the kinds of things that individuals who became followers of Jesus in the early church needed. Having become followers of Jesus, they did not need to learn what was necessary for salvation as much as how to allow the knowledge they had already acquired to shape their new life. Dahl explains, "Those who have been led to faith and have re-

---

[31] 2 Tim 4:18; 2 Pet 3:18; Rev 1:5–6; *Acts John* 77; *Acts Paul* 42; *Acts Pet.* 20; 39; Melito, *Peri Pascha* 10, 45, 65, 105; and also in Hippolytus, Origen, and Tertullian. Ibid., 135.

[32] Luke 2:14; Rev 19:1. Christological use of this formula is seen in the Apocryphal Acts (*Acts John* 43; 78; *Acts Thom.* 59; 60; 80; 153; *Acts Andr.* 29:1) and *Odes Sol.* 17:17.

[33] On the didactic significance of this formulation see the discussion of the hymns of Rev 4–5 in the following chapter.

[34] Deichgräber, *Gotteshymnus und Christushymnus*, 116.

[35] Other kinds of classifications are possible as well. Schille attempts to classify material according to content and liturgical function (Gottfried Schille, *Frühchristliche Hymnen* [Berlin: Evangelische Verlagsanstalt, 1965], 15–22).

[36] Nils Alstrup Dahl, *Jesus in the Memory of the Early Church: Essays* (Minneapolis: Augsburg, 1976), 25.

ceived baptism know already what is necessary for salvation. From that moment, they need only to recall their initiation and permit this memory to shape their conduct."[37] He suggests that many of the hymnic passages about Christ in the epistles served to meet this need of remembering what the Christians already accepted. He points out,

> Passages such as Phil 2:6–11; Col 1:9–15; 1 Tim 3:16; 1 Peter 1:18–21; 2:21–25; 3:18–22 reflect hymnic style, but they have an epistolary function and serve to recall the memory of Christ in the communities where the letters are read. Their antecedents may be homiletical as well as liturgical.[38]

Whether the antecedents are homiletical or liturgical or both, in either case we are able to discern a heavy didactic impulse in these concise and dense passages about the person and work of Jesus.

Taking a specific example, Dahl notes Phil 2:6–11. He claims, "Here we do not have a confession of faith; we could say it is an 'anamnesis of Christ,' a commemoration of Christ."[39] While Dahl may be overstating the case to say that Phil 2:6–11 is not a confession (note the verb "confess" in v. 11), as we will see in our study of this hymn he is undoubtedly correct to note the commemorative character of this passage. The central point here is Dahl's observation that a hymnic passage plays a key role in the memory of the early believers. Hymnic confession enables believers to remember what they have been taught, as well as to remember what Jesus had accomplished for them.

Longenecker presents a slightly more nuanced understanding of the function of these confessional materials in New Testament letters. In his view, the memory of Jesus is not the primary reason for citing these in the epistles. Rather, the confessions serve several purposes relative to the occasion of the letter and the situation the author is aiming to address. These include establishing rapport with their audiences, summarizing their presentation, showing the validity of their arguments, or, more often, as the basis for the argument that would follow.[40] In this view, the confessional materials are used as part of an argument to bolster the claims of the letter, particularly with regard to the persuasive aims of the author. In particular, the confessional materials play a significant role in the letter writers' attempts to instruct or to refute false teaching.[41] In the analysis of specific examples of New Testament hymns below we will see how Longenecker's thesis is borne out: the hymnic passages serve a significant rhetorical function in achieving the aims of the letter, particularly with regard to instruct-

---

[37] Ibid., 16.
[38] Ibid., 20 n. 45.
[39] Ibid., 20.
[40] Longenecker, *New Wine*, 48.
[41] Ibid., 49.

ing believers in Jesus as to how they ought to order their lives in light of the good news about Jesus.

Like the Jewish, Greek, and Roman didactic hymns we examined, we will see that these carefully composed hymnic passages paint a vivid portrait of reality that the reader is invited to embrace and in which the way of life espoused by the author makes sense. In the case of both Phil 2:6–11 and Col 1:15–20, the portrait of reality is in marked contrast to the portrait of reality offered by the ideology of the Roman Empire.

C. Didactic Aspects of New Testament Christological Hymns

As we have noted, the christological hymns of the New Testament represent a subset of the broader category of early Christian confessions. Christological hymns are the most fully developed form of confessional statement; they tend to be longer than the single statement affirmations and reflect a narrative framework. Because of their length together with the ways they are used in epistolary contexts, christological hymns have a significant didactic function. This section will explore two christological hymns (Phil 2:6–11 and Col 1:15–20) in order to explore the extent to which they may be considered didactic hymns and assess their didactic functions. We will see that these passages can be considered hymns in the sense that they participate in a number of Jewish and Greco-Roman hymnic conventions that have been identified in this study. Further, these hymns are didactic both in terms of their own content (what they teach about Jesus) as well as their use within the epistolary context (what they teach about the circumstances facing the recipients of the letters). Common to both hymns is the dynamic use of multiple temporal and spatial registers in a primarily narratival composition that paints a vivid portrait of Jesus as Lord. Understood in context, this grand vision teaches the understanding of ultimate reality in which the remainder of the teaching of the epistle is grounded.

It should be noted here that the identification of hymnic passages within the letters of the New Testament is a task which has come under criticism by some scholars.[42] The nature of the critiques and the range of arguments

---

[42] For example, see Daniel Boyarin, "The Gospel of the *Memra*: Jewish Binitarianism and the Prologue to John," *HTR* 94 (2001): 243–284; Ralph Brucker, *'Christushymnen' oder 'epideiktische Passagen'?: Studien zum Stilwechsel im Neuen Testament und seiner Umwelt* (FRLANT 176; Göttingen: Vandenhoeck & Ruprecht, 1997); Gordon D. Fee, "Philippians 2:5–11: Hymn or Exalted Pauline Prose," *BBR* 2 (1992): 29–46; Stephen E. Fowl, *Philippians* (The Two Horizons New Testament Commentary; Grand Rapids: Eerdmans, 2005), 108–113; N. T. Wright, "Poetry and Theology in Colossians 1:15–20," *NTS* 36 (1990): 444–468.

generally suggest that the identification of hymnic passages in the New Testament employs a flawed methodology, from a literary and form-critical standpoint, that results in conclusions that are highly speculative. Further, the critics hold that even if the methodology and its results were valid, the findings would be of very limited value in interpreting the letters of the New Testament. Since the focus of this chapter is on the didactic emphasis of these passages, the methodological and theoretical arguments would take us too far afield if we were to attempt a full-scale analysis of the issues.[43] Instead, we simply note here that caution is in order in this exercise. Where possible we can respond to warnings that have been suggested as these have direct bearing on the concerns of this chapter. In examining these hymns, it will be important to keep in mind the nature of these materials.

Along these lines, Longenecker has identified four qualities in particular that seem to be shared by Christological hymns within the New Testament. These texts are: 1) devotional in nature; 2) narrative in content; 3) functional in focus; and 4) use current language and metaphors. Early confessional materials in the New Testament are devotional in nature in the sense that they are "expressing the early Christians praise of God and adoration of Christ in the context of corporate worship."[44] As a result of this devotional emphasis Longenecker suggests they are, by nature, imprecise: "It attempts to inspire adoration, not to explicate doctrinal nuances. . . . It is therefore not always philosophically precise, philologically exact, or theologically correct – perhaps at times not even logically coherent."[45] This is in marked contrast to what we will see in some of the christological hymns of the second century. In those later hymns philosophical terminology and, at times, advanced cosmological schema are utilized to reflect as accurately as possible the reality of the advent of Christ in terms and frameworks that would make sense to educated second-century Christians. The devotional nature of these New Testament passages will thus be important to bear in mind as we analyze the content of each one. In spite of the devotional nature of these hymns, however, we will keep in mind that in the

---

[43] A general summary of the methodology for identifying both hymns and confessional material is found in Longenecker, *New Wine*, 10–11, 15–16. Unfortunately, Longenecker does not address the major lines of critique that have been offered; a detailed methodological outline is still needed. Longenecker essentially summarizes the earlier work of W. Hulitt Gloer, "Homologies and Hymns in the New Testament: Form, Content and Criteria for Identification," *PRS* 11 (1984): 115–132. My comments on the Johannine prologue in response to Daniel Boyarin address some of those concerns as well: Matthew E. Gordley, "The Johannine Prologue and Jewish Didactic Hymn Traditions: A New Case for Reading the Prologue as a Hymn," *JBL* 128 (2009): 781–802.

[44] Longenecker, *New Wine*, 28.

[45] Ibid., 29.

context of the letters they play a significant role in the argumentation and rhetorical impact of the letter. We can thus attend to the message of the hymn itself (its didactic content) as well as its function within the letter (its didactic use).

D. Philippians 2:6–11

One of two major hymns in the letters of Paul, this passage has received a massive amount of scholarly attention.[46] In spite of the complexity of the history of interpretation of this hymn, we would do well to keep in mind the devotional nature of the New Testament hymns and to be careful to keep their primary point in focus, even as we delve into detailed matters of scholarship. Neither in this hymn nor any New Testament hymn can we expect to find a fully developed and carefully articulated christology. Such statements and their hymnic reflection will come only later, as we will see in a later chapter. In the present context we will aim to observe the teaching of the hymn and consider its use in its context in the letter. We will see that the Philippian hymn shows that the Jesus of the cross is to be identified with the exalted Lord of all, and as such is worthy of the worship of all creatures. The hymn maintains that the cross was not a sign of defeat, but rather a means of triumph and exaltation. This teaching is conveyed through a narratival development that: 1) moves from mythic past, to events of the recent past, to the present and future, and 2) references multiple spatial realities (heaven, earth, and under the earth). As a poetic composition it paints a grand portrait of ultimate reality that the reader is invited to embrace. It is this portrait of reality in which the ethical and theological directives of Paul's letter make sense.

The arguments that Phil 2:6–11 is a poetic composition have been well covered in the scholarship on this hymn. Ralph Martin has made the most

---

[46] Major and recent works include Brucker, *Christushymnen*; Charles B. Cousar, "The Function of the Christ-hymn (2.6–11) in Philippians," in *The Impartial God: Essays in Biblical Studies in Honor of Jouette M. Bassler* (ed. Calvin J. Roetzel, Robert L. Foster, and Jouette M. Bassler; Sheffield: Sheffield Phoenix Press, 2007), 212–218; idem., *Philippians and Philemon: A Commentary* (Louisville, Ky.: Westminster John Knox, 2009), 50–59; Fowl, *Story of Christ*; Otfried Hofius, *Der Christushymnus Philipper 2, 6–11: Untersuchungen zu Gestalt und Aussage eines urchristlichen Psalms* (2nd ed.; WUNT 17; Tübingen: Mohr, 1991); Martin, *Hymn of Christ*; John Reumann, *Philippians: A New Translation with Introduction and Commentary* (AB 33B; New Haven: Yale University, 2008), 333–377; Thomas Tobin, "The World of Thought in the Philippians Hymn (Philippians 2:6–11)," in *The New Testament and Early Christian Literature in Greco-Roman Context: Studies in Honor of David E. Aune* (ed. John Fotopoulos; Leiden: Brill, 2006), 91–104.

extensive case for reading the passage as a preexisting hymn of the early church.[47] He points to the form, the context, and the content of the passage, as being indicative of its hymnic nature. With regard to form, the composition shows a number of features that are typical of Semitic style poetry. Specifically, the passage contains parallelism both at the line level and the strophe level. With regard to the context, the hymn disrupts the argument that is in process in Phil 2:1–5. Though part of the hymn is relevant to the argument (the verses about Christ's humility), the second part of the verse (about Christ's exaltation) does not support the argument Paul is making. Further, marking off the passage from its context, the passage begins (as do other confessional materials in the NT) with the relative pronoun ὅς (v. 6), and is followed by a resumptive ὥστε (v. 12) where Paul resumes his argument. Moreover, in contrast to the surrounding verses, within the passage there is a high concentration of participles (v. 6 ὑπάρχων, v. 7 λαβών, γενόμενος, v. 8 γενόμενος) and relative clauses. The vocabulary of the passage can be shown to be uncharacteristic of Paul as well, though of course, that can be explained in a number of ways.[48] None of these observations are conclusive proof that the passage is a hymn. Nevertheless, the presence of these features does require an explanation. The thesis that the passage is a preexisting hymn has proven to be a convincing hypothesis for many scholars.

In addition to matters of form and style, the content reflects a hymnic emphasis as it speaks of Christ's exaltation and humiliation. The passage shares general content and themes that are common to other passages that are thought to be christological hymns. These include the preexistence of Christ; Christ's pre-temporal activity; Christ's role as cosmological Lord; and Christ's receiving homage of all the orders of creation in heaven, earth, and the underworld. Further, the narrative about Christ's humiliation and exaltation is set in a cosmic context. Finally, the person of Christ is viewed in relation to his work. In other words, it is not just his deeds or just his person that are considered significant. Both are significant and can only be understood in relation to one another.

Since its content focuses on praise of Christ as an exalted figure, it may be placed in the broad category "hymn to Christ" in the sense employed by Deichgräber above.[49] Recently, Adela Yarbro Collins has argued that this

---

[47] For all of the major arguments see especially the preface to the 1997 edition of Martin, *Hymn of Christ*, lv–lxv. More recently see the discussion in Reumann, *Philippians*, 361–376. Reumann agrees that the composition is a preexisting praise composition but prefers to call it an *encomion* rather than a hymn (esp. 361–366).

[48] The passage meets many of the standard criteria for detecting confessional material. These have been articulated by Stauffer, *New Testament Theology*, 338–339.

[49] Walter, Reinmuth, and Lampe eschew the terms hymn or psalm altogether, focusing instead on the content and calling it a didactic poem (Lehrgedicht) focusing on the way

passage may be seen to fit well the ancient category of prose hymn or prose encomium, since it is does not conform to any Greek metrical pattern.[50] She notes that though the passage may be poetic in the sense of Jewish psalmody, in terms of the Greek style it can best be considered rhythmic prose. The combination of rhythmic prose and praise of Christ as an exalted being make it reasonable to call this passage a "hymn" provided that one recognizes the need to define that term in the broadest sense.[51]

It is not surprising that, even among those who view the passage as a hymn, conclusions about the structure and the original content of the hymn (apart from Pauline interpolations) are widely debated. Ralph Martin argues that Paul may have added explanatory glosses that would highlight the key elements of the hymn. Following the lead of earlier scholars he proposed that the following phrases be seen as Pauline additions:

8c – θανάτου δὲ σταυροῦ.
10b – ἐπουρανίων καὶ ἐπιγείων καὶ καταχθονίων,
11c – εἰς δόξαν θεοῦ πατρός.[52]

That these are Pauline additions is suggested by the fact that each one aligns closely with Paul's theological concerns (more so than the contents of the rest of the passage) and that their presence disrupts the balance one might expect from such a carefully planned composition. This is of course not to say that the passage as a whole does not align with Paul's theology, but rather that these phrases correspond with special emphases of Paul. Further, it is often argued that removal of such phrases does not disrupt the hymn itself.

While the general idea that an author would gloss a quotation with his own material makes good intuitive sense, not all scholars have been convinced by these suggestions. O. Hofius has argued cogently for the unity of

---

of Christ (Nikolaus Walter, Eckart Reinmuth, and Peter Lampe, *Die Briefe an die Philipper, Thessalonicher und an Philemon* [NTD 8/2; Göttingen: Vandenhoeck & Ruprecht, 1998], 56–57).

[50] Collins, "The Psalms and the Origins of Christology," 119–123.

[51] In response to these standard lines of argumentation, Gordon Fee has offered eight counter-arguments in an attempt to demonstrate that Phil 2:6–11 should be read as exalted Pauline prose. Fee, "Philippians 2:5–11: Hymn or Exalted Pauline Prose," 29–46. In response to the argument about the presence of parallelism, he observes, "[Paul's] own rhetorical style is simply replete with examples of balanced structures, parallelism, chiasmus, etc." He adds that just because one finds this to be exalted prose, one cannot conclude that it is a hymn. Further, Fee claims that this passage is nothing like the hymns of the ancient Greeks. Fee also cites the general failure of scholars to agree on a strophic arrangement of the passage, concluding that the whole exercise is a futile one at best. For a response to Fee's position see Martin, *Hymn of Christ*, xliii–xliv.

[52] Martin, *Hymn of Christ*, 25–38.

the hymn as it is preserved in Phil 2:6–11.[53] My arrangement of the hymn below follows the lead of Hofius in seeing the lines noted above (8c, 10b, and 11c) as integral parts of the hymn. In particular, in the arrangement that follows, the phrase "death on a cross" is in the climactic central portion of the hymn. In English translation, the hymn reads:

Who, existing in the form of God,
did not consider equality with God a thing to be seized,

but emptied himself, taking the nature of a servant,
being born in human likeness.

And being found in appearance as a human, he humbled himself,
becoming obedient unto death – even death on a cross.

Therefore God highly exalted him,
and gave him the name that is above every name,

that at the name of Jesus every knee should bow
in heaven and on earth and under the earth,

And every tongue confess
that Jesus Christ is Lord
to the glory of God the Father. (vv. 6–11)

This arrangement in six stanzas reflects the parallelism from line to line as well as from the first three stanzas to the last three stanzas. One important result of viewing the hymn in this way is the centrality of the phrase "even death on a cross (θανάτου δὲ σταυροῦ)." The thematic and positional centrality of the phrase makes it difficult to envision this as a Pauline interpolation. Rather, in this view it is crucial to the teaching of the hymn.

It is difficult to identify one primary theological influence that serves as the dominant metaphor for the Philippian hymn. The hymn seems to bring together a number of elements of christological reflection which are not necessarily related to one another.[54] Martin has drawn attention to this fact and points out that the author

seems to draw into his picture of the pre-existent, humiliated and victorious Lord many strands of Christological speculation and theory. He is dependent upon a variety of categories as he sets forth the meaning of the incarnation, the *kenosis* and the glorification of Christ. It is not surprising that scholars have been able to detect a bewildering array of

---

[53] Hofius, *Christushymnus*, 1–17.

[54] Reumann lists fourteen different proposals with regard to the history of religions background of Phil 2:6–11, noting that no one proposal does justice to the variety of traditions represented in this passage (Reumann, *Philippians*, 335–338).

categories, so that the verses of this short tribute appear like a Christological miscellany with many contributions.[55]

This "bewildering" variety of influences is present in each of the longer New Testament christological hymns, though not all strands of influence are present in each case. These poetic reflections on the person and work of Christ thus stand at the crossroads of a number of theological currents of Judaism and early Christianity. Looking back at the early Church from our vantage point it is difficult to appreciate how revolutionary or how traditional the ideas would have seemed. In spite of shared traditions, each hymn does have its own unique emphasis – a perspective which the final writer deemed suitable for its deployment in the setting in which it is found.

What role does the hymn play in the context in which it is cited and commented upon? It is widely recognized that Philippians is a letter in which example plays a key role.[56] Paul cites himself as an example (3:17; 4:9), and also draws on some of his associates such as Timothy and Epaphroditus as individuals who embody the traits Paul is calling on the Philippians to embrace (2:19–30). Paul models a Christian attitude toward hardship, suffering, and death. He models rejoicing in trials, trusting in God's ability to work through all circumstances, and persevering until the end. The clearest example in Philippians, however, is the model of Christ. Paul presents Christ as an example of humility and obedience that Christians should imitate. Yet the hymn as a whole is more than simply an example to imitate. It functions on several levels to reinforce some key concepts of the letter as a whole. The emphasis on humility is really only part of the first half of the hymn. The second half of the hymn focuses on the exaltation of the crucified Christ.

Fowl has sought to articulate a different understanding of the function of the Philippians hymn. He uses the idea of an exemplar to claim that Paul uses the story about Christ as a basis from which to draw an analogy that is applicable to his audience.[57] He explains that, with regard to Paul's argument in Philippians, Christ does not offer a model to be imitated. Rather, "This hymnic passage supports Paul's position by means of its analogous

---

[55] Martin, *Hymn of Christ*, 296–297. Among the ideas that may contribute to the development of the hymn Martin lists: "a Son of Man dogmatic; oriental or Greek mythology; the first-second Adam speculation of Jewish thought; Hellenistic Jewish concepts of Wisdom; the Servant of Yahweh concept, a 'Paidology'; an Emperor motif; a divine Hero, theios aner, Christology; an enthronement ritual of an oriental monarch; an Iranian or Gnostic redemption myth; all these categories have been suggested with varying degrees of plausibility" (297).

[56] Carolyn Osiek, *Philippians, Philemon* (Nashville: Abingdon Press, 2000), 31.

[57] Fowl, *Story of Christ*, 77–101.

relationship to various aspects of the Philippians' situation."[58] In this reading Paul uses the tradition about Christ to speak to the present reality facing the Philippians. Though this is surely a part of the dynamic of how the hymn functions in Philippians, there is still more that can be said.

Cousar has recently argued against both the simple ethical model and the related exemplar reading of Fowl in which the narrative of the hymn provides an analogy that is then applied to the situation facing the addressees in Philippi.[59] The problem with both readings, he claims, is that they do not adequately take into account the overall force of the hymn, the idea that Christ is now the exalted Lord of all. For this reason, Cousar prefers to follow an approach similar to Kasemann's, in which the point of the hymn is the divine saga of the redeemer. Cousar, as others have done, connects the hymn with Isa 45 showing that the "name above all names" is the name of the Lord (YHWH).[60] It is this grand vision about Christ that contains the force of the citation. Cousar also argues that the confession of Jesus as Lord "places the Philippian readers in a subversive role in relation to their Roman context."[61] This idea has been more fully developed by Heen, who argues that the phrase in v. 6 referred to the practice of receiving divine honors.[62] In contrast to the Emperor, a false claimant to divine honors, the Philippian hymn identifies Jesus as the true Lord. By embracing this view of reality, the Philippians would be emboldened to live their life of faith in spite of the challenges that faced them in the present.[63]

---

[58] Ibid., 101.

[59] Cousar, "Function of the Christ-hymn"; Cousar, *Philippians and Philemon*, 55–59.

[60] Cf. Martin, *Hymn of Christ*, 237, 245–246. Martin makes the connection with Isa 45:23 and Isa 42:8.

[61] Cousar, "Function of the Christ-hymn," 218.

[62] Erik M. Heen, "Phil 2:6–11 and Resistance to Local Timocratic Rule: Isa theō and the Cult of the Emperor in the East," in *Paul and the Roman Imperial Order* (ed. Richard A Horsley; Harrisburg, Pa.: Trinity Press International, 2004), 125–153. He writes, "Phil 2:6–11 does appropriate for Jesus the honorific tradition of the ruler cult. The status claimed for the emperor (*to einai isa theō*) in the civic religions of the Greek cities of the East has been reassigned to Jesus in the early Christian hymn. The honor associated with the term in the public discourse is retained but redirected to one who is, from the perspective of the Pauline subaltern community, legitimately worthy of its claims" (149). See also the discussion in Efraín Agosto, "The Letter to the Philippians," in *A Postcolonial Commentary on the New Testament Writings* (ed. Fernando F. Segovia and R. S. Sugirtharajah; London: T & T Clark, 2007), 281–293, esp. 286–287.

[63] For another possible way of reading the Philippians hymn in light of empire see Adela Yarbro Collins, "The Worship of Jesus and the Imperial Cult," in *The Jewish Roots of Christological Monotheism: Papers from the St. Andrews Conference on the Historical Origins of the Worship of Jesus* (eds. Carey C. Newman, James R. Davila and Gladys S. Lewis; Leiden: Brill, 1999), 234–257.

Taking Cousar's approach we can utilize our notion of Phil 2:6–11 as a didactic hymn to explore the instructional impact of this hymn for the Philippians. First, of all, the hymn reflects ideas that the Philippian believers already accept; in that sense it is a reminder. Second, the hymn puts those ideas into concise, memorable form; a form which might be considered an extended confession in itself. Third, Paul is using it as an example of the kind of humility they need to live out (cf. Phil 2:5), but the confession as a whole has to do with much more than humility. Fourth, more than an example of humility, the hymn affirms a distinct view of reality that must be taken by faith. The hymn crafts a portrait of the world (embracing past, present, and future) in which the Jesus of the cross is also the Lord of all (including heaven, earth, and the underworld). It is in such a world that a life of Christ-like humility makes sense. Fifth, inherent in this picture of the world under the lordship of the humble-yet-exalted Lord is an implicit contrast between us and them (spelled out more in the rest of chapter 2). In this contrast the "we" of Paul and the Philippians are seen to be like Jesus, the true Lord. "They" are like Caesar, their lord, the false lord.

Like other didactic hymns the Philippians hymn conveys its teaching in complex ways. It taps into multiple temporal and spatial registers, offering a narrative portrait of Christ for a human audience which is in view primarily in the context of the hymn rather than explicitly being mentioned in the hymn itself. The Philippians hymn has to do then with: 1) essentials of the story of Jesus in poetic form, primarily in a narratival rather than attributive or descriptive style; 2) communal identity in light of those basic but crucial facts, especially in its context in the letter; 3) eschatological teaching as it taps into multiple temporal registers (cf. the future tense verbs in vv. 10–11).

A world in which Jesus is Lord of all is the world in which the pattern of life advocated in Philippians makes sense. Only in a world where Jesus Christ is Lord does it make sense for Paul to regard his prestigious heritage as rubbish in comparison with knowing Christ (3:7–8). The fact that Christ is now exalted in heaven has a direct bearing on who "we" are. Paul spells this out in 3:20–4:1 connecting his comments about the coming of Christ with the themes of humiliation and glorification. Because Christ is exalted, the Philippian believers have a citizenship in heaven with Christ, and because of that, they have assurance that the savior will return from heaven for them with life-altering results. At that time Christians will participate in the exaltation which Christ has already experienced (4:21). This understanding is part of the motivation that will enable the Philippians to "stand firm in the Lord" (4:1).

In another sense then, the Philippian hymn helps define "us" against "them." The citizenship in heaven (3:20) is explicitly contrasted with those whose minds and bodies are tied to the things of earth (3:18–19). Those who, like Paul, seek to know and imitate the humiliated and exalted Christ of the Philippian hymn, have a confidence for this life and the next that nothing else can provide (1:6; 2:1; 3:3, 10–11, 21; 4:7, 19). We have observed a similar dynamic in the didactic hymns at Qumran which placed a great deal of emphasis on the unique identity of the covenant people of God.

Because of who Christ is, what he has done, and what he will do, the Philippians can and should persevere in trials, rejoice in suffering, live blameless lives in unity with one another. Apart from the power and reality of the exalted Christ, such attitudes and actions make no sense. The rehearsal of the humiliation and exaltation of Christ in these terms is thus an example, a confession, and a source of encouragement to continue on in the way that Paul has outlined.

By way of comparison with other confessions and christological hymns, Martin notes that here, for the first time in Christian literature, three distinct epochs in the work of Christ are identified. First, Christ is hailed and confessed as preexistent (in the form of God). Second, Christ is portrayed as incarnate and humiliated (taking the form of a servant). Third, Christ is shown to be triumphant (exalted by the father and receiving the homage of all orders of creation).[64] Later christological hymns and confessions will include these aspects as well, though not necessarily with the same degree of emphasis.

Along these lines Tobin has recently compared the preexistence of the Philippians hymn with the more cosmologically-oriented preexistence expressed in John 1:1–18, Heb 1:1–3, and Col 1:15–20. In contrast to those later passages, in Phil 2:6–11 the preexistent Christ is not said to be involved in creation; rather he is able to think, to choose, and to act. Tobin argues that the Philippians hymn represents an early attempt to connect Jesus with the "heavenly man" tradition rather than directly with the Logos as was done in the later hymnic passages.[65] This suggestion is intriguing and suggests that by comparing New Testament christological hymns with one another, it may be possible to gain greater insight into trajectories of development in first-century christology.

As we will see, the imagery and expressions of the Philippians hymn will continue to impact Christian hymnody well into the second century CE. Its focus on the humiliation and exaltation of Christ is later reflected directly in hymnic form in *Odes Sol.* 41.

---

[64] Martin, *Hymn of Christ*, 22–25.
[65] Tobin, "World of Thought," 104.

E. Colossians 1:15–20

While clearly related to the Philippians hymn in terms of its focus on the person and work of Jesus including his death and resurrection, the Colossian hymn presents a number of unique features for consideration. First, while the Philippian hymn hinted at the preexistence of Christ, the Colossian hymn unequivocally addresses his preexistence. Second, this hymn places considerable emphasis on the supremacy of Christ in creation, particularly with regard to creating and sustaining all things. Third, it places a strong emphasis on the redemptive work of Christ as a work of reconciliation of all things. Fourth, it portrays Christ as the agent of God in both creation and redemption. In the context of the letter to the Colossians this carefully crafted statement about Christ serves as the basis for Paul's exhortation to the Colossian believers to continue in him (Col 2:6). The following analysis of a variety of features of the hymn will highlight its didactic function within the letter.

As was the case with the Philippian hymn, among those who interpret this as a preexisting poetic unit there is disagreement about the existence of or extent of interpolations and emendations by the author of the epistle, as well as the structure of the original hymn.[66] These issues are further complicated by the question of whether Colossians is a pseudonymous letter.[67] A related question concerns the existence of opponents at Colossae along with the nature of competing views that were undermining the faith of the Colossian believers.[68] For purposes of this discussion, and to avoid being sidetracked by innumerable technical details, I will briefly state the context and the manner in which I read the Colossian hymn.[69] First, arguments to the contrary notwithstanding, I take Colossians to be a genuine Pauline epistle written to address the concerns of Christians in Colossae.

---

[66] See the recent surveys of proposals in Matthew E. Gordley, *The Colossian Hymn in Context: An Exegesis in Light of Jewish and Greco-Roman Hymnic and Epistolary Conventions* (WUNT 2.228; Tübingen: Mohr Siebeck, 2007), 5–16; Vincent A. Pizzuto, *A Cosmic Leap of Faith: An Authorial, Structural, and Theological Investigation of the Cosmic Christology in Col. 1:15–20* (CBET 41; Leuven: Peeters, 2006).

[67] Pizzuto argues that it is pseudonymous, though this position is not universally accepted. Pizzuto, *Cosmic Leap of Faith*, 73–93. Most recently Jerry Sumney argues that Colossians was written in the early 60's CE shortly after the death of Paul (Jerry L. Sumney, *Colossians: A Commentary* [Louisville, Ky.: Westminster John Knox, 2008]).

[68] For a variety of views and review of the history of research see Clinton E. Arnold, *The Colossian Syncretism: The Interface between Christianity and Folk Belief at Colossae* (WUNT 2.77; Tübingen: Mohr (Siebeck), 1995); Troy W. Martin, *By Philosophy and Empty Deceit: Colossians as Response to a Cynic Critique* (JSNTSup 118; Sheffield: Sheffield Academic Press, 1996); R. McL. Wilson, *Colossians and Philemon: A Critical and Exegetical Commentary* (London: T & T Clark, 2005), 35–58.

[69] These conclusions are elaborated and defended in my earlier volume noted above.

Second, whether or not there were actual opponents of Paul in Colossae, Paul was at least addressing areas of concern that he felt could potentially threaten the faith of the Colossians. Third, while the stylistic, linguistic, and related evidence suggests that in Col 1:15–20 Paul is citing a preexisting composition, whether or not Paul himself was the author of that composition is not possible to determine. Fourth, the contents of the hymn reflect a synthesis of Jewish psalm style, Second Temple Jewish Wisdom theology, and Greco-Roman hymnic conventions. Fifth, the hymn functions in its context as a theological and christological foundation for the exhortations that follow. In short, the Colossian hymn utilizes hymnic conventions to paint a vivid picture of Christ, Christians, and the world in which the life, practices, and beliefs prescribed by Paul in the letter make sense.

Several indicators are frequently referenced to show that the author is citing earlier material. These have been recognized for many generations now.[70] The features discussed in the following paragraphs are among the more important.[71] No single indicator is sufficient in and of itself to establish the earlier existence of the passage. However, taken together, the collective force of the arguments makes it a reasonable conclusion. If the passage is not a preexisting composition of some kind, another thesis would need to be proposed in order to account for the stylistic, contextual, verbal and content oriented reasons listed below.

A major factor in this instance is the way that vv. 15–20 disrupt the flow of the larger passage. Col 1:3–14 are written in such a way that they address the Colossian Christians directly in the second person. Col 1:21 is likewise in the second person as are the verses that follow. Only vv. 15–20 are in the third person. The abrupt switch from second to third person and then back to second person lends support to the view that this passage may be some kind of traditional material cited by the author.[72]

Second, the style of the passage reflects a more elevated prose than the epistle in which it is found. The use of parallelism and other poetic features suggests that this passage was composed very deliberately and carefully and not simply in the moment of the writing of the epistle.[73] Stettler

---

[70] Much of this work related to Colossians can be traced back to Norden, *Agnostos Theos*, 250–254.

[71] Many of these connect with the criteria for creedal formulae identified by Gloer, "Homologies and Hymns," 115–132.

[72] This switch from second to third person and then back is also a feature of the Philippians hymn.

[73] Luis Carlos-Reyes, "The Structure and Rhetoric of Colossians 1:15–20," *FN* 12 (1999): 139–154.

concurs that this passage was composed in "solemn, liturgical-elevated language" and that its style is reflective of a Jewish psalm style.[74]

Third, the fact that it begins with the relative pronoun ὅς, links it with other confessional materials in the New Testament. We observed this as a feature of the Philippian hymn already (Phil 2:6). It is likewise a feature of 1 Tim 3:16b. Though not conclusive in itself, this feature at least makes a strong connection between several passages with a shared thematic focus and style.[75]

Fourth, the contents of the passage suggest that this is not typical Pauline epistolary prose. The passage is set apart from its context by the grand cosmic scale of the subject matter and its predications about the person and work of Christ using philosophically oriented terminology.[76] Other features of the passage have been suggested as well to bolster the case that this is a preexisting hymn of some kind.[77] When taken together, these observations lend weight to the view that this is traditional material.

Nevertheless, some scholars prefer to view the passage as composed by the author of Colossians in the process of writing the letter. Pizzuto, for example, suggests that a disciple of Paul wrote the epistle and the hymn together.[78] This explains, for him, the differences from Paul's other letters, as well as the way the hymn appears to be so carefully integrated into the remainder of the letter. Pizzuto still refers to the passage as a hymn, however, and suggests that it was intended for the recipients to use the hymn in their corporate gatherings. The real issue here is thus not whether it is a hymn, but a question of who composed it and when. Without resolving that issue right here, it is enough to note that even in Pizzuto's dissenting view, the features of the passage still justify calling it a hymn and suggesting that it was created for liturgical purposes. Pizzuto rightly points out that while the recognition of observable differences in style, content, diction, form, etc., is agreed upon, it is the interpretation of these observations that is open to question.[79]

---

[74] Christian Stettler, *Der Kolosserhymnus: Untersuchungen zu Form, traditionsgeschichtlichem Hintergrund und Aussage von Kol 1,15–20* (WUNT 2.131; Tübingen: Mohr Siebeck, 2000), 79–81.

[75] Wilson, *Colossians and Philemon*, 126–127.

[76] E.g., the emphasis on "all things" (*ta panta*) as well as the use of prepositions reflective of the prepositional metaphysics of Middle Platonic philosophers. Note also the claim about Christ as "image" (*eikōn*) and the use of that term in philosophical writings; cf. Hans Hübner, *An Philemon, an die Kolosser, an die Epheser* (HNT 12; Tübingen: Mohr Siebeck, 1997), 57–58.

[77] See Gordley, *Colossian Hymn in Context*, 170–202.

[78] Pizzuto, *Cosmic Leap of Faith*, 268.

[79] Stettler leaves the possibility open that Paul could have composed it for an earlier occasion (Stettler, *Kolosserhymnus*, 347).

Many scholars have observed the parallelism between what appears to be a first and a second strophe, and this observation forms the basis for most reconstructions of an original hymn.[80] Typically, those who reconstruct an original hymn have recourse to supposed interpolations and editorial comments by the author of the epistle.[81] These enable scholars to reconstruct a more balanced and aesthetically pleasing composition. In some cases the proposals for what the original hymn may have looked like are quite drastically different than the text as we have it.[82] A major critique of all interpolation theories is that there is no good reason to expect that an early Christian hymn would have exact symmetry between its parts or that every aspect in one strophe would be reflected in a second or third strophe. Though Lohse recognizes two phrases as interpolations, he cautions, "It is hardly probable that a primitive Christian hymn would have consisted of regularly constructed verses and strophes; rather, the individual strophes probably differed in structure and were composed in the free rhythm of hymnic prose."[83] The likelihood of finding perfectly metrical lines in an early Christian hymn is further diminished when one considers the importance of Jewish psalmody for the earliest Christians. As we have seen, structural conventions for Jewish psalms differed considerably from those of Greek metrical hymns. These observations remind us that one should be very careful about proposing glosses to an original hymn merely for the sake of balance or form. Some scholars have therefore opted to arrange the text solely on the basis of what is there.[84]

Even so, recent attention to the rhythmical patterns found in the Colossian hymn suggests that a strophic arrangement that recognizes some interpretive glosses may not be as unfounded as critics claim. In the arrangement that follows, a Greek metrical pattern consisting of a series of spondaic *metra* marks the ending of each strophe. Attention to rhythmic patterning also suggests that part of v. 16 is a later interpretive comment added to the hymn:[85]

Strophe (vv. 15–18a)
He is the image of the invisible God,
the firstborn over all creation.

---

[80] Following Norden, *Agnostos Theos*, 250–254.

[81] For example, see Eduard Lohse, *Colossians and Philemon: A Commentary on the Epistles to the Colossians and to Philemon* (Philadelphia: Fortress Press, 1971), 42–44.

[82] See Jerome Murphy-O'Connor, *Paul: A Critical Life* (Oxford: Clarendon Press, 1996), 240–246.

[83] Lohse, *Colossians*, 44.

[84] See, for example, Pizzuto, *Cosmic Leap of Faith*; Stettler, *Kolosserhymnus*; Wright, "Poetry and Theology in Colossians 1:15–20."

[85] For the arrangement that follows, and the arguments for it, see Gordley, *Colossian Hymn in Context*, 176–196.

For by him all things were created:*
all things were created through him and for him.
And he is before all things,
And all things hold together in him.
And he is the head of the
body, the church.

Anti-strophe (vv. 18b–20a)
He is the beginning firstborn from among the dead,
so that in all things he might have the supremacy.
For he [God] was pleased
to have all his fullness dwell in him,
and through him to reconcile
all things to himself
making peace through the
blood of his cross –

Epode (v. 20b)
through him, whether things on earth
or things in heaven.

*Redactional material removed from v. 16:
things in heaven and on earth, visible and invisible,
whether thrones or powers or rulers or authorities.

The reconstruction proposed here leads to several insights about the focus and major point of the hymn. First, as noted by many scholars, the first strophe has its focus on creation. But specifically, Christ is hailed as the agent of God in God's work of creation. Verse 15 provides the primary assertion of the strophe, and the remainder of the strophe provides the justification for that claim. It is Christ who is the εἰκὼν τοῦ θεοῦ precisely because of his role in the process of creation, the sustaining of creation, and as the end of creation. In addition, the fact that he is the head of the body, the church, lends support to the primary claim of the strophe. The final phrase of the strophe also shifts the focus from the cosmic realm of creation to the more limited sphere of humanity, setting the stage for the second strophe. Further, the strophe as a whole has a varying temporal focus which moves present reality to mythic past and then back to the present.

The second strophe's primary claim is that Christ is the beginning of the new creation. This claim of v. 18b is supported by the remainder of the strophe which points out that the fullness of God was pleased to dwell in him, and to reconcile all things to him, and to make peace through the blood of his cross. These clauses are evidence in support of the primary assertion of the strophe. The incarnation, death, and resurrection of Christ thus are provided in this strophe (though not in that order) in support of the claim that Christ is the beginning of the new creation. The temporal focus of this strophe is on present reality and events of the recent past in the incarnation.

The epode serves as a refrain that summarize the hymn's overarching main point: all things are through him, whether things in heaven or things on earth. Creation of the cosmos is through him, and the reconciliation and redemption of humanity is through him. The phrase "through him" is one that was present in both strophes. Its presence in the epode emphasizes the comprehensive picture that all things occur and exist "through him." Interestingly, the epode does not use the term "all things" though it was used in both strophes. Instead, the epode more concretely describes all things as including the things of the heavenly realm and the earthly realm, tapping into two spatial registers that emphasize the complete supremacy of Christ.

The redactional material (part of v. 16) serves the role, for the author of Colossians, of clarifying precisely what "all things" refers to. Rather than waiting until the epode, the author of the epistle considered it vital to clarify the precise extent of this concept for the reader as early as possible. Presumably the insertion of these phrases gives us a glimpse as to the nature of the main issues confronting the Colossian Christians. In some way, the sufficiency of Christ for the Colossian believers was under attack. The clarification that Christ created and is therefore superior over "things in heaven and on earth, visible and invisible, whether thrones or powers or rulers or authorities" is thus critical to what the author aims to teach the Colossians through citing the hymn.

As the structure shows, the hymn makes strong claims about the person and work of Christ: he is the unique agent of God in the spheres of God's creative work and his redemptive work. He is thus superior to all created beings both in heaven and on earth. How do these claims fit within the first-century religious context and what light does this shed on the didactic function of this hymn?

The best reading of the hymn is that which takes into account the complex and varied nature of Second Temple Judaism as the primary context of the hymn. The hymn represents continuity with many of the central aspects of Second Temple Jewish theology. Certainly OT psalm traditions and styles as well as traditions about personified Wisdom are foundational to reading the hymn and hearings its overtones.[86] As important as these elements are for understanding the Colossian hymn, readers who stop with the Jewish background are neglecting several other important pieces of information about the context and content of the Colossian hymn. Hellenistic philosophical terminology mediated through Hellenized aspects of Judaism plays a significant role in the hymn. This can be seen in the specialized use of prepositions that reflects the prepositional metaphysics discussed by

---

[86] Stettler, *Kolosserhymnus*, 338–339.

Stoic and Middle-Platonic philosophers.[87] Surprisingly, most often over-looked are Greco-Roman conventions for praising the divine.

How would these claims have been heard and understood by the original audience? What terms and ideas would have stood out to them and con-nected with their cultural situation? What connections would they have made? Certainly the audience would have picked up on philosophical ter-minology that permeates the hymn: image of the invisible God; all things were created in him, through him, and to him; head of the body; emphasis on "all things;" etc. Although they would not necessarily have been pre-pared to search out the nuances of each phrase, the "feel" of the hymn would have brought to mind philosophical discussions which were current, and perhaps controversial, in their community.

Further, they would have noticed the hymnic style and thus recognized the exalted position that was being ascribed to Christ. In many ways the kinds of claims being made about Christ were not unlike claims made for other deities such as Isis or Zeus. Other gods were praised for their active role in creation as well as for their benefactions and good gifts on behalf of humanity. Over against whatever claims were being made in Colossae for other supernatural beings, forces, angels, or personified figures, Christ is clearly being placed above any competitors. The audience would surely not have missed this fact.

One of the main competitors for these claims would be none other than the emperor. It has been shown that much of the language of Colossians as a whole (including the hymn) reflects some sense of response to or reac-tion to the claims of the imperial ideology of the Roman Empire.[88] Accord-ingly, the claims of the hymn go beyond theological or philosophical asser-tions. In the context of the Roman world, they would have been considered to be political claims as well.[89] This observation raises the question of the extent to which the Colossian hymn and its claims represent a critique of imperial ideology. Did the author of the hymn and/or the author of the epistle aim to provide a vision of reality in hymnic form that was subver-sive of imperial claims? It is to this question that we briefly turn now. We will see that the Colossian hymn actually reinforces key Roman values

---

[87] Gregory E. Sterling, "Prepositional Metaphysics in Jewish Wisdom Speculation and Early Christological Hymns," in *Wisdom and Logos: Studies in Jewish Thought in Honor of David Winston* (ed. D. T. Runia and Gregory E. Sterling; Atlanta: Scholars Press, 1997), 219–238.

[88] Harry O. Maier, "A Sly Civility: Colossians and Empire," *JSNT* 27 (2005): 323–349.

[89] Gordon Zerbe and Muriel Orevillo-Montenegro, "The Letter to the Colossians," in *A Postcolonial Commentary on the New Testament Writings* (ed. Fernando F. Segovia and R. S. Sugirtharajah; London: T & T Clark, 2007), 294–303, esp. 299–302.

(power, honor, universal peace) even as it claims that Christ is the one who embodies these ideals.

When one looks at the Colossian hymn in light of this first-century imperial context that we have discussed earlier, one can see that the status and power of Christ are of primary importance. In the hymn, through honorific titles and the description of Christ's mediation of creation and redemption it becomes clear that this beloved son has authority and power that are unmatched in the realm of humanity. Power is not downplayed in the Colossian hymn; rather, power (divine power), is emphasized.

Interestingly, for our purposes, we must acknowledge that the power of the emperor is in no way denied or diminished in the hymn; he is not directly mentioned at all. Rather, the emperor is indirectly (or by extension) placed under the authority of Christ who, as the unique agent of God, is the one through whom God created and sustains all things, whether things in heaven or things on earth. If there is any critique of imperial ideology here, it is not by way of argument that the emperor does not have power. Of course he did. But the Colossian hymn is a reminder to the readers that there is one greater than Caesar. The hymn represents the status and power of Christ as supreme and without competition.

In the ancient world there was no question that honor was due to those with power and authority.[90] As we have seen, recent scholarship places the imperial cult at the apex of a pyramid of potential honors.[91] The Colossian hymn is silent about who should or should not receive honors of any kind. It does not critique the system of imperial honors or argue against it as the Philippian hymn perhaps does, by presenting the picture of the humble servant, Christ, who does not seek divine honors and whom God the Father exalts. Instead, the Colossian hymn itself models proper praise of Christ, honoring Christ by the ascription of titles and description of his praiseworthy deeds. Later in the epistle, at 3:16, the Colossians are urged to let the

---

[90] Heen suggests this is an issue in Philippians, not just in terms of the emperor but also the local clients of the imperial cult; the elite expected reverence: "While they were in public – in whatever context – the elite expected ritualized deference from their inferiors. This script was basic to the public discourse of antiquity, and it did not allow much room for critical revision" (Heen, "Phil 2:6–11 and Resistance," 129). He adds, "When the early clients of Christ criticized the cult of the emperor, they included the pretensions of the local elite in their line of sight. A critique of the emperor implied a critique of his local clients" (151). While the Colossian hymn does not necessarily have the local elite in view, it does affirm the Roman value of giving honor to one who is worthy.

[91] Davies, *Rome's Religious History: Livy, Tacitus, and Ammianus on their Gods*, 183. Davies has recently explored early Roman historians' comments on the imperial cult. He claims that, in Tacitus for example, one can observe the ways that the imperial cult and the awarding of divine honours reflects a negotiation of power. "Tacitus' rendering of imperial cult reflects this negotiation of power, rather than any broad criticism of whether the cult had any validity" (177).

logos tou Christou, "discourse about Christ", dwell in them richly as they "sing psalms, hymns, and spiritual songs with gratitude in their hearts to God." The tone is altogether positive in this regard about honoring God through grateful song that centers on the message about Christ. In Colossians there is nothing wrong with giving honor where honor is due. It is appropriate, and particularly appropriate to honor Christ in this way.

While perhaps encroaching on some of the honor and power normally ascribed to the emperor, we have not observed any explicit critique of the imperial cult thus far. In fact, in terms of two central Roman values, power and the giving of honor to those whose status requires it, Colossians reinforces and buys in to those values. However, by ascribing power and honor that exceeds that of the emperor to someone other than the emperor, there is at least the implication that the Roman ideology is inadequate in what it affirms about reality.[92]

In addition to these general thematic connections, there is at least one aspect of the Colossian hymn, one specific detail, which indicates a far more specific similarity between claims about Christ and claims about Caesar. Maier points to the language of reconciliation and pacification in Col 1:20 and following, as being in contact with language of peace-making used about the emperor. One famous inscription of 9 BCE claims:

> We could justly hold it [the birthday of Caesar] to be equivalent to the beginning of all things, and he has restored at least to serviceability, if not to its natural state, every form that had become imperfect and fallen into misfortune; and he has given a different aspect to the whole world, which blithely would have embraced its own destruction if Caesar had not been born for the common benefit of all.[93]

Philo of Alexandria can claim of Caesar: "This is he who gave freedom to every city, who brought disorder into order, who civilized and made obedient and harmonious, nations which before his time were unsociable, hostile, and brutal."[94] Thus, in Col 1:20 where it is through Christ that God "reconciles all things to himself making peace," a case can be made that work that is normally claimed as an accomplishment of the Roman emperor is now ascribed to Christ. The verses that follow the hymn take up this idea and continue with discourse that brings to mind claims of universal peace and prosperity that were a result of Caesar's reign.

---

[92] Sumney teases out some of the implications of this understanding in his recent commentary (Sumney, *Colossians*, 68).

[93] *OGI* 2, 458, decree of Paulus Fabius Maximus, proconsul of Asia, cited in Allan Chester Johnson et al., *Ancient Roman Statutes: A Translation, with Introduction, Commentary, Glossary, and Index* (The Corpus of Roman Law 2; Austin: University of Texas, 1961 repr. 2003), 119.

[94] Philo, *Legat.* 147 (trans. Yonge).

Nevertheless, even in the appropriation of this specific language for Christ, in no case is the work of the emperor downplayed or even directly confronted. Interestingly, again, a Roman value (universal peace and harmony) is affirmed in the Colossian hymn, although in the perspective of the hymn it is Christ who is the one who is able to make the ideal a reality.

At this point it is possible to ask, to what extent do these thematic parallels point to a sustained and intentional critique or subversion of the imperial cult specifically or the imperial ideology in general? I have suggested that several key Roman values are affirmed in the hymn. Whether or not the emperor embodies these values is not at issue. The hymn points out that Christ is the supreme and ultimate embodiment of these values and the one whose accomplishments make the values real for those who recognize him.

But what about the emperor? Do the imperial themes in the hymn not suggest that some kind of critique is intended? It is possible to go line by line through the claims made about Christ in the Colossian hymn and identify parallel claims made about the emperor in ancient literary sources, decrees, and inscriptions (see Table 1).

While the chart suggests that there is a good deal of resonance with imperial themes, two points should be noted. First, many of the sources listed are parallels only in a very broad sense. In no case is there any verbal dependence, and there is actually very little verbal correspondence as well. The most that can be said is that the Colossian hymn touches on themes that were relevant in the imperial cult. It ascribes actions and powers to Christ that were held in high value by the Romans. Second, there are several significant sections of the Colossian hymn with no parallels at all in ancient discussions of kingship or decrees relating to the imperial cult (note the empty spaces in the right column).

When one looks at the sections of the hymn which are without parallel in imperial sources, one is confronted with a set of ideas that is foreign to praise of human rulers. There are three primary areas for which there is no verbal or conceptual parallel: Christ as agent of creation of all things, Christ as firstborn from the dead, and the idea of the blood of the cross as the means of peacemaking. If the rest of the hymn is in implicit dialogue with claims of Caesar, what are these lines doing here?

What is claimed for Christ but not for the emperor causes us to consider another plane of discourse: hymnic praise of the divine. This does not negate the imperial overtones, but complements them and takes the discourse to another level. In the extant examples of ancient hymns as well as in the ancient rhetorical handbooks and *progymnasmata* with their instructions for composing hymns, one encounters several common elements that were suggested for inclusion in hymnic compositions. These include, among

*Table 1: Colossians 1:15–20 and Select Ancient Witnesses
to Roman Imperial Ideology*

[15]He is the image of the invisible God,	Plutarch, *Themistocles* 27.4.4–5; Ecphantes, *On Kingship* 80.3–7; 81.9–13; various inscriptions
the firstborn over all creation.	Letter of the Proconsul of Asia in Praise of Caesar, 1–12 (*OGI* 2, 458)
[16]For by him all things were created: things in heaven and on earth, visible and invisible, whether thrones or powers or rulers or authorities; all things were created by him and for him. [17]He is before all things,	
and in him all things hold together.	Aristides, *Or.* 23.76–78; Seneca, *Clem.* 1.1.2; 1.3.4
[18]And he is the head of the body, the church.	Lucian, *Apology* 13; Seneca, *Clem.* 1.3.4; 1.5.1; 1.13.4; 2.2.1–2
He is the beginning	Letter of the Proconsul of Asia, 1–12 (*OGI* 2, 458)
and the firstborn from among the dead,	
so that in all things he might have the supremacy.	Lucian, *Apology* 13
[19]For God was pleased to have all his fullness dwell in him, [20]and through him to reconcile all things to himself making peace	Ecphantes, *On Kingship* 80.3–7; 81.9–13; Calpurnius Siculus, *Ecl.* 4.142–146 Pliny, *Panegyricus*, 80.1–2 *Res Gestae* 13.42–43; 26.11–12; Cassius Dio 44.49.2
through the blood of his cross –	
through him, whether things on earth or things in heaven.	Plutarch, *Fort. Rom.* 2.316e–317c; *Princ. iner.* 5.781f–82a; Suetonius, *Augustus* 98.2–3

other things, mention of the area of supremacy of the god, elaboration of the historical deeds of the god, and mention of the benefactions of the deity on behalf of humanity. These categories are not completely different from the categories used to praise a human, even an exalted human like the emperor. As Theon noted in the first-century CE in his *progymnasmata*,

Encomion is language revealing the greatness of virtuous actions and other good qualities belonging to a particular person. The term is now specifically applied to praise of living persons whereas praise of the dead is called an *epitaphios* and praise of the gods a hymn; but whether one praises the living or the dead or heroes or gods, the method of speaking is one and the same.[95]

Parallels with ancient psalms and hymns could be adduced to show that the Colossian hymn participates to a large degree in Greco-Roman hymnic conventions. Christ's area of supremacy is all things; his work in history includes the creating and sustaining of all things; his benefactions to humanity include reconciling and making peace. In light of those comparisons, and its context in a paraenetic letter of exhortation,[96] I believe the hymn is best described as a quasi-philosophical prose hymn. Other scholars disagree and have placed this hymn much more fully in a Jewish context based primarily on the contents of the hymn and their likely origins.

However, regardless of the origin of the ideas in the Colossian hymn, its themes and its form suggest that not only the emperor falls under the authority of Christ but so do other beings who claim divine status and authority. In view of the claims of the Colossian hymn, not even popular and beneficent gods and goddesses such as Isis or Asclepius can compare with Christ who is the agent of God in both creation and redemption of all things.

Thus far, it is clear that there are indeed imperial overtones in the language of the Colossian hymn. It is also apparent that there are claims in the hymn that take it beyond the praise of an exalted human, and cause one to consider this hymn as praising Christ as the preexistent agent of God. We must conclude by asking about the didactic deployment of such themes in this hymn. To answer this question we must consider the context of the hymn.

The author of Colossians makes his purpose clear both in his opening prayer and in the appeals that follow the citation of the hymn. The epistle is addressed to those who are followers of Christ already with the goal that they would continue in Him. The opening prayer asks that they would be filled with knowledge so that they can lead lives worthy of the Lord; that they would be made strong and able to endure everything with patience and thanksgiving (1:9–12). The verses following the hymn urge them to continue without shifting (1:23); not be deceived (2:4); continue to live their lives in him (2:6); and not be taken captive through philosophy and empty deceit (2:8).

The writer's desires include a positive and a negative: do this (i.e., continue in him) and not this (i.e., don't be deceived). What the Colossian believers are in danger of being deceived by has been the subject of much

---

[95] Kennedy, *Progymnasmata*, 50.

[96] For this claim see Walter T. Wilson, *The Hope of Glory: Education and Exhortation in the Epistle to the Colossians* (NovTSup 88; New York: Brill, 1997), 229–254.

debate and does not need to concern us here.[97] But in light of these twin purposes of affirmation and dissuasion, the hymn must be seen as painting a picture of the ultimate nature of reality in which those commands make sense. The hymn does this by recognizing that in all things Christ is supreme. Christ is above the emperor; Christ is above angels and spiritual powers. In light of that reality, the Colossians should continue with him and not be led astray to think they need to appease other beings or forces as well.

That the Colossians would defy Rome or resist the imperial cult in any sense does not appear to be in view in this epistle or in the hymn. In fact it is well known that elsewhere in Colossians the recipients are urged to conduct their households in light of accepted imperial norms, reflecting yet another Roman value: order.

Does the Colossian hymn, then, subvert or resist the empire? On the one hand, Roman values are affirmed: power, status, honor, peace, and order. On the other hand, someone more supreme than Caesar is in focus. Further, though we have not discussed this, the means of Christ's peacemaking work mentioned in the hymn (the cross and the resurrection) suggest that Roman methods of achieving universal peace are off-target, to say the least.

In light of all this it makes sense to view the hymn as an example of "worldview resistance" or, perhaps, "worldview reinforcement."[98] The specific worldview emphasized in Colossians takes into account the belief that all powers are subject to Christ; accordingly, believers in Colossae should not be deceived into thinking that there is anything missing from the life that is offered in Christ. Further, the good news about Jesus had universal implications; this good news required expression in universal terms which captured the scope of the works of Christ and the implications of being "in him." The form of expression this takes in Col 1:15–20 does resonate with imperial ideology; it also resonates with worship of the divine as well as with Jewish wisdom traditions. The hymnic form is thus a very effective way of communicating the universal significance of the message about Christ since it communicates on a number of levels both by its content and by its form.

---

[97] See the essential study, Morna Dorothy Hooker, "Were there False Teachers in Colossae?," in *Christ and Spirit in the New Testament* (ed. Barnabas Lindars and Stephen S. Smalley; Cambridge: Cambridge University Press, 1973), 315–331.

[98] Walsh and Keesmaat speak of Colossians as "a worldview book" (98): "As a worldview text, Colossians weaves for its readers and hearers a vision of life. It tells us who rules the world, where the world has come from and where it is going, where wisdom is ultimately to be found, and even which community of people holds the promise and destiny of the world in its hearts and lives" (Walsh and Keesmaat, *Colossians Remixed*, 99).

But for all of this resonance the Colossian hymn is not aimed at Caesar, or any other entity specifically. It is intended to portray the cosmic significance and authority of Christ in order to urge the Colossians to continue "in him." The emperor only incidentally falls under the authority of Christ as does anyone else who would make claims about their power and authority apart from Christ.

Pizzuto's point about confessional, creedal, and liturgical functions is worth considering here. He explains,

When we consider the polemical intent of the epistle, it seems as though the exalted style of Col 1:15–20 was intended also as a creedal statement of faith, directed against the threat of syncretism. . . . Thus the function of Col 1:15–20 is at once confessional (psalm-like) and creedal (pedagogical), confessing in poetic (hymnic) form, that Christ is Lord of the cosmos.[99]

As noted above, Longenecker has observed that confessional materials are usually used for one of three purposes: to establish rapport with the audience, to summarize the essence of their discussion, or, most commonly, as a basis for the argument and appeal which follows.[100] It can be argued that the Colossian hymn serves each of these functions.

The universal scope, elevated style, and thematic emphases of the Colossian hymn make it a passage which has attracted careful attention by scholars in light of its literary, cultural, and theological contexts. This chapter has shown the ways that it is profitable to read the passage as an early Christian hymn which recounts the work of God in creation and redemption through his agent, the beloved son. As a hymn the passage shares features with other ancient hymns of praise, both Jewish and Greco-Roman. As a hymn recounting the work of God in creation and redemption the passage shows a number of connections with major themes of the Old Testament and Second Temple Jewish literature. With its focus on the agent of God, some of the closest connections are with passages that reflect on the role of personified Wisdom, though the claims of the Colossian hymn go beyond the claims of the Wisdom literature. In the first-century Roman world, the claims of the hymn and of the epistle as a whole appear to reflect the claims of the imperial ideology that was promoted through the empire. Christ, not Caesar, is the one through whom the blessings of peace come into the world. Christ, the unique and only agent of God in the creation of all things is also the unique and only agent of God in making peace and reconciling all things to God. This peace-making and reconciling work is accomplished not through force of power but through the blood of the cross. As an early Christian hymn, the passage serves as a focal

---

[99] Pizzuto, *Cosmic Leap of Faith*, 110–111.
[100] Longenecker, *New Wine*, 48.

point for painting a picture of the visible and invisible world in which the followers of Christ live, and in which the imperatives of the epistle make sense. It also corrects other alternatives, implying that they are inadequate in light of the person and work of Christ.

F. Conclusions

In this chapter we have sought to understand the place of didactic hymnody within the letters of the New Testament noting that the passages most reflective of hymnic traditions are a subset of a larger category of confessional materials. This broader category includes a wide range of statements mostly having to do with the person and work of Jesus Christ. These confessional materials played a significant role in the corporate gatherings of the early Christians. Though we cannot know much about their exact use in those settings, we are able to consider their use within the letters of the New Testament.

The analysis in this chapter suggests that the christological hymns of the New Testament functioned on numerous interrelated levels as didactic hymns. First, they encapsulated key components of the developing Christian view of the person and work of Jesus. Accordingly, they provided a means of remembering Christ in a particular way. In the case of Colossians and Philippians this particular way of remembering Christ was primarily narrative and also all-encompassing in terms of both temporal and spatial register. This way of remembering Christ reflects the dynamics of cultural memory, and likely served to unite the early Christian communities around a shared understanding of their savior. Second, the ideas highlighted in these hymns reflected Christ's place within the trajectory of Jewish belief in the Second Temple period. In this way, the memory of Christ was joined to the memory of God's work in the history of Israel as remembered in the Jewish Scriptures. Third, by expressing these truths in hymnic and/or poetic form, the expression of these truths themselves took on a more sacred tone – Christ was being remembered with terms and styles of speaking appropriate only to God. Fourth, the hymns played a significant role in the formation of a worldview in which the practical lifestyle promoted by the early Christian letter writers makes sense. This last point was somewhat complicated in that it worked on several levels. We have observed, for example, that central ideas and concepts of both the Philippian hymn and the Colossian hymn resonated with and called into question central claims of the Roman imperial ideology.

Hymnody played an important role as the summary of distinctive Christian beliefs about Jesus and as one part of a theological foundation for

Christian living within the Roman Empire. In Philippians and Colossians in particular, hymns composed for multiple purposes took on a function that may be considered largely didactic as they served as both a reminder of teaching already accepted and a foundation for the practical appeals to be made in the rest of the letter.

Chapter 9

Didactic Hymns in New Testament Narratives and the Apocalypse

A. Introduction

Having observed the importance of hymnody as an instructional and formational tool embedded within the earliest Christian epistles, it is not surprising that hymnody should play a similar role in the earliest Christian literary works: the Gospels and the apocalypse. We have already seen the widespread use of hymnic passages as a significant feature in early Jewish narratives. Likewise we have observed that human and heavenly praise both played a role in Jewish apocalyptic literature. Hymnody provided a form and a medium through which an author could provide his readers with a larger perspective on events that had happened or were happening in the readers' day. Rather than directly stating propositions about the ultimate reality, poets painted a verbal portrait of ultimate reality through their hymns and psalms. In this way they invited their audiences to see themselves and their circumstances within that vision. In narrative settings in particular we observed that didactic hymns functioned to provide an eternal perspective in a temporal situation even as they model an appropriate response to an awareness of God's presence in history. In light of these dynamics, this chapter explores the ways that Christian writers of the first century utilized hymnody within their compositions for didactic purposes. Specifically, this chapter treats the hymns of the infancy narratives in Luke's Gospel, the prologue to John's Gospel, and the hymns in Revelation 4–5.

One thread which is woven through the materials studied in this chapter is the idea of hymnody as a contributor to social memory. The discipline of mnemohistory was addressed in the introduction to this volume and has been an important tool for this study, particularly in dealing with didactic hymns that address the past.[1] As we will see, the hymns in each of the

---

[1] Recall Jan Assmann's definition: "Unlike history proper, mnemohistory is concerned not with the past as such, but only with the past as it is remembered. It surveys the story-lines of tradition, the webs of intertextuality, the diachronic continuities and discontinuities of reading the past," Assmann, *Moses the Egyptian*, 9.

larger literary works in this chapter concern themselves, at least to some extent, with the proper understanding of events that occurred in the first half of the first century CE. Yet the compositions themselves date from the latter half of that century and have been composed for communities of readers that were attempting to make sense of their current contexts in light of the traditions they had received about Jesus. Mnemohistory enables us to consider how the way the past is remembered (social memory) helps to shape the present for any given community. While the dynamics of cultural memory are not the only common feature of the materials we will encounter in this chapter, attention to these dynamics will be important for identifying both commonalities and differences in the hymns of Luke, John, and Revelation.

B. Didactic Hymns in the Infancy Narrative of Luke's Gospel

As with many Jewish narratives of the biblical and Second Temple eras the author of the Gospel of Luke presented an account which incorporated hymnic compositions as a part of his compositional strategy. The opening two chapters of Luke's Gospel contain a large portion of hymnic materials in the well-known Magnificat (1:46–55), Benedictus (1:68–79), Gloria in excelsis (2:14), and Nunc Dimittis (2:29–32). The larger narrative of Luke-Acts is punctuated by song or references to praise in other key moments as well.[2] The response of joyous praise on the part of characters within Luke-Acts has been identified as a prominent feature in discerning the structure and emphasis of the two-volume work.[3] In this section we will limit our focus to considering the hymns of the infancy narratives as didactic hymnody.

The hymns of the infancy narratives have been the subject of scholarly attention for many years and scholars have identified a number of functions of this material as they have examined its form and content.[4] These passages are frequently identified within the tradition of declarative psalms of praise whose content is rooted in concepts from the Jewish scriptures

---

[2] E.g., Luke 19:37–38; 24:52–53; Acts 2:42; 3:9; 4:21.

[3] Cf. De Long, *Surprised by God.*

[4] Raymond Edward Brown, *The Birth of the Messiah: A Commentary on the Infancy Narratives in Matthew and Luke* (ABRL; New York: Doubleday, 1993); Mark Coleridge, *The Birth of the Lukan Narrative: Narrative as Christology in Luke 1–2* (JSNTSup 88; Sheffield: JSOT Press, 1993); Stephen Farris, *The Hymns of Luke's Infancy Narratives: Their Origin, Meaning and Significance* (JSNTSup 9; Sheffield: JSOT Press, 1985); Ulrike Mittmann-Richert, *Magnifikat und Benediktus: die ältesten Zeugnisse der judenchristlichen Tradition von der Geburt des Messias* (WUNT 2.90; Tübingen: Mohr Siebeck, 1996).

and expressed in terminology influenced by the LXX. In terms of their function, Farris views them as "the overture which sets out certain motifs which will recur in the body of the composition."[5] Among these motifs are the major themes of promise and fulfillment and the restoration of Israel.

Though the terms are not used in the songs, the Greek words for fulfill (πληρόω; πληροφορέω) are used in pivotal places in Luke's Gospel (1:1; 4:21; 24:44). The idea of fulfillment frames the narrative as a whole from the opening dedication (1:1) to the final words of Jesus (24:44). It also marks the beginning of the public ministry of Jesus. After reading aloud from Isaiah, his first publicly spoken statement was the claim that Isaiah's prophecy was being fulfilled right before the eyes and ears of his audience (Luke 4:21). The songs supplement this theme of fulfillment, harmonizing with it as they give praise to God that, with the birth of Jesus, God was fulfilling what he had promised in ancient times.

Taken as a whole the infancy narratives present themselves as a continuation of the Scriptures of Israel through their setting, characters, content, themes, allusive use of biblical language, and style.[6] In this way the story of Jesus and the worldwide spread of the gospel are to be understood as the latest phase in the merciful acts of the God of Israel in history on behalf of his people. The four hymnic passages within the infancy narrative contribute to this dynamic explicitly through their contents and implicitly through their form. Like the narrative as a whole the hymns contain many allusions to important biblical texts as they strike key thematic notes that resonate with the broader purposes of Luke's Gospel. Further, as we have seen in earlier chapters, hymnic praise on the mouths of devout individuals is a regular feature of early Jewish narrative and apocalyptic. By having devout and exemplary Jews affirm in biblical hymnic style the realities of God's salvific work for both Jews and Gentiles through Jesus, the infancy narratives invite the reader to see the story of Jesus as part of the story of God's continuing redemptive mercy. The reader is also invited to see himself or herself as a recipient of this mercy, which extends to both Jews and Gentiles. As we will see, though the language and imagery is somewhat different in the hymn to the Logos in John 1, that hymn shares a similar function as it orients the reader to the coming narrative, showing that the events recorded in the narrative must be understood within the context of God's redemptive work throughout history.

Even a cursory reading of the four hymns of the infancy narratives reveals similarities in theme and outlook among them all, particularly among the three longer passages. With the exception of the very brief angelic ac-

---

[5] Farris, *Hymns*, 151.
[6] David Ravens, *Luke and the Restoration of Israel* (JSNTSup 119; Sheffield: Sheffield Academic Press, 1995), 28–29.

clamation (2:14), the remaining three songs emphasize God's carrying out his promises together with God's mercy as demonstrated by his saving acts on behalf of his people. These songs show faithful Jews recognizing in the births of John and Jesus that God was bringing about what he had promised through the scriptures of Israel. In this section we review the contents of each hymn highlighting its unique features and its didactic role in the unfolding development of Luke's Gospel.

1. The Magnificat (Luke 1:46–55)

The Magnificat is Mary's song of rejoicing in response to the exclamation of her cousin Elizabeth (Luke 1:41–45). There is general agreement among interpreters that her song is modeled to some extent on Hannah's song in 1 Sam 2:1–10. For example, Luke 1:46 introduces Mary's song with the same verb the LXX uses in 1 Sam 2:1; there is an emphasis in both instances on the woman as a humble servant of the Lord (Luke 1:48; 1 Sam 1:11 LXX); both songs emphasize divine reversal (1 Sam 2:4–8; Luke 1:52–53). Nevertheless, Hannah's song is not the sole model for this song. Rather, it is more significant that Mary is portrayed in Luke 1 as a participant in a larger tradition of birth narratives, a tradition which includes Sarah, Rebecca, Leah, Rachel, the mother of Samson, Hannah, as well as personified Zion/Jerusalem (cf. Isa 54:1).[7] In this line of tradition Mary's praise is appropriate as a response to the mighty work that God has done relative to her miraculous pregnancy. But it is also appropriate as praise for God's eschatological restoration of his people as pictured with the language of personified Zion's barrenness and birth in passages like Isa 54:1. The expectation that God's salvific work would be met by responses of praise is seen in a number of other prophetic texts, including Joel 2:26–27, Zeph 3:14–15, Zech 9:9–10, and Isa 66:7–11. In other words, when the restoration of Israel began, praise was to be a part of the experience. By capitalizing on these kinds of expectations and precedents, the content and setting of Mary's praise suggest that in the events of the narrative the long expected restoration has begun.[8]

In terms of the form of this passage, Farris identifies this and the other major hymns as declarative psalms of praise in which an individual offers a word of praise (often an imperative, but not always) and then a reason for the praise (usually some way that God has acted).[9] Brown suggests that the

---

[7] For an explanation of the connections and their significance, see De Long, *Surprised by God*, 168–173.

[8] Ibid., 160–161.

[9] They may also be considered eschatological in that they deal with the coming victory of God from the perspective of the narrative. From the perspective of Luke and his

Magnificat embodies features of both the individual hymn of praise (especially in vv. 46–50) and the communal hymn of praise (in vv. 51–55).[10] In terms of its content the Magnificat divides easily into two distinct sections. A first strophe, vv. 46–50, provides the hymnic opening and Mary's personal praise for what God has done for her. The text reads, in English translation:

And Mary said:
My soul magnifies the Lord
And my spirit has found joy in God my Savior,
Because he considered the humble state of his servant.
For behold, from now on all generations will consider me blessed.
Because the Mighty One performed great things for me,
And holy is his name.
And his mercy is from generation to generation to those fearing him. (vv. 46–50)

Though these lines reflect specifically on what God has done for Mary personally in a narratival style, they also tie in those deeds with a larger picture of God's attributes of holiness and mercy to all generations using a descriptive style (v. 50). But as Nolland notes, these characteristics are not abstract qualities but are directly tied to what God is accomplishing in and through Mary in the coming birth of the Messiah.[11] In other words, God's mercy is now to be experienced by all generations through the specific events about to be narrated in Luke-Acts. Narrative and attributive descriptions are joined together in this strophe in such a way that one reinforces the other.

The second strophe (vv. 51–55) continues with that larger perspective and takes on a much more general feel with a series of aorist verbs describing God's deeds in the past and extending into the future. The text reads:

He performed mighty deeds with his arm,
He scattered the arrogant in the thought of their heart
He pulled down rulers from thrones
but raised up the humble.
He filled the hungry with good things
but the rich he sent away empty
He has come to the aid of Israel his child
In remembrance of his mercy
Just as he said to our fathers,
To Abraham and to his seed forever. (vv. 51–55)

While the aorist verbs point to the deeds of God in the past, the context suggests that the decisive saving work of God is still to come in the birth

---

readers, however, the decisive eschatological event is now past in the events described in Luke 1–2. Farris, *Hymns*, 11–12, 88.

[10] Brown, *Birth of the Messiah*, 355–357.

[11] John Nolland, *Luke 1–9:20* (WBC 35A; Dallas: Word Books, 1989), 76.

of the savior. In this way the hymn taps into multiple temporal registers at once as part of its artistic envisioning of reality. Ravens suggests that this feature demonstrates Luke's use of ambivalence to make two related points:

> The aorists direct the reader to God's past help for Israel and the form of the hymn alludes to Samuel. But it is the context of the hymn, rather than the content, that tells us that Israel's new prophet and Judge is about to be born, one who will fulfill the promises to Abraham and hence show God's constancy towards his people.[12]

As we have seen with the *Barkhi Nafshi* hymns at Qumran, the use of biblically-styled language can have several layers of meaning as it places current or recent events in the framework of biblical history. This dynamic seems to be at work in the Magnificat as well.

In both sections of the Magnificat, scripturesque language is a significant feature. Scholars have documented numerous instances of biblical allusion and intertextuality.[13] In this regard Nolland correctly observes,

> The Magnificat (vv. 46–55) is at times marked by specific OT allusions, but more commonly OT motifs and language are used in fresh coinage which evokes more generally the whole thought world of OT faith and declares its eschatological fulfillment, at least in principle, in God's present activity with Mary.[14]

Whether or not Luke's readers could identify each specific allusion within the song, it is certainly conceivable that both the overtones from the scriptures of Israel, together with the motif of the mother's song of praise would have been clear enough. The thematic content of the song thus stakes its ground within the thought-world of the scriptures of Israel. The coming birth of Jesus is thereby remembered in a biblically-styled way.

Taken together both sections praise God for his favor and mercy, his reversal of fortunes for the powerful and lowly, and for the fact that he has helped Israel in remembrance of his mercy and promise to Abraham. Allusions to several passages within Isaiah are significant, particularly as several of these will ultimately be seen to play a role in the theology and thought that underlie the climactic song of Simeon as well. Mittmann-Richert suggests that the Magnificat and Benedictus both can be best understood in the context of Isaianic praise for God's salvation through the birth of the Messiah.[15] In this view the Magnificat is a song in the tradition of Isa 12, which is a song in praise of God for his coming salvation. Mittmann-Richert notes, "The Isaianic birth cycle provides a solution in itself as an interpretive key for an understanding of the Magnificat and

---

[12] Ravens, *Luke and the Restoration of Israel*, 36.
[13] Brown, *Birth of the Messiah*, 358–360.
[14] Nolland, *Luke 1–9:20*, 74.
[15] Mittmann-Richert, *Magnifikat und Benediktus*, 144–153.

Benedictus."[16] The key passages in this regard are 7:14, 9:1–6, 11:1–10, and the song of praise in 12:1–6. This thesis is supported by several factors within the text. First, within the infancy narrative there are clear and direct allusions to these early chapters of Isaiah, particularly in the Benedictus with its clear reference to Isa 9:2 (cf. Luke 1:79). Second, the narrative context of the Magnificat emphasizes the birth of the Messiah to the virgin (cf. Isa 7:14). Third, the Magnificat itself places an emphasis on divine reversal which is also a significant feature of the passages in the Isaianic birth cycle (cf. Isa 9:1). Though this view does not exhaust the possibilities for hearing intertextual echoes within the Magnificat and Benedictus, it does suggest a level of connection with ideas in Isaiah that go beyond mere verbal echo. These thematic connections will become even more significant when we look at the song of Simeon, in which the universal salvation of Isa 11:10–12 and Isa 40–52 come into clearer view.

Another passage which has been shown to echo in the praise of Mary (and also of Zechariah and Simeon) is Ps 97:1–3 LXX. De Long has shown that several aspects of this passage correspond to the praise that Mary offers in the Magnificat.[17] For example, Ps 97:1 LXX mentions God's great deeds and mighty arm. Verse 2 mentions the salvation of the Lord, while v. 3 indicates that God remembers his mercy and his promise to Israel. Given that Ps 97 LXX is an eschatological psalm (cf. v. 9), with similar themes and language to the Magnificat, it is easy to see Mary's song as a song in this tradition. In fact, it is possible to see that the praise manifested in Mary's song fulfills expectations for joyous praise at the time of God's eschatological salvation.[18] The fact that the Benedictus and the Nunc Dimittis also show connections with Ps 97 LXX further strengthens the likelihood that the author had Ps 97 in view when composing each of these hymns.

From our vantage point it is not possible to say with certainty which set of allusions, if any, were primary in the mind of the author of the Magnificat. Nevertheless, Ps 97 LXX and songs of praise in the Isaianic birth cycle both share the foundational perspective that God will act decisively on behalf of his people (Isa 12:1–3; Ps 97:1–3 LXX) and that this will result in joyful song and praise (Isa 12:4–6; Ps 97:4–9). These overarching themes are prominent in the Magnificat and reflect idea that are seen in both the prophets and the psalms.

In terms of the didactic function of this song within the narrative, like the other songs we will look at, the Magnificat provides the reader with a

---

[16] Ibid., 145, trans. mine.

[17] De Long, *Surprised by God*, 160.

[18] Ibid.

larger perspective on the events of the narrative.[19] Wolter notes that Luke allows Mary to supply the interpretation of the events of the narrative in light of the election history of Israel. Further, Luke allows her to do this with the kinds of words with which Israel had always praised their God as they celebrated his intervention on their behalf.[20] The Magnificat is the most general of the songs and so connects very clearly with its Jewish background, containing nothing distinctly Christian in its content. The remaining songs will evidence more and more specificity, showing that the birth of John and Jesus are part of the unfolding of the eschatological salvation-plan of God.

More than just supplying the interpretation to the narrative, however, the Magnificat is also an important part of the narrative itself. De Long has noted several inter-related functions of the hymns of the infancy narratives. First, as they interpret the narrative for the reader, they invite the reader to embrace the view held by the characters: that the events in the narrative represent the divine visitation. Second, they describe this visitation and restoration using scriptural language. Third, as suggested above, their presence in the narrative fulfills scriptural expectations that praise would break forth at the dawn of the time of restoration. De Long explains, "Praise in the infancy narrative asserts that the divine visitation has begun."[21]

Taking a larger view, we can also see that the song strikes key notes that will be important throughout Luke's Gospel. For example, the kind of reversal depicted in the song is "announced by Jesus in his Beatitudes and woes (6:20–26), and is enacted by him in the narrative of his ministry."[22] Further, joyous praise in response to divine visitation is a major theme of Luke-Acts as a whole.[23] When we turn to the Benedictus, we will observe similar dynamics as praise fulfills scriptural expectations for the time of restoration, as it provides an interpretation for events in the narrative, and as it provides the interpretation in scriptural language and categories.

2. The Benedictus (Luke 1:68–79)

The Benedictus continues these same themes as Zechariah, filled with the Holy Spirit, prophesies in 1:68–79 following the naming of John and the restoration of Zechariah's voice. Just as Mary's song had a more specific strophe and a more general one, so does Zechariah's. His begins, however,

---

[19] Luke Timothy Johnson, *The Gospel of Luke* (SP 3; Collegeville, Minn.: Liturgical Press, 1991), 43.

[20] Michael Wolter, *Das Lukasevangelium* (HNT 5; Tübingen: Mohr Siebeck, 2008), 100.

[21] De Long, *Surprised by God*, 179.

[22] Johnson, *The Gospel of Luke*, 44.

[23] De Long, *Surprised by God*, 134.

with the more general (vv. 68–75) before moving to the more specific lines about John (vv. 76–77) and then back to the more general (vv. 78–79). The themes of this song are similar to those of Mary's as well: God's favor, mercy, rescue, and redemption through the promised savior. New themes or new variations are seen in the specific discussion of John as prophet of the Most High, and in the added themes of light, guidance, and peace. Peace will be mentioned again in the song of the angels and in the song of Simeon. Light will be a theme of the song of Simeon. With each new song in the infancy narratives, previous themes are reinforced and related themes or elements are introduced.

As with the Magnificat, each line of the song can be seen to be rich with allusions to themes and phrases from the Jewish scriptures.[24] Connections with Ps 97:1–3 LXX have already been mentioned in the discussion of the Magnificat. In the case of the Benedictus, De Long has identified thematic connections between the coming of salvation (Luke 1:69, 77; Ps 97:2 LXX) and the idea that God has shown mercy and remembered his covenant (Luke 1:72–73; Ps 97:3 LXX).[25] Though these connections may be valid, a strong case can also be made for connections with two historical psalms: Pss 105 and 106.[26] The idea that God remembers his covenant with Abraham is clearly spelled out in Ps 105:8–9 and 42 (cf. also Ps 106:45). Further, an allusion to Ps 106:4 may be seen in Luke 1:69 with the idea that God has visited his people. Finally, the mention of salvation from enemies in v. 71 seems to be a clear allusion to the exodus as described in Ps 106:10. In this case the biblical allusions reflect the idea that the events of the narrative should be seen as part of the history of God's redemptive work on behalf of his people: the Benedictus clearly references David, Moses and the exodus, and the covenant with Abraham.[27]

The Benedictus begins with the notice that Zechariah was filled with the Holy Spirit, and that he "prophesied saying" (1:67):

Blessed be the Lord the God of Israel,
Because he visited and brought about redemption for his people,
And raised a horn of salvation for us
In the house of his servant David.
Just as he said through the mouth of his holy prophets from ages long past.
Salvation from our enemies and from the hand of all who hate us,
To make mercy according to our fathers
And to remember his holy covenant,

---

[24] For a concise listing of parallels see Brown, *Birth of the Messiah*, 386–389.

[25] De Long, *Surprised by God*, 160–161.

[26] Stephen Farris, "The Canticles of Luke's Infancy Narrative: The Appropriation of a Biblical Tradition," in *Into God's Presence: Prayer in the New Testament* (ed. Richard N. Longenecker; Grand Rapids: Eerdmans, 2001), 91–112, here 107–108.

[27] Farris, *Hymns*, 138.

An oath which he swore to Abraham our father.
To grant us, without fear, rescued from the hand of enemies,
To serve him in holiness and righteousness
Before him all our days. (vv. 68–75)

This section includes the introductory word of praise (v. 68a) and the first strophe which provides the justification for the praise (vv. 68b–75). Whatever may be said about the primary scriptural allusions here, references to the history of Israel (David, the exodus, Abraham) are clearly placed in the foreground as the hymn strikes chords that relate to the distant past of Israel.

In the second strophe (vv. 76–79) the temporal register and focus switch to a prophesy directed to Zechariah's son John. The second strophe reads:

And you, child, will be called a prophet of the Most High.
For you will go before the Lord to prepare his way,
To give knowledge of salvation to his people
through the forgiveness of sins,
According to the compassionate mercy of our God
In which dawn will visit us from on high,
To shine on those in darkness and residing in the shadow of death,
To direct our feet in the way of peace. (vv. 76–79)

Allusions to the prophesies of Isaiah, Malachi, and other prophets are readily apparent in this strophe (cf. Isa 40:3; Mal 3:1; Zech 3:8; 6:6). The emphasis here is that in the coming births and ministries of John and Jesus, God is remembering and fulfilling his ancient promises in a way that results in knowledge of salvation, forgiveness of sins, light, and peace.[28]

As with the Magnificat, Luke uses this song to add to the narrative and supplement it with additional perspective. The issue of worship is one that the song raises both explicitly (vv. 68 and 74) and implicitly by Zechariah's model. The idea expressed in the phrase "worship/serve him fearlessly" reveals Luke's view of the church as a worshipping community.[29]

---

[28] The clear focus on John has led scholars to propose that the Benedictus, or at least portions of it, derive from the circle of followers of John the Baptist, and that Luke has incorporated it into his narrative, perhaps with the addition of some lines. Dillon, for example, identifies vv. 69–70 as Lukan additions to an original that referred only to John the Baptist (Richard J. Dillon, "The Benedictus in Micro- and Macrocontext," *CBQ* 68 [2006]: 457–80, here 458). The issue of whether Luke used a preexisting source is surely significant in terms of our understanding of the role and place of didactic hymnody in early Christianity. However for the purposes of this section, we are considering the collective impact of the four hymns in their current contexts. We will thus have to set aside the teaching and instructional use of the hymn in a pre-Lukan setting, except to note again the complexity that arises when considering hymnic passages that may have been used in a setting other than the one in which we find them preserved.

[29] Johnson, *The Gospel of Luke*, 47. Cf. Luke 24:52–53; Acts 2:42–47; 4:23–31; 13:1–3; 20:7–12.

Johnson points out, "Luke has thereby made the experience of Zechariah a miniature enactment of his own canticle: God's mercy liberates the people to worship fearlessly; Zechariah's release from muteness is expressed in praise."[30] This idea that the song itself is an enactment of the reality it describes represents a significant function of the hymns as a whole.

Further, the hymn serves a significant role in authenticating and articulating the significance of the births of both John and Jesus. Through a blameless and upright Israelite who was filled with the Holy Spirit, the eternal perspective on these temporal births is provided.[31] In the form of a hymn of praise the reader is invited to embrace the view of Zechariah who, filled with the Spirit, sees the birth of John as the initiation of the coming restoration as prophesied by Isaiah (Isa 40:3) and Malachi (Mal 3:1).

In many ways the Benedictus exemplifies the dynamics of social memory. Its web of historical and intertextual allusions relative to the history of Israel embodies Assmann's observation about the ways that the present is "haunted" by the past.[32] The births of John and Jesus, in the historical past from the perspective of Luke and his readers, are portrayed by Zechariah as participating in the even more distant historical work of God on behalf of his people – a history that extends back through David, Moses, and Abraham. As these biblical figures are remembered by Zechariah, Luke enables his audience to remember Jesus and John as part of that same history. With this song Luke thus educates his readers with regard to how to remember Jesus as part of the history of Israel.

3. Gloria (Luke 2:14)

In the brief Gloria in excelsis (2:14) we glimpse the song of the angels and a key proclamation of the plan of God for humanity. With this third song we may now observe something about the progression of speakers/singers of these songs. First, Mary, a humble servant of the Lord who finds favor with God, speaks her own response of praise in the tradition of many great mothers within Israel. Second, Zechariah, a devout and upright priest who prophesies by the Holy Spirit, offers God's prophetic perspective on the births in the language of the prophets of Israel. And now, the angels, heavenly messengers, offer praise to God for the news of the birth of the savior who is Christ the Lord. The songs are progressively more focused, even as the ones who vocalize the songs represent a closer and closer connection to the presence of God.

---

[30] Ibid.

[31] Wolter, *Das Lukasevangelium*, 212.

[32] Assmann, *Moses the Egyptian*, 9.

The angelic song follows the announcement of the angel of the Lord to the shepherds in 2:8–12. After the angelic birth announcement a multitude of the heavenly host appears with the first angel. Their song is introduced by indicating that they were "praising God and saying" (2:13):

Glory to God in the highest
And upon earth peace among men with whom he is pleased. (2:14)[33]

This brief angelic hymn of praise is a direct response to the birth annunciation in 2:10–12 which indicated that a savior, Christ the Lord, had been born. Just as angels praised God for what he had done in the work of creation (cf. *Jub.* 2:2–3), so in Luke's Gospel they glorify God for his work of sending the Messiah to be born.[34] As Brown notes, "Luke is telling us that the angels of heaven recognized at the beginning of Jesus' life what the disciples came to know only at the end, namely, the presence of the Messiah King who comes in the name of the Lord."[35] The angels are thus included as witnesses to the birth of the Messiah and to its heavenly significance. Their song joins the didactic purposes of the other hymns in the infancy narrative to convey Luke's message with great force and clarity.

The angelic praise reminds the reader that peace is an important theme of the infancy hymns and of the gospel as a whole. Zechariah has prophesied that John would direct the feet of the Israelites on the path of peace (1:79). Simeon will ask to be dismissed in peace (2:29). The song of the angels is echoed by the crowds as they shout "peace in heaven" in 19:38. Jesus greets his disciples with peace in his final appearance to them (24:36). The divine visitation results in the peace promised in the prophetic writings of Israel.[36]

Aside from the content of the angelic song, its very presence in the narrative creates a certain ethos. Johnson observes, "The opening of the heavens and the disclosure of angelic worship (2:13) establish for the reader both that this is a narrative with transcendental dimensions (events in heaven and on earth impinge each on the other), and that traffic can move both ways between these realms."[37] In this way the hymn and its context draw attention to heavenly and earthly space, showing that in the birth of Christ both spaces are connected. Though not a major emphasis of Luke, the worship of God in heavenly space is a central focus of Revelation as we will see below.

---

[33] The translation and arrangement of this brief angelic hymn is widely debated. I read it as a bicolon following Brown, *Birth of the Messiah*, 404–405.

[34] Ibid., 426.

[35] Ibid., 427.

[36] E.g., Isa 9:6–7; 52:7; 57:19.

[37] Johnson, *The Gospel of Luke*, 52.

4. The Nunc Dimittis (Luke 2:29–32)

The Nunc Dimittis quite clearly shares much in terms of outlook and style
with the preceding songs. Thematically it shows two close connections
with earlier songs: a focus on Israel as the people of God (cf. 1:54, 68;
2:32); and a focus on salvation and/or God as a savior (cf. 1:47, 68;
2:30).[38] Like the other songs it also shows a style which echoes many passages of the Jewish Scriptures.

And he blessed God and said:
Now dismiss your servant, Master,
According to your word, in peace.
For my eyes have seen your salvation,
Which you prepared before all the peoples,
A light for revelation to the Gentiles
And glory for your people Israel. (vv. 28b–32)

Though the similarities are important, differences in the song of Simeon
are also noticeable and are significant to the development of the narrative.
First, his is directed directly to God in the second-person, in contrast to the
third-person style of the Magnificat and the Benedictus. Coleridge notes
that this is the first instance of praise spoken directly to God rather than
about God in the birth narrative.[39] Second, Simeon was not a family member nor are we told that he was a recipient of an angelic visitation, both of
which were true about Mary and Zechariah. Yet, Simeon did have a word
from the Lord by means of the Holy Spirit, so he, like the others, was
awaiting the fulfillment of God's word to him. Third, his song introduces
yet another theme that was not yet explicit in the others: the inclusion of
the Gentiles in the mercy and favor of God. Like the theme of fulfillment,
the inclusion of the Gentiles in the salvation plan of God is another theme
which is echoed in the final verses of Luke's Gospel (24:47). It is also
echoed throughout the entire two-volume work and is prominent in the
concluding verses of Acts (cf. Acts 28:28).

    Allusions to Isa 40–52 are a major feature of this short song and suggest
that the function of the song in Luke's narrative has to do with witnessing
to the fulfillment of those Isaianic prophesies. Direct allusions can be seen
in the following concepts: eyes seeing the salvation of God (Luke 2:30; Isa
40:5; 52:10); light of revelation to the Gentiles (Luke 2:32; Isa 42:6; 49:6);
the concept of preparation (Luke 2:31; Isa 40:3); and glory for Israel (Luke
2:32; Isa 45:26 LXX). Even the narrative introduction that sets the stage
for song suggests connections with Isa 40–52. In Luke 2:25 we are told
that Simeon was waiting for the consolation of Israel, a clear allusion to

---

[38] Wolter, *Das Lukasevangelium*, 138.
[39] Coleridge, *Birth of the Lukan Narrative*, 167.

Isa 40:1 and 49:13. Though it is of course possible that these themes came to Luke through other sources (they are prominent themes in other early Jewish writings), the number and quality of connections with the Isaianic passages suggest that the author of the Nunc Dimittis was very intentionally drawing on those specific traditions.[40]

Berger has identified five elements which show the particular significance of Isa 40–52 for the song of Simeon. First, the language of Isa 40–52 is filled with an abundance of rhetorical expressions and metaphors, making it quite suitable for reception and imitation in a hymn. Second, the universal eschatology of these chapters is significant for Luke as is seen in the allusions noted above. Third, God is represented among humans in these chapters by his servant/prophet. Fourth, the chapters in Isaiah represent the radical newness of what God will do in the day of salvation (cf. 42:9; 43:19). Finally, these chapters of Isaiah contain particularly comprehensive salvation concepts which are able to describe salvation within the new covenant.[41] As Wolter explains, the salvation prophecies of deutero-Isaiah provide Luke with a profile of an Israel-centric universalism, in which God's salvation acts for Israel gain universal dimensions.[42]

Taken on its own, the song of Simeon echoes Isaiah and indicates that those prophecies are coming to pass in the person of Jesus who is explicitly identified as "your salvation" (2:30). It makes direct and explicit claims and thereby teaches about God's plans to be accomplished through Jesus. Taken together with the other hymns, it can be seen to be the final expression of the gradual unfolding of the significance of the birth narratives. The climactic final song echoes the themes of salvation and fulfillment, and shows that the salvation which will be wrought through Jesus extends beyond Israel to all nations.[43] As Berger observed, both earlier hymns clearly represent Jesus as the Messiah of Israel; the special goal of these passages however lies in their giving a foundational orientation regarding the role of Jesus for Israel and for the Gentiles.[44]

As was the case with the Magnificat, Benedictus, and the Gloria in excelsis, the Nunc Dimittis provides interpretation to the narrative in scripturesque language, on the lips of a credible, devout Israelite. De Long notes, "The characters who voice this praise are broadly representative of Israel. Male and female, young and old, they are humble, pious, and right-

---

[40] For a discussion of the connections with the Isaiah passages and other early Jewish literature see Brown, *Birth of the Messiah*, 458–459.

[41] Klaus Berger, "Das Canticum Simeonis (Lk 2:29–32)," *NovT* 27 (1985): 27–39, here 35–36.

[42] Wolter, *Das Lukasevangelium*, 140.

[43] Coleridge, *Birth of the Lukan Narrative*, 168–169.

[44] Berger, "Das Canticum Simeonis," 39.

eous Jews, upright but low in station: they are exactly the sort of people expected to greet the divine visitation with their praise."[45] The Nunc Dimittis fulfills these same eschatological expectations even as it interprets the events of the birth narratives.

5. Imperial Overtones in the Lukan Hymns

Having considered the major themes and vocabulary of Roman imperial ideology in an earlier chapter, it is easy to see that Luke's Gospel, and the infancy narratives in particular, are set in an imperial context. The events of Luke-Acts are carefully situated within the Roman imperial context both in terms of time and space. Time is marked according to the dates of various Roman rulers and administrators (e.g., 1:5; 2:1–2; 3:1; etc.). Space is marked by an expansion from the land of Israel (in Luke) to the city of Rome (in Acts). Issues of the scope and authority of imperial rule are also addressed directly (e.g., Luke 20:20–26). While the Roman Empire is a significant factor in Luke-Acts, just exactly how the Roman Empire is significant for Luke is open to debate.[46]

In the hymns, terminology and ideas related to Roman imperial ideology are readily recognizable. Kim traces some of these motifs and ideas through Luke-Acts showing that Luke is indeed concerned to present Jesus in implicit contrast to Caesar.[47] One primary piece of evidence is an *inclusio* between the beginning of Luke and the end of Acts. Kim summarizes,

By constructing a sort of inclusio between Luke 2:1–14 and Acts 28:30–31, Luke deliberately contrasts Jesus the Messianic king/lord to Caesar Augustus, and implicitly claims that Jesus is the true *kyrios* and *sotēr*, the true bearer of the kingship of God, and that he will bring the true *pax* on earth, replacing the false *pax* brought about by the military conquests of Caesar, a false *kyrios* and *sotēr*.[48]

---

[45] De Long, *Surprised by God*, 178.

[46] For a discussion of the variety of views see, among others, Christopher Bryan, *Render to Caesar: Jesus, the Early Church, and the Roman Superpower* (New York: Oxford University Press, 2005), 95–105; Virginia Burrus, "The Gospel of Luke and the Acts of the Apostles," in *A Postcolonial Commentary on the New Testament Writings* (ed. Fernando F. Segovia and R. S. Sugirtharajah; London: T & T Clark, 2007), 133–155; Brigitte Kahl, "Acts of the Apostles: Pro(to)-Imperial Script and Hidden Transcript," in *In the Shadow of Empire: Reclaiming the Bible as a History of Faithful Resistance* (ed. Richard A. Horsley; Louisville, Ky.: Westminster John Knox, 2008), 137–156; Seyoon Kim, *Christ and Caesar: The Gospel and the Roman Empire in the Writings of Paul and Luke* (Grand Rapids: Eerdmans, 2008), 75–190.

[47] Kim, *Christ and Caesar*, 77–93.

[48] Ibid., 80–81.

This is an important observation, one that indicates the importance of the imperial context for understanding Luke's message and his use of hymnody.

Within the hymns themselves, we can note several themes which may reflect on the reality of the omnipresent Roman Empire for Luke and his readers. First, the theme of reversal in the Magnificat brings into view the idea that God "has brought down the powerful from their thrones" (Luke 1:52). Second, the Benedictus speaks of a mighty savior being raised up in the house of David (1:69) and emphasizes being saved from their enemies (1:71, 74). Third, the song of Simeon places an emphasis on the universal reach of God's salvation (2:31–32). While none of these themes must necessarily be read as anti-Roman, each one can be seen to have the potential to place itself in contrast to Roman claims and values. However, when the vast web of scriptural echoes noted in earlier sections are considered, it becomes clear that the point of the hymns is not military conquest, revolution, or even resistance. The language of reversal, of a Davidic savior, and of the universal reach of God's salvation serve primarily to place the birth and life of Jesus in the larger context of God's redemptive work for humanity. The Roman Empire, while it is the temporal and physical context for the events narrated in Luke's Gospel, is not the ultimate context. The hymns of the infancy narrative let the reader know that this is ultimately God's story, and that it is an ancient one at that.[49]

Nevertheless, a number of scholars take the language of implicit contrast and read it in such a way that Jesus' mission is understood as direct opposition to Roman rule. For example, Richard Horsley writes,

That Jesus' mission stood in direct opposition to Roman imperial domination is dramatically displayed in his death by crucifixion and the circumstances of his birth, Augustus's decree, and Herod's massacre. . . Indeed, his whole mission, which focused on renewal of Israel, was also opposition to Roman rule and its effects.[50]

For Horsley the birth narratives themselves are a primary place where the early followers of Jesus show that they understood him to be challenging the Roman imperial order.[51] Not all scholars have accepted Horsley's view, however, suggesting that the totality of the evidence presents a more complex picture.[52]

---

[49] Bryan, *Render to Caesar*, makes a similar point on pp. 97–98.

[50] Richard A. Horsley, "Jesus and Empire," in *In the Shadow of Empire: Reclaiming the Bible as a History of Faithful Resistance* (ed. Richard A. Horsley; Louisville, Ky.: Westminster John Knox, 2008), 75–96, here 95.

[51] Ibid., 84–85.

[52] Burrus rightly notes the complexity of the "haunting ambiguity of Luke's political stance" (Burrus, "Gospel of Luke," 133).

In spite of the implicit contrast that develops in Luke-Acts between Christ and Caesar, Luke's broader point appears to be that the claims of Christ and his message are emphatically not in direct conflict with Rome, so that the Christian message should not be considered treason.[53] Certainly in Acts, it is clear that Luke aims to present a "public transcript" that would be "safe" in the context of Roman security concerns.[54] Paul, for example, is identified as a Roman citizen and himself comes under the protection of Rome (Acts 22:23–29; Acts 24:12–35).[55] Further, Gentiles are portrayed quite favorably, at times, in Luke's Gospel.[56] In light of these and other factors it seems that Luke aims to show that Jesus does not advocate a nationalistic agenda but a universal one that includes Jews and Gentiles – all nations. Based on this kind of evidence Kim argues that Luke

does not actually present Jesus' redemptive work in terms of altering the political, economic, and social structures of the day to bring Israel political freedom, economic prosperity, and social justice. Rather, he presents it in terms of healing and exorcism, bringing relief for the poor and oppressed; forgiveness, restoration, and transformation of sinners; formation of a new community of the righteous.[57]

Without much difficulty the contents of the hymns of the infancy narratives can be read in support of this position.[58]

This interpretation is further supported by looking at a more striking example of conflict with the imperial ideology in the hymns of Revelation. The author of Revelation clearly urges Christians to withdraw from the Roman Empire and to resist its ideology. Such an attitude or approach is not to be seen in Luke. As Kim observes, it is Luke's "dialectical attitude" which "recognizes the fundamentally diabolic nature of the empire and yet, for the sake of Christian mission, is willing to cooperate with it and use its facilities."[59] For now it is sufficient to note that an anti-imperial message, though implicit to some degree in the proclamation of Christ as the unique savior of all nations, is not at the center of Luke's teaching. His larger con-

---

[53] Kim, *Christ and Caesar*, 113.

[54] Kahl, "Acts of the Apostles," 148–49.

[55] Bryan, *Render to Caesar*, 103.

[56] Ibid., 101–102. Cf. Luke 7:1–10; 23:47; and Acts 10:1–48; 13:4–12.

[57] Kim, *Christ and Caesar*, 114.

[58] Taking a different approach, Kahl has argued that the anti-imperial message of Jesus can still be heard in Luke, despite the attempt by Luke to present the early Christian message in a way that would be acceptable in light of Roman concerns with security (Kahl, "Acts of the Apostles," 149). While Kahl raises an intriguing point, the question of the degree of correspondence between the message of Luke and the teaching of Jesus is one that falls outside the scope of this chapter.

[59] Kim, *Christ and Caesar*, 190. For further comparison between the attitudes toward empire in Luke and Revelation see Kim's discussion on pp. 180–190.

cerns result in a somewhat ambivalent stance regarding the conduct of Christians relative to the empire.

6. Conclusions about the Hymns of the Infancy Narrative

The hymns of the Lukan infancy narrative strike key notes that are important to Luke and his larger purposes. Accordingly they, together with the infancy narratives, provide the reader with a reflective perspective from which to view the events of the Gospel as a whole. Taken on their own the hymns teach nothing that is outside the realm of early Jewish thought. God has favor and mercy on his people. God remembers his promises and his covenant. God brings salvation to his people. God's salvation will extend to all the nations of the earth. Yet in the context of the story about Jesus they take on very strong Christian overtones as they affirm that in the birth and ministries of John and Jesus God is acting decisively and salvifically toward his people and towards all nations.

Further, these hymns, more than other didactic hymns that we have looked at, model a joyous response to the fulfillment of God's promises. This joyous response itself indicates that the time of eschatological visitation is happening, as the prophets taught that joyous praise would be part of the time of the Lord's salvation. The narrative setting in which these songs are found enables this issue to come to the forefront.

In addition to what they teach in this narrative context, the Lukan hymns also suggest that in order to fully understand the life and ministry of Jesus, one must see them within the context of the work of God throughout the history of Israel. Apart from such a perspective, the message about Jesus is incomplete. Thus we can conclude this section with the final words of Jesus in Luke's Gospel:

These are my words which I spoke to you while I was still with you, that it was necessary that all the things written about me in the law of Moses and the prophets and psalms would be fulfilled. (24:44)

Thus it is written that the Christ would suffer and rise from the dead on the third day, and repentance for the forgiveness of sins would be preached in his name to all nations. (24:46, 47)

Here the themes of the hymns are reiterated and spelled out: fulfillment of the scriptural promises about the Messiah, and the fundamental nature of the work of the Messiah accomplishing a redemptive and restorative work for a universal audience. As hymns expressing these themes, the hymns of the infancy narrative make a unique contribution to Luke's Gospel, enriching it and deepening its perspective on the significance of the life of Christ through the medium of song. In them the reader is enabled and invited to

remember Jesus as part of the larger story of God's work in Israel throughout history.

C. The Johannine Prologue and Didactic Hymnody

It is well known that many scholars regard the opening 18 verses of John's
Gospel as something of an early Christian hymn that has been adapted to
serve as a prologue to the Gospel as a whole.[60] While critiques of this view
are raised from time to time, scholars continue to discuss the prologue as a
hymn.[61] It is also widely agreed that the hymn falls in the line of tradition
of Jewish psalmody and reflects the thought-world of Second Temple Judaism and the Wisdom tradition in particular.[62] A number of scholars see
the prologue providing a review of the work of the Logos in history from
pre-creation all the way through to the Johannine community's experience
of the resurrected Christ.[63] In this section I will explore the Johannine prologue in light of the didactic hymn traditions we have been examining
throughout this volume. After providing a strophic arrangement of the passage, I will examine the major teachings of the hymn and consider how it
functioned within the larger literary context of the Gospel as a whole. We
will see that, when read as a hymn in the tradition of Jewish didactic hymnody, it is possible to see the thematic emphasis and instructional strategy
that the author has used to address significant ongoing issues within his
community.

Many proposals have been made regarding the form of the underlying
hymn on which the prologue of the Fourth Gospel is based. No consensus

---

[60] For a classic statement of the view see Raymond Edward Brown, *The Gospel According to John* (2 vols.; 2nd ed.; AB 29, 29A; Garden City, N.Y.: Doubleday, 1986). Of
the many scholarly treatments of the prologue, among the more recent see Gordley, "The
Johannine Prologue"; Elizabeth Harris, *Prologue and Gospel: The Theology of the
Fourth Evangelist* (New York: T & T Clark, 2004); Martin Hengel, "The Prologue of the
Gospel of John as the Gateway to Christological Truth" in *The Gospel of John and Christian Theology* (ed. Richard Bauckham and Carl Mosser; Grand Rapids: Eerdmans, 2008),
265–293; Peter M. Phillips, *The Prologue of the Fourth Gospel: A Sequential Reading*
(LNTS 294; London: T&T Clark, 2006); Hartwig Thyen, *Das Johannesevangelium* (HNT
6; Tübingen: Mohr Siebeck, 2005), 63–109.

[61] For a recent statement of the view that the prologue is *not* a hymn, see Boyarin,
"The Gospel of the *Memra*."

[62] Thomas Tobin, "The Prologue of John and Hellenistic Jewish Speculation," *CBQ*
52 (1990): 252–269.

[63] Hartmut Gese, *Essays on Biblical Theology* (Minneapolis: Augsburg, 1981). This
dynamic is recognized by those who see the passage as a hymn and by those who see the
passage as something else. Boyarin, "The Gospel of the *Memra*," 271; Hengel, "The Prologue of the Gospel of John," 268.

has emerged, however, with the result that, though the hymnic nature of the passage is generally agreed on, its original form and the existence of possible editorial additions by the final editor continue to be widely debated.[64] Below I provide an arrangement of the hymn in the tradition of Jewish didactic hymns that review the history of God's creative and redemptive work in the world. The following outline presents a hymnic review of history in seven strophes:

1. The Logos before creation (1:1–2);
2. The Logos involved in creation (1:3–4);
3. The Logos in the world (1:5, 9); [John the Baptist Interlude 1 (vv. 6–8)]
4. The rejection of the Logos in Israel's history (1:10–11);
5. The reception of the Logos in Israel's history (1:12–13);
6. The Logos made flesh and seen by the community (1:14); [John the Baptist Interlude 2 (v. 15)]
7. The community's reception of grace and truth through Jesus Christ (1:16–17).

Though space does not permit me to provide a thorough defense for this arrangement, I will briefly sketch the rationale in broad strokes.[65] First, on any reading it is evident that the prologue begins with the Logos before creation (the timeless past), and ends with the present community's experience of the Logos incarnate in Jesus Christ (the present). Thus it is clear that the prologue is, at the very least, chronologically framed. This observation suggests the possibility of a chronological reading of the entire passage.

Second, scholars have noted that the John the Baptist material in vv. 6–8 and v. 15 is something of an interruption to the flow and focus of the prologue. If we bracket these out as later additions to an earlier hymn, then the remaining composition is a more unified whole.[66]

---

[64] For an extensive (though now dated) review of a variety of scholarly proposals on the hymn see Michael Theobald, *Die Fleischwerdung des Logos: Studien zum Verhältnis des Johannesprologs zum Corpus des Evangeliums und zu 1 Joh* (NTAbh 20; Münster: Aschendorff, 1988), 3–161.

[65] For an extended defense of this arrangement see Gordley, "The Johannine Prologue," 786–802.

[66] Following the approach of Rudolf Schnackenburg, this arrangement excludes the John the Baptist portions (vv. 6–8 and v. 15) from the hypothetical original hymn. Cf. Rudolf Schnackenburg, *The Gospel According to St. John: Volume 1* (trans. Kevin Smyth; HTKNT; New York: Herder & Herder, 1968), 223. This view continues to find widespread support. For example, Martin Hengel recently noted, "I am convinced that this hymn corresponds to the text of the Prologue and that only the two passages about John the Baptist in vv. 6–8 and 15 – written in the same style as the hymn – have been inserted to clamp it to the Gospel." Hengel, "The Prologue of the Gospel of John," 268. Likewise, v. 18 can be considered as an editorial edition that summarized the hymn and served as a transition to the Gospel itself, as seen in Ernst Haenchen, *John: A Commen-*

Third, by investigating what is left both in terms of style, content, and thematic development we can see that each strophe or unit reflects a different period of history, and a different aspect of the Logos in history. In this view v. 14 is rightly seen as the first mention of the incarnation of the Logos. Prior to v. 14 the hymn treats events in the history of Israel and the history of the world more generally.

Finally, one stylistic feature which supports the validity of this arrangement is the way that the last line of each strophe leads naturally into the first line of the following strophe. In each case the last and first lines are connected by means of shared concepts (note the allusion to Gen 1:1 at the end of strophe 1 and beginning of strophe 2; reference to birth at the end of strophe 5 and strophe 6) or shared vocabulary (especially vocabulary relating to light, the world, receiving, and fullness). This dynamic can be clearly observed in the English translation of the hymn below:

First Strophe (vv. 1–2): The Logos before Creation
In the beginning was the Logos,
and the Logos was with God,
and the Logos was God.
He was in the beginning with God.

Second Strophe (vv. 3–4): The Logos Involved in Creation
All things came into being through him,
and without him nothing came into being.
What came to be in him was life,
and the life was the light of men;

Third Strophe (vv. 5, 9): The Logos in the World
The light shines in the darkness,
and the darkness has not overcome it.
The true light,
which enlightens every person,
was coming into the world.

Fourth Strophe (vv. 10–11): The Rejection of the Logos in Israel's History
He was in the world,
and the world came into being through him,
but the world did not know him.
He came to his own,
but his own did not receive him.

Fifth Strophe (vv. 12–13): The Reception of the Logos in Israel's History
But to as many as received him,
he gave them authority
to become children of God.
To those who believed in his name.

---

tary on the Gospel of John (trans. Robert W. Funk; Hermeneia; Philadelphia: Fortress Press, 1984), 121.

Those not of blood
neither of the will of flesh
nor of the will of man
but born of God.

Sixth Strophe (v. 14): The Logos Made Flesh and Seen by the Community
And the Logos became flesh
and tented among us,
and we have beheld his glory,
glory as an only begotten from the father,
full of grace and truth.

Seventh Strophe (vv. 16–17): The Community's Reception of Grace through Jesus Christ
For out of his fullness
we all received,
even grace upon grace.
For the law was given through Moses,
grace and truth
came through Jesus Christ.

This arrangement brings into view the way the author taps into multiple temporal registers to create a comprehensive vision of reality. The first two strophes address the mythic past of pre-creation and creation. Strophes 3–5 address the distant past (with ongoing implications as the light continues to shine), describing the past work of the Logos in the world, in general, and among the Israelites in particular ("he came to his own"). Finally strophes 6 and 7 address events of the recent past in the incarnation of the Logos and his ongoing benefactions of grace and truth to the author and his community.

1. Claims of the Hymn

In this chronological reading, the hymn may be seen to participate in conventions of earlier Jewish psalms that reviewed history in light of a particular theological agenda.[67] At this point then, the kinds of questions we might consider are questions like: What explicit claims is the text making with these historical events? What implicit theological frame of reference is the hymn working from? What competing ideas does the hymn challenge? How does this way of remembering the events of Jewish history play a role in promoting the specific vision of the author?

The primary claims of the hymn relate to the nature and work of the Logos who is ultimately identified with the figure of Jesus Christ in the

---

[67] For example, consider Pss 105 and 106, Wis 10 or Sir 45–50. We also observed this dynamic in the *Pss. Sol.* and *Hel. Syn. Pr.* Though none of these are models for the Johannine prologue, per se, all of these texts review periods and events in the history of the Jewish people for the purpose of making theological claims about the present.

final line of the hymn. The Logos is celebrated for his role as God's agent
in creation in the mythic past. The Logos is also acclaimed for his more
recent role in the redemption of humanity. In this process of redemption,
the Logos comes into the world (in the historical past of Israel), takes on
flesh (in the incarnation), reveals the glory of the father, reveals grace and
truth, and grants the authority to become children of God. These claims
about the Logos are made within the framework of central tenets of early
Judaism as seen in the Hebrew Bible and other Jewish literature of the Second Temple period. Specifically, the creative, redemptive, and revelatory
work of the Logos is spelled out in the context of clear allusions to creation traditions, wisdom traditions, and Moses and Sinai traditions. The
striking result is a series of incredible claims about Jesus Christ and the
way his early followers understood the significance of his person, life, and
work.

The first claim one encounters in the hymn is an assertion that calls to
mind the creation traditions of the Torah and their reverberations in the
Psalms and Wisdom writings. The expression ἐν ἀρχῇ (v. 1) in this context
must surely be understood as a not so subtle reference to Gen 1:1 LXX.[68]
Not only is the author wanting to bring to mind the biblical creation accounts, he is apparently beginning a poem that could be seen to bring with
it all the weight and impact of the Torah itself. This may be seen, from one
point of view, as more than a little audacious. But this emotional element
should not be placed in the foreground initially. At the point of v. 1 we
must simply keep in mind that what follows may in some way be a retelling or re-writing of the Torah – or at least an updated presentation of it
for the author's community. The terminology, expression, and content in
this opening strophe bring the reader to the beginning of human history to
observe the divine Logos.

As the first claim of the prologue unfolds the reader is introduced more
fully to the Logos and his work in history. The strophes reveal that: the
Logos has a mediating function in the process of creation (v. 3); the Logos
has a life-giving and light-giving function in creation (vv. 4–5); the Logos,
whose work is in time past, has an illuminating and enlightening function
(v. 9); the Logos is rejected by some and received by others in the course
of history (vv. 11–12); the Logos in history makes people into children of
God (vv. 12–13); the Logos in flesh reveals glory and is the mediator of
grace and truth (vv. 14, 17); Jesus Christ is the Logos in flesh (v. 17).

Much has been written about the Logos in John and in Philo, and new
evaluations of the connections between the two authors continue to
emerge. Philonic scholars are able to point to shades of similarity and dif-

---

[68] Thyen, *Das Johannesevangelium*, 63–64.

ference between the prologue and the writings of Philo.[69] On the other hand, scholars like Daniel Boyarin point to other origins for the background of the Logos terminology in the prologue. Though he does not read the prologue as a hymn, Boyarin makes a compelling case for understanding the Logos in the Jewish tradition of the *memra*, a tradition which is well represented in the Targumim in this time period.[70] In a related but distinct approach, Peder Borgen finds its origin in the Targumic equating of word and light.[71] It is difficult to deny the possibility of any one of these explanations. The term Logos was in wide use in the first century in a number of different contexts and with a number of different implications.[72] It is thus a multi-faceted term that is well-suited for its context and its purpose in the Prologue. The wisdom connections are impressive and convincing, and when one considers the equation of wisdom with Torah in Second Temple Judaism, one is clearly moving in the right direction as indicated by the prologue itself with its concentration of wisdom terminology and Sinai allusions.[73]

Aside from the startling claim that a person is the embodiment of the Logos, what is most interesting is the combination of major themes of early Judaism that coalesce in the hymn. As noted above one can observe creation traditions, wisdom traditions, and Sinai traditions not in the background but in the foreground. In what stream of tradition do the contents of the hymn then belong?

It is useful here to consider the notion of various traditions of discourse associated with key Jewish figures. Hindy Najman discusses the concept of

---

[69] Cf. Tobin, "The Prologue of John and Hellenistic Jewish Speculation," 252–269. More recently see the essays by Leonhardt-Balzer and Folker Siegert: Jutta Leonhardt-Balzer, "Der Logos und die Schöpfung: Streiflichter bei Philo (Op 20–25) und im Johannesprolog (Joh 1,1–18)" in *Kontexte des Johannesevangeliums: das vierte Evangelium in religions- und traditionsgeschichtlicher Perspektive* (ed. Jörg Frey and Udo Schnelle; Tübingen: Mohr Siebeck, 2004), 295–319; Folker Siegert, "Der Logos, 'älterer Sohn' des Schöpfers und 'zweiter Gott.' Philons Logos und der Johannesprolog," in *Kontexte des Johannesevangeliums: das vierte Evangelium in religions- und traditionsgeschichtlicher Perspektive* (ed. Jörg Frey and Udo Schnelle; Tübingen: Mohr Siebeck, 2004), 277–293.

[70] Boyarin, "The Gospel of the *Memra*."

[71] Peder Borgen, "The Prologue of John – As Exposition of the Old Testament," in *Philo, John, and Paul: New Perspectives on Judaism and Early Christianity* (ed. Peder Borgen; Atlanta: Scholars Press, 1987), 75–102.

[72] For an exhaustive review of contemporary uses of the term, see Phillips, *Prologue of the Fourth Gospel*, 77–141. He concludes, "The point is not that λόγος picks up one tradition, but that it points to an ambiguous amalgam of different traditions. . . The role of the lexeme here is to allow different readers the opportunity of finding a point of access into this text, to cross the threshold on what seems to be familiar terms" (138–139).

[73] See also Martin Scott, *Sophia and the Johannine Jesus* (Sheffield: JSOT Press, 1992).

an ongoing tradition of "Mosaic discourse" that developed in the Second
Temple period and served as a way of presenting updated interpretations of
authoritative texts for use by the present community. In her view Mosaic
discourse is marked by a number of specific indicators including how the
new text: 1) claims the same authority as older texts in the tradition by re-
interpreting them in an authoritative way, 2) indicates its status as an authentic expression of Torah, 3) emphasizes a connection with the revelation event on Sinai, and 4) claims close association with or even authorship
by the founding figure, Moses.[74] Further, Najman suggests that there are
modes of discourse tied to other foundational figures as well.[75]

Though Najman does not discuss the Fourth Gospel in her work, one
might ask to what extent it can be argued that the prologue participates in
Mosaic discourse or some other kind of discourse associated with a significant, authoritative figure. Given her four criteria, it can be argued that the
prologue satisfies three of them with regard to Moses. First, even the brief
analysis offered here suggests that the prologue reworks and expands older
traditions through interpretation, thereby claiming for itself the authority
that attaches with those traditions (criteria one). Second, by opening with
the phrase ἐν ἀρχῇ and focusing on the creative work of God through a
word, the prologue implicitly ascribes to itself something of the status of
Torah, as noted above (criteria two). Third, as with other participants in
Mosaic discourse, the prologue re-presents the revelatory experience of
Sinai (criteria three). This can be seen especially in the language of John
1:14–18 with its numerous allusions to the Sinai event.[76] The one factor
relating to Najman's concept of Mosaic discourse that is not present in the
prologue is the claim of Mosaic authorship. Yet such an observation does
not disqualify the prologue from participating in the discourse of Moses.
Najman cites the writings of Philo as participating in this tradition of discourse, but in a different way than those texts which claim Mosaic authorship (e.g., Deuteronomy, *Jubilees*, and 11QTemple).[77] Certainly the references to creation along with the Sinai elements weigh heavily in favor of
the idea that some degree of Mosaic discourse is in view.

Can we also identify connections with other traditions of discourse? Interestingly, while there are wisdom elements in the prologue, these do not
necessarily suggest the idea of a tradition of Solomonic discourse. Rather
they lend further support to the contention that this is a form of Mosaic

---

[74] Hindy Najman, *Seconding Sinai: The Development of Mosaic Discourse in Second Temple Judaism* (JSJSup 77; Leiden; Boston: Brill, 2003), 13–19.

[75] Ibid.

[76] Craig A. Evans, *Word and Glory: On the Exegetical and Theological Background of John's Prologue* (JSNTSup 89; Sheffield: JSOT, 1993), 79–83.

[77] Najman, *Seconding Sinai*, 18.

discourse. However, it is Mosaic discourse viewed through the lens of Jewish wisdom traditions. Wisdom had long been identified with Torah (cf. Sir 24:23), making it possible that the prologue is seeking to make a stronger link between wisdom and the Logos.[78] Glasson claims, "We thus have in the Prologue a transference to Christ of what had been ascribed to the Torah. This is indeed one of the ruling motifs of the Gospel as a whole."[79] In light of Najman's conception of Mosaic discourse, we may expand Glasson's observation to claim that in the prologue there is an attempt to utilize a kind of Mosaic discourse to support a particular view of Jesus as the ultimate and ideal mediator of God's grace to humanity.

One aspect of this Mosaic discourse is thus seen in a major theme of the prologue of John's Gospel, and the Gospel itself: that Jesus is the ideal broker, go between, or mediator, between God and humanity.[80] Though it was common in Second Temple Jewish sources to regard Moses as the ideal mediator, the prologue shifts this role to Christ.[81] The prologue advances this view by demonstrating that Jesus Christ is the one being who has moved in both worlds. Specifically, it can be argued that in John's prologue, the unique agent of God in creation (1:3, 10) is also the unique agent of God in God's work of redemption (1:12, 17). This central idea is shared with other Christological hymns of the New Testament, where the agent of creation is also the agent of redemption (cf. Col 1:15–20). What is perhaps most significant is that the salvific effect of the work of God's agent is integrally connected with the agent's identity as God's agent in creation.

Ultimately, through explicit and implicit claims the prologue places the story of Jesus Christ within the context of God's creative and redemptive work throughout history. It invites the reader to draw the conclusion that the coming of Christ and the establishment of communities of his followers is not simply a recent historical phenomenon. Rather it is rooted in the life-creating and light-giving nature of God himself, which has been experienced by humanity in a number of ways throughout history. This conclusion in itself, while a high claim for an individual human, is not outside the realm of possibility in Second Temple Judaism. However, there is a further inescapable conclusion that is brought into focus in the final line of the hymn – a conclusion that might rightly be called scandalous. The scandal

---

[78] T. F. Glasson, *Moses in the Fourth Gospel* (Naperville, Ill.: A. R. Allenson, 1963), 87.

[79] Ibid., 88.

[80] Jerome Neyrey, "'I Am the Door' (John 10:7, 9): Jesus the Broker in the Fourth Gospel," *CBQ* 69 (2007): 271–291.

[81] Evans, *Word and Glory*, 135–143. For a variety of themes associated with Moses in Second Temple Jewish sources see Wayne A. Meeks, *The Prophet-King: Moses Traditions and the Johannine Christology* (Leiden: Brill, 1967).

of the prologue is not that the life and work of Jesus Christ should be viewed as the latest part of God's creative and redemptive work in the world; the scandal of the prologue is the claim that the work of God in creation and salvation should all be understood in light of Jesus Christ.

The composer of this hymn to Christ the Logos would have the Jewish Christians in Asia Minor see all of their Jewish history and heritage under the oversight of the work of Jesus Christ, the Logos, in history. This claim is quite startling, particularly in light of the social setting of the Johannine community.[82] For a community in the midst of a significant conflict between Jews and Jewish-Christians, John offers this poetic and hymnic vision, perhaps as a means of strengthening the faith of the Christians. He may also have hoped to show both Jewish and gentile-Christians the extent to which the life of Christ must be understood within the larger framework of Jewish history and theology.

2. Conflict about Moses?

This raises the question of the extent to which a tension between followers of Moses and followers of Jesus is attested in the hymn that underlies the prologue. Judging from the Gospel as a whole, there is a great deal of tension between the two communities. But does the hymn behind the prologue attest to such a tension as well?

In order to answer this question two strophes of the original hymn must be considered. In the fourth strophe (vv. 10–11) the Logos is rejected by his own. At first glance this may seem to suggest the rejection of Jesus during his earthly ministry or perhaps his rejection by many Jews in the Johannine community. Yet in the context of the entire hymn, this strophe should not be understood as the rejection of the incarnate Logos; in this chronological reading the Logos incarnate does not enter the scene until the sixth strophe (v. 14). Rather, vv. 10–11 describe the rejection of the Logos earlier in the history of God's people. These verses most likely refer to the rejection of God's wisdom or perhaps of the Torah by God's people

---

[82] On the Johannine community see especially Marinus de Jonge, "The Gospel and the Epistles of John Read against the Background of the History of the Johannine Communities," in *What We Have Heard from the Beginning: The Past, Present, and Future of Johannine Studies* (ed. Tom Thatcher; Waco, Tex.: Baylor University Press, 2007), 127–144; J. Louis Martyn, "The Johannine Community among Jewish and other Early Christian Communities," in *What We Have Heard from the Beginning: The Past, Present, and Future of Johannine Studies* (ed. Tom Thatcher; Waco, Tex.: Baylor University Press, 2007), 183–190. On related issues of the contexts of the Fourth Gospel, see the review of the scholarly research in Jörg Frey, "Auf der Suche nach dem Kontext des vierten Evangeliums: Eine forschungsgeschichtliche Einführung," in *Kontexte des Johannesevangeliums: das vierte Evangelium in religions- und traditionsgeschichtlicher Perspektive* (ed. Jörg Frey and Udo Schnelle; Tübingen: Mohr Siebeck, 2004), 3–45.

in their long history.[83] Regardless of the tensions the Johannine community experienced, this particular passage deals with the rejection of the Logos in the past, not the present.

The seventh strophe (vv. 16–17) may also suggest tension between followers of Moses and followers of Jesus within the present tense of the Johannine community. It makes an explicit comparison between the two central figures, though this comparison need not be read as a negative one.[84] In fact, viewed in light of the entire hymn, it should most certainly be read as a positive comparison. The seventh strophe pictures the giving of the law through Moses as a gracious outpouring from the fullness of the Logos; in a similar way the creation and manifestation of grace and truth through Jesus Christ is also an expression of God's redemptive purposes.

This positive interpretation of the comparison of Jesus and Moses is supported by careful attention to the verb used in v. 17. The precise phrase used in v. 17 (ἡ χάρις καὶ ἡ ἀλήθεια διὰ Ἰησοῦ Χριστοῦ ἐγένετο) connects strongly with the similar expression in v. 3 (πάντα δι' αὐτοῦ ἐγένετο) and also in v. 10. This allusion to v. 3 must be considered in interpreting this final portion of the hymn. The use of the same verb in both places for the act of bringing into existence suggests that grace and truth (v. 17) were part of the "all things" (v. 3) that came into being through him in creation in the past. Grace and truth are not things that have come into being through Jesus Christ only in the incarnation; they came into being through him at the very beginning (v. 3). Accordingly, though the incarnation itself occurs much later than the giving of the Law through Moses, the grace and truth which are experienced through the incarnate Jesus Christ are here shown to be in reality *prior* to that of Moses. There is thus both a degree of continuity and a measure of contrast between Moses and Christ. The giving of the Law through Moses can be viewed as one historical manifestation of the grace and truth which originally came into being through Jesus Christ at creation. The latest historical manifestation of that grace and truth, however, is the incarnation of the Logos himself, in the person of Jesus Christ.

It seems then that reading v. 17 as a simple contrast between the two (Law came through Moses, *but* grace and truth came later through Jesus Christ) is inadequate to capture the dynamics of all that has preceded in the passage.[85] Rather, in v. 17 the reader is hurtled back through history from the incarnation of Christ in the recent past of the community, back to the giving of the Law through Moses, and ultimately back to the time of creation. Jesus Christ, the physical manifestation of the Logos (v. 14), through whom all things were made (v. 10), is the pre-creation source of grace and

---

[83] Evans, *Word and Glory*, 89. cf. Bar 3:12; Ps 105[106]:24–25.

[84] Schnackenburg, *The Gospel According to St. John*, 277.

[85] Haenchen, for example, reads it simply as a contrast. Haenchen, *John*, 120.

truth (vv. 3, 17). Life and light have been available through him throughout history, though many have not accepted him. The Law given through
Moses is seen here as one instance of God's gracious redemptive work in
history. The hymnist's conclusion, however, is that all of the gracious redemptive works of God in history must now be seen in light of the coming
of Jesus Christ.

The prologue invites the reader to the opening of the Torah ("In the beginning") and brings the reader through a tour of the work of the Logos, in
its various manifestations, throughout history. The prologue ends with the
person of Jesus Christ whose revealing and redeeming work is seen
through the lens of the Sinai experience, but whose origins are in the beginning. The original hymn thus runs from pre-creation to the hymn-
writer's present, with the present viewed as, in some respects, a seconding
of Sinai – another manifestation in history of that which Sinai represented,
namely, God's gracious redemptive work on behalf of his people. But instead of the coming of Jesus Christ seconding Sinai, Sinai is itself seen to
be a seconding of creation. What happened at Sinai is also, in this picture,
one of several concrete ways that the Logos has revealed himself to humanity in history. Read in this way no denigration of Moses or the Law
can be found in this review of redemptive history.[86]

Of course, this is not to say that the message of the prologue would not
have been seen as an affront by Jews that did not accept its claims about
Jesus. But for those that did, it would appear that such an articulation of
the relationship between Jesus Christ the Logos and their Jewish history
could affirm both their faith in Christ and their Jewish heritage.

Along these lines it is important to note that the hymn is not entirely focused on the person and work of Christ. The range of human responses to
the Logos is also in view, from ignorance (v. 10) and outright rejection (v.
11) to acceptance and belief (v. 12). This focus on human response to the
Logos is seen most clearly in vv. 12–13 where we learn that those who
welcome the Logos and believe in his name experience a transformation in
which they become children of God. With this kind of language and expression the hymn invites the hearers to become participants in the story
(or remain participants in the story) as they embrace the Logos, becoming
a child of God and experiencing the grace and truth that came through Jesus Christ (v. 17). Regardless of how we interpret the form and structure of
the Johannine hymn it is clear that it has a dual emphasis on christological
understanding and on human response. Who Jesus was and how his incar-

---

[86] On the complexities of the ambiguous place of Moses in the Johannine community
see especially chapter 5, "Jesus, the Jews and Moses," in Raimo Hakola, *Identity Matters: John, the Jews, and Jewishness* (Supplements to Novum Testamentum 118; Leiden:
Brill, 2005), 146–176.

nation is to be understood by the community were primary aspects of the hymn.

3. Function of the Prologue

In a recent study it has been proposed that the Johannine prologue can be best understood within the tradition of *prooimia* in Greek drama.[87] Harris outlines the function and purposes of dramatic prologues and suggests that the author and readers of John's gospel would have been well aware of this Greek literary practice.

While an intriguing hypothesis, Harris' study faces some significant challenges. Most significant is that the language of the prologue connects very strongly with Second Temple Jewish concepts and ideas, and very little with ideas of a purely Greek nature. The term *logos* may be most clearly Greek in its conception, but even this term is developed and used in a very Jewish context. Second, the poetic nature of the prologue is a function of Jewish poetic conventions such as parallelism as opposed to Greek conventions such as meter. Taken together these two observations do not make Harris's suggestion impossible, but they do suggest that as a primary backdrop, Jewish (even Hellenistic-Jewish) literary precedents should be considered. As we have observed, didactic hymnody played a significant role in Jewish narrative and other literary contexts, so it is likely that this is a more significant factor for the Johannine prologue than Greek drama.

Nevertheless, if Harris's study were expanded beyond the realm of Greek drama to include ancient Greek hymnody more broadly, it may be possible to argue for a closer connection with some of these traditions of *prooimia*. Surprisingly, Harris omits any mention of epic poetry such as the Homeric hymns, poems of Hesiod, or other traditions related to ancient hymnic preludes. Including these ancient compositions within her study might lead to a stronger case and also more insight into the function of the prologue.

In light of what we have observed in earlier chapters of this volume, the following six connections between the prologue and Greek didactic hymnody could be plausibly argued. First, as the prologue began "in the beginning," so Greek hymnic preludes reflected a concern with the right place to begin. Here we may consider, for example, the proem to Hesiod's *Theogony* ("Let us begin to sing . . ." line 1). Second, a prominent feature of the most ancient hymnic preludes was the appearance of the god together with a specific instance of non-recognition by humans (e.g., *Homeric Hymn to Demeter*; *Homeric Hymn to Dionysus*). In the Johannine prologue we can observe a related dynamic in vv. 10–11 where the world, though made by

---

[87] Harris, *Prologue and Gospel*, 189–191.

him, did not know him and where his people, though he came to them, did not receive him. Third, and often related, is the idea of the appearance of the god with a scene of revelation of identity and glory (seen also in the *Hymn to Demeter* and the *Hymn to Dionysus*). The Logos is finally fully revealed and seen in glory in v. 14 of the prologue. Fourth, a common feature of Greek hymnic preludes was a narration of the gifts of the god to humanity (e.g., *Hymn to Demeter*; proem to *Works and Days*). The gifts of the Logos are a focal point of the Johannine prologue. These included life, light, grace, and truth, as well as the right to become children of God. Fifth, we can note the function of Greek hymns as a proem/prelude to a larger work. This is most clear in the hymns that open the *Theogony* and the *Works and Days*. But this may also have been the case with the Homeric hymns, which themselves could have served as preludes for recitation of epic poetry. Later Aratus, Lucretius, and other writers in later periods will imitate this way of beginning a larger didactic work. Certainly the Johannine prologue functions in an analogous way as it previews the main themes of the larger work to follow.[88] Finally, as ancient Greek hymnic preludes provided their underlying theology inscribed in narrative form rather than detailed exposition, so does the prologue, particularly when read as a chronological account of the work of the Logos in history from creation to the community's present. In addition to statements about the Logos, it is his work in history that reveals his character and his full identity.

Though John's gospel is thoroughly rooted in Jewish ideas and biblical concepts, the observations noted above show that it can be seen to reflect at least some of the dynamics of ancient hymnic preludes such as the Homeric Hymns and the opening sections of Hesiod's *Theogony* and *Works and Days*. The comparisons I made here are not aimed to imply that the Evangelist modeled his prologue after any of these precedents. Yet the similarities suggest ways that the very presence of a hymnic prologue with these kinds of themes might have been understood by educated readers or listeners in the religious world of antiquity.

4. Conclusions Regarding the Johannine Prologue and Didactic Hymnody

Given the rich influences and ideas present in the prologue it is likely that this carefully crafted statement functions on a number of complementary levels relative to the rest of the gospel. Certainly one important function

---

[88] In a similar vein, Phillips claims that the prologue "resembles a dramatic prologue in introducing the context of the ensuing drama, in giving the audience the rough outline of what is to come, in enabling them to engage with the story which follows" (Phillips, *Prologue of the Fourth Gospel*, 45).

suggested by this analysis is that the prologue initiates the participation in creation discourse, wisdom discourse, and Mosaic discourse. Accordingly it places the story of Jesus Christ within the context of God's creative and redemptive work throughout history. More importantly it implies that all of the creative and redemptive work of God in history should be understood in light of Jesus Christ. Indeed, it is this theological claim promoted in hymnic form that may have contributed to tension between the Johannine community and the faithful Jews who did not accept this message.

In a world filled with hymns and songs, the author of the prologue crafted a poem that presented a vision of reality on a grand, cosmic scale. This vision, like many others, encompassed key events in the course of history from eternity past to the present. This vision of reality is, to a large extent, in line with the Jewish practices of offering sweeping overviews of history for theological purposes. At the same time, its primary teaching focuses on the identity and work of an individual whose exact status is disputed.

For the author of the prologue, hymnody provided a medium through which the Christian teacher could inspire, instruct, and invite the reader into participation with the realities that were central to Christian faith as he understood it. Hymnody also contributed to a social setting in which an understanding of basic Christian claims was disputed. In John's community the identity and work of Jesus Christ were being called into question. John's prologue responded to this question as it set the stage for the details of the life of Christ that would follow in his gospel, and gave the framework in which those details should be read and understood. While the author of the Fourth Gospel utilized narrative to make the case for his view of Christ, he went a step further here and utilized hymnic styles of expression in strategic and creative ways to encapsulate and promote his understanding of the Christian faith for his community.

D. Didactic Hymns in Revelation 4–5

Scholars have long been fascinated with the hymnic aspects of Revelation, and many ways of identifying and classifying the hymnic passages of the Apocalypse have been proposed.[89] These hymns, doxologies, and acclama-

---

[89] Klaus-Peter Jörns identified sixteen passages within the narrative vision descriptions of Revelation that are generally accepted as hymnic (Klaus-Peter Jörns, *Das hymnische Evangelium: Untersuchungen zu Aufbau, Funktion und Herkunft der hymnischen Stücke in der Johannesoffenbarung* [SNT 5; Gütersloh: G. Mohn, 1971], 19). By combining several of these and adding two more passages, Josephine Massyngberde Ford identified ten sections of Revelation that could be considered hymnic. These included: 4:8b–

tions have received attention from scholars in terms of their form, contents, and function within Revelation as a whole, and also with regard to their place in early Christian worship.[90] In this section I examine the hymns in Rev 4–5, an important segment of Revelation that marks the transition from the letters to the seven churches to the unfolding of the coming eschatological events. In the narrative development of the vision of John these hymns are given in the context of heavenly worship. They are offered straightforwardly as the verbal content of the worship of God and the Lamb. But as we have seen elsewhere, hymns in narrative and other literary contexts often play a role in communicating something to the human audience of the larger composition. This is true whether the hymns were composed for their literary context or were already extant and/or used in liturgical settings.[91] Accordingly we can explore these as instances of didactic hymns: praise passages whose primary purpose goes beyond simply praising the divine to include teaching important theological truths to a human audience. In this section we will consider not just what these passages say but also what they do.

We will see that these hymns play a role in constructing the portrait of reality which is a major aim of the Apocalypse as a whole. This portrait is one that is in close dialogue with Jewish visions of God's ultimate purposes for the world. It is also in implicit conversation and even dispute with the Roman imperial vision of reality. As Brian Blount argues, the hymns of Revelation are "a celebration of confrontational resistance."[92] The hymns of Rev 4–5, and of the entire Apocalypse, play an important role in the process of communal formation for an early Christian community in Roman Asia.

11; 5:9–10, 12, 13b; 7:10, 12, 15–17; 11:15, 17, 18; 12:10–12; 14:3–5; 15:3–4; 16:5–7; 18:2–3, 4–8, 10, 14, 16, 19–23; 19:1a–8 (Josephine Massyngbaerde Ford, "The Christological Function of the Hymns in the Apocalypse of John," *AUSS* 56 [1998]: 207–229, here 212).

[90] Deichgräber, *Gotteshymnus und Christushymnus*, 44–59; Lucetta Mowry, "Revelation 4–5 and Early Christian Liturgical Usage," *JBL* 71 (1952): 75–84; John J. O'Rourke, "The Hymns of the Apocalypse," *CBQ* 30 (1968): 399–409. The question of the extent to which the hymns of the Apocalypse reflect an early Christian liturgy are addressed most recently in Russo, "Behind the Heavenly Door."

[91] This is a debated issue. I follow David Aune's view that these passages are likely not taken over from the early church's liturgical practice, though they are certainly reflective of early Christian worship practices (Aune, *Revelation 1–5*, 315–317). Accordingly, the author is not quoting early Christian sources, but rather crafting these expressions of praise according to the custom of early Christians for the purposes of his larger composition.

[92] Brian K. Blount, *Revelation: A Commentary* (Louisville, Ky.: Westminster John Knox, 2009), 98.

1. Social Setting of Revelation

A key factor for interpreting the import and significance of the hymnic materials of Revelation is a proper understanding of the setting of the composition as a whole. The social setting of the book of Revelation has been reconstructed in a number of different ways.[93] Most scholars would agree that, given the limited evidence, a precise dating of the book is not possible. Further, while internal and external evidence points to a date during the reign of Domitian (81–96 CE), some interpreters have noted that some indicators point to an earlier date shortly after the reign of Nero and before the destruction of the temple (66–70 CE). David Aune's proposal takes into account both sets of evidence, suggesting a final version from the reign of Domitian that incorporated earlier oral and written apocalyptic materials going back a generation earlier.[94] Along these lines Friesen sees the final form of the book reflecting a Christian community in Roman Asia at the end of the first century.[95] Rather than reflecting a time of intense persecution under Domitian, Revelation seems to reflect a social setting in which the Christian response to imperial society and its pressures was in dispute. Thompson explains, "The conflict and crisis in the Book of Revelation between Christian commitment and the social order derive from John's perspective on Roman society rather than from significant hostilities in the social environment."[96] In this view, the conflict that plays out in Revelation reflects that author's attempt to dramatize what he sees as the inherent conflict between Christian reality and the social world of Asia.

If we base our understanding of the social setting of Revelation as a whole on internal evidence (e.g., what we see in the letters to the seven churches in Rev 2–3) it is clear that Christians in Asia Minor were not necessarily excluded from Roman society as outsiders. In fact, these letters indicate that Christians could be found in a number of socio-economic levels and with a variety of responses to current issues in their cities. Churches (some poor, some rich; some in conflict, some not) were not dealing with systematic persecution as much as false teaching, contested practices, complacency, compromise and issues of how they relate to the surrounding society.[97] Whether each church was aware of it or not, the letters indicate

---

[93] Akira Satake, *Die Offenbarung des Johannes* (KEK 16; Göttingen: Vandenhoeck & Ruprecht, 2008), 45–58.

[94] Aune, *Revelation 1–5*, lviii. cf. Blount, *Revelation*, 8.

[95] Friesen, *Imperial Cults*, 150. This view corresponds with Aune's proposal that portions of Revelation could have been composed earlier and passed on orally or in written form.

[96] Leonard L. Thompson, *The Book of Revelation: Apocalypse and Empire* (New York: Oxford University Press, 1990), 175.

[97] Blount, *Revelation*, 8–14.

that there was a range of ways that these first-century congregations were dealing with what it means to overcome, that is, endure in faith holding onto the word of God and the testimony of Jesus (1:2, 9). In the eyes of John, some churches, like Pergamum, Thyatira, and Laodicea, had it wrong. The church in Philadelphia was perhaps the paradigm for obedient endurance as they have "kept my word and have not denied my name" (3:9). Though the pattern was uneven at the time of writing, the letters indicate that a time of intense persecution was on the horizon (2:10) and that this was going to be God's judgment on the whole world, including those who hold to false teaching.

Thus a major issue in Revelation is the question of how the church should relate to the world.[98] More specifically, in the context of the Roman Empire, Christians were dealing with the questions of who is worthy of worship, what is the nature of the kingdom of Christ, and how believers should live as Christians in relation to their society.[99] Along these lines Knight explains,

> The author wants his readers to *perceive* a crisis, and thus to take a responsible course of action, when in fact the lives of at least the wealthier members of the churches may have been strikingly free of apprehension. By reworking apocalyptic traditions, John calls his churches to action and threatens the security of their existence. He does this from the conviction that they had become too comfortable in their world and needed decisive action to return to their calling as a priestly people.[100]

The letters create a portrait of a social setting in which the issue of what it means to live as a faithful believer in a larger pagan society is at issue.[101] The vision that follows in the context of these letters paints a portrait of the unseen world and reveals the true nature of the kingdom of God and the kingdom of Satan.

This brief study of the hymns in Revelation will proceed on the view that the book of Revelation portrays a crisis of belief and practice in which Christians in Asia Minor are being called to endure and, to some extent, suffer as they worship God and the Lamb. The extent to which this call to

---

[98] Jonathan Knight, *Revelation* (Sheffield: Sheffield Academic Press, 1999), 24–25.

[99] Friesen, *Imperial Cults*, 209.

[100] Knight, *Revelation*, 27.

[101] Stephen D. Moore, "The Revelation to John," in *A Postcolonial Commentary on the New Testament Writings* (ed. Fernando F. Segovia and R. S. Sugirtharajah; London: T & T Clark, 2007), 436–455, here 449–451. On the issue of the imperial cult as reflected in Revelation and specifically in the letters to the seven churches see Jörg Frey, "The Relevance of the Roman Imperial Cult for the Book of Revelation: Exegetical and Hermeneutical Reflections on the Relation between the Seven Letters and the Visionary Main Part of the Book," in *The New Testament and Early Christian Literature in Greco-Roman Context: Studies in Honor of David E. Aune* (ed. John Fotopoulos; Leiden: Brill, 2006), 231–255.

suffering relates to actual threats of martyrdom or the author's expectation of increasing threats in the near future, or both, will be set aside for the moment.

2. Narrative Setting of the Hymns

The hymns of Rev 4–5 are embedded in an important narrative that reveals first the worship of God on his heavenly throne (chapter 4) and then the praiseworthy identity of the Lamb (chapter 5). Within the larger structure of Revelation, these two chapters set the stage for all of the eschatological drama that will follow (6–22). In their immediate context they provide the occasion for the opening of the seals and the revelation of eschatological judgments that begin in chapter 6.[102]

In terms of physical setting, John portrays a heavenly throne room that in many ways reflects the model of human rulers of the ancient near east.[103] Though the actions that unfold are related to worship, the setting is related to the reign of a king, enabling the narrative to strike both religious and political chords.[104] Further, the setting suggests a scene of judgment. Even though the scroll is not mentioned until 5:1, it does not suddenly enter the picture in chapter 5; it is part of the unified judgment scene which is composed of chapters 4–5 together.[105]

The characters (fantastic creatures, elders, angels, and one seated upon a throne) align largely with other ancient Jewish visions of the heavenly throne, with the exception of the twenty-four elders.[106] As we follow the narrative development of Rev 4–5 we will see that the participants in worship are constantly increasing. The first to offer verbal praise are the four living creatures (4:8). The twenty-four elders then respond in worship (4:9–11). Then both groups together sing a new song (5:8–10). The scope of worship then expands beyond these to include thousands upon thousands of angels (5:11–12). Finally, every creature everywhere sings praise to God and the Lamb (5:13). Thus a major feature of Rev 4–5 is the dynamic expansion of the scope of worship both in terms of who is worshipped and who is doing the worshiping.

---

[102] For a review of scholarship on how these chapters fit into the larger context of Revelation see Russell S. Morton, *One upon the Throne and the Lamb: A Tradition Historical/Theological Analysis of Revelation 4–5* (New York: Peter Lang, 2007), 39–82.

[103] David E. Aune, "The Influence of Roman Imperial Court Ceremonial on the Apocalypse of John," *BR* 28 (1983): 5–26; Aune, *Revelation 1–5*, 313; Mowry, "Revelation 4–5 and Early Christian Liturgical Usage," 77.

[104] Moore, "Revelation," 442–443.

[105] Jörns, *Das hymnische Evangelium*, 31–32.

[106] Aune, *Revelation 1–5*, 313.

If chapter four is descriptive of the scene of heavenly worship, the narrative of chapter five introduces a conflict into that setting: who is worthy to open the scroll (5:2)? The remainder of the chapter provides the heavenly celebration of the one who was able to open the scroll. In Rev 4–5 then, we are introduced to heavenly worship of God which expands from four living creatures around the throne to include every creature everywhere. We are also introduced to worship that expands its focus to include not only God but also the Lamb, and concludes in praise of God and the Lamb together. Further, as we will see in the hymns themselves, temporally the focus of worship extends from the distant past of creation, to the recent past of redemption, to the present and future of the redeemed, to the eternal worship of God and the Lamb. The hymnic praise is one means that John uses to paint a vision of past, present, and future in which the Christians of Asia Minor can locate themselves, form their communal identity, and live accordingly.

3. The Hymns and their Contents

Five discrete hymnic passages can be found within Rev 4–5. These include: 1) the trishagion (Rev 4:8b); 2) a second-person acclamation of God's worthiness (4:11); 3) a second-person acclamation of the Lamb's worthiness (5:9); 4) a third-person acclamation of the Lamb's worthiness (5:12); and 5) a doxology (5:13b). We will discuss their contents briefly before looking at their collective significance.

The hymns in chapter four have their sole focus on the Lord God Almighty (κύριος ὁ θεὸς ὁ παντοκράτωρ). In the first acclamation, the trishagion, it is God's holiness and eternal nature that are singled out by the four living creatures:

Holy, Holy, Holy Lord God Almighty,
the one who was and who is and who is to come. (4:8b)

This verse strikes two notes that were already sounded in the opening verses of Revelation, and that resound throughout the Apocalypse. The notion of God as "Almighty" is introduced in 1:8. God as the one who was and is and is to come is seen in 1:4 and 8. One can see a similar expression in 11:17 which joins "the Almighty" with "who was and who is." The phrase "Lord God Almighty" is seen again in 15:3 with a combination of expressions from the Psalms, Isaiah, and Jeremiah (cf. 16:7; 19:6, 15). The connections of each of these phrases with earlier Jewish literature have been widely discussed.[107] That the first line of this two-line hymn reflects Isa 6:3 and the second line reflects Jewish exegetical traditions relating to Ex-

---

[107] Jörns, *Das hymnische Evangelium*, 24–31. Cf. Aune, *Revelation 1–5*, 302–307.

od 3:14 and Deut 32:39 is generally accepted.[108] For our purposes, it is sufficient to note that the heavenly worship begins in a way that is vitally connected with the language and thought of Second Temple Jewish theology.

In the second song of chapter four it is God's work in the creation of all things that is identified as a reason for praise:

You are worthy, our Lord and our God,
to receive the glory and the honor and the power,
for you created all things,
and according to your will they exist and were created. (4:11)

This brief hymn of praise is addressed directly to God and is sung by the twenty-four elders. As was the case with the previous hymn, this hymnic passage likewise shows strong connections with early Jewish thought, with no distinctly Christian content.[109] Second person acclamations are somewhat rare in the New Testament but occur frequently in the *Didache*.[110] Expressions of praise for God's work in creation are common in hymnic texts, and, though often connected with the mediating work of Christ in New Testament christological hymns (e.g., John 1:3, 10; Col 1:16), that connection does not appear to be in view here.

Jörns has suggested that chapter four is integral in setting up the major theme which is that of God's coming judgment. The trishagion introduces the idea that God is the one who is to come. The thrones suggest apocalyptic scenes of judgment. In this view, the antiphone of 4:9–11 is in reference to the judgment that is about to begin and is still future.[111] The result is that the heavenly liturgy of chapter four can be seen to be constructed to set up the judgment that will be described in the remainder of the book beginning with chapter six. Regardless of one's view of the praise in 4:9–11 as past, present or still to come, it is clear that the entire throne room scene does indeed set the stage for all of the judgment events that follow.[112]

It is important to note that the hymnic portions of chapter four, together with the description of the setting and the posture of those involved in worship, direct the focus of the chapter to God as the center of all things. Not only so, but this passage teaches that worship is the appropriate response in the presence of God. At this point we cannot identify any explicit

---

[108] Jörns, *Das hymnische Evangelium*, 26–27.

[109] Deichgräber, *Gotteshymnus und Christushymnus*, 51.

[110] Cf. *Did.* 8:2; 9:3–4; 10:2, 4, and 5. For a fuller discussion of connections with early Jewish and Christian writings see Jörns, *Das hymnische Evangelium*, 34–37.

[111] Ibid., 30–42.

[112] Aune, *Revelation 1–5*, 313. Aune notes, "The longest throne-room scene in 4:1–5:14 serves not only to introduce the narrative of the seven seals (6:1–8:1) but also to introduce the entire series of visions that constitute the body of Revelation" (313).

critique of Jewish or Roman practices, although we might see an implicit critique of imperial practices through the use of royal court imagery.[113] Nevertheless, through this focus on the centrality of the throne of God, the possibility of any suggestion that any other being or person should be considered the center of the world or should receive worship is eliminated.

As the narrative moves to chapter five the Lamb comes into focus and receives hymnic praise in a scene that has been identified as the investiture of the Lamb.[114] While God is worthy to receive praise for his role as creator, the Lamb is worthy for his redemptive work among humanity. He was slain, he purchased people for God with his blood, and he made them into a kingdom and priests who will rule upon the earth. Because of all this he is also worthy to open the scroll in which the eschatological secrets are sealed. This complex of ideas is then summarized and reiterated in the simple expression "Worthy is the Lamb that was slain."

The first hymn of chapter five (vv. 9–10) is described as a "new song" and is sung by the four living creatures and the twenty-four elders together. With this kind of introduction and participation it seems to be a further development of the worship that began in chapter four.

You are worthy to take the book and to open its seals,
for you were slain and purchased for God by your blood
those from every tribe and tongue and people and ethnic group,
and made them a kingdom and priests to our God,
and they will rule upon the earth. (5:9–10)

Whereas God was worthy for his creative work, the Lamb is worthy for his redemptive work – a work that is universal in scope (cf. the universal dimension in the Song of Simeon in Luke 2:29–32 discussed above). The proclamation of worthiness here is not merely a declaration of praise but is directly in answer to the question of the angel (5:2).[115] The Lamb's redemptive work is what has demonstrated that he is worthy to open the scroll. His work is described in both past and future tenses in language that has been described as "liturgical prose." He was slain, purchased people, and made them a kingdom and priests. This much is accomplished already. Still to come is the future aspect of this redemption: they will rule upon the earth. This brief hymn thus taps into a multitude of temporal registers as did the hymns of Rev 4.

This new song moves into the next hymn which is offered by thousands and thousands of angels around the throne:

---

[113] See the discussion of the way that Revelation "though passionately resistant to Roman imperial ideology, paradoxically and persistently reinscribes its terms" in Moore, "Revelation," 451–452.

[114] Aune, *Revelation 1–5*, 332.

[115] Deichgräber, *Gotteshymnus und Christushymnus*, 51.

Worthy is the Lamb that was slain
to receive the power and wealth and wisdom
and strength and honor and glory and blessing. (5:12)

Just as in 4:11 the one upon the throne was worthy (ἄξιος), so here the Lamb is declared to be worthy of receiving a multitude of honorific expressions. Like the one on the throne, the Lamb is worthy to receive glory, honor, and power (5:12; 4:11). The Lamb is worthy also to receive wealth, wisdom, strength, and blessing. The expansion of praise attributes has the effect of indicating that the Lamb is truly and fully worthy, just as the one on the throne was.

The throne narrative reaches its conclusion with God and the Lamb receiving the same praise from every creature everywhere:

To the one seated upon the throne and to the lamb
be the blessing and the honor and the glory and the power forever and ever (5:13b)

With language and form reflective of all that has already transpired, all creatures praise God and the Lamb together. This short doxology adds one new element to what has already been said: power (κράτος).[116] The final praises of Rev 5 take the focus that has already been established and extend it into the eternal future by adding "forever and ever." The ultimate response to this acclamation of praise is a verbal "amen" from the four living beings (5:14) and a physical act of falling and worshipping by the elders.

4. What do the Hymns of Rev 4–5 Teach?

The hymns of Rev 4–5 teach a number of significant lessons both through their contents and their placement in the narrative. These will be summarized here under the headings of worship of God, critique of empire, christology, and communal formation.

First and foremost these hymns teach that worship of God is the ultimate and lasting reality. In chapter four, the God of Israel is praised in traditional Jewish language and style. The traditional apocalyptic imagery and setting shows that the heavenly world centers around the throne of God who is the eternal sovereign of the universe. By setting the remainder of the visions in this context of heavenly worship John has shown the priority of the worship of God.

Further, in chapter five we learn that Christ, the agent of God in the redemption of humanity, is also worthy of divine worship. This is taught both through the content of the songs (5:9–10, 12) and through their

---

[116] Jörns, *Das hymnische Evangelium*, 55. The praise of God in 4:11 and of the Lamb in 5:12 use the term δύναμις rather than κράτος. Cf. 1 Tim 6:16; 1 Pet 4:11; 5:11; and Rev 1:6.

placement in the narrative. Without explaining how this can be, the legitimacy of praising Christ along with God is demonstrated as normative for the people of God. Friesen explains that the forward movement of the worship throughout these two chapters serves to "draw together the One seated on the throne and the Lamb as the two beings uniquely worthy of worship."[117] Along these lines Bauckham has observed that apocalyptic imagery centering around the throne of God was perhaps the best way to present this high christology in the language and thought-world of first-century Jews.[118] Certainly the author of the Apocalypse has found a way of presenting a very high view of Christ in a way that is unique among the writings of the New Testament. Hymnody afforded an ideal medium for conveying this kind of teaching.

Closely related to the issue of worship of God is the implicit critique of human empires in these chapters. In his discussion of the Apocalypse and the Roman imperial cult, Freisen discusses the way that Augustus and later emperors were brought into close association with Zeus, as we have seen in earlier chapters. In the case of Rev 4–5, Jesus is brought into close association with the one God of Israel.[119] The heavenly worship of God and the Lamb in the setting of a throne room may be seen to be in stark contrast to the earthly worship of human rulers and all that it entailed. This visual image sets the stage for a more explicit critique that will follow as John portrays the Roman Empire as a satanic imitation of the kingdom of God. The idolatrous worship of the beast was a major issue for the community (cf. Rev 13).

But the critique of Roman practices goes beyond just the idea of who is worthy of worship and who is not. The one who is worthy in Rev 5 is the Lamb that was slain. Friesen is helpful for painting the contrast between a kingdom marked by suffering and endurance and a kingdom marked by power and domination. He writes,

> The authority of the Lamb, then, was based on his execution of God's will and in his execution. His kingdom had been won not by inflicting suffering but by enduring suffering. Such a view was so at odds with dominant views of reality that it could best be expressed in paradoxical imagery: the king of beasts as a slaughtered lamb that shepherds the nations.[120]

---

[117] Friesen, *Imperial Cults*, 198. He adds, "John did not attempt to work out the relationship between the Lamb and the One on the throne through discussions of ontology or through abstract reasoning. His vision report works through the logic of worship and of apocalyptic symbol" (198).

[118] Richard Bauckham, *The Climax of Prophecy: Studies on the Book of Revelation* (Edinburgh: T&T Clark, 1993), 118–149.

[119] Friesen, *Imperial Cults*, 198.

[120] Ibid., 201.

This particular lesson, which is conveyed clearly through the imagery of the songs of Rev 4–5, is developed more fully throughout the book of Revelation as believers are likewise called to suffer and endure (cf. Rev 14:12). This implicit critique of Roman power and domination leads to another teaching of the hymns: the memory of Christ and what he accomplished on the cross.

As with the hymns of Philippians and Colossians, the hymns of Rev 4–5 summarize several key components of the early Christian witness about Jesus. In particular, they memorialize the death of Christ as the Lamb who was slain. The slaughter of Christ is mentioned explicitly three times in chapter five (vv. 6, 9, 12), twice in hymnic passages (vv. 9, 12). The death of Christ is portrayed as the means by which people from all nations were ransomed for God (5:10). The author would have the readers join with the heavenly creatures and elders in remembering what Christ had done through his death.

The concept of social memory can be noted here to help us grasp the significance of the way that Christ's work is remembered. Fentress and Wickham explain, "In principle, we can usually regard social memory as an expression of collective experience: social memory identifies a group, giving it a sense of its past and defining its aspirations for the future."[121] Further, they point out that social memory is not merely passive but can be an active force, one that enables a community collectively to make sense of its present circumstances: "It is not a passive receptacle, but instead a process of active restructuring, in which elements may be retained, reordered, or suppressed."[122] In a similar vein, Assmann observes,

Memory is not simply the storage of past 'facts' but the ongoing work of reconstructive imagination. In other words, the past cannot be stored but always has to be 'processed' and mediated. This mediation depends on the semantic frames and needs of a given individual or society within a given present.[123]

Undoubtedly, the way that Christ's death is remembered in these songs is not incidental, but can be seen to be related to the present concerns facing the readers. Christ's death was remembered and celebrated in the imagery of a lamb being slaughtered. This idea of a sacrificial lamb surely strikes some overtones with the Jewish sacrificial system.[124] More generally, it evokes the idea that God's kingdom is brought about not through force but through the willing submission of the sacrificial victim. This way of remembering Christ is significant for the author of the Apocalypse who

---

[121] Fentress and Wickham, *Social Memory*, 25.

[122] Ibid., 40.

[123] Assmann, *Moses the Egyptian*, 14.

[124] See the variety of views on the significance of the lamb imagery in Russo, "Behind the Heavenly Door," 195–204; Satake, *Die Offenbarung des Johannes*, 208–210.

wants believers to hold fast, endure, and conquer by following the way of the Lamb and his word.

Finally, we might note the ways that this form of social memory, preserved in hymnic passages, contributes to a process of communal formation. As Assmann has noted in his discussion of social memory, what is remembered and how and when it is remembered is part of "the ongoing process of shaping an identity by reconstructing its past."[125] As we have seen, these hymns teach a good deal about who God is and who Christ is, even as they serve as part of a larger critique of other false claimants to divine worship. But the portrait of reality these hymns portray also says something about who the community is, both in the past and in the future. They are those ransomed by the blood of the Lamb (5:9), from every nation (5:9), made into a kingdom and priests serving God (5:10). Further, as to their future they will reign on earth (5:10). These hymns thus have something to say not just about the one being praised but also about those who are doing the praising within the earthly community. The hymn to the Lamb summarizes in succinct form who Christians are, what their status is, and what their ultimate destiny is. Over against competing ideas of what it means to live as a Christian within the Roman Empire (a variety of possibilities are represented in the letters to the seven churches in Rev 2–3), the hymns of Rev 4–5 make a claim that the true nature of the Christian life is a life marked by devoted service to the kingdom of God, the kingdom of the slain Lamb. The hymns themselves, reflecting elements of early Christian liturgy, model the kind of jubilant response that belongs to God and the Lamb at all times. Each of these aspects of Christian communal formation are supported by the hymns, even as they are developed throughout the remainder of the Apocalypse.

The fact that these hymns are found in the first and longest throne room vision is also important as it sets the stage for the remainder of the book, establishing some fundamental realities that affect how the message of the book as a whole is understood. Though we have only looked at the hymns of Rev 4–5, the importance of hymns throughout the book as a whole is well documented. As Massyngbaerde Ford notes, "The hymns carry the 'story line' of the Apocalypse, and through them the work gradually moves into a crescendo and reaches a climax which becomes the proclamation of the establishment of the kingdom of God and the enthronement of the Lamb."[126]

---

[125] Assmann, *Moses the Egyptian*, 14.
[126] Ford, "Christological Function of the Hymns," 208.

E. Conclusions

We are now in a position to review the role of didactic hymnody in early Christian narratives and in the Apocalypse. The hymns in the infancy narratives of Luke's Gospel were part of a strategy of progressively unfolding the significance of the coming of Jesus as the Messiah. Further, they were part of a strategy of using a range of credible Jewish and angelic voices to witness to this event as part of a fulfillment of God's covenant promises to Israel. These hymns featured earthly voices joined with the angels to proclaim the significance of the coming of the Messiah. That significance entailed the salvation of all humanity, Jew and Gentile alike. Remembering the birth of Jesus Christ in this way was a part of the larger strategy of presenting the ultimate significance of the life and ministry of Jesus for the readers of Luke's Gospel.

In John 1 we encountered a complex and rich review of history in Jewish didactic hymn style. This hymnic review of history focused on the work of God in history through the Logos, and ultimately showed that the birth of Jesus was the latest and fullest embodiment of the Logos in human history. Further, the prologue taught that the significance of the life of Jesus can only be fully understood within that historical and theological frame. As a hymnic review of history the prologue not only enabled the community to remember the life of Jesus but also to collectively remember the history of Israel in a way that placed Christ in the middle of it all.

In Revelation, particularly chapters 4–5, heavenly liturgy in the Jewish liturgical and apocalyptic tradition likewise expressed christological insight, but primarily by means of angelic and supernatural voices. Yet ultimately the voices of all creatures joined in as well. The hymns in this context instructed early Christians in the area of christological understanding for the purposes of shaping a view of ultimate reality for Christians living within the context of the Roman Empire.

In each instance it can be argued that these didactic hymns functioned at the nexus of a conflict within the early Christian communities. This is most clear in Revelation where conflict is explicitly identified within the Christian community (e.g., Rev 2:14–16; 2:20–25) and also between Christians and the broader society (Rev 2:13). The conflicts represented in Luke-Acts and also in John are more subtle but are nonetheless present. Competing views of Jesus's identity and mission are readily observed in both compositions, where Jews and Gentiles alike struggle to accept the Christian message, and also where competing views of Christian faith and life are attested within early Christian circles (Paul; John the Baptist). How does hymnody speak into these kinds of situations?

Hymnody, as a poetic art, has the ability to convey its meaning through metaphor, imagery, allusion and carefully styled development. Rather than providing a logical step-by-step argument, hymnody evokes a certain ethos even as it brings into view lofty claims about its subject matter. The familiarity of the language along with its sacred status allows the hymn to bring the world of the human and the world of the divine into proximity with one another. By creating a verbal portrait of reality, the author invites the reader to see the big picture, and to embrace it.

Further, hymnody is a medium that is well-suited to preserve and revise social memory as it remembers the past in light of the concerns of the present. As we have examined the use of hymnody in Luke, John, and Revelation some clear patterns have emerged. First, expressions of praise directed to God or at least focused on God and his work are also directed to the reader. Rather than simply reporting what happened, the authors of these works have carefully chosen each element of their compositions in order to contribute to their overall instructional aims. These hymns in narrative contexts have much to teach the reader.

Second, the hymnic passages have been carefully presented in terms of their setting and their contents. This was clearly the case with the hymns of the infancy narratives in Luke's Gospel, which set the stage of praise of God for his fulfillment of his promises which extend blessing to Jews and Gentiles – a major theme of the entire two-volume work of Luke-Acts. It was also the case with the Johannine prologue which laid out the framework within which the rest of the gospel should be read. In Revelation the hymnic praise of God and the Lamb likewise focused on key themes of the work as a whole. In all cases the hymns contributed to the ethos and the meaning of their literary settings.

Third, in all cases the form and content of these early Christian hymns showed very strong connections with the Jewish theological heritage. Accordingly, it can be argued that this was a major function of these early Christian hymns: they grounded the Christian message in Jewish theology and history. Not only so, they grounded their christology in those traditions as well. Whether this was for the sake of Jewish-Christians or Gentile-Christians is a debated issued which must be addressed individually in each case.

Fourth, through modifications or additions to traditional Jewish hymnody the early Christian hymns added a new dimension to what is conveyed through didactic hymnody in the Jewish tradition. Even as Jewish traditions are appropriated, alluded to, or remembered, they are also transformed in the service of the Christian message about Jesus.

Naturally, in spite of similarities of content and function, these hymns in larger compositions showed some variety as they contributed to the different purposes of their authors. Some were arguably preexisting hymns that were modified or adapted to their present location. Others were likely composed for their current literary purpose. The existence of both kinds of materials reflects the reality that hymnody played a significant role in early Christianity in a number of areas: worship, teaching, letter-writing, and literary compositions. In each case, what was affirmed in hymnic compositions can be seen to play a role in helping the early Christians address issues that were facing their communities.

Chapter 10

Didactic Hymns in Early Christian Writings

A. Introduction

Around the year 200 CE, the author of the work *Against Artemon* sought to refute the teaching of Artemon by citing earlier and more reliable witnesses with regard to the nature of Christ. Within the few lines of this work preserved by Eusebius is the following rhetorical question: "For who is ignorant of the books of Irenaeus, Melito, and the rest who proclaim Christ as God and man, and how many psalms and odes, written from the beginning by brothers in the faith, hymn Christ, the word of God, proclaiming him as a god?"[1] While it is no great surprise that the early Christians made continued use of psalms and hymns for the purposes of honoring their God and their savior, it is interesting to observe that psalms and odes were appealed to early on as a source of theological teaching. Drawing on the canonical book of Psalms as both an example of sacred song and a source of prophecy about the Messiah, the Christian practice of hymnody was, to a large extent, in line with Jewish practices of the day.[2] As we have seen, Jews of the Second Temple period continued composing psalms, hymns, and prayers using them for purposes of praise as well as a means of promoting a theological understanding of their circumstances. Moreover the Christians (whether Jewish or gentile), like their Jewish contemporaries, were part of a society that itself made significant use of hymns and prayers in the service of religion, philosophy, and even politics.

In addition to these influences, the Christians of the second century CE had other factors influencing their use of hymnic traditions. On the one hand, the second-century Christians inherited the traditions of first-century followers of Christ as preserved in the earliest Christian writings that would later be collected and called the New Testament. On the other hand,

---

[1] *Hist. eccl.* 5.28.5. Trans. mine based on the Greek text in Eusebius, *Histoire Ecclésiastique: Livres V–VII* (trans. Gustave Bardy; 4th ed.; SC 41; Paris: Éditions du Cerf, 1994).

[2] On the place of the Psalms in early Christian worship see Hengel, "The Song about Christ," 227–291. But note also the cautions voiced earlier with regard to assuming too much of a direct correspondence between early Christian and Jewish singing practices. Cf. Jeffery, "Philo's Impact on Christian Psalmody," 147–187.

second-century Christians represented a diversity that, in the eyes of some, exceeded the boundaries of acceptable Christian teaching and practice.[3] The struggles between competing understandings of Christian faith and life find reflection in many of the writings of second-century Christians. In light of these factors, this chapter will examine the development and use of hymns and psalms as illustrated in second-century Christian writings. In light of the focus of this volume, the specific focus will be on the kinds of teaching that was conveyed through the medium of didactic hymnody.

As with earlier chapters, we can observe that hymnic passages with strongly didactic emphases are found in a wide range of compositions. These include letters (epistles of Ignatius of Antioch), collections of psalms (*Odes of Solomon*), narratives (*Acts of Thomas*), treatises (Hippolytus, *Refutatio omnium haeresium*), and explicitly instructional writings (Clement of Alexandria's *Paedagogus*). The contents and themes of these hymnic passages cover a broad range of topics from the incarnation and christological concerns, to Gnostic theology and cosmology, to issues of Christian discipleship. We begin this chapter with the epistles of Ignatius of Antioch. In his writings at the beginning of the second century, we find further development of the New Testament trajectory of the use of musical imagery and of the use of hymnic styles. From Ignatius we move to the few Gnostic hymns that are cited by Hippolytus, then to the *Odes of Solomon*. We conclude this chapter at the end of the second century with the hymn that Clement of Alexandria wrote to conclude the *Paedagogus*.

Though we cannot necessarily trace a straight line of development or influence from one text to the next, these compositions do help give us a sense of both the continuity and the development of didactically oriented hymnic praise in the second century.

B. Ignatius of Antioch

Outside of the New Testament, the hymns and hymnic fragments cited in the epistles of Ignatius are the earliest of the second-century hymns, dating to the early part of the century.[4] Hymnic passages are found in the epistle

---

[3] On the composition and use of hymns by a number of groups deemed "heretical" by their opponents, as well as its impact on the ongoing composition of Christian hymns, see Hengel, "The Song about Christ," 240–244.

[4] Though the dating is debated, a date of composition between 100 and 118 CE arguably fits with the internal and external evidence (William R. Schoedel, *Ignatius of Antioch: A Commentary on the Letters of Ignatius of Antioch* [Hermeneia; Philadelphia: Fortress Press, 1985], 4–5). Pierre Thomas Camelot follows the date given by Eusebius, 107 CE, for the martyrdom of Ignatius (Ignatius, *Lettres* [trans. Pierre Thomas Camelot; Repr. of the 4th rev. and corr. ed.; SC 10bis; Paris: Éd. du Cerf, 1998], 13).

to the Ephesians (Ign. *Eph.* 7:2 and 19:2–3) and the epistle to Polycarp (Ign. *Pol.* 3:2). In addition his letters contain several creed-like statements about the life, death, and resurrection of Christ (Ign. *Trall.* 9:1–2, Ign. *Smyrn.* 1:1–2, and Ign. *Magn.* 11:1).[5] As was the case with hymnic and confessional materials in the letters of the New Testament, it is probable that these passages are reflective of the language and expressions used in early Christian worship. Moreover, some scholars claim that several of these reflect the actual language of early Christian baptismal and eucharistic ceremonies.[6] Ignatius' elaborate use of musical imagery and references to praise in these letters adds support to the view that these letters reflect an early Christian worship setting.[7] Regardless of how much we may be able to learn about early Christian worship from the letters of Ignatius, in this section our interest is in examining the hymnic portions of his letters in order to gain insight into how Ignatius utilized hymnic forms for didactic and hortatory purposes.

Though in earlier chapters we have already addressed the issue of what constitutes a "didactic hymn," it will be valuable here to review our definition in light of the kinds of hymnic materials we find embedded in the letters of Ignatius. Didactic hymns, prayers, and religious poetry are those compositions which employ the stylistic and/or formal conventions of praise and prayer, but whose primary purpose was to convey a lesson, idea, or theological truth to a human audience. In some instances we have observed that the content of a hymn allows us to identify it as didactic, particularly when it explicitly claims a teaching role (e.g., Ps 78:1) or, more often, when its message is directed toward a human audience in addition to a deity (e.g., Aristotle's *Hymn to Virtue*). In other cases, a hymn demonstrates a didactic function through its inclusion in another context such as a narrative (e.g., the hymns of Luke 1–2), a larger didactic poem (e.g., the hymns in Lucretius, *De rerum natura*), or an epistle (e.g., Col 1:15–20). In such a context the hymn can be considered didactic to the extent that the author employs it in support of the instructional aims of the larger composition. It is in this latter sense that we consider the hymnic passages in Ignatius to be didactic hymns: their inclusion in his letters lends support to the teaching the author wishes to convey and also constructs a picture of ultimate reality which supports the claims made in the remainder of his let-

---

[5] Ignatius, *Lettres*, 25. Schoedel refers to these as "quasi-creedal materials" and "semi-creedal statements" (cf. Schoedel, *Ignatius*, 129, 152, 220). Aune refers to these passages as "creedal formulas summarizing correct belief," (David E. Aune, "Ignatius, Letters of," in *The Westminster Dictionary of New Testament and Early Christian Literature and Rhetoric* [Louisville, Ky.: Westminster John Knox, 2003], 225–228, here 228).

[6] Ignatius, *Lettres*, p. 101 on Ign. *Trall.* 9:1–2; p. 64 on Ign. *Eph.* 7:2. Cf. Deichgräber, *Gotteshymnus und Christushymnus*, 159–160.

[7] For musical imagery see Ign. *Eph.* 4:1–2, Ign. *Phld.* 1:2, and Ign. *Rom.* 2:2.

ters. As we will see, these hymns are particularly valuable in responding to the emerging challenges of docetism faced by Ignatius and the churches of Asia Minor.

1. The Star Hymn in Ignatius' Epistle to the Ephesians

The longest hymnic passage (Ign. *Eph.* 19:2–3), known as the "Star Hymn," describes the incarnation of Christ metaphorically as the appearance of a star in heaven and provides the reaction of the other cosmic entities. Christ is not named in the hymn (unlike Phil 2:6–11 or John 1:1–18) but the context makes it clear that this hymn is about the mystery of the revelation of Christ in the world (cf. 18:2–19:1).[8] Like earlier christological hymns this is not a metrical hymn, though it is possible to divide this hymn into four distinct strophes: 1) describing the appearance of the star (lines 1–4); 2) the reaction of the celestial bodies to the star (lines 5–9); 3) the workings of the star (lines 10–15); and 4) a concluding theological commentary on the first three strophes (lines 16–18).[9] The hymn reads, in English translation:

A star shone forth in heaven
brighter than all the stars,
and its light was unspeakable
and its newness caused astonishment. (lines 1–4)

All the other stars
with the sun and the moon
gathered in chorus round this star,
and it far exceeded them all in its light.
There was perplexity, whence came this new thing, so unlike them. (lines 5–9)

By this all magic was dissolved
and every bond of wickedness disappeared;
ignorance was removed
and the old kingdom was destroyed,
for God was revealed as man
for the newness of eternal life. (lines 10–15)

That which had been prepared by God received its beginning.
Hence all things were disturbed
because the abolition of death was being planned. (lines 16–18)[10]

While Stander's arrangement above has much to commend it, consideration of metrical patterns and repetition of a key term in lines 4, 9, and 15

---

[8] Deichgräber, *Gotteshymnus und Christushymnus*, 157.
[9] H. F. Stander, "The Star-Hymn in the Epistle of Ignatius to the Ephesians (19:2–3)," *VC* 43 (1989): 209–214. For a variety of other arrangements see Deichgräber, *Gotteshymnus und Christushymnus*, 157–158.
[10] Translation from Stander, "Star-Hymn," 210.

leads to a slight correction: strophe 4, as a theological comment on the first three strophes, should not be considered part of the hymn. Strophes 1–3 are united by two important features that distinguish them from the fourth strophe. First, the final line of each of these strophes utilizes the key word "newness" (καινότης). Secondly, each of these strophes ends with a pattern of three long syllables (– – –).[11] By contrast, the final line of the fourth strophe ends with four short syllables in the word κατάλυσιν (∪∪∪∪), and contains no mention of newness or anything related to it. These observations may be added to the perception of Schoedel that the last three lines are somewhat "shapeless" in contrast to the preceding section.[12] For these reasons it is preferable to view the final strophe as the theological comment of Ignatius added to three carefully constructed strophes about the incarnation of Christ and its cosmic impact.

Viewed in this way, the comments of Ignatius on the hymn are quite interesting. Each of the three lines of lines 16–18 comments on and summarizes the point of one strophe of the hymn. "That which had been prepared by God received its beginning" (line 16) explains the meaning of the first strophe and the appearance of the star (i.e., the birth of Christ): his appearance in the world marked the beginning of the eschatological salvation planned and prepared by God himself. "Hence all things were disturbed" (line 17) summarizes the response of the "powers" represented by stars, sun, and moon in the second strophe. This idea of the disturbance of the powers stands together with the hidden descent of Christ in other early Christian writings as well.[13] Finally, the phrase "because the abolition of death was being planned" (line 18) connects with strophe three summarizing the redemptive work of Christ elaborated in that strophe under the general idea of the abolition of death. This final line reminds us that this hymn is primarily focused on the incarnation, at which point we see only the beginning of the unfolding of God's redemptive plan through Christ. In 20:1

---

[11] More specifically, lines 4 and 15 end with the pattern ∪ – – –. Line 9, the conclusion of the second strophe ends with – – – –, two spondees. For the use of spondaic rhythm as a solemn rhythm appropriate to libation prayers see M. L. West, *Greek Metre* (Oxford: Clarendon Press, 1982), 55–56.

[12] Schoedel, *Ignatius*, 88. Schoedel actually argues against the whole composition being a hymn (in spite of its many unique terms and several poetic figures of speech) and claims instead that it is "a product of Ignatius' rhetorical methods" (88). Schoedel cites uneven line lengths and the fact that it "often seems too awkward for a hymn" (88). Nevertheless, as we observed in the earliest christological hymns (not to mention Jewish psalms), it is not necessary to work off of the assumption that line lengths are the determinative factor in identifying a hymn.

[13] For the connection between stars, angels, and powers, cf. *1 En.* 18:12–19:3; 21:1–10; 72:3; 75:1, 3; 82:10–20; Clement Alex., *Exc. ex Theod.* 69–75; Origen, *Cels.* 8.67 (Ibid., 92).

Ignatius indicates that he hopes to write to them about the suffering and resurrection of Christ in a later letter. The hymn and its interpretation thus provide a concise and compelling metaphorical picture of the incarnation and its God-intended results.

The hymn itself, with the rich mythical metaphor and expressions, strongly reflects a Hellenistic background.[14] It also connects with earlier christological hymns in emphasizing both the coming of Christ as well as the positive redemptive effects of his incarnation. The hymn is perhaps closest in outlook to Col 1:15–20 (with its cosmic christology and emphasis on the reconciling work of Christ) and John 1:1–18 (with its emphasis on light and on the life-giving work of Christ). The final line of the third strophe ("for the newness of eternal life") suggests a strong connection with Rom 6:4.[15] The guiding image of the star suggests a reference to the birth of Christ in Matt 2:1–12.[16] Nevertheless, the hymn goes well beyond the New Testament precedents and utilizes more extensive mythological imagery, an exegetical tradition associating stars with angels and powers (noted above), and references to the power of magic, bonds, ignorance, and an old kingdom.

The *Sitz im Leben* of the hymn prior to its use in this epistle is not known. It is possible that the hymn is purely a literary creation and thus would not have had a liturgical use.[17] Regardless, we are on sure footing if we attempt to understand how this passage contributes to the larger purposes of the epistle rather than how it *may* have contributed to an early Christian worship setting. Set in an epistolary context that includes warnings against false teaching (cf. 16:1) the hymn supplements Ignatius' attempt to encourage the readers to not be deceived. In support of that aim Ignatius draws on New Testament texts (in 17:1–18:1) and also cites quasi-creedal statements about the birth of Christ (cf. 18:2). In 19:2–3 Ignatius cites the hymn to further justify the christological picture he presents elsewhere.

We may agree with the assessment of Schoedel who concludes that this passage "represents esoteric teaching based primarily on apocalyptic tradition enriched by legends about the birth of Christ."[18] We might also add that Ignatius' choice of a hymnic passage to present this kind of developing christological reflection is reflective of the era in which he wrote. We will observe the continuing development of this phenomenon of hymnic

---

[14] Deichgräber, *Gotteshymnus und Christushymnus*, 159.

[15] Ignatius, *Lettres*, 76. Cf. Schoedel, *Ignatius*, 93 n. 43.

[16] Schoedel, *Ignatius*, 92.

[17] Deichgräber, *Gotteshymnus und Christushymnus*, 159.

[18] Schoedel, *Ignatius*, 94.

reflection about Christ as we continue through the Christian hymns of the second century.

2. Shorter Hymnic Passages in Ignatius

The shorter passages (Ign. *Eph.* 7:2 and Ign. *Pol.* 3:2) offer a series of paradoxes that reflect on aspects of the person and work of Christ. Both deal primarily with issues related to the incarnation, although the final line of the citation in the letter to Polycarp points to the passion of Christ as well. Both passages are found in the context of warnings about false teachers (cf. Ign. *Eph.* 7:1 and Ign. *Pol.* 3:1). In English translation these passages read,

> There is one physician,
> both fleshly and spiritual
> begotten and unbegotten,
> come in flesh, God,
> in death, true life,
> both of Mary and of God,
> first passible and then impassible,
> Jesus Christ, our Lord. (Ign. *Eph.* 7:2)

> Look for him who is above time –
> non-temporal,
> invisible,
> for our sakes visible,
> intangible,
> impassible,
> for our sakes passible,
> one who endured in every way for our sakes. (Ign. *Pol.* 3:2)[19]

Though clearly christologically oriented in their subject matter, these passages are unlike earlier christological hymns in that they lack a narrative about Christ, focusing primarily instead on attributes. The kind of terminology used to discuss these paradoxical aspects of the incarnation is markedly philosophical.[20] At the same time, as with the Star Hymn, in spite of their uniqueness, these passages show multiple levels of contact with the New Testament. Many of the expressions can be traced to New Testament reflections about the person and work of Christ (cf. Rom 1:3–4, 20; John 1:14, 18; Col 1:15; 1 Tim 1:17; Heb 11:27).

The opening line of Ign. *Eph.* 7:2 ("There is one healer") reflects a development of the εἷς-acclamation formula that was common in the New Testament and also used elsewhere in Ignatius (cf. Ign. *Eph.* 15:1).[21] What

---

[19] Translations are from Schoedel, *Ignatius*, 59, 266.

[20] Ignatius, *Lettres*, 27–28. Schoedel shares this assessment (Schoedel, *Ignatius*, 61).

[21] Deichgräber, *Gotteshymnus und Christushymnus*, 155, cf. 115–116.

is unique is the use of the term "healer" rather than Lord or God or teacher, and also the fact that the εἷς-acclamation form is expanded here by the addition of a series of six paradoxes. The pairs of terms used in the paradoxes contrast the human and divine aspects of Christ's nature. In each case the first pair focuses on an aspect of the incarnate Christ stressing the humility of this reality, while the second term reflects the idea that Christ is indeed God. Such a deliberate use of stark opposites marks this passage (and Ign. *Pol.* 3:2) as particularly Hellenistic.[22]

Another feature of Ign. *Eph.* 7:2 that shows a strong connection with the New Testament is the series of lines composed of two parts. This was a prominent feature in the early christological hymn in 1 Tim 3:16 and also occurred on a smaller scale in 1 Pet 3:18b. Deichgräber suggests that there is a very close relationship between these passages, so much so that Ignatius may have known these specific texts.[23] While Ignatius clearly draws on precedents found in the writings of the New Testament, these passages reflect on Christ's incarnation in ways that move beyond the New Testament descriptions of the incarnation.[24]

The hymnic passage in Ign. *Pol.* 3:2, though similar to Ign. *Eph.* 7:2, is also marked by some unique features. Its most distinctive feature is its use of "negative" theology; that is, it focuses on negative attributes of Christ. The negative terms include references to his impassibility, non-temporality, intangibility, and invisibility. These terms were common in Hellenistic discussions of the divine, but are used here in connection with their opposites (visibility, passibility, enduring) in support of Ignatius' christological understanding.[25] Through the use of these kinds of terms, the passage portrays an even more educated and philosophical tone than the other hymns of Ignatius.

In each of these examples of hymns in Ignatius, we can observe something of a close connection with the New Testament christological hymns and their tendency to focus on presenting the person and work of Christ in poetic language. The innovations in the hymns of Ignatius are seen with regard to the kinds of imagery that he chooses and with the metaphysical language he uses to express christological concepts. Though the precise social setting of these letters is debated, it is at least clear that the hymnic passages in Ignatius serve as a means of affirming and supporting Ignatius'

---

[22] Ibid., 156.
[23] Ibid.
[24] Schoedel, *Ignatius*, 267–268.
[25] Ibid., 266–268.

vision of what he considered to be correct christological understanding in the face of alternative or competing views.[26]

C. Gnostic Hymns

From the middle to late second century we have several surviving examples of what have been called Gnostic hymns.[27] These hymns are remarkable in that they are the first hymns in the Christian tradition to be composed in Greek metrical form.[28] The third-century writer Hippolytus preserves these hymns in his *Refutatio omnium haeresium*, a massive treatise in which he discusses a variety of Gnostic teachers, providing summaries of their teachings and occasional citations of their writings.[29] Hippolytus preserves a hymn of Valentinus from the mid second century (*Haer.* 6.37.7) and two hymns of the Naassenes from the late second or early third century (*Haer.* 5.10.2; 5.4.8), all of which are quite unlike the psalms of the LXX or the Christ-hymns of the New Testament. In this section we will examine the Valentinian poem, a hymn that uses terminology and ideas which resonate with late antique philosophical-theological speculation.[30] Of the two Naassene hymn fragments, one reflects the syncretistic tendencies of the period offering praise to the divine through many names (*Haer.* 5.4.8). The one that we will explore below describes the revealing work of Christ within the framework of Gnostic cosmology and thus conveys a much more strongly didactic character. Hippolytus can cite these hymns as examples in the context of his own work precisely because they were effective as didactic hymns. They paint a vivid picture of ultimate reality as seen by these particular communities.

---

[26] For an extended discussion of the social setting of these letters and the conflicts in which Ignatius is involved see Ibid., 10–17.

[27] On the problematic nature of the term "Gnostic" see Christoph Markschies, *Gnosis: An Introduction* (trans. John Bowden; London: T & T Clark, 2003), 1–27. He discusses the problems associated with using the term "Gnosticism" as an interpretive category for a number of wide-ranging philosophical and religious movements on antiquity.

[28] Hengel, "The Song about Christ," 252–253.

[29] For a concise introduction to Hippolytus and a summary of *Refutatio omnium haeresium* see Claudio Moreschini and Enrico Norelli, *Early Christian Greek and Latin Literature: A Literary History* (2 vols.; Peabody, Mass.: Hendrickson, 2005), 1:232–239.

[30] See the discussion of such terminology in Thielko Wolbergs, *Griechische religiöse Gedichte der ersten nachchristlichen Jahrhunderte* (Beiträge zur klassischen Philologie 40; Meisenheim am Glan: A. Hain, 1971), 24.

1. The Psalm of Valentinus

The psalm of Valentinus preserved in Hippolytus is the only poetry of Valentinus that has been preserved.[31] It is possible that this text belongs to the corpus of Gnostic Psalms referenced by several early Christian writers.[32] The poem can be dated to the middle of the second century CE when Valentinus was at the height of his influence.[33] In English translation the hymn reads:

All things suspended in air by spirit I see,
And all things wafted by spirit I perceive:
Flesh from soul suspended,
and soul from air projected,
and air suspended from aether,
and from the deep fruits brought forth,
and from the womb a baby brought forth.[34]

The seven-line psalm is carefully constructed in dactylic tetrameters, a popular meter that resulted in a psalm structure that was easily remembered. This meter was particularly common for sailor songs and drinking songs.[35] Such a catchy arrangement lends support to the idea that this psalm could have been accompanied by music and sung in the context of a communal gathering.[36] In addition to its metrical style which places this very much within the Greek tradition of song, the psalm also connects with features of Jewish poetry and the canonical psalms. The marks of Jewish psalm style are evident in the parallelism of "all things" and "by the spirit" (lines 1 and 2), and the verb "brought fourth" (lines 6 and 7).[37] Other elements of parallelism are present as well (e.g., the verb "suspended" at the end of lines 3 and 5). Between the meter and the parallelism, it is safe to consider that this is a unified and complete composition.

---

[31] For text and commentary of eleven fragments of Valentinus preserved in other contexts see Christoph Markschies, *Valentinus Gnosticus?: Untersuchungen zur valentinianischen Gnosis mit einem Kommentar zu den Fragmenten Valentins* (WUNT 65; Tübingen: J. C. B. Mohr, 1992), 11–290.

[32] Tertullian (*De carne Christi* 17:20), Muratorian Fragment, and Origen (*Hom. Job* 21:12; *PG* 17.80.12–15) (cf. Wolbergs, *Griechische religiöse Gedichte*, 24). For additional bibliography on Gnostic hymns see the entries in Michael Lattke, *Hymnus: Materialen zu einer Geschichte der antiken Hymnologie* (NTOA 19; Göttingen: Vandenhoeck & Ruprecht, 1991), 254–260.

[33] Wolbergs, *Griechische religiöse Gedichte*, 24.

[34] Translation adapted from *ANF*, vol. 5, p. 91 and the German translation in Markschies, *Valentinus Gnosticus?*, 218. My adaptation follows the Greek word order more closely so that the parallelism from line to line can be more readily perceived.

[35] Ibid., 220–221.

[36] Ibid., 223–225.

[37] Ibid., 225–227.

With regard to its teaching, we may note at the outset that the first two lines portray the teaching that follows as the visionary perception of the teacher (presumably Valentinus). The first five lines together emphasize that all things depend ultimately on Spirit, which in Valentinian thought could refer to Sophia who was at times called the Holy Spirit.[38] The last two lines shift the focus to the deep (Bythos), which in the Valentinian system is the supreme God.[39] The final line may refer to the procession of the divine Word particularly in the incarnation.[40] Read in this way the hymn provides a reference to the preexistent savior.[41]

When we consider the teaching of the hymn, we are once again confronted with the issue of a text that has at least two contexts in which it could be interpreted. Its original context is that of the community for which the song was written and which would have (presumably) recited it together. Its secondary context is the context in which we know it: it is cited by Hippolytus as a succinct summary of Valentinus's system of belief. This psalm certainly qualifies as a "twice-used song" though its first and second uses are quite a bit further apart from one another in terms of meaning and purpose than many of the twice-used songs of the Hebrew Bible. If we are able to talk about what this hymn teaches, it is likely that the understanding of the significance of this hymn would be quite different depending on which of the two contexts were being considered.

For Hippolytus the psalm summarizes the heretical teaching of Valentinus. Hippolytus interprets the hymn himself in the lines following his citation of it, explaining that flesh, soul, air, and aether are representative of elements of Gnostic cosmology. "Flesh" is matter, "soul" is the Demiurge, "air" is Achamoth, and "aether" is Sophia in the Pleroma.[42] Scholars rightly question the extent to which Hippolytus' third-century allegorical interpretation of the psalm corresponds to the meaning intended by Valentinus when he composed the psalm.[43] Nevertheless, it is quite likely that the teachers in the Valentinian school continued to develop the teaching of Valentinus so that by the third century, the hymn could have been used to express a distinctly Valentinian Gnostic cosmology.[44]

---

[38] Birger A. Pearson, *Ancient Gnosticism: Traditions and Literature* (Minneapolis, Minn.: Fortress Press, 2007), 151–152.

[39] Markschies, *Gnosis*, 90.

[40] Bentley Layton, *The Gnostic Scriptures: A New Translation with Annotations and Introductions* (ABRL; New York: Doubleday, 1995), 246.

[41] Pearson, *Ancient Gnosticism*, 152.

[42] Wolbergs, *Griechische religiöse Gedichte*, 31.

[43] Layton, *Gnostic Scriptures*, 249.

[44] On the history of Valentinus and the Valentinians see Kurt Rudolph, *Gnosis: The Nature and History of Gnosticism* (San Francisco: Harper & Row, 1983), 317–325.

Reading the psalm in its mid-second century context as opposed to its third-century context, it is possible to see it as an expression of developing Christian theology within the context of second century Platonic philosophy. Markschies argues from biblical parallels as well as from contemporary philosophical discussions that this psalm represents an attempt on the part of Valentinus to present a cosmology that was grounded in Jewish thought while at the same time expressed in the language of contemporary philosophy. Specifically, the cosmology of this hymn can be shown to be rooted in Hellenistic-Jewish concepts of the Spirit, but expressed in a way that resonated with contemporary philosophical speculation.[45] This interpretation, one that does not overstate the distance between Valentinus and developing Christian theology, fits well with a view of Valentinus who was for many years a respected Christian teacher in Rome, before leaving for Cyprus in 160 CE.[46]

Interestingly, the christological hymns and confessions cited by Ignatius at the beginning of the century do not concern themselves with cosmology. Ignatius certainly knows the New Testament tradition of the involvement of Christ in creation. In Ign. *Eph.*15:1 he claims that Christ is the one who "spoke and it was so," a reading that places Christ in the creation account of Gen 1.[47] Nevertheless, the hymns cited by Ignatius center on the human and divine nature of Christ, his incarnation, his suffering, and the benefits of his redemptive work for humanity. The psalm of Valentinus, by contrast, concerns itself almost entirely with cosmology, with the exception of the possible mention of the incarnation in line 7.

Read in this way the psalm illustrates Markschies' claims about the Valentinian theological project in general: "The Valentinians attempted – to use a graphic metaphor – to make Christianity more competitive in the market of opinions, philosophies, and forms of religion by 'expanding' Christian theology, adding a prehistory and a sequel to the Bible."[48] The psalm encapsulates one aspect of that teaching – a cosmological development – in a concise and memorable form. The compelling manner of expression was no doubt partly responsible for the currency of this psalm from the time Valentinus composed it until the time when Hippolytus quoted it roughly seventy years later.

---

[45] Markschies, *Valentinus Gnosticus?* , 258–259.
[46] Rudolph, *Gnosis: The Nature and History of Gnosticism*, 318.
[47] Schoedel, *Ignatius*, 77–78.
[48] Markschies, *Gnosis*, 93.

2. The Naassene Hymn

In contrast to the ambiguity of the Gnostic orientation of the psalm of Valentinus, the Naassene hymn, preserved in Hippolytus, shows a much closer connection with Gnostic thinking and has been called "a masterpiece of Gnostic hymnology."[49] This twenty-one line poem contains thirty key Gnostic terms, and culminates with the climactic last word, "Gnosis."[50] In English translation the hymn reads:

The universal law of the All was the First-born Mind [Nous];
the second one after First-born was the outpoured Chaos,
while the Soul [Psyche] got the third rank, with the duty to fulfill the law.
For that reason she put on the form of a hind
and started toiling as a captive, being a game for Death.
Sometimes she would live in a royal palace and look at the light,
but sometimes she is being thrown in a den, and there she weeps.

[Sometimes she rejoices; sometimes she weeps aloud;
sometimes she is a judge, sometimes she is being judged;
sometimes she dies, sometimes she is being born.]

Finally, she – wretched in her sorrows –
in her wanderings entered the exitless Labyrinth.
Then Jesus said: "Look, Father:
this prey to evils is wandering away to Earth,
far from Thy spirit (*or* breath)!
And she seeks to escape the bitter Chaos,
but knows not how to win through.

For that reason send Me, Father!
Bearing the seals I will descend;
I will pass through all the Aeons;
I will reveal all the mysteries
and show the form of the gods.
I will transmit the secrets of the holy way,
calling them Gnosis." (lines 1–21)[51]

This hymn provides a clear delineation of a three-part Gnostic system involving Nous, Chaos, and Psyche (lines 1–3).[52] More significantly, in narrative form it describes the redemptive work of Christ in Gnostic terms in lines 8–21. Thus it addresses cosmological concerns as well as christological and soteriological issues.

For purposes of this study it is instructive to compare the portrayal of the redemptive work of Christ in this hymn with what we have encountered

---

[49] Giovanni Filoramo, *A History of Gnosticism* (Cambridge, Mass.: Blackwell, 1992).

[50] Miroslav Marcovich, "The Naassene Psalm in Hippolytus," in *Studies in Graeco-Roman Religions and Gnosticism* (Leiden: Brill, 1988), 80–88, here 85.

[51] Translation by Marcovich in Ibid., 81.

[52] Ibid., 85.

in earlier Christian hymnody. The greatest contrast may be seen in the actions that Jesus undertakes. In this psalm he intends to descend (line 16), pass through the aeons (line 17), reveal mysteries (line 18), show the form of the gods (line 19), and transmit secrets (i.e., Gnosis) (lines 20–21).

By contrast, in the hymns and hymnic fragments preserved in Ignatius from the early second century, Jesus is a physician (Ign. *Eph.* 7:2), a destroyer of magic, God revealed as a human, bringing newness of life (Ign. *Eph.* 19:3), and one who endured (Ign. *Pol.* 3:2). In the New Testament Christological hymns we find references to his incarnation (Phil 2:7; John 1:14), death on the cross (Phil 2:8; Col 1:18, 20), his resurrection (Phil 2:9; Col 1:18), and his work of reconciliation (Col 1:20). There are also references to Christ's work of revealing grace and truth (John 1:17–18), though the revelatory aspects of the incarnation appear to be less central than the redemptive aspects.

This Naassene hymn highlights the revelatory aspect of the work of Christ, to the exclusion of other aspects. There is no reference to the death of Christ, his suffering, or his resurrection. The hymn teaches both the problem with humanity (lines 1–9) and the solution proposed and brought about by Jesus (lines 10–21). Both aspects of the hymn's teaching can be seen to fit well within a Gnostic system of thought. By tapping into temporal registers of the timeless past (rather than of the recent past in the incarnation) and highlighting Gnostic understandings of heavenly and earthly planes, the hymn offers a distinctly Gnostic vision of reality.

In sum, the Gnostic hymns cited in Hippolytus are evidence of the widespread use of hymns as didactic tools for communities of faith. As the New Testament christological hymns dealt with cosmology and christology, so did these Gnostic hymns. Yet their terminology and orientation reflects the move toward a more philosophical form of expression that we observed in the hymns preserved in the letters of Ignatius. They also reflect a move away from the common narrative events of the New Testament hymns and a move toward the idea of Christ as a revealer of secret knowledge. The fact that Hippolytus can cite these in the third decade of the third century attests to the power of these songs to convey instruction and summarize systems of belief in succinct and memorable form.

D. Odes of Solomon

The *Odes of Solomon* is a collection of forty-two Syriac psalms, hymns, and meditations commonly regarded as an early Jewish-Christian hymnbook. The precise date and place of origin of the *Odes* is uncertain and scholars have proposed dates from the early second century to the ear-

ly third century.[53] The background of the *Odes* has also been debated.
James H. Charlesworth has made a strong case for ruling out a Gnostic
background to the *Odes*, while at the same time indicating they were a
likely tributary to Gnosticism.[54] The *Odes* reflect earlier Jewish and Christian influences and ideas in terms of content, form, and style, but they also
contain a number of distinctive characteristics which make it impossible to
classify the *Odes* according to any one schema.[55]

Among its unique features the *Odes of Solomon* contains many psalms
and hymns that are infused with a revelatory emphasis. This idea of revealed knowledge is made explicit through references to the inspiration of
the singer in numerous places.[56] For example, in *Odes Sol.* 16:5 the odist
claims, "I will open my mouth and his Spirit will speak by me." This prophetic theme is related to another unique feature of the *Odes*: in numerous
places the singer identifies himself directly with Christ and speaks to the
congregation on his behalf.[57] So clear is the revelatory nature of these
hymns that Aune has described the collection as a "distinctive type of prophetic hymnbook."[58] While Aune is surely correct to note the pervading
prophetic theme, other features must be considered as well.

---

[53] See the recent summary and analysis of these issues in Michael Lattke and Harold
W. Attridge, *Odes of Solomon: A Commentary* (trans. Marianne Ehrhardt; Hermeneia;
Minneapolis: Fortress Press, 2009), 1–26. On the dating see also Michael Lattke, "Dating
the Odes of Solomon," in *Die Oden Salomos in ihrer Bedeutung für Neues Testament und
Gnosis* (Göttingen: Vandenhoeck & Ruprecht, 1998), 113–132. H. J. W. Drijvers, "Odes
of Solomon and Psalms of Mani. Christians and Manichaeans in Third-Century Syria," in
East of Antioch: Studies in Early Syriac Christianity (London: Variorum Reprints, 1984),
117–130. Lattke argues for the earlier dating while Drijvers argues for the later date.

[54] James H. Charlesworth, "The Odes of Solomon – Not Gnostic," *CBQ* 31 (1969):
357–369.

[55] Franzmann lists the following classifications that have been proposed for the Odes
as a whole: Grichische Dichtungen; Semitische Poesie in griechischen Gewande;
Psalmen; Songs; Hymns of the Catechumens/Hymns of the newly baptized; Griechische
Gedichte in Nachahmung hebräischer poetischer Satzordnung; Hymnes antiochiennes;
Prophetic hymns; Hymnisch-enthusiastische Lobpreisungen der Erlösung; Didactic poet-
ry of a religious nature; "Inspirierte"/ "geistgewirkte" Liederdichtungen. Majella Franz-
mann, *The Odes of Solomon: An Analysis of the Poetical Structure and Form* (NTOA 20;
Göttingen: Vandenhoeck & Ruprecht, 1991), 8.

[56] The appeals to inspiration suggest these are inspired, prophetic utterances (6:1–2;
10:1–3; 11:4–6; 12:1–2; 15:3–4; 16:5; 42:6). Aune, *Prophecy in Early Christianity*, 296.
See the extended discussion in David E. Aune, "The *Odes of Solomon* and Early Christian Prophecy," in *Apocalypticism, Prophecy, and Magic in Early Christianity* (Tübingen: Mohr Siebeck, 2006), 320–346.

[57] These include *Odes Sol.* 8:8–21; 10:4–6; 17:6–15; 22:1–12; 28:8–19; 31:6–13;
36:3–8; 41:8–10; 42:3–20. See Aune, "The *Odes of Solomon* and Early Christian Prophecy," 332–334.

[58] Idem, *Prophecy in Early Christianity*, 299.

In addition to the emphasis on revealed knowledge, the *Odes of Solomon* as a whole has a strongly didactic character. References to learning (7:6; 13:2), teaching (3:10; 14:7), knowledge (8:8; 12:3), and truth (1:2; 8:8, 11; 9:8; 11:3, 5; 12:1, 12–13; 14:7; 33:8) are scattered throughout. Blaszczak has identified several of the *Odes* as "odes of instruction" (39; 34; 23:1–4) and suggested that *Odes Sol.* 24 and 23:5–22 are "didactic story odes."[59] Reflecting this didactic emphasis, in *Odes Sol.* 33:8 the "perfect Virgin" calls out to sons and daughters of men using imagery reminiscent of Wisdom calling out in Prov 8: "And I will enter into you, and bring you forth from destruction, and make you wise in the ways of truth."[60] Drijvers refers to the *Odes* as a whole as "didactic poetry of a religious nature."[61] He makes fruitful comparisons between the Jewish-Christian *Odes* and the Jewish Wisdom of Solomon, suggesting that the title ascribing the *Odes* to Solomon is given because of the similarities between the way that true knowledge is received in both writings.[62] Connecting the inspiration of the *Odes* with the didactic emphasis Drijvers explains, "The singer functions as teacher and revealer of God's saving plans for the world which he knows because God's Spirit dwells in him."[63] It is likely that the prophetic and didactic concerns of the *Odes of Solomon* complement one another, with the prophetic speech being supported by the teaching of the *Odes*, and the teaching of the *Odes* being given authority because of the revelatory nature of the *Odes*.

Within the collection a variety of kinds of compositions have been distinguished.[64] Numerous efforts have been made to classify the *Odes*, whether according to Gunkel's Old Testament Psalm *Gattungen*, or a classification scheme that emphasizes the liturgical function of groups of *Odes*.[65] Since our interest in this study is the kinds of instruction conveyed through hymnic compositions, it will be most helpful here to examine *Odes* that have been specifically identified as hymns, but that also have clear di-

---

[59] Gerald R. Blaszczak, *A Formcritical Study of Selected Odes of Solomon* (Harvard Semitic Monographs 36; Atlanta: Scholars Press, 1985), 99.

[60] Except for the translations of *Odes Sol.* 16 and 41 below, translations are taken from James H. Charlesworth, *The Odes of Solomon* (Texts and Translations 13; Missoula, Mont.: Scholars Press for Society of Biblical Literature, 1977).

[61] H. J. W. Drijvers, "Solomon as Teacher: Early Syriac Didactic Poetry," in *IV Symposium Syriacum 1984: Literary Genres in Syriac literature (Groningen – Oosterhesselen, 10–12 September)* (Roma: Pont. Institutum Studiorum Orientalium, 1987), 123–134, here 128.

[62] See the details of the argument in Ibid., 129–134.

[63] Drijvers, "Solomon as Teacher," 128.

[64] Michael Lattke, "Formen/Gattungen in den *Oden Salomos*," in *Die Oden Salomos in ihrer Bedeutung für Neues Testament und Gnosis* (Göttingen: Vandenhoeck & Ruprecht, 1998), 151–159.

[65] Blaszczak, *Formcritical Study*, 4–6.

dactic emphases. Hymns or hymnic portions of *Odes* have been identified in *Odes Sol.* 6, 11, 16, 18, 20, 21, 26, 40, and 41.[66] In this section we will look at two specific hymnic *Odes* with clear didactic tendencies: *Odes Sol.* 16, a hymn that teaches about the works of the Word in creation, and *Odes Sol.* 41 a hymn that addresses the life-giving work of the Savior.

1. Odes of Solomon *16*

Odes of Solomon 16 is a hymn that unfolds in 8 stanzas and focuses on the works of the Word of God.[67] Though this ode may not follow the precise form-critical definition for a hymn in the tradition of the psalms, it surely reflects a hymnic style as it calls itself a hymn (vv. 1, 2, and 4) and has as its focus the recitation of the deeds of God in the context of praise. The first two stanzas begin with the speaker's declaration of intent to praise:

As the work of the ploughman is the plough-share,
And the work of the helmsman the steering of the ship;
So also my work is the psalm of the Lord in his praises.
My skill and my service are in his praises;
Because his love nourished my heart,
And up to my lips it poured forth fruits.
For my love is the Lord;
Because of this I will sing to him.
For I am strengthened in his praises,
And I have faith in him.

I will open my mouth and his Spirit will speak by me;
The glory of the Lord and his beauty,
The work of his hands and the service of his fingers,
The multitude of his mercy and the power of his Word. (vv. 1–7)[68]

The first two stanzas serve as a hymnic introduction to the body of the hymn which goes on to teach about the works of God. Lattke identifies this section as "Hymnologische Selbstbeschreibung" on the part of the singer.[69] In v. 5 we see that the singer sees his work of verbal praise as being inspired by the Spirit, a motif that is common in the *Odes* as we noted above. This opening introduction ends with a reference to the creative power of the Word, suggesting the focus on the Word and creation which will follow in stanzas three to seven.

---

[66] Franzmann, *The Odes of Solomon*, 305–306; Lattke, "Formen/Gattungen in den Oden Salomos," 156; Lattke and Attridge, *Odes of Solomon*, 15.

[67] See the extensive commentary on this ode in Lattke and Attridge, *Odes of Solomon*, 217–232.

[68] Translations of *Odes Sol.* 16 and 41 adapted from Franzmann, *The Odes of Solomon*. Line 6 from Blaszczak, *Formcritical Study*.

[69] Michael Lattke, *Oden Salomos: Text, Übersetzung, Kommentar. Teil 2. Oden 15–28* (NTOA 41/2; Göttingen: Vandenhoeck & Ruprecht, 2001), 20.

In the second major section of the poem (vv. 8–20) we encounter what Blaszczak calls a "longer didactic poem,"[70] and what Lattke refers to as "a didactic poem on aspects of creation."[71] Stanza four, picking up on the antecedent "the Word of the Lord" from the third stanza, begins the instructional portion and declares:

He himself spread the land out widely and placed the waters in the sea;
He stretched out the heaven and fixed the stars;
And he fixed the creation and set it up.
And he was at rest from his works. (vv. 10–12)

In language strongly reminiscent of the Johannine prologue, the seventh stanza reads:

And there is nothing outside of the Lord,
Because he himself was before everything was.
And the aeons were by his Word,
And by the thought of his heart. (vv. 18–19)

Lattke refers to these stanzas on creation as a "Schopfungslehre," a component of several other odes as well.[72] Blaszczak refers to the entire section of vv. 18–20 as a didactic poem.[73] The hymn closes with a doxology similar to what is found at the end of *Odes Sol.* 11, 17, 18, and 20:

Glory and honour to his name.
Allelluia. (v. 20)

Similarities to the prologue of John were mentioned above and have been noted by scholars for decades.[74] Charlesworth notes that the "he" in line 10 refers back to the Word so that lines 10–19 reflect the thought pattern of John 1:1–18 with the preexistent word, God's agent of creation who was identified with light. He connects vv. 18–19 with John 1:1–3 in particular.[75] Other connections between the Johannine prologue and the *Odes of Solomon* have been identified as well.[76]

Another important angle of comparison is between this ode and some of the ideas found in other second-century hymns, particularly the *Hymn to*

---

[70] Blaszczak, *Formcritical Study*, 29–30.

[71] Lattke and Attridge, *Odes of Solomon*, 223.

[72] Cf. *Odes Sol.* 4:15; 7:8–9, 24; 8:18–20b (Lattke, "Formen/Gattungen in den *Oden Salomos*," 158).

[73] Blaszczak, *Formcritical Study*, 29–30.

[74] Cf. Ibid., 38–39.

[75] Charlesworth, *The Odes of Solomon*, 72–73.

[76] See James H. Charlesworth and R. Alan Culpepper, "The Odes of Solomon and the Gospel of John," *CBQ* 35 (1973): 298–322, esp. 300–315; Jack T. Sanders, *The New Testament Christological Hymns: Their Historical Religious Background* (SNTSMS 15; Cambridge: Cambridge University Press, 1971), 101–104.

Christ the Savior of Clement of Alexandria.[77] For example, both the image of the ploughman and the helmsman in *Odes Sol.* 16:1 are found in Clement's hymn (lines 3 and 19). Likewise, the appropriateness of the response of praise is emphasized in both compositions (Clement, lines 7–9, 40, 54–66). Clement calls Christ "the Word" (lines 12, 30, 35, 51). The Spirit is mentioned in both compositions as well (Clement, line 53; *Odes Sol.* 16:5). Mercy is an attribute of the word (Clement, line 38). Outside of this ode, references to breast-milk (e.g., *Odes Sol.* 19; 35:5) connect with similar imagery in lines 42–53 of Clement's hymn.

While the similarities are instructive, so are the differences between these two songs. *Odes Sol.* 16 is spoken by an individual and addressed to the community, not directly to the Lord who is the subject. Clement's hymn is addressed to Christ, until in line 54 the author turns to exhort the community to join in praise. Further, in Clement's hymn the address is specifically to Christ, who is named throughout. In this ode, Christ is not named, as is the case with the rest of the *Odes of Solomon* as well. As we have seen, this was the case with some other earlier christological hymns as well (Col 1:15–20; 1Tim 3:16; Ign. *Eph.* 19:2–3).

2. Odes of Solomon *41*

Turning our focus to *Odes Sol.* 41, we can note that it has a similar structure to *Odes Sol.* 16 with an opening section of praise (stanzas 1–3), a teaching section (stanza 5), and a closing doxology (stanza 6). Unlike *Odes Sol.* 16 it also includes a stanza that is understood to be the word of Christ to the community (stanza 4; vv. 8–10). The particular focus of the teaching of this hymn is on the Savior and his work including his work in history from the present back to pre-creation (stanza 5).

Here we may consider the christological teaching of this ode which is made explicit in the fifth stanza:

And his Word (is) with us in all our way;
The saviour who gives life,
and does not reject our souls;
the man who humbled himself,
and was lifted up by his own righteousness.
The Son of the Most High was seen
in the perfection of his Father.
And light sprang forth from the Word,
the one who was before in him.
The Messiah in truth is one.
And he was known before the foundation of the world,
that he might give life to souls forever by the truth of his name. (vv. 11–16a)

---

[77] *Paed.* 3.12.101.4. See below.

This short passage shows a number of close connections with New Testament hymns and descriptions of Christ.[78] Charlesworth noted the affinity of v. 12 ("The man who humbled himself, but was exalted because of his own righteousness") with the similar manner of speaking about Christ in the Philippian hymn.[79] We may note also the way that line provides a paradoxical contrast similar to what we observed in Ign. *Eph.* 7:2 and Ign. *Pol.* 3:2 above. The difference here is that this paradox is only one aspect of the whole stanza; paradoxical contrasts are not the primary focus here as they were in those two Ignatian hymnic confessions. Also similar to what we find in Ignatius is the emphasis on life noticeable in the second and in the last lines of the fifth stanza. In the Star Hymn of Ignatius we saw that the whole purpose of the incarnation was "to bring newness of eternal life" (Ign. *Eph.* 19:3).

Connections with the Johannine prologue are again apparent in this ode (children; appearance of the son; eternal preexistence; light; grace and truth; etc.). The idea that the savior "gives life" and "does not reject" is reflected in a similar way in John 6:33, 37. The idea that the savior existed before the foundation of the world is echoed in the Johannine prologue as well as in John 17:5 and 17:24.[80] The hymns in Ignatius do not emphasize the preexistence of Christ, but the paradoxical contrasts of Ign. *Pol.* 3:2 do refer to Christ as "above time" and "non-temporal."

Love is emphasized in *Odes Sol.* 41:2, 6, and 16. Interestingly, the odist appears to echo and revise Ps 1:2, replacing the "law" with "his love" (v. 6). By adapting an earlier psalm, the author reveals a primary emphasis of his teaching in this hymn.

Of particular interest here is the way that *Odes Sol.* 41 begins with the present and moves back in time with each successive verse, tapping into multiple temporal registers as part of the hymn's didactic strategy. For the present community the Word is present with them, the savior who gives life and will not reject them (v. 11). Verse 12 goes back to refer to the death and resurrection of the savior who was humbled and exalted. Verse 13 goes back further to refer to the incarnation of the son. Verse 14 goes back to the time of the creation of light by a word (cf. Gen 1:3 and John 1:4–5). Verse 15 indicates that the one Messiah was known even before the foundation of the world (cf. Gen 1:1–2 and John 1:1–3; 17:5, 24). The conclusion of this review of the work of the savior in history is that all of

---

[78] Lattke and Attridge, *Odes of Solomon*, 576–581. Lattke goes so far as to note, "If the third part of *Ode* 41 had made its way into the New Testament there would hardly be a voice raised in objection" (576). For further connections with the New Testament see Lattke's analysis of the entire ode on pp. 565–581.

[79] Charlesworth, *The Odes of Solomon*, 142–143.

[80] Charlesworth and Culpepper, "The Odes of Solomon and the Gospel of John," 309.

this happened for the purpose of giving eternal life by the truth of his name (cf. John 1:4; 3:16; 20:31).

If this chronological reading is correct, then vv. 11–16 of *Odes Sol.* 41 provides a chronological hymnic reflection related to the Messiah and his life-giving and light-giving work. Unlike earlier Christian hymns that reviewed history from the past to the present (e.g., Col 1:15–20; John 1:1–18; Phil 2:5–11; Ign. *Eph.* 19:2–3; the Naassene psalm) this one works backwards from the present to the pre-creation past. This dynamic thus marks a unique development in the composition of hymns that convey christological instruction.

Comparing *Odes Sol.* 41 to Clement's *Hymn to Christ the Savior*, we can immediately note some similarities. In both compositions the followers of Christ are children (*Odes Sol.* 41:2) and babes (*Odes Sol.* 41:1). Also as with Clement's hymn, praise is the fitting response to his love (*Odes Sol.* 41:5–7). Nevertheless, as we will see below, Clement's hymn moves well beyond the earlier hymns (including *Odes Sol.* 41) as it employs new imagery for the relationship of Christ to his children.

Both of these didactic hymns (*Odes Sol.* 16 and 41) emphasize the deeds and works of the Word, his existence before the foundation of the world, the fitting response of praise, and the love of the Lord. Unlike Clement's hymn there is little concern with ethical teaching, holy living, or other aspects of Christian life outside of the presentation of the identity and works of the Word. Ethical concerns are addressed in several other *Odes of Solomon* (e.g., 20:5–8) but do not suggest themselves as a prominent theme of the *Odes*.[81]

This brief review of two of the *Odes* highlights the fact that the *Odes of Solomon* do indeed have a didactic emphasis. Of the songs in this collection that might be considered didactic hymns (whether formally or through their contents and style) much of their teaching appears to center around the savior and his deeds, especially within the context of revelatory speech. If scholars were able to identify an original setting with greater certainty, there would be immense value in considering how the remembrance of the savior in these specific ways contributed to the needs facing the community responsible for these *Odes*. For example, if Charlesworth is correct in associating the *Odes* with the same community that produced the Gospel of John, then a closer comparison of themes in the Johannine hymn and the *Odes* might shed further light on issues facing Christians in that community at the end of the first century and beginning of the second century. On the other hand, if Drijvers is correct in placing the *Odes* in the third century and seeing them as originating in the same area as the Coptic Manichaean Psalm-Book, then the teaching of some of the *Odes* could be read in di-

---

[81] For ethical concerns of the *Odes* see Charlesworth, *OTP* II, 730–731.

rect in opposition to the teaching of Mani.[82] Since we cannot adjudicate that debated issue here, we will simply note that the dispute itself attests to our lack of solid information about second-century Christian movements. Nevertheless, it is certainly of value to observe the way that one Christian group quite skillfully continued the first-century Christian practice of teaching through psalms, hymns, and spiritual odes.

E. Clement of Alexandria's *Hymn to Christ the Savior*

As we have seen, there is no question that Christians in the second century continued the first-century New Testament practice of singing psalms, hymns, and spiritual songs. Clement of Alexandria (ca.150–220 CE) reminds us of this fact in book seven of the *Stromata* where he discusses the prayer and praise habits of believers who praise as they plow and sing hymns as they sail (*Strom.* 7.7.35.6). Likewise he exhorts Christians in *To the Newly Baptized* to make time for prayers and hymns to God, and to take delight in divine words and hymns.[83] In the *Paedagogus* he cautions Christians to sing psalms and hymns to God in appropriate ways – ways that contrast with the musical customs of the Greeks and Romans (*Paed.* 2.4.43.1–44.5).[84] While we are certain that the composing, singing, and reciting of songs of praise continued in the second century, we have very few representatives of these songs that would allow us to say much about the nature of Christian hymnody in this period. One hymn that has survived from the end of the second century (dating to ca. 190 CE) is a *Hymn to Christ the Savior* that comes to us in the manuscripts of Clement's *Paedagogus* (3.12.101.4). In this section we will examine the hymn in light of earlier hymnic traditions with particular regard to its form, contents and function. A look at these aspects of the hymn will allow us to say something of the didactic qualities of this hymn.

Clement of Alexandria was facing some unique challenges in Alexandria at the end of the second century.[85] Representing an earlier generation

---

[82] Drijvers, "Odes of Solomon and Psalms of Mani," 129–130.

[83] Clement, "To the Newly Baptized," in *Clement of Alexandria* (trans. G.W. Butterworth; Cambridge, Mass.: Harvard University Press, 1979), 368–377, 375.

[84] For a full discussion of musical imagery and thought in Clement see Charles H. Cosgrove, "Clement of Alexandria and Early Christian Music," *JECS* 14 (2006): 255–282.

[85] For the issues in Alexandria see Eric Francis Osborn, *Clement of Alexandria* (Cambridge: Cambridge University Press, 2005), 1–23. See also the discussions in John Ferguson, "Introduction," in *Stromateis. Books 1–3* (trans. John Ferguson; Washington, D.C.: Catholic University of America Press, 1991), 3–19, esp. 4–10, and Moreschini and Norelli, *Early Christian Greek and Latin Literature*, 1:248–267.

of scholarship, Henry Chadwick noted, "Alexandrian Christianity before his time is shrouded in mist, but what evidence there is suggests the powerful influence of gnostic thought and a tendency for the dividing line between heresy and orthodoxy to be less clearly drawn in Egypt than in Italy or Asia Minor."[86] Though it is commonplace nowadays to question the appropriateness of the terms orthodoxy and heresy in this time period, it is nevertheless clear that in Clement's day there were contested understandings of what the Christian life was about. As a Christian teacher in Alexandria, Clement aimed to show that his vision of the Christian faith was authoritative and authentic, while other competing versions, notably those of the Gnostics, were not legitimate.[87] In Clement's own writings we can see that he was addressing challenges from at least two distinct groups, but probably more.[88] Within the Christian community were those who were "orthodox" but not highly intelligent.[89] These were perhaps resistant to philosophical reflection and education, and needed to be spurred on toward a greater understanding of their faith as a means of growing in the knowledge of Christ. A different challenge came from the Gnostics: "On the other side stand educated Christians deeply influenced and attracted by Valentinian Gnosticism with its generous fusion of Christianity, Platonism, and almost everything else as well."[90] In this context Clement aimed to show that the believer in Christ who accepted the traditions of the apostles was the true gnostic.[91]

---

[86] Henry Chadwick, *Early Christian Thought and the Classical Tradition: Studies in Justin, Clement, and Origen* (Oxford: Clarendon Press, 1966 repr. 1984), 33.

[87] See for example, Denise Kimber Buell, *Making Christians: Clement of Alexandria and the Rhetoric of Legitimacy* (Princeton: Princeton University Press, 1999), 12. She writes, "Clement employs language that naturalizes and authorizes his own speaking position, while also differentiating him from his competitors. Specifically, he asserts himself as a rightful heir to a tradition of knowledge and interpretation that he depicts as having emerged from a single source" (12).

[88] Ronald Heine notes four specific groups that Clement appears to address in the course of his writings. Ronald E. Heine, "The Alexandrians," in *The Cambridge History of Early Christian Literature* (ed. Frances M. Young, Lewis Ayres, and Andrew Louth; Cambridge: Cambridge University Press, 2004), 117–130, here 119. On the make-up of the Christian community in Alexandria see Osborn, *Clement of Alexandria*, 22–23.

[89] See the discussion in *Strom.* 1.43–45 (GCS 15); Clement refers to the orthodox believers in 1.45.6 (GCS 15).

[90] Chadwick, *Early Christian Thought*, 34.

[91] Along these lines see *Strom.* 7, esp. 104.2 (GCS 17): "The life of the Gnostic is in my view no other than works and words which correspond to the tradition of the Lord." Rudolph cites this verse and explains that Clement "sought to take up in a positive way the legitimate concerns of Gnosis and to reconcile them with the basic Christian affirmations in an original fashion" (16). In this sense Clement attempted to not only deny the claims of false gnosis, but to use gnosis in a positive sense meaning "Christian knowledge of truth" (Rudolph, *Gnosis: The Nature and History of Gnosticism*, 16). On

Clement's only known hymn, the *Hymn to Christ the Savior*, is found at the end of the *Paedagogus*, a treatise for young Christians on the subject of learning from Christ the instructor regarding Christian faith and conduct.[92] That the epilogue to this work is a hymn is clear from several indicators. First, in the manuscripts it is called a hymn in its title. Second, the hymn is carefully composed in Greek meter. Third, its contents include several calls to Christians to join in praising Christ. Fourth, it includes a number of series of epithets and poetic descriptions of Christ which reflect the traditional language of earlier Greek poems and hymns.[93]

The *Hymn to Christ the Savior* is a sixty-six line metrical Greek hymn that addresses Christ directly with multiple epithets and requests, and ends with a series of exhortations to the congregation. The hymn may be analyzed as a well-balanced collection of couplets of anapestic lines, which have a rather free character and may reflect a semi-popular feel.[94] The *Hymn* is thus quite different from the earliest Christian hymnody we encountered in the New Testament where the hymnic style reflected to a large extent the Jewish tradition of psalmody. Clement's *Hymn* reflects more directly the influence and impact of Greek hymnody both in its form as well as its expressions. While some scholars in the past have argued that the form and content can be differentiated and shown to reflect two distinct worldviews, more recent scholarship has maintained that the hymn is a witness to the complex inter-relationship of Greek and biblical elements.[95] Accordingly, it is not merely the case that Clement expresses biblical ideas in Greek hymnic form. Rather, as part of Clement's larger theological program, the hymn is representative of the ways that biblical truth is reflected in the manner of expression of the Greek poets and philosophers.[96] Further,

---

this idea see the comments by Marrou in his introduction to Clement, *Le Pédagogue: Livre I* (trans. Marguerite Harl; introduction and notes by Henri-Irénée Marrou; SC 70; Paris: Éditions du Cerf, 1983), 29–34.

[92] GCS 12:291–292. The fact that the hymn is missing from one of the primary manuscripts of *Paedagogus* leads some scholars to question whether the hymn is a secondary addition. See the summary and discussion in Cosgrove, "Clement of Alexandria and Early Christian Music," 266–268. The present study interprets the hymn in its current literary context.

[93] For a fuller development of these points, see the commentary and discussion by Marrou in Clement, *Le Pédagogue: Livre III* (trans. Claude Mondesert and Chantal Matray; notes by Henri-Irenee Marrou.; SC 158; Paris: Éditions du Cerf, 1970), 257–273; Gerhard May, "Der Christushymnus des Clemens von Alexandrien," *Liturgie und Dichtung* 1 (1983): 257–273; Annewies van den Hoek, "Hymn of the Holy Clement to Christ the Saviour," in *Prayer from Alexander to Constantine: A Critical Anthology* (ed. Mark Christopher Kiley; London: Routledge, 1997), 296–303.

[94] Clement, *Le Pédagogue: Livre III*, 204.

[95] May, "Christushymnus," 260.

[96] Ibid., 258.

the hymn points to Clement's social setting as it reflects some of the characteristics of second-century Gnostic hymns.[97] In view of this complexity we will see that the form of the early Christian hymn has developed to serve a different function in Clement than in the New Testament, and that its contents also reflect that new purpose.

The opening lines of the hymn reveal just how different this is compared with the Johannine prologue or other New Testament Christological hymns:

Bridle-bit of foals unschooled in worldly ways
Wing of birds that do not go astray
Sure rudder-handle of ships
Shepherd of royal lambs
Gather together
Your simple children
To sing praise in a holy way
To hymn – in a guileless way
With innocent mouths –
Christ, guide of children. (lines 1–10)[98]

While one of the latest New Testament hymns, the Johannine prologue, begins in the beginning (John 1:1), Clement begins with poetic imagery reflecting the present moment where Christians may be gathering for worship. While John focused primarily on the work of the Logos in the past, Clement's descriptive epithets for Christ have their focus on the present aspect of the relationship between Christ and the believer. Christ actively guides, shepherds, and directs his children. The remainder of the hymn develops in a similar manner as these initial epithets are developed further and as new epithets and images are introduced.

Though scholars agree that Clement (or some other early Christian) has written this metrical hymn in a Greek style, there is no agreement as to the precise structure of the hymn.[99] Part of the difficulty lies in the way that imagery introduced earlier in the hymn is taken up and expanded on later in the hymn, so that it is possible to show that each of the distinct sections are still closely connected. Thus Wolbergs, for example, divides the hymn into two main sections (lines 1–32 and 33–66). The outline I provide here is based primarily on the implicit functions and the explicit themes that change in some way from one section to the next, resulting in seven distinct but inter-connected strophes:

---

[97] Wolbergs, *Griechische religiöse Gedichte*, 84.

[98] Translation is mine based on the Greek text in SC 158.

[99] Ferguson, Marrou, and May each propose different outlines, and point to still other possibilities as well. Clement, *Le Pédagogue: Livre III*, 206–207; John Ferguson, *Clement of Alexandria* (New York: Twayne Publishers, 1974), 105; May, "Christushymnus," 263.

First Strophe (1–10): Invocation
Second Strophe (11–18): Epithets in praise of Christ
Third Strophe (19–28): Epithets and descriptive interlude
Fourth Strophe (29–34): Prayer to the Holy Shepherd
Fifth Strophe (35–41): Epithets in praise of Christ
Sixth Strophe (42–53): Epithet and descriptive interlude
Seventh Strophe (54–66): Triple exhortation

Even if Clement did not compose this with seven distinct strophes in mind, it is still clear that each of these divisions represents a shift in subject matter, emphasis, or addressee. For our purposes, in addition to seeing how the hymn develops over these strophes, it is also significant to note what is absent from this hymn: there is no reference to any aspect of the narrative about Christ that is so prominent in the New Testament christological hymns. One looks in vain for references to the incarnation, the cross, or the resurrection. Instead, the focus is on expressing praise to Christ through imagery and metaphors that capture the current relationship of Christ to his people. It will be useful here to examine the strophes in a little more detail to note the kinds of imagery that Clement utilizes as this hymn unfolds.

As we have seen, the first strophe begins with a series of epithets in praise of Christ (lines 1–4), followed by a request that he gather his children that they may sing praise to him (lines 5–10). The epithets in 1–4 are varied and can each be traced to Clement's discussion about Christians as the children needing to be educated in chapter five of book one of the *Paedagogus*. There Clement discusses the notion that Christians are referred to in Scripture by a number of images including colts, birds, lambs, and children.[100] Each of these images can also be traced to philosophical writings.[101] Taken together the epithets point to the supremacy of the Logos on earth, in heaven, and in the deep.[102] Christ is not identified, however, until line 10 where he is hailed as "Christ, the guide of children." In this epithet we see a striking instance of Clement's use of pagan motifs for his own Christian purposes. Marrou notes that this epithet is used by Homer and also applied as an epithet to Zeus, Apollo, and Aphrodite. At the same time the expression is a poetic equivalent of the term *paidagogos*, thus

---

[100] On the Christians as children see *Paed.* 1.5.12.1–13.4. On the children of Christ as birds see *Paed.* 1.5.14.3–5 where Clement cites Matt 23:37: "In that sense we are young birds, a name which graphically and mystically describes the simplicity of soul belonging to childhood" (14.5). On Christians being described under the figure of a colt see *Paed.* 1.5.15.1–3 where Clement cites Zech 9:9 and Gen 49:11. On Christians as lambs Clement cites Isa 40:11 explaining, "Once again he uses the more innocent class of sheep, lambs, as a figure for simplicity" (*Paed.* 1.5.15.4). Clement will draw on the characteristics of these animals, particularly guilelessness and simplicity, in the *Hymn* in lines 9 and 60.
[101] Wolbergs, *Griechische religiöse Gedichte*, 86–88.
[102] May, "Christushymnus," 265–266.

connecting the hymn closely to the work that precedes it.[103] In the first strophe then, Christ is hailed using a variety of epithets which resonate with Greek hymnic traditions as well as with book one of the *Paedagogus*, culminating in his being named as the guide of children. The request in this first strophe is that Christ would gather his children to offer pure and sincere praise to Christ.

The second strophe develops the kingly imagery that was hinted at in line 4 where Christ was hailed as "shepherd of royal lambs." In line 11 Christ is called the "King of saints," an expression not found in the New Testament but certainly derived from the New Testament use of kingly imagery for Christ.[104] The kingship of Christ will be a recurring motif of the hymn (cf. lines 31 and 55). The second strophe also introduces new concepts into the hymn. The term *pandamator* in line 12 ("all-taming word") is one of several expressions that reflect Clement's intentional use of Greek poetic style.[105] The term is used by Homer, though not in the Homeric Hymns.[106] The expression also introduces the idea of Christ as the Logos, which will be reflected later in lines 30 and 51. In line 14 Christ is "ruler of wisdom," an expression in line with Clement's earlier discussions about Christ as the Wisdom of the Father (*Paed.* 1.2.6.2; 1.11.97.3; 3.12.98.1) and expressing the development of a Pauline idea (cf. Col 2:3). Wisdom likewise figures later in the hymn (line 47).

As was the case with the second strophe, the third strophe also returns to imagery introduced in the first strophe mentioning helm, bridle, heavenly wing in sequence before moving on to a new image: Christ as fisher of men (line 24). Though not a prominent image for Clement, he does use this metaphor in *Paed.* 3.12.99.2 where man is caught as though he were a fish, and it is the Logos who fashions the rod. The unique feature of this strophe is that it moves from a list of epithets to a description of one of the deeds of Christ. He saves the fish from the sea of evil and lures them with the promise of life (lines 24–28). It is here that we find a glimpse of the teaching of the hymn as this image of fisher of men is unpacked to a small extent. May suggests that Clement applies the image of fisher of men directly to the Logos, noting that he leads men to the truth in many ways (cf. *Strom.* 7.95.3).[107] Wolbergs points to the use of the concept in Greek phi-

---

[103] Clement, *Le Pédagogue: Livre III*, 194.

[104] May, "Christushymnus," 266. The image does not figure prominently in the *Paedagogus*, though Christ is identified as king in *Paed.* 2.8.73.3–6. Cf. *Strom.* 1.159.5–6 where Clement refers to "Christ our king," citing part of the Philippian hymn (Phil 2:10–11).

[105] Ibid.

[106] *Il.* 24.5; *Od.* 9.373.

[107] May, "Christushymnus," 267.

losophers and poets as well as in the Hebrew Bible (cf. Hab 1:14).[108] Regardless of the ways it may have resonated with Greek readers, the image strongly suggests two clear teachings: 1) that the world is hostile and evil, and 2) that Christ saves his children from that environment offering them something better, namely, life. The concept of "life" is referenced twice more in the later strophes of the hymn (lines 40 and 59). As we have observed, the life-giving work of Christ has been a repeated theme in second-century christological hymns.[109]

It is interesting to note the wide range of imagery and epithets that are used thus far in the hymn. At the same time it is fascinating to see how Clement introduces key concepts and expressions that he will allude to later in the hymn: shepherd, king, Logos, wisdom, and life. Though he developed the fisher of men imagery more than others, this is one image that is not reiterated later in the hymn. However, the "life" which Christ offers these fish is referred to again in line 59 as the "teaching of life."

The fourth strophe returns to the shepherd imagery introduced in the first strophe. In direct address the singer asks the shepherd and king to lead the children on the path marked out by Christ, which is the path to heaven.

Holy shepherd
of sheep of the *Logos*,
lead, O king,
the unharmed children;
the footprints of Christ,
are the path to heaven. (lines 29–34)[110]

May suggests that this prayer is the central aspect of the hymn, as the guiding of the Logos is the central teaching of the *Paedagogus* as a whole.[111] In spite of textual difficulties and proposed emendations,[112] the prayer calls for the king, Christ, to lead his children on the path to heaven, and metaphorically, to lead the sheep of the Logos (or the rational sheep), as a shepherd leads his sheep. Here Clement connects the imagery of children and sheep earlier in the hymn (lines 3–5), and also earlier in the *Paedagogus* (cf. *Paed.* 1.5.14.1–2). We can note here in particular *Paed.* 1.4.11.2 where Clement cites Plato (*Laws* VII 808D) on the need of sheep for a shepherd and children for a *paidagogos*. As the central strophe of the

---

[108] Wolbergs, *Griechische religiöse Gedichte*, 91–92. He also suggests a baptismal overtone.

[109] Cf. Ign. *Eph.* 19:3; *Odes Sol.* 41:11–16a.

[110] Translations of Clement's hymn from this point on are from van den Hoek, "Hymn of the Holy Clement," 296–297.

[111] May, "Christushymnus," 267.

[112] See a variety of views in Clement, *Le Pédagogue: Livre III*, 196; May, "Christushymnus," 267; Wolbergs, *Griechische religiöse Gedichte*, 11.

hymn, this prayer encapsulates the desire of Clement that Christians be led in the education that only Christ offers, an education leading to heaven.

The fifth strophe returns to the style of praise through epithets. Marrou points out the subtle play between nominative and vocative, as the hymn opens with the vocative and continues in this manner through line 28. After the prayer in the fourth strophe, the fifth strophe switches to the nominative case.

Ever-flowing word,
unlimited age,
everlasting light,
source of mercy,
artisan of virtue
of those who praise God
with their holy life. (lines 35–41)

After this the sixth strophe will return to the vocative with Christ Jesus in line 42.[113] While lines 35–36 continue the theme of eternal life referenced in lines 26 and 34, Marrou suggests they may also represent a philosophical explication of the first verse of the Logos hymn, John 1:1. May sees these lines as a statement that responds to Gnostic thought regarding the Aeon. Here Clement claims not only that the Logos is eternal but also that the Logos himself is the Aeon (line 36).[114] Further, in this strophe the Logos is also divine light (cf. *Paed.* 1.28.2).[115] The strophe ends, however, with a focus on what the children of the Logos do, hymning God with their lives. This picks up the image from strophe one (lines 7–10), an idea which will be the focus of the exhortations in strophe seven.

The sixth strophe (lines 42–53) introduces another new image into the hymn: the idea that Christ Jesus is heavenly milk that nurtures the infants.

Christ Jesus,
heavenly milk
pressed from the sweet breasts
of the bride,
gracious gifts
of your wisdom.
The tiny infants
with tender mouths,
suckled
at the nipple of the *logos*
and filled
with the dewy Spirit. (lines 42–53)

---

[113] Clement, *Le Pédagogue: Livre III*, 198, 206.

[114] May, "Christushymnus," 268.

[115] Wolbergs points to this understanding in the NT, Wisdom of Solomon, and elsewhere in Clement (Wolbergs, *Griechische religiöse Gedichte*, 94).

While new to the hymn that concludes the *Paedagogus*, the concept is hardly new to the larger composition. Chapter six of book one (*Paed.* 1.6.34.3–52.3) contains an extended discussion of the milk of the Word drawing extensively on passages such as 1 Cor 3:1–2, Exod 3:8, 17, John 6:57, and 1 Peter 2:1–3. Similar imagery is found in the *Odes of Solomon* as well.[116] Buell explores Clement's use of lactation imagery in light of other ancient discussions of the practice, noting its use as a metaphor for both salvation and character formation. She claims, "In developing this metaphor of nursing to depict the activity of the divine toward Christians, Clement resonates with traditions known to virtually everyone in his audience, whether through religious iconography, literature, or discussions of *paideia*."[117] Though the imagery was widely known, Buell's study shows that Clement's specific application of the metaphor to the Logos and the process of Christian instruction is unique to his context and is in implicit competition with other understandings of the Christian life.[118] This metaphor is a complex one and, as May points out, the milk is understood by Clement as the Logos himself in some of his discussions or the teaching and proclamation of the Church in other places.[119] In fact, Clement can use lactation imagery for a number of different purposes within his larger project. Though a full discussion of this motif goes beyond the scope of the present study, for our purposes here it is important to note two points. First, the imagery was widespread in the second century and so would have been appreciated by Clement's audience. Second, the inclusion of this kind of language in the hymn in condensed form relates to an extensive discussion of the topic elsewhere in the *Paedagogus*.[120]

The final strophe (lines 54–66) consists of three exhortations directed to the Christian audience using a variety of images. They are called to sing together to Christ the king (lines 54–55), to escort the son as a mighty chorus (lines 60–63), and to "sing songs together to the God of peace" (lines 65–66). As Clement suggests in the *Paedagogus* and elsewhere, this simple and pure praise of God and Christ are the obligation of those who have been instructed by the Logos.

Having sketched the contents we can now consider the purpose of this fascinating hymn. The original function of the hymn is debated, as there is no witness to the hymn's use in Clement's day. In this regard, our discussion of function is similar to the discussion about the function of Cle-

---

[116] Cf. *Odes Sol.* 8:14; 19:1–5.

[117] Buell, *Making Christians*, 127.

[118] See Buell's extended discussion of *Paed.* 1.34.3–1.50.2 on pp. 119–179.

[119] May, "Christushymnus," 270.

[120] See *Odes Sol.* 8:14 and 19:1–4 for other second century hymns that employ images of nurture through breast milk.

anthes' *Hymn to Zeus*, a composition that, in the form of praise, presented key precepts of the philosophical program and at the same time made requests of the deity culminating in the call to praise. As we saw with the *Hymn to Zeus* one can imagine some of the ways these hymns may have been used in their communities, but the results must necessarily be hypothetical. Still, in the case of Clement's *Hymn to Christ the Savior* it is most likely that the hymn was used in some kind of a communal setting. Its contents, which very directly refer to the act of singing and praising on behalf of the followers of Christ, suggest that the hymn was not merely literary ornamentation for Clement's *Paedagogus*.[121]

As far as the strategy of the hymn and the way it conveys its teaching, a few more comments can be made. First, as the conclusion to the *Paedagogus* we have seen that the *Hymn to Christ the Savior* expresses many of the central ideas of the larger work, particularly as it uses specific phrases and images that were critical to the larger composition. In light of the larger composition the didactic and instructional aspects of the hymn can be much more clearly seen. Second, in light of this, the hymn can be seen as a hymnic summary of the teaching of the *Paedagogus*. Though it does not capture every aspect of the larger composition, it strikes the central chords of the work as it praises Christ, asking him to lead his children, and as it exhorts the children to bring sincere and pure praise to the one who has saved and nourished them. Third, since the hymn is marked by the piling up of descriptive epithets rather than narrative or even expository sections, the teaching of the hymn is somewhat unique. Rather than focusing on the deeds of Christ in the past, the hymn focuses on the relationship of the individual child or collective group of children to the Instructor in the present. The imagery suggests the ways that Christ relates to his children, and also the appropriate response of his children to Christ. Christ leads, rescues, guides, tames, shepherds, and so forth. His children are marked by simplicity, holiness, artlessness, and wisdom with the result that they sing hymns and psalms of praise to Christ. The *Hymn to Christ the Savior* also teaches the value of appropriate songs of praise, even as Clement discussed these in *Paed.* 2.4.43.1–44.4. But as the hymn moves beyond the model of early Jewish psalms and the model of the New Testament, it shows how the educated Greek believer can offer up songs of praise in a fitting way that draws on the best of Greek, Jewish, and Christian thought.

We are unaware of whether or not Clement wrote other hymns or songs. Having other hymns with which to compare this one would enable many more fruitful conclusions about the development of early Christian hymnody in Alexandria. Nevertheless, in this one passage we see a vivid testimony to one early Christian's quest to express his teaching in light of the

---

[121] May, "Christushymnus," 263–265.

best of Greek culture. Along these lines Robert Wilken wrote, "Among early Christian writers Clement is the most Greek, the most literary, a savant so immersed in the high culture of the Hellenistic world that he effortlessly cited hundreds of passages from poets, philosophers, playwrights, and historians in his writings."[122] In these few verses of the *Hymn to Christ the Savior* we can see evidence of the creativity and breadth of Clement, who could draw on such a wide range of ideas and styles to compose a simple yet profound hymn in praise of Christ.

F. Conclusions

Though our evidence is limited, it is clear that the Christian hymnody of the second century indicates an increasing level of sophistication among the poets and teachers who composed and used this medium of instruction and reflection. This claim is suggested first of all by the greater instances of the use philosophical terminology together with Hellenistic philosophical styles of expression (e.g., the paradoxes of Ign. *Eph.* 7:2 and the negative theology of Ign. *Pol.* 3:2). Second, it is suggested by the move to compose poems in Greek meter (as seen in the Gnostic hymns and in Clement of Alexandria's *Hymn to Christ the Savior*). Third, it is seen in a move beyond the simpler contents of the christological hymns of the New Testament, while at the same time continuing to develop further the kinds of specific issues they raised (e.g., cosmology, the incarnation, the effects of the redemptive work of Christ, etc.). Along with the increasing sophistication of second-century Christian hymnody and its didactic emphases, the practice of singing hymns of praise continued in full force among Christian communities of diverse beliefs. The preservation of one particular hymnbook, the *Odes of Solomon*, illustrates both the devout and joyous nature of hymnic praise, as well as the development of christological and theological thought that occurred in the second century CE.

The second-century Christian didactic hymns we have examined confirm once again the perceived effectiveness of hymnic praise to convey truth to human audiences. Particularly in the context of the developing christologies of the second century, hymnic reflection about Christ and hymnic description of his redemptive work was a fruitful means of theological expression as well as a useful tool for passing on one's teaching.[123] It was also a useful tool for assessing and evaluating the teaching of others,

---

[122] Robert Louis Wilken, *The Spirit of Early Christian Thought: Seeking the Face of God* (New Haven: Yale University Press, 2003), 54.

[123] Cf. the quote preserved in Eusebius (*Hist. eccl.* 5.28.5) and cited at the beginning of this chapter.

as the citations and comments in the third-century writings of Hippolytus make clear.

Chapter 11

Didactic Hymns and the Communities
that Treasured Them

As a kind of discourse that bridges the world of the human and the divine, hymns, psalms, and prayers manifest multiple and complex communicative dynamics. On the one hand, any hymn can communicate praise (or thanks or requests) to the god or exalted human who is the subject of that composition. On the other hand, that same hymn can also communicate messages to the human audience that hears, recites, or reads it. In this latter sense, one can examine almost any hymn and consider what it conveys about the one being praised, the nature of the task of praise, or the nature and needs of the community offering the praise. The present study, however, has focused on a subset of ancient psalms, hymns, and prayers: those for which the element of teaching and instructing a human audience was a primary focus. These texts were both hymnically styled and oriented around instruction. We have referred to these throughout as didactic hymns, a shorthand term for hymns, prayers and religious poetry that, through their contents and contexts, reflect a concern for shaping the perceptions of an earthly audience.

This extensive survey of didactic hymns in antiquity has shown that, for Greeks, Romans, Jews and Christians, didactic hymns provided a way of viewing events, circumstances, and oneself (individually or communally) in the context of a larger view of reality. They invited their audiences to embrace a particular picture of the world as a means of understanding the reader's place in that world. In this way they can be said to have played a role in the process of formation of communal identity. To facilitate the reinforcement of a particular communal identity, didactic hymns drew on well-understood traditions of praise to create a verbal portrait of a reality that was larger than the poet, the audience, or the community. These compositions used praise (of gods, of humans, of virtues, of ideals) to direct the focus of the audience (reader, hearer, participant, observer) to a subject matter that was in many ways beyond the audience but that also directly related to the current life circumstances of that audience.

We have not suggested that the poets who wrote these compositions had a carefully thought out philosophy of instruction. Rather, poets and writers of many times and places sensed the transcendent nature of their subjects and knew intuitively that they required a treatment and presentation that went beyond a straightforward, clinical rehearsal of factual information. Hymns and hymnic styles of expression provided an already existing language and form in which to present a vision of the world that looked beyond the present to see it in light of the remembered past or beyond the visible to see it in light of the imagined invisible or beyond historical circumstances to the divine forces at work behind them.

As we have seen, the didactic functions of hymns and prayers among Greeks, Romans, Jews, and Christians are diffuse and varied. Nevertheless, in each hymn that may be considered didactic to any significant degree, we saw that the author drew on important and abiding traditions to paint a picture of ultimate reality that would be relevant and significant for his or her community. This is arguably the common thread of didactic hymnody across cultures and times: hymns provide a medium for reflecting on ultimate realities using traditional language for a contemporary audience. In this final chapter we review the ways in which didactic hymnody contributed to each of the major cultural and religious groups we have examined, making some connections and highlighting some features of the various uses of didactic hymns in the ancient world.

A. Didactic Hymnody in the Greco-Roman World

Having shown that didactic hymns, songs, and poems played a significant role in the process of cultural formation and transformation in the Greco-Roman world, we will briefly review the texts we encountered and consider the insights we gained from analyzing the didactic function of these hymns.

In chapter two we examined three of the Homeric Hymns as well as the proem of Hesiod's *Theogony* and the prelude to his *Works and Days*. In the Homeric Hymns we observed that ancient poets utilized both narrative and direct statements to address issues of relevance in the performative context of their songs. The *Hymn to Demeter* grounded the Eleusinian mysteries in the mythical past through the hymnic recounting of the story of Demeter and Persephone. It also offered direct instruction about both Demeter and the mysteries themselves through direct claims made within the hymn. The *Hymn to Apollo* taught about Apollo's gifts to humanity as it recounted in narrative how two specific oracular sites were chosen. It also offered clear teaching about Apollo through direct claims about the nature of prophecy. The *Hymn to Hermes* taught directly about the gifts of Hermes and Apollo, while at the same time offering through its narrative a model for young men of a young god who negotiated a place among the established gods through his cunning. In each case we observed how the hymn's narrative together with its pan-Hellenic outlook would have reinforced important values and perspectives within a possible performative context.

When we turned to the poetry of Hesiod, we observed that hymnic preludes opened both the *Theogony* and the *Works and Days*. Though functioning somewhat differently in each case, both preludes served a didactic role as they conveyed to the reader certain ideas that were central to the teaching of the larger composition. Like the Homeric Hymns, these hymnic preludes painted a picture of a world in which Zeus reigns supreme. By emphasizing the supremacy of Zeus these hymns implicitly downplayed the traditions of local deities presenting instead a pan-Hellenic outlook. In a move beyond what we observed in the Homeric Hymns, Hesiod's preludes taught about his own role as divinely inspired poet and prophet. We thus saw in Hesiod the use of hymnic forms to teach lessons not just about the way the gods interact with the world of humanity, but also about the divine aspect of poetic performance.

In our examination of philosophical hymns in chapter three, we observed the ongoing influence of both Homer and Hesiod in the hymnic works of philosophers who conveyed their teaching in hymnic forms. We explored two independent hymns (Aristotle's *Hymn to Virtue* and Cleanthes' *Hymn to Zeus*) and several hymns embedded in larger works (the prelude of Aratus's *Phaenomena* and hymnic passages in Lucretius's *On the Nature of the Universe*). In each instance traditional forms were utilized in innovative ways to convey a particular way of viewing the world. Aristotle and Cleanthes demonstrated several strategies related to teaching central values and ideas of their philosophies in a form and style that was readily accepted as a means of praising the divine. Without a specific performative context for either hymn, we were still able to observe the central teachings of these hymns on their own merit. With the philosophical hymns of Aratus and Lucretius we could consider the ways that the hymnic form contributed to the teaching of the larger compositions in which they were found. In the case of Lucretius, in particular, we observed that hymnic praise of Venus and of Epicurus supported the teaching of the larger work that, in the end, would do away with hymnic praise. In this regard, Lucretius offered one of the most striking examples of didactic hymnody as he used the medium of praise in an innovative way to undermine the traditional view of the gods.

In chapter four we observed that hymnic compositions provided an opportunity to teach not just about the gods or about philosophy but also about human subjects. Poets and writers from Pindar in the fifth century BCE to Pliny at the end of the first century CE used their craft to honor praiseworthy individuals and to instruct their audiences about the realities

they were experiencing. Since praises of exalted humans were often closely tied with specific historical and cultural contexts, we were able to consider how the contents of a given composition in praise of a human ruler
contributed to the audience's perception of both the ruler and the audience.
Through a number of different strategies, human rulers were shown to be
gifts of the gods and were associated with the realm of the divine even
more so than the realm of humanity. At times, poets praising human rulers
also sought to instruct the one being praised (or his progeny) with regard to
what it meant to be a praiseworthy ruler. In the Roman era in particular,
poets and political advisors found in hymns, odes, and encomia a powerful
means of promoting a view of ultimate reality in which the emperor ruled
the world as a divinely chosen and empowered benefactor of humanity.
Their compositions invited audiences to embrace that view of reality and
order their own lives accordingly.

A common denominator to the diverse didactic hymns, poems, and
songs of the Greco-Roman world can be seen in the need to negotiate the
relationship between the human and divine world. A question that lies below the surface of many of the hymns we looked at may be expressed in
this way: Who are "we" and how do we relate to the powerful forces at
work in the world? In the Homeric Hymns and hymnic passages in Hesiod
we saw that traditional Greek religious discourse answered this underlying
question with stories of the gods and their temples and the establishment of
the cult. In philosophical hymns from Aristotle to Lucretius we observed
that philosophers answered this larger question with systems of thought
expressed in universal terms. Rulers and their court poets answered this
question with a picture of a divinely empowered leader through whom
peace and prosperity were possible. In all cases didactic hymns and poems
played a role in crafting a vision of who "we" are, where ultimate power
lies, and how a community can relate in that context. Participation in a cult
or ritual, acceptance of a particular philosophy, or dutiful submission and
deference to the divinely appointed ruler were variously promoted by these
hymns as ways of negotiating life within their world.

In cases where the use of a hymn within a particular social setting was
known, it was possible to delve more deeply into the dynamics of communal formation that the hymn fostered. This was particularly the case with
some of the court poetry in praise of Greek and Roman rulers. But even for
those texts whose precise use was uncertain (e.g., the Homeric Hymns;
Cleanthes' *Hymn to Zeus*) we could perceive important values and ideals
that were inscribed into a given hymn through the choice of subject matter
and through comments directed specifically to the human audience (often
in the Homeric Hymns) or to the deity about the human audience (as in
Cleanthes' *Hymn to Zeus*). By attending to instructional emphases of each

hymn, both explicit instruction and implicit teaching, we were able to appreciate how the hymn contributed to an ongoing process of formation of and reinforcement of a particular communal identity focused on values and ideals that were central to that community.

B. Didactic Hymns in Jewish Traditions

Like the Greeks and Romans, early Jewish poets and writers used their hymns and prayers to shape the thoughts and perceptions of their communities. While many early Jewish psalms served as models to be imitated by later generations, some psalms and hymns made teaching and instruction a primary focus, thus fitting our description of didactic hymns. Here we briefly review the texts we examined in section two and place these findings within the context of our larger study.

We saw in chapter five that the Hebrew Bible contained a wealth of psalms and prayers that utilized a wide range of instructional strategies suited to their diverse literary contexts. Some didactic hymns were found as independent, self-standing psalms within a larger collection: the book of Psalms. We examined Pss 34, 49, and 105, and saw that, whether or not we consider these in the formal category of Wisdom psalms, they clearly showed a primary purpose of conveying instruction to a human audience. These psalms introduced us to a variety of strategies didactic hymns could employ including: claims about teaching; direct claims about God and the world; narrative and review of historical events with their implicit lessons; and the use of multiple temporal and/or spatial registers to convey the grandeur of their vision of reality. Our examination of these didactic Psalms also provided a foundation for exploring the didactic impact of psalms and hymns found in other literary contexts. The remainder of chapter five explored select didactic hymns in the Wisdom literature (Prov 8), narratives (Exod 15; Deut 32), and prophetic writings of the Hebrew Bible (Isa 40–55; Dan 3:31–33; 4:31–32). Though these hymns centered on a range of themes (the character of God; the Wisdom of God; God's deeds in history on behalf of his people; the future of God's people) a common feature was the way that they used verbal imagery in hymnic style to paint a portrait of reality in which the reading community could picture itself and find meaning in its present circumstances.

Jewish writers of the Second Temple period drew on the earlier biblical traditions of didactic hymnody and utilized them for teaching lessons that were relevant in a new historical context. In chapter six we saw that, as in the Hebrew Bible, didactic hymns were found in hymn collections (*Psalms of Solomon, Hellenistic Synagogue Prayers*), Wisdom writings (Wisdom of

Solomon; Wisdom of Ben Sira), narratives (Tobit; Baruch), and prophet-ic/apocalyptic writings (*1 Enoch*; *4 Ezra*; *2 Baruch*; *Apocalypse of Abraham*). Their themes continued to center on the character of God, his control of history, and the nature of the people of God. In some cases we observed that recent events could be recounted in biblically styled language, ena-bling the audience to see their own history as part of the larger story of Is-rael. In addition, some hymns showed an increased interest in dealing with issues of the suffering of God's people (theodicy), explaining some of the circumstances of the Jews as the judgment of God for forsaking his ways. On a related note, some didactic hymns showed greater focus on wisdom, and, in particular, wisdom embodied in the Law of God.

Chapter seven reviewed several didactic hymns from Qumran, showing how they created a portrait of reality in which the Qumran community was in direct continuity with the traditions of the Bible. Their recent history was recounted in ways that connected it with biblical history by use of bib-lically-styled language and literary allusion (*Barkhi Nafshi*). Similarly, their future was imagined in a way that it would be a fulfillment of biblical promises (the War Scroll). A number of hymns taught about the nature of humanity and the mercy of God in revealing his mysteries to at least one member of the community, the Teacher of Righteousness (Hodayot). By reciting hymns that offered a distinct Qumran view of the individual as weak and wicked, and of God as rich in mercy, the community members could embrace an identity that saw themselves as the people of God among whom his promises were being and would be fulfilled.

How did these diverse Jewish hymns and prayers teach? In the first place, whether intended this way or not, in their hymnic prayers early Jew-ish writers modeled an ideal human response to the working of God in the world and in their lives (as in the Song of Judith). Often this response was one of gratitude for the kindness of God which they had experienced (as in the Song of Tobit). At other times it was a response of confidence and re-affirmation of belief that God's purposes would prevail (as in apocalyptic hymns). Faithful Jewish writers could also respond to their circumstances with lament, complaint, or questioning (as in the *Psalms of Solomon*). At times the response was one of humility, recognizing the greatness of God and the finitude of humanity (as in the Hodayot). In each of these respons-es the psalmist taught by example, and the community learned from this example how they might also respond to God within the midst of the cir-cumstances of their lives.

But the instructional import of many Jewish psalms and hymns went far beyond the provision of a model to be imitated and embraced. While all hymns in the Jewish tradition conveyed through their contents a theologi-cal message (at least to some extent), in didactic hymns in particular this theological lesson became a primary focus. Through their didactic hymns, poets and psalmists aimed to foster within their communities a particular way of understanding God, the world, and/or the people of Israel.

Wisdom psalms and hymns conveyed teaching through their praises of wisdom and their promotion of the principles of the wisdom tradition. Other didactic hymns drew on the events of biblical history to draw out lessons as to how God has acted and would continue to act on behalf of his people. Still others expressed their theological understanding more directly in the form of direct assertions and claims about the nature of God. In yet another instructional approach some Jewish poets utilized biblical allusion and styles of expression to portray their own personal or communal experiences as in line with the deeds and plans of God in the Hebrew Scriptures. Didactic hymns of this kind enabled devout Jews to see themselves as participants in the ongoing development of the story of the God of Israel.

One function that pervades all of this Jewish didactic poetry is that of orienting the writer or reader to his or her place in the divine story. Naturally, communities in diverse times and locations had somewhat varied needs in terms of finding their place in the divine story. Didactic hymns and psalms were a means of providing that sense of identity that united them with Jews of time past and also helped them make sense of their present circumstances. In this regard didactic psalms, hymns, and prayers preserved cultural memory and also shaped the way the past was remembered in light of the present. Didactic hymns activated the power of memory for a new generation with its concerns as they put the past, present, and future on display creating a "deictic moment" for the audience. The vision of reality seen through the eyes of faith most often provided hope regarding the larger purposes of God in what appeared to be uncertain and challenging times.

C. Didactic Hymns in Early Christian Traditions

We were not surprised to see that the early Christians' use of psalms and hymns for didactic purposes aligned closely with Jewish practice. Hymns and prayers recorded in the Jewish Scriptures and in Second Temple Jewish writings served as models for later Christians to emulate in their response to God within their circumstances. Just as devout men and women in the Jewish Scriptures sang psalms and hymns in response to the miraculous works of God, so did the men and women who inhabit the pages of the New Testament. In this practice the Christian writings followed the precedent of the Jewish writings using their hymns to teach. Further, it was not just the fact that a hymn was sung that was important; the contents of these hymns and psalms were of strategic instructional significance.

Interestingly, we observed that, because of the nature of the development of the early Christian communities, the Christian hymns functioned somewhat differently than the Jewish ones. The Christian hymns tended to shift the focus from the plan of God for his people Israel and place the focus instead on the plan of God brought to reality in and through the person of his agent, Jesus Christ. Even the hymns that maintained a strongly Jewish outlook such as the hymns of the Lukan infancy narrative, were placed into the service of a narrative that taught the significance of the life and ministry of Jesus. Further, hymns that were specifically christologically oriented were included in all genres of early Christian writings including epistles (see chapter eight along with the discussion of the epistles of Ignatius in chapter ten), gospels and apocalypse (see chapter nine), as well as a hymnbook (*Odes of Solomon*), apologetic writings (Hippolytus), and instructional texts (on these latter genres in the second century see chapter ten). The widespread presence of didactic hymns in the surviving early Christian literature indicates that they were a major force early on in the development of Christian thinking and practice.

While the focus in Christian didactic hymnody shifted to the agent of God and his redemptive work, the forms of the hymns and their major motifs still revealed their Jewish roots in many ways. Reviews of history still found a prominent place (e.g., John 1:1–18; *Odes Sol.* 41). Eschatological and political themes also remained of high importance (e.g., Phil 2 and the hymns of Revelation). Likewise, biblical imagery and allusions were prominent in all of the didactic hymns of the New Testament.

New themes were emphasized as well, however: themes that resonated with the Greco-Roman world into which the Christian missionaries and evangelists went. In Clement's *Hymn to Christ the Savior* we observed a Christian vision of ultimate reality that was congruent with the picture of reality reflected in the New Testament but that presented it in a novel way for a new cultural context as christological reflection was wedded with the form and style of classical Greek poetry. In the psalm of Valentinus and the Naassene Hymns we observed hymnic summaries of the teaching of early Christian groups that sought to understand the significance of Christ in ways that resonated with philosophical and religious reflection of the second century CE. Though Hippolytus and other second-century Christians viewed these hymnic presentations of Christ as deficient and potentially dangerous, the way in which they could readily be used to showcase the doctrine of these teachers suggests both their availability and their effectiveness as didactic hymns. In addition to new forms and new ideas, another novelty of the early Christian didactic hymns was their presentation of a view of the world that was in implicit (and sometimes explicit) dialogue with the worldview advocated in Roman imperial ideology (cf. Phil 2:5–11; Col 1:15–20; Rev 4–5).

If one major aim of Jewish didactic poetry was to orient the writer or reader to his or her place in the divine story, the Christian aim was not completely different. Yet the Christian didactic hymns focused more on orienting the reader to the person and work of God's agent, and, secondarily, how that understanding should impact one's own existence. This shift of focus arose in part because of the contested nature of the early Christian claims about Jesus. In the process of formulating and promoting a distinctly Christian vision of community in Greco-Roman society and in the context of Jewish traditions, it was necessary to articulate a clear view of who Christ was and what God had done for humanity through him. Or rather, it was a particular view of Christ and his significance that led to the formation of a distinctly Christian vision of community. The christological hymns crystallized these understandings utilizing existing forms of discourse and using the language and categories of Greco-Roman and Jewish religious thought. It is the values, ideals, and presuppositions inscribed in the Christian understanding of Christ that then work their way out into the ethics, practices, and customs of the early believers. Nevertheless, our study reminds us as well that these early Christian hymnic reflections on Christ were not monolithic or uniform in their understanding of the Christian savior. In our survey we observed that this process of reflecting on the person and work of Christ and drawing out the implications of these reflections for Christian life and faith was still very much ongoing in the second century CE.

It is well known that the early Christians used personal witness, oral proclamation, scripture reading and interpretation, letter writing, and the composition of narratives and other literary works to promote their understanding of the latest phase of the redemptive work of God in history. The findings of this study indicate that didactic hymnody should be considered more prominently as a major vehicle that was used for creating, promoting, and affirming a Christian understanding of reality. As we have seen, the use of hymnody for instructional purposes was not a new or distinctly Christian phenomenon. The Jewish precedents are unmistakable as are the Greco-Roman uses of this kind of strategy. What was new and distinctly Christian was the focus of this hymnic acclamation and hymnic proclamation on a person – and, notably, a person who was not the emperor.

D. Summary and Conclusion

As defined here, didactic hymns, prayers, and religious poetry are those compositions which employ the stylistic and/or formal conventions of praise and prayer, but whose primary purpose was to convey a lesson, idea, or theological truth to a human audience. We have seen that didactic hymns are complex, artistic creations that use a variety of approaches to show forth a vision of reality that goes beyond what the audience could observe in the world around them. Hymns were particularly well-suited to bring into focus the work of the divine in the context of the earthly. Through this kind of teaching, didactic hymns contributed to a process of identity formation within a given community. By tracing didactic hymnody within specific traditions, it has been possible to see the development of religious, theological, philosophical and even political thought over time, as new or more fully developed ideas were given expression in traditional language and in traditional styles for new generations.

It has also been possible to see instances where one tradition appropriated the language, form, or styles of another tradition in order to confront challenges from that tradition. The Qumran community composed and preserved hymns that placed the history of that specific community (and no other) as the locus of the fulfillment of the promises of God in earlier Jewish writings. Lucretius appropriated the form of Greek hymns in praise of gods in order to promote the idea among a Roman audience that the gods are uninvolved in human affairs. Clement, in his *Hymn to Christ the Savior*, joined the content and ideas of early Christian hymns, with their roots in Jewish psalm styles, with the form and language of classical Greek hymns, in part to combat the views of other Christian teachers regarding the central ideas of the Christian faith. The New Testament christological hymns likewise used the language and forms of earlier and contemporary Jewish psalmody to remember Jesus in light of God's creative and redemptive work in the world. Teaching through song (as broadly defined here) was a phenomenon that was able to be adapted and utilized in a wide variety of contexts and cultures.

In short, we saw that Greek and Roman poets employed didactic hymnody as one part of a strategy of negotiating between the community and its benefactors, whether divine or human. In this regard it also served as a means of reconciling disparate traditions and new ideas in an ongoing process of cultural formation and transformation. Jewish poets and writers employed didactic psalms, hymns, and prayers in the service of the formation of communal identity in specific contexts. Their didactic hymns served as a vehicle for reflecting on their place in the divine story as they considered their identity in light of the collective weight of tradition together with the challenges facing Jewish communities in the present. Like their fellow Jews, the earliest followers of Jesus inscribed their understanding of their place in the divine story within their hymnic and psalm-like compositions as part of the process of communal formation. In a distinctly Christian turn, early hymnody among communities of followers of Jesus demonstrated an overwhelming interest in teaching the reader to see the past, present, and future in light of the life, death, and resurrection of the agent of God, Jesus Christ.

In most general terms then, didactic hymnody was widely employed in antiquity to engage the imagination of a human audience as it invited that audience to see the world in a particular way in light of the broader tradition and current setting in which the writer and his or her community found themselves. Didactic hymnody also appears to have been particularly well-suited for bridging the human world and the realm of the divine. Recognition of these widespread practices of didactic hymnody observed in this study, together with increased attention to the potential of ancient hymnody for engaging the issues and challenges of a given community, suggest great promise for ongoing research on the beliefs, values, and self-understanding of ancient Jews, Christians, Greeks, and Romans. If we are to continue to deepen our understanding of these ancient cultures, the wealth of material readily available for study in the didactic hymns, poems, and prayers of antiquity will require further examination and careful study from scholars in diverse fields of study utilizing a variety of approaches. That kind of interdisciplinary research on hymns will surely bear new insights into antiquity, as well as into some of the ancient texts that continue to shape the minds and thoughts of many people in our own day.

Bibliography

Agosto, Efraín. "The Letter to the Philippians." Pages 281–293 in *A Postcolonial Commentary on the New Testament Writings*. The Bible and Postcolonialism. Edited by Fernando F. Segovia and R. S. Sugirtharajah. London: T & T Clark, 2007.

Albrecht, Michael von and Gareth L. Schmeling. *A History of Roman Literature: From Livius Andronicus to Boethius*. Translated by Ruth R. Caston and Francis R. Schwartz. 2 vols. Leiden: Brill, 1997.

Allen, T. W., W. R. Halliday, and E. E. Sikes. *The Homeric Hymns*. Reprint of 1936 ed. Amsterdam: Adolf M. Hakkert, 1980.

Alter, Robert. *The Art of Biblical Poetry*. Edinburgh: T&T Clark, 1990.

Ando, Clifford. *Imperial Ideology and Provincial Loyalty in the Roman Empire*. Classics and Contemporary Thought 6. Berkeley, Calif.: University of California, 2000.

Aratus. "Phaenomena." Pages 183–299 in *Callimachus, Hymns and Epigrams; Lycophron; Aratus*. Loeb Classical Library LCL 129. Translated by A. W. Mair and G. R. Mair. Cambridge, Mass.: Harvard University Press, 1977.

Arnim, H. von. *Stoicorum Veterum Fragmenta*. 3 vols. Stuttgart: B.G. Teubner, 1964.

Arnold, Clinton E. *The Colossian Syncretism: The Interface between Christianity and Folk Belief at Colossae*. WUNT 2.77. Tübingen: Mohr (Siebeck), 1995.

Asmis, Elizabeth. "Lucretius' Venus and Stoic Zeus." Pages 88–103 in *Lucretius*. Edited by Monica Gale. Oxford: Oxford University Press, 2007.

Assmann, Jan. *Moses the Egyptian: The Memory of Egypt in Western Monotheism*. Cambridge, Mass.: Harvard University Press, 1997.

Atkinson, Kenneth. *An Intertextual Study of the Psalms of Solomon*. Lewiston, N.Y.: E. Mellen Press, 2001.

–. *I Cried to the Lord: A Study of the Psalms of Solomon's Historical Background and Social Setting*. JSJSup 84. Leiden; Boston: Brill, 2004.

Attridge, Harold W. and Margot E. Fassler. *Psalms in Community: Jewish and Christian Textual, Liturgical, and Artistic Traditions*. Atlanta: Society of Biblical Literature, 2003.

Aune, David E. "The Influence of Roman Imperial Court Ceremonial on the Apocalypse of John." *BR* 28 (1983): 5–26.

–. *Prophecy in Early Christianity and the Ancient Mediterranean World*. Grand Rapids: Eerdmans, 1983.

–. "Romans as a Logos Protreptikos." Pages 278–296 in *The Romans Debate*. Edited by Karl P. Donfried. Peabody, Mass.: Hendrickson, 1991.

–. *Revelation 1–5*. WBC 52a. Dallas: Word, 1997.

–. "Ignatius, Letters of." Pages 225–228 in *The Westminster Dictionary of New Testament and Early Christian Literature and Rhetoric*. Louisville, Ky.: Westminster John Knox, 2003.

–. "The *Odes of Solomon* and Early Christian Prophecy." Pages 320–346 in *Apocalypticism, Prophecy, and Magic in Early Christianity*. 199. Tübingen: Mohr Siebeck, 2006.

Bakker, Egbert J. *Pointing at the Past: From Formula to Performance in Homeric Poetics*. Washington, D.C.: Center for Hellenic Studies, 2005.

Baltzer, Klaus. *Deutero-Isaiah: A Commentary on Isaiah 40–55*. Hermeneia. Minneapolis, Minn.: Fortress Press, 2001.

Bartsch, Shadi. *Actors in the Audience: Theatricality and Doublespeak from Nero to Hadrian*. Revealing Antiquity 6. Cambridge, Mass.: Harvard University Press, 1994.

Bauckham, Richard. *The Climax of Prophecy: Studies on the Book of Revelation*. Edinburgh: T&T Clark, 1993.

–. *Jesus and the God of Israel: God Crucified and Other Studies on the New Testament's Christology of Divine Identity*. Grand Rapids: Eerdmans, 2009.

Berger, Klaus. "Das Canticum Simeonis (Lk 2:29–32)." *NovT* 27 (1985): 27–39.

Bernstein, Moshe J. "Scriptures: Quotation and Use." Pages 839–842 in *Encyclopedia of the Dead Sea Scrolls*. Edited by Lawrence H. Schiffman and James C. VanderKam. 2 vols. New York: Oxford University Press, 2000.

Blaszczak, Gerald R. *A Formcritical Study of Selected Odes of Solomon*. Harvard Semitic Monographs 36. Atlanta: Scholars Press, 1985.

Blenkinsopp, Joseph. *The Pentateuch: An Introduction to the First Five Books of the Bible*. ABRL. New York: Doubleday, 1992.

Blount, Brian K. *Revelation: A Commentary*. Louisville, Ky.: Westminster John Knox, 2009.

Borgen, Peder. "The Prologue of John – As Exposition of the Old Testament." Pages 75–102 in *Philo, John, and Paul: New Perspectives on Judaism and Early Christianity*. 131. Edited by Peder Borgen. Atlanta: Scholars Press, 1987.

Bowra, C. M. *Problems in Greek Poetry*. Oxford: Clarendon Press, 1953.

Boyarin, Daniel. "The Gospel of the *Memra*: Jewish Binitarianism and the Prologue to John." *HTR* 94 (2001): 243–284.

Bradshaw, Paul F. *The Search for the Origins of Christian Worship: Sources and Methods for the Study of Early Liturgy*. 2nd ed. New York: Oxford University Press, 2002.

–. *Reconstructing Early Christian Worship*. London: SPCK, 2009.

Brown, Raymond Edward. *The Gospel According to John*. 2nd ed. AB 29, 29A. 2 vols. Garden City, N.Y.: Doubleday, 1986.

–. *The Birth of the Messiah: A Commentary on the Infancy Narratives in Matthew and Luke*. ABRL. New York: Doubleday, 1993.

Brucker, Ralph. *'Christushymnen' oder 'epideiktische Passagen'? : Studien zum Stilwechsel im Neuen Testament und seiner Umwelt*. FRLANT 176. Göttingen: Vandenhoeck & Ruprecht, 1997.

Brunschwig, Jacques and D. N. Sedley. "Hellenistic Philosophy." Pages 151–183 in *The Cambridge Companion to Greek and Roman Philosophy*. Edited by D. N. Sedley. Cambridge: Cambridge University Press, 2003.

Bryan, Christopher. *Render to Caesar: Jesus, the Early Church, and the Roman Superpower*. New York: Oxford University Press, 2005.

Buell, Denise Kimber. *Making Christians: Clement of Alexandria and the Rhetoric of Legitimacy*. Princeton: Princeton University Press, 1999.

Burrus, Virginia. "The Gospel of Luke and the Acts of the Apostles." Pages 133–155 in *A Postcolonial Commentary on the New Testament Writings*. The Bible and Postcolonialism 13. Edited by Fernando F. Segovia and R. S. Sugirtharajah. London: T & T Clark, 2007.

Carlos-Reyes, Luis. "The Structure and Rhetoric of Colossians 1:15–20." *FN* 12 (1999): 139–154.

Carne-Ross, D. S. *Pindar*. New Haven: Yale University Press, 1985.

Ceresko, A. R. "The Sage in the Psalms." Pages 217–30 in *The Sage in Israel and the Ancient Near East*. Edited by John G. Gammie and Leo G. Perdue. Winona Lake, Ind.: Eisenbrauns, 1990.

Chadwick, Henry. *Early Christian Thought and the Classical Tradition: Studies in Justin, Clement, and Origen*. Oxford: Clarendon Press, 1966. Reprinted, 1984.

Charlesworth, James H. "The Odes of Solomon – Not Gnostic." *CBQ* 31 (1969): 357–369.

–. *The Odes of Solomon*. Texts and Translations 13. Missoula, Mont.: Scholars Press for Society of Biblical Literature, 1977.

–. "Jewish Hymns, Odes, and Prayers (ca 167 BCE–135 CE)." Pages 411–436 in *Early Judaism and its Modern Interpreters*. Philadelphia: Fortress Press, 1986.

Charlesworth, James H. and R. Alan Culpepper. "The Odes of Solomon and the Gospel of John." *CBQ* 35 (1973): 298–322.

Chazon, Esther Glickler. "A 'Prayer Alleged to be Jewish' in the *Apostolic Constitutions*." Pages 261–277 in *Things Revealed: Studies in Early Jewish and Christian Literature in Honor of Michael E. Stone*. Supplements to the Journal for the Study of Judaism 89. Edited by Esther G. Chazon, David Satran and Ruth A. Clements. Leiden: Brill, 2004.

–. "Hymns and Prayers in the Dead Sea Scrolls." Pages 244–270 in *Dead Sea Scrolls after Fifty Years: A Comprehensive Assessment*. Edited by James C. VanderKam and Peter W. Flint. Leiden: Brill, 1998.

Childs, Brevard S. *Memory and Tradition in Israel*. Naperville, Ill.: A. R. Allenson, 1962.

–. *The Book of Exodus: A Critical, Theological Commentary*. OTL. Philadelphia: Westminster Press, 1976.

Clay, Diskin. "The Sources of Lucretius' Inspiration." Pages 18–47 in *Lucretius*. Edited by Monica Gale. Oxford: Oxford University Press, 2007.

Clay, Jenny Strauss. *Hesiod's Cosmos*. Cambridge: Cambridge University Press, 2003.

–. *The Politics of Olympus: Form and Meaning in the Major Homeric Hymns*. 2nd ed. Bristol Classical Paperbacks. London: Bristol Classical, 2006.

Clement. *Le Pédagogue: Livre III*. Translated by Claude Mondesert and Chantal Matray; notes by Henri-Irénée Marrou. SC 158. Paris: Éditions du Cerf, 1970.

–. "To the Newly Baptized." Pages 368–377 in *Clement of Alexandria*. Loeb Classical Library LCL 92. Translated by G.W. Butterworth. Cambridge, Mass.: Harvard University Press, 1979.

–. *Le Pédagogue: Livre I*. Translated by Marguerite Harl; introduction and notes by Henri-Irénée Marrou. SC 70. Paris: Éditions du Cerf, 1983.

Coats, G. W. "The Song of the Sea." *CBQ* 31 (1969): 1–17.

Coleridge, Mark. *The Birth of the Lukan Narrative: Narrative as Christology in Luke 1–2*. JSNTSup 88. Sheffield: JSOT Press, 1993.

Collins, Adela Yarbro. "The Worship of Jesus and the Imperial Cult." Pages 234–257 in *The Jewish Roots of Christological Monotheism: Papers from the St. Andrews Conference on the Historical Origins of the Worship of Jesus*. Edited by Carey C. Newman, James R. Davila and Gladys S. Lewis. Leiden: Brill, 1999.

–. "The Psalms and the Origins of Christology." Pages 113–123 in *Psalms in Community: Jewish and Christian Textual, Liturgical, and Artistic Traditions*. Edited by Harold W. Attridge and Margot E. Fassler. Atlanta: Society of Biblical Literature, 2003.

Collins, John Joseph. *Daniel: A Commentary on the Book of Daniel*. Hermeneia. Minneapolis, Minn.: Fortress Press, 1993.

–. *Jewish Wisdom in the Hellenistic Age*. OTL. Louisville, Ky.: Westminster John Knox, 1997.

–. *The Apocalyptic Imagination: An Introduction to Jewish Apocalyptic Literature*. 2nd ed. The Biblical Resource Series. Grand Rapids: Eerdmans, 1998.

Cosgrove, Charles H. "Clement of Alexandria and Early Christian Music." *JECS* 14 (2006): 255–282.

Cousar, Charles B. "The Function of the Christ-hymn (2.6–11) in Philippians." Pages 212–218 in *The Impartial God: Essays in Biblical Studies in Honor of Jouette M. Bassler*. Edited by Calvin J. Roetzel, Robert L. Foster and Jouette M. Bassler. Sheffield: Sheffield Phoenix Press, 2007.

–. *Philippians and Philemon: A Commentary*. Louisville, Ky.: Westminster John Knox, 2009.

Crenshaw, James. *Education in Ancient Israel*. ABRL. New York: Doubleday, 1998.

–. *Old Testament Wisdom: An Introduction*. Louisville, Ky.: Westminster John Knox, 1998.

–. "Wisdom Psalms?" *Currents in Biblical Research* 8 (2000): 9–17.

–. "Gold Dust or Nuggets? A Brief Response to J. Kenneth Kuntz." *Currents in Biblical Research* 1 (2003): 155–158.

Crook, Zeba A. and Philip A. Harland. *Identity and Interaction in the Ancient Mediterranean: Jews, Christians and Others: Essays in Honour of Stephen G. Wilson*. New Testament Monographs 18. Sheffield: Sheffield Phoenix Press, 2007.

Cross, Frank Moore and David Noel Freedman. *Studies in Ancient Yahwistic Poetry*. New ed. The Biblical Resource Series. Grand Rapids: Eerdmans, 1997.

Currie, Bruno. *Pindar and the Cult of Heroes*. Oxford: Oxford University Press, 2005.

Dahl, Nils Alstrup. *Jesus in the Memory of the Early Church: Essays*. Minneapolis: Augsburg, 1976.

Danker, Frederick W. *Benefactor: Epigraphic Study of a Graeco-Roman and New Testament Semantic Field*. St. Louis, Mo.: Clayton Pub. House, 1982.

Darnell, D. R. "Hellenistic Synagogal Prayers: Translation." Pages 677–97 in *The Old Testament Pseudepigrapha, Vol. 2*. Edited by James H. Charlesworth. New York: Doubleday, 1985.

Davies, Jason P. *Rome's Religious History: Livy, Tacitus, and Ammianus on their Gods*. Cambridge: Cambridge University Press, 2004.

Davies, Philip R. *1QM, the War Scroll from Qumran: Its Structure and History*. Biblica et orientalia 32. Rome: Biblical Institute Press, 1977.

–. "Didactic Stories." Pages 99–133 in *Justification and Variegated Nomism. Vol. 1, The Complexities of Second Temple Judaism*. Edited by D. A. Carson, Peter T. O'Brien and Mark A. Seifrid. Grand Rapids: Baker Academic, 2001.

de Jonge, Marinus. "The Gospel and the Epistles of John Read against the Background of the History of the Johannine Communities." Pages 127–144 in *What We Have Heard from the Beginning: The Past, Present, and Future of Johannine Studies*. Edited by Tom Thatcher. Waco, Tex.: Baylor University Press, 2007.

De Long, Kindalee Pfremmer. *Surprised by God: Praise Responses in the Narrative of Luke-Acts*. BZNW 166. Berlin: Walter de Gruyter, 2009.

Deichgräber, Reinhard. *Gotteshymnus und Christushymnus in der frühen Christenheit*. SUNT 5. Göttingen: Vandenhoek & Ruprecht, 1967.

Deissmann, Adolf. *Light from the Ancient East*. Translated by Lionel R. M. Strachan. New and completely rev. ed. Grand Rapids: Baker Book House, 1927. Reprinted, 1978.

Des Places, Édouard. "Hymnes grecs au seuil de l'ère chrétienne." *Bib* 38 (1957): 113–129.

Dihle, Albrecht. *Greek and Latin Literature of the Roman Empire: From Augustus to Justinian*. London: Routledge, 1994.

–. *A History of Greek Literature: From Homer to the Hellenistic Period.* London: Routledge, 1994.

Dillon, Richard J. "The Benedictus in Micro- and Macrocontext." *CBQ* 68 (2006): 457–80.

Dozeman, Thomas. "The Song of the Sea and Salvation History." Pages 96–113 in *On the Way to Nineveh: Studies in Honor of George M. Landes.* Edited by Stephen L. Cook, George M. Landes and Sara C. Winter. Atlanta: Scholars Press, 1999.

Drijvers, H. J. W. "Odes of Solomon and Psalms of Mani. Christians and Manichaeans in Third-Century Syria." Pages 117–130 in *East of Antioch: Studies in Early Syriac Christianity.* 198. London: Variorum Reprints, 1984.

–. "Solomon as Teacher: Early Syriac Didactic Poetry." Pages 123–134 in *IV Symposium Syriacum 1984: Literary Genres in Syriac literature (Groningen - Oosterhesselen, 10–12 September).* 229. Roma: Pont. Institutum Studiorum Orientalium, 1987.

Du Quesnay, I. M. Le M. "Horace, *Odes* 4.5: *Pro Reditu Imperatoris Caesaris Divi Filii Augusti.*" Pages 128–187 in *Homage to Horace: A Bimillenary Celebration.* Edited by S. J. Harrison. Oxford: Clarendon Press, 1995.

Duhaime, Jean. "War Scroll." Pages 80–141 in *The Dead Sea Scrolls: Hebrew, Aramaic, and Greek Texts with English Translations. Volume 2: Damascus Document, War Scroll, and Related Documents.* PTSDSSP 2. Edited by James Charlesworth. Tübingen: Mohr (Siebeck), 1995.

–. *The War Texts: 1QM and Related Manuscripts.* Companion to the Qumran Scrolls 6. London: T & T Clark, 2004.

Egger-Wenzel, Renate. *Ben Sira's God: Proceedings of the International Ben Sira Conference, Durham, Upshaw College 2001.* Berlin: Walter de Gruyter, 2002.

Endo, Masanobu. *Creation and Christology: A Study on the Johannine Prologue in the Light of Early Jewish Creation Accounts.* Tübingen: Mohr Siebeck, 2002.

Enns, Peter. *Exodus Retold: Ancient Exegesis of the Departure from Egypt in Wisdom 10:15–21 and 19:1–9.* Atlanta: Scholars Press, 1997.

Eusebius. *Histoire Ecclésiastique: Livres V–VII.* Translated by Gustave Bardy. 4 ed. SC 41. Paris: Éditions du Cerf, 1994.

Evans, Craig A. *Word and Glory: On the Exegetical and Theological Background of John's Prologue.* JSNTSup 89. Sheffield: JSOT, 1993.

Fakas, Christos. *Der hellenistische Hesiod: Arats Phainomena und die Tradition der antiken Lehrepik.* Serta Graeca 11. Wiesbaden: Reichert, 2001.

Falk, Daniel K. *Daily, Sabbath, and Festival Prayers in the Dead Sea Scrolls.* STDJ 27. Leiden: Brill, 1998.

Fantuzzi, Marco and R. L. Hunter. *Tradition and Innovation in Hellenistic Poetry.* Cambridge: Cambridge University Press, 2004.

Farris, Stephen. *The Hymns of Luke's Infancy Narratives: Their Origin, Meaning and Significance.* JSNTSup 9. Sheffield: JSOT Press, 1985.

–. "The Canticles of Luke's Infancy Narrative: The Appropriation of a Biblical Tradition." Pages 91–112 in *Into God's Presence: Prayer in the New Testament.* McMaster New Testament Studies. Edited by Richard N. Longenecker. Grand Rapids: Eerdmans, 2001.

Fee, Gordon D. "Philippians 2:5–11: Hymn or Exalted Pauline Prose." *BBR* 2 (1992): 29–46.

Fentress, James and Chris Wickham. *Social Memory.* Oxford, UK: Blackwell, 1992.

Ferguson, John. *Clement of Alexandria.* New York: Twayne Publishers, 1974.

–. "Introduction." Pages 3–19 in *Stromateis. Books 1–3.* Translated by John Ferguson. Washington, D.C.: Catholic University of America Press, 1991.

Fiensy, David A. "Hellenistic Synagogal Prayers: Introduction." Pages 671–76 in *The Old Testament Pseudepigrapha, Vol. 2*. Edited by James H. Charlesworth. New York: Doubleday, 1985.

–. *Prayers Alleged to Be Jewish: An Examination of the Constitutiones Apostolorum*. BJS 65. Chico, Calif.: Scholars Press, 1985.

Filoramo, Giovanni. *A History of Gnosticism*. Cambridge, Mass.: Blackwell, 1992.

Fischer, Georg. "Das Schilfmeerlied Exodus 15 in seinem Kontext." *Bib* 77 (1996): 32–47.

Fishwick, Duncan. *The Imperial Cult in the Latin West: Studies in the Ruler Cult of the Western Provinces of the Roman Empire*. Études préliminaires aux religions orientales dans l'Empire Romain. 2 vols. Leiden: Brill, 1987.

Fitzmyer, Joseph A. *Tobit*. Commentaries on Early Jewish Literature. Berlin: Walter de Gruyter, 2003.

Flusser, David. "Psalms, Hymns, and Prayers." Pages 551–577 in *Jewish Writings of the Second Temple Period: Apocrypha, Pseudepigrapha, Qumran Sectarian Writings, Philo, Josephus*. Edited by Michael E. Stone. Philadelphia: Fortress Press, 1984.

Fokkelman, J. P. *Major Poems of the Hebrew Bible: At the Interface of Hermeneutics and Structural Analysis: Vol. 1: Ex. 15, Deut. 32, and Job 3*. SSN 37. Assen, Netherlands: Van Gorcum, 1998.

Foley, Helene P. *The Homeric Hymn to Demeter: Translation, Commentary, and Interpretive Essays*. Princeton: Princeton University Press, 1994.

Ford, Josephine Massyngbaerde. "The Christological Function of the Hymns in the Apocalypse of John." *AUSS* 56 (1998): 207–229.

Fowl, Stephen E. *The Story of Christ in the Ethics of Paul: An Analysis of the Function of the Hymnic Material in the Pauline Corpus*. JSNTSup 36. Sheffield: Sheffield Academic Press, 1990.

–. *Philippians*. The Two Horizons New Testament Commentary. Grand Rapids: Eerdmans, 2005.

Franzmann, Majella. *The Odes of Solomon: An Analysis of the Poetical Structure and Form*. NTOA 20. Göttingen: Vandenhoeck & Ruprecht, 1991.

Frey, Jörg. "Auf der Suche nach dem Kontext des vierten Evangeliums: Eine forschungsgeschichtliche Einführung." Pages 3–45 in *Kontexte des Johannesevangeliums: das vierte Evangelium in religions- und traditionsgeschichtlicher Perspektive*. WUNT 175. Edited by Jörg Frey and Udo Schnelle. Tübingen: Mohr Siebeck, 2004.

–. "The Relevance of the Roman Imperial Cult for the Book of Revelation: Exegetical and Hermeneutical Reflections on the Relation between the Seven Letters and the Visionary Main Part of the Book." Pages 231–255 in *The New Testament and Early Christian Literature in Greco-Roman Context: Studies in Honor of David E. Aune*. Edited by John Fotopoulos. Leiden: Brill, 2006.

Frey, Jörg, Daniel R. Schwartz, and Stephanie Gripentrog. *Jewish Identity in the Greco-Roman World = Jüdische Identität in der griechisch-römischen Welt*. Leiden: Brill, 2007.

Friesen, Steven J. *Imperial Cults and the Apocalypse of John: Reading Revelation in the Ruins*. New York: Oxford University Press, 2001.

Fuhrer, Therese. "Hymnus III. The Christian Hymn." Columns 622–625 in *Brill's New Pauly*. 6. Edited by Hubert Cancik and Helmuth Schneider. Boston: Brill, 2005.

Furley, William D. and Jan Maarten Bremer. *Greek Hymns: Selected Cult Songs from the Archaic to the Hellenistic Period*. STAC 9–10. 2 vols. Tübingen: Mohr Siebeck, 2001.

Gale, Monica. *Myth and Poetry in Lucretius*. Cambridge Classical Studies. Cambridge: Cambridge University Press, 1994.

–. "Introduction." Pages 1–17 in *Lucretius*. Edited by Monica Gale. Oxford: Oxford University Press, 2007.

–. "Lucretius and Previous Poetic Traditions." Pages 59–75 in *The Cambridge Companion to Lucretius*. Edited by Stuart Gillespie and Philip R. Hardie. Cambridge: Cambridge University Press, 2007.

Galinsky, Karl. *Augustan Culture: An Interpretive Introduction*. Princeton: Princeton University Press, 1996.

García Martínez, Florentino and Eibert J. C. Tigchelaar. *The Dead Sea Scrolls Study Edition*. 2 vols. Leiden: Brill, 1997.

Gese, Hartmut. *Essays on Biblical Theology*. Minneapolis: Augsburg, 1981.

Gilbert, Maurice, Núria Calduch-Benages, and J. Vermeylen. *Treasures of Wisdom: Studies in Ben Sira and the Book of Wisdom: Festschrift M. Gilbert*. BETL 143. Leuven: Leuven University Press, 1999.

Giles, Terry and William Doan. *Twice Used Songs: Performance Criticism of the Songs of Ancient Israel*. Peabody, Mass.: Hendrickson, 2009.

Gillespie, Stuart and Philip R. Hardie. "Introduction." Pages 1–15 in *The Cambridge Companion to Lucretius*. Edited by Stuart Gillespie and Philip R. Hardie. Cambridge: Cambridge University Press, 2007.

Gillingham, S. E. *The Poems and Psalms of the Hebrew Bible*. Oxford Bible Series. Oxford: Oxford University Press, 1994.

Glasson, T. F. *Moses in the Fourth Gospel*. Naperville, Ill.: A. R. Allenson, 1963.

Gloer, W. Hulitt. "Homologies and Hymns in the New Testament: Form, Content and Criteria for Identification." *PRS* 11 (1984): 115–132.

Goff, Matthew J. "Reading Wisdom at Qumran: 4QInstruction and the Hodayot." *DSD* 11 (2004): 263–288.

Goldingay, John. *Daniel*. WBC 30. Dallas, Tex.: Word Books, 1989.

–. *Psalms 1–41*. Baker Commentary on the Old Testament: Wisdom and Psalms. Grand Rapids: Baker Academic, 2006.

Goldingay, John and David F. Payne. *Isaiah 40–55: Volume 1*. ICC. London: T&T Clark, 2006.

Gordley, Matthew E. *The Colossian Hymn in Context: An Exegesis in Light of Jewish and Greco-Roman Hymnic and Epistolary Conventions*. WUNT 2.228. Tübingen: Mohr Siebeck, 2007.

–. "The Johannine Prologue and Jewish Didactic Hymn Traditions: A New Case for Reading the Prologue as a Hymn." *JBL* 128 (2009): 781–802.

Goulder, Michael. "Deutero-Isaiah of Jerusalem." *JSOT* 28 (2004): 351–362.

Gowing, Alain M. *Empire and Memory: The Representation of the Roman Republic in Imperial Culture*. Cambridge: Cambridge University Press, 2005.

Gradel, Ittai. *Emperor Worship and Roman Religion*. Oxford Classical Monographs. Oxford: Clarendon Press, 2002.

Grandjean, Yves. *Une Nouvelle Arétalogie d'Isis à Maronée*. EPRO 49. Leiden: Brill, 1975.

Grant, J. A. "Wisdom Poem." Pages 891–894 in *Dictionary of the Old Testament: Wisdom, Poetry & Writings*. Edited by Tremper Longman and Peter Enns. Downers Grove, Ill.: IVP Academic, 2008.

Gunkel, Hermann and Joachim Begrich. *Introduction to Psalms: The Genres of the Religious Lyric of Israel*. Translated by James D. Nogalski. MLBS. Macon, Ga.: Mercer University Press, 1998.

Haenchen, Ernst. *John: A Commentary on the Gospel of John*. Translated by Robert W. Funk. Hermeneia. Philadelphia: Fortress Press, 1984.

Hakola, Raimo. *Identity Matters: John, the Jews, and Jewishness*. Supplements to Novum Testamentum 118. Leiden: Brill, 2005.

Harkins, Angela Kim. "Observations on the Editorial Shaping of the So-Called Community Hymns from 1QH^a and 4QH^a (4Q427)." *DSD* 12 (2005): 233–256.

Harland, Philip A. *Dynamics of Identity in the World of the Early Christians: Associations, Judeans, and Cultural Minorities.* New York: T & T Clark, 2009.

Harris, Elizabeth. *Prologue and Gospel: The Theology of the Fourth Evangelist.* New York: T & T Clark, 2004.

Harrison, S. J., ed. *Homage to Horace: A Bimillenary Celebration.* Oxford: Clarendon Press, 1995.

Heen, Erik M. "Phil 2:6–11 and Resistance to Local Timocratic Rule: Isa theō and the Cult of the Emperor in the East." Pages 125–153 in *Paul and the Roman Imperial Order.* Edited by Richard A Horsley. Harrisburg, Pa.: Trinity Press International, 2004.

Heine, Ronald E. "The Alexandrians." Pages 117–130 in *The Cambridge History of Early Christian Literature.* Edited by Frances M. Young, Lewis Ayres and Andrew Louth. Cambridge: Cambridge University Press, 2004.

Hengel, Martin. "Hymns and Christology." Pages 78–96 in *Between Jesus and Paul.* London: Fortress Press, 1983.

–. "The Song about Christ in Earliest Worship." Pages 227–291 in *Studies in Early Christology.* Edinburgh: T&T Clark, 1995.

–. "The Prologue of the Gospel of John as the Gateway to Christological Truth " Pages 265–293 in *The Gospel of John and Christian Theology.* Edited by Richard Bauckham and Carl Mosser. Grand Rapids: Eerdmans, 2008.

Hoek, Annewies van den. "Hymn of the Holy Clement to Christ the Saviour." Pages 296–303 in *Prayer from Alexander to Constantine: A Critical Anthology.* Edited by Mark Christopher Kiley. London: Routledge, 1997.

Hofius, Otfried. *Der Christushymnus Philipper 2, 6–11: Untersuchungen zu Gestalt und Aussage eines urchristlichen Psalms.* 2nd ed. WUNT 17. Tübingen: Mohr, 1991.

Holm-Nielsen, Svend. "The Importance of Late Jewish Psalmody for the Understanding of Old Testament Psalmodic Tradition." *ST* 14 (1960): 1–53.

–. "The Exodus Traditions in Psalm 105." *ASTI* 11 (1962–63):

Holmberg, Bengt and Mikael Winninge. *Identity Formation in the New Testament.* WUNT 227. Tübingen Germany: Mohr Siebeck, 2008.

Hook, LaRue van. *Isocrates. In Three Volumes.* LCL 373. Cambridge, Mass.: Harvard University Press, 1968.

Hooker, Morna Dorothy. "Were there False Teachers in Colossae?" Pages 315–331 in *Christ and Spirit in the New Testament.* Edited by Barnabas Lindars and Stephen S. Smalley. Cambridge: Cambridge University Press, 1973.

Horace. *The Odes and Epodes.* Translated by Charles E. Bennett. Rev. ed. LCL 33. Cambridge, Mass.: Harvard University Press, 1927. Reprinted, 1978.

Hornblower, Simon. *Thucydides and Pindar: Historical Narrative and the World of Epinikian Poetry.* Oxford: Oxford University Press, 2004.

Hornblower, Simon and Catherine Morgan. *Pindar's Poetry, Patrons, and Festivals: From Archaic Greece to the Roman Empire.* Oxford: Oxford University Press, 2007.

Horsley, G. H. R. "A Personalized Aretalogy of Isis." *NewDocs* 6 (1981): 10–23.

Horsley, Richard A. *Paul and Empire: Religion and Power in Roman Imperial Society.* Harrisburg, Pa.: Trinity Press International, 1997.

–. "Jesus and Empire." Pages 75–96 in *In the Shadow of Empire: Reclaiming the Bible as a History of Faithful Resistance.* Edited by Richard A. Horsley. Louisville, Ky.: Westminster John Knox, 2008.

Horst, Pieter W. van der and Judith H. Newman. *Early Jewish Prayers in Greek.* Commentaries on Early Jewish Literature. Berlin: Walter de Gruyter, 2008.

Horst, Pieter W. van der. "Was the Synagogue a Place of Sabbath Worship?" Pages 55–82 in *Japheth in the Tents of Shem: Studies on Jewish Hellenism in Antiquity*. Leuven: Peeters, 2002.

Hübner, Hans. *An Philemon, an die Kolosser, an die Epheser*. HNT 12. Tübingen: Mohr Siebeck, 1997.

—. *Die Weisheit Salomons*. ATDA 4. Göttingen: Vandenhoeck & Ruprecht, 1999.

Hughes, Julie. *Scriptural Allusions and Exegesis in the Hodayot*. STDJ 59. Leiden: Brill, 2006.

Hunter, R. L. *Theocritus: Encomium of Ptolemy Philadelphus*. Berkeley: University of California Press, 2003.

—. "Introduction and Notes." *Idylls*. Oxford World's Classics. Oxford: Oxford University Press, 2008.

Hurowitz, Victor. "Additional Elements of Alphabetical Thinking in Psalm xxxiv." *VT* 52 (2002): 326–333.

Hurtado, Larry W. *At the Origins of Christian Worship: The Context and Character of Earliest Christian Devotion*. Grand Rapids: Eerdmans, 2000.

Ignatius. *Lettres*. Translated by Pierre Thomas Camelot. Repr. of the 4th rev. and corr. ed. SC 10bis. Paris: Éd. du Cerf, 1998.

Isaac, E. "1 (Ethiopic Apocalypse of) Enoch." Pages 5–89 in *The Old Testament Pseudepigrapha, Vol. 1, Apocalyptic Literature and Testaments*. Edited by James H. Charlesworth. Garden City, N.Y.: Doubleday, 1983.

James, A. W. "The Zeus Hymns of Cleanthes and Aratus." *Antichthon* 6 (1972): 28–38.

Jeffery, Peter. "Philo's Impact on Christian Psalmody." Pages 147–187 in *Psalms in Community: Jewish and Christian Textual, Liturgical, and Artistic Traditions*. Edited by Harold W. Attridge and Margot E. Fassler. Atlanta: Society of Biblical Literature, 2003.

Johnson, Allan Chester, Paul R. Coleman-Norton, Frank Card Bourne, and Clyde Pharr. *Ancient Roman Statutes: A Translation, with Introduction, Commentary, Glossary, and Index*. The Corpus of Roman Law 2. Austin: University of Texas, 1961. Reprinted, 2003.

Johnson, Luke Timothy. *The Gospel of Luke*. SP 3. Collegeville, Minn.: Liturgical Press, 1991.

Johnson, Timothy S. *A Symposion of Praise: Horace Returns to Lyric in Odes IV*. Wisconsin Studies in Classics. Madison, Wisc.: University of Wisconsin Press, 2004.

Johnston, Sarah Iles. "Myth, Festival, and Poet: *The Homeric Hymn to Hermes* and Its Performative Context." *CPh* 97 (2002): 109–132.

Jörns, Klaus-Peter. *Das hymnische Evangelium: Untersuchungen zu Aufbau, Funktion und Herkunft der hymnischen Stücke in der Johannesoffenbarung*. SNT 5. Gütersloh: G. Mohn, 1971.

Juel, Donald. *Messianic Exegesis: Christological Interpretation of the Old Testament in Early Christianity*. Philadelphia: Fortress Press, 1988.

Kahl, Brigitte. "Acts of the Apostles: Pro(to)-Imperial Script and Hidden Transcript." Pages 137–156 in *In the Shadow of Empire: Reclaiming the Bible as a History of Faithful Resistance*. Edited by Richard A. Horsley. Louisville, Ky.: Westminster John Knox, 2008.

Kearns, Emily. "The Gods in the Homeric Epics." Pages 59–73 in *The Cambridge Companion to Homer*. Edited by Robert Fowler. Cambridge: Cambridge University Press, 2004.

Keck, Leander. "The Poor Among the Saints in Jewish Christianity and Qumran." *ZNW* 57 (1966): 54–78.

Kennedy, George Alexander. *Progymnasmata: Greek Textbooks of Prose Composition and Rhetoric*. SBLWGRW 10. Atlanta: Society of Biblical Literature, 2003.

Kenney, E. J. "Lucretian Texture: Style, Metre and Rhetoric in the *De rerum natura.*" Pages 92–110 in *The Cambridge Companion to Lucretius*. Edited by Stuart Gillespie and Philip R. Hardie. Cambridge: Cambridge University Press, 2007.

Kidd, Douglas. *Aratus: Phaenomena.* Cambridge Classical Texts and Commentaries 34. Cambridge: Cambridge University Press, 1997.

Kim, Seyoon. *Christ and Caesar: The Gospel and the Roman Empire in the Writings of Paul and Luke*. Grand Rapids: Eerdmans, 2008.

Kittel, Bonnie Pedrotti. *The Hymns of Qumran: Translation and Commentary*. Missoula, Mont.: Scholars Press, 1980.

Klijn, A. F. J. "2 (Syriac Apocalypse of) Baruch." Pages 621–652 in *The Old Testament Pseudepigrapha. Vol. 1, Apocalyptic Literature and Testaments*. Edited by James H. Charlesworth. Garden City, N.Y.: Doubleday, 1983.

Kloppenborg, John S. "Isis and Sophia in the Book of Wisdom." *HTR* 75 (1982): 57–84.

Knight, Jonathan. *Revelation*. Sheffield: Sheffield Academic Press, 1999.

Knohl, Israel. "Between Voice and Silence: The Relationship between Prayer and Temple Cult." *JBL* 115 (1996): 17–30.

Korpel, Marjo C. A. "The Demarcation of Hymns and Prayers in the Prophets (2)." Pages 141–157 in *Psalms and Prayers: Papers Read at the Joint Meeting of the Society of Old Testament Study and Het Oudtestamentische Werkgezelschap in Nederland en België, Apeldoorn August 2006*. Edited by Bob Becking and Eric Peels. Leiden: Brill, 2007.

–. "The Demarcation of Hymns and Prayers in the Prophets (1)." Pages 114–145 in *The Impact of Unit Delimitation on Exegesis*. Edited by Raymond de Hoop, Marjo C. A. Korpel, and Stanley E. Porter. Leiden: Brill, 2009.

Kraemer, Ross Shepard. *Her Share of the Blessings: Women's Religions among Pagans, Jews and Christians in the Greco-Roman World*. New York: Oxford University Press, 1992.

Krentz, Edgar. "Epideiktik and Hymnody: The New Testament and Its World." *BR* 40 (1995): 50–97.

Kroll, Josef. *Die christliche Hymnodik bis zu Klemens von Alexandria*. 2nd ed. Darmstadt: Wissenschaftliche Buchgesellschaft, 1968.

Kugel, James L. *The Idea of Biblical Poetry: Parallelism and its History*. New Haven: Yale University Press, 1981.

–. "Some Thoughts on Future Research into Biblical Style: Addenda to The Idea of Biblical Poetry." *JSOT* 28 (1984): 108–117.

Kuntz, J. Kenneth. "Reclaiming Biblical Wisdom Psalms: A Response to Crenshaw." *Currents in Biblical Research* 1 (2003): 145–154.

Lattke, Michael. *Hymnus: Materialen zu einer Geschichte der antiken Hymnologie*. NTOA 19. Göttingen: Vandenhoeck & Ruprecht, 1991.

–. "Dating the Odes of Solomon." Pages 113–132 in *Die Oden Salomos in ihrer Bedeutung für Neues Testament und Gnosis*. 25/4. Göttingen: Vandenhoeck & Ruprecht, 1998.

–. "Formen/Gattungen in den *Oden Salomos*." Pages 151–159 in *Die Oden Salomos in ihrer Bedeutung für Neues Testament und Gnosis*. 25/4. Göttingen: Vandenhoeck & Ruprecht, 1998.

–. *Oden Salomos: Text, Übersetzung, Kommentar. Teil 2. Oden 15–28*. NTOA 41/2. Göttingen: Vandenhoeck & Ruprecht, 2001.

Lattke, Michael and Harold W. Attridge. *Odes of Solomon: A Commentary*. Translated by Marianne Ehrhardt. Hermeneia. Minneapolis: Fortress Press, 2009.

Layton, Bentley. *The Gnostic Scriptures: A New Translation with Annotations and Introductions*. ABRL. New York: Doubleday, 1995.

Leonhard, Jutta. *Jewish Worship in Philo of Alexandria.* TSAJ 84. Tübingen: Mohr Siebeck, 2001.

Leonhardt-Balzer, Jutta. "Der Logos und die Schöpfung: Streiflichter bei Philo (Op 20–25) und im Johannesprolog (Joh 1,1–18) " Pages 295–319 in *Kontexte des Johannesevangeliums: das vierte Evangelium in religions- und traditionsgeschichtlicher Perspektive.* WUNT 175. Edited by Jörg Frey and Udo Schnelle. Tübingen: Mohr Siebeck, 2004.

Leuchter, Mark. "Why is the Song of Moses in Deuteronomy?" *VT* 57 (2007): 295–317.

Liesen, Jan. *Full of Praise: An Exegetical Study of Sir 39, 12–35.* JSJSup 64. Boston: Brill, 2000.

Lohse, Eduard. *Colossians and Philemon: A Commentary on the Epistles to the Colossians and to Philemon.* Philadelphia: Fortress Press, 1971.

Long, Anthony A. "Roman Philosophy." Pages 184–210 in *The Cambridge Companion to Greek and Roman Philosophy.* Edited by D. N. Sedley. Cambridge: Cambridge University Press, 2003.

–. *The Cambridge Companion to Early Greek Philosophy.* Cambridge Companions to Philosophy. Cambridge: Cambridge University Press, 2006.

Longenecker, Richard N. *New Wine into Fresh Wineskins: Contextualizing the Early Christian Confessions.* Peabody, Mass.: Hendrickson, 1999.

Lowrie, Michèle. *Horace's Narrative Odes.* Oxford: Oxford University Press, 1997.

Lucretius. *On the Nature of the Universe.* Translated by Ronald Melville; notes and introduction by Don Fowler and Peta Fowler. Oxford: Oxford University Press, 1999.

Lührmann, Dieter. "Paul and the Pharisaic Tradition." *JSNT* 36 (1989): 75–94.

Mack, Burton L. *Wisdom and the Hebrew Epic: Ben Sira's Hymn in Praise of the Fathers.* Chicago Studies in the History of Judaism. Chicago: University of Chicago Press, 1985.

Maier, Harry O. "A Sly Civility: Colossians and Empire." *JSNT* 27 (2005): 323–349.

Mair, A. W. *Callimachus, Hymns and Epigrams. Lycophron.* LCL 129. Cambridge, Mass.: Harvard University Press, 1977.

Mansoor, Menahem. *The Thanksgiving Hymns.* STDJ 3. Leiden: Brill, 1961.

Marcovich, Miroslav. "The Naassene Psalm in Hippolytus." Pages 80–88 in *Studies in Graeco-Roman Religions and Gnosticism.* Leiden: Brill, 1988.

Markschies, Christoph. *Valentinus Gnosticus?: Untersuchungen zur valentinianischen Gnosis mit einem Kommentar zu den Fragmenten Valentins.* WUNT 65. Tübingen: J. C. B. Mohr, 1992.

–. *Gnosis: An Introduction.* Translated by John Bowden. London: T & T Clark, 2003.

Martin, Ralph P. *A Hymn of Christ: Philippians 2:5–11 in Recent Interpretation and in the Setting of Early Christian Worship.* Downers Grove, IL: InterVarsity Press, 1997.

Martin, Troy W. *By Philosophy and Empty Deceit: Colossians as Response to a Cynic Critique.* JSNTSup 118. Sheffield: Sheffield Academic Press, 1996.

Martyn, J. Louis. "The Johannine Community among Jewish and other Early Christian Communities." Pages 183–190 in *What We Have Heard from the Beginning: The Past, Present, and Future of Johannine Studies.* Edited by Tom Thatcher. Waco, Tex.: Baylor University Press, 2007.

May, Gerhard. "Der Christushymnus des Clemens von Alexandrien." *Liturgie und Dichtung* 1 (1983): 257–273.

McKay, Heather A. *Sabbath and Synagogue: The Question of Sabbath Worship in Ancient Judaism.* RGRW. Leiden: Brill, 1994.

McKnight, Edgar V. *Postmodern Use of the Bible: the Emergence of Reader-Oriented Criticism.* Nashville: Abingdon Press, 1988.

Meeks, Wayne A. *The Prophet-King: Moses Traditions and the Johannine Christology.* Leiden: Brill, 1967.

Mendels, Doron. *Memory in Jewish, Pagan, and Christian Societies of the Graeco-Roman World.* LSTS 45. London: T & T Clark, 2004.

Metzger, Bruce M. "Fourth Ezra." Pages 525–559 in *The Old Testament Pseudepigrapha. Vol. 1, Apocalyptic Literature and Testaments.* Edited by James H. Charlesworth. Garden City, N.Y.: Doubleday, 1983.

Meyer, Marvin W. *The Ancient Mysteries: A Sourcebook.* Philadelphia: University of Pennsylvania Press, 1999.

Miller, Andrew M. *From Delos to Delphi: A Literary Study of the Homeric Hymn to Apollo.* Mnemosyne 93. Leiden: Brill, 1986.

Mittmann-Richert, Ulrike. *Magnifikat und Benediktus: die ältesten Zeugnisse der judenchristlichen Tradition von der Geburt des Messias.* WUNT 2.90. Tübingen: Mohr (Siebeck), 1996.

Moore, Carey A. *Daniel, Esther and Jeremiah: The Additions.* AB 44. New York: Doubleday, 1985.

–. *Tobit: A New Translation with Introduction and Commentary.* AB 40A. New York: Doubleday, 1996.

Moore, Stephen D. "The Revelation to John." Pages 436–455 in *A Postcolonial Commentary on the New Testament Writings.* The Bible and Postcolonialism. Edited by Fernando F. Segovia and R. S. Sugirtharajah. London: T & T Clark, 2007.

Moreschini, Claudio and Enrico Norelli. *Early Christian Greek and Latin Literature: A Literary History.* 2 vols. Peabody, Mass.: Hendrickson, 2005.

Morton, Russell S. *One upon the Throne and the Lamb: A Tradition Historical/Theological Analysis of Revelation 4–5.* New York: Peter Lang, 2007.

Most, Glenn W. *Hesiod: Theogony, Works and Days, Testimonia.* LCL 57. Cambridge, Mass.: Harvard University Press, 2006.

–. "The Poetics of Early Greek Philosophy." Pages 332–362 in *The Cambridge Companion to Early Greek Philosophy.* Edited by Anthony A. Long. Cambridge: Cambridge University Press, 2006.

–. "Religion and Philosophy." Pages 300–321 in *The Cambridge Companion to Greek and Roman Philosophy.* Edited by D. N. Sedley. Cambridge: Cambridge University Press, 2003.

Mowinckel, S. "Psalms and Wisdom." Pages 205–224 in *Wisdom in Israel and in the Ancient Near East.* Supplements to Vetus Testamentum. Edited by M. Noth and D. Winton Thomas. Leiden: Brill, 1955.

–. *The Psalms in Israel's Worship.* Translated by D. R. Ap-Thomas. Reprint of 1962 ed. 2 vols. Grand Rapids: Eerdmans, 2004.

Mowry, Lucetta. "Revelation 4–5 and Early Christian Liturgical Usage." *JBL* 71 (1952): 75–84.

Murphy-O'Connor, Jerome. *Paul: A Critical Life.* Oxford: Clarendon Press, 1996.

Murphy, Roland. "A Consideration of the Classification 'Wisdom Psalms' " Pages 456–467 in *Studies in Ancient Israelite Wisdom.* Edited by James L. Crenshaw. New York: Ktav Pub. House, 1976.

Myers, Jacob Martin. *I and II Esdras.* AB 42. Garden City, N.Y.: Doubleday, 1974.

Nagy, Gregory. "Ancient Greek Poetry, Prophecy, and Concepts of Theory." Pages 56–64 in *Poetry and Prophecy: The Beginnings of a Literary Tradition.* Edited by James L. Kugel. Ithaca, N.Y.: Cornell University Press, 1990.

–. *Greek Mythology and Poetics.* Myth and Poetics. Ithaca, N.Y.: Cornell University Press, 1990.

–. "Hesiod and the Ancient Biographical Traditions." *Brill Companion to Hesiod.* Edited by A. Rengakos and Ch. Tsagalis. Leiden: Brill, 2008.

–. *Homer the Preclassic*: University of California, 2009.

Najman, Hindy. *Seconding Sinai: The Development of Mosaic Discourse in Second Temple Judaism*. JSJSup 77. Leiden; Boston: Brill, 2003.

Nelson, Richard D. *Joshua: A Commentary*. The Old Testament Library. Louisville, Ky.: Westminster John Knox, 1997.

Newman, Carey C., James R. Davila, and Gladys S. Lewis. *The Jewish Roots of Christological Monotheism: Papers from the St. Andrews Conference on the Historical Origins of the Worship of Jesus*. JSJSup 63. Leiden; Boston: Brill, 1999.

Newman, Judith H. "Holy, Holy, Holy: The Use of Isaiah 6.3 in *Apostolic Constitutions* 7.35.1–10 and 8.12.6–27." Pages 2:123–134 in *Of Scribes and Sages: Early Jewish Interpretation and Transmission of Scripture*. Library of Second Temple Studies 50–51. Edited by Craig A. Evans. 2 vols. London: T & T Clark, 2004.

Newsom, Carol A. "Woman and the Discourse of Patriarchal Wisdom." Pages 116–131 in *Reading Bibles, Writing Bodies: Identity and the Book*. Edited by Timothy K. Beal and D. M. Gunn. New York: Routledge, 1997.

–. *The Self as Symbolic Space: Constructing Identity and Community at Qumran*. STDJ 52. Leiden: Brill, 2004.

Neyrey, Jerome. "'I Am the Door' (John 10:7, 9): Jesus the Broker in the Fourth Gospel." *CBQ* 69 (2007): 271–291.

Nickelsburg, George W. E. *1 Enoch 1: A Commentary on the Book of 1 Enoch, Chapters 1–36; 81–108*. Hermeneia. Minneapolis: Fortress Press, 2001.

–. *Jewish Literature between the Bible and the Mishnah: A Historical and Literary Introduction*. 2nd ed. Minneapolis: Fortress, 2005.

Nickelsburg, George W. E. and James C. VanderKam. *1 Enoch: A New Translation: Based on the Hermeneia Commentary*. Minneapolis: Fortress Press, 2004.

Nitzan, Bilha. *Qumran Prayer and Religious Poetry*. STDJ 12. Leiden: Brill, 1994.

Nolland, John. *Luke 1–9:20*. WBC 35A. Dallas: Word Books, 1989.

Norden, Eduard. *Agnostos Theos: Untersuchungen zur Formengeschichte religiöser Rede*. Stuttgart: B.G. Teubner, 1956.

O'Rourke, John J. "The Hymns of the Apocalypse." *CBQ* 30 (1968): 399–409.

Osborn, Eric Francis. *Clement of Alexandria*. Cambridge: Cambridge University Press, 2005.

Osiek, Carolyn. *Philippians, Philemon*. Nashville: Abingdon Press, 2000.

Parker, R. C. T. "Hymns (Greek)." Pages 735–736 in *Oxford Classical Dictionary*. Oxford: Oxford University Press, 2003.

Pearson, Birger A. *Ancient Gnosticism: Traditions and Literature*. Minneapolis, Minn.: Fortress Press, 2007.

Perdue, Leo G. *Wisdom and Creation: The Theology of Wisdom Literature*. Nashville: Abingdon, 1994.

–. *The Sword and the Stylus: An Introduction to Wisdom in the Age of Empires*. Grand Rapids: Eerdmans, 2008.

Pfeiff, Karl Arno, Gerd von der Gönna, and Erika Simon. *Homerische Hymnen*. Tübingen: Stauffenburg, 2002.

Phillips, Peter M. *The Prologue of the Fourth Gospel: A Sequential Reading*. LNTS 294. London: T&T Clark, 2006.

Pindar. *Olympian Odes; Pythian Odes*. Translated by William H. Race. LCL 56. Cambridge, Mass.: Harvard University Press, 1997.

Pizzuto, Vincent A. *A Cosmic Leap of Faith: An Authorial, Structural, and Theological Investigation of the Cosmic Christology in Col. 1:15–20*. CBET 41. Leuven: Peeters, 2006.

Pliny. *Letters and Panegyricus*. Translated by Betty Radice. LCL 59. Cambridge: Heinemann, 1969.

Pohlenz, M. *Die Stoa: Geschichte einer geistigen Bewegung.* Göttingen: Vandenhoeck & Ruprecht, 1948.

Pokorný, Petr. *Colossians: A Commentary.* Peabody, Mass.: Hendrickson, 1991.

Pötscher, Walter. "Das Selbstverständnis des Dichters in der homerischen Poesie." *Literaturwissenschaftliches Jahrbuch* 27 (1986): 9–22.

Price, S. R. F. *Rituals and Power: The Roman Imperial Cult in Asia Minor.* Cambridge: Cambridge University Press, 1986.

Puech, Émile. "Hodayot." Pages 365–369 in *Encyclopedia of the Dead Sea Scrolls.* Edited by Lawrence H. Schiffman and James C. VanderKam. 2 vols. New York: Oxford University Press, 2000.

Putnam, Michael C. J. *Artifices of Eternity: Horace's Fourth Book of Odes.* Ithaca: Cornell University Press, 1986.

Quintilian. *The Orator's Education.* Translated by D. A. Russell. LCL 124–127, 494. Cambridge, Mass.: Harvard University Press, 2001.

Race, William H. *Style and Rhetoric in Pindar's Odes.* Atlanta: Scholars Press, 1990.

Rad, Gerhard von. *Wisdom in Israel.* Translated by James D. Martin. Nashville: Abingdon Press, 1972.

Ravens, David. *Luke and the Restoration of Israel.* JSNTSup 119. Sheffield: Sheffield Academic Press, 1995.

Reese, James M. *Hellenistic Influence on the Book of Wisdom and Its Consequences.* Analecta Biblica, 41. Rome: Biblical Institute Press, 1970.

Reif, Stefan C. *Judaism and Hebrew Prayer: New Perspectives on Jewish Liturgical History.* Cambridge: Cambridge University Press, 1993.

Reumann, John. *Philippians: A New Translation with Introduction and Commentary.* AB 33B. New Haven: Yale University, 2008.

Richardson, N. J. *The Homeric Hymn to Demeter.* Oxford: Clarendon Press, 1974.

Rubinkiewicz, R. and H. G. Lunt. "The Apocalypse of Abraham." Pages 781–705 in *The Old Testament Pseudepigrapha. Vol. 1, Apocalyptic Literature and Testaments.* Edited by James H. Charlesworth. Garden City, N.Y.: Doubleday, 1983.

Rudolph, Kurt. *Gnosis: The Nature and History of Gnosticism.* San Francisco: Harper & Row, 1983.

Russell, Brian D. *The Song of the Sea: The Date of Composition and Influence of Exodus 15, 1–21.* Studies in Biblical Literature, 101. New York: Peter Lang, 2007.

Russell, D. A. "Aristides and the Prose Hymn." Pages 199–216 in *Antonine Literature.* Edited by D. A. Russell. Oxford: Clarendon Press, 1990.

Russo, Ardea. "Behind the Heavenly Door: Earthly Liturgy and Heavenly Worship in the Apocalypse of John." PhD Diss., University of Notre Dame, 2009.

Sandbach, F. H. *The Stoics.* 2nd ed. Bristol: Bristol Press, 1989.

Sanders, Jack T. *The New Testament Christological Hymns: Their Historical Religious Background.* SNTSMS 15. Cambridge: Cambridge University Press, 1971.

Satake, Akira. *Die Offenbarung des Johannes.* KEK 16. Göttingen: Vandenhoeck & Ruprecht, 2008.

Sawyer, Deborah F. *God, Gender, and the Bible.* London: Routledge, 2002.

Schiesaro, Alessandro. "Lucretius and Roman Politics and History." Pages 41–58 in *The Cambridge Companion to Lucretius.* Edited by Stuart Gillespie and Philip R. Hardie. Cambridge: Cambridge University Press, 2007.

Schille, Gottfried. *Frühchristliche Hymnen.* Berlin: Evangelische Verlagsanstalt, 1965.

Schmitt, Von Armin. "Struktur, Herkunft und Bedeutung der Beispielreihe in Weish 10." *BZ* 21 (1977): 1–22.

Schnackenburg, Rudolf. *The Gospel According to St. John: Volume 1.* Translated by Kevin Smyth. HTKNT. New York: Herder & Herder, 1968.

Schoedel, William R. *Ignatius of Antioch: A Commentary on the Letters of Ignatius of Antioch*. Hermeneia. Philadelphia: Fortress Press, 1985.

Schuller, Eileen M. "Some Reflections on the Function and Use of Poetical Texts among the Dead Sea Scrolls." Pages 173–189 in *Liturgical Perspectives: Prayer and Poetry in Light of the Dead Sea Scrolls*. Studies on the Texts of the Desert of Judah. Edited by Esther G. Chazon. Leiden: Brill, 2003.

Schultz, Brian. *Conquering the World: The War Scroll (1QM) Reconsidered*. STDJ 76. Leiden: Brill, 2009.

Schüpphaus, Joachim. *Die Psalmen Salomos: ein Zeugnis Jerusalemer Theologie und Frömmigkeit in der Mitte des vorchristlichen Jahrhunderts*. ALGHJ 7. Leiden: Brill, 1977.

Schwabl, Hans. "Aus der Geschichte der Hymnischen Prooimien: Homer, Hesiod, art, Lukrez – und ein Blick auf den Zeushymnus des Kleanthes." *Wiener humanistische Blätter* 43 (2001): 39–105.

Scott, Martin. *Sophia and the Johannine Jesus*. Sheffield: JSOT Press, 1992.

Scott, R. B. Y. *Proverbs, Ecclesiastes*. AB 18. Garden City, N.Y.: Doubleday, 1965.

Sedley, D. N. *The Cambridge Companion to Greek and Roman Philosophy*. Cambridge Companions to Philosophy. Cambridge: Cambridge University Press, 2003.

–. "The Empedoclean Opening." Pages 48–87 in *Lucretius*. Edited by Monica Gale. Oxford: Oxford University Press, 2007.

Seely, David and Moshe Weinfeld. "Barkhi Nafshi." Pages 255–334 in *Qumran Cave 4.XX: Poetical and Liturgical Texts, Part 2*. DJD XXIX. Edited by Esther G. Chazon et al. Oxford: Clarendon Press, 1999.

Segal, Charles. "Bard and Audience in Homer." Pages 113–141 in *Singers, Heroes, and Gods in the Odyssey*. Edited by Charles Segal. Ithaca, N.Y.: Cornell University Press, 1994.

Siegert, Folker. "Der Logos, 'älterer Sohn' des Schöpfers und 'zweiter Gott.' Philons Logos und der Johannesprolog." Pages 277–293 in *Kontexte des Johannesevangeliums: das vierte Evangelium in religions- und traditionsgeschichtlicher Perspektive*. WUNT 175. Edited by Jörg Frey and Udo Schnelle. Tübingen: Mohr Siebeck, 2004.

Signer, Michael A. *Memory and History in Christianity and Judaism*. Notre Dame, Ind.: University of Notre Dame, 2001.

Skehan, Patrick W. "Borrowings from the Psalms in the Book of Wisdom." *CBQ* 10 (1948): 384–97.

Skehan, Patrick W. and Alexander A. Di Lella. *The Wisdom of Ben Sira: A New Translation with Notes and Commentary*. AB 39. New York: Doubleday, 1987.

Smith, J. A. "The Ancient Synagogue, the Early Church, and Singing." *Music and Letters* 65 (1984): 1–16.

Sommer, Benjamin D. *A Prophet Reads Scripture: Allusion in Isaiah 40–66*. Stanford, Calif: Stanford University Press, 1998.

Stander, H. F. "The Star-Hymn in the Epistle of Ignatius to the Ephesians (19:2–3)." *VC* 43 (1989): 209–214.

Stauffer, Ethelbert. *New Testament Theology*. Translated by John Marsh. London: SCM Press, 1955.

Stegemann, Hartmut, Eileen M. Schuller, and Carol A. Newsom. *1QHodayot^a: With Incorporation of 1QHodayot^b and 4QHodayot^{a-f}*. DJD 40. Oxford: Clarendon Press, 2009.

Sterling, Gregory E. "Prepositional Metaphysics in Jewish Wisdom Speculation and Early Christological Hymns." Pages 219–238 in *Wisdom and Logos: Studies in Jewish Thought in Honor of David Winston*. Studia philonica 9. Edited by D. T. Runia and Gregory E. Sterling. Atlanta: Scholars Press, 1997.

Stettler, Christian. *Der Kolosserhymnus: Untersuchungen zu Form, traditionsgeschichtlichem Hintergrund und Aussage von Kol 1,15–20.* WUNT 2.131. Tübingen: Mohr Siebeck, 2000.

Steudel, Annette. "The Eternal Reign of the People of God: Collective Expectations in Qumran Texts (4Q246 and 1QM)." *RevQ* 17 (1996): 507–525.

Stone, Michael E. "Apocalyptic Literature." Pages 383–441 in *Jewish Writings of the Second Temple Period: Apocrypha, Pseudepigrapha, Qumran, Sectarian Writings, Philo, Josephus.* Edited by Michael E. Stone. Assen, Netherlands; Philadelphia: Van Gorcum; Fortress Press, 1984.

–. *Jewish Writings of the Second Temple Period: Apocrypha, Pseudepigrapha, Qumran, Sectarian Writings, Philo, Josephus.* CRINT. Section 2, Literature of the Jewish People in the Period of the Second Temple and the Talmud 2. Assen, Netherlands; Philadelphia: Van Gorcum; Fortress Press, 1984.

–. *Fourth Ezra: A Commentary on the Book of Fourth Ezra.* Hermeneia. Minneapolis: Fortress Press, 1990.

Suetonius. *Suetonius.* Translated by John Carew Rolfe. Rev. ed. LCL 38. Cambridge, Mass.: Harvard University Press, 1998.

Sumney, Jerry L. *Colossians: A Commentary.* Louisville, Ky.: Westminster John Knox, 2008.

Sutherland, Elizabeth H. *Horace's Well-Trained Reader: Toward a Methodology of Audience Participation in the Odes.* Studien zur klassischen Philologie 136. Frankfurt am Main: Peter Lang, 2002.

Terrien, Samuel L. "Wisdom in the Psalter." Pages 51–72 in *In Search of Wisdom: Essays in Memory of John G. Gammie.* Edited by Leo G. Perdue, Bernard Brandon Scott, and William Johnston Wiseman. Louisville, Ky.: Westminster/John Knox, 1993.

–. *The Psalms: Strophic Structure and Theological Commentary.* The Eerdmans Critical Commentary. Grand Rapids: Eerdmans, 2003.

Theobald, Michael. *Die Fleischwerdung des Logos: Studien zum Verhältnis des Johannesprologs zum Corpus des Evangeliums und zu 1 Joh.* NTAbh 20. Münster: Aschendorff, 1988.

Theocritus. *Idylls.* Translated by Anthony Verity. New ed. Oxford World's Classics. Oxford: Oxford University Press, 2008.

Thom, Johan C. *Cleanthes' Hymn to Zeus.* STAC 33. Tübingen: Mohr Siebeck, 2005.

Thompson, Leonard L. *The Book of Revelation: Apocalypse and Empire.* New York: Oxford University Press, 1990.

Thyen, Hartwig. *Das Johannesevangelium.* HNT 6. Tübingen: Mohr Siebeck, 2005.

Tigay, Jeffrey Howard. *Deuteronomy: The Traditional Hebrew Text with the New JPS Translation.* The JPS Torah Commentary. Philadelphia: Jewish Publication Society, 1996.

Tobin, Thomas. "The Prologue of John and Hellenistic Jewish Speculation." *CBQ* 52 (1990): 252–269.

–. "The World of Thought in the Philippians Hymn (Philippians 2:6–11)." Pages 91–104 in *The New Testament and Early Christian Literature in Greco-Roman Context: Studies in Honor of David E. Aune.* Edited by John Fotopoulos. Leiden: Brill, 2006.

Toohey, Peter. *Epic Lessons: An Introduction to Ancient Didactic Poetry.* London: Routledge, 1996.

Towner, W. Sibley. "The Poetic Passages in Daniel 1–6." *CBQ* 31 (1969): 317–326.

VanderKam, James C. *Enoch: A Man for All Generations.* Studies on Personalities of the Old Testament. Columbia, S.C.: University of South Carolina Press, 1995.

–. *An Introduction to Early Judaism.* 2nd ed. Grand Rapids: Eerdmans, 2003.

Vanderlip, Vera Frederika. *The Four Greek Hymns of Isidorus and the Cult of Isis.* ASP 12. Toronto: A. M. Hakkert, 1972.

Verdenius, Willem Jacob. *A Commentary on Hesiod: Works and Days, vv. 1–382.* Mnemosyne. Supplementum 86. Leiden: Brill, 1985.

Walsh, Brian J. and Sylvia C. Keesmaat. *Colossians Remixed: Subverting the Empire.* Downers Grove, Ill.: InterVarsity Press, 2004.

Walter, Nikolaus, Eckart Reinmuth, and Peter Lampe. *Die Briefe an die Philipper, Thessalonicher und an Philemon.* NTD 8/2. Göttingen: Vandenhoeck & Ruprecht, 1998.

Waltke, Bruce K. *The Book of Proverbs: Chapters 1–15.* NICOT. ser. Ed. Robert L. Hubbard, Jr. Grand Rapids: Eerdmans, 2004.

Watts, James W. *Psalm and Story: Inset Hymns in Hebrew Narrative.* JSOTSup 139. Sheffield: JSOT Press, 1992.

Weitzman, Steven. *Song and Story in Biblical Narrative: The History of a Literary Convention in Ancient Israel.* Indiana Studies in Biblical Literature. Bloomington: Indiana University Press, 1997.

Wenthe, Dean O. "The Use of the Hebrew Scriptures in 1QM." *DSD* 5 (1998): 290–319.

West, M. L. *Hesiod: Works and Days.* Oxford: Clarendon Press, 1978.

–. *Greek Metre.* Oxford: Clarendon Press, 1982.

–. *Hesiod: Theogony.* Oxford: Clarendon Press, 1997.

–. *Homeric Hymns, Homeric Apocrypha, Lives of Homer.* LCL 496. Cambridge, Mass.: Harvard University Press, 2003.

Westermann, Claus. *Isaiah 40–66: A Commentary.* OTL. London: SCM Press, 1976.

Wilken, Robert Louis. *The Spirit of Early Christian Thought: Seeking the Face of God.* New Haven: Yale University Press, 2003.

Wilks, John G. F. "The Prophet as Incompetent Dramatist." *VT* 53 (2003): 530–543.

Willcock, M. M. *Pindar: Victory Odes.* CGLC. Cambridge: Cambridge University Press, 1995.

Williams, Gordon Willis. *Horace.* Greece & Rome. New Surveys in the Classics 6. Oxford: Clarendon Press, 1972.

Wilson, R. McL. *Colossians and Philemon: A Critical and Exegetical Commentary.* London: T & T Clark, 2005.

Wilson, Stephen G. "Music in the Early Church." Pages 390–401 in *Common Life in the Early Church: Essays Honoring Graydon F. Snyder.* Edited by Julian V. Hills and Richard B. Gardner. Harrisburg, Pa.: Trinity Press International, 1998.

Wilson, Walter T. *The Hope of Glory: Education and Exhortation in the Epistle to the Colossians.* NovTSup 88. New York: Brill, 1997.

Winston, David. *The Wisdom of Solomon: A New Translation with Introduction and Commentary.* AB 43. Garden City, N.Y.: Doubleday and Company, 1979.

Wise, Michael Owen. "The Concept of a New Covenant in the Teacher Hymns from Qumran (1QH^A X–XVII)." Pages 99–128 in *The Concept of the Covenant in the Second Temple Period.* Supplements to the Journal for the Study of Judaism 71. Edited by Stanley E. Porter and Jacqueline C. R. De Roo. Leiden: Brill, 2003.

Wolbergs, Thielko. *Griechische religiöse Gedichte der ersten nachchristlichen Jahrhunderte.* Beiträge zur klassischen Philologie 40. Meisenheim am Glan: A. Hain, 1971.

Wolter, Michael. *Das Lukasevangelium.* HNT 5. Tübingen: Mohr Siebeck, 2008.

Wright, N. T. "Poetry and Theology in Colossians 1:15–20." *NTS* 36 (1990): 444–468.

–. "Worship and the Spirit in the New Testament." Pages 3–24 in *The Spirit in Worship, Worship in the Spirit.* Edited by Teresa Berger and Bryan D. Spinks. Collegeville, Minn.: Liturgical Press, 2009.

Wright, R. B. "Psalms of Solomon: A New Translation and Introduction." Pages 639–70 in *The Old Testament Pseudepigrapha, Vol. 2.* Edited by James H. Charlesworth. New York: Doubleday, 1985.

Yadin, Yigael. *The Scroll of the War of the Sons of Light against the Sons of Darkness.* London: Oxford University Press, 1962.

Zerbe, Gordon and Muriel Orevillo-Montenegro. "The Letter to the Colossians." Pages 294–303 in *A Postcolonial Commentary on the New Testament Writings*. The Bible and Postcolonialism 13. Edited by Fernando F. Segovia and R. S. Sugirtharajah. London: T & T Clark, 2007.

Index of Ancient Sources

1. Hebrew Bible

2. Apocrypha and Pseudepigrapha

3. Dead Sea Scrolls

4. New Testament

5. Early Christian Writings

6. Greek and Roman Authors

7.1–21	102		1.81–98	103
7.16–21	103		1.92–100	23
			1.92–98	107
Nemean Odes			1.94–98	205
2.1	31		1.99–100	103, 107
3.6–12	103		2.15–17	205
6.1–6	103		2.21–24	205
6.28–30	103		10.22–29	103
7.1–9	102			
7.9–16	103		Plato	
7.54–58	103		*Ion*	34
7.61–79	103			
9.6–7	103		Pliny	
9.44–47	103		*Epistulae*	
10.1–3	205		3.13.1	139
10.4–18	205		10.96.7	272
Olympian Odes			*Panegyricus*	
2.53–80	103		1.3	140
8.12–14	103		2.3	140
12.1–14	102		4.1	139
			5.1–2	140
Pythian Odes			11.2	141
1	22, 104, 108		47.1	143
1.1–12	104–105, 107		48.3	143
1.5	105		52.2	140, 142
1.6–10	105		52.6	140, 142
1.10–12	105		53.1	143
1.12–28	105		53.2	144
1.13–28	104		80.1–2	298
1.15	107		80.3	24, 141
1.28	105		80.4–5	141
1.29	105		87.1	145
1.29–33	105		90.5–6	143
1.32–33	104		93.1	145
1.33–38	106		93.3	26, 143–144
1.39–40	106			
1.41–42	103, 107		Plutarch	
1.47–57	106		*Ad principem ineruditum*	
1.48	107		5.781f–82a	298
1.50	107			
1.56–57	107		*Adversus Colotem*	
1.58–61	106		1117b–c	95
1.59	104			
1.61–66	106		*De fortuna Romanorum*	
1.67–68	107		2.316e–317c	298
1.67–72	106			
1.70	107		*Themistocles*	
1.73–80	106		27.4.4–5	298
1.80	107			

7. Papyri and Inscriptions

Index of Modern Authors

Index of Subjects

Wissenschaftliche Untersuchungen zum Neuen Testament

Alphabetical Index of the First and Second Series

Becker, Michael and *Markus Öhler* (Ed.): Apokalyptik als Herausforderung neutestamentlicher Theologie. 2006. *Vol. II/214.*

Bell, Richard H.: Deliver Us from Evil. 2007. *Vol. 216.*

– The Irrevocable Call of God. 2005. *Vol. 184.*

– No One Seeks for God. 1998. *Vol. 106.*

– Provoked to Jealousy. 1994. *Vol. II/63.*

Bennema, Cornelis: The Power of Saving Wisdom. 2002. *Vol. II/148.*

Bergman, Jan: see *Kieffer, René*

Bergmeier, Roland: Das Gesetz im Römerbrief und andere Studien zum Neuen Testament. 2000. *Vol. 121.*

Bernett, Monika: Der Kaiserkult in Judäa unter den Herodiern und Römern. 2007. *Vol. 203.*

Betz, Otto: Jesus, der Messias Israels. 1987. *Vol. 42.*

– Jesus, der Herr der Kirche. 1990. *Vol. 52.*

Beyschlag, Karlmann: Simon Magus und die christliche Gnosis. 1974. *Vol. 16.*

Bieringer, Reimund: see *Koester, Craig.*

Bittner, Wolfgang J.: Jesu Zeichen im Johannesevangelium. 1987. *Vol. II/26.*

Bjerkelund, Carl J.: Tauta Egeneto. 1987. *Vol. 40.*

Blackburn, Barry Lee: Theios Aner and the Markan Miracle Traditions. 1991. *Vol. II/40.*

Blanton IV, Thomas R.: Constructing a New Covenant. 2007. *Vol. II/233.*

Bock, Darrell L.: Blasphemy and Exaltation in Judaism and the Final Examination of Jesus. 1998. *Vol. II/106.*

– and *Robert L. Webb* (Ed.): Key Events in the Life of the Historical Jesus. 2009. *Vol. 247.*

Bockmuehl, Markus: The Remembered Peter. 2010. *Vol. 262.*

– Revelation and Mystery in Ancient Judaism and Pauline Christianity. 1990. *Vol. II/36.*

Bøe, Sverre: Cross-Bearing in Luke. 2010. *Vol. II/278.*

– Gog and Magog. 2001. *Vol. II/135.*

Böhlig, Alexander: Gnosis und Synkretismus. Vol. 1 1989. *Vol. 47* – Vol. 2 1989. *Vol. 48.*

Böhm, Martina: Samarien und die Samaritai bei Lukas. 1999. *Vol. II/111.*

Börstinghaus, Jens: Sturmfahrt und Schiffbruch. 2010. *Vol. II/274.*

Böttrich, Christfried: Weltweisheit – Menschheitsethik – Urkult. 1992. *Vol. II/50.*

– and *Herzer, Jens* (Ed.): Josephus und das Neue Testament. 2007. *Vol. 209.*

Bolyki, János: Jesu Tischgemeinschaften. 1997. *Vol. II/96.*

Bosman, Philip: Conscience in Philo and Paul. 2003. *Vol. II/166.*

Bovon, François: New Testament and Christian Apocrypha. 2009. *Vol. 237.*

– Studies in Early Christianity. 2003. *Vol. 161.*

Brändl, Martin: Der Agon bei Paulus. 2006. *Vol. II/222.*

Braun, Heike: Geschichte des Gottesvolkes und christliche Identität. 2010. *Vol. II/279.*

Breytenbach, Cilliers: see *Frey, Jörg.*

Broadhead, Edwin K.: Jewish Ways of Following Jesus Redrawing the Religious Map of Antiquity. 2010. *Vol. 266.*

Brocke, Christoph vom: Thessaloniki – Stadt des Kassander und Gemeinde des Paulus. 2001. *Vol. II/125.*

Brunson, Andrew: Psalm 118 in the Gospel of John. 2003. *Vol. II/158.*

Büchli, Jörg: Der Poimandres – ein paganisiertes Evangelium. 1987. *Vol. II/27.*

Bühner, Jan A.: Der Gesandte und sein Weg im 4. Evangelium. 1977. *Vol. II/2.*

Burchard, Christoph: Untersuchungen zu Joseph und Aseneth. 1965. *Vol. 8.*

– Studien zur Theologie, Sprache und Umwelt des Neuen Testaments. Ed. by D. Sänger. 1998. *Vol. 107.*

Burnett, Richard: Karl Barth's Theological Exegesis. 2001. *Vol. II/145.*

Byron, John: Slavery Metaphors in Early Judaism and Pauline Christianity. 2003. *Vol. II/162.*

Byrskog, Samuel: Story as History – History as Story. 2000. *Vol. 123.*

Cancik, Hubert (Ed.): Markus-Philologie. 1984. *Vol. 33.*

Capes, David B.: Old Testament Yaweh Texts in Paul's Christology. 1992. *Vol. II/47.*

Caragounis, Chrys C.: The Development of Greek and the New Testament. 2004. *Vol. 167.*

– The Son of Man. 1986. *Vol. 38.*

– see *Fridrichsen, Anton.*

Carleton Paget, James: The Epistle of Barnabas. 1994. *Vol. II/64.*

– Jews, Christians and Jewish Christians in Antiquity. 2010. *Vol. 251.*

Carson, D.A., O'Brien, Peter T. and *Mark Seifrid* (Ed.): Justification and Variegated Nomism.

Vol. 1: The Complexities of Second Temple Judaism. 2001. *Vol. II/140.*

Vol. 2: The Paradoxes of Paul. 2004. *Vol. II/181.*

Chae, Young Sam: Jesus as the Eschatological Davidic Shepherd. 2006. *Vol. II/216.*

Chapman, David W.: Ancient Jewish and Christian Perceptions of Crucifixion. 2008. *Vol. II/244.*

Chester, Andrew: Messiah and Exaltation. 2007. *Vol. 207.*

Chibici-Revneanu, Nicole: Die Herrlichkeit des Verherrlichten. 2007. *Vol. II/231.*

Ciampa, Roy E.: The Presence and Function of Scripture in Galatians 1 and 2. 1998. *Vol. II/102.*

Classen, Carl Joachim: Rhetorical Criticsm of the New Testament. 2000. *Vol. 128.*

Colpe, Carsten: Griechen – Byzantiner – Semiten – Muslime. 2008. *Vol. 221.*

– Iranier – Aramäer – Hebräer – Hellenen. 2003. *Vol. 154.*

Cook, John G.: Roman Attitudes Towards the Christians. 2010. *Vol. 261.*

Coote, Robert B. (Ed.): see *Weissenrieder, Annette.*

Coppins, Wayne: The Interpretation of Freedom in the Letters of Paul. 2009. *Vol. II/261.*

Crump, David: Jesus the Intercessor. 1992. *Vol. II/49.*

Dahl, Nils Alstrup: Studies in Ephesians. 2000. *Vol. 131.*

Daise, Michael A.: Feasts in John. 2007. *Vol. II/229.*

Deines, Roland: Die Gerechtigkeit der Tora im Reich des Messias. 2004. *Vol. 177.*

– Jüdische Steingefäße und pharisäische Frömmigkeit. 1993. *Vol. II/52.*

– Die Pharisäer. 1997. *Vol. 101.*

Deines, Roland and *Karl-Wilhelm Niebuhr* (Ed.): Philo und das Neue Testament. 2004. *Vol. 172.*

Dennis, John A.: Jesus' Death and the Gathering of True Israel. 2006. *Vol. 217.*

Dettwiler, Andreas and *Jean Zumstein* (Ed.): Kreuzestheologie im Neuen Testament. 2002. *Vol. 151.*

Dickson, John P.: Mission-Commitment in Ancient Judaism and in the Pauline Communities. 2003. *Vol. II/159.*

Dietzfelbinger, Christian: Der Abschied des Kommenden. 1997. *Vol. 95.*

Dimitrov, Ivan Z., James D.G. Dunn, Ulrich Luz and *Karl-Wilhelm Niebuhr* (Ed.): Das Alte Testament als christliche Bibel in orthodoxer und westlicher Sicht. 2004. *Vol. 174.*

Dobbeler, Axel von: Glaube als Teilhabe. 1987. *Vol. II/22.*

Docherty, Susan E.: The Use of the Old Testament in Hebrews. 2009. *Vol. II/260.*

Dochhorn, Jan: Schriftgelehrte Prophetie. 2010. *Vol. 268.*

Downs, David J.: The Offering of the Gentiles. 2008. *Vol. II/248.*

Dryden, J. de Waal: Theology and Ethics in 1 Peter. 2006. *Vol. II/209.*

Dübbers, Michael: Christologie und Existenz im Kolosserbrief. 2005. *Vol. II/191.*

Dunn, James D.G.: The New Perspective on Paul. 2005. *Vol. 185.*

Dunn , James D.G. (Ed.): Jews and Christians. 1992. *Vol. 66.*

– Paul and the Mosaic Law. 1996. *Vol. 89.*

– see *Dimitrov, Ivan Z.*

–, *Hans Klein, Ulrich Luz,* and *Vasile Mihoc* (Ed.): Auslegung der Bibel in orthodoxer und westlicher Perspektive. 2000. *Vol. 130.*

Ebel, Eva: Die Attraktivität früher christlicher Gemeinden. 2004. *Vol. II/178.*

Ebertz, Michael N.: Das Charisma des Gekreuzigten. 1987. *Vol. 45.*

Eckstein, Hans-Joachim: Der Begriff Syneidesis bei Paulus. 1983. *Vol. II/10.*

– Verheißung und Gesetz. 1996. *Vol. 86.*

Ego, Beate: Im Himmel wie auf Erden. 1989. *Vol. II/34.*

Ego, Beate, Armin Lange and *Peter Pilhofer* (Ed.): Gemeinde ohne Tempel – Community without Temple. 1999. *Vol. 118.*

– and *Helmut Merkel* (Ed.): Religiöses Lernen in der biblischen, frühjüdischen und frühchristlichen Überlieferung. 2005. *Vol. 180.*

Eisele, Wilfried: Welcher Thomas? 2010. *Vol. 259.*

Eisen, Ute E.: see *Paulsen, Henning.*

Elledge, C.D.: Life after Death in Early Judaism. 2006. *Vol. II/208.*

Ellis, E. Earle: Prophecy and Hermeneutic in Early Christianity. 1978. *Vol. 18.*

– The Old Testament in Early Christianity. 1991. *Vol. 54.*

Elmer, Ian J.: Paul, Jerusalem and the Judaisers. 2009. *Vol. II/258.*

Endo, Masanobu: Creation and Christology. 2002. *Vol. 149.*

Ennulat, Andreas: Die 'Minor Agreements'. 1994. *Vol. II/62.*

Ensor, Peter W.: Jesus and His 'Works'. 1996. *Vol. II/85.*

Eskola, Timo: Messiah and the Throne. 2001. *Vol. II/142.*

– Theodicy and Predestination in Pauline Soteriology. 1998. *Vol. II/100.*

Farelly, Nicolas: The Disciples in the Fourth Gospel. 2010. *Vol. II/290.*
Fatehi, Mehrdad: The Spirit's Relation to the Risen Lord in Paul. 2000. *Vol. II/128.*
Feldmeier, Reinhard: Die Krisis des Gottessohnes. 1987. *Vol. II/21.*
– Die Christen als Fremde. 1992. *Vol. 64.*
Feldmeier, Reinhard and *Ulrich Heckel* (Ed.): Die Heiden. 1994. *Vol. 70.*
Finnern, Sönke: Narratologie und biblische Exegese. 2010. *Vol. II/285.*
Fletcher-Louis, Crispin H.T.: Luke-Acts: Angels, Christology and Soteriology. 1997. *Vol. II/94.*
Förster, Niclas: Marcus Magus. 1999. *Vol. 114.*
Forbes, Christopher Brian: Prophecy and Inspired Speech in Early Christianity and its Hellenistic Environment. 1995. *Vol. II/75.*
Fornberg, Tord: see *Fridrichsen, Anton.*
Fossum, Jarl E.: The Name of God and the Angel of the Lord. 1985. *Vol. 36.*
Foster, Paul: Community, Law and Mission in Matthew's Gospel. *Vol. II/177.*
Fotopoulos, John: Food Offered to Idols in Roman Corinth. 2003. *Vol. II/151.*
Frank, Nicole: Der Kolosserbrief im Kontext des paulinischen Erbes. 2009. *Vol. II/271.*
Frenschkowski, Marco: Offenbarung und Epiphanie. Vol. 1 1995. *Vol. II/79* – Vol. 2 1997. *Vol. II/80.*
Frey, Jörg: Eugen Drewermann und die biblische Exegese. 1995. *Vol. II/71.*
– Die johanneische Eschatologie. Vol. I. 1997. *Vol. 96.* – Vol. II. 1998. *Vol. 110.* – Vol. III. 2000. *Vol. 117.*
Frey, Jörg and *Cilliers Breytenbach* (Ed.): Aufgabe und Durchführung einer Theologie des Neuen Testaments. 2007. *Vol. 205.*
– *Jens Herzer, Martina Janßen* and *Clare K. Rothschild* (Ed.): Pseudepigraphie und Verfasserfiktion in frühchristlichen Briefen. 2009. *Vol. 246.*
– *Stefan Krauter* and *Hermann Lichtenberger* (Ed.): Heil und Geschichte. 2009. *Vol. 248.*
– and *Udo Schnelle (Ed.):* Kontexte des Johannesevangeliums. 2004. *Vol. 175.*
– and *Jens Schröter* (Ed.): Deutungen des Todes Jesu im Neuen Testament. 2005. *Vol. 181.*
– Jesus in apokryphen Evangelienüberlieferungen. 2010. *Vol. 254.*
–, *Jan G. van der Watt,* and *Ruben Zimmermann* (Ed.): Imagery in the Gospel of John. 2006. *Vol. 200.*

Freyne, Sean: Galilee and Gospel. 2000. *Vol. 125.*
Fridrichsen, Anton: Exegetical Writings. Edited by C.C. Caragounis and T. Fornberg. 1994. *Vol. 76.*
Gadenz, Pablo T.: Called from the Jews and from the Gentiles. 2009. *Vol. II/267.*
Gäbel, Georg: Die Kulttheologie des Hebräerbriefes. 2006. *Vol. II/212.*
Gäckle, Volker: Die Starken und die Schwachen in Korinth und in Rom. 2005. *Vol. 200.*
Garlington, Don B.: 'The Obedience of Faith'. 1991. *Vol. II/38.*
– Faith, Obedience, and Perseverance. 1994. *Vol. 79.*
Garnet, Paul: Salvation and Atonement in the Qumran Scrolls. 1977. *Vol. II/3.*
Gemünden, Petra von (Ed.): see *Weissenrieder, Annette.*
Gese, Michael: Das Vermächtnis des Apostels. 1997. *Vol. II/99.*
Gheorghita, Radu: The Role of the Septuagint in Hebrews. 2003. *Vol. II/160.*
Gordley, Matthew E.: The Colossian Hymn in Context. 2007. *Vol. II/228.*
– Teaching through Song in Antiquity. 2011. *Vol. II/302.*
Gräbe, Petrus J.: The Power of God in Paul's Letters. 2000, ²2008. *Vol. II/123.*
Gräßer, Erich: Der Alte Bund im Neuen. 1985. *Vol. 35.*
– Forschungen zur Apostelgeschichte. 2001. *Vol. 137.*
Grappe, Christian (Ed.): Le Repas de Dieu / Das Mahl Gottes. 2004. *Vol. 169.*
Gray, Timothy C.: The Temple in the Gospel of Mark. 2008. *Vol. II/242.*
Green, Joel B.: The Death of Jesus. 1988. *Vol. II/33.*
Gregg, Brian Han: The Historical Jesus and the Final Judgment Sayings in Q. 2005. *Vol. II/207.*
Gregory, Andrew: The Reception of Luke and Acts in the Period before Irenaeus. 2003. *Vol. II/169.*
Grindheim, Sigurd: The Crux of Election. 2005. *Vol. II/202.*
Gundry, Robert H.: The Old is Better. 2005. *Vol. 178.*
Gundry Volf, Judith M.: Paul and Perseverance. 1990. *Vol. II/37.*
Häußer, Detlef: Christusbekenntnis und Jesusüberlieferung bei Paulus. 2006. *Vol. 210.*
Hafemann, Scott J.: Suffering and the Spirit. 1986. *Vol. II/19.*

– Paul, Moses, and the History of Israel. 1995.
Vol. 81.

Hahn, Ferdinand: Studien zum Neuen Testament.
Vol. I: Grundsatzfragen, Jesusforschung, Evangelien. 2006. *Vol. 191.*
Vol. II: Bekenntnisbildung und Theologie in urchristlicher Zeit. 2006. *Vol. 192.*

Hahn, Johannes (Ed.): Zerstörungen des Jerusalemer Tempels. 2002. *Vol. 147.*

Hamid-Khani, Saeed: Relevation and Concealment of Christ. 2000. *Vol. II/120.*

Hannah, Darrel D.: Michael and Christ. 1999.
Vol. II/109.

Hardin, Justin K.: Galatians and the Imperial Cult? 2007. *Vol. II /237.*

Harrison; James R.: Paul's Language of Grace in Its Graeco-Roman Context. 2003.
Vol. II/172.

Hartman, Lars: Text-Centered New Testament Studies. Ed. von D. Hellholm. 1997.
Vol. 102.

Hartog, Paul: Polycarp and the New Testament. 2001. *Vol. II/134.*

Hays, Christopher M.: Luke's Wealth Ethics. 2010. *Vol. 275.*

Heckel, Theo K.: Der Innere Mensch. 1993.
Vol. II/53.

– Vom Evangelium des Markus zum viergestaltigen Evangelium. 1999. *Vol. 120.*

Heckel, Ulrich: Kraft in Schwachheit. 1993.
Vol. II/56.

– Der Segen im Neuen Testament. 2002.
Vol. 150.

– see *Feldmeier, Reinhard.*

– see *Hengel, Martin.*

Heemstra, Marius: The Fiscus Judaicus and the Parting of the Ways. 2010. *Vol. II/277.*

Heiligenthal, Roman: Werke als Zeichen. 1983.
Vol. II/9.

Heininger, Bernhard: Die Inkulturation des Christentums. 2010. *Vol. 255.*

Heliso, Desta: Pistis and the Righteous One. 2007. *Vol. II/235.*

Hellholm, D.: see *Hartman, Lars.*

Hemer, Colin J.: The Book of Acts in the Setting of Hellenistic History. 1989. *Vol. 49.*

Hengel, Martin: Jesus und die Evangelien. Kleine Schriften V. 2007. *Vol. 211.*

– Die johanneische Frage. 1993. *Vol. 67.*

– Judaica et Hellenistica. Kleine Schriften I. 1996. *Vol. 90.*

– Judaica, Hellenistica et Christiana. Kleine Schriften II. 1999. *Vol. 109.*

– Judentum und Hellenismus. 1969, ³1988.
Vol. 10.

– Paulus und Jakobus. Kleine Schriften III. 2002. *Vol. 141.*

– Studien zur Christologie. Kleine Schriften IV. 2006. *Vol. 201.*

– Studien zum Urchristentum. Kleine Schriften VI. 2008. *Vol. 234.*

– Theologische, historische und biographische Skizzen. Kleine Schriften VII. 2010.
Vol. 253.

– and *Anna Maria Schwemer:* Paulus zwischen Damaskus und Antiochien. 1998.
Vol. 108.

– Der messianische Anspruch Jesu und die Anfänge der Christologie. 2001. *Vol. 138.*

– Die vier Evangelien und das eine Evangelium von Jesus Christus. 2008. *Vol. 224.*

Hengel, Martin and *Ulrich Heckel* (Ed.): Paulus und das antike Judentum. 1991. *Vol. 58.*

– and *Hermut Löhr* (Ed.): Schriftauslegung im antiken Judentum und im Urchristentum. 1994. *Vol. 73.*

– and *Anna Maria Schwemer* (Ed.): Königsherrschaft Gottes und himmlischer Kult. 1991. *Vol. 55.*

– Die Septuaginta. 1994. *Vol. 72.*

–, *Siegfried Mittmann* and *Anna Maria Schwemer* (Ed.): La Cité de Dieu / Die Stadt Gottes. 2000. *Vol. 129.*

Hentschel, Anni: Diakonia im Neuen Testament. 2007. *Vol. 226.*

Hernández Jr., Juan: Scribal Habits and Theological Influence in the Apocalypse. 2006.
Vol. II/218.

Herrenbrück, Fritz: Jesus und die Zöllner. 1990.
Vol. II/41.

Herzer, Jens: Paulus oder Petrus? 1998.
Vol. 103.

– see *Böttrich, Christfried.*

– see *Frey, Jörg.*

Hill, Charles E.: From the Lost Teaching of Polycarp. 2005. *Vol. 186.*

Hoegen-Rohls, Christina: Der nachösterliche Johannes. 1996. *Vol. II/84.*

Hoffmann, Matthias Reinhard: The Destroyer and the Lamb. 2005. *Vol. II/203.*

Hofius, Otfried: Katapausis. 1970. *Vol. 11.*

– Der Vorhang vor dem Thron Gottes. 1972.
Vol. 14.

– Der Christushymnus Philipper 2,6–11. 1976, ²1991. *Vol. 17.*

– Paulusstudien. 1989, ²1994. *Vol. 51.*

– Neutestamentliche Studien. 2000. *Vol. 132.*

– Paulusstudien II. 2002. *Vol. 143.*

Konradt, Matthias: Israel, Kirche und die Völker im Matthäusevangelium. 2007. *Vol. 215.*

Kooten, George H. van: Cosmic Christology in Paul and the Pauline School. 2003. *Vol. II/171.*

– Paul's Anthropology in Context. 2008. *Vol. 232.*

Korn, Manfred: Die Geschichte Jesu in veränderter Zeit. 1993. *Vol. II/51.*

Koskenniemi, Erkki: Apollonios von Tyana in der neutestamentlichen Exegese. 1994. *Vol. II/61.*

– The Old Testament Miracle-Workers in Early Judaism. 2005. *Vol. II/206.*

Kraus, Thomas J.: Sprache, Stil und historischer Ort des zweiten Petrusbriefes. 2001. *Vol. II/136.*

Kraus, Wolfgang: Das Volk Gottes. 1996. *Vol. 85.*

– see *Karrer, Martin.*

– see *Walter, Nikolaus.*

– and *Martin Karrer* (Hrsg.): Die Septuaginta – Texte, Theologien, Einflüsse. 2010. *Bd. 252.*

– and *Karl-Wilhelm Niebuhr* (Ed.): Frühjudentum und Neues Testament im Horizont Biblischer Theologie. 2003. *Vol. 162.*

Krauter, Stefan: Studien zu Röm 13,1-7. 2009. *Vol. 243.*

– see *Frey, Jörg.*

Kreplin, Matthias: Das Selbstverständnis Jesu. 2001. *Vol. II/141.*

Kuhn, Karl G.: Achtzehngebet und Vaterunser und der Reim. 1950. *Vol. 1.*

Kvalbein, Hans: see *Ådna, Jostein.*

Kwon, Yon-Gyong: Eschatology in Galatians. 2004. *Vol. II/183.*

Laansma, Jon: I Will Give You Rest. 1997. *Vol. II/98.*

Labahn, Michael: Offenbarung in Zeichen und Wort. 2000. *Vol. II/117.*

Lambers-Petry, Doris: see *Tomson, Peter J.*

Lange, Armin: see *Ego, Beate.*

Lampe, Peter: Die stadtrömischen Christen in den ersten beiden Jahrhunderten. 1987, ²1989. *Vol. II/18.*

Landmesser, Christof: Wahrheit als Grundbegriff neutestamentlicher Wissenschaft. 1999. *Vol. 113.*

– Jüngerberufung und Zuwendung zu Gott. 2000. *Vol. 133.*

Lau, Andrew: Manifest in Flesh. 1996. *Vol. II/86.*

Lawrence, Louise: An Ethnography of the Gospel of Matthew. 2003. *Vol. II/165.*

Lee, Aquila H.I.: From Messiah to Preexistent Son. 2005. *Vol. II/192.*

Lee, Pilchan: The New Jerusalem in the Book of Relevation. 2000. *Vol. II/129.*

Lee, Sang M.: The Cosmic Drama of Salvation. 2010. *Vol. II/276.*

Lee, Simon S.: Jesus' Transfiguration and the Believers' Transformation. 2009. *Vol. II/265.*

Lichtenberger, Hermann: Das Ich Adams und das Ich der Menschheit. 2004. *Vol. 164.*

– see *Avemarie, Friedrich.*

– see *Frey, Jörg.*

Lierman, John: The New Testament Moses. 2004. *Vol. II/173.*

– (Ed.): Challenging Perspectives on the Gospel of John. 2006. *Vol. II/219.*

Lieu, Samuel N.C.: Manichaeism in the Later Roman Empire and Medieval China. ²1992. *Vol. 63.*

Lindemann, Andreas: Die Evangelien und die Apostelgeschichte. 2009. *Vol. 241.*

Lincicum, David: Paul and the Early Jewish Encounter with Deuteronomy. 2010. *Vol. II/284.*

Lindgård, Fredrik: Paul's Line of Thought in 2 Corinthians 4:16–5:10. 2004. *Vol. II/189.*

Livesey, Nina E.: Circumcision as a Malleable Symbol. 2010. *Vol. II/295.*

Loader, William R.G.: Jesus' Attitude Towards the Law. 1997. *Vol. II/97.*

Löhr, Gebhard: Verherrlichung Gottes durch Philosophie. 1997. *Vol. 97.*

Löhr, Hermut: Studien zum frühchristlichen und frühjüdischen Gebet. 2003. *Vol. 160.*

– see *Hengel, Martin.*

Löhr, Winrich Alfried: Basilides und seine Schule. 1995. *Vol. 83.*

Lorenzen, Stefanie: Das paulinische Eikon-Konzept. 2008. *Vol. II/250.*

Luomanen, Petri: Entering the Kingdom of Heaven. 1998. *Vol. II/101.*

Luz, Ulrich: see *Alexeev, Anatoly A.*

– see *Dunn, James D.G.*

Mackay, Ian D.: John's Raltionship with Mark. 2004. *Vol. II/182.*

Mackie, Scott D.: Eschatology and Exhortation in the Epistle to the Hebrews. 2006. *Vol. II/223.*

Magda, Ksenija: Paul's Territoriality and Mission Strategy. 2009. *Vol. II/266.*

Maier, Gerhard: Mensch und freier Wille. 1971. *Vol. 12.*

– Die Johannesoffenbarung und die Kirche. 1981. *Vol. 25.*

Markschies, Christoph: Valentinus Gnosticus? 1992. *Vol. 65.*

Marshall, Jonathan: Jesus, Patrons, and Benefactors. 2009. *Vol. II/259.*

Marshall, Peter: Enmity in Corinth: Social Conventions in Paul's Relations with the Corinthians. 1987. *Vol. II/23.*

Martin, Dale B.: see *Zangenberg, Jürgen.*

Maston, Jason: Divine and Human Agency in Second Temple Judaism and Paul. 2010. *Vol. II/297.*

Mayer, Annemarie: Sprache der Einheit im Epheserbrief und in der Ökumene. 2002. *Vol. II/150.*

Mayordomo, Moisés: Argumentiert Paulus logisch? 2005. *Vol. 188.*

McDonough, Sean M.: YHWH at Patmos: Rev. 1:4 in its Hellenistic and Early Jewish Setting. 1999. *Vol. II/107.*

McDowell, Markus: Prayers of Jewish Women. 2006. *Vol. II/211.*

McGlynn, Moyna: Divine Judgement and Divine Benevolence in the Book of Wisdom. 2001. *Vol. II/139.*

Meade, David G.: Pseudonymity and Canon. 1986. *Vol. 39.*

Meadors, Edward P.: Jesus the Messianic Herald of Salvation. 1995. *Vol. II/72.*

Meißner, Stefan: Die Heimholung des Ketzers. 1996. *Vol. II/87.*

Mell, Ulrich: Die „anderen" Winzer. 1994. *Vol. 77.*

– see *Sänger, Dieter.*

Mengel, Berthold: Studien zum Philipperbrief. 1982. *Vol. II/8.*

Merkel, Helmut: Die Widersprüche zwischen den Evangelien. 1971. *Vol. 13.*

– see *Ego, Beate.*

Merklein, Helmut: Studien zu Jesus und Paulus. Vol. 1 1987. *Vol. 43.* – Vol. 2 1998. *Vol. 105.*

Merkt, Andreas: see *Nicklas, Tobias*

Metzdorf, Christina: Die Tempelaktion Jesu. 2003. *Vol. II/168.*

Metzler, Karin: Der griechische Begriff des Verzeihens. 1991. *Vol. II/44.*

Metzner, Rainer: Die Rezeption des Matthäusevangeliums im 1. Petrusbrief. 1995. *Vol. II/74.*

– Das Verständnis der Sünde im Johannesevangelium. 2000. *Vol. 122.*

Mihoc, Vasile: see *Dunn, James D.G.*

– see *Klein, Hans.*

Mineshige, Kiyoshi: Besitzverzicht und Almosen bei Lukas. 2003. *Vol. II/163.*

Mittmann, Siegfried: see *Hengel, Martin.*

Mittmann-Richert, Ulrike: Magnifikat und Benediktus. 1996. *Vol. II/90.*

– Der Sühnetod des Gottesknechts. 2008. *Vol. 220.*

Miura, Yuzuru: David in Luke-Acts. 2007. *Vol. II/232.*

Moll, Sebastian: The Arch-Heretic Marcion. 2010. *Vol. 250.*

Morales, Rodrigo J.: The Spirit and the Restorat. 2010. *Vol. 282.*

Mournet, Terence C.: Oral Tradition and Literary Dependency. 2005. *Vol. II/195.*

Mußner, Franz: Jesus von Nazareth im Umfeld Israels und der Urkirche. Ed. von M. Theobald. 1998. *Vol. 111.*

Mutschler, Bernhard: Das Corpus Johanneum bei Irenäus von Lyon. 2005. *Vol. 189.*

– Glaube in den Pastoralbriefen. 2010. *Vol. 256.*

Myers, Susan E.: Spirit Epicleses in the Acts of Thomas. 2010. *Vol. 281.*

Nguyen, V. Henry T.: Christian Identity in Corinth. 2008. *Vol. II/243.*

Nicklas, Tobias, Andreas Merkt und *Joseph Verheyden* (Ed.): Gelitten – Gestorben – Auferstanden. 2010. *Vol. II/273.*

– see *Verheyden, Joseph*

Niebuhr, Karl-Wilhelm: Gesetz and Paränese. 1987. *Vol. II/28.*

– Heidenapostel aus Israel. 1992. *Vol. 62.*

– see *Deines, Roland.*

– see *Dimitrov, Ivan Z.*

– see *Klein, Hans.*

– see *Kraus, Wolfgang.*

Nielsen, Anders E.: "Until it is Fullfilled". 2000. *Vol. II/126.*

Nielsen, Jesper Tang: Die kognitive Dimension des Kreuzes. 2009. *Vol. II/263.*

Nissen, Andreas: Gott und der Nächste im antiken Judentum. 1974. *Vol. 15.*

Noack, Christian: Gottesbewußtsein. 2000. *Vol. II/116.*

Noormann, Rolf: Irenäus als Paulusinterpret. 1994. *Vol. II/66.*

Norin, Stig: see *Hultgård, Anders.*

Novakovic, Lidija: Messiah, the Healer of the Sick. 2003. *Vol. II/170.*

Obermann, Andreas: Die christologische Erfüllung der Schrift im Johannesevangelium. 1996. *Vol. II/83.*

Öhler, Markus: Barnabas. 2003. *Vol. 156.*

– see *Becker, Michael.*

Okure, Teresa: The Johannine Approach to Mission. 1988. *Vol. II/31.*

Onuki, Takashi: Heil und Erlösung. 2004. *Vol. 165.*

Oropeza, B. J.: Paul and Apostasy. 2000. *Vol. II/115.*

Ostmeyer, Karl-Heinrich: Kommunikation mit Gott und Christus. 2006. *Vol. 197.*

– Taufe und Typos. 2000. *Vol. II/118.*

Pao, David W.: Acts and the Isaianic New Exodus. 2000. *Vol. II/130.*

Park, Eung Chun: The Mission Discourse in Matthew's Interpretation. 1995. *Vol. II/81.*

Park, Joseph S.: Conceptions of Afterlife in Jewish Insriptions. 2000. *Vol. II/121.*

Parsenios, George L.: Rhetoric and Drama in the Johannine Lawsuit Motif. 2010. *Vol. 258.*

Pate, C. Marvin: The Reverse of the Curse. 2000. *Vol. II/114.*

Paulsen, Henning: Studien zur Literatur und Geschichte des frühen Christentums. Ed. von Ute E. Eisen. 1997. *Vol. 99.*

Pearce, Sarah J.K.: The Land of the Body. 2007. *Vol. 208.*

Peres, Imre: Griechische Grabinschriften und neutestamentliche Eschatologie. 2003. *Vol. 157.*

Perry, Peter S.: The Rhetoric of Digressions. 2009. *Vol. II/268.*

Philip, Finny: The Origins of Pauline Pneumatology. 2005. *Vol. II/194.*

Philonenko, Marc (Ed.): Le Trône de Dieu. 1993. *Vol. 69.*

Pilhofer, Peter: Presbyteron Kreitton. 1990. *Vol. II/39.*

– Philippi. Vol. 1 1995. *Vol. 87.* – Vol. 2 ²2009. *Vol. 119.*

– Die frühen Christen und ihre Welt. 2002. *Vol. 145.*

– see *Becker, Eve-Marie.*

– see *Ego, Beate.*

Pitre, Brant: Jesus, the Tribulation, and the End of the Exile. 2005. *Vol. II/204.*

Plümacher, Eckhard: Geschichte und Geschichten. 2004. *Vol. 170.*

Pöhlmann, Wolfgang: Der Verlorene Sohn und das Haus. 1993. *Vol. 68.*

Poirier, John C.: The Tongues of Angels. 2010. *Vol. II/287.*

Pokorný, Petr and *Josef B. Souček:* Bibelauslegung als Theologie. 1997. *Vol. 100.*

– and *Jan Roskovec* (Ed.): Philosophical Hermeneutics and Biblical Exegesis. 2002. *Vol. 153.*

Popkes, Enno Edzard: Das Menschenbild des Thomasevangeliums. 2007. *Vol. 206.*

– Die Theologie der Liebe Gottes in den johanneischen Schriften. 2005. *Vol. II/197.*

Porter, Stanley E.: The Paul of Acts. 1999. *Vol. 115.*

Prieur, Alexander: Die Verkündigung der Gottesherrschaft. 1996. *Vol. II/89.*

Probst, Hermann: Paulus und der Brief. 1991. *Vol. II/45.*

Puig i Tàrrech, Armand: Jesus: An Uncommon Journey. 2010. *Vol. II/288.*

Rabens, Volker: The Holy Spirit and Ethics in Paul. 2010. *Vol. II/283.*

Räisänen, Heikki: Paul and the Law. 1983, ²1987. *Vol. 29.*

Rehkopf, Friedrich: Die lukanische Sonderquelle. 1959. *Vol. 5.*

Rein, Matthias: Die Heilung des Blindgeborenen (Joh 9). 1995. *Vol. II/73.*

Reinmuth, Eckart: Pseudo-Philo und Lukas. 1994. *Vol. 74.*

Reiser, Marius: Bibelkritik und Auslegung der Heiligen Schrift. 2007. *Vol. 217.*

– Syntax und Stil des Markusevangeliums. 1984. *Vol. II/11.*

Reynolds, Benjamin E.: The Apocalyptic Son of Man in the Gospel of John. 2008. *Vol. II/249.*

Rhodes, James N.: The Epistle of Barnabas and the Deuteronomic Tradition. 2004. *Vol. II/188.*

Richards, E. Randolph: The Secretary in the Letters of Paul. 1991. *Vol. II/42.*

Riesner, Rainer: Jesus als Lehrer. 1981, ³1988. *Vol. II/7.*

– Die Frühzeit des Apostels Paulus. 1994. *Vol. 71.*

Rissi, Mathias: Die Theologie des Hebräerbriefs. 1987. *Vol. 41.*

Röcker, Fritz W.: Belial und Katechon. 2009. *Vol. II/262.*

Röhser, Günter: Metaphorik und Personifikation der Sünde. 1987. *Vol. II/25.*

Rose, Christian: Theologie als Erzählung im Markusevangelium. 2007. *Vol. II/236.*

– Die Wolke der Zeugen. 1994. *Vol. II/60.*

Roskovec, Jan: see *Pokorný, Petr.*

Rothschild, Clare K.: Baptist Traditions and Q. 2005. *Vol. 190.*

– Hebrews as Pseudepigraphon. 2009. *Vol. 235.*

– Luke Acts and the Rhetoric of History. 2004. *Vol. II/175.*

– see *Frey, Jörg.*

Rüegger, Hans-Ulrich: Verstehen, was Markus erzählt. 2002. *Vol. II/155.*

Rüger, Hans Peter: Die Weisheitsschrift aus der Kairoer Geniza. 1991. *Vol. 53.*

Ruf, Martin G.: Die heiligen Propheten, eure Apostel und ich. 2011. *Vol. II/300.*

Sänger, Dieter: Antikes Judentum und die Mysterien. 1980. *Vol. II/5.*

– Die Verkündigung des Gekreuzigten und Israel. 1994. *Vol. 75.*

– see *Burchard, Christoph*

– and *Ulrich Mell* (Ed.): Paulus und Johannes. 2006. *Vol. 198.*

Salier, Willis Hedley: The Rhetorical Impact of the Semeia in the Gospel of John. 2004. *Vol. II/186.*

Salzmann, Jorg Christian: Lehren und Ermahnen. 1994. *Vol. II/59.*

Sandnes, Karl Olav: Paul – One of the Prophets? 1991. *Vol. II/43.*

Sato, Migaku: Q und Prophetie. 1988. *Vol. II/29.*

Schäfer, Ruth: Paulus bis zum Apostelkonzil. 2004. *Vol. II/179.*

Schaper, Joachim: Eschatology in the Greek Psalter. 1995. *Vol. II/76.*

Schimanowski, Gottfried: Die himmlische Liturgie in der Apokalypse des Johannes. 2002. *Vol. II/154.*

– Weisheit und Messias. 1985. *Vol. II/17.*

Schlichting, Günter: Ein jüdisches Leben Jesu. 1982. *Vol. 24.*

Schließer, Benjamin: Abraham's Faith in Romans 4. 2007. *Vol. II/224.*

Schnabel, Eckhard J.: Law and Wisdom from Ben Sira to Paul. 1985. *Vol. II/16.*

Schnelle, Udo: see *Frey, Jörg.*

Schröter, Jens: Von Jesus zum Neuen Testament. 2007. *Vol. 204.*

– see *Frey, Jörg.*

Schutter, William L.: Hermeneutic and Composition in I Peter. 1989. *Vol. II/30.*

Schwartz, Daniel R.: Studies in the Jewish Background of Christianity. 1992. *Vol. 60.*

Schwemer, Anna Maria: see *Hengel, Martin*

Scott, Ian W.: Implicit Epistemology in the Letters of Paul. 2005. *Vol. II/205.*

Scott, James M.: Adoption as Sons of God. 1992. *Vol. II/48.*

– Paul and the Nations. 1995. *Vol. 84.*

Shi, Wenhua: Paul's Message of the Cross as Body Language. 2008. *Vol. II/254.*

Shum, Shiu-Lun: Paul's Use of Isaiah in Romans. 2002. *Vol. II/156.*

Siegert, Folker: Drei hellenistisch-jüdische Predigten. Teil I 1980. *Vol. 20* – Teil II 1992. *Vol. 61.*

– Nag-Hammadi-Register. 1982. *Vol. 26.*

– Argumentation bei Paulus. 1985. *Vol. 34.*

– Philon von Alexandrien. 1988. *Vol. 46.*

Simon, Marcel: Le christianisme antique et son contexte religieux I/II. 1981. *Vol. 23.*

Smit, Peter-Ben: Fellowship and Food in the Kingdom. 2008. *Vol. II/234.*

Snodgrass, Klyne: The Parable of the Wicked Tenants. 1983. *Vol. 27.*

Söding, Thomas: Das Wort vom Kreuz. 1997. *Vol. 93.*

– see *Thüsing, Wilhelm.*

Sommer, Urs: Die Passionsgeschichte des Markusevangeliums. 1993. *Vol. II/58.*

Sorensen, Eric: Possession and Exorcism in the New Testament and Early Christianity. 2002. *Vol. II/157.*

Souček, Josef B.: see *Pokorný, Petr.*

Southall, David J.: Rediscovering Righteousness in Romans. 2008. *Vol. 240.*

Spangenberg, Volker: Herrlichkeit des Neuen Bundes. 1993. *Vol. II/55.*

Spanje, T.E. van: Inconsistency in Paul? 1999. *Vol. II/110.*

Speyer, Wolfgang: Frühes Christentum im antiken Strahlungsfeld. Vol. I: 1989. *Vol. 50.*

– Vol. II: 1999. *Vol. 116.*

– Vol. III: 2007. *Vol. 213.*

Spittler, Janet E.: Animals in the Apocryphal Acts of the Apostles. 2008. *Vol. II/247.*

Sprinkle, Preston: Law and Life. 2008. *Vol. II/241.*

Stadelmann, Helge: Ben Sira als Schriftgelehrter. 1980. *Vol. II/6.*

Stein, Hans Joachim: Frühchristliche Mahlfeiern. 2008. *Vol. II/255.*

Stenschke, Christoph W.: Luke's Portrait of Gentiles Prior to Their Coming to Faith. *Vol. II/108.*

Sterck-Degueldre, Jean-Pierre: Eine Frau namens Lydia. 2004. *Vol. II/176.*

Stettler, Christian: Der Kolosserhymnus. 2000. *Vol. II/131.*

– Das letzte Gericht. 2011. *Vol. II/299.*

Stettler, Hanna: Die Christologie der Pastoralbriefe. 1998. *Vol. II/105.*

Stökl Ben Ezra, Daniel: The Impact of Yom Kippur on Early Christianity. 2003. *Vol. 163.*

Strobel, August: Die Stunde der Wahrheit. 1980. *Vol. 21.*

Stroumsa, Guy G.: Barbarian Philosophy. 1999. *Vol. 112.*

Stuckenbruck, Loren T.: Angel Veneration and Christology. 1995. *Vol. II/70.*

–, *Stephen C. Barton* and *Benjamin G. Wold*
(Ed.): Memory in the Bible and Antiquity.
2007. *Vol. 212.*

Stuhlmacher, Peter (Ed.): Das Evangelium und
die Evangelien. 1983. *Vol. 28.*

– Biblische Theologie und Evangelium. 2002.
Vol. 146.

Sung, Chong-Hyon: Vergebung der Sünden.
1993. *Vol. II/57.*

Svendsen, Stefan N.: Allegory Transformed.
2009. *Vol. II/269.*

Tajra, Harry W.: The Trial of St. Paul. 1989.
Vol. II/35.

– The Martyrdom of St.Paul. 1994. *Vol. II/67.*

Tellbe, Mikael: Christ-Believers in Ephesus.
2009. *Vol. 242.*

Theißen, Gerd: Studien zur Soziologie des Ur-
christentums. 1979, ³1989. *Vol. 19.*

Theobald, Michael: Studien zum Corpus Iohan-
neum. 2010. *Vol. 267.*

– Studien zum Römerbrief. 2001. *Vol. 136.*

– see *Mußner, Franz.*

Thornton, Claus-Jürgen: Der Zeuge des Zeugen. 1991. *Vol. 56.*

Thüsing, Wilhelm: Studien zur neutestamentlichen Theologie. Ed. von Thomas Söding.
1995. *Vol. 82.*

Thurén, Lauri: Derhethorizing Paul. 2000.
Vol. 124.

Thyen, Hartwig: Studien zum Corpus Iohan-
neum. 2007. *Vol. 214.*

Tibbs, Clint: Religious Experience of the Pneu-
ma. 2007. *Vol. II/230.*

Toit, David S. du: Theios Anthropos. 1997.
Vol. II/91.

Tolmie, D. Francois: Persuading the Galatians.
2005. *Vol. II/190.*

Tomson, Peter J. and *Doris Lambers-Petry*
(Ed.): The Image of the Judaeo-Christians
in Ancient Jewish and Christian Literature.
2003. *Vol. 158.*

Toney, Carl N.: Paul's Inclusive Ethic. 2008.
Vol. II/252.

Trebilco, Paul: The Early Christians in Ephesus
from Paul to Ignatius. 2004. *Vol. 166.*

Treloar, Geoffrey R.: Lightfoot the Historian.
1998. *Vol. II/103.*

*Troftgruben, Troy M.: A Conclusion Unhinde-
red. 2010. Vol. II/280.*

Tso, Marcus K.M.: Ethics in the Qumran Community. 2010. *Vol. II/292.*

Tsuji, Manabu: Glaube zwischen Vollkommen-
heit und Verweltlichung. 1997. *Vol. II/93.*

Twelftree, Graham H.: Jesus the Exorcist. 1993.
Vol. II/54.

Ulrichs, Karl Friedrich: Christusglaube. 2007.
Vol. II/227.

Urban, Christina: Das Menschenbild nach dem
Johannesevangelium. 2001. *Vol. II/137.*

Vahrenhorst, Martin: Kultische Sprache in den
Paulusbriefen. 2008. *Vol. 230.*

Vegge, Ivar: 2 Corinthians – a Letter about
Reconciliation. 2008. *Vol. II/239.*

Verheyden, Joseph, Korinna Zamfir and *Tobias
Nicklas* (Ed.): Prophets and Prophecy in
Jewish and Early Christian Literature. 2010.
Vol. II/286.

– see *Nicklas, Tobias*

Visotzky, Burton L.: Fathers of the World. 1995.
Vol. 80.

Vollenweider, Samuel: Horizonte neutestamentlicher Christologie. 2002. *Vol. 144.*

Vos, Johan S.: Die Kunst der Argumentation bei
Paulus. 2002. *Vol. 149.*

Waaler, Erik: The *Shema* and The First
Commandment in First Corinthians. 2008.
Vol. II/253.

Wagener, Ulrike: Die Ordnung des „Hauses
Gottes". 1994. *Vol. II/65.*

Wagner, J. Ross: see *Wilk, Florian.*

Wahlen, Clinton: Jesus and the Impurity of
Spirits in the Synoptic Gospels. 2004.
Vol. II/185.

Walker, Donald D.: Paul's Offer of Leniency
(2 Cor 10:1). 2002. *Vol. II/152.*

Walter, Nikolaus: Praeparatio Evangelica. Ed.
von Wolfgang Kraus und Florian Wilk.
1997. *Vol. 98.*

Wander, Bernd: Gottesfürchtige und Sympathi-
santen. 1998. *Vol. 104.*

Wardle, Timothy: The Jerusalem Temple and
Early Christian Identity. 2010. *Vol. II/291.*

Wasserman, Emma: The Death of the Soul in
Romans 7. 2008. *Vol. 256.*

Waters, Guy: The End of Deuteronomy in the
Epistles of Paul. 2006. *Vol. 221.*

Watt, Jan G. van der: see *Frey, Jörg*

– see *Zimmermann, Ruben*

Watts, Rikki: Isaiah's New Exodus and Mark.
1997. *Vol. II/88.*

Webb, Robert L.: see *Bock, Darrell L.*

Wedderburn, Alexander J.M.: Baptism and
Resurrection. 1987. *Vol. 44.*

– Jesus and the Historians. 2010. *Vol. 269.*

Wegner, Uwe: Der Hauptmann von Kafarnaum.
1985. *Vol. II/14.*

Weiß, Hans-Friedrich: Frühes Christentum und
Gnosis. 2008. *Vol. 225.*

Weissenrieder, Annette: Images of Illness in the Gospel of Luke. 2003. Vol. II/164.

–, and *Robert B. Coote* (Ed.): The Interface of Orality and Writing. 2010. *Vol. 260.*

–, *Friederike Wendt* and *Petra von Gemünden* (Ed.): Picturing the New Testament. 2005. *Vol. II/193.*

Welck, Christian: Erzählte ‚Zeichen'. 1994. *Vol. II/69.*

Wendt, Friederike (Ed.): see *Weissenrieder, Annette.*

Wiarda, Timothy: Peter in the Gospels. 2000. *Vol. II/127.*

Wifstrand, Albert: Epochs and Styles. 2005. *Vol. 179.*

Wilk, Florian and *J. Ross Wagner* (Ed.): Between Gospel and Election. 2010. *Vol. 257.*

– see *Walter, Nikolaus.*

Williams, Catrin H.: I am He. 2000. *Vol. II/113.*

Wilson, Todd A.: The Curse of the Law and the Crisis in Galatia. 2007. *Vol. II/225.*

Wilson, Walter T.: Love without Pretense. 1991. *Vol. II/46.*

Winn, Adam: The Purpose of Mark's Gospel. 2008. *Vol. II/245.*

Winninge, Mikael: see *Holmberg, Bengt.*

Wischmeyer, Oda: Von Ben Sira zu Paulus. 2004. *Vol. 173.*

Wisdom, Jeffrey: Blessing for the Nations and the Curse of the Law. 2001. *Vol. II/133.*

Witmer, Stephen E.: Divine Instruction in Early Christianity. 2008. *Vol. II/246.*

Wold, Benjamin G.: Women, Men, and Angels. 2005. *Vol. II/2001.*

Wolter, Michael: Theologie und Ethos im frühen Christentum. 2009. *Vol. 236.*

– see *Stuckenbruck, Loren T.*

Wright, Archie T.: The Origin of Evil Spirits. 2005. *Vol. II/198.*

Wucherpfennig, Ansgar: Heracleon Philologus. 2002. *Vol. 142.*

Yates, John W.: The Spirit and Creation in Paul. 2008. *Vol. II/251.*

Yeung, Maureen: Faith in Jesus and Paul. 2002. *Vol. II/147.*

Zamfir, Corinna: see *Verheyden, Joseph*

Zangenberg, Jürgen, Harold W. Attridge and *Dale B. Martin* (Ed.): Religion, Ethnicity and Identity in Ancient Galilee. 2007. *Vol. 210.*

Zimmermann, Alfred E.: Die urchristlichen Lehrer. 1984, ²1988. *Vol. II/12.*

Zimmermann, Johannes: Messianische Texte aus Qumran. 1998. *Vol. II/104.*

Zimmermann, Ruben: Christologie der Bilder im Johannesevangelium. 2004. *Vol. 171.*

– Geschlechtermetaphorik und Gottesverhältnis. 2001. *Vol. II/122.*

– (Ed.): Hermeneutik der Gleichnisse Jesu. 2008. *Vol. 231.*

– and *Jan G. van der Watt* (Ed.): Moral Language in the New Testament. Vol. II. 2010. *Vol. II/296.*

– see *Frey, Jörg.*

– see *Horn, Friedrich Wilhelm.*

Zugmann, Michael: „Hellenisten" in der Apostelgeschichte. 2009. *Vol. II/264.*

Zumstein, Jean: see *Dettwiler, Andreas*

Zwiep, Arie W.: Christ, the Spirit and the Community of God. 2010. *Vol. II/293.*

– Judas and the Choice of Matthias. 2004. *Vol. II/187.*

For a complete catalogue please write to the publisher
Mohr Siebeck • P.O. Box 2030 • D-72010 Tübingen/Germany
Up-to-date information on the internet at www.mohr.de